Financial accounting

Financial accounting

William W. Pyle ▪ Kermit D. Larson

 1980

RICHARD D. IRWIN, INC. Homewood, Illinois 60430
Irwin-Dorsey Limited Georgetown, Ontario L7G 4B3

© RICHARD D. IRWIN, INC., 1980

All rights reserved. No part of this publication may be
reproduced, stored in a retrieval system, or transmitted,
in any form or by any means, electronic, mechanical,
photocopying, recording, or otherwise, without the prior
written permission of the publisher.

ISBN 0-256-02259-3
Library of Congress Catalog Card No. 79–88780

Printed in the United States of America

2 3 4 5 6 7 8 9 0 K 7 6 5 4 3 2 1

Preface

Financial Accounting is designed for use in a one-semester course at the college and university level. Its focus is on the generally accepted accounting principles that guide the accumulation and presentation of accounting data. Emphasis is placed on the pronouncements of authoritative bodies such as the Accounting Principles Board, the Financial Accounting Standards Board, and the Securities and Exchange Commission; and the discussion is consistently oriented toward helping students understand, interpret, and use financial accounting data, especially periodic financial statements.

Financial Accounting builds a solid foundation for later courses in accounting and finance. It thus meets the needs of both students who will make accountancy a career and students who will use accounting as a tool in other fields of specialization or in their personal affairs. Its authors assume that the student's previous business contacts, vocabulary, and understanding of business practices are limited. Consequently, all new terms, business practices, and accounting principles are fully explained when first introduced.

Highlights of the book and its supplementary materials

1. The book is organized into 16 chapters that allow complete coverage in a concentrated one-semester financial accounting course, or selective coverage in a more moderately paced course.
2. Primary reliance in the early chapters is on the easily understood single proprietorship. However, the book also begins in the first chapter to build the vocabulary and knowledge necessary for an understanding of corporations and their accounting. Consequently, by the time chapters are devoted exclusively to corporation accounting, students are comfortable with this form of business organization.
3. Important accounting concepts and principles are integrated into the topical discussions rather than being placed in an isolated separate chapter. As a result, students are able to see the practical importance of each concept or principle immediately upon learning its definition and conceptual significance.

4. Both the conceptual significance of each accounting principle and the procedures used in its application are presented. Thus both the *why* and the *how to apply* of each principle are explained.

5. To focus the student's attention on important areas of expected achievement, learning objectives stated in terms of specific activities the student should master are enumerated at the beginning of each chapter. Also, each chapter's discussion ends with a glossary of new words and terms to be understood.

6. The latest relevant pronouncements of authorative bodies such as the Financial Accounting Standards Board and the Securities and Exchange Commission are presented and footnoted throughout the book.

7. A full chapter is devoted to a comprehensive coverage of what frequently is called the most significant accounting problem today, the problem of accounting for price-level changes.

8. An example of corporate financial statements including footnotes is presented in an appendix at the end of the book. The financial statements show the real-world applicability of many of the principles discussed. They also suggest to the student the relevance of further study in accounting.

9. Questions, exercises, and problems at the end of each chapter provide a wide range of assignment material, both in terms of length of assignment and degree of difficulty. An alternate set of problems allows variability in assignments from semester to semester, or planned repetition of selected problem types. In addition, one or two "Provocative Problems" are provided and may be used to help students analyze the material in a somewhat more complex or uncertain context as would be true in the real world.

10. A complete set of supporting materials that supplement the text is provided. The materials include:

Working papers   A booklet of working papers for solutions to the problems and alternate problems is provided. To eliminate much of the tedious "busy work" in completing assigned problems, account titles and beginning account balances are provided in the working papers. Also, account titles and, where possible, account balances are entered on the work sheet forms.

Study guide   A comprehensive study guide that provides specific study hints, an outline of major points, and a variety of self-testing questions and short problems with answers is available.

Practice set   The set, Lee Hardware Store, Inc., is designed to illustrate accounting for a small merchandising business organized as a corporation. It uses columnar journals and may be assigned after the completion of Chapter 7 and the appendix following the chapter.

Check figures   This list of key figures gives students an indication of possible errors in their solutions to the problems and alternate problems. The check figures are available in quantity from the publisher.

Solutions manual   The instructor's manual contains complete solutions to all of the questions, exercises, and problems in the text, with the estimated time required by an average student to complete each problem solution.

Booklet of examination materials   This booklet contains a large number of questions and problems of various types that an instructor can draw from in preparing examinations and quizzes.

Transparencies   A set of transparencies of the solutions to all exercises, problems, and alternate problems is provided free to adopters. Included with the transparencies of the problem and exercise solutions is a set of additional transparencies for use by the instructor in illustrating classroom lectures.

December 1979   William W. Pyle
                                                               Kermit D. Larson

Contents

7 Accounts and notes receivable, 232

8 Inventories and cost of goods sold, 278

part six
Financial statements,
interpretation and modifications

Financial accounting

part one
Introduction

CHAPTER 1 Accounting, an introduction to
its concepts.

1

Accounting, an introduction to its concepts

After studying Chapter 1, you should be able to:

- Tell the function of accounting and the nature and purpose of the information it provides.
- List the main fields of accounting and tell the kinds of work carried on in each field.
- List the accounting concepts and principles introduced and tell the effect of each on accounting records and statements.
- Describe the purpose of a balance sheet and of an income statement and tell the kinds of information presented in each.
- Recognize and be able to indicate the effects of transactions on the elements of an accounting equation.
- Prepare simple financial statements.
- Tell in each case the extent of the responsibility of a business owner for the debts of a business organized as a single proprietorship, a partnership, or a corporation.
- Define or explain the words and phrases listed in the chapter Glossary.

Accounting is a service activity. Its function is to provide quantitative information about economic entities. The information is primarily financial in nature and is intended to be useful in making economic decisions.[1] If the entity for which the information is provided is a business, for example, the information is used by its management in answering questions such as: What are the resources of the business? What debts does it owe? Does it have earnings? Are expenses too large in relation to sales? Is too little or too much merchandise being kept? Are amounts owed by customers being collected rapidly? Will the business be able to meet its own debts as they mature? Should the plant be expanded? Should a new product be introduced? Should selling prices be increased?

In addition, grantors of credit such as banks, wholesale houses, and manufacturers use accounting information in answering such questions as: Are the customer's earning prospects good? What is his debt-paying ability? Has he paid his debts promptly in the past? Should he be granted additional credit?[2] Likewise, governmental units use accounting information in regulating businesses and collecting taxes, labor unions use it in negotiating working conditions and wage agreements, and investors make wide use of accounting data in investment decisions.

WHY STUDY ACCOUNTING

Information for use in answering questions like the ones listed is conveyed in accounting reports. If a person is to use these reports effectively, he or she must have some understanding of how their data were gathered and the figures put together. He or she must appreciate the limitations of the data and the extent to which portions are based on estimates rather than precise measurements, and must under-

---

[1] Accounting Principles Board, "Basic Concepts and Accounting Principles Underlying Financial Statements of Business Enterprises," *APB Statement No. 4* (New York: AICPA, October 1970), par. 9.

[2] Obviously, women as well as men are customers—and students and accountants. In this discussion as in others not referring to a specific person, the pronouns *he, his,* and *him* are used in their generic sense and should be understood to include both men and women.

stand accounting terms and concepts. Needless to say, these understandings are gained in a study of accounting.

Another reason to study accounting is to make it one's lifework. A career in accounting can be very interesting and highly rewarding.

ACCOUNTANCY AS A PROFESSION

Over the past half century accountancy as a profession has attained a stature comparable with that of law or medicine. All states license *certified public accountants* or *CPAs* just as they license doctors and lawyers. The licensing helps ensure a high standard of professional service. Only individuals who have passed a rigorous examination of their accounting and related knowledge, met other education and experience requirements, and have received a license may designate themselves as certified public accountants.

The requirements for the CPA certificate or license vary with the states. In general an applicant must be a citizen, 21 years of age, of unquestioned moral character, and a college graduate with a major concentration in accounting. Also the applicant must pass a rigorous three-day examination in accounting theory, accounting practice, auditing, and business law. The three-day examination is uniform in all states and is given on the same days in all states. It is prepared by the American Institute of Certified Public Accountants (AICPA) which is the national professional organization of CPAs. In addition to the examination, many states require an applicant to have one or more years of work experience in the office of a CPA or the equivalent before the certificate is granted. However, some states do not require the work experience and some states permit the applicant to substitute one or more years of experience for the college level education requirement. On this score the AICPA's Committee on Education and Experience Requirements for CPAs expressed the opinion that at least five years of college study are necessary to obtain the body of knowledge needed to be a CPA. For those meeting this standard, it recommends that no previous work experience should be required.[3] However, it will be several years before all states accept this recommendation. In the meantime, interested students can learn the requirements of any state in which they are interested by writing to its state board of accountancy.

THE WORK OF AN ACCOUNTANT

Accountants are commonly employed in three main fields: (1) in public accounting, (2) in private accounting, or (3) in government.

---

[3] *Report of the Committee on Education and Experience Requirements for CPAs* (New York, 1969), p. 11.

Public accounting

Public accountants are individuals who offer their professional services and those of their employees to the public for a fee, in much the same manner as a lawyer or a consulting engineer.

Auditing The principal service offered by a public accountant is auditing. Banks commonly require an *audit* of the financial statements of a company applying for a sizable loan, with the audit being performed by a CPA who is not an employee of the audited concern but an independent professional person working for a fee. Companies whose securities are offered for sale to the public generally must also have such an audit before the securities may be sold. Thereafter additional audits must be made periodically if the securities are to continue being traded.

The purpose of an audit is to lend credibility to a company's financial statements. In making the audit the auditor carefully examines the company's statements and the accounting records from which they were prepared. In the examination, the auditor makes sure the statements fairly reflect the company's financial position and operating results and were prepared in accordance with generally accepted accounting principles from records kept in accordance with such principles. Banks, investors, and others rely on the information in a company's financial statements in making loans, granting credit, and in buying and selling securities. They depend on the auditor to verify the dependability of the information the statements contain.

Management advisory services In addition to auditing, accountants commonly offer *management advisory services*. An accountant gains from an audit an intimate knowledge of the audited company's accounting procedures and its financial position. He or she is thus in an excellent position to offer constructive suggestions for improving the procedures and strengthening the position. Clients expect these suggestions as a useful audit by-product. They also commonly engage certified public accountants to conduct additional investigations for the purpose of determining ways in which their operations may be improved. Such investigations and the suggestions growing from them are known as management advisory services.

Management advisory services include the design, installation, and improvement of a client's general accounting system and any related information system it may have for determining and controlling costs. They also include the application of machine methods to these systems, plus advice in financial planning, budgeting, forecasting, and inventory control. In fact, they include all phases of information systems and related matters.

Tax services In this day of increasing complexity in income and other tax laws and continued high tax rates, few important business decisions are made without consideration being given to their tax effect.

A certified public accountant, through training and experience, is well qualified to render important service in this area. The service includes not only the preparation and filing of tax returns but also advice as to how transactions may be completed so as to incur the smallest tax.

Private accounting

When an accountant is employed by a single enterprise, he or she is said to be in private accounting. A small business may employ only one accountant or it may depend upon the services of a public accountant and employ none. A large business, on the other hand, may have more than a hundred employees in its accounting department. They commonly work under the supervision of a chief accounting officer, commonly called the *controller*, who is often a CPA. The title, controller, results from the fact that one of the chief uses of accounting data is to control the operations of a business.

The one accountant of the small business and the accounting department of a large concern do a variety of work, including general accounting, cost accounting, budgeting, and internal auditing.

General accounting   *General accounting* has to do primarily with recording transactions and preparing financial and other reports for the use of management, owners, creditors, and governmental agencies. The private accountant may design or help the public accountant design the system used in recording the transactions. He or she will also supervise the clerical or data processing staff in recording the transactions and preparing the reports.

Cost accounting   The phase of accounting that has to do with collecting, determining, and controlling costs, particularly costs of producing a given product or service, is called *cost accounting*. A knowledge of costs and controlling costs is vital to good management. Therefore, a large company may have a number of accountants engaged in this activity.

Budgeting   Planning business activities before they occur is called *budgeting*. The objective of budgeting is to provide management with an intelligent plan for future operations. Then after the budget plan has been put into effect, it provides summaries and reports that can be used to compare actual accomplishments with the plan. Many large companies have a number of people who devote all their time to this phase of accounting.

Internal auditing   In addition to an annual audit by a firm of certified public accountants, many companies maintain a staff of internal auditors. The internal auditors constantly check the records prepared and maintained in each department or company branch. It is their responsibility to make sure that established accounting procedures and management directives are being followed throughout the company.

Governmental accounting

Furnishing governmental services is a vast and complicated operation in which accounting is just as indispensable as in business. Elected and appointed officials must rely on data accumulated by means of accounting if they are to complete effectively their administrative duties. Accountants are responsible for the accumulation of these data. Accountants also check and audit the millions of income, payroll, and sales tax returns that accompany the tax payments upon which governmental units depend. And finally, federal and state agencies, such as the Interstate Commerce Commission, Securities and Exchange Commission, and so on, use accountants in many capacities in their regulation of business.

ACCOUNTING AND BOOKKEEPING

Many people confuse *accounting* and *bookkeeping* and look upon them as one and the same. In effect they identify the whole with one of its parts. Actually, bookkeeping is only part of accounting, the record-making part. To keep books is to record transactions, and a bookkeeper is one who records transactions. The work is often routine and primarily clerical in nature. The work of an accountant goes far beyond this, as a rereading of the previous section will show.

ACCOUNTING STATEMENTS

Accounting statements are the end product of the accounting process, but a good place to begin the study of accounting. They are used to convey a concise picture of the profitability and financial position of a business. The two most important are the income statement and the balance sheet.

The income statement

A company's *income statement* (see Illustration 1–1) is perhaps more important than its balance sheet. It shows whether or not the business achieved or failed to achieve its primary objective—earning a "profit" or net income. A *net income* is earned when revenues exceed expenses, but a *net loss* is incurred if the expenses exceed the revenues. An income statement is prepared by listing the revenues earned during the period, listing the expenses incurred in earning the revenues, and subtracting the expenses from the revenues to determine if a net income or a net loss was incurred.

Revenues are inflows of cash or other properties received in exchange for goods or services provided to customers. Rents, dividends,

Coast Realty
Income Statement for Year Ended December 31, 19—

Revenues:

Commissions earned	$31,450	
Property management fees	1,200	
Total revenues		$32,650

Operating expenses:

Salaries expense	$ 7,800	
Rent expense	2,400	
Utilities expense	315	
Telephone expense	560	
Advertising expense	2,310	
Total operating expenses		13,385
Net income		$19,265

Illustration 1–1

and interest earned are also revenues. Coast Realty of Illustration 1–1 had revenue inflows from services which totaled $32,650.

Expenses are goods and services consumed in operating a business or other economic unit. Coast Realty consumed the services of its employees (salaries expense), the services of a telephone company, and so on.

The heading of an income statement tells the name of the business for which it is prepared and the time period covered by the statement. Both bits of information are important. However, the time covered is extremely significant, since the items on the statement must be interpreted in relation to the period of time. For example, the item "Commissions earned, $31,450" on the income statement of Illustration 1–1 has little significance until it is known that the amount represents one year's commissions and not the commissions of a week or a month.

The balance sheet

The purpose of a *balance sheet* is to show the financial position of a business on a specific date. It is often called a *position statement*. Financial position is shown by listing the *assets* of the business, its *liabilities* or debts, and the *equity of the owner or owners*. The name of the business and the date are given in the balance sheet heading. It is understood that the item amounts shown are as of the close of business on that date.

Before a business manager, investor, or other person can make effective judgments based on balance sheet information, he or she must gain several concepts and understandings. To illustrate, assume that on August 3, Joan Ball began a new business, called World Travel Agency. During the day she completed these transactions in the name of the business:

Aug. 3 Invested $18,000 of her personal savings in the business.
 3 Paid $15,000 of the agency's cash for a small office building and the land on which it was built (cost of the building, $10,000, and cost of the land, $5,000).
 3 Purchased on *credit* from Office Equipment Company office equipment costing $2,000. (Purchased on credit means purchased with a promise to pay at a later date.)

A balance sheet reflecting the effects of these transactions appears in Illustration 1–2. It shows that after completing the transactions the agency has four assets, a $2,000 debt, and that its owner has an $18,000 equity in the business.

World Travel Agency
Balance Sheet, August 3, 19—

Assets		*Liabilities*	
Cash	$ 3,000	Accounts payable	$ 2,000
Office equipment	2,000		
Building	10,000		
Land	5,000	*Owner's Equity*	
		Joan Ball, capital	18,000
Total assets	$20,000	Total equities	$20,000

Illustration 1–2

Observe that the two sides of the balance sheet are equal. This is where it gets its name. Its two sides must always be equal because one side shows the resources of the business and the other shows who supplied the resources. For example, World Travel Agency has $20,000 of resources (assets) of which $18,000 were supplied by its owner and $2,000 by its creditors. (*Creditors* are individuals and organizations to whom the business owes debts.)

ASSETS, LIABILITIES, AND OWNER'S EQUITY

The assets of a business are, in general, the properties or economic resources owned by the business. They include cash, amounts owed to the business by its customers for goods and services sold to them on credit (called *accounts receivable*), merchandise held for sale by the business, supplies, equipment, buildings, and land. Assets may also include such intangible rights as those granted by a patent or copyright.

The liabilities of a business are its debts. They include amounts owed to creditors for goods and services bought on credit (called *accounts payable*), salaries and wages owed employees, taxes payable, notes payable, and mortgages payable.

When a business is owned by one person, the owner's interest or equity in the assets of the business is shown on a balance sheet by listing the person's name, followed by the word "capital," and then the amount of the equity. The use of the word "capital" comes from the idea that the owner has furnished the business with resources or "capital" equal to the amount of the equity.

Liabilities are also sometimes called *equities*. An equity is a right, claim, or interest; and a liability represents a claim or right to be paid. The law recognizes this right. If a business fails to pay its creditors, the law gives the creditors the right to force the sale of the assets of the business to secure money to meet creditor claims. Furthermore, if the assets are sold, the creditors are paid first, with any remainder going to the business owner. Obviously, then, by law creditor claims take precedence over those of a business owner.

Since creditor claims take precedence over those of an owner, an owner's equity in a business is always a residual amount. Creditors recognize this. When they examine the balance sheet of a business, they are always interested in the share of its assets furnished by creditors and the share furnished by its owner or owners. The creditors recognize that if the business must be liquidated and its assets sold, the shrinkage in converting the assets into cash must exceed the equity of the owner or owners before the creditors will lose.

GENERALLY ACCEPTED ACCOUNTING PRINCIPLES

An understanding of financial statement information requires a knowledge of the generally accepted accounting principles that govern the accumulation and presentation of the data appearing on such statements. A common definition of the word "principle" is: "A broad general law or rule adopted or professed as a guide to action; a settled ground or basis of conduct or practice. . . ." Consequently, generally accepted accounting principles may be described as broad rules adopted by the accounting profession as guides in measuring, recording, and reporting the financial affairs and activities of a business. They consist of a number of concepts, principles, and procedures which are first discussed at the points shown in the following list. They also are referred to again and again throughout this text in order to increase your understanding of the information conveyed by accounting data.

	First introduced	
	Chapter	Page
Generally accepted concepts:		
1. Business entity concept	1	14
2. Continuing-concern concept	1	16
3. Stable-dollar concept	1	16
4. Time-period concept	3	79
Generally accepted principles:		
1. Cost principle	1	15
2. Objectivity principle	1	15
3. Realization principle	1	22

Generally accepted procedures:
These specify the ways data are processed and reported and are described and discussed throughout the text.

SOURCE OF ACCOUNTING PRINCIPLES

Generally accepted accounting principles are not natural laws in the sense of the laws of physics and chemistry. They are man-made rules that depend for their authority upon their general acceptance by the accounting profession. They have evolved from the experience and thinking of members of the accounting profession, aided by such groups as the American Institute of Certified Public Accountants, the Financial Accounting Standards Board, the American Accounting Association, and the Securities and Exchange Commission.

The American Institute of Certified Public Accountants (AICPA) has long been influential in describing and defining generally accepted accounting principles. During the years from 1939 to 1959 it published a series of *Accounting Research Bulletins* which were recognized as expressions of generally accepted accounting principles. In 1959 it established an 18-member Accounting Principles Board (APB) composed of practicing accountants, educators, and representatives of industry, and gave the board authority to issue opinions that were to be regarded by members of the AICPA as authoritative expressions of generally accepted accounting principles. During the years 1962 through 1973 the Board issued 31 such opinions. Added importance was given to these opinions beginning in 1964 when the AICPA ruled that its members must disclose in footnotes to published financial statements of the companies they audit any departure from generally accepted accounting principles as set forth in the *Opinions of the Accounting Principles Board.*

In 1973, after 11 years of activity, the Accounting Principles Board was terminated. Its place was taken by a seven-member Financial Accounting Standards Board (FASB). The seven members serve full time, receive salaries, and must resign from accounting firms and other employment. They must have a knowledge of accounting, finance, and business, but are not required to be CPAs. This differs from the Accounting Principles Board, all members of which were CPAs, who served part time, without pay, and continued their affiliations with accounting firms and other employment. The FASB issues *Statements of the Financial Accounting Standards Board* which like the *Opinions of the Accounting Principles Board* must be considered as authoritative expressions of generally accepted accounting principles. Both the *State-*

ments and *Opinions* are referred to again and again throughout this text.

The American Accounting Association, an organization with strong academic ties, has also been influential in describing and defining generally accepted accounting principles. It has sponsored a number of research studies and has published many articles dealing with accounting principles. However, its influence has not been as great as the AICPA, since it has no power to impose its views on the accounting profession but must depend upon the prestige of its authors and the logic of their arguments.

The Securities and Exchange Commission (SEC) plays a prominent role in financial reporting. The SEC is an independent quasi-judicial agency of the federal government. It was established to administer the provisions of various securities and exchange acts dealing with the distribution and sale of securities. Such securities, to be sold, must be registered with the SEC. This requires the filing of audited financial statements prepared in accordance with the rules of the SEC. Furthermore, the information contained in the statements must be kept current by filing additional audited annual reports. The SEC does not appraise the registered securities. However, it attempts to safeguard investors by requiring that all material facts affecting the worth of the securities be made public and that no important information be withheld. Its rules carry over into the annual reports of large companies and have contributed to the usefulness of these reports. In a real sense, the SEC should be viewed as the dominant authority in respect to the establishment of accounting principles. However, it has relied on the accounting profession, particularly the AICPA and the FASB, to determine and enforce accepted accounting principles. At the same time it has pressured the accounting profession to reduce the number of acceptable accounting procedures.

UNDERSTANDING ACCOUNTING PRINCIPLES

Your authors believe that an understanding of *accounting principles* is best conveyed with examples illustrating the application of each principle. The examples must be such that a student can understand at his or her level of experience. Consequently, three *accounting concepts* and two accounting principles are introduced here. Discussions of the others are delayed until later in the text when meaningful examples of their application can be developed.

Business entity concept

Under the *business entity concept*, for accounting purposes, every business is conceived to be and is treated as a separate entity, separate and distinct from its owner or owners and from every other business.

Businesses are so conceived and treated because, insofar as a specific business is concerned, the purpose of accounting is to record its transactions and periodically report its financial position and profitability. Consequently, the records and reports of a business should not include either the transactions or assets of another business or the personal assets and transactions of its owner or owners. To include either distorts the financial position and profitability of the business. For example, the personally owned automobile of a business owner should not be included among the assets of the owner's business. Likewise, its gas, oil, and repairs should not be treated as an expense of the business, for to do so distorts the reported financial position and profitability of the business.

Cost principle

In addition to the *business entity concept,* an accounting principle called the *cost principle* should be borne in mind when reading financial statements. Under this principle all goods and services purchased are recorded at cost and appear on the statements at cost. For example, if a business pays $50,000 for land to be used in carrying on its operations, the purchase should be recorded at $50,000. It makes no difference if the owner and several competent outside appraisers thought the land "worth" at least $60,000. It cost $50,000 and should appear on the balance sheet at that amount. Furthermore, if five years later, due to booming real estate prices, the land's market value has doubled, this makes no difference either. The land cost $50,000 and should continue to appear on the balance sheet at $50,000 even though its estimated market value is twice that.

In applying the *cost principle,* costs are measured on a cash or cash-equivalent basis. If the consideration given for an asset or service is cash, cost is measured at the entire cash outlay made to secure the asset or service. If the consideration is something other than cash, cost is measured at the cash-equivalent value of the consideration given or the cash-equivalent value of the thing received, whichever is more clearly evident.[4]

Why are assets and services recorded at cost and why are the balance sheet amounts for the assets not changed from time to time to reflect changing market values? The *objectivity principle* and the *continuing-concern concept* supply answers to these questions.

Objectivity principle

The *objectivity principle* supplies the reason transactions are recorded at cost, since it requires that transaction amounts be objectively

---

[4] APB, "Accounting for Nonmonetary Transactions," *APB Opinion No. 29* (New York: AICPA, 1973), par. 18.

established. Whims and fancies plus, for example, something like an opinion of management that an asset is "worth more than it cost" have no place in accounting. To be fully useful, accounting information must be based on objective data. As a rule, costs are objective, since they normally are established by buyers and sellers, each striking the best possible bargain for themselves.

Continuing-concern concept

Balance sheet amounts for assets used in carrying on the operations of a business are not changed from time to time to reflect changing market values. A balance sheet is prepared under the assumption that the business for which it is prepared will continue in operation, and as a continuing or going concern the assets used in carrying on its operations are not for sale. In fact, they cannot be sold without disrupting the business. Therefore, since the assets are for use in the business and are not for sale, their current market values are not particularly relevant and need not be shown. Also, without a sale, their current market values usually cannot be objectively established, as is required by the *objectivity principle.*

The *continuing-concern or going-concern concept* applies in most situations. However, if a business is about to be sold or liquidated, the *continuing-concern concept* and the *cost and objectivity principles* do not apply in the preparation of its statements. In such cases amounts other than costs, such as estimated market values, become more useful and informative.

The stable-dollar concept

In our country accounting transactions are measured, recorded, and reported in terms of dollars. In the measuring, recording, and reporting process the dollar has been treated as a stable unit of measure, like a gallon, an acre, or a mile. However, unfortunately the dollar, like other currencies, is not a stable unit of measure. When the general price level (the average of all prices) changes, the value of money (its purchasing power) also changes. For example, during the past 10 years the general price level has approximately doubled, which means that over these years the purchasing power of the dollar has declined from 100 cents to approximately 50 cents.

Nevertheless, although the instability of the dollar is recognized, accountants in their reports continue to add and subtract items acquired in different years with dollars of different sizes. In effect they ignore changes in the size of the measuring unit. For example, assume a company purchased land some years ago for $10,000 and sold it today for $20,000. If during this period the purchasing power of the dollar declined from 100 cents to 50 cents, it can be said that the company is no better off for having purchased the land for $10,000 and sold it for $20,000 because the $20,000 will buy no more goods and services today than the $10,000 at the time of the purchase. Yet, using the dollar to measure both transactions, the accountant reports a $10,000 gain from the purchase and sale.

The instability of the dollar as a unit of measure is recognized. Therefore, the question is should the amounts shown on financial statements be adjusted for changes in the purchasing power of the dollar. Techniques have been devised to convert the historical dollars of statement amounts into dollars of current purchasing power. Such statements are called *price-level-adjusted statements*. Also, by consulting catalogs and securing current prices from manufacturers and wholesalers, it is possible to determine replacement costs for various assets owned. As a result, such costs could be used in preparing financial statements. However, financial statements showing current replacement costs and also price-level-adjusted statements require subjective judgments in their preparation. Consequently, most accountants are of the opinion that the traditional statements based on the *stable-dollar concept* are best for general publication and use. Nevertheless, they also recognize that the information conveyed by traditional statements can be made more useful if accompanied by replacement cost and/or price-level-adjusted information. This is discussed in Chapter 16.

From the discussions of the *cost principle,* the *continuing-concern concept,* and *stable-dollar concept,* it should be recognized that in most instances a balance sheet does not show the amounts at which the listed assets can be sold or replaced. Nor does it show the "worth" of the business for which it was prepared, since some of the listed assets may be salable for much more or much less than the dollar amounts at which they are shown.

BUSINESS ORGANIZATIONS

Accounting is applicable to all economic entities such as business concerns, schools, churches, fraternities, and so on. However, this text will focus on accounting for business concerns organized as single proprietorships, partnerships, and corporations.

Single proprietorships

An unincorporated business owned by one person is called a *single proprietorship.* Small retail stores and service enterprises are commonly operated as single proprietorships. There are no legal requirements to be met in starting a single proprietorship business. Furthermore, single proprietorships are the most numerous of all business concerns.

In accounting for a single proprietorship, the *business entity concept* is applied and the business is treated as a separate entity, separate and distinct from its owner. However, insofar as the debts of the business are concerned, no such legal distinction is made. The owner of a single proprietorship business is personally responsible for its debts. As a result, if the assets of such a business are not sufficient to pay its debts, the personal assets of the proprietor may be taken to satisfy the claims of the business creditors.

Partnerships

When a business is owned by two or more people as partners, it is called a *partnership*. Like a single proprietorship, there are no special legal requirements to be met in starting a partnership business. All that is required is for two or more people to enter into an agreement to operate a business as partners. The agreement becomes a contract and may be either oral or written, but to avoid disagreements, a written contract is preferred.

For accounting purposes a partnership business is treated as a separate entity, separate and distinct from its owners. However, just as with a single proprietorship, insofar as the debts of the business are concerned no such legal distinction is made. A partner is personally responsible for all the debts of the partnership, both his or her own share and the shares of any partners who are unable to pay. Furthermore, the personal assets of a partner may be taken to satisfy all the debts of a partnership if other partners cannot pay.

Corporations

A business incorporated under the laws of a state or the federal government is called a *corporation*. Unlike a single proprietorship or partnership, a corporation is a separate legal entity, separate and distinct from its owners. The owners are called *stockholders* or *shareholders* because their ownership is evidenced by shares of the corporation's *capital stock* which may be sold and transferred from one shareholder to another without affecting the operation of the corporation.

Separate legal entity is the most important characteristic of a corporation. It makes a corporation responsible for its own acts and its own debts and relieves its stockholders of liability for either. It enables a corporation to buy, own, and sell property in its own name, to sue and be sued in its own name, and to enter into contracts for which it is solely responsible. In short, separate legal entity enables a corporation to conduct its business affairs as a legal person with all the rights, duties, and responsibilities of a person. However, unlike a person, it must act through agents.

A corporation is created by securing a charter from one of the 50 states or the federal government. The requirements for obtaining a charter vary; but in general call for filing an application with the proper governmental official and paying certain fees and taxes. If the application complies with the law and all fees and taxes have been paid, the charter is granted and the corporation comes into existence. At that point the corporation's organizers and perhaps others buy the corporation's stock and become stockholders. Then, as stockholders they meet and elect a board of directors. The board then meets, appoints the corporation's president and other officers, and makes them responsible for managing the corporation's business affairs.

Lack of stockholder liability and the ease with which stock may be sold and transferred have enabled corporations to multiply, grow, and become the dominant form of business organization in our country. Nevertheless, because of its simplicity, it is best to begin the study of accounting with a single proprietorship.

THE BALANCE SHEET EQUATION

As previously stated, a balance sheet is so called because its two sides must always balance. The sum of the assets shown on the balance sheet must equal liabilities plus the equity of the owner or owners of the business. This equality may be expressed in equation form for a single proprietorship business as follows:

$$\text{Assets} = \text{Liabilities} + \text{Owner's Equity}$$

When balance sheet equality is expressed in equation form, the resulting equation is called the *balance sheet equation*. It is also known as the *accounting equation,* since all double-entry accounting is based on it. And, like any mathematical equation, its elements may be transposed and the equation expressed:

$$\text{Assets} - \text{Liabilities} = \text{Owner's Equity}$$

The equation in this form illustrates the residual nature of the owner's equity. An owner's claims are secondary to the creditors' claims.

EFFECTS OF TRANSACTIONS ON THE ACCOUNTING EQUATION

A *business transaction* is an exchange of goods or services, and business transactions affect the elements of the accounting equation. However, regardless of what transactions a business completes, its accounting equation always remains in balance. Also, its assets always equal the combined claims of its creditors and its owner or owners. This may be demonstrated with the transactions of the law practice of Larry Owen, a single proprietorship business, which follow.

On July 1 Larry Owen began a new law practice by investing $2,500 of his personal cash, which he deposited in a bank account opened in the name of the business, Larry Owen, Attorney. After the investment, the one asset of the new business and the equity of Owen in the business are shown in the following equation:

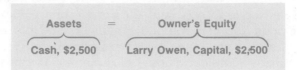

Assets	=	Owner's Equity
Cash, $2,500		Larry Owen, Capital, $2,500

Observe that after its first transaction the new business has one asset, cash, $2,500. Therefore, since it has no liabilities, the equity of Owen in the business is $2,500.

To continue the illustration, after the investment, (2) Owen used $600 of the business cash to pay the rent for three months in advance on suitable office space and (3) $1,200 to buy office equipment. These transactions were exchanges of cash for other assets. Their effects on the accounting equation are shown in color in Illustration 1–3. Observe that the equation remains in balance after each transaction.

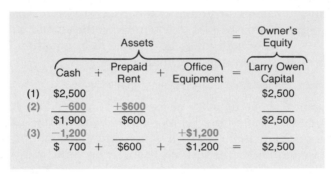

	Cash	+	Prepaid Rent	+	Office Equipment	=	Larry Owen Capital
(1)	$2,500						$2,500
(2)	−600		+$600				
	$1,900		$600				$2,500
(3)	−1,200				+$1,200		
	$ 700	+	$600	+	$1,200	=	$2,500

Illustration 1–3

Continuing the illustration, assume that Owen needed office supplies and additional equipment in the law office. However, he felt he should conserve the cash of the law practice. Consequently, he purchased on credit from Alpha Company office equipment costing $300 and office supplies that cost $60. The effects of this transaction (4) are shown in Illustration 1–4. Note that the assets were increased by the purchase. However, Owen's equity did not change because Alpha Company acquired a claim against the assets equal to the increase in the assets. The claim or amount owed Alpha Company is called an account payable.

A primary objective of a business is to increase the equity of its owner or owners by earning a profit or a net income. Owen's law practice will accomplish this objective by providing legal services to its clients on a fee basis. Of course, the practice will earn a net income only if legal fees earned are greater than the expenses incurred in

		Assets			=	Liabilities	+	Owner's Equity
	Cash +	Prepaid Rent +	Office Supplies +	Office Equipment	=	Accounts Payable	+	Larry Owen, Capital
(1)	$2,500							$2,500
(2)	−600	+600						
	$1,900	$600						$2,500
(3)	−1,200			+$1,200				
	$ 700	$600						$2,500
(4)			+$60	+300		+$360		
	$ 700 +	$600 +	$60 +	$1,500	=	$360	+	$2,500

Illustration 1–4

earning the fees. Legal fees earned and expenses incurred affect the elements of an accounting equation. To illustrate their effects, assume that on July 12 Larry Owen completed legal work for a client (transaction 5) and immediately collected $400 in cash for the services rendered. Also, the same day (transaction 6) he paid the salary of the office secretary for the first two weeks of July, a $250 expense of the business. The effects of these transactions are shown in Illustration 1–5.

Observe first the effects of the legal fee. The $400 fee is a revenue, an inflow of assets from the sale of services. Note that the revenue not only increased the asset cash but also caused a $400 increase in Owen's equity. Owen's equity increased because total assets increased without an increase in liabilities.

Next observe the effects of paying the secretary's $250 salary, an

		Assets			=	Liabilities	+	Owner's Equity
	Cash +	Prepaid Rent +	Office Supplies +	Office Equipment	=	Accounts Payable	+	Larry Owen, Capital
(1)	$2,500							$2,500
(2)	−600	+$600						
	$1,900	$600						$2,500
(3)	−1,200			+$1,200				
	$ 700	$600		$1,200				$2,500
(4)			+$60	+300		+$360		
	$ 700	$600	$60	$1,500		$360		$2,500
(5)	+400							+400
	$1,100	$600	$60	$1,500		$360		$2,900
(6)	−250							−250
	$ 850 +	$600 +	$60 +	$1,500	=	$360	+	$2,650

Illustration 1–5

expense. Note that the effects are opposite those of a revenue. Expenses are goods and services consumed in the operation of a business. In this instance the business consumed the secretary's services. When the services were paid for, both the assets and Owen's equity in the business decreased. Owen's equity decreased because cash decreased without an increase in other assets or a decrease in liabilities.

Now note this about earning a net income. A business earns a net income when its revenues exceed its expenses, and the income increases both net assets and the equity of the owner or owners. (*Net assets* are the excess of assets over liabilities.) Net assets increase because more assets flow into the business from revenues than are consumed and flow out for expenses. The equity of the owner or owners increases because net assets increase. A net loss has opposite effects.

To simplify the material and emphasize the actual effects of revenues and expenses on owner's equity, in this first chapter revenues are added directly to and expenses are deducted from the owner's capital. However, this is not done in actual practice. In actual practice revenues and expenses are first accumulated in separate categories. They are then combined, and their combined effect, the net income or loss, is added to or deducted from owner's capital. A further discussion of this is deferred to later chapters.

REALIZATION PRINCIPLE

In transaction 5 the revenue inflow was in the form of cash. However, revenue inflows are not always in cash because of the *realization prin-*

		Assets					=	Liabilities	+	Owner's Equity
	Cash +	Accounts Receivable +	Prepaid Rent +	Office Supplies +	Office Equipment	=	Accounts Payable	+	Larry Owen, Capital
(1)	$2,500								$2,500
(2)	−600		+$600						
	$1,900		$600						$2,500
(3)	−1,200				+$1,200				
	$ 700		$600		$1,200				$2,500
(4)				+$60	+300		+$360		
	$ 700		$600	$60	$1,500		$360		$2,500
(5)	+400								+400
	$1,100		$600	$60	$1,500		$360		$2,900
(6)	−250								−250
	$ 850		$600	$60	$1,500		$360		$2,650
(7)		+750							+750
	$ 850	$750	$600	$60	$1,500		$360		$3,400
(8)	+750	−750							
	$1,600 +	0 +	$600 +	$60 +	$1,500		$360		$3,400

Illustration 1–6

ciple (also called the *recognition principle*), which governs the recognition of revenue. This principle (1) defines a revenue as an inflow of assets (not necessarily cash) in exchange for goods or services. (2) It requires that the revenue be recognized (entered in the accounting records as revenue) at the time, but not before, it is earned (which generally is at the time title to goods sold is transferred or services are rendered). (3) It also requires that the amount of revenue recognized be measured by the cash received plus the cash equivalent (fair value) of any other asset or assets received.

To demonstrate the recognition of a revenue inflow in a form other than cash, assume that (transaction 7) Larry Owen completed legal work for a client and sent the client a $750 bill for the services rendered. Also assume that ten days later the client paid in full (transaction 8) for the services rendered. The effects of the two transactions are shown in Illustration 1–6.

Observe in transaction 7 that the asset flowing into the business was the right to collect $750 from the client, an account receivable. Compare transactions 5 and 7 and note that they differ only as to the type of asset received. Next observe that the receipt of cash (ten days after the services were rendered) is nothing more than an exchange of assets, cash for the right to collect from the client. Also note that the receipt of cash did not affect Owen's equity because the revenue was recognized in accordance with the *realization principle* and Owen's equity was increased upon completion of the services rendered.

	Cash	+	Accounts Receivable	+	Prepaid Rent	+	Office Supplies	+	Office Equipment	=	Accounts Payable	+	Larry Owen, Capital
													Assets ... *= Liabilities + Owner's Equity*
(1)	$2,500												$2,500
(2)	−600				+$600								
	$1,900				$600								$2,500
(3)	−1,200								+$1,200				
	$ 700				$600				$1,200				$2,500
(4)							+$60		+300		+$360		
	$ 700				$600		$60		$1,500		$360		$2,500
(5)	+400												+400
	$1,100				$600		$60		$1,500		$360		$2,900
(6)	−250												−250
	$ 850				$600		$60		$1,500		$360		$2,650
(7)			+$750										+750
	$ 850		$750		$600		$60		$1,500		$360		$3,400
(8)	+750		−750										
	$1,600		0		$600		$60		$1,500		$360		$3,400
(9)	−100										−100		
	$1,500 +				$600 +		$60 +		$1,500 =		$260 +		$3,400

Illustration 1–7

As a final transaction assume that on July 30 Larry Owen paid Alpha Company $100 of the $360 owed for the equipment and supplies purchased in transaction 4. This transaction reduced in equal amounts both assets and liabilities, and its effects are shown in Illustration 1–7 on the previous page.

IMPORTANT TRANSACTION EFFECTS

Look again at Illustration 1–7 and observe that every transaction affected at least two items in the equation; and in each case, after the effects were entered in the columns, the equation remained in balance. The accounting system you are beginning to study is called a *double-entry system*. It is based on the fact that every transaction affects two or more items in an accounting equation such as that in Illustration 1–7 and requires a "double entry" or, in other words, entries in two or more places. Also, the fact that the equation remained in balance after each transaction is important, for this is a proof of the accuracy with which the transactions were recorded.

BASES OF REVENUE RECOGNITION

Returning to the discussion of revenue recognition, the Accounting Principles Board ruled that revenue is realized and in most cases should be recognized in the accounting records upon the completion of a sale or when services have been performed and are billable.[5] This is known as the *sales basis of revenue recognition*. Under it a sale is considered to be completed when assets such as cash or the right to collect cash within a short period of time are received in exchange for goods sold or services rendered. Theoretically, revenue is earned throughout the entire performance of a service or throughout the whole process of securing goods for sale, taking a customer's order, and delivering the goods.[6] Yet, until all steps are completed and there is a right to collect the sale price, the requirements of the *objectivity principle* are not fulfilled and revenue is not recognized.

An exception to the required use of the sales basis is made for installment sales when payments are to be made over a relatively long period of time and there is considerable doubt as to the amounts that ultimately will be collected. For such sales, when collection of the full sale price is in doubt, revenue may be recognized as it is collected in cash.[7] This is known as the *cash basis of revenue recognition*.

A second exception to the required use of the sales basis applies

---

[5] APB, "Omnibus Opinion—1966," *APB Opinion No. 10* (New York: AICPA, December 1966), par. 12.

[6] *APB Statement No. 4*, par. 149.

[7] *APB Opinion No. 10*, par. 12.

to construction firms. Large construction jobs often take two or more years to complete. Consequently, if a construction firm has only a few jobs in process at any time and it recognizes revenue on a sales basis (upon the completion of each job), it may have a year in which no jobs are completed and no revenue is recognized even though the year is one of heavy activity. As a result, construction firms may and do recognize revenue on a *percentage-of-completion basis.* Under this basis, for example, if a firm has incurred 40% of the estimated cost to complete a job, it may recognize 40% of the job's contract price as revenue.

Space does not permit a full discussion of the cash basis and the percentage-of-completion basis of revenue recognition. This must be reserved for a more advanced text.

GLOSSARY

Accounting. The art of recording, classifying, reporting, and interpreting the financial data of an organization.

Accounting concept. An abstract idea that serves as a basis in the interpretation of accounting information.

Accounting equation. An expression in dollar amounts of the equivalency of the assets and equities of an enterprise, usually stated Assets = Liabilities + Owner's Equity. Also called a *balance sheet equation.*

Accounting principle. A broad rule adopted by the accounting profession as a guide in measuring, recording, and reporting the financial affairs and activities of a business.

Account payable. A debt owed to a creditor for goods or services purchased on credit.

Account receivable. An amount receivable from a debtor for goods or services sold on credit.

AICPA. American Institute of Certified Public Accountants, the professional association of certified public accountants in the United States.

APB. Accounting Principles Board, a committee of the AICPA that was responsible for formulating accounting principles.

Asset. A property or economic resource owned by an individual or enterprise.

Audit. A critical exploratory review by a public accountant of the business methods and accounting records of an enterprise, made to enable the accountant to express an opinion as to whether the financial statements of the enterprise fairly reflect its financial position and operating results.

Balance sheet. A financial report showing the assets, liabilities, and owner equity of an enterprise on a specific date. Also called a *position statement.*

Balance sheet equation. Another name for the *accounting equation.*

Bookkeeping. The record-making phase of accounting.

Budgeting. The phase of accounting dealing with planning the activities of an enterprise and comparing its actual accomplishments with the plan.

Business entity concept. The idea that a business is separate and distinct from its owner or owners and from every other business.

Business transaction. An exchange of goods, services, money, and/or the right to collect money.

Capital stock. Ownership equity in a corporation resulting from the sale of shares of the corporation's stock to its stockholders.

Continuing-concern concept. The idea that a business is a going concern that will continue to operate, using its assets to carry on its operations and, with the exception of merchandise, not offering the assets for sale.

Controller. The chief accounting officer of a large business.

Corporation. A business incorporated under the laws of a state or other jurisdiction.

Cost accounting. The phase of accounting that deals with collecting and controlling the costs of producing a given product or service.

Cost principle. The accounting rule that requires assets and services plus any resulting liabilities to be taken into the accounting records at cost.

CPA. Certified public accountant, an accountant who has met legal requirements as to age, education, experience, residence, and moral character and is licensed to practice public accounting.

Creditor. A person or enterprise to whom a debt is owed.

Debtor. A person or enterprise that owes a debt.

Equity. A right, claim, or interest in property.

Expense. Goods or services consumed in operating an enterprise.

FASB. Financial Accounting Standards Board, the seven-member board which replaced the Accounting Principles Board and has the authority to formulate rules governing the practice of accounting.

General accounting. That phase of accounting dealing primarily with recording transactions and preparing financial statements.

Going-concern concept. Another name for the *continuing-concern concept.*

Income statement. A financial statement showing revenues earned by a business, the expenses incurred in earning the revenues, and the resulting net income or net loss.

Internal auditing. A continuing examination of the records and procedures of a business by its own internal audit staff to determine if
established procedures and management directives are being followed.

Liability. A debt owed.

Management advisory services. The phase of public accounting dealing with the design, installation, and improvement of a client's
accounting system, plus advice on planning, budgeting, forecasting, and all other phases of accounting.

Net assets. Assets minus liabilities.

Net income. The excess of revenues over expenses.

Net loss. The excess of expenses over revenues.

Objectivity principle. The accounting rule requiring that wherever
possible the amounts used in recording transactions be based on
objective evidence rather than on subjective judgments.

Owner's equity. The equity of the owner (or owners) of a business
in the assets of the business.

Partnership. A business owned by two or more people as partners.

Position statement. Another name for the *balance sheet.*

Price-level-adjusted statements. Financial statements showing
amounts adjusted for changes in the purchasing power of money.

Realization principle. The accounting rule that defines a revenue
as an inflow of assets, not necessarily cash, in exchange for goods
or services and requires the revenue to be recognized at the time,
but not before, it is earned.

Recognition principle. Another name for the *realization principle.*

Revenue. An inflow of assets, not necessarily cash, in exchange for
goods and services sold.

Shareholder. A person or enterprise owning a share or shares of stock
in a corporation. Also called a *stockholder.*

Single proprietorship. A business owned by one individual.

Stable-dollar concept. The idea that the purchasing power of the unit
of measure used in accounting, the dollar, does not change.

Stockholder. Another name for a *shareholder.*

Tax services. The phase of public accounting dealing with the preparation of tax returns and with advice as to how transactions may
be completed in a way as to incur the smallest tax liability.

QUESTIONS FOR CLASS DISCUSSION

1. What is the nature of accounting and what is its function?
2. How does a business executive use accounting information?
3. Why do the states license certified public accountants?

4. What is the purpose of an audit? What do certified public accountants do when they make an audit?
5. A public accountant may provide management advisory services. Of what does this consist?
6. What do the tax services of a public accountant include beyond preparing tax returns?
7. Differentiate between accounting and bookkeeping.
8. What does an income statement show?
9. As the word is used in accounting, what is a revenue? An expense?
10. Why is the period of time covered by an income statement of extreme significance?
11. What does a balance sheet show?
12. Define (a) asset, (b) liability, (c) equity, and (d) owner's equity.
13. Why is a business treated as a separate entity for accounting purposes?
14. What is required by the cost principle? Why is such a principle necessary?
15. Why are not balance sheet amounts for the assets of a business changed from time to time to reflect changes in market values?
16. A business shows office stationery on its balance sheet at its $50 cost, although the stationery can be sold for not more than $0.25 as scrap paper. What accounting principle and concept justify this?
17. In accounting, transactions are measured, recorded, and reported in terms of dollars and the dollar is assumed to be a stable unit of measure. Is the dollar a stable unit of measure?
18. What are generally accepted accounting principles?
19. Why are the *Statements* of the Financial Accounting Standards Board and the *Opinions* of the Accounting Principles Board of importance to accounting students?
20. How does separate legal entity affect the responsibility of a corporation's stockholders for the debts of the corporation? Does this responsibility or lack of responsibility for the debts of the business apply to the owner or owners of a single proprietorship or partnership business?
21. What is the balance sheet equation? What is its importance to accounting students?
22. Is it possible for a transaction to increase or decrease a single liability without affecting any other asset, liability, or owner's equity item?
23. In accounting, what does the realization principle require?

CLASS EXERCISES

Exercise 1-1

On May 31 of the current year the balance sheet of Hillside Shop, a single proprietorship, showed the following:

Cash	1,500
Other assets	30,000
Accounts payable	15,000
Jack Hill, capital	16,500

On that date Jack Hill sold the "Other assets" for $20,000 in preparation for ending and liquidating the business of Hillside Shop.

Required:

1. Prepare a balance sheet for the shop as it would appear immediately after the sale of the assets.
2. Tell how the shop's cash should be distributed in ending the business and why.

Exercise 1–2

Determine the missing amount on each of the following lines:

	Assets	=	*Liabilities*	+	*Owner's Equity*
a.	$32,600		$8,400		$?
b.	28,800		?		16,500
c.	?		7,200		12,500

Exercise 1–3

Describe a transaction that will—

a. Increase an asset and decrease an asset.
b. Increase an asset and increase a liability.
c. Decrease an asset and decrease a liability.
d. Increase an asset and increase owner's equity.
e. Decrease an asset and decrease owner's equity.

Exercise 1–4

A business had the following assets and liabilities at the beginning and at the end of a year:

	Assets	*Liabilities*
Beginning of the year	$65,000	$20,000
End of the year	70,000	10,000

Determine the net income or net loss of the business during the year under each of the following unrelated assumptions:

a. The owner of the business made no additional investments in the business and no withdrawals of assets from the business during the year.
b. The owner made no additional investments in the business during the year but had withdrawn $1,500 per month to pay personal living expenses.
c. During the year the owner had made no withdrawals but had made a $20,000 additional investment in the business.
d. The owner had withdrawn $1,000 from the business each month to pay personal living expenses and near the year-end had invested an additional $10,000 in the business.

Exercise 1–5

Jane Ball began the practice of dentistry and during a short period completed these transactions:

a. Invested $3,000 in cash and dental equipment having a $2,000 fair value in a dental practice.
b. Paid the rent on suitable office space for two months in advance, $1,200.
c. Purchased additional dental equipment for cash, $500.
d. Completed dental work for a patient and immediately collected $100 cash for the work.
e. Completed dental work for a patient on credit, $600.
f. Purchased additional dental equipment on credit, $400.
g. Paid the dental assistant's wages, $300.
h. Collected $200 of the amount owed by the patient of transaction (e).
i. Paid for the equipment purchased in transaction (f).

Required:

Arrange the following asset, liability, and owner's equity titles in an equation form like Illustration 1–7: Cash; Accounts Receivable; Prepaid Rent; Dental Equipment; Accounts Payable; and Jane Ball, Capital. Then show by additions and subtractions the effects of the transactions on the elements of the equation. Show new totals after each transaction.

Exercise 1–6

On October 1 of the current year Ted Lee began the practice of law, and on October 31 his records showed the following asset, liability, and owner's equity items including revenues earned and expenses. From the information, prepare an income statement for the month and a month-end balance sheet like Illustration 1–2. Head the statements Ted Lee, Attorney. (The October 31, $2,500 amount for Lee's capital is the amount of his capital after it was increased and decreased by the October revenues and expenses shown.)

Cash	$ 600	Ted Lee, capital	$2,500
Accounts receivable	200	Legal fees earned	1,200
Prepaid rent	300	Rent expense	300
Law library	1,500	Salaries expense	400
Accounts payable	100	Telephone expense	50

PROBLEMS

Problem 1–1

Sue Davis began the practice of dentistry and during a short period completed the following transactions:

a. Sold for $18,765 a personal investment in General Electric stock, which she had inherited, and deposited $18,000 of the proceeds in a bank account opened in the name of the practice.
b. Purchased for $50,000 a small building to be used as an office. She paid $15,000 in cash and signed a mortgage contract promising to pay the balance over a period of years.

c. Took dental equipment, which she had purchased in college, from home for use in the practice. The equipment has a $500 fair value.
d. Purchased dental supplies for cash, $400.
e. Purchased dental equipment on credit, $6,000.
f. Completed dental work for a patient and immediately collected $150 for the work done.
g. Paid the local newspaper $25 for a small notice of the opening of the practice.
h. Completed $135 of dental work for a patient, for which the patient paid $35 in cash and promised to pay the balance within a few days.
i. Made a $500 installment payment on the equipment purchased on credit in transaction (e).
j. The patient of transaction (h) paid $50 of the amount he owed.
k. Paid the dental assistant's wages, $300.
l. Sue Davis withdrew $200 from the bank account of the dental practice to pay personal living expenses.

Required:

1. Arrange the following asset, liability, and owner's equity titles in an equation like Illustration 1–7: Cash; Accounts Receivable; Dental Supplies; Dental Equipment; Building; Accounts Payable; Mortgage Payable; and Sue Davis, Capital.
2. Show by additions and subtractions, as in Illustration 1–7, the effects of each transaction on the elements of the equation. Show new totals after each transaction.

Problem 1–2

Ned Hall, a young lawyer, began the practice of law and completed these transactions during August of the current year:

Aug. 1 Transferred $3,000 from his personal savings account to a checking account opened in the name of the law practice, Ned Hall, Attorney.
  1 Rented the furnished office of a lawyer who was retiring, and paid cash for three months' rent in advance, $900.
  1 Purchased the law library of the retiring lawyer for $2,000, paying $500 in cash and agreeing to pay the balance within one year.
  3 Purchased office supplies for cash, $50.
  8 Completed legal work for a client and immediately collected $150 in cash for the work done.
  9 Purchased law books on credit, $300.
  14 Completed legal work for Guaranty Bank on credit, $600.
  18 Purchased office supplies on credit, $25.
  19 Paid for the law books purchased on August 9.
  22 Completed legal work for Apex Realty on credit, $750.
  24 Received $600 from Guaranty Bank for the work completed on August 14.
  31 Paid the office secretary's salary, $800.
  31 Paid the monthly utility bills, $80.

Aug. 31   Recognized that one month's rent on the office had expired and become an expense. (Reduce the prepaid rent and the owner's equity.)

31   Took an inventory of unused office supplies and determined that $25 of supplies had been used and had become an expense.

Required:

1.   Arrange the following asset, liability, and owner's equity titles in an equation like Illustration 1–7: Cash; Accounts Receivable; Prepaid Rent; Office Supplies; Law Library; Accounts Payable; and Ned Hall, Capital.
2.   Show by additions and subtractions the effects of each transaction on the items of the equation. Show new totals after each transaction.
3.   Prepare for the law practice an August 31 balance sheet like Illustration 1–2.
4.   Analyze the increases and decreases in the last column of the equation and prepare an August income statement for the practice.

Problem 1–3

The records of June Cole's accounting practice show the following assets and liabilities as of the ends of 1980 and 1981:

	December 31	
	1980	*1981*
Cash	$1,100	$ 600
Accounts receivable	3,800	5,300
Prepaid rent	500	
Office supplies.............	200	100
Prepaid insurance	400	500
Office equipment	4,200	4,800
Land		15,000
Building		35,000
Accounts payable	500	600
Note payable...............		2,500
Mortgage payable		40,000

During the last week of December 1981, Ms. Cole purchased in the name of the accounting practice, June Cole, CPA, a small office building and moved the practice from rented quarters to the new building. The building and the land it occupied cost $50,000. The practice paid $10,000 in cash and assumed a mortgage liability for the balance. Ms. Cole had to invest an additional $6,000 in the practice to enable it to pay the $10,000. The practice earned a satisfactory net income during 1981, which enabled Ms. Cole to withdraw $1,500 per month from the business to pay her personal living expenses.

Required:

1.   Prepare balance sheets for the practice as of the ends of 1980 and 1981.
2.   Calculate the amount of net income earned by the practice during 1981.

Problem 1–4

Gary Blake graduated from college in June of the current year with a degree in architecture and on July 1 began the practice of his profession by investing $3,000 in cash in the business. He then completed these additional transactions:

July 1 Rented the furnished office and equipment of an architect who was retiring, paying $1,500 cash for three months' rent in advance.
     1 Purchased drafting supplies for cash, $65.
     2 Purchased insurance protection for one year in advance for cash by paying the premiums on two policies, $360.
     4 Completed architectural work for a client and immediately collected $150 cash for the work done.
     8 Completed architectural work for Valley Realty on credit, $750.
    15 Paid the salary of the draftsman, $400.
    18 Received payment in full for the work completed for Valley Realty on July 8.
    19 Completed architectural work for Western Contractors on credit, $450.
    20 Purchased additional drafting supplies on credit, $25.
    23 Completed architectural work for Dale West on credit, $500.
    27 Purchased additional drafting supplies on credit, $40.
    29 Received payment in full from Western Contractors for the work completed on July 19.
    30 Paid for the drafting supplies purchased on July 20.
    31 Paid the July telephone bill, $25.
    31 Paid the July utilities expense, $35.
    31 Paid the salary of the draftsman, $400.
    31 Recognized that one month's office rent had expired and become an expense. (Reduce the prepaid rent and owner's equity to record the expense.)
    31 Recognized that one month's prepaid insurance, $30, had expired.
    31 Took an inventory of drafting supplies and determined that $60 of drafting supplies had been used and had become an expense.

Required:
1. Arrange the following asset, liability, and owner's equity titles in an equation like Illustration 1–7: Cash; Accounts Receivable; Prepaid Rent; Prepaid Insurance; Drafting Supplies; Accounts Payable; and Gary Blake, Capital.
2. Show the effects of the transactions on the elements of the equation by recording increases and decreases in the appropriate columns. Indicate an increase with a + and a decrease with a − before the amount. *Do not determine new totals for the items of the equation after each transaction.*
3. After recording the last transaction, determine and insert on the next line the final total for each item of the equation and determine if the equation is in balance.
4. Prepare a July 31 balance sheet for the practice like the one in Illustration 1–2. Head the statement Gary Blake, Architect.

5. Analyze the items in the last column of the equation and prepare a July income statement for the practice.

ALTERNATE PROBLEMS

Problem 1–1A

Sue Davis began the practice of dentistry and during a short period completed these transactions:

a. Sold a personal investment in IBM stock that she had inherited for $19,250 and deposited $19,000 of the proceeds in a bank account opened in the name of the practice.
b. Purchased the office building and dental equipment of a dentist who was retiring. The building had a $48,000 fair value, and the equipment had a $12,000 fair value. Paid the retiring dentist $15,000 in cash and signed a mortgage contract promising to pay the balance over a period of years.
c. Purchased dental supplies for cash, $350.
d. Purchased additional dental equipment on credit, $500.
e. Completed dental work for a patient and immediately collected $100 for the work done.
f. Paid the local newspaper $50 for a small notice of the opening of the practice.
g. Completed dental work for a patient on credit, $350.
h. Made a $250 installment payment on the equipment purchased in transaction (d).
i. Completed $300 of dental work for a patient. The patient paid $150 cash and promised to pay the balance within a short period.
j. The patient of transaction (g) paid in full for her dental work.
k. Paid the dental assistant's wages, $400.
l. Sue Davis withdrew $250 from the bank account of the practice to pay personal expenses.

Required:

1. Arrange the following asset, liability, and owner's equity titles in an equation like Illustration 1–7: Cash; Accounts Receivable; Dental Supplies; Dental Equipment; Building; Accounts Payable; Mortgage Payable; and Sue Davis, Capital.
2. Show by additions and subtractions, as in Illustration 1–7, the effects of each transaction on the elements of the equation. Show new totals after each transaction.

Problem 1–2A

Ned Hall began the practice of law and completed these transactions during October of the current year.

Oct. 2   Sold a personal investment in Xerox stock for $2,650 and deposited $2,500 of the proceeds in a bank account opened in the name of the law practice, Ned Hall, Attorney.
      2   Rented the furnished office of a lawyer who was retiring, and paid cash for two months' rent in advance, $550.

Oct. 2 Moved from home to the law office law books acquired in college. (In other words, invested the books in the practice.) The books had a $500 fair value.

4 Purchased office supplies for cash, $65.

6 Purchased additional law books on credit, $600.

8 Completed legal work for a client and immediately collected $125 in cash for the work done.

12 Completed legal work for Valley Bank on credit, $650.

16 Made a $200 installment payment on the law books purchased on October 6.

21 Completed legal work for Vista Realty on credit, $550.

22 Received $650 from Valley Bank for the work completed on October 12.

31 Paid the salary of the office secretary, $700.

31 Paid the October telephone bill, $25.

31 Recognized that one month's rent on the office had expired and become an expense. (Reduce the prepaid rent and the owner's equity.)

31 Took an inventory of unused office supplies and determined that $30 of supplies had been used and had become an expense.

Required:

1. Arrange the following asset, liability, and owner's equity titles in an equation like Illustration 1–7: Cash; Accounts Receivable; Prepaid Rent; Office Supplies; Law Library; Accounts Payable; and Ned Hall, Capital.
2. Show by additions and subtractions the effects of each transaction on the items of the equation. Show new totals after each transaction.
3. Prepare an October 31 balance sheet for the law practice like the one in Illustration 1–2.
4. Analyze the increases and decreases in the last column of the equation and prepare an October income statement for the practice.

Problem 1–3A

The records of Teresa Juarez's dental practice show the following assets and liabilities as of the ends of 1980 and 1981:

	December 31	
	1980	*1981*
Cash	$1,400	$ 500
Accounts receivable	3,200	3,600
Prepaid rent	600	
Office supplies............	300	200
Prepaid insurance	500	800
Office equipment	8,700	9,100
Land		20,000
Building		65,000
Accounts payable	300	800
Note payable		5,000
Mortgage payable		60,000

During the last week of December 1981, Dr. Juarez purchased in the name of the dental practice, Teresa Juarez, DDS, a small office building and moved her practice from rented quarters to the new building. The building and the land it occupies cost $85,000. The practice paid $25,000 in cash and assumed a mortgage liability for the balance. Dr. Juarez had to borrow $5,000 in the name of the practice, signing a $5,000 note payable, and invest an additional $15,000 in the practice to enable it to pay the $25,000. The practice earned a satisfactory net income during 1981, which enabled Dr. Juarez to withdraw $1,500 per month from the practice to pay her personal living expenses.

Required:

1. Prepare balance sheets for the practice as of the ends of 1980 and 1981.
2. Prepare a calculation to show the amount of net income earned by the practice during 1981.

Problem 1–4A

Gary Blake received his degree in architecture in June of the current year and on July 1 began the practice of his profession by investing $2,500 in cash in the practice. He then completed these additional transactions:

July 1 Rented the office and equipment of an architect who was retiring, paying $1,200 cash for three months' rent in advance.
    1 Purchased insurance protection for one year by paying the premium on two policies, $300.
    2 Purchased drafting supplies for cash, $75.
    5 Completed a short architectural assignment for a client and immediately collected $100 cash for the work done.
    8 Purchased additional drafting supplies on credit, $35.
    10 Completed architectural work for Ajax Contractors on credit, $650.
    15 Paid the salary of the draftsman, $350.
    18 Paid for the drafting supplies purchased on July 8.
    20 Received payment in full from Ajax Contractors for the work completed on July 10.
    23 Completed architectural work for Valley Realtors on credit, $450.
    26 Purchased additional drafting supplies on credit, $40.
    30 Completed additional architectural work for Ajax Contractors on credit, $500.
    31 Paid the salary of the draftsman, $350.
    31 Paid the July telephone bill, $20.
    31 Paid the July electric bill, $65.
    31 Recognized that one month's office rent had expired and become an expense. (Reduce the prepaid rent and the owner's equity to record the expense.)
    31 Recognized that one month's prepaid insurance, $25, had expired.
    31 Took an inventory of the unused drafting supplies and determined that supplies costing $60 had been used and had become an expense.

Required:

1. Arrange the following asset, liability, and owner's equity titles in an equation like Illustration 1–7: Cash; Accounts Receivable; Prepaid Rent; Prepaid Insurance; Drafting Supplies; Accounts Payable; and Gary Blake, Capital.

2. Show the effects of the transactions on the elements of the equation by recording increases and decreases in the appropriate columns. Indicate an increase with a + and a decrease with a − before the amount. *Do not determine new totals for the items after each transaction.*
3. After recording the last transaction, determine and enter on the next line the final total for each item and determine if the equation is in balance.
4. Prepare a July 31 balance sheet for the practice like the one in Illustration 1–2. Head the statement Gary Blake, Architect.
5. Analyze the items in the last column of the equation and prepare a July income statement for the practice.

PROVOCATIVE PROBLEMS

Provocative problem 1–1
Annual homecoming

Jerry Marsh invested $500 in a short-term enterprise, the sale of soft drinks during the annual homecoming celebration in his small town. He paid the town $100 for the exclusive right to sell soft drinks in the town park, the center of the celebration, and constructed a stand from which to make his sales, at a cost of $45 for lumber and crepe paper, none of which had any value at the end of the celebration. He bought ice for which he paid $40, and purchased soft drinks costing $500. At that point he had only $315 in cash and could not pay in full for the drinks, but since his credit rating was good, the soft drink company accepted $300 in cash and the promise that he would pay the balance the day after the celebration. During the celebration he collected $925 in cash from sales and at the end of the day paid $20 each to two boys hired to help with the sales. He also had soft drinks left over that cost $35 and could be returned to the soft drink company. Assemble the information in a manner that will enable you to prepare a balance sheet like that in Illustration 1–2 for Jerry Marsh as of the end of the celebration and an income statement showing the results of the day's operations.

Provocative problem 1–2
Speedway Service

Bob Hill ran out of money during his sophomore year in college and had to go to work. He could not find a satisfactory job; and since he owned a Honda motorcycle having an $1,800 fair value, he decided to go into business for himself. Consequently, he began Speedway Service with no assets other than the motorcycle. He kept no accounting records; and now, at the year-end, he has engaged you to determine the net income earned by the service during its first partial year of 45 weeks. You find that the service has a year-end bank balance of $800 plus $25 of undeposited cash, and local stores owe the service $150 for delivering packages during the past month. The service still owns the Honda, but from use it has depreciated $300 during the past 45 weeks. In addition the service has a new delivery truck that cost $6,200 and has depreciated $500 since its purchase, and on which the service still owes the finance company $3,500. When the truck was purchased, Bob Hill borrowed $1,000 from his father to help make the down payment. The loan was made to the delivery service, was interest free, and has not been repaid. Finally, since the service has been profitable from the beginning, Bob Hill has withdrawn $100 of its earnings each week for personal expenses.

Determine the net income earned by the service during the 45 weeks of its operations. Present figures to prove your answer.

part two
Processing accounting data

2

Recording transactions

After studying Chapter 2, you should be able to:

- Explain the mechanics of double-entry accounting and tell why transactions are recorded with equal debits and credits.
- State the rules of debit and credit and apply the rules in recording transactions.
- Tell the normal balance of any asset, liability, or owner's equity account.
- Record transactions in a General Journal, post to the ledger accounts, and prepare a trial balance to test the accuracy of the recording and posting.
- Define or explain the words and phrases listed in the chapter Glossary.

Transactions are the raw material of the accounting process. The process consists of identifying transactions, recording them, and summarizing their effects on periodic reports for the use of management and other decision makers.

Some years ago almost all concerns used pen and ink in recording transactions. However, today only small concerns use this method, concerns small enough that their bookkeeping can be done by one person working as bookkeeper a part of his or her day. Larger, modern concerns use electric bookkeeping machines, computers, punched cards, and magnetic tape in recording transactions.

Nevertheless, most students begin their study of accounting by learning a double-entry accounting system based on pen and ink. There are several reasons for this. First, since accounting reports evolved from and are based on double entry, the effective use of these reports requires some understanding of the system. Second, there is little lost motion from learning the system, since almost everything about it is applicable to machine methods. Primarily the machines replace pen and ink as the recording medium, taking the drudgery out of the recording process. And last, for the student who will start, manage, or own a small business, one small enough to use a pen-and-ink system, the system applies as it is taught.

BUSINESS PAPERS

Business papers provide evidence of transactions completed and are the basis for accounting entries to record the transactions. For example, when goods are sold on credit, two or more copies of an invoice or sales ticket are prepared. One copy is enclosed with the goods or is delivered to the customer. The other is sent to the accounting department where it becomes the basis for an entry to record the sale. Also, when goods are sold for cash, the sales are commonly "rung up" on a cash register that prints the amount of each sale on a paper tape locked inside the register. At the end of the day, when the proper key is depressed, the register prints on the tape the total cash sales for the day. The tape is then removed and becomes the basis for an entry to record the sales. Also, when an established business purchases assets, it normally buys on credit and receives an invoice that becomes the basis for an entry to record the purchase. Likewise, when the invoice is paid, a check is issued and the check or a carbon copy becomes the basis for an entry to record the payment. Obviously then, business papers are the starting point in the accounting process. Furthermore, verifiable business papers, particularly those originating outside the business, are also objective evidence of transactions completed and the amounts at which they should be recorded, as required by the *objectivity principle*.

ACCOUNTS

A concern with an accounting system based on pen and ink or electric bookkeeping machines uses *accounts* in recording its transactions. A number of accounts are normally required, with a separate account being used for summarizing the increases and decreases in each asset, liability, and owner's equity item appearing on the balance sheet and each revenue and expense appearing on the income statement.

In its most simple form an account looks like the letter "T," is called a *T-account,* and appears as follows:

(Place for the Name of the Item Recorded in This Account)	
(Left side)	(Right side)

Note that the "T" gives the account a left side, a right side, and a place for the name of the item, the increases and decreases of which are recorded therein.

When a T-account is used in recording increases and decreases in an item, the increases are placed on one side of the account and the decreases on the other. For example, if the increases and decreases in the cash of Larry Owen's law practice of the previous chapter are recorded in a T-account, they appear as follows:

Cash			
Investment	2,500	Prepayment of rent	600
Legal fee earned	400	Equipment purchase	1,200
Collection of account		Salary payment	250
receivable	750	Payment on account	
		payable	100

The reason for putting the increases on one side and the decreases on the other is that this makes it easy to add the increases and then add the decreases. The sum of the decreases may then be subtracted from the sum of the increases to learn how much of the item recorded in the account the company has, owns, or owes. For example, the increases in the cash of the Owen law practice were:

Investment	$2,500
Legal fee earned	400
Collection of an account receivable ..	750
Sum of the increases	$3,650

And the decreases were:

Prepayment of office rent	$ 600
Equipment purchase	1,200
Salary payment	250
Payment on account payable ..	100
Sum of the decreases ..	$2,150

And when the sum of the decreases is subtracted from the sum of the increases,

Sum of the increases	$3,650
Sum of the decreases	2,150
Balance of cash remaining ..	$1,500

the subtraction shows the law practice has $1,500 of cash remaining.

Balance of an account

When the increases and decreases recorded in an account are separately added and the sum of the decreases is subtracted from the sum of the increases, the procedure is called determining the *account balance*. The balance of an account is the difference between its increases and decreases. It is also the amount of the item recorded in the account that the company has, owns, or owes at the time the balance is determined.

ACCOUNTS COMMONLY USED

A business uses a number of accounts in recording its transactions. However, the specific accounts used vary from one concern to another, depending upon the assets owned, the debts owed, and the information to be secured from the accounting records. Nevertheless, although the specific accounts vary, the accounts that are discussed beginning on the next page are common.

Asset accounts

If useful records of a concern's assets are to be kept, an individual account is needed for each kind of asset owned. Some of the more common assets for which accounts are maintained are as follows:

Cash   Increases and decreases in cash are recorded in an account called Cash. The cash of a business consists of money or any medium of exchange that a bank will accept at face value for deposit. It includes coins, currency, checks, and postal and bank money orders. The balance of the Cash account shows both the cash on hand in the store or office and that on deposit in the bank.

Notes receivable   A formal written promise to pay a definite sum of money at a fixed future date is called a *promissory note.* When amounts due from others are evidenced by promissory notes, the notes are known as notes receivable and are recorded in a Notes Receivable account.

Accounts receivable   Goods and services are commonly sold to customers on the basis of oral or implied promises of future payment. Such sales are known as sales on credit or sales on account; and the oral or implied promises to pay are known as accounts receivable. Accounts receivable are increased by sales on credit and are decreased by customer payments. Since it is necessary to know the amount currently owed by each customer, a separate record must be kept of each customer's purchases and payments. However, a discussion of this separate record is deferred until Chapter 7, and for the present all increases and decreases in accounts receivable are recorded in a single account called Accounts Receivable.

Prepaid insurance   Fire, liability, and other types of insurance protection are normally paid for in advance. The amount paid is called a premium and may give protection from loss for from one to five years. As a result, a large portion of each premium is an asset for a considerable time after payment. When insurance premiums are paid, the asset "prepaid insurance" is increased by the amount paid. The increase is normally recorded in an account called Prepaid Insurance. Day by day, insurance premiums expire. Consequently, at intervals the insurance that has expired is calculated and the balance of the Prepaid Insurance account is reduced accordingly.

Office supplies   Stamps, stationery, paper, pencils, and like items are known as office supplies. They are assets when purchased, and continue to be assets until consumed. As they are consumed, the amounts consumed become expenses. Increases and decreases in the asset "office supplies" are commonly recorded in an account called Office Supplies.

Store supplies   Wrapping paper, cartons, bags, string, and similar items used by a store are known as store supplies. Increases and decreases in store supplies are recorded in an account of that name.

Other prepaid expenses   Prepaid expenses are items that are assets at the time of purchase but become expenses as they are consumed or used. Prepaid insurance, office supplies, and store supplies are examples. Other examples are prepaid rent, prepaid taxes, and prepaid wages. Each is accounted for in a separate account.

Equipment   Increases and decreases in such things as typewriters, desks, chairs, and office machines are commonly recorded in an account called Office Equipment. Likewise, changes in the amount of counters, showcases, cash registers, and like items used by a store are recorded in an account called Store Equipment.

Buildings   A building used by a business in carrying on its operations may be a store, garage, warehouse, or factory. However, regardless of use, an account called Buildings is commonly employed in recording the increases and decreases in the buildings owned by a business and used in carrying on its operations.

Land   An account called Land is commonly used in recording increases and decreases in the land owned by a business. Land and the buildings placed upon it are inseparable in physical fact. Nevertheless, it is usually desirable to account for land and its buildings in separate accounts because buildings depreciate and wear out but land does not.

Liability accounts

Most companies do not have as many liability accounts as asset accounts; however, the following are common:

Notes payable   Increases and decreases in amounts owed because of promissory notes given to creditors are accounted for in an account called Notes Payable.

Accounts payable   An account payable is an amount owed to a creditor. Accounts payable result from the purchase of merchandise, supplies, equipment, and services on credit. Since it is necessary to know the amount owed each creditor, an individual record must be kept of the purchases from and the payments to each. However, a discussion of this individual record is deferred until Chapter 7, and for the present all increases and decreases in accounts payable are recorded in a single Accounts Payable account.

Unearned revenues   The *realization principle* requires that revenue be earned before it is recognized as revenue. Therefore, when a company collects for its products or services before delivery, the amounts collected are unearned revenue. An unearned revenue is a liability that will be extinguished by delivering the product or service paid for in advance. Subscriptions collected in advance by a magazine publisher, rent collected in advance by a landlord, and legal fees collected in advance by a lawyer are examples. Upon receipt, the amounts collected are recorded in liability accounts such as Unearned Subscriptions, Unearned Rent, and Unearned Legal Fees. When earned by delivery, the amounts earned are transferred to the revenue accounts, Subscriptions Earned, Rent Earned, and Legal Fees Earned.

Other short-term payables   Wages payable, taxes payable, and interest payable are illustrations of other short-term liabilities for which individual accounts must be kept.

Mortgage payable   A *mortgage payable* is a long-term debt for which the creditor has a secured prior claim against some one or more of the debtor's assets. The mortgage gives the creditor the right to force the sale of the mortgaged assets through a foreclosure if the mortgage debt is not paid when due. An account called Mortgage Payable is commonly used in recording the increases and decreases in the amount owed on a mortgage.

Owner's equity accounts

Several kinds of transactions affect the equity of a business owner. In a single proprietorship these include the investment of the owner, his or her withdrawals of cash or other assets for personal use, revenues earned, and expenses incurred. In the previous chapter all such transactions were entered in a column under the name of the owner. This simplified the material of the chapter but made it necessary to analyze the items entered in the column in order to prepare an income statement. Fortunately such an analysis is not necessary. All that is required to avoid it is a number of accounts, a separate one for each owner's equity item appearing on the balance sheet and a separate one for each revenue and expense on the income statement. Then as each transaction affecting owner's equity is completed, it is recorded in the proper account. Among the accounts required are the following:

Capital account   When a person invests in a business of his or her own, the investment is recorded in an account carrying the owner's name and the word "Capital." For example, an account called Larry Owen, Capital is used in recording the investment of Larry Owen in his law practice. In addition to the original investment, the *capital account* is used for any permanent additional increases or decreases in owner's equity.

Withdrawals account   Usually a person invests in a business to earn income. However, income is earned over a period of time, say a year. Often during this period the business owner must withdraw a portion of the earnings to pay living expenses or for other personal uses. These withdrawals reduce both assets and owner's equity. To record them, an account carrying the name of the business owner and the word "Withdrawals" is used. For example, an account called Larry Owen, Withdrawals is used to record the withdrawals of cash by Larry Owen from his law practice. The *withdrawals account* is also known as the *personal account* or *drawing account*.

An owner of a small unincorporated business often withdraws a fixed amount each week or month for personal living expenses, and often thinks of these withdrawals as a salary. However, in a legal sense they are not a salary because the owner of an unincorporated business cannot enter into a legally binding contract with himself to hire himself and pay himself a salary. Consequently, in law and custom it is recognized that such withdrawals are neither a salary nor an expense of the business but are withdrawals in anticipation of earnings.

Revenue and expense accounts   When an income statement is prepared, it is necessary to know the amount of each kind of revenue earned and each kind of expense incurred during the period covered by the statement. To accumulate this information, a number of revenue and expense accounts are needed. However, all concerns do not have the same revenues and expenses. Consequently, it is impossible to list all revenue and expense accounts to be encountered. Nevertheless, Revenue from Repairs, Commissions Earned, Legal Fees Earned, Rent Earned, and Interest Earned are common examples of revenue accounts. And Advertising Expense, Store Supplies Expense, Office Salaries Expense, Office Supplies Expense, Rent Expense, Utilities Expense, and Insurance Expense are common examples of expense accounts. It should be noted that the kind of revenue or expense recorded in each above-mentioned account is evident from its title. This is generally true of such accounts.

Real and nominal accounts

To add to your vocabulary, it may be said here that balance sheet accounts are commonly called *real accounts*. Presumably this is because the items recorded in these accounts exist in objective form. Likewise, income statement accounts are called *nominal accounts* because items recorded in these accounts exist in name only.

THE LEDGER

A business may use from two dozen to several thousand accounts in recording its transactions. Each account is placed on a separate page in a bound or loose-leaf book, or on a separate card in a tray of cards. If the accounts are kept in a book, the book is called a *ledger*. If they are kept on cards in a file tray, the tray of cards is a ledger. Actually, as used in accounting, the word "ledger" means a group of accounts.

DEBIT AND CREDIT

As previously stated, a T-account has a left side and a right side. However, in accounting the left side is called the *debit* side, abbreviated "Dr."; and the right side is called the *credit* side, abbreviated "Cr." Furthermore, when amounts are entered on the left side of an account, they are called *debits,* and the account is said to be *debited.* When amounts are entered on the right side, they are called *credits,* and the account is said to be *credited.* The difference between the total debits and the total credits recorded in an account is the *balance of the account.* The balance may be either a *debit balance* or a *credit balance.* It is a debit balance when the sum of the debits exceeds the sum of the credits and a credit balance when the sum of the credits exceeds the sum of the debits. An account is said to be *in balance* when its debits and credits are equal.

The words "to debit" and "to credit" should not be confused with "to increase" and "to decrease." To debit means simply to enter an amount on the left side of an account. To credit means to enter an amount on the right side. Either may be an increase or a decrease. This may readily be seen by examining the way in which the investment of Larry Owen is recorded in his Cash and capital accounts which follow:

Cash	Larry Owen, Capital
Investment 2,500	Investment 2,500

When Owen invested $2,500 in his law practice, both the business cash and Owen's equity were increased. Observe in the accounts that the increase in cash is recorded on the left or debit side of the Cash account, while the increase in owner's equity is recorded on the right or credit side. The transaction is recorded in this manner because of the mechanics of *double-entry accounting.*

MECHANICS OF DOUBLE-ENTRY ACCOUNTING

The mechanics of double-entry accounting are such that every transaction affects and is recorded in two or more accounts with equal debits and credits. Transactions are so recorded because equal debits and credits offer a means of proving the recording accuracy. The proof is, if every transaction is recorded with equal debits and credits, then the debits in the ledger must equal the credits.

The person who first devised double-entry accounting based the system on the accounting equation, $A = L + OE$. He assigned the recording of increases in assets to the debit sides of asset accounts. He then recognized that equal debits and credits were possible only if increases in liabilities and owner's equity were recorded on the opposite or credit sides of liability and owner's equity accounts. In other words, he recognized that if increases in assets were to be recorded as debits, then increases and decreases in all accounts would have to be recorded as follows:

Assets		=	Liabilities		+	Owner's Equity	
Debit for increases	Credit for decreases		Debit for decreases	Credit for increases		Debit for decreases	Credit for increases

From the T-accounts it is possible to formulate rules for recording transactions under a double-entry system. The rules are:

1. Increases in assets are debited to asset accounts; consequently, decreases must be credited.
2. Increases in liability and owner's equity items are credited to liability and owner's equity accounts; consequently, decreases must be debited.

At this stage, beginning students will find it helpful to memorize these rules. They should also note that in a single proprietorship there are four kinds of owner's equity accounts: (1) the capital account, (2) the withdrawals account, (3) revenue accounts, and (4) expense accounts. Furthermore, for transactions affecting these accounts, students should observe these additional points:

1. The original investment of the owner of a business plus any more or less permanent changes in the investment are recorded in the capital account.
2. Withdrawals of assets for personal use, including cash to pay personal expenses, decrease owner's equity and are debited to the owner's withdrawals account.
3. Revenues increase owner's equity and are credited in each case to a revenue account that shows the kind of revenue earned.
4. Expenses decrease owner's equity and are debited in each case to an expense account that shows the kind of expense incurred.

TRANSACTIONS ILLUSTRATING THE RULES OF DEBIT AND CREDIT

The following transactions of Larry Owen's law practice illustrate the application of debit and credit rules. They also show how transactions are recorded in the accounts. The number preceding each transaction is used throughout the illustration to identify the transaction in the accounts. Note that most of the transactions are the same ones used in Chapter 1 to illustrate the effects of transactions on the accounting equation.

To record a transaction, it must be analyzed to determine what items are increased and decreased. The rules of debit and credit are then applied to determine the debit and credit effects of the increases or decreases. An analysis of each of the following transactions is given in order to demonstrate the process.

1. On July 1 Larry Owen invested $2,500 in a new law practice.

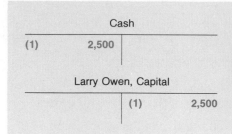

Analysis of the transaction: The transaction increased the cash of the practice and at the same time it increased the equity of Owen in the business. Increases in assets are debited, and increases in owner's equity are credited. Consequently, to record the transaction, Cash should be debited and Larry Owen, Capital should be credited for $2,500.

2. Paid the office rent for three months in advance, $600.

Cash		
(1) 2,500	(2)	600

Prepaid Rent	
(2) 600	

Analysis of the transaction: The asset prepaid rent, the right to occupy the office for three months, is increased; and the asset cash is decreased. Increases in assets are debited, and decreases are credited. Therefore, to record the transaction, debit Prepaid Rent and credit Cash for $600.

3. Purchased office equipment for cash, $1,200.

Cash		
(1) 2,500	(2)	600
	(3)	1,200

Office Equipment	
(3) 1,200	

Analysis of the transaction: The asset office equipment is increased, and the asset cash is decreased. Debit Office Equipment and credit Cash for $1,200.

4. Purchased on credit from Alpha Company office supplies, $60, and office equipment, $300.

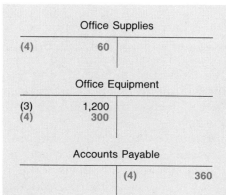

Analysis of the transaction: This transaction increased the assets office equipment and office supplies, but it also created a liability. Increases in assets are debits, and increases in liabilities are credits; therefore, debit Office Supplies for $60 and Office Equipment for $300 and credit Accounts Payable for $360.

5. Completed legal work for a client and immediately collected a $400 fee.

Cash			
(1)	2,500	(2)	600
(5)	400	(3)	1,200

Legal Fees Earned	
	(5) 400

Analysis of the transaction: This revenue transaction increased both assets and owner's equity. Increases in assets are debits, and increases in owner's equity are credits. Therefore, Cash is debited; and in order to show the nature of the increase in owner's equity and at the same time accumulate information for the income statement, the revenue account Legal Fees Earned is credited.

6. Paid the secretary's salary for the first two weeks of July, $250.

Cash			
(1)	2,500	(2)	600
(5)	400	(3)	1,200
		(6)	250

Office Salaries Expense	
(6) 250	

Analysis of the transaction: The secretary's salary is an expense that decreased both assets and owner's equity. Debit Office Salaries Expense to decrease owner's equity and also to accumulate information for the income statement, and credit Cash to record the decrease in cash.

7. Signed a contract with Coast Realty to do its legal work on a fixed-fee basis for $100 per month. Received the fee for the first month and a half in advance, $150.

Cash			
(1)	2,500	(2)	600
(5)	400	(3)	1,200
(7)	150	(6)	250

Unearned Legal Fees	
	(7) 150

Analysis of the transaction: The $150 inflow increased cash, but the inflow is not a revenue until earned. Its acceptance before being earned created a liability, the obligation to do the client's legal work for the next month and a half. Consequently, debit Cash to record the increase in cash and credit Unearned Legal Fees to record the liability increase.

8. Completed legal work for a client on credit and billed client $750 for the services rendered.

Accounts Receivable		
(8)	750	

Legal Fees Earned		
	(5)	400
	(8)	750

Analysis of the transaction: Completion of this revenue transaction gave the law practice the right to collect $750 from the client, and thus increased assets and owner's equity. Consequently, debit Accounts Receivable for the increase in assets and credit Legal Fees Earned to increase owner's equity and at the same time accumulate information for the income statement.

9. Paid the secretary's salary for the second two weeks of the month.

Cash			
(1)	2,500	(2)	600
(5)	400	(3)	1,200
(7)	150	(6)	250
		(9)	250

Office Salaries Expense		
(6)	250	
(9)	250	

Analysis of the transaction: An expense that decreased assets and owner's equity. Debit Office Salaries Expense to accumulate information for the income statement and credit Cash.

10. Larry Owen withdrew $200 from the law practice to pay personal expenses.

Cash			
(1)	2,500	(2)	600
(5)	400	(3)	1,200
(7)	150	(6)	250
		(9)	250
		(10)	200

Larry Owen, Withdrawals		
(10)	200	

Analysis of the transaction: This transaction reduced in equal amounts both assets and owner's equity. Cash is credited to record the asset reduction; and the Larry Owen, Withdrawals account is debited for the reduction in owner's equity.

11. The client paid the $750 legal fee billed in transaction 8.

	Cash		
(1)	2,500	(2)	600
(5)	400	(3)	1,200
(7)	150	(6)	250
(11)	750	(9)	250
		(10)	200

Analysis of the transaction: One asset was increased, and the other decreased. Debit Cash to record the increase in cash, and credit Accounts Receivable to record the decrease in the account receivable, or the decrease in the right to collect from the client.

	Accounts Receivable		
(8)	750	(11)	750

12. Paid Alpha Company $100 of the $360 owed for the items purchased on credit in transaction 4.

	Cash		
(1)	2,500	(2)	600
(5)	400	(3)	1,200
(7)	150	(6)	250
(11)	750	(9)	250
		(10)	200
		(12)	100

Analysis of the transaction: Payments to creditors decrease in like amounts both assets and liabilities. Decreases in liabilities are debited, and decreases in assets are credited. Debit Accounts Payable and credit Cash.

	Accounts Payable		
(12)	100	(4)	360

13. Paid the July telephone bill, $30.
14. Paid the July electric bill, $35.

	Cash		
(1)	2,500	(2)	600
(5)	400	(3)	1,200
(7)	150	(6)	250
(11)	750	(9)	250
		(10)	200
		(12)	100
		(13)	30
		(14)	35

Analysis of the transactions: These expense transactions are alike in that each decreased cash; they differ in each case as to the kind of expense involved. Consequently, in recording them, Cash is credited; and to accumulate information for the income statement, a different expense account, one showing the nature of the expense in each case, is debited.

	Telephone Expense	
(13)	30	

	Heating and Lighting Expense	
(14)	35	

THE ACCOUNTS AND THE EQUATION

In Illustration 2–1 the transactions of the Owen law practice are shown in the accounts, with the accounts brought together and classified under the elements of an accounting equation.

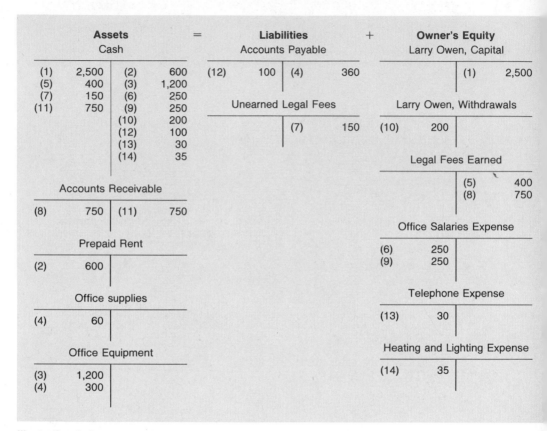

Assets	=	**Liabilities**	+	**Owner's Equity**

Cash

(1)	2,500	(2)	600
(5)	400	(3)	1,200
(7)	150	(6)	250
(11)	750	(9)	250
		(10)	200
		(12)	100
		(13)	30
		(14)	35

Accounts Receivable

| (8) | 750 | (11) | 750 |

Prepaid Rent

| (2) | 600 |

Office supplies

| (4) | 60 |

Office Equipment

| (3) | 1,200 |
| (4) | 300 |

Accounts Payable

| (12) | 100 | (4) | 360 |

Unearned Legal Fees

| | | (7) | 150 |

Larry Owen, Capital

| | | (1) | 2,500 |

Larry Owen, Withdrawals

| (10) | 200 |

Legal Fees Earned

| | | (5) | 400 |
| | | (8) | 750 |

Office Salaries Expense

| (6) | 250 |
| (9) | 250 |

Telephone Expense

| (13) | 30 |

Heating and Lighting Expense

| (14) | 35 |

Illustration 2–1

PREPARING A TRIAL BALANCE

As previously stated, in a double-entry accounting system every transaction is recorded with equal debits and credits so that the equality of the debits and credits may be tested as a proof of the recording accuracy. This equality is tested at intervals by preparing a *trial balance*. A trial balance is prepared by (1) determining the balance of each account in the ledger; (2) listing the accounts having balances, with the debit balances in one column and the credit balances in another (as in Illustration 2–2); (3) adding the debit balances; (4) adding the credit balances; and then (5) comparing the sum of the debit balances with the sum of the credit balances.

Larry Owen, Attorney
Trial Balance, July 31, 19—

Cash	$1,135	
Prepaid Rent	600	
Office supplies	60	
Office equipment	1,500	
Accounts payable		$ 260
Unearned legal fees		150
Larry Owen, capital		2,500
Larry Owen, withdrawals	200	
Legal fees earned		1,150
Office salaries expense	500	
Telephone expense	30	
Heating and lighting expense ..	35	
Totals	$4,060	$4,060

Illustration 2–2

The illustrated trial balance was prepared from the accounts in Illustration 2–1. Note that its column totals are equal, or in other words, the trial balance is in balance. When a trial balance is in balance, debits equal credits in the ledger and it is assumed that no errors were made in recording transactions.

THE PROOF OFFERED BY A TRIAL BALANCE

If when a trial balance is prepared it does not balance, an error or errors have been made. The error or errors may have been either in recording transactions, in determining the account balances, in copying the balances on the trial balance, or in adding the columns of the trial balance. On the other hand, if a trial balance balances, it is assumed that no errors have been made. However, a trial balance that balances is not absolute proof of accuracy. Errors may have been made that did not affect the equality of its columns. For example, an error in which a correct debit amount is debited to the wrong account or a correct credit amount is credited to the wrong account will not cause a trial balance to be out of balance. Likewise, an error in which a wrong amount is both debited and credited to the right accounts will not cause a trial balance to be out of balance. Consequently, a trial balance in balance is only presumptive proof of recording accuracy.

STANDARD ACCOUNT FORM

T-accounts like the ones shown thus far are commonly used in text-book illustrations and also in accounting classes for blackboard demon-strations. In both cases their use eliminates details and permits the student to concentrate on ideas. However, although widely used in textbooks and in teaching, T-accounts are not used in business for recording transactions. In recording transactions, accounts like the one in Illustration 2–3 are generally used. (Note the year in the date column of the illustrated account. Throughout the remainder of this text, years will be designated 198A, 198B, 198C, and so forth. In all such situations, 198A is the earliest year, 198B is the succeeding year, and so on through the series.)

DATE	EXPLANATION	POST REF.	DEBIT	CREDIT	BALANCE
198A July 1		G1	2500 00		2500 00
1		G1		600 00	1900 00
3		G1		1200 00	700 00
12		G1	400 00		1100 00

Cash   ACCOUNT NO. 1

Illustration 2–3

The account of Illustration 2–3 is called a *balance column account.* It differs from a T-account in that it has columns for specific information about each debit and credit entered in the account. Also, its Debit and Credit columns are placed side by side and it has a third or Balance column. In this Balance column the account's new balance is entered each time the account is debited or credited. As a result, the last amount in the column is the account's current balance. For example, on July 1 the illustrated account was debited for the $2,500 investment of Larry Owen, which caused it to have a $2,500 debit balance. It was then credited for $600, and its new $1,900 balance was entered. On July 3 it was credited again for $1,200, which reduced its balance to $700. Then on July 12 it was debited for $400 and its balance was increased to $1,100.

When a balance column account like that of Illustration 2–3 is used, the heading of the Balance column does not tell whether the balance is a debit balance or a credit balance. However, this does not create a problem because an account is assumed to have its normal kind of balance, unless the contrary is indicated. Furthermore, an accountant is expected to know the normal balance of any account. Fortunately this too is not difficult because the balance of an account normally results from recording in it a larger sum of increases than decreases. Consequently, if increases are recorded as debits, the account normally has a debit balance. Likewise, if increases are recorded as credits, the account normally has a credit balance. Or, increases are recorded in an account in each of the following classifications as shown, and its normal balance is:

Account classification	Increases are recorded as—	And the normal balance is—
Asset	Debits	Debit
Contra asset*	Credits	Credit
Liability	Credits	Credit
Owner's equity:		
Capital	Credits	Credit
Withdrawals	Debits	Debit
Revenue	Credits	Credit
Expense	Debits	Debit
* Explained in the next chapter.		

When an unusual transaction causes an account to have a balance opposite from its normal kind of balance, this opposite from normal kind of balance is indicated in the account by entering it in red or entering it in black and encircling the amount. Also when a debit or credit entered in an account causes the account to have no balance, some bookkeepers place a -0- in the Balance column on the line of the entered amount. Other bookkeepers and bookkeeping machines write 0.00 in the column to indicate the account does not have a balance.

NEED FOR A JOURNAL

It is possible to record transactions by entering debits and credits directly in the accounts, as was done earlier in this chapter. However, when this is done and an error is made, the error is difficult to locate, because even with a transaction having only one debit and one credit, the debit is entered on one ledger page or card and the credit on another, and there is nothing to link the two together.

Consequently, to link together the debits and credits of each transaction and to provide in one place a complete record of each transaction, it is the universal practice in pen-and-ink systems to record all transactions in a *journal*. The debit and credit information about each transaction is then copied from the journal to the ledger accounts. These procedures are important when errors are made, since the journal record makes it possible to trace the debits and credits into the accounts and to see that they are equal and properly recorded.

The process of recording transactions in a journal is called journalizing transactions. Also, since transactions are first recorded in a journal and their debit and credit information is then copied from the journal to the ledger, a journal is called a *book of original entry* and a ledger a *book of final entry*.

THE GENERAL JOURNAL

The simplest and most flexible type of journal is a *General Journal*. For each transaction it provides places for recording (1) the transaction date, (2) the names of the accounts involved, and (3) an explanation of the transaction. It also provides a place for (4) the account numbers of the accounts to which the transaction's debit and credit information is copied and (5) the transaction's debit and credit effect on the accounts named. A standard ruling for a general journal page with two of the transactions of the Owen law practice recorded therein is shown in Illustration 2–4.

	GENERAL JOURNAL			PAGE /
DATE	ACCOUNT TITLES AND EXPLANATION	POST. REF.	DEBIT	CREDIT
198A July 5	Office Supplies		60 00	
	Office Equipment		300 00	
	Accounts Payable			360 00
	Purchased supplies and equipment on credit.			
12	Cash		400 00	
	Legal Fees Earned			400 00
	Collected a legal fee.			

Illustration 2–4

The first entry in Illustration 2–4 records the purchase of supplies and equipment on credit, and three accounts are involved. When a transaction involves three or more accounts and is recorded with a general journal entry, a compound entry is required. A *compound journal entry* is one involving three or more accounts. The second entry records a legal fee earned.

RECORDING TRANSACTIONS IN A GENERAL JOURNAL

To record transactions in a General Journal:

1. The year is written in small figures at the top of the first column.

2. The month is written on the first line in the first column. The year and the month are not repeated except at the top of a new page or at the beginning of a new month or year.

3. The day of each transaction is written in the second column on the first line of the transaction.

4. The names of the accounts to be debited and credited and an explanation of the transaction are written in the Account Titles and Explanation column. The name of the account debited is written first, beginning at the left margin of the column. The name of the account credited is written on the following line, indented about one inch. The explanation is placed on the next line, indented about a half inch from the left margin. The explanation should be short but sufficient to explain the transaction and set it apart from every other transaction.

5. The debit amount is written in the Debit column opposite the name of the account to be debited. The credit amount is written in the Credit column opposite the account to be credited.

6. A single line is skipped between each journal entry to set the entries apart.

At the time transactions are recorded in the General Journal, nothing is entered in the *Posting Reference (Post. Ref.) column*. However, when the debits and credits are copied from the journal to the ledger, the account numbers of the ledger accounts to which the debits and credits are copied are entered in this column. The Posting Reference column is sometimes called the *Folio column*.

POSTING TRANSACTION INFORMATION

The process of copying journal entry information from the journal to the ledger is called *posting*. Normally, near the end of a day all transactions recorded in the journal that day are posted. In the posting procedure, journal debits are copied and become ledger account debits and journal credits are copied and become ledger account credits.

The posting procedures for a journal entry are shown in Illustration 2–5, and they may be described as follows. To post a journal entry:

For the debit:

1. Find in the ledger the account named in the debit of the entry.

2. Enter in the account the date of the entry as shown in the journal, the *journal page number* from which the entry is being posted, and in the Debit column the debit amount. Note the letter "G" preceding the journal page number in the Posting Reference column of the account. The letter indicates that the amount was posted from the General Journal. Other journals are introduced in Chapter 7, and each is identified by a letter.

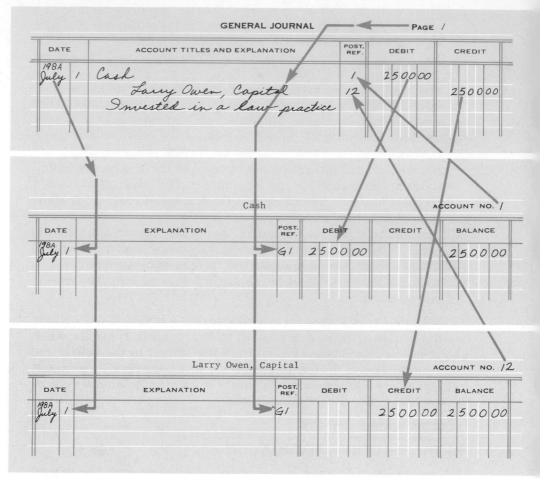

Illustration 2–5

3. Determine the effect of the debit on the account balance and enter the new balance.
4. Enter in the Posting Reference column of the journal the account number of the account to which the amount was posted.

For the credit:

Repeat the foregoing steps, with the exception that the credit amount is entered in the Credit column and has a credit effect on the account balance.

Observe that the last step (Step 4) in the posting procedure for either the debit or the credit of an entry is to insert the account number in the Posting Reference column of the journal. Inserting the account number in this column serves two purposes: (1) The account number in the journal and the journal page number in the account act as a cross-reference when it is desired to trace an amount from one record to the other. And, (2) writing the account number in the journal as a last step in posting indicates that posting is completed. If posting is interrupted, the bookkeeper, by examining the journal's Posting Reference column, can easily see where posting stopped.

LOCATING ERRORS

When a trial balance does not balance, an error or errors are indicated. To locate the error or errors, check the journalizing, posting, and trial balance preparation steps in their reverse order. First check the addition of the columns in the trial balance to see that no error in addition was made. Then check to see that the account balances were correctly copied from the ledger. Then recalculate the account balances. If at this stage the error or errors have not been found, check the posting and then the original journalizing of the transactions.

CORRECTING ERRORS

When an error is discovered in either the journal or the ledger, it must be corrected. Such an error is never erased, for this seems to indicate an effort to conceal something. However, the method of correction will vary with the nature of the error and the stage in the accounting procedures at which it is discovered.

If an error is discovered in a journal entry before the error is posted, it may be corrected by ruling a single line through the incorrect amount or account name and writing in above the correct amount or account name. Likewise, a posted error or an error in posting in which only the amount is wrong may be corrected in the same manner. However, when a posted error involves a wrong account, it is considered best to correct the error with a correcting journal entry. For example, the following journal entry to record the purchase of office supplies was made and posted:

Oct.	14	Office Furniture and Fixtures	15.00	
		Cash		15.00
		To record the purchase of office supplies.		

Obviously, the debit of the entry is to the wrong account; consequently, the following entry is needed to correct the error:

Oct.	17	Office Supplies	15.00	
		Office Furniture and Fixtures		15.00
		To correct the entry of October 14 in which the Office Furniture and Fixtures account was debited in error for the purchase of office supplies.		

The debit of the second entry correctly records the purchase of supplies, and the credit cancels the error of the first entry. Note the full explanation of the correcting entry. Such an explanation should always be full and complete so that anyone can see exactly what has occurred.

BOOKKEEPING TECHNIQUES

Commas and decimal points in dollar amounts

When amounts are entered in a journal or a ledger, commas to indicate thousands of dollars and decimal points to separate dollars and cents are not necessary. The ruled lines accomplish this. However, when statements are prepared on unruled paper, the decimal points and commas are necessary.

Dollar signs

Dollar signs are not used in journals or ledgers but are required on financial reports prepared on unruled paper. On such reports, a dollar sign is placed (1) before the first amount in each column of figures and (2) before the first amount appearing after a ruled line that indicates an addition or a subtraction. Examine Illustration 3–5, page 94, for examples of the use of dollar signs on a financial report.

Omission of zeros in the cents columns

When an amount to be entered in a ledger or a journal is an amount of dollars and no cents, some bookkeepers will use a dash in the cents column in the place of two zeros to indicate that there are no cents. They feel that the dash is easier and more quickly made than the two zeros. This is a matter of choice in journal and ledger entries. However, on financial reports the two zeros are preferred because they are neater in appearance.

Often in this text, where space is limited, exact dollar amounts are used in order to save space. Obviously, in such cases, neither zeros nor dashes are used to show that there are no cents involved.

GLOSSARY

Account. An accounting device used in recording and summarizing the increases and decreases in a revenue, an expense, asset, liability, or owner's equity item.

Account balance. The difference between the increases and decreases recorded in an account.

Account number. An identifying number assigned to an account.

Balance column account. An account having a column for entering the new account balance after each debit or credit is posted to the account.

Book of final entry. A ledger to which amounts are posted.

Book of original entry. A journal in which transactions are first recorded.

Business paper. A sales ticket, invoice, check, or other document arising in and evidence of the completion of a transaction.

Capital account. An account used to record the more or less permanent changes in the equity of an owner in his or her business.

Compound journal entry. A journal entry having more than one debit or more than one credit.

Credit. The right-hand side of a T-account.

Debit. The left-hand side of a T-account.

Double-entry accounting. An accounting system in which each transaction affects and is recorded in two or more accounts with equal debits and credits.

Drawing account. Another name for the *withdrawals account.*

Folio column. Another name for the *Posting Reference column.*

General Journal. A book of original entry in which any type of transaction can be recorded.

Journal. A book of original entry in which transactions are first recorded and from which transaction amounts are posted to the ledger accounts.

Journal page number. A posting reference number entered in the Posting Reference column of each account to which an amount is posted and which shows the page of the journal from which the amount was posted.

Ledger. A group of accounts used by a business in recording its transactions.

Mortgage payable. A debt, usually long term, that is secured by a special claim against one or more assets of the debtor.

Nominal accounts. The income statement accounts.

Normal balance of an account. The usual kind of balance, either debit or credit, that a given account has and which is a debit balance if increases are recorded in the account as debits and a credit balance if increases are recorded as credits.

Personal account. Another name for the *withdrawals account.*

Posting. Transcribing the debit and credit amounts from a journal to the ledger accounts.

Posting Reference (Post. Ref.) column. A column in a journal and in each account for entering posting reference numbers. Also called a *folio column.*

Posting reference numbers. Journal page numbers and ledger account numbers used as a cross-reference between amounts entered in a journal and posted to the ledger accounts.

Promissory note. An unconditional written promise to pay a definite sum of money on demand or at a fixed or determinable future date.

Real accounts. The balance sheet accounts.

T-account. An abbreviated account form, two or more of which are used in illustrating the debits and credits required in recording a transaction.

Trial balance. A list of accounts having balances in the ledger, the debit or credit balance of each account, the total of the debit balances, and the total of the credit balances.

Withdrawals account. The account used to record the withdrawals from a business by its owner of cash or other assets intended for personal use. Also known as *personal account* or *drawing account.*

QUESTIONS FOR CLASS DISCUSSION

1. What is an account? What is a ledger?
2. What determines the number of accounts a business will use?
3. What are the meanings of the following words and terms: *(a)* debit, *(b)* to debit, *(c)* credit, and *(d)* to credit?
4. Does debit always mean increase and credit always mean decrease?
5. A transaction is to be entered in the accounts. How do you determine the accounts in which amounts are to be entered? How do you determine whether a particular account is to be debited or credited?
6. Why is a double-entry accounting system so called?
7. Give the rules of debit and credit for *(a)* asset accounts and *(b)* for liability and owner's equity accounts.
8. Why are the rules of debit and credit the same for both liability and owner's equity accounts?
9. List the steps in the preparation of a trial balance.
10. Why is a trial balance prepared?

11. Why is a trial balance considered to be only presumptive proof of recording accuracy? What types of errors are not revealed by a trial balance?
12. What determines whether the normal balance of an account is a debit or a credit balance?
13. Can transaction debits and credits be recorded directly in the ledger accounts? What is gained by first recording transactions in a journal and then posting to the accounts?
14. In recording transactions in a journal, which is written first, the debit or the credit? How far is the name of the account credited indented? How far is the explanation indented?
15. What is a compound entry?
16. Are dollar signs used in journal entries? In the accounts?
17. If decimal points are not used in journal entries to separate dollars from cents, what accomplishes this purpose?
18. Define or describe each of the following:
    a. Journal.
    b. Ledger.
    c. Book of original entry.
    d. Book of final entry.
    e. Folio column.
    f. Posting.
    g. Posting Reference column.
    h. Posting reference numbers.
19. Entering in the Posting Reference column of the journal the account number to which an amount was posted is the last step in posting the amount. What is gained by making this the last step?

CLASS EXERCISES

Exercise 2–1

Prepare the following columnar form. Then (1) indicate the treatment for increases and decreases by entering the words "debited" and "credited" in the proper columns. (2) Indicate the normal balance of each kind of account by entering the word "debit" or "credit" in the last column of the form.

Kind of Account	Increases	Decreases	Normal Balance
Asset			
Liability			
Owner's capital			
Owner's withdrawals			
Revenue			
Expense			

Exercise 2–2

Place the following T-accounts on a sheet of notebook paper: Cash; Accounts Receivable; Office Supplies; Office Equipment; Accounts Payable; Carl Wells,

Capital; Revenue from Services; and Utilities Expense. Then record these transactions by entering debits and credits directly in the accounts. Use the transaction letters to identify amounts in the accounts.

a. Carl Wells began a service business, called Quick Service, by investing
$1,000 in the business.
b. Purchased office supplies for cash, $50.
c. Purchased office equipment on credit, $300.
d. Earned revenue by rendering services for a customer for cash, $100.
e. Paid for the office equipment purchased in transaction (c).
f. Earned revenue by rendering services for a customer on credit, $200.
g. Paid the monthly utility bills, $25.
h. Collected $150 of the amount owed by the customer of transaction (f).

Exercise 2–3

After recording the transactions of Exercise 2–2, prepare a trial balance
for Quick Service. Use the current date.

Exercise 2–4

Prepare a form on notebook paper with the following three column headings: (1) Error, (2) Amount Out of Balance, and (3) Column Having Larger
Total. Then for each of the following errors: (1) list the error by letter in
the first column, (2) tell the amount it will cause the trial balance to be out
of balance in the second column, and (3) tell in the third column which trial
balance column will have the larger total as a result of the error. If the error
does not affect the trial balance, write "none" in each of the last two columns.

a. A $70 debit to Office Supplies was debited to Office Equipment.
b. A $90 credit to Office Equipment was credited to Sales.
c. A $60 credit to Sales was credited to the Sales account twice.
d. A $40 debit to Office Supplies was posted as a $45 debit.
e. A $35 debit to Office Supplies was not posted.
f. A $11 credit to Sales was posted as a $110 credit.

Exercise 2–5

A trial balance did not balance. In looking for the error, the bookkeeper
discovered that a transaction for the purchase of a calculator on credit for
$350 had been recorded with a $350 debit to Office Equipment and a $350
debit to Accounts Payable. Answer each of the following questions, giving
the dollar amount of the misstatement, if any.

a. Was the balance of the Office Equipment account overstated, understated,
or correctly stated in the trial balance?
b. Was the balance of the Accounts Payable account overstated, understated,
or correctly stated in the trial balance?
c. Was the debit column total of the trial balance overstated, understated,
or correctly stated?

d. Was the credit column total of the trial balance overstated, understated, or correctly stated?

e. If the credit column total of the trial balance was $96,000 before the error was corrected, what was the total of the debit column?

Exercise 2–6

A careless bookkeeper prepared the following trial balance which does not balance, and you have been asked to prepare a corrected trial balance. In examining the records of the concern you discover the following: (1) The debits to the Cash account total $13,200, and the credits total $10,750. (2) A $75 receipt of cash from a customer in payment of the customer's account was not posted to Accounts Receivable. (3) A $25 purchase of shop supplies on credit was entered in the journal but was not posted to any account. (4) Two digits in the balance of the Revenue from Services account, as shown on the trial balance of the bookkeeper, were transposed in copying the balance from the ledger to the trial balance. The correct amount is $12,100

RED ROCK COMPANY
Trial Balance, September 30, 19—

Cash	$ 2,550	
Accounts receivable		$ 3,175
Shop supplies	300	
Shop equipment	1,500	
Accounts payable	550	
Wages payable	50	
Joe Sims, capital	3,175	
Joe Sims, withdrawals	7,200	
Revenue from services		11,200
Rent expense		1,200
Advertising expense	125	
Totals	$15,450	$15,575

PROBLEMS

Problem 2–1

Mary Hall began a new real estate agency called Phoenix Realty, and during a short period completed these transactions:

a. Began business by investing the following assets at their fair values: cash, $3,500; office equipment, $1,500; automobile, $3,000; land, $15,000; and building, $45,000. Security Bank holds a $30,000 mortgage on the land and building.

b. Purchased office supplies, $50, and office equipment, $175, on credit.

c. Collected a $3,500 commission from the sale of property for a client.

d. Purchased additional office equipment on credit, $150.

e. Paid cash for advertising that had appeared in the local paper, $75.

f. Traded the company automobile and $4,500 in cash for a new automobile.

g.   Paid the office secretary's salary, $350.
h.   Paid for the supplies and equipment purchased in transaction *(b)*.
i.   Completed a real estate appraisal for a client on credit, $200.
j.   Paid for the equipment purchased in transaction *(d)*.
k.   The client of transaction *(i)* paid $100 of the amount the client owed.
l.   Paid the secretary's salary, $350.
m.   Paid $125 cash for newspaper advertising that had appeared.
n.   Mary Hall withdrew $500 from the business to pay personal expenses.

Required:

1. Open the following T-accounts: Cash; Accounts Receivable; Office Supplies; Office Equipment; Automobile; Land; Building; Accounts Payable; Mortgage Payable; Mary Hall, Capital; Mary Hall, Withdrawals; Commissions Earned; Appraisal Fees Earned; Office Salaries Expense; and Advertising Expense.
2. Record the transactions by entering debits and credits directly in the accounts. Use the transaction letters to identify each debit and credit amount.
3. Prepare a trial balance using the current date.

Problem 2–2

Susan Kent began a public accounting practice and completed these transactions during October of the current year.

Oct. 1   Invested $3,500 cash in a public accounting practice begun this day.
      1   Paid cash for three months' office rent in advance, $900.
      2   Purchased office supplies, $60, and office equipment, $2,100, on credit.
      3   Paid the premium on two insurance policies, $375.
      8   Completed accounting work for Mary Hall and collected $150 cash therefor.
    13   Completed accounting work for Valley Bank on credit, $350.
    15   Purchased additional office supplies on credit, $25.
    23   Received $350 from Valley Bank for the work completed on October 13.
    25   Made a $250 installment payment on the supplies and equipment purchased on October 2.
    30   Susan Kent wrote a $45 check on the bank account of the accounting practice to pay the electric bill of her personal residence.
    31   Completed accounting work for Evans Company on credit, $300.
    31   Paid the monthly utility bills of the accounting office, $30.

Required:

1. Open the following accounts: Cash; Accounts Receivable; Prepaid Rent; Prepaid Insurance; Office Supplies; Office Equipment; Accounts Payable; Susan Kent, Capital; Susan Kent, Withdrawals; Accounting Revenue; and Utilities Expense. Number the accounts beginning with 1.
2. Prepare general journal entries to record the transactions, post to the accounts, and prepare a trial balance. Head the trial balance Susan Kent, CPA.

Problem 2–3

Fred Oaks began a new business called A–1 Dirt Digger, and during a short period completed these transactions:

a. Began business by investing $18,000 in cash and office equipment having a $500 fair value.
b. Purchased for $10,000 land to be used as an office site and for parking equipment. Paid $3,000 in cash and signed a promissory note for the balance.
c. Purchased excavating equipment costing $22,500. Paid $7,500 in cash and signed promissory notes for the balance.
d. Paid $5,000 cash for the erection of a quonset-type office building.
e. Paid the premiums on several insurance policies, $875.
f. Completed an excavating job and collected $825 cash in payment therefor.
g. Completed $1,200 of excavating work for Tri-City Contractors on credit.
h. Paid the wages of the equipment operator, $750.
i. Paid $225 cash for repairs to excavating equipment.
j. Received $1,200 from Tri-City Contractors for the work of transaction (g).
k. Completed $650 of excavating work for Ralph Sims on credit.
l. Recorded as an account payable a bill for rent of a special machine used on the Ralph Sims job, $75.
m. Purchased additional excavating equipment on credit, $850.
n. Fred Oaks withdrew $50 from the business for personal use.
o. Paid the wages of the equipment operator, $1,000.
p. Paid the account payable resulting from renting the machine of transaction (l).
q. Paid for gas and oil consumed by the excavating equipment, $175.

Required:

1. Open the following T-accounts: Cash; Accounts Receivable; Prepaid Insurance; Office Equipment; Excavating Equipment; Building; Land; Notes Payable; Accounts Payable; Fred Oaks, Capital; Fred Oaks, Withdrawals; Excavating Revenue; Equipment Repairs Expense; Wages Expense; Equipment Rentals Expense; and Gas and Oil Expense.
2. Record the transactions by entering debits and credits directly in the T-accounts. Use the transaction letters to identify amounts in the accounts.
3. Prepare a trial balance using the current date.

Problem 2–4

Ann Evans began the practice of architecture and completed these transactions during October of the current year:

Oct. 2 Opened a bank account in the name of the practice, Ann Evans, Architect, and deposited $2,500 therein.
2 Rented suitable office space and paid two months' rent in advance, $600.
3 Purchased $3,800 of office and drafting equipment under an agreement calling for a $500 down payment and the balance in monthly installments. Paid the down payment.

Oct. 3 Purchased drafting supplies for cash, $250.

9 Delivered a set of building plans to a contractor and collected $500 in full payment therefor.

10 Paid the premiums on fire and liability insurance policies, $525.

11 Purchased additional drafting supplies, $40, and drafting equipment, $100, on credit.

16 Completed and delivered a set of plans to Lakeside Developers on credit, $900.

16 Paid the salary of the draftsman, $500.

22 Received $900 from Lakeside Developers for the plans delivered on October 16.

22 Paid for the supplies and equipment purchased on October 11.

26 Completed additional architectural work for Lakeside Developers on credit, $250.

28 Paid $125 cash for blueprinting expense.

30 Ann Evans withdraw $500 cash for personal expenses.

31 Paid the monthly utility bills, $65.

31 Paid the salary of the draftsman, $500.

Required:

1. Open the following accounts, numbering them beginning with 1: Cash; Accounts Receivable; Prepaid Rent; Drafting Supplies; Prepaid Insurance; Office and Drafting Equipment; Accounts Payable; Ann Evans, Capital; Ann Evans, Withdrawals; Architectural Fees Earned; Salaries Expense; Blueprinting Expense; and Utilities Expense.

2. Prepare general journal entries to record the transactions, post to the accounts, and prepare a trial balance.

Problem 2–5

Ned Lake graduated from college with a law degree in June of the current year, and during July he completed these transactions:

July 1 Began the practice of law by investing $2,000 in cash and law books acquired in college and having a $600 fair value.

1 Rented the furnished office of a lawyer who was retiring due to illness, and paid two months' rent in advance, $800.

1 Paid the premium on a liability insurance policy giving one year's protection, $480.

2 Purchased office supplies on credit, $40.

8 Completed legal work for a client and immediately collected $200 cash for the work.

12 Paid for the office supplies purchased on July 2.

15 Completed legal work for Evans Realty on credit, $650.

22 Completed legal work for Security Bank on credit, $500.

25 Received $650 from Evans Realty for the work completed on July 15.

27 Ned Lake wrote a $25 check on the bank account of the legal practice to pay his home telephone bill, $25.

29 Purchased additional office supplies on credit, $30.

July 31 Paid the July telephone bill of the office, $35.
   31 Paid the salary of the office secretary, $600.
   31 Recognized that one month's rent on the office had expired and had become an expense. (Make a general journal entry to transfer the amount of the expense from the asset account to the Rent Expense account.)
   31 Recognized that one month's insurance had expired and become an expense.
   31 Took an inventory of the unused office supplies and determined that supplies costing $25 had been used and had become an expense.

Required:

1. Open the following accounts, numbering them beginning with 1: Cash; Accounts Receivable; Prepaid Rent; Prepaid Insurance; Office Supplies; Law Library; Accounts Payable; Ned Lake, Capital; Ned Lake, Withdrawals; Legal Fees Earned; Rent Expense; Salaries Expense; Telephone Expense; Insurance Expense; and Office Supplies Expense.
2. Prepare general journal entries to record the transactions, post to the accounts, and prepare a trial balance headed Ned Lake, Attorney.
3. Analyze the trial balance and prepare a July 31 balance sheet and a July income statement for the practice. (The $2,600 trial balance amount of capital for Ned Lake is his July 1 beginning-of-the-month capital. To determine the July 31 balance sheet amount of his capital, remember that the net income increased his equity and the withdrawal decreased it. Show his ending equity as in Illustration 1–2.)

ALTERNATE PROBLEMS

Problem 2–1A

Mary Hall began business as a real estate agent. She called her agency Red Rock Realty, and during a short period completed these transactions:

a. Invested $12,000 in cash and office equipment having a $2,500 fair value in the agency.
b. Purchased land valued at $18,000 and a small office building valued at $32,000, paying $10,000 cash and signing a mortgage contract to pay the balance over a period of years.
c. Purchased office supplies on credit, $75.
d. Took her personal automobile, which had a $5,500 fair value, for exclusive use in the business.
e. Purchased additional office equipment on credit, $400.
f. Paid the office secretary's salary, $300.
g. Collected a $2,500 commission from the sale of property for a client.
h. Paid cash for newspaper advertising that had appeared, $65.
i. Paid for the supplies purchased in transaction (c).
j. Gave a typewriter carried in the accounting records at $110 and $650 cash for a new typewriter.
k. Completed a real estate appraisal for a client on credit, $150.

  l. Paid the secretary's salary, $300.
  m. Received payment in full for the appraisal of transaction *(k)*.
  n. Mary Hall withdrew $250 from the business to pay personal living expenses.

Required:

1. Open the following T-accounts: Cash; Accounts Receivable; Office Supplies; Office Equipment; Automobile; Land; Building; Accounts Payable; Mortgage Payable; Mary Hall, Capital; Mary Hall, Withdrawals; Commissions Earned; Appraisal Fees Earned; Office Salaries Expense; and Advertising Expense.
2. Record the transactions by entering debits and credits directly in the accounts. Use the transaction letters to identify each debit and credit amount.
3. Prepare a trial balance using the current date.

Problem 2–2A

Susan Kent, CPA, completed the following transactions during August of the current year:

Aug. 2 Began a public accounting practice by investing $2,000 in cash and office equipment having a $3,500 fair value.
  2 Purchased on credit office supplies, $50, and office equipment, $250.
  2 Paid two months' rent in advance on suitable office space, $700.
  5 Completed accounting work for a client and immediately collected $100 cash therefor.
  9 Completed accounting work for Valley Bank on credit, $500.
  11 Paid for the items purchased on credit on August 2.
  12 Paid the premium on an insurance policy, $525.
  19 Received $500 from Valley Bank for the work completed on August 9.
  25 Susan Kent withdrew $200 from the practice for personal expenses.
  29 Completed accounting work for Dennis Realty on credit, $350.
  30 Purchased additional office supplies on credit, $35.
  31 Paid the August utility bills, $85.

Required:

1. Open the following accounts: Cash; Accounts Receivable; Prepaid Rent; Prepaid Insurance; Office Supplies; Office Equipment; Accounts Payable; Susan Kent, Capital; Susan Kent, Withdrawals; Accounting Revenue; and Utilities Expense. Number the accounts beginning with 1.
2. Prepare general journal entries to record the transactions, post to the accounts, and prepare a trial balance. Head the trial balance Susan Kent, CPA.

Problem 2–3A

Fred Oaks began business as an excavating contractor and during a short period completed these transactions:

a. Began business under the firm name of Dirt Mover by investing cash, $12,500; office equipment, $650; and excavating equipment, $28,500.

b. Purchased land for use as an office site and for parking equipment. Paid $2,500 cash and signed a $5,000 promissory note for the balance of the $7,500 total cost.

c. Purchased for cash a small prefabricated building and moved it onto the land for use as an office, $5,000.

d. Paid the premiums on two insurance policies, $550.

e. Completed an excavating job and collected $800 cash in payment therefor.

f. Purchased additional excavating equipment costing $5,000. Gave $1,000 in cash and signed a promissory note for the balance.

g. Completed excavating work for Western Contractors on credit, $1,100.

h. Purchased additional excavating equipment on credit, $350.

i. Completed an excavating job for Barry Fox on credit, $725.

j. Received and recorded as an account payable a bill for rent on a special machine used on the Barry Fox job, $100.

k. Received $1,100 from Western Contractors for the work of transaction (g).

l. Paid the wages of the equipment operator, $600.

m. Paid for the equipment purchased in transaction (h).

n. Paid $150 cash for repairs to excavating equipment.

o. Fred Oaks wrote a check on the bank account of the business for repairs to his personal automobile, $60. (The car is not used for business purposes.)

p. Paid the wages of the equipment operator, $600.

q. Paid for gas and oil consumed by the excavating equipment, $125.

Required:

1. Open the following T-accounts: Cash; Accounts Receivable; Prepaid Insurance; Office Equipment; Excavating Equipment; Building; Land; Notes Payable; Accounts Payable; Fred Oaks, Capital; Fred Oaks, Withdrawals; Excavating Revenue; Equipment Repairs Expense; Wages Expense; Equipment Rentals Expense; and Gas and Oil Expense.

2. Record the transactions by entering debits and credits directly in the accounts, and prepare a trial balance. (Use the transaction letter to identify each amount in the accounts. Use the current date for the trial balance.)

Problem 2–4A

Ann Evans completed these transactions during October of the current year:

Oct. 1 Began the practice of architecture by investing cash, $2,000; drafting supplies, $125; and office and drafting equipment, $3,450.

1 Paid two months' rent in advance on suitable office space, $800.

2 Purchased drafting equipment, $325, and drafting supplies, $35, on credit.

2 Paid the premium on an insurance policy taken out in the name of the practice, $475.

8 Delivered a set of plans to a contractor and collected $300 in full payment therefor.

Oct. 15   Completed and delivered a set of plans to Phoenix Contractors on credit, $600.

15   Paid the draftsman's salary, $450.

17   Paid for the equipment and supplies purchased on October 2.

18   Purchased drafting supplies on credit, $45.

24   Received payment in full from Phoenix Contractors for the plans delivered on October 15.

26   Ann Evans withdrew $75 from the practice for personal expenses.

28   Paid for the supplies purchased on October 18.

30   Completed architectural work for Sears Realty on credit, $350.

31   Paid the draftsman's salary, $450.

31   Paid the October utility bills, $65.

31   Paid the blueprinting expense for October, $55.

Required:

1.   Open the following accounts, numbering them beginning with 1: Cash; Accounts Receivable; Prepaid Rent; Drafting Supplies; Prepaid Insurance; Office and Drafting Equipment; Accounts Payable; Ann Evans, Capital; Ann Evans, Withdrawals; Architectural Fees Earned; Salaries Expense; Blueprinting Expense; and Utilities Expense.

2.   Prepare general journal entries to record the transactions, post to the accounts, and prepare a trial balance. Use as the name of the business Ann Evans, Architect.

PROVOCATIVE PROBLEMS

Provocative problem 2–1
Lake Pleasant

Jed Monroe has just completed the first summer's operation of a concession on Lake Pleasant at which he rents boats and sells hamburgers, soft drinks, and candy. He began the summer's operation with $2,500 in cash and a five-year lease on a boat dock and small concession building on the lake. The lease calls for a $1,000 annual rental, although the concession is open only from May 15 to September 15. On opening day Jed paid the first year's rent in advance and also purchased four boats at $300 each, paying cash. He estimated the boats would have a five-year life, after which he could sell them for $50 each.

During the summer he purchased food, soft drinks, and candy costing $4,175, all of which was paid for by summer's end, excepting food costing $150 which was purchased during the last week's operations. He also paid electric bills, $165, and wages of a part-time helper, $800; and he withdrew $200 of the earnings of the concession each week for 16 weeks for personal expenses.

He took in $1,450 in boat rentals during the summer and sold $9,650 of food and drinks, all of which was collected in cash, except $125 he had not collected from Hill Company for food and drinks for an employees' party.

When he closed for the summer, he was able to return to the soft drink company several cases of soft drinks for which he received a $40 cash refund.

However, he had to take home for consumption by his family a number of candy bars and some hamburger and buns which cost $15 and could have been sold for $45.

Prepare an income statement showing the results of the summer's operations and a September 15 balance sheet. Head the statements Lake Pleasant Concession. Determine Jed Monroe's ending equity by subtracting the liability from the assets. Then prepare a different caculation to prove the amount of the equity. (T-accounts will be helpful in organizing the data.)

Provocative problem 2–2
Valley Glass Service

Ed Cook began a window cleaning service by depositing $500 in a bank account opened in the name of the business, Valley Glass Service. He then made a $250 down payment and signed a promissory note payable to purchase a secondhand truck priced at $800; and he spent $150 for detergents, sponges, and other supplies to be used in the business. He also paid $50 for newspaper advertising through which he gained a number of customers who together agreed to pay him approximately $250 per week for his services.

After six months, on June 30, 19—, Ed's records showed that he had collected $5,800 in cash from customers for services and that other customers owed him $300 for washing their windows. He had bought additional supplies for cash, $350, which brought the total supplies purchased during the six months to $500; however, supplies that had cost $100 were on hand unused at the period end. He spent $275 for gas and oil used in the truck and through payments had reduced the balance owed on the truck to $250; but through use the truck had worn out and depreciated an amount equal to one fourth of its cost. Also, he had withdrawn sufficient cash from the business each week to pay his personal living expenses.

Under the assumption the business had a total of $400 of cash at the period end, determine the amount of cash Ed had withdrawn from the business. Prepare an income statement for the six months and a balance sheet as of the period end. Determine Ed Cook's end-of-the-period equity by subtracting the balance owed on the note payable from the total of the assets. Then prepare a calculation to prove in another way the amount of the ending equity. (T-accounts will be useful in organizing the data.)

3

Adjusting the accounts and preparing the statements

After studying Chapter 3, you should be able to:

- ■ Explain why the life of a business is divided into accounting periods of equal length and why the accounts of a business must be adjusted at the end of each accounting period.
- ■ Prepare adjusting entries for prepaid expenses, accrued expenses, unearned revenues, accrued revenues, and depreciation.
- ■ Prepare entries to dispose of accrued revenue and expense items in the new accounting period.
- ■ Explain the difference between the cash and accrual bases of accounting.
- ■ Explain the importance of comparability in the financial statements of a business, period after period; and tell how the realization principle and the matching principle contribute to comparability.
- ■ Define each asset and liability classification appearing on a balance sheet, classify balance sheet items, and prepare a classified balance sheet.
- ■ Define or explain the words and phrases listed in the chapter Glossary.

The life of a business often spans many years, and its activities go on without interruption over the years. However, taxes based on annual income must be paid governmental units, and the owners and managers of a business must have periodic reports on its financial progress. Consequently, a *time-period concept* of the life of a business is required in accounting for its activities. This concept results in a division of the life of a business into time periods of equal length, called *accounting periods*. Accounting periods may be a month, three months, or a year in length. However, *annual accounting periods*, periods one year in length, are the norm.

An accounting period of any 12 consecutive months is known as a *fiscal year*. A fiscal year may coincide with the calendar year and end on December 31 or it may follow the *natural business year*. When accounting periods follow the natural business year, they end when inventories are at their lowest point and business activities are at their lowest ebb. For example, in department stores the natural business year begins on February 1, after the Christmas and January sales, and ends the following January 31. Consequently, the annual accounting periods of department stores commonly begin on February 1 and end the following January 31.

NEED FOR ADJUSTMENTS AT THE END OF AN ACCOUNTING PERIOD

As a rule, at the end of an accounting period, after all transactions are recorded, several of the accounts in a concern's ledger do not show proper end-of-the-period balances for preparing the statements. This is true even though all transactions were correctly recorded. The balances are incorrect for statement purposes, not through error but because of the expiration of costs brought about by the passage of time. For example, the second item on the trial balance of Owen's law practice, as prepared in Chapter 2 and reproduced again on the next page, is "Prepaid rent, $600." This $600 represents the rent for three months paid in advance on July 1. However, by July 31, $600 is not the balance sheet amount for this asset because one month's rent, or $200, has expired and become an expense and only $400 remains as an asset. Likewise, a portion of the office supplies as repre-

Larry Owen Attorney
Trial Balance, July 31, 19—

Cash	$1,135	
Prepaid rent	600	
Office supplies	60	
Office equipment	1,500	
Accounts payable		$ 260
Unearned legal fees		150
Larry Owen, capital		2,500
Larry Owen, withdrawals	200	
Legal fees earned		1,150
Office salaries expense	500	
Telephone expense	30	
Heating and lighting expense	35	
Totals	$4,060	$4,060

Illustration 3–1

sented by the $60 debit balance in the Office Supplies account has been used, and the office equipment has begun to wear out and depreciate. Obviously, then, the balances of the Prepaid Rent, Office Supplies, and Office Equipment accounts as they appear on the trial balance do not reflect the proper amounts for preparing the July 31 statements. The balance of each and the balances of the Office Salaries Expense and Legal Fees Earned accounts must be *adjusted* before they will show proper amounts for the July 31 statements.

ADJUSTING THE ACCOUNTS

Prepaid expenses

As the name implies, a *prepaid expense* is an expense that has been paid for in advance of its use. At the time of payment an asset is acquired that will be used or consumed, and as it is used or consumed, it becomes an expense. For example:

On July 1 the Owen law practice paid three months' rent in advance and obtained the right to occupy a rented office for the following three months. On July 1 this right was an asset valued at its $600 cost. However, day by day the agency occupied the office, and each day a portion of the prepaid rent expired and became an expense. On July 31 one month's rent, valued at one third of $600, or $200, had expired. Consequently, if the agency's July 31 accounts are to reflect proper asset and expense amounts, the following adjusting entry is required:

July	31	Rent Expense	200.00	
		Prepaid Rent		200.00
		To record the expired rent.		

Posting the adjusting entry has the following effect on the accounts:

Prepaid Rent				Rent Expense	
July 1	600	July 31	200	July 31	200

After the entry is posted, the Prepaid Rent account with a $400 balance and the Rent Expense account with a $200 balance show proper statement amounts.

To continue, early in July, the Owen law practice purchased some office supplies and placed them in the office for use. Each day the secretary used a portion. The amount used or consumed each day was an expense that daily reduced the supplies on hand. However, the daily reductions were not recognized in the accounts because day-by-day information as to amounts used and remaining was not needed. Also, bookkeeping labor could be saved if only a single amount, the total of all supplies used during the month, was recorded.

Consequently, if on July 31 the accounts are to reflect proper statement amounts, it is necessary to record the amount of office supplies used during the month. However, to do this, it is first necessary to learn the amount used. To learn the amount used, it is necessary to count or inventory the unused supplies remaining and to deduct their cost from the cost of the supplies purchased. If, for example, $45 of unused supplies remain, then $15 ($60 − $45 = $15) of supplies have been used and have become an expense. The following entry is required to record this:

July	31	Office Supplies Expense	15.00	
		Office Supplies		15.00
		To record the supplies used.		

The effect of the adjusting entry on the accounts is:

Office Supplies				Office Supplies Expense	
July 5	60	July 31	15	July 31	15

Often, unlike in the two previous examples, items that are prepaid expenses at the time of purchase are both bought and fully consumed within a single accounting period. For example, a company pays its rent in advance on the first day of each month. Each month the amount paid results in a prepaid expense that is entirely consumed before the month's end and before the end of the accounting period. In such cases, it is best to ignore the fact that an asset results from each prepayment, because an adjustment can be avoided if each prepayment is originally recorded as an expense.

Other prepaid expenses that are handled in the same manner as prepaid rent and office supplies are prepaid insurance, store supplies, and factory supplies.

Depreciation

An item of equipment used in carrying on the operations of a business in effect represents a "quantity of usefulness." Also, since the equipment will eventually wear out and be discarded, the cost of its "quantity of usefulness" must be charged off as an expense over the useful life of the equipment. This is accomplished by recording *depreciation.*

Depreciation is an *expense* just like the expiration of prepaid rent. For example, if a company purchases a machine for $4,500 that it expects to use for four years, after which it expects to receive $500 for the machine as a trade-in allowance on a new machine, the company has purchased a $4,000 quantity of usefulness ($4,500 − $500 = $4,000). Furthermore, this quantity of usefulness expires or the machine depreciates at the rate of $1,000 per year [($4,500 − $500) ÷ 4 years = $1,000]. Actually, when depreciation is compared to the expiration of a prepaid expense, the primary difference is that since it is often impossible to predict exactly how long an item of equipment will be used or how much will be received for it at the end of its useful life, the amount it depreciates each accounting period is only an estimate.

Estimating and apportioning depreciation can be simple, as in the foregoing example, or it can become complex. A discussion of more complex situations is unnecessary at this point and is deferred to Chapter 9. However, to illustrate the recording of depreciation, assume that on July 31 the Owen law practice estimated its office equipment had depreciated $20 during the month. The depreciation reduced the assets and increased expenses, and the following adjusting entry is required:

July	31	Depreciation Expense, Office Equipment	20.00	
		Accumulated Depreciation,		
		Office Equipment		20.00
		To record the July depreciation.		

The effect of the entry on the accounts is:

	Office Equipment		Depreciation Expense, Office Equipment	
July 3	1,200		July 31	20
5	300			

	Accumulated Depreciation, Office Equipment	
	July 31	20

After the entry is posted, the Office Equipment account and its related Accumulated Depreciation, Office Equipment account together show the July 31 balance sheet amounts for this asset. The Depreciation Expense, Office Equipment account shows the amount of depreciation expense that should appear on the July income statement.

In most cases a decrease in an asset is recorded with a credit to the account in which the asset is recorded. However, note in the illustrated accounts that this procedure is not followed in recording depreciation. Rather, depreciation is recorded in a *contra account,* the Accumulated Depreciation, Office Equipment account. (A contra account is an account the balance of which is subtracted from the balance of an associate account to show a more proper amount for the item recorded in the associated account.)

There are two good reasons for using contra accounts in recording depreciation. First, although based on objective evidence whenever possible, at its best depreciation is only an estimate. Second, the use of contra accounts better preserves the facts in the lives of items of equipment. For example, in this case the Office Equipment account preserves a record of the equipment's cost, and the Accumulated Depreciation, Office Equipment account shows its depreciation to date.

A better understanding of the second reason for using contra accounts, along with an appreciation of why the word "accumulated" is used in the account name, can be gained when it is pointed out that depreciation is recorded at the end of each accounting period in a depreciating asset's life. As a result, at the end of the third month in the life of the law practice's office equipment, the Office Equipment and its related accumulated depreciation account will look like this:

	Office Equipment		Accumulated Depreciation, Office Equipment	
July 3	1,200		July 31	20
5	300		Aug. 31	20
			Sept. 30	20

And the equipment's cost and three months' *accumulated depreciation* will be shown on its September 30 balance sheet thus:

Office equipment	$1,500	
Less accumulated depreciation	60	$1,440

Accumulated depreciation accounts are sometimes found in ledgers and on statements under titles such as "Allowance for Depreciation, Store Equipment" or the totally unacceptable caption, "Reserve for Depreciation, Office Equipment." However, more appropriate terminology is "Accumulated Depreciation, Store Equipment" and "Accumulated Depreciation, Office Equipment." The "Accumulated" terminology is better because it is more descriptive of the depreciation procedure.

Accrued expenses

Most expenses are recorded during an accounting period at the time they are paid. However, when a period ends there may be expenses that have been incurred but have not been paid and recorded because payment is not due. These unpaid and unrecorded expenses for which payment is not due are called *accrued expenses*. Earned but unpaid wages are a common example. To illustrate:

The Owen law practice has a part-time secretary who is paid $25 per day or $125 per week for a week that begins on Monday and ends on Friday. The secretary's wages are due and payable every two weeks on Friday; and during July they were paid on the 12th and 26th and recorded as follows:

Cash			Office Salaries Expense		
July 12	250		July 12	250	
26	250		26	250	

If the calendar for July appears as illustrated and the secretary worked on July 29, 30, and 31, then at the close of business on Wednesday, July 31, the secretary has earned three days' wages that are not paid and recorded because payment is not due. However, this $75 of earned but unpaid wages is just as much a part of the July expenses as the $500 of wages that have been paid. Furthermore, on July 31, the unpaid wages are a liability. Consequently, if the accounts are to show the correct amount of wages for July and all liabilities owed on July 31, then an adjusting entry like the following must be made:

JULY						
S	M	T	W	T	F	S
	1	2	3	4	5	6
7	8	9	10	11	12	13
14	15	16	17	18	19	20
21	22	23	24	25	26	27
28	29	30	31			

July	31	Office Salaries Expense	75.00	
		Salaries Payable		75.00
		To record the earned but unpaid wages.		

The effect of the entry on the accounts is:

Office Salaries Expense			Salaries Payable	
July 12	250		July 31	75
26	250			
31	75			

Unearned revenues

An *unearned revenue* results when payment is received for goods or services in advance of their delivery. For instance, on July 15 Larry Owen entered into an agreement with Coast Realty to do its legal work on a fixed-fee basis for $100 per month. On that date Owen received $150 in advance for services during the remainder of July and the month of August. The fee was recorded with this entry:

July	15	Cash	150.00	
		Unearned Legal Fees....................		150.00
		Received a legal fee in advance.		

Acceptance of the fee in advance increased the cash of the law practice and created a liability, the obligation to do Coast Realty's legal work for the next month and a half. However, by July 31 the law practice has discharged $50 of the liability and earned that much income, which according to the *realization principle* should appear on the July income statement. Consequently, on July 31 the following entry is required:

July	31	Unearned Legal Fees........................	50.00	
		Legal Fees Earned		50.00
		To record legal fees earned.		

Posting the entry has this effect on the accounts:

Unearned Legal Fees				Legal Fees Earned		
July 31	50	July 15	150		July 12	400
					19	750
					31	50

The effect of the entry is to transfer the $50 earned portion of the fee from the liability account to the revenue account. It reduces the liability and records as a revenue the $50 that has been earned.

Accrued revenues

An *accrued revenue* is a revenue that has been earned but has not been collected because payment is not due. For example, assume that on July 15 Larry Owen also entered into an agreement with Guaranty Bank to do its legal work on a fixed-fee basis for $150 per month to be paid monthly. Under this assumption, by July 31 the law practice has earned half of a month's fee, $75, which according to the *realization principle* should appear on its July income statement. Therefore the following entry is required:

July	31	Accounts Receivable	75.00	
		Legal Fees Earned		75.00
		To record legal fees earned.		

Posting the entry has this effect on the accounts:

Accounts Receivable				Legal Fees Earned		
July 19	750	July 29	750		July 12	400
31	75				19	750
					31	50
					31	75

THE ADJUSTED TRIAL BALANCE

A trial balance prepared before adjustments is known as an *unadjusted trial balance,* or simply a trial balance. One prepared after adjustments is known as an *adjusted trial balance*. A July 31 adjusted trial balance for the law practice appears in Illustration 3–2.

Larry Owen, Attorney
Adjusted Trial Balance, July 31,19—

Cash	$1,135	
Accounts receivable	75	
Prepaid rent	400	
Office supplies	45	
Office equipment	1,500	
Accumulated depreciation, office equipment		$ 20
Accounts payable		260
Salaries payable		75
Unearned legal fees		100
Larry Owen, capital		2,500
Larry Owen, withdrawals	200	
Legal fees earned		1,275
Office salaries expense	575	
Telephone expense	30	
Heating and lighting expense	35	
Rent expense	200	
Office supplies expense	15	
Depreciation expense, office equipment	20	
Totals	$4,230	$4,230

Illustration 3–2

PREPARING STATEMENTS FROM THE ADJUSTED TRIAL BALANCE

An adjusted trial balance shows proper balance sheet and income statement amounts. Consequently, it may be used in preparing the statements. When it is so used, the revenue and expense items are arranged into an income statement, as in Illustration 3–3. Likewise, the asset, liability, and owner's equity items are arranged into a balance sheet as in Illustration 3–4.

When the statements are prepared, the income statement is normally prepared first because the net income, as calculated on the income statement, is needed in completing the balance sheet's owner's equity section. Observe in Illustration 3–4 how the net income is combined with the withdrawals and the excess is added to Owen's July 1 capital. The income increased Owen's equity, and the withdrawals reduced it. Consequently, when the excess of the income over the withdrawals is added to the beginning equity, the result is the ending equity.

Larry Owen, Attorney
Adjusted Trial Balance, July 31, 19—

Cash	$1,135	
Accounts receivable	75	
Prepaid rent	400	
Office supplies	45	
Office equipment	1,500	
Accumulated depreciation, office equipment		$ 20
Accounts payable		260
Salaries payable		75
Unearned legal fees		100
Larry Owen, capital		2,500
Larry Owen, withdrawals	200	
Legal fees earned		1,275
Office salaries expense	575	
Telephone expense	30	
Heating and lighting expense	35	
Rent expense	200	
Office supplies expense	15	
Depreciation expense, office equipment	20	
Totals	$4,230	$4,230

PREPARING THE INCOME STATEMENT FROM THE ADJUSTED TRIAL BALANCE

Larry Owen, Attorney
Income Statement for Month Ended July 31, 19—

Revenue:		
Legal fees earned		$1,275
Operating expenses:		
Office salaries expense	$575	
Telephone expense	30	
Heating and lighting expense	35	
Rent expense	200	
Office supplies expense	15	
Depreciation expense, office equipment	20	
Total operating expense		875
Net income		$ 400

Illustration 3–3

PREPARING THE BALANCE SHEET
FROM THE ADJUSTED TRIAL BALANCE

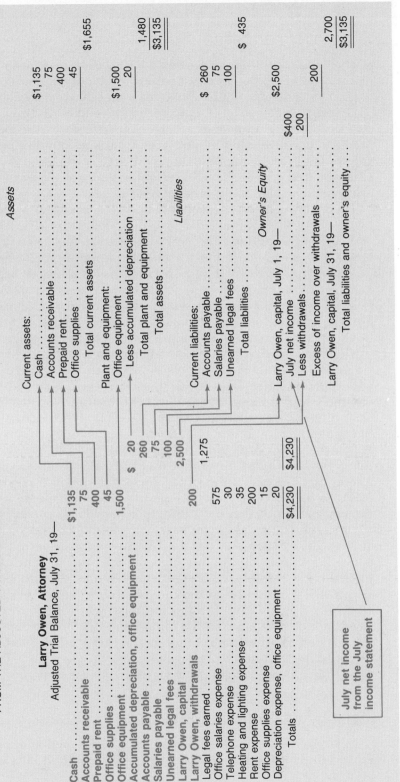

Larry Owen, Attorney
Adjusted Trial Balance, July 31, 19—

Cash	$1,135	
Accounts receivable	75	
Prepaid rent	400	
Office supplies	45	
Office equipment	1,500	
Accumulated depreciation, office equipment		$ 20
Accounts payable		260
Salaries payable		75
Unearned legal fees		100
Larry Owen, capital		2,500
Larry Owen, withdrawals	200	
Legal fees earned		1,275
Office salaries expense	575	
Telephone expense	30	
Heating and lighting expense	35	
Rent expense	200	
Office supplies expense	15	
Depreciation expense, office equipment	20	
Totals	$4,230	$4,230

Larry Owen, Attorney
Balance Sheet, July 31, 19—

Assets

Current assets:
Cash	$1,135	
Accounts receivable	75	
Prepaid rent	400	
Office supplies	45	
Total current assets		$1,655

Plant and equipment:
Office equipment	$1,500	
Less accumulated depreciation	20	
Total plant and equipment		1,480
Total assets		$3,135

Liabilities

Current liabilities:
Accounts payable	$ 260	
Salaries payable	75	
Unearned legal fees	100	
Total liabilities		$ 435

Owner's Equity

Larry Owen, capital, July 1, 19—		$2,500
July net income	$400	
Less withdrawals	200	
Excess of income over withdrawals		200
Larry Owen, capital, July 31, 19—		2,700
Total liabilities and owner's equity		$3,135

July net income from the July income statement

Illustration 3–4

THE ADJUSTMENT PROCESS

The *adjustment process* described in this chapter arises from recognition that the operation of a business results in a continuous stream of transactions. Some of the transactions affect several accounting periods. And, the objective of the process is to allocate to each period that portion of a transaction's effects applicable to the period. For example, if a revenue is earned over several accounting periods, the adjustment process apportions and credits to each period its fair share. Likewise, if an expense benefits several periods, the adjustment process charges a fair share to each benefited period.

The adjustment process is based on two accounting principles, the *realization principle* and the *matching principle*. The *realization principle* requires that revenue be assigned to the accounting period in which it is earned, rather than to the period it is collected in cash. The *matching principle* requires that revenues and expenses be matched. As for matching revenues and expenses, it is recognized that a business incurs expenses in order to earn revenues. Consequently, it is only proper that expenses be matched with (deducted on the income statement from) the revenues they helped to produce.

The basic purpose behind the adjustment process, the *realization principle,* and the *matching principle* is to make the information on accounting statements comparable from period to period. For example, the Owen law practice paid its rent for three months in advance on July 1 and debited the $600 payment to Prepaid Rent. Then at the end of July it transferred $200 of this amount to its Rent Expense account and the $200 appeared on its July income statement as the July rent expense. At the end of August it will transfer another $200 to rent expense, and at the end of September it will transfer the third $200. As a result, the amounts shown for rent expense on its July, August, and September income statements will be comparable.

An unsatisfactory alternate procedure would be to debit the entire $600 to Rent Expense at the time of payment and permit the entire amount to appear on the July income statement as rent expense for July. However, if this were done, the July income statement would show $600 of rent expense and the August and September statements would show none. Thus the income statements of the three months would not be comparable. In addition, the July net income would be understated $400 and the net incomes of August and September would be overstated $200 each. As a result, a person seeing only the fluctuations in net income might draw an incorrect conclusion.

ARRANGEMENT OF THE ACCOUNTS IN THE LEDGER

Normally the accounts of a business are classified and logically arranged in its ledger. This serves two purposes: (1) it aids in locating any account and (2) it aids in preparing the statements. Obviously, statements can be prepared with the least difficulty if accounts are arranged in the ledger in the order of their statement appearance. This causes the accounts to appear on the adjusted trial balance in their statement order, which aids in rearranging the adjusted trial balance items into a balance sheet and an income statement. Consequently, the balance sheet accounts beginning with Cash and ending with the owner's equity accounts appear first in the ledger. These are followed by the revenue and expense accounts in the order of their income statement appearance.

DISPOSING OF ACCRUED ITEMS

Accrued expenses

Several pages back the July 29, 30, and 31 accrued wages of the secretary were recorded as follows:

July	31	Office Salaries Expense	75.00	
		Salaries Payable		75.00
		To record the earned but unpaid wages.		

When these wages are paid on Friday, August 9, the following entry is required:

Aug.	9	Salaries Payable	75.00	
		Office Salaries Expense	175.00	
		Cash		250.00
		Paid two weeks' wages.		

The first debit in the August 9 entry cancels the liability for the three days' wages accrued on July 31. The second debit records the wages of August's first seven working days as an expense of the August accounting period. The credit records the amount paid the secretary.

Accrued revenues

On July 15 Larry Owen entered into an agreement to do the legal work of Guaranty Bank on a fixed-fee basis for $150 per month. On July 31 the following entry was made to record one-half month's revenue earned under this contract:

July	31	Accounts Receivable	75.00	
		Legal Fees Earned		75.00
		To record legal fees earned.		

And when payment of the first month's fee is received on August 15, the following entry will be made:

Aug.	15	Cash	150.00	
		Accounts Receivable		75.00
		Legal Fees Earned		75.00
		Received legal fees earned.		

The first credit in the August 15 entry records the collection of the fee accrued at the end of July. The second credit records as revenue the fee earned during the first half of August.

CASH AND ACCRUAL BASES OF ACCOUNTING

For income tax purposes an individual or a business in which inventories are not a factor may report income on either a *cash basis* or an *accrual basis.* Under the cash basis no adjustments are made for prepaid, unearned, and accrued items. Revenues are reported as being earned in the accounting period in which they are received in cash. Expenses are deducted from revenues in the accounting period in which cash is disbursed in their payment. As a result, under the cash basis, net income is the difference between revenue receipts and expense disbursements. Under the accrual basis, on the other hand, adjustments are made for accrued and deferred (prepaid and unearned) items. Under this basis revenues are credited to the period in which earned, expenses are matched with revenues, and no consideration is given to when cash is received and disbursed. As a result, net income is the difference between revenues earned and the expenses incurred in earning the revenues.

The cash basis of accounting is satisfactory for individuals and a few concerns in which accrued and deferred items are not important. However, it is not satisfactory for most concerns since it results in accounting reports that are not comparable from period to period. Consequently, most businesses keep their records on an accrual basis.

CLASSIFICATION OF BALANCE SHEET ITEMS

The balance sheets in the first two chapters were simple ones, and no attempt was made to classify the items. However, a balance sheet becomes more useful when its assets and liabilities are classified into significant groups, because a reader of a *classified balance sheet* can better judge the adequacy of the different kinds of assets used in the business. The reader can also better estimate the probable availability of funds to meet the various liabilities as they become due.

Accountants are not in full agreement as to the best way in which to classify balance sheet items. As a result, they are classified in several ways. A common way classifies assets into (1) current assets, (2) long-term investments, (3) plant and equipment, and (4) intangible assets. It classifies liabilities into (1) current liabilities and (2) long-term liabilities.

Of the four asset classifications listed, only two, current assets and plant and equipment, appear on the balance sheet of Valley Store, Illustration 3–5 on the next page. The store is small and has no long-term investments and intangible assets.

Current assets

Current assets are primarily those to which current creditors (current liabilities) may look for payment. As presently defined, current assets consist of cash and assets that are reasonably expected to be realized in cash or be sold or consumed within one year or within one *operating cycle of the business*, whichever is longer. The accounts and notes receivable of Illustration 3–5 are expected to be realized in cash. The merchandise (merchandise inventory) is expected to be sold either for cash or accounts receivable that will be realized in cash. The prepaid insurance and supplies are to be consumed.

The operating cycle of a business is the average period of time between its acquisition of merchandise or raw materials and the realization of cash from the sale of the merchandise or the sale of the products manufactured from the raw materials. In many concerns this interval is less than one year, and as a result these concerns use a one-year period in classifying current assets. However, due to an aging process or other cause, some concerns have an operating cycle longer than one year. For example, distilleries must age some products for several years before the products are ready for sale. Consequently, in such concerns inventories of raw materials, manufacturing supplies, and products being processed for sale are classified as current assets, although the products made from the inventories will not be ready for sale for more than a year.

Such things as prepaid insurance, office supplies, and store supplies are called *prepaid expenses*. Until consumed they are classified as current assets. An AICPA committee said: "Prepaid expenses are not current assets in the sense that they will be converted into cash but in the sense that, if not paid in advance, they would require the use of

Valley Store
Balance Sheet, December 31, 198A

Assets

Current assets:

Cash................................		$ 1,050	
Notes receivable		300	
Accounts receivable		3,961	
Merchandise inventory		10,248	
Prepaid insurance		109	
Office supplies		46	
Stores supplies...........................		145	
Total current assets			$15,859

Plant and equipment:

Office equipment	$ 1,500		
Less accumulated depreciation	300	$ 1,200	
Store equipment	$ 3,200		
Less accumulated depreciation	800	2,400	
Buildings	$25,000		
Less accumulated depreciation	7,400	17,600	
Land.....................................		4,200	
Total plant and equipment			25,400
Total assets			$41,259

Liabilities

Current liabilities:

Notes payable	$ 3,000		
Accounts payable	2,715		
Wages payable	112		
Mortgage payable (current portion)	1,200		
Total current liabilities		$ 7,027	

Long-term liabilities:

First mortgage payable, secured by a mortgage on land and buildings		8,800	
Total liabilities			$15,827

Owner's Equity

Samuel Jackson, capital, January 1, 198A		$23,721	
Net income for the year	$19,711		
Less withdrawals	18,000		
Excess of income over withdrawals		1,711	
Samuel Jackson, capital, December 31, 198A..			25,432
Total liabilities and owner's equity ..			$41,259

Illustration 3–5

current assets during the operating cycle."[1] This means that if the prepaid expense items were not already owned, current assets would be required for their purchase during the operating cycle.

The prepaid expenses of a business, as a total, are seldom a major

[1] Committee on Accounting Procedure, "Accounting Research Bulletin No. 43," *Accounting Research and Terminology Bulletins, Final Edition* (New York: AICPA, 1961), p. 20.

item on its balance sheet. As a result, instead of listing them individually, as in Illustration 3–5, they are commonly totaled and only the total is shown under the caption "Prepaid expenses."

Long-term investments

The second balance sheet classification is long-term investments. Stocks, bonds, and promissory notes that will be held for more than one year or one cycle appear under this classification. Also, such things as land held for future expansion but not now being used in the business operations appear here.

Plant and equipment

Plant assets are relatively long-lived assets of a tangible nature that are held for use in the production or sale of other assets or services. Examples are items of equipment, buildings, and land. The key words in the definition are "long-lived" and "held for use in the production or sale of other assets or services." Land held for future expansion is not a plant asset. It is not being used to produce or sell other assets, goods, or services.

The words "Plant and equipment" are commonly used as a balance sheet caption. More complete captions are "Property, plant, and equipment" and "Land, buildings, and equipment." However, all three captions are long and unwieldy. As a result, items of plant and equipment will be called plant assets in this book.

The order in which plant assets are listed within the balance sheet classification is not uniform. However, they are often listed from the ones of least permanent nature to those of most permanent nature.

Intangible assets

Intangible assets are assets having no physical nature. Their value is derived from the rights conferred upon their owner by possession. Goodwill, patents, and trademarks are examples.

Current liabilities

Current liabilities are debts or other obligations that must be paid or liquidated within one year or one operating cycle, using presently listed current assets. Common current liabilities are notes payable, accounts payable, wages payable, taxes payable, interest payable, and unearned revenues. Also, that portion of a long-term debt due within one year or one operating cycle, for example, the $1,200 portion of the mortgage debt shown in Illustration 3–5, is a current liability. The order of their listing within the classification is not uniform. Often notes payable are listed first because notes receivable are listed first after cash in the current asset section.

Unearned revenues are classified as current liabilities because current assets will normally be required in their liquidation. For example, payments for future delivery of merchandise will be earned and the obligation for delivery will be liquidated by delivering merchandise, a current asset.

Long-term liabilities

The second main liability classification is long-term liabilities. Liabilities that are not due and payable for a comparatively long period, usually more than one year, are listed under this classification. Common long-term liability items are mortgages payable, bonds payable, and notes payable due more than a year after the balance sheet date.

OWNER'S EQUITY ON THE BALANCE SHEET

Single proprietorship

The equity of the owner of a single proprietorship business may be shown on a balance sheet as follows:

Owner's Equity		
James Gibbs, capital, January 1, 198A		$23,152
Net income for the year	$10,953	
Withdrawals	12,000	
Excess of withdrawals over income		(1,047)
James Gibbs, capital, December 31, 198A		$22,105

The withdrawals of James Gibbs exceeded his net income, and in the equity section the excess is enclosed in parentheses to indicate that it is a negative or subtracted amount. Negative amounts are commonly shown in this way on financial statements.

The illustrated equity section shows the increases and decreases in owner's equity resulting from earnings and withdrawals. Some accountants prefer to put these details on a supplementary schedule attached to the balance sheet and called a *statement of owner's equity*. When this is done, owner's equity is shown on the balance sheet as follows:

Owner's Equity	
James Gibbs, capital (see schedule attached)	$22,105

Partnerships

Changes in partnership equities resulting from earnings and withdrawals are commonly shown in a statement of partners' equities. Then, only the amount of each partner's equity and the total of the equities as of the statement date are shown on the balance sheet, as follows:

Partners' Equities

John Reed, capital $16,534
Robert Burns, capital 18,506
    Total equities of the partners...... $35,040

Corporations

Corporations are regulated by state corporation laws. These laws require that a distinction be made between amounts invested in a corporation by its stockholders and the increase or decrease in stockholders' equity due to earnings, losses, and dividends. Consequently, stockholders' equity is commonly shown on a corporation balance sheet as follows:

Stockholders' Equity

Common stock $500,000
Retained earnings 64,450
    Total stockholders' equity ... $564,450

If a corporation issues only one kind of stock (others are discussed later), it is called *common stock*. The $500,000 amount shown here for this item is the amount originally invested in this corporation by its stockholders through the purchase of the corporation's stock. The $64,450 of *retained earnings* represents the increase in the stockholders' equity resulting from earnings that exceeded any losses and any *dividends* paid to the stockholders. (A dividend is a distribution of assets made by a corporation to its stockholders. A dividend of cash reduces corporation assets and the equity of its stockholders in the same way a withdrawal reduces assets and owner's equity in a single proprietorship.)

ARRANGEMENT OF BALANCE SHEET ITEMS

The balance sheet of Illustration 1–2 in the first chapter, with the liabilities and owner's equity placed to the right of the assets, is called an *account form balance sheet*. Such an arrangement emphasizes that assets equal liabilities plus owner's equity. Account form balance sheets are often reproduced on a double page with the assets on the left-hand page and the liabilities and owner's equity on the right-hand page.

The balance sheet of Illustration 3–5 is called a *report form balance sheet*. Its items are arranged vertically and better fit a single page. Both forms are commonly used, and neither is preferred.

CLASSIFICATION OF INCOME STATEMENT ITEMS

An income statement, like a balance sheet, is more useful with its items classified. However, the classifications used depend upon the type of business for which the statement is prepared and the nature of its costs and expenses; consequently, a discussion of this is deferred to Chapter 5, after more income statement items are introduced.

GLOSSARY

Account form balance sheet. A balance sheet with the assets on the left and the liability and owner's equity items on the right.

Accounting period. The time interval over which the transactions of a business are recorded and at the end of which its financial statements are prepared.

Accrual basis of accounting. The accounting basis in which revenues are assigned to the accounting period in which earned regardless of whether or not received in cash and expenses incurred in earning the revenues are deducted from the revenues regardless of whether or not cash has been disbursed in their payment.

Accrued expense. An expense which has been incurred during an accounting period but which has not been paid and recorded because payment is not due.

Accrued revenue. A revenue that has been earned during an accounting period but has not been received and recorded because payment is not due.

Accumulated depreciation. The cumulative amount of depreciation recorded against an asset or group of assets during the entire period of time the asset or assets have been owned.

Adjusted trial balance. A trial balance showing account balances brought up to date by recording appropriate adjusting entries.

Adjusting entries. Journal entries made to assign revenues to the period in which earned and to match revenues and expenses.

Adjustment process. The end-of-the-period process of recording appropriate adjusting entries to assign revenues to the period in which earned and to match revenues and expenses.

Cash basis of accounting. The accounting basis in which revenues are reported as being earned in the accounting period received in cash and expenses are deducted from revenues in the accounting period in which cash is disbursed in their payment.

Classified balance sheet. A balance sheet with assets and liabilities classified into significant groups.

Common stock. The name given to a corporation's stock when it issues only one kind or class of stock.

Contra account. An account the balance of which is subtracted from the balance of an associated account to show a more proper amount for the item recorded in the associated account.

Current asset. Cash or an asset that may reasonably be expected to be realized in cash or be consumed within one year or one operating cycle of the business, whichever is longer.

Current liability. A debt or other obligation that must be paid or liquidated within one year or one operating cycle, and the payment or liquidation of which will require the use of presently classified current assets.

Depreciation. The expiration of a plant asset's "quantity of usefulness."

Depreciation expense. The expense resulting from the expiration of a plant asset's "quantity of usefulness."

Dividend. A distribution of cash or other assets made by a corporation to its stockholders.

Fiscal year. A period of any 12 consecutive months used as an accounting period.

Intangible asset. An asset having no physical existence but having value because of the rights conferred as a result of its ownership and possession.

Matching principle. The accounting rule that all expenses incurred in earning a revenue be deducted from the revenue in determining net income.

Natural business year. Any 12 consecutive months used by a business as an accounting period, at the end of which the activities of the business are at their lowest point.

Operating cycle of a business. The average period of time between the acquisition of merchandise or materials by a business and the realization of cash from the sale of the merchandise or product manufactured from the materials.

Plant and equipment. Tangible assets having relatively long lives that are used in the production or sale of other assets or services.

Prepaid expense. An asset that will be consumed in the operation of a business, and as it is consumed it will become an expense.

Report form balance sheet. A balance sheet prepared on one page, at the top of which the assets are listed, followed down the page by the liabilities and owner's equity.

Retained earnings. Stockholders' equity in a corporation resulting from earnings in excess of losses and dividends declared.

Time-period concept. The idea that the life of a business is divisible into time periods of equal length.

Unadjusted trial balance. A trial balance prepared after transactions are recorded but before any adjustments are made.

Unearned revenue. Payment received in advance for goods or services to be delivered at a later date.

QUESTIONS FOR CLASS DISCUSSION

1. Why are the balances of some of a concern's accounts normally incorrect for statement purposes at the end of an accounting period even though all transactions were correctly recorded?
2. Other than to make the accounts show proper statement amounts, what is the basic purpose behind the end-of-the-period adjustment process?
3. A prepaid expense is an asset at the time of its purchase or prepayment. When is it best to ignore this and record the prepayment as an expense? Why?
4. What is a contra account? Give an example.
5. What contra account is used in recording depreciation? Why is such an account used?
6. What is an accrued expense? Give an example.
7. How does an unearned revenue arise? Give an example of an unearned revenue.
8. What is the balance sheet classification of an unearned revenue?
9. What is an accrued revenue? Give an example.
10. When the statements are prepared from an adjusted trial balance, why should the income statement be prepared first?
11. The adjustment process results from recognizing that some transactions affect several accounting periods. What is the objective of the process?
12. When are a concern's revenues and expenses matched?
13. Why should the income statements of a concern be comparable from period to period?
14. What is the usual order in which accounts are arranged in the ledger?
15. Differentiate between the cash and the accrual bases of accounting?
16. What is a classified balance sheet?
17. What are the characteristics of a current asset? What are the characteristics of an asset classified as plant and equipment?
18. What are current liabilities? Long-term liabilities?
19. The equity section of a corporation balance sheet shows two items, common stock and retained earnings. What does the sum of the items represent? How did each item arise?

CLASS EXERCISES

Exercise 3–1

A company has two shop employees who together earn a total of $100 per day for a five-day week that begins on Monday and ends on Friday. They were paid for the week ended Friday, December 26, and both worked full days on Monday, Tuesday, and Wednesday, December 29, 30, and 31. January 1 of the next year was an unpaid holiday and none of the employees worked, but all worked a full day on Friday, January 2. Give in general journal form the year-end adjusting entry to record the accrued wages and the entry to pay the employees on January 2.

Exercise 3–2

Give in general journal form the year-end adjusting entry for each of the following situations:

a. The Shop Supplies account had a $225 debit balance on January 1; $340 of supplies were purchased during the year; and a year-end inventory showed $120 of unconsumed supplies on hand.

b. The Prepaid Insurance account had a $765 debit balance at the end of the accounting period before adjustment for expired insurance. An examination of insurance policies showed $410 of insurance expired.

c. The Prepaid Insurance account had a $880 debit balance at the end of the accounting period before adjustment for expired insurance. An examination of insurance policies showed $315 of unexpired insurance.

d. Depreciation on shop equipment was estimated at $625 for the accounting period.

e. Three months' property taxes, estimated at $320, have accrued but are unrecorded at the accounting period end.

Exercise 3–3

Assume that the required adjustments of Exercise 3–2 were not made at the end of the accounting period and tell for each adjustment the effect of its omission on the income statement and balance sheet prepared at that time.

Exercise 3–4

Determine the amounts indicated by the question marks in the columns below. The amounts in each column constitute a separate problem.

	(a)	(b)	(c)	(d)
Supplies on hand on January 1	$235	$140	$375	$?
Supplies purchased during the year	450	530	?	630
Supplies remaining at the year-end	165	?	215	240
Supplies consumed during the year	?	480	670	560

Exercise 3–5

A company paid the $900 premium on a three-year insurance policy on June 1, 198A.

a. How many dollars of the premium should appear on the 198A income statement as an expense?
b. How many dollars of the premium should appear on the December 31, 198A, balance sheet as an asset?
c. Under the assumption that the Prepaid Insurance account was debited in recording the premium payment, give the December 31, 198A, adjusting entry to record the expired insurance.
d. Under the assumption that the bookkeeper incorrectly debited the Insurance Expense account for $900 in recording the premium payment, give the December 31, 198A, adjusting entry. (Hint: Did the bookkeeper's error change the answers to questions [a] and [b] of this exercise?)

Exercise 3–6

a. A tenant rented space in a building on November 1 at $300 per month, paying six months' rent in advance. The building owner credited Unearned Rent to record the $1,800 received. Give the year-end adjusting entry of the building owner.
b. Another tenant rented space in the building at $400 per month on October 1. The tenant paid the rent on the first day of October and again on the first day of November; but by December 31 the December rent had not yet been paid. Give the required adjusting entry of the building owner.
c. Assume the foregoing tenant paid the rent for December and January on January 2 of the new year. Give the entry to record the receipt of the $800.

PROBLEMS

Problem 3–1

The following information for adjustments was available on December 31, the end of a yearly accounting period. Prepare an adjusting journal entry for each unit of information.

a. The Store Supplies account had a $125 debit balance at the beginning of the year, $560 of supplies were purchased during the year, and an inventory of unused store supplies at the year-end totaled $135.
b. An examination of insurance policies showed three policies, as follows:

Policy	Date of purchase	Life of policy	Cost
1	October 1 of previous year	3 years	$720
2	April 1 of current year	2 years	480
3	August 1 of current year	1 year	180

Prepaid Insurance was debited for the cost of each policy at the time of its purchase. Expired insurance was correctly recorded at the end of the previous year.

c. The company's two office employees earn $40 per day and $50 per day, respectively. They are paid each Friday for a five-day workweek that begins on Monday. This year December 31 falls on Tuesday, and the employees both worked on Monday and Tuesday.

d. The company owns a building that it completed and occupied for the first time on June 1 of the current year. The building cost $288,000, has an estimated 40-year life, and is not expected to have any salvage value at the end of that time.

e. The company occupies most of the space in its building but it also rents space to two tenants. One tenant rented a small amount of space on September 1 at $120 per month. The tenant paid the rent on the first day of each month September through November, and the amounts paid were credited to Rent Earned. However, the tenant has not paid the rent for December, although on several occasions the tenant said the rent would be paid the next day. (f) The second tenant agreed on November 1 to rent a small amount of space at $150 per month, and on that date paid three months' rent in advance. The amount paid was credited to the Unearned Rent account.

Problem 3–2

A trial balance of the ledger of Rockhill Realty at the end of its annual accounting period carried these items:

ROCKHILL REALTY

Trial Balance, December 31, 19—

Cash	$ 2,940	
Prepaid insurance	815	
Office supplies	290	
Office equipment	3,250	
Accumulated depreciation, office equipment		$ 920
Automobile	6,780	
Accumulated depreciation, automobile		1,150
Accounts payable		225
Unearned management fees		420
Alice Hall, capital		6,745
Alice Hall, withdrawals	15,600	
Sales commissions earned		34,210
Office salaries expense	10,300	
Advertising expense	830	
Rent expense	2,400	
Telephone expense	465	
Totals	$43,670	$43,670

Required:

1. Open the accounts of the trial balance plus these additional ones: Accounts Receivable; Office Salaries Payable; Management Fees Earned; Insurance Expense; Office Supplies Expense; Depreciation Expense, Office Equipment; and Depreciation Expense, Automobile. Enter the trial balance amounts in the accounts.

2. Use the following information to prepare and post adjusting journal entries:
   a. An examination of insurance policies showed $585 of expired insurance.
   b. An inventory showed $75 of unused office supplies on hand.
   c. The year's depreciation on office equipment was estimated at $325 and (d) on the automobile at $1,100.
   e. and (f) Rockhill Realty offers property management services and has two contracts with clients. In the first contract (e) it agreed to manage an office building beginning on November 1. The contract called for a $140 monthly fee, and the client paid the fees for the first three months in advance at the time the contract was signed. The amount paid was credited to the Unearned Management Fees account. In the second contract (f) it agreed to manage an apartment building for a $100 monthly fee payable at the end of each quarter. The contract was signed on October 15, and two and a half months' fees have accrued.
   g. The one office employee is paid weekly, and on December 31 three days' wages at $40 per day have accrued.
3. After posting the adjusting entries, prepare an adjusted trial balance, an income statement, and a classified balance sheet.

Problem 3–3

A trial balance of the ledger of Phoenix Moving and Storage Service carried these items:

PHOENIX MOVING AND STORAGE SERVICE
Trial Balance, December 31, 19—

Cash	$ 1,240	
Accounts receivable	590	
Prepaid insurance	1,580	
Office supplies	220	
Office equipment	2,650	
Accumulated depreciation, office equipment		$ 680
Trucks	24,200	
Accumulated depreciation, trucks		8,540
Buildings	68,000	
Accumulated depreciation, buildings		8,600
Land	7,500	
Unearned storage fees		730
Mortgage payable		37,500
Ted Lee, capital		35,290
Ted Lee, withdrawals	13,000	
Revenue from moving services		56,860
Storage fees earned		3,770
Office salaries expense	8,580	
Movers' wages expense	18,730	
Gas, oil, and repairs	2,680	
Mortgage interest expense	3,000	
Totals	$151,970	$151,970

Required:

1. Open the accounts of the trial balance plus these additional ones: Wages Payable; Insurance Expense; Office Supplies Expense; Depreciation Expense, Office Equipment; Depreciation Expense, Trucks; and Depreciation Expense, Buildings. Enter the trial balance amounts in the accounts.
2. Use this information to prepare and post adjusting journal entries:
    a. An examination of insurance policies showed $1,270 of expired insurance.
    b. An inventory of office supplies showed $60 of unused supplies on hand.
    c. Estimated depreciation on office equipment, $240; *(d)* trucks, $3,000; and *(e)* buildings, $2,400.
    f. The company credits the storage fees of customers who pay in advance to the Unearned Storage Fees account. Of the $730 credited to this account during the year, $420 had been earned by the year-end.
    g. Accrued storage fees earned but unrecorded in the accounts and uncollected at the year-end totaled $160.
    h. There were $540 of accrued movers' wages at the year-end.
3. After posting the adjusting journal entries, prepare an adjusted trial balance, an income statement, and a classified balance sheet. A $2,500 installment on the mortgage is due within one year.

Problem 3–4

After all its transactions had been recorded at the end of its annual accounting period, a trial balance of the ledger of RV Trailer Park carried these items:

RV TRAILER PARK
Trial Balance, December 31, 19—

Cash	$ 3,540	
Prepaid insurance	825	
Office supplies	260	
Office equipment	1,450	
Accumulated depreciation, office equipment		$ 420
Buildings and improvements	72,000	
Accumulated depreciation, buildings and improvements ..		8,350
Land	85,000	
Unearned rent		480
Mortgage payable		108,000
Jane Wells, capital		35,635
Jane Wells, withdrawals	10,500	
Rent earned		39,865
Wages expense	8,120	
Utilities expense	525	
Property taxes expense	2,115	
Interest expense	8,415	
Totals	$192,750	$192,750

Required:

1. Open the accounts of the trial balance plus these additional ones: Accounts Receivable; Wages Payable; Property Taxes Payable; Interest Payable; Insurance Expense; Office Supplies Expense; Depreciation Expense, Office Equipment; and Depreciation Expense, Buildings and Improvements.
2. Use the following information to prepare and to post adjusting journal entries:

   a. An examination of insurance policies showed $650 of insurance expired.

   b. An office supplies inventory showed $110 of unused supplies on hand.

   c. Estimated depreciation of office equipment, $125; and *(d)* on the buildings and improvements, $2,450.

   e. RV Trailer Park follows the practice of crediting the Unearned Rent account for rents paid in advance by tenants, and an examination revealed that $360 of the balance of this account had been earned by year-end.

   f. A tenant is a month in arrears on rent payments, and this $75 of accrued revenue was unrecorded at the time the trial balance was prepared.

   g. The one employee works a five-day week at $30 per day. The employee was paid last week but has worked two days this week for which no pay was received.

   h. Three months' property taxes expense, totaling $700, has accrued but is unrecorded.

   i. One month's interest on the mortgage, $765, has accrued but is unrecorded.
3. After posting the adjusting journal entries, prepare an adjusted trial balance, an income statement, and a classified balance sheet. A $3,000 installment on the mortgage is due within one year.

Problem 3–5

The 198A and 198B balance sheets of a company showed the following asset and liability amounts at the end of each year:

	December 31	
	198A	*198B*
Prepaid insurance	$600	$300
Interest payable	400	100
Unearned property management fees	200	500

The concern's records showed the following amounts of cash disbursed and received for these items during 198B:

Cash disbursed to pay insurance premiums	$1,600
Cash disbursed to pay interest	1,200
Cash received for managing property	2,300

Required:

Present calculations to show the amounts to be reported on the 198B income statements for *(a)* insurance expense, *(b)* interest expense, and *(c)* property management fees earned.

ALTERNATE PROBLEMS

Problem 3–1A

The following information for adjustments was available on December 31, the end of an annual accounting period. Prepare an adjusting journal entry for each unit of information.

a. The Office Supplies account showed the following items:

Office Supplies

Jan. 1	Balance	85	
Feb. 9	Purchase	140	
Oct. 4	Purchase	65	

The year-end office supplies inventory showed $75 of unused supplies on hand.

b. The Prepaid Insurance account showed these items:

Prepaid Insurance

Jan. 1	Balance	280	
June 1		540	
Aug. 1		720	

The January 1 balance represents the unexpired premium on a one-year policy purchased on June 1 of the previous year. The June 1 debit resulted from paying the premium on a one-year policy, and the August 1 debit represents the cost of a three-year policy.

c. The company's three office employees earn $24, $32, and $40 per day, respectively. They are paid each Friday for a five-day workweek that begins on Monday. They were paid last week and have worked Monday, Tuesday, and Wednesday, December 29, 30, and 31, this week.

d. The company owns and occupies a building that was completed and occupied for the first time on March 1 of the current year. Previously the company had rented quarters. The building cost $360,000, has an estimated 40-year useful life, and is not expected to have any salvage value at the end of its life.

e. The company rents portions of the space in its building to two tenants. One tenant agreed beginning on September 1 to rent a small amount of space at $125 per month, and on that date the tenant paid six months' rent in advance. The $750 payment was credited to the Unearned Rent account.

f. The other tenant pays $150 rent per month on the space occupied by the tenant. During the months May through November the tenant paid the rent each month on the first day of the month, and the amounts paid were credited to Rent Earned. However, recently the tenant experienced financial difficulties and has not as yet paid the rent for the month of December.

Problem 3–2A

A trial balance of the ledger of Hillside Realty at the end of its annual accounting period carried these items:

HILLSIDE REALTY

Trial Balance, December 31, 19—

Cash	$ 2,940	
Prepaid insurance	815	
Office supplies	290	
Office equipment	3,250	
Accumulated depreciation, office equipment....		$ 920
Automobile.................................	6,780	
Accumulated depreciation, automobile		1,150
Accounts payable		225
Unearned management fees		420
Alice Hall, capital		6,745
Alice Hall, withdrawals	15,600	
Sales commissions earned		34,210
Office salaries expense	10,300	
Advertising expense	830	
Rent expense	2,400	
Telephone expense..........................	465	
Totals	$43,670	$43,670

Required:

1. Open the accounts of the trial balance plus these additional ones: Accounts Receivable; Office Salaries Payable; Management Fees Earned; Insurance Expense; Office Supplies Expense; Depreciation Expense, Office Equipment; and Depreciation Expense, Automobile. Enter the trial balance amounts in the accounts.
2. Use the following information to prepare and post adjusting journal entries:
   a. An examination of insurance policies showed $210 of unexpired insurance.
   b. An office supplies inventory showed $120 of unused supplies on hand.
   c. Depreciation for the year on the office equipment was estimated at $400, and (d) it was estimated at $1,150 on the automobile.
   e. The company offers property management services and has two clients under contract. It agreed to manage an apartment building for the first client for a $60 monthly fee payable at the end of each quarter.

The contract with this client was signed on November 1, and two months' fees have accrued.

f. For the second client it agreed to manage an office building for a $70 monthly fee. The contract with this client was signed on October 15, and at that time the client paid six months' fees in advance, which were credited on receipt to the Unearned Management Fees account.

g. The office secretary is paid weekly, and on December 31 four days' wages at $40 per day have accrued.

h. The December telephone bill, $45, arrived in the mail on December 31. It has not been recorded or paid.

3. After posting the adjusting entries, prepare an adjusted trial balance, an income statement, and a classified balance sheet.

Problem 3–3A

At the end of its annual accounting period Carefree Moving and Storage Service prepared the following trial balance:

CAREFREE MOVING AND STORAGE SERVICE
Trial Balance, December 31, 19—

Cash	$ 1,240	
Accounts receivable	590	
Prepaid insurance	1,580	
Office supplies	220	
Office equipment	2,650	
Accumulated depreciation, office equipment....		$ 680
Trucks	24,200	
Accumulated depreciation, trucks		8,540
Buildings	68,000	
Accumulated depreciation, buildings		8,600
Land	7,500	
Unearned storage fees		730
Mortgage payable		37,500
Ted Lee, capital		35,290
Ted Lee, withdrawals	13,000	
Revenue from moving services		56,860
Storage fees earned		3,770
Office salaries expense	8,580	
Movers' wages expense	18,730	
Gas, oil, and repairs expense	2,680	
Mortgage interest expense	3,000	
Totals	$151,970	$151,970

Required:

1. Open the accounts of the trial balance plus these additional ones: Wages Payable; Insurance Expense; Office Supplies Expense; Depreciation Expense, Office Equipment; Depreciation Expense, Trucks; and Depreciation

Expense, Buildings. Enter the trial balance amounts in the accounts.

2. Use this information to prepare and post adjusting journal entries:

a. An examination of insurance policies showed that $1,310 of insurance had expired.

b. An inventory of office supplies showed $40 of unused supplies on hand.

c. Estimated depreciation on office equipment, $285; *(d)* trucks, $4,200; and *(e)* buildings, $2,800.

f. The company credits the storage fees of customers who pay in advance to the Unearned Storage Fees account. Of the $730 credited to this account during the year, $380 had been earned by the year-end.

g. Accrued storage fees earned but unrecorded in the accounts and uncollected at the year-end totaled $130.

h. There were $490 of earned but unpaid movers' wages at the year-end.

3. After posting the adjusting journal entries, prepare an adjusted trial balance, an income statement, and a classified balance sheet. A $3,500 installment on the mortgage is due within one year.

Problem 3–4A

An inexperienced bookkeeper prepared the first of the following income statements but forgot to adjust the accounts before its preparation. However, the oversight was discovered, and the second correct statement was prepared. Analyze the two statements and prepare the adjusting journal entries that were made between their preparation. Assume that one fourth of the additional property management fees resulted from recognizing accrued management fees and three fourths resulted from previously recorded unearned fees that were earned by the time the statements were prepared. (You will need only general journal paper for the solution of this problem. You may use the paper provided for Problems 3–4 or 3–4A or for any other unassigned problem.)

ACTION REALTY

Income Statement for Year Ended December 31, 19—

Revenues:		
Commissions earned		$31,540
Property management fees earned		2,235
Total revenues		$33,775
Operating expenses:		
Rent expense	$3,025	
Salaries expense	8,280	
Advertising expense.....................	1,315	
Utilities expense	675	
Telephone expense	545	
Gas, oil, and repairs expense	925	
Total operating expenses		14,765
Net income		$19,010

ACTION REALTY
Income Statement for Year Ended December 31, 19—

Revenues:
Commissions earned $31,540
Property management fees earned   2,875
    Total revenues $34,415

Operating expenses:
Rent expense $3,300
Salaries expense   8,345
Advertising expense.....................   1,380
Utilitics expense   675
Telephone expcnsc   545
Gas, oil, and repairs expense   940
Office supplies expense   215
Insurance expense   985
Depreciation expense, office equipment....   420
Depreciation expense, automobile   1,210
Taxes expense   185
    Total operating expenses   18,200
Net income $16,215

Problem 3–5A

Robert Snell, a lawyer, has always kept his accounting records on a cash basis; and at the end of 198B he prepared the following cash basis income statement:

ROBERT SNELL, ATTORNEY
Income Statement for Year Ended December 31, 198B

Revenues $46,400
Expenses   22,300
Net income $24,100

In preparing the income statement, the following amounts of accrued and deferred items were ignored at the ends of 198A and 198B:

	End of	
	198A	*198B*
Prepaid expenses........	$1,215	$ 840
Accrued expenses	2,240	1,925
Unearned revenues	1,370	1,535
Accrued revenues	1,860	1,490

Required:

Assume that the 198A prepaid and unearned items became expenses or were earned in 198B, the ignored 198A accrued items were either received in cash or were paid in 198B, and prepare a condensed 198B accrual basis income statement for Robert Snell. Attach to your income statement calculations showing how you arrived at each income statement amount.

PROVOCATIVE PROBLEMS

Provocative problem 3-1
Andy Handy

On January 2 of this year Andy Handy began a small business he calls Handy Repair Shop. He has kept no formal accounting records, but he does file any unpaid invoices for things purchased by impaling them on a nail in the wall over his workbench. He has kept a good check stub record of the year's receipts and payments, which shows the following:

	Receipts	Payments
Investment	$ 3,000	
Shop equipment		$ 2,000
Repair parts and supplies		3,220
Rent expense		1,950
Insurance premiums		470
Newspaper advertising		250
Utilities		340
Helper's wages		6,180
Andy Handy for personal uses		13,900
Revenue from repairs	26,890	
Subtotals	$29,890	$28,310
Cash balance, December 31, 19—		1,580
Totals	$29,890	$29,890

Andy wants to know how much his business actually earned during its first year, and he would like for you to prepare an accrual basis income statement and a year-end classified balance sheet. You learn that the shop equipment has an estimated ten-year life, after which it will be worthless. There is a $275 unpaid invoice on the nail over Andy's workbench for supplies received, and an inventory shows $330 of unused supplies on hand. The shop space rents for $150 per month on a five-year lease. The lease contract requires payment for the first and last months' rents in advance, which were paid. The insurance premiums paid for two policies taken out on January 2. The first is a one-year policy that cost $110, and the second is a two-year policy that cost $360. There are $60 of accrued wages payable to the helper, and customers owe the shop $415 for services they have received.

Provocative problem 3-2
Dale's TV Service

Dale West began a new business on January 2 of this year. He calls the business Dale's TV Service, and he has asked you for help in determining the results of its first year's operations and its year-end financial position. He feels that the business has done a lot of work, but the bank has begun to dishonor its checks, its creditors are dunning the business and it is unable to pay, and he just cannot understand why.

You find the service's accounting records, such as they are, have been kept

by Dale West's wife, who has had no formal training in record keeping. However she has prepared the following statement of cash receipts and disbursements for your inspection:

DALE'S TV SERVICE
Cash Receipts and Disbursements
For Year Ended December 31, 19—

Receipts:
Investment .... $ 5,000
Received from customers for services.... 34,490 $39,490

Disbursements:
Rent expense........................ $ 2,600
Repair equipment purchased 4,200
Service truck expense 6,975
Wages expense 19,240
Insurance expense 890
Repair parts and supplies 5,650   39,555
Bank overdraft .... $ (65)

There were no errors in the statement and you learn these additional facts:

1. The lease contract for the shop space runs for five years and requires
    rent payments of $200 per month, with the first and last months' rent to
    be paid in advance. All required payments were made on time.
2. The repair equipment purchased has an estimated six-year life, after which
    it will be valueless. It has been used for the full year.
3. The service truck expense consists of $6,100 paid for the truck on January
    2, plus $875 paid for gas, oil, and repairs to the truck. Mr. West expects
    to use the truck four years, after which he thinks he will get $2,100 for
    it as a trade-in on a new truck.
4. The wages expense consists of $6,240 paid the service's one employee
    since he was hired on June 1 plus $250 per week withdrawn by Mr. West
    for personal living expenses. In addition, $100 is owed the one employee
    on December 31 for wages earned since the employee's last payday.
5. The $890 of insurance expense resulted from paying the premiums on
    two insurance policies on January 2. One policy cost $170 and gave protec-
    tion for one year, and the other policy cost $720 for two years' protection.
6. In addition to the $5,650 of repair parts and supplies paid for during
    the year, creditors are dunning the business for $515 for parts and supplies
    purchased and delivered, but not paid for. Also, an inventory shows there
    are $985 of unused parts and supplies on hand.
7. Mrs. West reports that the business does most of its work for cash, but
    customers do owe $450 for repair work done on credit.

Prepare an income statement showing the results of the first year's operations of the business and a classified balance sheet showing its financial position
as of the year-end.

The work sheet and closing the accounts of proprietorships, partnerships, and corporations

After studying Chapter 4, you should be able to:

■ Explain why a work sheet is prepared and be able to prepare a work sheet for a service-type business.

■ Explain why it is necessary to close the revenue and expense accounts at the end of each accounting period.

■ Prepare entries to close the temporary accounts of a service business and prepare a post-closing trial balance to test the accuracy of the end-of-the-period adjusting and closing procedures.

■ Explain the nature of the retained earnings item on corporation balance sheets.

■ Explain why a corporation with a deficit cannot pay a legal dividend.

■ Prepare entries to close the Income Summary account of a corporation and to record the declaration and payment of a dividend.

■ List the steps in the accounting cycle in the order in which they are completed.

■ Define or explain the words and phrases listed in the chapter Glossary.

As an aid in their work, accountants prepare numerous memoranda, analyses, and informal papers that serve as a basis for the formal reports given to management or to their clients. These analyses and memoranda are called *working papers* and are invaluable tools of the accountant. The work sheet described in this chapter is such a working paper. It is prepared solely for the accountant's use. It is not given to the owner or manager of the business for which it is prepared but is retained by the accountant. Normally it is prepared with a pencil, which makes changes and corrections easy as its preparation progresses.

WORK SHEET IN THE ACCOUNTING PROCEDURES

In the accounting procedures described in the previous chapter, at the end of an accounting period, as soon as all transactions were recorded, recall that adjusting entries were entered in the journal and posted to the accounts. Then an adjusted trial balance was prepared and used in making an income statement and balance sheet. For a very small business these are satisfactory procedures. However, if a company has more than a very few accounts and adjustments, errors in adjusting the accounts and in preparing the statements are less apt to be made if an additional step is inserted in the procedures. The additional step is the preparation of a *work sheet*. A work sheet is a tool of accountants upon which they (1) achieve the effect of adjusting the accounts before entering the adjustments in the accounts, (2) sort the adjusted acccount balances into columns according to whether the accounts are used in preparing the income statement or balance sheet, and (3) calculate and prove the mathematical accuracy of the net income. Then after the work sheet is completed, (4) accountants use the work sheet in preparing the income statement and balance sheet and in preparing adjusting journal entries.

PREPARING A WORK SHEET

The Owen law practice of previous chapters does not have sufficient accounts or adjustments to warrant the preparation of a work sheet. Nevertheless, since its accounts and adjustments are familiar, they are used here to illustrate the procedures involved.

During July, the Owen law practice completed a number of transactions. On July 31, after these transactions were recorded but *before any adjusting entries were prepared and posted,* a trial balance of its ledger appeared as in Illustration 4–1.

Larry Owen, Attorney
Trial Balance, July 31, 19—

Cash	$1,135	
Prepaid rent	600	
Office supplies......................	60	
Office equipment	1,500	
Accounts payable		$ 260
Unearned legal fees		150
Larry Owen, capital		2,500
Larry Owen, withdrawals	200	
Legal fees earned		1,150
Office salaries expense	500	
Telephone expense	30	
Heating and lighting expense	35	
Totals	$4,060	$4,060

Illustration 4–1

Notice that the trial balance is an *unadjusted trial balance.* The accounts have not been adjusted for expired rent, supplies consumed, depreciation, and so forth. Nevertheless, this unadjusted trial balance is the starting point in preparing the work sheet for the law practice. The work sheet is shown in Illustration 4–2.

Note that the work sheet has five pairs of money columns and that the first pair is labeled "Trial Balance." In this first pair of columns is copied the unadjusted trial balance of the law practice. Often when a work sheet is prepared, the trial balance is prepared for the first time in its first two money columns.

The second pair of work sheet columns is labeled "Adjustments." The adjustments are entered in these columns. Note they are, with one exception, the same adjustments for which adjusting journal entries were prepared and posted in the previous chapter. The one exception is the last one, *(e),* in which the two adjustments affecting the Legal Fees Earned account are combined into one compound adjustment. They were combined because both result in credits to the same account.

Note that the adjustments on the illustrated work sheet are keyed together with letters. When a work sheet is prepared, after it is completed, the adjusting entries still have to be entered in the journal and posted to the ledger. At that time the key letters help identify each adjustment's related debits and credits. Explanations of the adjustments on the illustrated work sheet are as follows:

Adjustment (a): To adjust for the rent expired.
Adjustment (b): To adjust for the office supplies consumed.

Larry Owen, Attorney
Work Sheet for Month Ended July 31, 19--

ACCOUNT TITLES	TRIAL BALANCE Dr.	TRIAL BALANCE Cr.	ADJUSTMENTS Dr.	ADJUSTMENTS Cr.	ADJUSTED TRIAL BALANCE Dr.	ADJUSTED TRIAL BALANCE Cr.	INCOME STATEMENT Dr.	INCOME STATEMENT Cr.	BALANCE SHEET Dr.	BALANCE SHEET Cr.
Cash	1,135 00				1,135 00				1,135 00	
Prepaid rent	600 00			(a)200 00	400 00				400 00	
Office supplies	60 00			(b) 15 00	45 00				45 00	
Office equipment	1,500 00				1,500 00				1,500 00	
Accounts payable		260 00				260 00				260 00
Unearned legal fees		150 00	(e) 50 00			100 00				100 00
Larry Owen, capital		2,500 00				2,500 00				2,500 00
Larry Owen, withdrawals	200 00				200 00				200 00	
Legal fees earned		1,150 00		(e)125 00		1,275 00		1,275 00		
Office salaries expense	500 00		(d) 75 00		575 00		575 00			
Telephone expense	30 00				30 00		30 00			
Heating & lighting expense	35 00				35 00		35 00			
	4,060 00	4,060 00								
Rent expense			(a)200 00		200 00		200 00			
Office supplies expense			(b) 15 00		15 00		15 00			
Depr. expense, office equip.			(c) 20 00		20 00		20 00			
Accum. depr., office equip.				(c) 20 00		20 00				20 00
Salaries payable				(d) 75 00		75 00				75 00
Accounts receivable			(e) 75 00		75 00				75 00	
			435 00	435 00	4,230 00	4,230 00	875 00	1,275 00	3,355 00	2,955 00
Net income							400 00			400 00
							1,275 00	1,275 00	3,355 00	3,355 00

Illustration 4-2

Adjustment (c):   To adjust for depreciation of the office equipment.
Adjustment (d):   To adjust for the accrued secretary's salary.
Adjustment (e):   To adjust for the unearned and accrued revenue.

Each adjustment on the illustrated work sheet required that one or two additional account names be written in below the original trial balance. These accounts did not have balances when the trial balance was prepared. Consequently, they were not listed in the trial balance. Often, when a work sheet is prepared, the effects of the adjustments are anticipated and any additional accounts required are provided without amounts in the body of the trial balance.

When a work sheet is prepared, after the adjustments are entered in the Adjustments columns, the columns are totaled to prove the equality of the adjustments.

The third set of work sheet columns is labeled "Adjusted Trial Balance." In preparing a work sheet, each amount in the Trial Balance columns is combined with its adjustment in the Adjustments columns, if any, and is entered in the Adjusted Trial Balance columns. For example, in Illustration 4–2 the Prepaid Rent account has a $600 debit balance in the Trial Balance columns. This $600 debit is combined with the $200 credit in the Adjustments columns to give Prepaid Rent a $400 debit in the Adjusted Trial Balance columns. Rent Expense has no balance in the Trial Balance columns, but it has a $200 debit in the Adjustment columns. Therefore, no balance combined with a $200 debit gives Rent Expense a $200 debit in the Adjusted Trial Balance columns. Cash, Office Equipment, and several other accounts have trial balance amounts but no adjustments. As a result, their trial balance amounts are carried unchanged into the Adjusted Trial Balance columns. Notice that the result of combining the amounts in the Trial Balance columns with the amounts in the Adjustments columns is an adjusted trial balance in the Adjusted Trial Balance columns.

After the combined amounts are carried to the Adjusted Trial Balance columns, the Adjusted Trial Balance columns are added to prove their equality. Then, the amounts in these columns are sorted to the proper Balance Sheet or Income Statement columns according to the statement on which they will appear. This is an easy task that requires only two decisions: (1) is the item to be sorted a debit or a credit and (2) on which statement does it appear. As to the first decision, an adjusted trial balance debit amount must be sorted to either the Income Statement debit column or the Balance Sheet debit column. Likewise, a credit amount must go into either the Income Statement credit or Balance Sheet credit column. In other words, debits remain debits and credits remain credits in the sorting process. As to the second decision, it is only necessary in the sorting process to remember that revenues and expenses appear on the income statement and assets, liabilities, and owner's equity items go on the balance sheet.

After the amounts are sorted to the proper columns, the columns are totaled. At this point, the difference between the totals of the Income Statement columns is the net income or loss. The difference is the net income or loss because revenues are entered in the credit column and expenses in the debit column. If the credit column total exceeds the debit column total, the difference is a net income. If the debit column total exceeds the credit column total, the difference is a net loss. In the illustrated work sheet, the credit column total exceeds the debit column total, and the result is a $400 net income.

After the net income is determined in the Income Statement columns, it is added to the total of the Balance Sheet credit column. The reason for this is that with the exception of the balance of the capital account, the amounts appearing in the Balance Sheet columns are "end-of-the-period" amounts. Therefore, it is necessary to add the net income to the Balance Sheet credit column total to make the Balance Sheet columns equal. Also, adding the income to this column has the effect of adding it to the capital account.

Had there been a loss, it would have been necessary to add the loss to the debit column. This is because losses decrease owner's equity, and adding the loss to the debit column has the effect of subtracting it from the capital account.

Balancing the Balance Sheet columns by adding the net income or loss is a proof of the accuracy with which the work sheet was prepared. When the income or loss is added in the Balance Sheet columns and the addition makes these columns equal, it is assumed that no errors were made in preparing the work sheet. However, if the addition does not make the columns equal, it is proof that an error or errors were made. The error or errors may have been either mathematical or an amount may have been sorted to a wrong column.

Although balancing the Balance Sheet columns with the net income or loss is a proof of the accuracy with which a work sheet was prepared, it is not an absolute proof. These columns will balance even when errors have been made if the errors are of a certain type. For example, an expense amount carried into the Balance Sheet debit column or an asset amount carried into the debit column of the income statement section will cause both of these columns to have incorrect totals. Likewise, the net income will be incorrect. However, when such an error is made, the Balance Sheet columns will balance, but with the incorrect amount of income. Therefore, when a work sheet is prepared, care must be exercised in sorting the adjusted trial balance amounts into the correct Income Statement or Balance Sheet columns.

WORK SHEET AND THE FINANCIAL STATEMENTS

As previously stated, the work sheet is a tool of the accountant and is not for management's use or publication. However, as soon as it is completed, the accountant uses it in preparing the income statement and balance sheet that are given to management. To do this the accountant rearranges the items in the work sheet's Income Statement columns into a formal income statement and rearranges the items in the Balance Sheet columns into a formal balance sheet.

WORK SHEET AND ADJUSTING ENTRIES

Entering the adjustments in the Adjustments columns of a work sheet does not get these adjustments into the ledger accounts. Consequently, after the work sheet and statements are completed, adjusting entries like the ones described in the previous chapter must still be entered in the General Journal and posted. The work sheet makes this easy, however, because its Adjustments columns provide the information for these entries. All that is needed is an entry for each adjustment appearing in the columns.

As for the adjusting entries for the illustrated work sheet, they are the same as the entries in the previous chapter, with the exception of the entry for adjustment (e). Here a compound entry having a $50 debit to Unearned Legal Fees, a $75 debit to Accounts Receivable, and a $125 credit to Legal Fees Earned is used.

CLOSING ENTRIES

After the work sheet and statements are completed, in addition to adjusting entries, it is also necessary to prepare and post *closing entries*. Closing entries clear and close the revenue and expense accounts. The accounts are cleared in the sense that their balances are transferred to another account. They are closed in the sense that they have zero balances after closing entries are posted.

WHY CLOSING ENTRIES ARE MADE

The revenue and expense accounts are cleared and closed at the end of each accounting period by transferring their balances to a summary account, called *Income Summary*. Their summarized amount, which is the net income or loss, is then transferred in a single proprietorship to the owner's capital account. These transfers are necessary because—

a. Revenues actually increase owner's equity and expenses decrease it.
b. However, throughout an accounting period these increases and decreases are accumulated in revenue and expense accounts rather than in the owner's capital account.
c. As a result, closing entries are necessary at the end of each accounting period to transfer the net effect of these increases and decreases out of the revenue and expense accounts and on to the owner's capital account.

In addition, closing entries also cause the revenue and expense accounts to begin each new accounting period with zero balances. This too is necessary because—

a. An income statement reports the revenues and expenses incurred during *one* accounting period and is prepared from information recorded in the revenue and expense accounts.

b. Consequently, these accounts must begin each new accounting period with zero balances if their end-of-the-period balances are to reflect just *one* period's revenues and expenses.

CLOSING ENTRIES ILLUSTRATED

At the end of July, after its adjusting entries were posted but before its accounts were cleared and closed, the owner's equity accounts of Owen's law practice had the balances shown in Illustration 4–3. (An

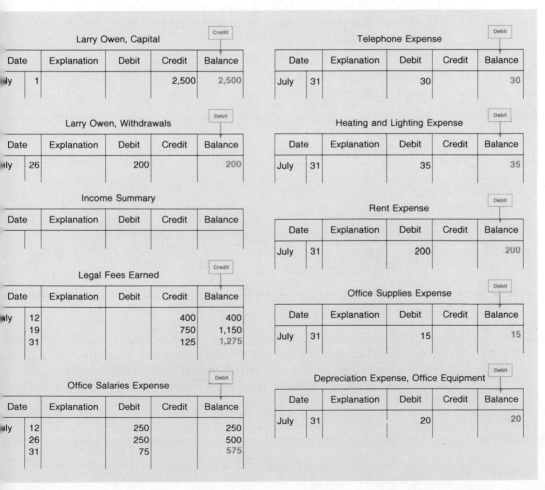

Larry Owen, Capital (Credit)

Date	Explanation	Debit	Credit	Balance
ly 1			2,500	2,500

Larry Owen, Withdrawals (Debit)

Date	Explanation	Debit	Credit	Balance
ly 26		200		200

Income Summary

Date	Explanation	Debit	Credit	Balance

Legal Fees Earned (Credit)

Date	Explanation	Debit	Credit	Balance
ly 12			400	400
19			750	1,150
31			125	1,275

Office Salaries Expense (Debit)

Date	Explanation	Debit	Credit	Balance
ly 12		250		250
26		250		500
31		75		575

Telephone Expense (Debit)

Date	Explanation	Debit	Credit	Balance
July 31		30		30

Heating and Lighting Expense (Debit)

Date	Explanation	Debit	Credit	Balance
July 31		35		35

Rent Expense (Debit)

Date	Explanation	Debit	Credit	Balance
July 31		200		200

Office Supplies Expense (Debit)

Date	Explanation	Debit	Credit	Balance
July 31		15		15

Depreciation Expense, Office Equipment (Debit)

Date	Explanation	Debit	Credit	Balance
July 31		20		20

account's Balance column heading as a rule does not tell the nature of an account's balance. However, in Illustration 4–3 and in the illustrations immediately following, the nature of each account's balance is shown as an aid to the student.)

Observe in Illustration 4–3 that Owen's capital account shows only its $2,500 July 1 balance. This is not the amount of Owen's equity on July 31. Closing entries are required to make this account show the July 31 equity.

Note also the third account in Illustration 4–3, the Income Summary account. This account is used only at the end of the accounting period in summarizing and clearing the revenue and expense accounts.

Closing revenue accounts

Before closing entries are posted, revenue accounts have credit balances. Consequently, to clear and close a revenue account an entry debiting the account and crediting Income Summary is required.

The Owen law practice has only one revenue account, and the entry to close and clear it is:

July	31	Legal Fees Earned	1,275.00	
		Income Summary		1,275.00
		To clear and close the revenue account.		

Posting the entry has this effect on the accounts:

	Legal Fees Earned				Credit		Income Summary				Credit
Date	Explanation	Debit	Credit	Balance		Date	Explanation	Debit	Credit	Balance
July 12			400	400		July 31			1,275	1,275
19			750	1,150						
31			125	1,275						
31		1,275		–0–						

Note that the entry clears the revenue account by transferring its balance as a credit to the Income Summary account. It also causes the revenue account to begin the new accounting period with a zero balance.

Closing expense accounts

Before closing entries are posted, expense accounts have debit balances. Consequently, to clear and close a concern's expense accounts, a compound entry debiting the Income Summary account and crediting each individual expense account is required. The Owen law practice has six expense accounts, and the compound entry to clear and close them is:

July	31	Income Summary	875.00	
		Office Salaries Expense..................		575.00
		Telephone Expense		30.00
		Heating and Lighting Expense		35.00
		Rent Expense		200.00
		Office Supplies Expense		15.00
		Depreciation Expense, Office Equipment ...		20.00
		To close and clear the expense accounts.		

Posting the entry has the effect shown in Illustration 4–4. Turn to Illustration 4–4 on the next page and observe that the entry clears the expense accounts of their balances by transferring the balances in a total as a debit to the Income Summary account. It also causes the expense accounts to begin the new period with zero balances.

Closing the Income Summary account

After a concern's revenue and expense accounts are cleared and their balances transferred to the *Income Summary account,* the balance of the Income Summary account is equal to the net income or loss. When revenues exceed expenses, there is a net income and the Income Summary account has a credit balance. On the other hand, when expenses exceed revenues, there is a loss and the account has a debit balance. But, regardless of the nature of its balance, the Income Summary account is cleared and its balance, the amount of net income or loss, is transferred to the capital account.

The Owen law practice earned $400 during July. Consequently, after its revenue and expense accounts are cleared, its Income Summary account has a $400 credit balance. This balance is transferred to the Larry Owen, Capital account with an entry like this:

July	31	Income Summary	400.00	
		Larry Owen, Capital		400.00
		To clear and close the Income Summary account.		

Posting this entry has the following effect on the accounts:

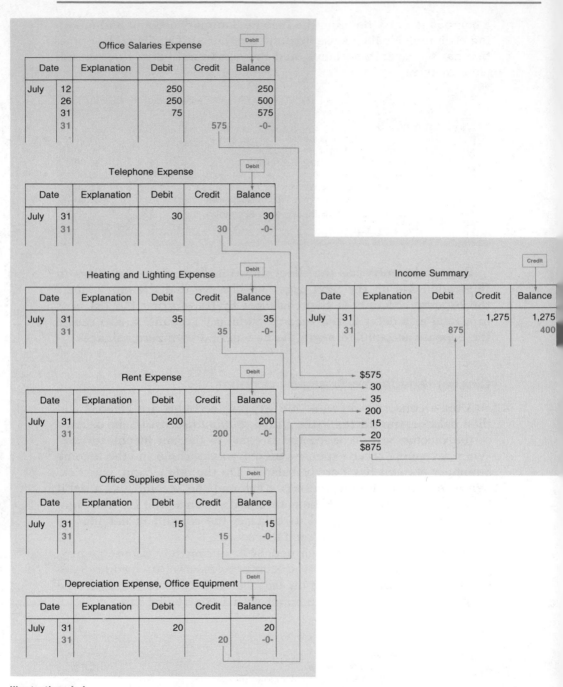

Illustration 4–4

Income Summary				Credit		Larry Owen, Capital				Credit
Date	Explanation	Debit	Credit	Balance	Date	Explanation	Debit	Credit	Balance
y 31			1,275	1,275	July 1				2,500	2,500
31		875		400	31				400	2,900
31		400		-0-					

Observe that the entry clears the Income Summary account, transferring its balance, the amount of the net income in this case, to the capital account.

Closing the withdrawals account

At the end of an accounting period the withdrawals account shows the owner's withdrawals. The account is closed, and its debit balance is transferred to the capital account with an entry like this:

July	31	Larry Owen, Capital	200.00	
		Larry Owen, Withdrawals		200.00
		To close and clear the withdrawals account.		

Posting the entry has this effect on the accounts:

Larry Owen, Withdrawals				Debit		Larry Owen, Capital				Credit
Date	Explanation	Debit	Credit	Balance	Date	Explanation	Debit	Credit	Balance
ly 26		200		200	July 1				2,500	2,500
31			200	-0-	31				400	2,900
					31		200			2,700

After the entry closing the withdrawals account is posted, observe that the two reasons for making closing entries are accomplished: (1) All revenue and expense accounts have zero balances. And (2) the net effect of the period's revenue, expense, and withdrawal transactions on the owner's equity is shown in the capital account.

Temporary accounts

Revenue and expense accounts plus the Income Summary and withdrawals accounts are often called *temporary accounts* because in a

sense the items recorded in these accounts are only temporarily recorded therein. At the end of each accounting period, through closing
entries their debit and credit effects are transferred out and on to
other accounts.

THE ACCOUNTS AFTER CLOSING

At this stage, after both adjusting and closing entries have been
posted, the Owen law practice accounts appear as in Illustration 4–
5. Observe in the illustration that the asset, liability, and the owner's

Cash   ACCOUNT NO. 1

DATE		EXPLANATION	POST. REF.	DEBIT	CREDIT	BALANCE
198A July	1		G1	2 5 0 0 00		2 5 0 0 00
	1		G1		6 0 0 00	1 9 0 0 00
	3		G1		1 2 0 0 00	7 0 0 00
	12		G1	4 0 0 00		1 1 0 0 00
	12		G1		2 5 0 00	8 5 0 00
	15		G1	1 5 0 00		1 0 0 0 00
	26		G2		2 5 0 00	7 5 0 00
	26		G2		2 0 0 00	5 5 0 00
	29		G2	7 5 0 00		1 3 0 0 00
	30		G2		1 0 0 00	1 2 0 0 00
	31		G2		3 0 00	1 1 7 0 00
	31		G2		3 5 00	1 1 3 5 00

Accounts Receivable   ACCOUNT NO. 2

DATE		EXPLANATION	POST. REF.	DEBIT	CREDIT	BALANCE
198A July	19		G2	7 5 0 00		7 5 0 00
	29		G2		7 5 0 00	– 0 –
	31		G3	7 5 00		7 5 00

Prepaid Rent   ACCOUNT NO. 3

DATE		EXPLANATION	POST. REF.	DEBIT	CREDIT	BALANCE
198A July	1		G1	6 0 0 00		6 0 0 00
	31		G3		2 0 0 00	4 0 0 00

Illustration 4–5

Office Supplies   ACCOUNT NO. 4

DATE	EXPLANATION	POST. REF.	DEBIT	CREDIT	BALANCE
198A July 5		G1	6 0 00		6 0 00
31		G3		1 5 00	4 5 00

Office Equipment   ACCOUNT NO. 5

DATE	EXPLANATION	POST. REF.	DEBIT	CREDIT	BALANCE
198A July 3		G1	1 2 0 0 00		1 2 0 0 00
5		G1	3 0 0 00		1 5 0 0 00

Accumulated Depreciation, Office Equipment   ACCOUNT NO. 6

DATE	EXPLANATION	POST. REF.	DEBIT	CREDIT	BALANCE
198A July 31		G3		2 0 00	2 0 00

Accounts Payable   ACCOUNT NO. 7

DATE	EXPLANATION	POST. REF.	DEBIT	CREDIT	BALANCE
198A July 5		G1		3 6 0 00	3 6 0 00
30		G2	1 0 0 00		2 6 0 00

Salaries Payable   ACCOUNT NO. 8

DATE	EXPLANATION	POST. REF.	DEBIT	CREDIT	BALANCE
198A July 31		G3		7 5 00	7 5 00

Unearned Legal Fees   ACCOUNT NO. 9

DATE	EXPLANATION	POST. REF.	DEBIT	CREDIT	BALANCE
198A July 15		G1		1 5 0 00	1 5 0 00
31		G3	5 0 00		1 0 0 00

Illustration 4–5 *(continued)*

Larry Owen, Capital — ACCOUNT NO. 10

DATE		EXPLANATION	POST. REF.	DEBIT	CREDIT	BALANCE
198A July	1		G1		2 5 0 0 00	2 5 0 0 00
	31		G3		4 0 0 00	2 9 0 0 00
	31		G3	2 0 0 00		2 7 0 0 00

Larry Owen, Withdrawals — ACCOUNT NO. 11

DATE		EXPLANATION	POST. REF.	DEBIT	CREDIT	BALANCE
198A July	26		G2	2 0 0 00		2 0 0 00
	31		G3		2 0 0 00	- 0 -

Income Summary — ACCOUNT NO. 12

DATE		EXPLANATION	POST. REF.	DEBIT	CREDIT	BALANCE
198A July	31		G3		1 2 7 5 00	1 2 7 5 00
	31		G3	8 7 5 00		4 0 0 00
	31		G3	4 0 0 00		- 0 -

Legal Fees Earned — ACCOUNT NO. 13

DATE		EXPLANATION	POST. REF.	DEBIT	CREDIT	BALANCE
198A July	12		G1		4 0 0 00	4 0 0 00
	19		G2		7 5 0 00	1 1 5 0 00
	31		G3		1 2 5 00	1 2 7 5 00
	31		G3	1 2 7 5 00		- 0 -

Office Salaries Expense — ACCOUNT NO. 14

DATE		EXPLANATION	POST. REF.	DEBIT	CREDIT	BALANCE
198A July	12		G1	2 5 0 00		2 5 0 00
	26		G2	2 5 0 00		5 0 0 00
	31		G3	7 5 00		5 7 5 00
	31		G3		5 7 5 00	- 0 -

Illustration 4–5 *(continued)*

Telephone Expense   ACCOUNT NO. 15

DATE	EXPLANATION	POST. REF.	DEBIT	CREDIT	BALANCE
198A July 31		G2	3 0 00		3 0 00
31		G3		3 0 00	- 0 -

Heating and Lighting Expense   ACCOUNT NO. 16

DATE	EXPLANATION	POST. REF.	DEBIT	CREDIT	BALANCE
198A July 31		G2	3 5 00		3 5 00
31		G3		3 5 00	- 0 -

Rent Expense   ACCOUNT NO. 17

DATE	EXPLANATION	POST. REF.	DEBIT	CREDIT	BALANCE
198A July 31		G3	2 0 0 00		2 0 0 00
31		G3		2 0 0 00	- 0 -

Office Supplies Expense   ACCOUNT NO. 18

DATE	EXPLANATION	POST. REF.	DEBIT	CREDIT	BALANCE
198A July 31		G3	1 5 00		1 5 00
31		G3		1 5 00	- 0 -

Depreciation Expense, Office Equipment   ACCOUNT NO. 19

DATE	EXPLANATION	POST. REF.	DEBIT	CREDIT	BALANCE
198A July 31		G3	2 0 00		2 0 00
31		G3		2 0 00	- 0 -

Illustration 4–5 *(concluded)*

capital accounts show their end-of-the-period balances. Observe also that the revenue and expense accounts have zero balances and are ready for recording the new accounting period's revenues and expenses.

THE POST-CLOSING TRIAL BALANCE

It is easy to make errors in adjusting and closing the accounts. Consequently, after all adjusting and closing entries are posted, a new trial balance is prepared to retest the equality of the accounts. This new, after-closing trial balance is called a *post-closing trial balance,* and for Owen's law practice appears as in Illustration 4–6.

Larry Owen, Attorney Post-Closing Trial Balance, July 31, 19—		
Cash	$1,135	
Accounts receivable	75	
Prepaid rent	400	
Office supplies	45	
Office equipment	1,500	
Accumulated depreciation, office equipment		$ 20
Accounts payable		260
Salaries payable		75
Unearned legal fees		100
Larry Owen, capital		2,700
Totals	$3,155	$3,155

Illustration 4–6

Compare Illustration 4–6 with the accounts having balances in Illustration 4–5. Note that only asset, liability, and the owner's capital accounts have balances in Illustration 4–5. Note also that these are the only accounts that appear on the post-closing trial balance. The revenue and expense accounts have been cleared and have zero balances at this point.

ACCOUNTING FOR PARTNERSHIPS AND CORPORATIONS

Partnership accounting

Accounting for a partnership is like accounting for a single proprietorship except for transactions directly affecting the partners' capital and withdrawal accounts. For these transactions there must be a capital account and a withdrawals account for each partner. Also, the Income Summary account is closed with a compound entry that allocates to each partner his or her share of the income or loss.

Corporation accounting

A corporation's accounting also differs from that of a single proprietorship for transactions affecting the accounts that show the equity of the corporation's stockholders in the assets of the corporation. The differences result because accounting principles require a corporation to distinguish between stockholders' equity resulting from amounts invested in the corporation by its stockholders and stockholders' equity resulting from earnings. This distinction is also important because in most states a corporation cannot pay a legal dividend unless it has stockholders' equity resulting from earnings. In making the distinction, two kinds of stockholder equity accounts are kept: (1) *contributed capital accounts* and (2) *retained earnings accounts*. Amounts invested in a corporation by its stockholders are shown in a contributed capital account such as the Common Stock account. Stockholders' equity resulting from earnings is shown in a retained earnings account.

To demonstrate corporation accounting, assume that five persons secured a charter for a new corporation. Each invested $10,000 in the corporation by buying 1,000 shares of its $10 par value common stock. The corporation's entry to record their investments is:

Jan.	5	Cash	50,000.00	
		Common Stock		50,000.00
		Sold and issued 5,000 shares of $10 par value common stock.		

If during its first year the corporation earned $8,000, the entry to close its Income Summary account is:

Dec.	31	Income Summary	8,000.00	
		Retained Earnings......................		8,000.00
		To close the Income Summary account.		

If these were the only entries affecting the stockholders' equity during the first year, the corporation's year-end balance sheet will show the equity as follows:

Stockholders' Equity

Common stock, $10 par value, 5,000 shares authorized and outstanding	$50,000	
Retained earnings	8,000	
Total stockholders' equity		$58,000

Since a corporation is a separate legal entity, the names of its stock-holders are of little or no interest to a balance sheet reader and are not shown in the equity section. However, in this case the section does show that the corporation's stockholders have a $58,000 equity in its assets, $50,000 of which resulted from their purchase of the corporation's stock and $8,000 from earnings. As to the equity from earnings, $8,000 more assets flowed into the corporation from revenues than flowed out for expenses. This not only increased the assets but also increased the stockholders' equity in the assets by $8,000.

Many beginning students have difficulty understanding the nature of the retained earnings item in the equity section of a corporation balance sheet. They would perhaps have less difficulty if the item were labeled "Stockholders' equity resulting from earnings." However, the retained earnings caption is common. Therefore, upon seeing it a stu-dent must recognize that it represents nothing more than stockholders' equity resulting from earnings. Furthermore, it does not represent a specific amount of cash or any other asset, since these are shown in the asset section of the balance sheet.

To continue, assume that on January 10 of the corporation's second year its board of directors met and by vote declared a $1 per share dividend payable on February 1 to the January 25 *stockholders of record* (stockholders according to the corporation's records). The en-tries to record the declaration and payment are as follows:

Jan.	10	Retained Earnings	5,000.00	
		Common Dividend Payable		5,000.00
		Declared a $1 per share dividend.		
Feb.	1	Common Dividend Payable	5,000.00	
		Cash		5,000.00
		Paid the dividend declared on January 10.		

Note in the two entries that the dividend declaration and payment together reduced corporation assets and stockholders' equity just as a withdrawal of cash by the owner of a single proprietorship reduces assets and the owner's equity.

A cash dividend is normally paid by mailing checks to the stockhold-ers. Also, as in this case, three dates are normally involved in a dividend declaration and payment: (1) the *date of declaration*, (2) the *date of record*, and (3) the *date of payment*. Since stockholders may sell their stock to new investors at will, the three dates give new stockholders an opportunity to have their ownership entered in the corporation's records in time to receive the dividend. Otherwise it would go to the old stockholders.

A dividend must be formally voted by a corporation's board of directors. Furthermore, courts have generally held that the board is the final judge of when if at all a dividend should be paid. Consequently, stockholders have no right to a dividend until declared. However, as soon as a cash dividend is declared, it becomes a liability of the corporation, normally a current liability, and must be paid. Furthermore, stockholders have the right to sue and force payment of a cash dividend once it is declared.

If during its second year the corporation of this illustration suffered a $7,000 net loss, the entry to close its Income Summary account is:

Dec.	31	Retained Earnings	7,000.00	
		Income Summary		7,000.00
		To close the Income Summary account.		

Posting the entry has the effect shown on the third line of the following Retained Earnings account.

Retained Earnings

Date		Explanation	Post Ref.	Debit	Credit	Balance
198A Dec.	31	Net income	G4		8.000.00	8,000.00
198B Jan.	10	Dividend declaration	G5	5,000.00		3,000.00
Dec.	31	Net loss	G9	7,000.00		4,000.00

After the entry was posted, due to the dividend and the net loss, the Retained Earnings account has a $4,000 debit balance. A debit balance in a Retained Earnings account indicates a negative amount of retained earnings, and a corporation with a negative amount of retained earnings is said to have a *deficit*. A deficit may be shown on a corporation's balance sheet as follows:

Stockholders' Equity

Common stock, $10 par value, 5,000 shares authorized and outstanding	$50,000	
Deduct retained earnings deficit	(4,000)	
Total stockholders' equity		$46,000

In most states it is illegal for a corporation with a deficit to pay a cash dividend. Such dividends are made illegal because as a separate legal entity a corporation is responsible for its own debts. Consequently, if its creditors are to be paid, they must be paid from the corporation's assets. Therefore, making a dividend illegal when there is a deficit helps prevent a corporation in financial difficulties from paying out all of its assets in dividends and leaving nothing for payment of its creditors.

THE ACCOUNTING CYCLE

Each accounting period in the life of a business is a recurring *accounting cycle*, beginning with transactions recorded in a journal and ending with a post-closing trial balance. All steps in the cycle have now been discussed. A knowledge of accounting requires that each step be understood and its relation to the others seen. The steps in the order of their occurrence are as follows:

1. *Journalizing* .... Analyzing and recording transactions in a journal.
2. *Posting* .... Copying the debits and credits of journal entries into the ledger accounts.
3. *Preparing a trial balance* ..... Summarizing the ledger accounts and testing the recording accuracy.
4. *Preparing a work sheet* .... Gaining the effects of the adjustments before entering the adjustments in the accounts. Then sorting the account balances into the balance sheet and income statement columns and finally determining and proving the income or loss.
5. *Preparing the statements* .... Rearranging the work sheet information into a balance sheet and an income statement.
6. *Adjusting the ledger accounts* .... Preparing adjusting journal entries from information in the Adjustments columns of the work sheet and posting the entries in order to bring the account balances up to date.

7. *Closing the temporary
accounts* . . . . Preparing and posting entries to
close the temporary accounts and
transfer the net income or loss to
the capital account or accounts in
a single proprietorship or partnership and to the Retained Earnings
account in a corporation.

8. *Preparing a post-closing
trial balance* . . . . Proving the accuracy of the adjusting and closing procedures.

GLOSSARY

Accounting cycle. The accounting steps that recur each accounting
period in the life of a business and which begin with the recording
of transactions and proceed through posting the recorded amounts,
preparing a trial balance, preparing a work sheet, preparing the
financial statements, preparing and posting adjusting and closing
entries, and preparing a post-closing trial balance.

Closing entries. Entries made to close and clear the revenue and expense accounts and to transfer the amount of the net income or
loss to a capital account or accounts or to the Retained Earnings
account.

Closing procedures. The preparation and posting of closing entries
and the preparation of the post-closing trial balance.

Contributed capital. Stockholders' equity in a corporation resulting
among other ways from amounts invested in the corporation by
its stockholders.

Date of declaration. Date on which a dividend is declared.

Date of payment. Date for the payment of a dividend.

Date of record. Date on which the stockholders who are to receive
a dividend is determined.

Deficit. A negative amount of retained earnings.

Income Summary account. The account used in the closing procedures to summarize the amounts of revenues and expenses, and
from which the amount of the net income or loss is transferred
to the owner's capital account in a single proprietorship, the partners' capital accounts in a partnership, or the Retained Earnings
account in a corporation.

Post-closing trial balance. A trial balance prepared after closing entries are posted.

Stockholders of record. A corporation's stockholders according to its
records.

Temporary accounts. The revenue, expense, Income Summary, and withdrawals accounts.

Working papers. The memoranda, analyses, and other informal papers prepared by accountants and used as a basis for the more formal reports given to clients.

Work sheet. A working paper used by an accountant to bring together in an orderly manner the information used in preparing the financial statements and adjusting entries.

QUESTIONS FOR CLASS DISCUSSION

1. A work sheet is a tool accountants use to accomplish three tasks. What are these tasks?
2. Is it possible to complete the statements and adjust and close the accounts without preparing a work sheet? What is gained by preparing a work sheet?
3. At what stage in the accounting process is a work sheet prepared?
4. From where are the amounts that are entered in the Trial Balance columns of a work sheet obtained?
5. Why are the adjustments in the Adjustments columns of a work sheet keyed together with letters?
6. What is the result of combining the amounts in the Trial Balance columns with the amounts in the Adjustments columns of a work sheet?
7. Why must care be exercised in sorting the items in the Adjusted Trial Balance columns to the proper Income Statement or Balance Sheet columns?
8. In extending the items in the Adjusted Trial Balance columns of a work sheet, what would be the effect on the net income of extending (a) an expense into the Balance Sheet debit column, (b) a liability into the Income Statement credit column, and (c) a revenue into the Balance Sheet debit column? Would each of these errors be automatically detected on the work sheet? Which would be automatically detected? Why?
9. Why are revenue and expense accounts called temporary accounts?
10. What two purposes are accomplished by recording closing entries?
11. What accounts are affected by closing entries? What accounts are not affected?
12. Explain the difference between adjusting and closing entries.
13. What is the purpose of the Income Summary account?
14. Why is a post-closing trial balance prepared?
15. An accounting student listed the item, "Depreciation expense, building, $1,800," on a post-closing trial balance. What did this indicate?
16. What two kinds of accounts are used in accounting for stockholders' equity in a corporation?
17. Explain how the retained earnings item found on corporation balance sheets arises.
18. What three dates are normally involved in the declaration and payment of a cash dividend?
19. Explain why the payment of a cash dividend by a corporation with a deficit is made illegal.

CLASS EXERCISES

Exercise 4–1

The balances of the following alphabetically arranged accounts appeared in the Adjusted Trial Balance columns of a work sheet. Copy the account numbers in a column on a sheet of note paper and beside each number indicate by letter the income statement or balance sheet column to which the account's balance would be sorted in completing the work sheet. Use the letter *a* to indicate the Income Statement debit column, *b* to indicate the Income Statement credit column, *c* to indicate the Balance Sheet debit column, and *d* to indicate the Balance Sheet credit column.

1. Accounts Payable.
2. Accounts Receivable.
3. Accumulated Depreciation, Repair Equipment.
4. Advertising Expense.
5. Cash.
6. Ted Lee, Capital.
7. Ted Lee, Withdrawals.
8. Prepaid Insurance.
9. Rent Expense.
10. Repair Equipment.
11. Repair Supplies.
12. Revenue from Repairs.
13. Wages Expense.

Exercise 4–2

The following item amounts are from the Adjustments columns of a work sheet. From the information prepare adjusting journal entries. Use December 31 as the date.

		Adjustments		
		Debit		*Credit*
Prepaid insurance			(a)	850
Office supplies			(b)	215
Accumulated depreciation, office equipment			(c)	540
Accumulated depreciation, delivery equipment ..			(d)	3,345
Office salaries expense	(e)	50		
Truck drivers' wages	(e)	280		
Insurance expense, office equipment	(a)	85		
Insurance expense, delivery equipment	(a)	765		
Office supplies expense	(b)	215		
Depreciation expense, office equipment	(c)	540		
Depreciation expense, delivery equipment	(d)	3,345		
Salaries and wages payable			(e)	330
Totals		5,280		5,280

Exercise 4–3

Copy the following T-accounts and their end-of-the-period balances on a sheet of note paper. Below the accounts prepare entries to close the accounts. Post to the T-accounts.

Dale Nash, Capital		
	Dec. 31	12,500

Rent Expense		
Dec. 31	2,400	

Dale Nash, Withdrawals		
Dec. 31	15,600	

Salaries Expense		
Dec. 31	10,200	

Income Summary	

Insurance Expense		
Dec. 31	800	

Commissions Earned		
	Dec. 31	32,600

Depreciation Expense, Equipment		
Dec. 31	500	

Exercise 4–4

Following is a list of trial balance accounts and their balances. All are normal balances. To save your time, the balances are in one- and two-digit numbers; however, to increase your skill in sorting adjusted trial balance amounts to the proper work sheet columns, the accounts are listed in alphabetical order.

TRIAL BALANCE ACCOUNTS AND BALANCES

Accounts payable	$2	Rent expense	$ 2
Accounts receivable	3	Revenue from repairs	18
Accumulated depreciation,		Robert Ross, capital	11
shop equipment	2	Robert Ross, withdrawals	2
Cash	5	Shop equipment	7
Notes payable	1	Shop supplies	4
Prepaid insurance	3	Wages expense	8

Required:

1. Prepare a work sheet form on notebook paper and enter the trial balance accounts and amounts on the work sheet in their alphabetical order.
2. Complete the work sheet using the following information:
    a. Estimated depreciation of shop equipment, $1.
    b. Expired insurance, $1.
    c. Unused shop supplies per inventory, $1.
    d. Earned but unpaid wages, $2.

Exercise 4–5

1. On a sheet of note paper open the following T-accounts: Cash, Accounts Receivable, Equipment, Notes Payable, Common Stock, Retained Earnings, Income Summary, Revenue from Services, and Operating Expenses.
2. Record directly in the T-accounts these transactions of a corporation:
    a. Sold and issued $10,000 of common stock for cash.
    b. Purchased $9,000 of equipment for cash.

      c. Sold and delivered $25,000 of services on credit.
      d. Collected $22,000 of accounts receivable.
      e. Paid $20,000 of operating expenses.
      f. Purchased $5,000 of additional equipment, giving $3,000 in cash and a $2,000 promissory note.
      g. Closed the Revenue from Services, Operating Expenses, and Income Summary accounts.
3. Answer these questions:
      a. Does the corporation have retained earnings?
      b. Does it have any cash?
      c. If the corporation has retained earnings, why does it not also have cash?
      d. Can the corporation declare a legal cash dividend?
      e. Can it pay the dividend?
      f. In terms of assets, what does the balance of the Notes Payable account represent?
      g. In terms of assets, what does the balance of the Common Stock account represent?
      h. In terms of assets, what does the balance of the Retained Earnings account represent?

PROBLEMS

Problem 4–1

Walter Jenkins, Paul Kern, and Ned Lang began a business on January 8, 198A, in which each man invested $25,000. During 198A the business lost $6,000, and during 198B it earned a $27,000 net income. On January 3, 198C, the three men agreed to pay out to themselves $15,000 of the accumulated earnings of the business, and on January 8 the $15,000 was paid out.

Required:

1. Under the assumption that the business is a partnership in which the partners share losses and gains equally, give the entries to record the investments and to close the Income Summary account at the end of 198A and again at the end of 198B. Under the further assumption that the partners shared equally in the $15,000 of earnings paid out, give the entry to record the withdrawals.
2. Under the assumption that the business is organized as a corporation and that each man invested in the corporation by buying 2,500 shares of its $10 par value common stock, give the entries to *(a)* record the investments, *(b)* close the Income Summary account at the end of 198A and again at the end of 198B, and *(c)* to record the declaration and payment of the $2 per share dividend. (Ignore corporation income taxes and assume that the three men are the corporation's board of directors.)

Problem 4–2

A trial balance of the ledger of Quick Repair Shop carried these amounts at the end of its annual accounting period:

QUICK REPAIR SHOP
Trial Balance, December 31, 19—

Cash	$ 1,125	
Prepaid insurance	415	
Repair supplies	1,550	
Repair equipment	4,220	
Accumulated depreciation, repair equipment		$ 1,120
Accounts payable		250
Perry Winkle, capital		3,665
Perry Winkle, withdrawals	12,000	
Revenue from repairs		23,475
Wages expense	7,775	
Rent expense	1,200	
Advertising expense	225	
Totals	$28,510	$28,510

Required:

1. Enter the trial balance amounts in the Trial Balance columns of a work
    sheet and complete the work sheet using the following information:
    a. Expired insurance, $265.
    b. A repair supplies inventory showed $380 of unused supplies on hand.
    c. Estimated depreciation on repair equipment, $650.
    d. Wages earned by the one employee but unpaid and unrecorded, $25.
2. From the work sheet prepare an income statement and a classified balance
    sheet.
3. Prepare adjusting journal entries and compound closing entries.

Problem 4–3
(Covers two accounting cycles)

On October 2 Mary Nash opened a real estate office she called Mary Nash
Realty, and during October she completed these transactions:

Oct. 2 Invested $2,500 in cash and an automobile having a $7,200 fair value
         in the real estate agency.
      2 Rented furnished office space and paid one month's rent, $325.
      3 Purchased office supplies for cash, $135.
     10 Sold a building lot and collected a $1,250 commission.
     15 Paid the biweekly salary of the office secretary, $350.
     16 Paid the premium on a one-year insurance policy, $480.
     29 Paid the biweekly salary of the office secretary, $350.
     31 Paid the October telephone bill, $55.
     31 Paid for gas and oil used in the agency car during October, $65.

Required work for October:

1. Open the following accounts: Cash; Prepaid Insurance; Office Supplies;
    Automobile; Accumulated Depreciation, Automobile; Salaries Payable;

Mary Nash, Capital; Mary Nash, Withdrawals; Income Summary; Commissions Earned; Rent Expense; Salaries Expense; Gas, Oil, and Repairs Expense; Telephone Expense; Insurance Expense; Office Supplies Expense; and Depreciation Expense, Automobile.

2. Prepare and post journal entries to record the transactions.
3. Prepare a trial balance in the Trial Balance columns of a work sheet form and complete the work sheet using the following information.
   a. One half of a month's insurance has expired.
   b. An inventory shows $110 of unused office supplies remaining.
   c. Estimated depreciation on the automobile, $100.
   d. Accrued but unpaid salary of the secretary, $70.
4. Prepare an October income statement and an October 31 classified balance sheet.
5. Prepare and post adjusting and closing journal entries.
6. Prepare a post-closing trial balance.

During November the real estate agency completed these transactions:

Nov. 1 Paid the November rent on the office space, $325.
      3 Purchased additional office supplies for cash, $25.
     12 Paid the biweekly salary of the office secretary, $350.
     14 Sold a house and collected a $4,200 commission.
     16 Withdrew $1,500 from the business to pay personal living expenses.
     26 Paid the biweekly salary of the office secretary, $350.
     30 Paid for gas and oil used in the agency car during November, $60.
     30 Paid the November telephone bill, $35.

Required work for November:
1. Prepare and post journal entries to record the transactions.
2. Prepare a trial balance in the Trial Balance columns of a work sheet form and complete the work sheet using the following information:
   a. One month's insurance has expired.
   b. An inventory of office supplies shows $115 of unused supplies remaining.
   c. Estimated depreciation on the automobile, $100.
   d. Accrued but unpaid secretary's salary, $140.
3. Prepare a November income statement and a November 30 classified balance sheet.
4. Prepare and post adjusting and closing journal entries.
5. Prepare a post-closing trial balance.

Problem 4–4

The ledger accounts of Leisure Alleys showing account balances as of the end of its annual accounting period appear in the booklet of working papers that accompanies this text and a trial balance of the ledger is reproduced on a work sheet form provided there. The trial balance has these items:

LEISURE ALLEYS
Trial Balance, December 31, 19—

Cash	$ 1,575	
Bowling supplies	2,420	
Prepaid insurance	575	
Bowling equipment	36,565	
Accumulated depreciation, bowling equipment		$ 9,640
Mortgage payable		10,000
Walter Hall, capital		14,025
Walter Hall, withdrawals	9,000	
Bowling revenue		35,500
Salaries expense	13,655	
Advertising expense	750	
Equipment repairs expense	420	
Rent expense	2,400	
Utilities expense	1,135	
Taxes expense	220	
Interest expense	450	
Totals	$69,165	$69,165

Required:

1. If the working papers are being used, complete the work sheet provided there for the solution of this problem, using the information that follows. If the working papers are not being used, enter the trial balance on a work sheet form and complete the work sheet.
    a. Bowling supplies inventory, $590.
    b. Expired insurance, $445.
    c. Estimated depreciation of bowling equipment, $3,875.
    d. Salaries earned but unpaid and unrecorded, $315.
    e. The lease contract on the building calls for an annual rental equal to 10% of the annual bowling revenue, with $200 payable each month on the first day of the month. The $200 was paid each month and debited to the Rent Expense account.
    f. Personal property taxes on the bowling equipment amounting to $85 have accrued but are unrecorded and unpaid.
    g. The mortgage debt was incurred on September 1, and interest on the debt is at the rate of 9% annually or $75 per month. The mortgage contract calls for the payment of $225 interest each three months in advance. Interest payments of $225 each were made on September 1 and December 1. The first payment on the mortgage principal is not due until two years after the date on which the debt was incurred.
2. Prepare an income statement and a classified balance sheet.
3. Prepare adjusting and closing journal entries.
4. Post the adjusting and closing entries and prepare a post-closing trial balance. (If the working papers are not being used, omit this last requirement.)

Problem 4–5

The accounts of A–1 Delivery Service showing balances as of the end of its annual accounting period appear in the booklet of working papers that accompanies this text, and a trial balance of the accounts is reproduced on a work sheet form provided there. The trial balance carries these items:

A-1 DELIVERY SERVICE
Trial Balance, December 31, 19—

Cash	$ 2,225	
Accounts receivable	470	
Prepaid insurance	1,275	
Office supplies	245	
Office equipment	2,460	
Accumulated depreciation, office equipment		$ 470
Delivery equipment	12,790	
Accumulated depreciation, delivery equipment		3,150
Accounts payable		290
Unearned delivery service revenue		450
Carl Bush, capital		9,855
Carl Bush, withdrawals	13,000	
Delivery service revenue		46,555
Office rent expense	600	
Telephone expense	245	
Office salaries expense	8,060	
Truck drivers' wages expense	16,320	
Gas, oil, and repairs expense	2,180	
Garage rent expense	900	
Totals	$60,770	$60,770

Required:
1. If the working papers are being used, complete the work sheet provided for the solution of this problem, using the following information. If the working papers are not being used, enter the trial balance on a work sheet form and complete the work sheet.
    a. Insurance expired on office equipment, $75; and on the delivery equipment, $915.
    b. An inventory showed $115 of unused office supplies on hand.
    c. Estimated depreciation on office equipment, $180; and *(d)* on delivery equipment, $2,345.
    e. Three stores entered into contracts with the delivery service in which they agreed to pay a fixed fee for having packages delivered. Two of the stores made advance payments on their contracts, and the amounts were credited to Unearned Delivery Service Revenue. An examination of their contracts shows $325 of the $450 paid in advance was earned by the accounting period end. The contract of the third store provides for a $150 monthly fee to be paid at the end of each month's service. It was signed on December 15, and a half month's revenue has accrued but is unrecorded.
    f. Office salaries, $70, and truck drivers' wages, $280, have accrued.
2. Prepare an income statement and a classified balance sheet.
3. Prepare adjusting and closing entries.
4. Post the adjusting and closing entries to the accounts and prepare a post-closing trial balance. (Omit this requirement if the working papers are not being used.)

ALTERNATE PROBLEMS

Problem 4–1A

On January 5, 198A, Fred Gage, Dale Hall, and Carl Russ began a business in which Fred Gage invested $15,000, Dale Hall invested $30,000, and Carl Russ invested $45,000. During 198A the business lost $6,000, and during 198B it earned a $30,000 net income. On January 4, 198C, the three men agreed to pay out to themselves $18,000 of the accumulated earnings of the business, and on January 12 the $18,000 was paid out.

Required:

1. Under the assumption the business is a partnership in which the partners share losses and gains in proportion to their investments, give the entries to record the investments and to close the Income Summary account at the end of 198A and again at the end of 198B. Under the further assumption that the partners paid out the $18,000 of accumulated earnings in proportion to their investments, give the entry to record the withdrawals.
2. Under the alternate assumption that the business is organized as a corporation and that the men invested in the corporation by buying its $10 par value common stock, with Fred Gage buying 1,500 shares, Dale Hall buying 3,000 shares, and Carl Russ buying 4,500 shares, give the entries to (a) record the investments, (b) close the Income Summary account at the end of 198A and again at the end of 198B, and (c) to record the declaration and payment of the $2 per share dividend. (Ignore corporation income taxes and assume the three men are the corporation's board of directors.)

Problem 4–2A

At the end of its annual accounting period a trial balance of the ledger of Sparkling Janitorial Service appeared as follows:

SPARKLING JANITORIAL SERVICE
Trial Balance, December 31, 19—

Cash	$ 835	
Accounts receivable	180	
Prepaid insurance	765	
Cleaning supplies	840	
Prepaid rent	225	
Cleaning equipment	2,830	
Accumulated depreciation, cleaning equipment		$ 1,220
Trucks	8,690	
Accumulated depreciation, trucks		3,610
Accounts payable		135
Unearned janitorial revenue		180
Timothy Watts, capital		6,870
Timothy Watts, withdrawals	10,400	
Janitorial revenue		28,730
Wages expense	14,700	
Rent expense	600	
Gas, oil, and repairs expense	680	
Totals	$40,745	$40,745

Required:

1. Enter the trial balance amounts on a work sheet form and complete the work sheet using the following information:
    a. Expired insurance, $625.
    b. An inventory of cleaning supplies showed $135 of unused cleaning supplies on hand.
    c. The cleaning service rents garage and equipment storage space. At the beginning of the year three months' rent was prepaid as shown by the debit balance of the Prepaid Rent account. Rents for the months April through November were paid on the first day of each month and debited to the Rent Expense account. The December rent was unpaid on the trial balance date.
    d. Estimated depreciation on cleaning equipment, $375; and *(e)* on the trucks, $1,500.
    f. On November 20 the janitorial service contracted and began cleaning the office of Western Realty for $90 per month. The realty company paid in advance for two months' service, and the amount paid was credited to Unearned Janitorial Revenue. The janitorial service also entered into a contract and began cleaning the office of Valley Insurance Agency on December 15. By the month's end a half month's revenue, $40, had been earned on this contract but was unrecorded.
    g. Employees' wages amounting to $120 had accrued but were unrecorded on the trial balance date.
2. From the work sheet prepare an income statement and a classified balance sheet.
3. Prepare adjusting and closing entries for the janitorial service.

Problem 4–3A
(Covers two accounting cycles)

On July 1 of the current year Mary Nash opened a new real estate office called Mary Nash Realty, and during the month she completed these transactions:

July 1 Invested $1,500 in cash and an automobile having a $6,500 fair value.
       2 Rented a furnished office and paid one month's rent, $350.
       2 Paid the premium on a one-year insurance policy, $420.
       3 Purchased office supplies for cash, $125.
      12 Sold a house and collected a $3,850 commission.
      15 Paid the biweekly salary of the office secretary, $300.
      29 Paid the biweekly salary of the office secretary, $300.
      31 Paid the July telephone bill, $50.
      31 Paid for gas and oil used in the agency car during July, $60.

Required work for July:

1. Open the following accounts: Cash; Prepaid Insurance; Office Supplies; Automobile; Accumulated Depreciation, Automobile; Salaries Payable; Mary Nash, Capital; Mary Nash, Withdrawals; Income Summary; Commissions Earned; Rent Expense; Salaries Expense; Gas, Oil, and Repairs Expense; Telephone Expense; Insurance Expense; Office Supplies Expense; and Depreciation Expense, Automobile.

2. Prepare and post journal entries to record the July transactions.
3. Prepare a trial balance in the Trial Balance columns of a work sheet form and complete the work sheet using the following information:
   a. One month's insurance has expired.
   b. An inventory shows $95 of unused office supplies remaining.
   c. Estimated depreciation on the automobile, $100.
   d. Accrued but unpaid salary of the secretary, $60.
4. Prepare a July income statement and a July 31 classified balance sheet.
5. Prepare and post adjusting and closing journal entries.
6. Prepare a post-closing trial balance.

During August the real estate agency completed these transactions:

Aug. 1. Paid the August rent on the office space, $350.
12   Paid the biweekly salary of the office secretary, $300.
14   Purchased additional office supplies for cash, $35.
17   Sold a building lot and collected a $1,200 commission.
26   Paid the biweekly salary of the office secretary, $300.
31   Paid for gas and oil used in the agency car, $55.
31   Paid the August telephone bill, $45.
31   Mary Nash withdrew $1,000 from the business to pay personal expenses.

Required work for August:

1. Prepare and post journal entries to record the August transactions.
2. Prepare a trial balance in the Trial Balance columns of a work sheet and complete the work sheet using the following information:
   a. One month's insurance has expired.
   b. An inventory shows $105 of unused office supplies remaining.
   c. Estimated depreciation on the automobile, $100.
   d. Accrued but unpaid salary of the secretary, $120.
3. Prepare an August income statement and an August 31 classified balance sheet.
4. Prepare and post adjusting and closing journal entries.
5. Prepare a post-closing trial balance.

Problem 4–4A

The ledger of Leisure Alleys showing account balances as of the end of its annual accounting period appears in the booklet of working papers that accompanies this text and a trial balance of the ledger is reproduced on a work sheet form provided there. The trial balance carries these items:

LEISURE ALLEYS
Trial Balance, December 31, 19—

Cash	$ 1,575	
Bowling supplies	2,420	
Prepaid insurance	575	
Bowling equipment	36,565	
Accumulated depreciation, bowling equipment		$ 9,640
Mortgage payable		10,000
Walter Hall, capital		14,025
Walter Hall, withdrawals	9,000	
Bowling revenue		35,500
Salaries expense	13,655	
Advertising expense	750	
Equipment repairs expense	420	
Rent expense	2,400	
Utilities expense	1,135	
Taxes expense	220	
Interest expense	450	
Totals	$69,165	$69,165

Required:

1. If the working papers are being used, complete the work sheet provided there for the solution of this problem, using the information that follows. If the working papers are not being used, enter the trial balance on a work sheet form and complete the work sheet.
   a. Bowling supplies inventory, $225.
   b. Expired insurance, $530.
   c. Estimated depreciation of bowling equipment, $3,850.
   d. Salaries accrued but unrecorded and unpaid on December 31, $240.
   e. The lease contract on the building calls for an annual rental equal to 8% of the annual bowling revenue, with $200 payable monthly on the first day of each month. The $200 was paid each month and debited to the Rent Expense account.
   f. On December 31 personal property taxes of $115 have accrued on the bowling equipment but are unrecorded and unpaid.
   g. The mortgage liability was incurred on May 1 of the current year, and interest on the debt is at the rate of 9% annually or $75 per month. The mortgage contract calls for annual payments of $1,000 on the anniversary date of the mortgage to reduce the amount of the debt. It also calls for quarterly interest payments of $225 each at the end of each quarter. Quarterly payments were made on July 31 and October 31.
2. Prepare an income statement and a classified balance sheet.
3. Prepare adjusting and closing entries.
4. Post the adjusting and closing entries and prepare a post-closing trial balance. (If the working papers are not being used, omit this last requirement.)

Problem 4–5A

The accounts of A–1 Delivery Service showing balances as of the end of its annual accounting period appear in the booklet of working papers that accompany this text, and a trial balance of the accounts is reproduced on a work sheet form provided there. The trial balance has these items:

A–1 DELIVERY SERVICE
Trial Balance, December 31, 19—

Cash	$ 2,225	
Accounts receivable	470	
Prepaid insurance	1,275	
Office supplies	245	
Office equipment	2,460	
Accumulated depreciation, office equipment		$ 470
Delivery equipment	12,790	
Accumulated depreciation, delivery equipment		3,150
Accounts payable		290
Unearned delivery service revenue		450
Carl Bush, capital		9,855
Carl Bush, withdrawals	13,000	
Delivery service revenue		46,555
Office rent expense	600	
Telephone expense..................................	245	
Office salaries expense	8,060	
Truck drivers' wages expense	16,320	
Gas, oil, and repairs expense	2,180	
Garage rent expense	900	
Totals	$60,770	$60,770

Required:

1. If the working papers are being used, complete the work sheet provided there for the solution of this problem, using the information that follows. If the working papers are not being used, enter the trial balance on a work sheet form and complete the work sheet.

    a. Insurance expired on office equipment, $90; and on delivery equipment, $975.

    b. An inventory showed $125 of unused office supplies on hand.

    c. Estimated depreciation on office equipment, $215; and *(d)* on delivery equipment, $2,420.

    e. Three stores entered into contracts with the delivery service in which they agreed to pay a fixed fee for having packages delivered. Two of the stores made advance payments on their contracts, and the amounts were credited to Unearned Delivery Service Revenue. An examination of their contracts shows that $280 of the $450 paid in advance was earned by the accounting period end. The contract of the third store provides for a $150 monthly fee to be paid at the end of each month's service. It was signed on December 10, and two thirds of a month's revenue has accrued but is unrecorded.

  f. A \$30 December telephone bill and a \$55 bill for repairs to one of the delivery trucks arrived in the mail on December 31. Neither bill was paid nor recorded on the trial balance date.

  g. Office salaries, \$50, and truck drivers' wages, \$170, have accrued but are unpaid and unrecorded.

2. Prepare an income statement and a classified balance sheet.

3. Prepare adjusting and closing entries.

4. Post the adjusting and closing entries to the accounts and prepare a post-closing trial balance. (If the working papers are not being used, omit this requirement.)

PROVOCATIVE PROBLEMS

Provocative problem 4–1
Susan Bell, Attorney

  During the first year-end closing of the accounts of Susan Bell's law practice the office secretary and bookkeeper was in an accident and is in the hospital in a coma. Ms. Bell is certain the secretary prepared a work sheet, income statement, and balance sheet, but she has only the income statement and cannot find either the work sheet or balance sheet. She does have a trial balance of the accounts of the law practice, and she wants you to prepare adjusting and closing entries from the following trial balance and income statement. She also wants you to prepare a classified balance sheet. She says she has no legal work in process on which fees have accrued, and that the \$600 of unearned fees on the trial balance represents a retainer fee paid by Security Bank. The bank retained Susan Bell on November 15 to do its legal work, agreeing to pay her \$300 per month for her service.

SUSAN BELL, ATTORNEY
Trial Balance, December 31, 19—

Cash	\$ 1,250	
Legal fees receivable	1,500	
Office supplies	400	
Prepaid insurance	625	
Furniture and equipment	5,500	
Accounts payable		\$ 200
Unearned legal fees		600
Susan Bell, capital		7,500
Susan Bell, withdrawals	15,000	
Legal fees earned		29,800
Rent expense	4,550	
Office salaries expense	9,025	
Telephone expense	250	
Totals	\$38,100	\$38,100

SUSAN BELL, ATTORNEY
Income Statement for Year Ended December 31, 19—

Revenue:
Legal fees earned $30,250

Operating expenses:
Rent expense $4,200
Office salaries expense 9,100
Telephone expense 295
Accrued property taxes expense 125
Office supplies expense 275
Insurance expense 425
Depreciation expense, furniture and equipment..... 700
Total operating expenses 15,120
Net income $15,130

Provocative problem 4–2
Majestic Dry Cleaners

During his second year in college, Gregory Moss, as the only heir, inherited Majestic Dry Cleaners, a cash-and-carry dry cleaning business, upon the death of his father. He immediately dropped out of school and took over management of the business. At the time he took over, Greg recognized he knew little about accounting, but he reasoned that if the business cash increased, the business was doing OK. Therefore, he was pleased as he watched the balance of the concern's cash grow from $2,630 when he took over at the beginning of the year to $7,455 at the year-end. Furthermore, at the year-end he reasoned that since he had withdrawn $16,500 from the business to buy a new car and pay personal living expenses, the business had earned $21,325 during the year. He arrived at the $21,325 by adding the $4,825 increase in cash to the $16,500 he had withdrawn from the business, and he was shocked when he received the following income statement and learned the business had earned less than the amounts withdrawn.

MAJESTIC DRY CLEANERS
Income Statement for Year Ended December 31, 19—

Cleaning revenue earned $51,690

Operating expenses:
Salaries and wages expense...................... $28,450
Cleaning supplies expense 840
Insurance expense 960
Depreciation expense, cleaning equipment 1,500
Depreciation expense, building 3,600
Property taxes expense 825
Total operating expenses 36,175
Net income $15,515

After mulling the statement over for several days, he has asked you to explain how in a year in which the cash increased $4,825 and he had withdrawn

$16,500, the business could have earned only $15,515. In examining the accounts of the business you note that accrued salaries and wages payable at the beginning of the year were $145, but had increased to $385 at the year's end. Also, the balance of the Cleaning Supplies account had decreased $160 between the beginning and the end of the year and the balance of the Prepaid Insurance account had decreased $310. However, except for the changes in these accounts, the change in cash, and the changes in the balances of the accumulated depreciation accounts, there were no other changes in the balances of the company's asset and liability accounts between the beginning and the end of the year. Back your explanation with a calculation accounting for the increase in cash.

5

Accounting for a merchandising concern organized as a corporation

After studying Chapter 5, you should be able to:

■ Explain the nature of each item entering into the calculation of cost of goods sold and be able to calculate cost of goods sold and gross profit from sales.

■ Prepare a work sheet and the financial statements for a merchandising business organized as a corporation and using a periodic inventory system.

■ Prepare adjusting and closing entries for a merchandising business organized as a corporation.

■ Define or explain the words and phrases listed in the chapter Glossary.

The accounting records and reports of the Owen law practice, as described in previous chapters, are those of a service enterprise. Other service enterprises are laundries, taxicab companies, barber and beauty shops, theaters, and golf courses. Each performs a service for a commission or fee, and the net income of each is the difference between fees or commissions earned and operating expenses.

A merchandising concern, on the other hand, whether a wholesaler or retailer, earns revenue by selling goods or merchandise. In such a concern a net income results when revenue from sales exceeds the cost of the goods sold plus operating expenses, as illustrated below:

XYZ Store
Condensed Income Statement

Revenue from sales	$100,000
Less cost of goods sold	60,000
Gross profit from sales	$ 40,000
Less operating expenses	25,000
Net income	$ 15,000

The store of the illustrated income statement sold for $100,000 goods that cost $60,000. It thereby earned a $40,000 gross profit from sales. From this it subtracted $25,000 of operating expenses to show a $15,000 net income.

Gross profit from sales, as shown on the illustrated income statement, is the "profit" before operating expenses are deducted. Accounting for the factors that enter into its calculation differentiates the accounting of a merchandising concern from that of a service enterprise.

Gross profit from sales is determined by subtracting cost of goods sold from the revenue resulting from their sale. However, before the subtraction can be made, both revenue from sales and cost of goods sold must be determined.

153

REVENUE FROM SALES

Revenue from sales consists of gross proceeds from merchandise sales less returns, allowances, and discounts. It may be reported on an income statement as follows:

Kona Sales, Incorporated
Income Statement for Year Ended December 31, 198B

Revenue from sales:		
Gross sales		$306,200
Less: Sales returns and allowances	$1,900	
Sales discounts	4,300	6,200
Net sales		$300,000

Gross sales

The gross sales item on the partial income statement is the total cash and credit sales made by the company during the year. Cash sales were "rung up" on a cash register as each sale was completed. At the end of each day the register total showed the amount of that day's cash sales, which was recorded with an entry like this:

Nov.	3	Cash	1,205.00	
		Sales		1,205.00
		To record the day's cash sales.		

In addition, an entry like this was used to record credit sales:

Nov.	3	Accounts Receivable	45.00	
		Sales		45.00
		Sold merchandise on credit.		

Sales returns and allowances

In most stores a customer is permitted to return any unsatisfactory merchandise purchased. Or the customer is sometimes allowed to keep the unsatisfactory goods and is given an allowance or an amount off its sales price. Either way, returns and allowances result from dissatisfied customers. Consequently, it is important for management to know the amount of such returns and allowances and their relation to sales. This information is supplied by the Sales Returns and Allowances account when each return or allowance is recorded as follows:

Nov.	4	Sales Returns and Allowances...............	20.00	
		Accounts Receivable (or Cash)		20.00
		Customer returned unsatisfactory merchandise.		

Sales discounts

When goods are sold on credit, the terms of payment are always made definite so there will be no misunderstanding as to the amount and time of payment. The *credit terms* normally appear on the invoice or sales ticket and are part of the sales agreement. Exact terms granted usually depend upon the custom of the trade. In some trades it is customary for invoices to become due and payable ten days after the end of the month *(EOM)* in which the sale occurred. Invoices in these trades carry terms, "n/10 EOM." In other trades invoices become due and payable 30 days after the invoice date and carry terms of "n/30." This means that the net amount of the invoice is due 30 days after the invoice date.

When credit periods are long, creditors usually grant discounts, called *cash discounts,* for early payments. This reduces the amount invested in accounts receivable and tends to decrease losses from uncollectible accounts. When discounts for early payment are granted, they are made part of the credit terms and appear on the invoice as, for example, "Terms: 2/10, n/60." Terms of 2/10, n/60 mean that the *credit period* is 60 days but that the debtor may deduct 2% from the invoice amount if payment is made within 10 days after the invoice date. The ten-day period is known as the *discount period.*

Since at the time of a sale it is not known if the customer will pay within the discount period and take advantage of a cash discount, normally sales discounts are not recorded until the customer pays. For example, on November 12, Kona Sales, Incorporated, sold $100 of merchandise to a customer on credit, terms 2/10, n/60, and recorded the sale as follows:

Nov.	12	Accounts Receivable	100.00	
		Sales		100.00
		Sold merchandise, terms 2/10, n/60.		

At the time of the sale the customer could choose either to receive credit for paying the full $100 by paying $98 any time before November 22, or to wait 60 days, until January 11, and pay the full $100. If the customer elected to pay by November 22 and take advantage of the cash discount, Kona Sales, Incorporated, would record the receipt of the $98 as follows:

Nov.	22	Cash	98.00	
		Sales Discounts	2.00	
		Accounts Receivable		100.00
		Received payment for the November 12 sale less the discount.		

Sales discounts are accumulated in the Sales Discounts account until the end of an accounting period. Their total is then deducted from gross sales in determining revenue from sales. This is logical. A sales discount is an "amount off" the regular price of goods that is granted for early payment. As a result, it reduces revenue from sales.

COST OF GOODS SOLD

An automobile dealer or an appliance store make a limited number of sales each day. Consequently, they can easily refer to their records at the time of each sale and record the cost of the car or appliance sold. A drugstore, on the other hand, would find this difficult. For instance, if a drugstore sells a customer a tube of toothpaste, a box of aspirin, and a magazine, it can easily record with a cash register the sale of these items at marked selling prices. However, it would be difficult to maintain records that would enable it to also "look up" and record as "cost of goods sold" the costs of the items sold. As a result, stores such as drug, grocery, and others selling a volume of low-priced items make no effort to record the cost of the goods sold at the time of each sale. Rather, they wait until the end of an accounting period, take a physical inventory, and from the inventory and their accounting records determine at that time the cost of all goods sold during the period.

The end-of-the-period inventories taken by drug, grocery, or like stores in order to learn the cost of the goods they have sold are called *periodic inventories.* Also, the system used by such stores in accounting for cost of goods sold is known as a *periodic inventory system.* Such a system is described and discussed in this chapter. The system used by a car or appliance dealer to record the cost of each car or appliance sold depends on a *perpetual inventory record* of cars or appliances in stock. As a result, it is known as a *perpetual inventory system of accounting for goods on hand and sold.* It is discussed in Chapter 8.

COST OF GOODS SOLD, PERIODIC INVENTORY SYSTEM

As previously said, a store using a periodic inventory system makes no effort to determine and record the cost of items sold as they are sold. Rather, it waits until the end of an accounting period and determines at one time the cost of all the goods sold during the period. And to do this, it must have information as to (1) the cost of the merchandise it had on hand at the beginning of the period, (2) the cost of the merchandise purchased during the period, and (3) the cost of the unsold goods on hand at the period end. With this information a store can, for example, determine the cost of the goods it sold during a period as follows:

Cost of goods on hand at beginning of period	$ 19,000
Cost of goods purchased during the period	232,000
Goods available for sale during the period	$251,000
Unsold goods on hand at the period end	21,000
Cost of goods sold during the period	$230,000

The store of the calculation had $19,000 of merchandise at the beginning of the accounting period. During the period it purchased additional merchandise costing $232,000. Consequently, it had available and could have sold $251,000 of merchandise. However, $21,000 of this merchandise was on hand unsold at the period end. Therefore, the cost of the goods it sold during the period was $230,000.

The information needed in calculating cost of goods sold is accumulated as follows:

Merchandise inventories

The merchandise on hand at the beginning of an accounting period is called the *beginning inventory* and that on hand at the end is the *ending inventory*. Furthermore, since accounting periods follow one after another, the ending inventory of one period always becomes the beginning inventory of the next.

When a periodic inventory system is in use, the ending inventory is determined by (1) counting the items on the shelves in the store and in the stockroom, (2) multiplying the count for each kind of goods by its cost, and (3) adding the costs of the different kinds.

After the cost of the ending inventory is determined in this manner, it is subtracted from the cost of the goods available for sale to determine cost of goods sold. Also, by means of an adjusting entry the ending inventory is posted to an account called Merchandise Inventory. It remains there throughout the succeeding accounting period as a record of the inventory at the end of the period ended and the beginning of the succeeding period.

It should be emphasized at this point that, other than to correct errors, entries are made in the Merchandise Inventory account only at the end of each accounting period. Furthermore, since some goods are soon sold and other goods purchased, the account does not long show the dollar amount of goods on hand. Rather, as soon as goods are sold or purchased, its balance becomes a historical record of the dollar amount of goods that were on hand at the end of the last period and the beginning of the new period.

Cost of merchandise purchased

Cost of merchandise purchased is determined by subtracting from purchases any discounts, returns, and allowances and then adding any freight charges on the goods purchased. However, before examining this calculation it is best to see how the amounts involved are accumulated.

Under a periodic inventory system, when merchandise is bought for resale, its cost is debited to an account called Purchases, as follows:

Nov.	5	Purchases	1,000.00	
		Accounts Payable		1,000.00
		Purchased merchandise on credit, invoice dated November 2, terms 2/10, n/30.		

The Purchases account has as its sole purpose the accumulation of the cost of all merchandise bought for resale during an accounting period. The account does not at any time show whether the merchandise is on hand or has been disposed of through sale or other means.

If a credit purchase is subject to a cash discount, payment within the discount period results in a credit to Purchases Discounts, as in the following entry:

Nov.	12	Accounts Payable	1,000.00	
		Purchases Discounts		20.00
		Cash		980.00
		Paid for the purchase of November 5 less the discount.		

When *purchases discounts* are involved, it is important that every invoice on which there is a discount be paid within the discount period, so that no discounts are lost. On the other hand, good cash management requires that no invoice be paid until the last day of its discount period. Consequently, to accomplish these objectives, every invoice must be

filed in such a way that it automatically comes to the attention of
the person responsible for its payment on the last day of its discount
period. A simple way to do this is to provide a file with 31 folders,
one for each day in a month. Then after an invoice is recorded, it is
placed in the file folder of the last day of its discount period. For
example, if the last day of an invoice's discount period is November
12, it is filed in folder number 12. Then on November 12 this invoice,
together with any other invoices in the same folder, are removed and
paid or refiled for payment without a discount on a later date.

Sometimes merchandise received from suppliers is not acceptable
and must be returned. Or, if kept, it is kept only because the supplier
grants an allowance or reduction in its price. When merchandise is
returned, purchasers "get their money back"; but from a managerial
point of view more is involved. Buying merchandise, receiving and
inspecting it, deciding that the merchandise is unsatisfactory, and returning it is a costly procedure that should be held to a minimum.
The first step in holding it to a minimum is to know the amount of
returns and allowances. To make this information available, returns
and allowances on purchases are commonly recorded in an account
called Purchases Returns and Allowances, as follows:

Nov.	14	Accounts Payable	65.00	
		Purchases Returns and Allowances		65.00
		Returned defective merchandise.		

When an invoice is subject to a cash discount and a portion of its
goods is returned before the invoice is paid, the discount applies to
just the goods kept. For example, if $500 of merchandise is purchased
and $100 of the goods are returned before the invoice is paid, any
discount applies only to the $400 of goods kept.

Sometimes a manufacturer or wholesaler pays transportation costs
on merchandise it sells. The total cost of the goods to the purchaser
then is the amount paid the manufacturer or wholesaler. Other times
the purchaser must pay transportation costs (freight-in). When this
occurs, such charges are a proper addition to the cost of the goods
purchased and may be recorded with a debit to the Purchases account.
However, more complete information is obtained if such costs are
debited to an account called Freight-in, as follows:

Nov.	24	Freight-In	22.00	
		Cash		22.00
		Paid express charges on merchandise purchased.		

When transportation charges are involved, it is important that the buyer and seller understand which party is responsible for the charges. Normally, in quoting a price, the seller makes this clear by quoting a price of, say $400, *FOB* factory. FOB factory means free on board or loaded on board the means of transportation at the factory free of loading charges. The buyer then pays transportation costs from there. Likewise, FOB destination means the seller will pay transportation costs to the destination of the goods.

Sometimes, when terms are FOB factory, the seller will prepay the transportation costs as a service to the buyer. In such a case, if a cash discount is involved, the discount does not apply to the transportation charges.

When a classified income statement is prepared, the balances of the Purchases, Purchases Returns and Allowances, Purchases Discounts, and Freight-In accounts are combined on it as follows to show the cost of the merchandise purchased during the period:

Purchases		$235,800
Less: Purchases returns and allowances	$1,200	
Purchases discounts	4,100	5,300
Net purchases		$230,500
Add: Freight-in		1,500
Cost of goods purchased		$232,000

Cost of goods sold

The last item in the foregoing calculation is the cost of the merchandise purchased during the accounting period. It is combined with the beginning and ending inventories to arrive at cost of goods sold as follows:

Cost of goods sold:			
Merchandise inventory, January 1, 198B			$ 19,000
Purchases		$235,800	
Less: Purchases returns and allowances....	$1,200		
Purchases discounts	4,100	5,300	
Net purchases		$230,500	
Add: Freight-in........................		1,500	
Cost of goods purchased			232,000
Goods available for sale			$251,000
Merchandise inventory, December 31, 198B ..			21,000
Cost of goods sold.....................			$230,000

Inventory losses

Under a periodic inventory system the cost of any merchandise lost through shrinkage, spoilage, or shoplifting is automatically included in cost of goods sold. For example, assume a store lost $500 of merchandise to shoplifters during a year. This caused its year-end inventory to be $500 less than it otherwise would have been, since these goods were not available for inclusion in the year-end count. Therefore, since the year-end inventory was $500 smaller because of the loss, the cost of the goods the store sold was $500 greater.

Many stores are troubled with shoplifting. Although under a periodic inventory system such losses are automatically included in cost of goods sold, it is often important to know their extent. Consequently, a way to estimate shoplifting losses is described in Chapter 8.

INCOME STATEMENT OF A MERCHANDISING CONCERN

A classified income statement for a merchandising concern has (1) a revenue section, (2) a cost of goods sold section, and (3) an operating expenses section. The first two sections have been discussed, but note in Illustration 5–1 (on the next page) how they are brought together to show gross profit from sales.

Observe also in Illustration 5–1 how operating expenses are classified as either "Selling expenses" or "General and administrative expenses." *Selling expenses* include expenses of storing and preparing goods for sale, promoting sales, actually making sales, and delivering goods to customers. *General and administrative expenses* include the general office, accounting, personnel, and credit and collection expenses.

Sometimes an expenditure should be divided or prorated part to selling expenses and part to general and administrative expenses. Kona Sales, Incorporated, divided the rent on its store building in this manner, as an examination of Illustration 5–1 will reveal. However, it did not prorate its insurance expense because the amount involved was so small the company felt the extra exactness did not warrant the extra work.

The last item subtracted in Illustration 5–1 is income taxes expense. This income statement was prepared for Kona Sales, Incorporated, a corporation. Of the three kinds of business organizations, corporations alone are subject to the payment of state and federal income taxes. Often on a corporation income statement, as in Illustration 5–1, the operating expenses are subtracted from gross profit from sales to arrive at income from operations, after which income taxes are deducted to arrive at net income.

Kona Sales, Incorporated
Income Statement for Year Ended December 31, 198B

Revenue from sales:			
Gross sales			$306,200
Less: Sales returns and allowances		$ 1,900	
Sales discounts		4,300	6,200
Net sales			$300,000
Cost of goods sold:			
Merchandise inventory, January 1, 198B		$ 19,000	
Purchases	$235,800		
Less: Purchases returns and allowances	$1,200		
Purchase discounts	4,100	5,300	
Net purchases		$230,500	
Add: Freight-in		1,500	
Cost of goods purchased		232,000	
Goods available for sale		$251,000	
Merchandise inventory, December 31, 198B		21,000	
Cost of goods sold			230,000
Gross profit from sales			$ 70,000
Operating expenses:			
Selling expenses:			
Sales salaries expense		$ 18,500	
Rent expense, selling space		8,100	
Advertising expense		700	
Store supplies expense		400	
Depreciation expense, store equipment		3,000	
Total selling expenses		$ 30,700	
General and administrative expenses:			
Office salaries expense		$ 25,200	
Rent expense, office space		900	
Insurance expense		600	
Office supplies expense		200	
Depreciation expense, office equipment		700	
Total general and administrative expenses		27,600	
Total operating expenses			58,300
Income from operations			$ 11,700
Income taxes expense			2,300
Net income			$ 9,400

Illustration 5–1

WORK SHEET OF A MERCHANDISING CONCERN

A concern selling merchandise, like a service-type company, uses a work sheet in bringing together the end-of-the-period information needed in preparing its income statement, balance sheet, and adjusting entries. Such a work sheet, that of Kona Sales, Incorporated, is shown in Illustration 5–2 (on pages 164 and 165).

Illustration 5–2 differs from the work sheet in the previous chapter in several ways, the first of which is that it was prepared for a corporation. This is indicated by the word "Incorporated" in the company name. It is also indicated by the appearance on the work sheet of the Common Stock and Retained Earnings accounts. Note on lines 13 and 14 how the balances of these two accounts are carried unchanged from the Trial Balance credit column into the Balance Sheet credit column.

Illustration 5–2 also differs in that it does not have any Adjusted Trial Balance columns. The experienced accountant commonly omits these columns from a work sheet in order to reduce the time and effort required in its preparation. He or she enters the adjustments in the Adjustments columns, combines the adjustments with the trial balance amounts, and sorts the combined amounts directly to the proper Income Statement or Balance Sheet columns in a single operation. In other words, the experienced accountant simply omits the adjusted trial balance in preparing a work sheet.

The remaining similarities and differences of Illustration 5–2 are best described column by column.

Account Titles column

Several accounts that do not have trial balance amounts are listed in the Account Titles column, with each being listed in the order of its appearance on the financial statements. These accounts receive debits and credits in making the adjustments. Entering their names on the work sheet in statement order at the time the work sheet is begun makes later preparation of the statements somewhat easier. If required account names are anticipated and listed without balances, as in Illustration 5–2, but later it is discovered that a name not listed is needed, it may be entered below the trial balance totals as was done in Chapter 4.

Trial Balance columns

The amounts in the Trial Balance columns of Illustration 5–2 are the unadjusted account balances of Kona Sales, Incorporated, as of the end of its annual accounting period. They were taken from the company's ledger after all transactions were recorded but before any end-of-the-period adjustments were made.

Note the $19,000 inventory amount appearing in the Trial Balance debit column on line 3. This is the amount of inventory the company had on January 1, at the beginning of the accounting period. The $19,000 was debited to the Merchandise Inventory account at the end of the previous period and remained in the account as its balance throughout the current accounting period.

KONA SALES, INCORPORATED

Work Sheet for Year Ended December 31, 198B

	ACCOUNT TITLES	TRIAL BALANCE DR.	TRIAL BALANCE CR.	ADJUSTMENTS DR.	ADJUSTMENTS CR.	INCOME STATEMENT DR.	INCOME STATEMENT CR.	BALANCE SHEET DR.	BALANCE SHEET CR.
1	Cash	820000						820000	
2	Accounts receivable	1120000						1120000	
3	Merchandise inventory	1900000		(b)2100000	(a)1900000			2100000	
4	Prepaid insurance	90000			(c)60000			30000	
5	Store supplies	60000			(d)40000			20000	
6	Office supplies	30000			(e)20000			10000	
7	Store equipment	2910000						2910000	
8	Accumulated depreciation, store equipment		250000		(f)300000				550000
9	Office equipment	440000						440000	
10	Accumulated depreciation, office equipment		60000		(g)70000				130000
11	Accounts payable		360000						360000
12	Income taxes payable				(h)10000				10000
13	Common stock		5000000						5000000
14	Retained earnings		460000						460000
15	Income summary			(a)1900000	(b)2100000	1900000	2100000		
16	Sales		30620000				30620000		
17	Sales returns and allowances	190000				190000			
18	Sales discounts	430000				430000			
19	Purchases	23580000				23580000			
20	Purchases returns and allowances		120000				120000		
21	Purchases discounts		410000				410000		
22	Freight-in	150000				150000			
23	Sales salaries expense	1850000				1850000			

#	Account							
24	Rent expense, selling space	810000			810000			
25	Advertising expense	70000			70000			
26	Store supplies expense		(d)40000		40000			
27	Depreciation expense, store equipment		(f)300000		300000			
28	Office salaries expense	2520000			2520000			
29	Rent expense, office space	90000			90000			
30	Insurance expense		(c)60000		60000			
31	Office supplies expense		(e)20000		20000			
32	Depreciation expense, office equipment		(g)70000		70000			
33	Income taxes expense	220000	(h)10000		230000			
34		37280000	37280000	4500000	32310000	33250000	7450000	6510000
35	Net income				940000			940000
36				4500000	33250000	33250000	7450000	7450000
37								
38								
39								
40								
41								
42								
43								
44								
45								
46								
47								
48								
49								

Illustration 5–2

Adjustments columns

Of the adjustments appearing on the illustrated work sheet, only those for inventories and for income taxes are new.

Inventory adjustments   The company of Illustration 5–2 determined that it had a $21,000 ending inventory by counting its items of unsold merchandise. It then made adjustments *(a)* and *(b)* on its work sheet, the effects of which are shown in T-accounts in Illustration 5–3. Observe that adjustment *(a)* removes the amount of the beginning inventory from the inventory account and charges (debits) it to Income Summary. Adjustment *(b)* then enters the amount of the ending inventory in the inventory account. (After the work sheet and statements are completed, the effects shown in Illustration 5–3 are obtained in the accounts by preparing and posting two adjusting entries.)

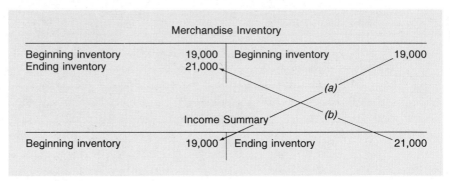

Illustration 5–3

Look again at the work sheet and observe that combining the amounts on line 3 results in the extension of the $21,000 ending inventory amount into the Balance Sheet debit column. This is as it should be. The company has a $21,000 ending inventory, and it should appear on the balance sheet as an asset of that amount.

Next observe on line 15 that both the $19,000 beginning inventory amount and the $21,000 ending inventory amount are extended from the Adjustments columns into the Income Statement columns. The beginning inventory is extended as a debit, and the ending inventory as a credit. Observe too that the balances of the Purchases, Purchases Returns and Allowances, Purchases Discounts, and Freight-In accounts are also extended into the Income Statement columns in the same debit and credit positions they occupy in the Trial Balance columns. These six items, which are emphasized in color in the Income Statement columns, are the items that enter into the calculation of cost of goods sold. Note in the following calculation that the sum of the three debit items minus the sum of the three credit items equals the $230,000 cost of goods sold amount shown in Illustration 5–1.

Debits	Credits
$ 19,000	$21,000
235,800	1,200
1,500	4,100
$256,300	$26,300
(26,300)	
$230,000	

Therefore, extending the six amounts into the Income Statement columns in effect extends cost of goods sold into these columns.

Income tax adjustment   As previously explained, a business organized as a corporation is subject to the payment of state and federal income taxes. As to the federal tax, near the beginning of each year a corporation must estimate the amount of income it expects to earn during the year. It must then pay in advance in installments an estimated tax on this income. The advance payments are debited to the Income Taxes Expense account as each installment is paid. Consequently, a corporation that expects to earn a profit normally reaches the end of the year with a debit balance in its Income Taxes Expense account. However, since the balance is an estimate and usually less than the full amount of the tax, an adjustment like that on lines 12 and 33 normally must be made to reflect the additional tax owed.

COMPLETING THE WORK SHEET

After all adjustments are entered on a work sheet like that of Illustration 5–2 and totaled, the amounts in the Trial Balance columns are combined with the amounts in the Adjustments columns and sorted to the proper Income Statement and Balance Sheet columns. In sorting each amount, two decisions are required: (1) Is the amount a debit or a credit and (2) on which statement does it appear? As to the first decision, debit amounts must be sorted to a debit column and credit amounts must go into a credit column. As to the second decision, revenue, cost of goods sold, and expense items go on the income statement. Asset, liability, and stockholders' (owners') equity items go on the balance sheet. After the amounts are sorted to the proper columns, the work sheet is completed in the manner described in the previous chapter.

PREPARING THE STATEMENTS

After the work sheet is completed, the items in its Income Statement columns are arranged into a formal income statement. The items in its Balance Sheet columns are then arranged into a formal balance sheet. A classified income statement prepared from information in the Income Statement columns of Illustration 5–2 is shown in Illustration 5–1. The balance sheet appears in Illustration 5–4. Observe that since none of the company's prepaid items are material in amount, they are totaled and shown as a single item on the balance sheet. The $14,000 retained earnings amount on the balance sheet is the sum of the $4,600 of retained earnings appearing on line 14 of the work sheet plus the company's $9,400 net income.

Kona Sales, Incorporated
Balance Sheet, December 31, 198B

Assets

Current assets:			
Cash		$ 8,200	
Accounts receivable		11,200	
Merchandise inventory		21,000	
Prepaid expenses		600	
Total current assets			$41,000
Plant and equipment:			
Store equipment	$29,100		
Less accumulated depreciation	5,500	$23,600	
Office equipment	$ 4,400		
Less accumulated depreciation	1,300	3,100	
Total plant and equipment			26,700
Total assets			$67,700

Liabilities

Current liabilities:			
Accounts payable		$ 3,600	
Income taxes payable		100	
Total current liabilities			$ 3,700

Stockholders' Equity

Common stock, $5 par value, 10,000 shares authorized and outstanding		$50,000	
Retained earnings		14,000	
Total stockholders' equity			64,000
Total liabilities and stockholders' equity			$67,700

Illustration 5–4

RETAINED EARNINGS STATEMENT

In addition to an income statement and a balance sheet, a third financial statement called a *retained earnings statement* is commonly prepared for a corporation. It reports the changes that have occurred in the corporation's retained earnings during the period and accounts for the difference between the retained earnings reported on balance sheets of successive accounting periods.

The retained earnings statement of Kona Sales, Incorporated, appears in Illustration 5–5. It shows that the company began the year with $8,600 of retained earnings, which is also the amount of retained earnings it reported on its previous year's balance sheet. Its retained earnings were reduced by the declaration of $4,000 of dividends and increased by the $9,400 net income to the $14,000 reported on its year-end balance sheet. Information as to the beginning retained earnings and the dividends declared were taken from the company's Retained Earnings account.

Kona Sales, Incorporated
Retained Earnings Statement
For Year Ended December 31, 198B

Retained earnings, January 1, 198B	$ 8,600
Add 198B net income	9,400
Total	$18,000
Deduct dividends declared	4,000
Retained earnings, December 31, 198B ..	$14,000

Illustration 5–5

ADJUSTING AND CLOSING ENTRIES

In a merchandising concern, as in a service-type business, after the work sheet and statements are completed, adjusting and closing entries must be prepared and posted. The entries for Kona Sales, Incorporated, are shown in Illustration 5–6. They differ from previously illustrated adjusting and closing entries in that an explanation for each entry is not given. Individual explanations may be given, but are unnecessary. The words "Adjusting entries" before the first adjusting entry and "Closing entries" before the first closing entry are sufficient to explain the entries.

DATE		ACCOUNT TITLES AND EXPLANATION	POST. REF.	DEBIT	CREDIT
198B		Adjusting entries:			
Dec.	31	Income Summary	313	1 9 0 0 0 00	
		Merchandise Inventory	113		1 9 0 0 0 00
	31	Merchandise Inventory	113	2 1 0 0 0 00	
		Income Summary	313		2 1 0 0 0 00
	31	Insurance Expense	653	6 0 0 00	
		Prepaid Insurance	115		6 0 0 00
	31	Store Supplies Expense	614	4 0 0 00	
		Store Supplies	116		4 0 0 00

Illustration 5–6

Dec.	31	Office Supplies Expense	651	2 0 0 00	
		Office Supplies	117		2 0 0 00
	31	Depreciation Expense, Store Equipment	615	3 0 0 00	
		Accumulated Depr., Store Equipment	132		3 0 0 00
	31	Depreciation Expense, Office Equipment	655	7 0 00	
		Accumulated Depr., Office Equipment	134		7 0 00
	31	Income Taxes Expense	711	1 0 0 00	
		Income Taxes Payable	213		1 0 0 00
		Closing entries:			
	31	Sales	411	30 6 2 0 0 00	
		Purchases Returns and Allowances	512	1 2 0 0 00	
		Purchases Discounts	513	4 1 0 0 00	
		Income Summary	313		31 1 5 0 0 00
	31	Income Summary	313	30 4 1 0 0 00	
		Sales Returns and Allowances	412		1 9 0 0 00
		Sales Discounts	413		4 3 0 0 00
		Purchases	511		23 5 8 0 0 00
		Freight-In	514		1 5 0 0 00
		Sales Salaries Expense	611		1 8 5 0 0 00
		Rent Expense, Selling Space	612		8 1 0 0 00
		Advertising Expense	613		7 0 0 00
		Store Supplies Expense	614		4 0 0 00
		Depreciation Expense, Store Equip.	615		3 0 0 00
		Office Salaries Expense	651		2 5 2 0 0 00
		Rent Expense, Office Space	652		9 0 0 00
		Insurance Expense	653		6 0 0 00
		Office Supplies Expense	654		2 0 0 00
		Depreciation Expense, Office Equip.	655		7 0 0 00
		Income Taxes Expense	711		2 3 0 0 00
	31	Income Summary	313	9 4 0 0 00	
		Retained Earnings	312		9 4 0 0 00

Illustration 5–6 *(continued)*

The effects of adjusting and closing entries on the accounts were illustrated in Chapters 3 and 4. However, since the inventory adjustments, as well as the closing entries, affect the Income Summary account of Kona Sales, Incorporated, the account is reproduced as Illustration 5–7. To aid understanding, each amount in the account is identified. However, such identifications are not required in the posting procedure. The nature of the account's balance after the second entry is determined by examining the relative sizes of the two inventory amounts.

Illustration 5–8 shows the company's Retained Earnings account after the last closing entry was posted. The company earned $8,600

			Income Summary		Account No. 313	
Date		Explanation	Post. Ref.	Debit	Credit	Balance
198B Dec.	31	Beginning inventory	G23	19,000		19,000
	31	Ending inventory	G23		21,000	2,000
	31	Sales, etc.	G23		311,500	313,500
	31	Expenses, etc.	G23	304,100		9,400
	31	Net income	G23	9,400		–0–

Illustration 5–7

during 198A, its first year in business, and it began 198B with that amount of retained earnings. It declared a $4,000 dividend in October and earned a $9,400 net income. The account is reproduced here so that its information may be compared with that in the company's retained earnings statement, Illustration 5–5.

			Retained Earnings		Account No. 312	
Date		Explanation	Post. Ref.	Debit	Credit	Balance
198A Dec.	31	198A net income	G10		8,600	8,600
198B Oct.	15	Dividend declared	G20	4,000		4,600
Dec.	31	198B net income	G23		9,400	14,000

Illustration 5–8

INCOME STATEMENT FORMS

The income statement in Illustration 5–1 is called a classified income statement because its items are classified into significant groups. It is also a *multiple-step income statement* because cost of goods sold and the expenses are subtracted in steps to arrive at net income. Another income statement form, the *single-step form*, is shown in Illustration 5–9. This form is commonly used for published statements. Also, although it need not be, its information is commonly condensed as shown. Note how cost of goods sold and the expenses are added together in the illustration and are subtracted in "one step" from net sales to arrive at net income, thus the name of the form.

Kona Sales, Incorporated
Income Statement for Year Ended December 31, 198B

Revenue from sales..........................		$300,000
Expenses:		
Cost of goods sold........................	$230,000	
Selling expenses	30,700	
General and administrative expenses	27,600	
Income taxes expense	2,300	
Total expenses		290,600
Net income		$ 9,400

Illustration 5–9

COMBINED INCOME AND RETAINED EARNINGS STATEMENT

Many companies combine their income and retained earnings statements into a single statement. Such a statement may be prepared in either single-step or multiple-step form. A single-step statement is shown in Illustration 5–10.

Kona Sales, Incorporated
Statement of Income and Retained Earnings
For Year Ended December 31, 198B

Revenue from sales		$300,000
Expenses:		
Cost of goods sold	$230,000	
Selling expenses	30,700	
General and administrative expenses	27,600	
Income taxes expense	2,300	
Total expenses		290,600
Net income		$ 9,400
Add retained earnings, January 1, 198B......		8,600
Total		$ 18,000
Deduct dividends declared		4,000
Retained earnings, December 31, 198B........		$ 14,000

Illustration 5–10

STATEMENT OF CHANGES IN FINANCIAL POSITION

In addition to the retained earnings statement, another very important financial statement commonly prepared for a corporation is the *statement of changes in financial position*. It shows where the concern secured funds and where it applied or used the funds, such as in the purchase of plant assets or the payment of dividends. A discussion of this statement is deferred until Chapter 14, after further discussion of corporation accounting.

BUSINESS PRACTICES

Taking an ending inventory

As previously stated, when a periodic inventory system is in use, the dollar amount of the ending inventory is determined by counting the items of unsold merchandise remaining in the store, multiplying the count for each kind by its cost, and adding the costs for all the kinds. In making the count, items are less apt to be counted twice or omitted from the count if prenumbered *inventory tickets* like the one in Illustration 5–11 are used. Before beginning the inventory, a sufficient number of the tickets, at least one for each kind of product on hand, is issued to each department in the store. Next a clerk counts the quantity of each product and from the count and the price tag attached to the merchandise fills in the information on the inventory ticket and attaches it to the counted items. After the count is completed, each department is examined for uncounted items. At this stage, inventory tickets are attached to all counted items. Consequently, any products without tickets attached are uncounted. After all items are counted and tickets attached, the tickets are removed and sent to the accounting department for completion of the inventory. To ensure that no ticket is lost or left attached to merchandise, all the prenumbered tickets issued are accounted for when the tickets arrive in the accounting department.

In the accounting department, the information on the tickets is copied on inventory summary sheets. The sheets are then completed by multiplying the number of units of each product by its unit cost.

```
INVENTORY
TICKET no.      786

Item

Quantity counted  |        |
Sales price       | $      |
Cost price        | $      |
Purchase date     |        |

Counted by_____
Checked by_____
```

Illustration 5–11

This gives the dollar amount of each product on hand, and the total for all products is the amount of the inventory.

Debit and credit memoranda

Merchandise purchased that does not meet specifications on delivery, goods received in damaged condition, goods received that were not ordered, goods received short of the amount ordered and billed, and invoice errors are matters for adjustment between the buyer and seller. In some cases the buyer can make the adjustment, and in others the adjustment is a subject for negotiation between the buyer and the seller. When there are invoice errors or when goods are received that were not ordered, the purchasing firm may make the adjustment. If it does, it must notify the seller of its action. It commonly does this by sending a *debit memorandum* or a *credit memorandum.*

A debit memorandum is a business form on which are spaces for the name and address of the concern to which it is directed and the printed words, "WE DEBIT YOUR ACCOUNT," followed by space for typing in the reason for the debit. A credit memorandum carries the words, "WE CREDIT YOUR ACCOUNT." To illustrate the use of a debit memorandum, assume a buyer of merchandise discovers an invoice error that reduces the invoice total by $10. For such an error the buyer notifies the seller with a debit memorandum reading: "WE DEBIT YOUR ACCOUNT to correct a $10 error on your November 17 invoice." A debit memorandum is sent because the correction reduces an account payable of the buyer, and to reduce an account payable requires a debit. In recording the purchase, the buyer normally marks the correction on the invoice and attaches a copy of the debit memorandum to show that the seller has been notified. The buyer then debits Purchases and credits Accounts Payable for the corrected amount.

Some adjustments, such as damaged merchandise or merchandise that does not meet specifications, normally require negotiations between the buyer and the seller. In such cases the buyer may debit Purchases for the full invoice amount and enter into negotiations with the seller for a return or a price adjustment. If the seller agrees to the return or adjustment, the seller notifies the buyer with a credit memorandum. A credit memorandum is used because the return or adjustment reduces an account receivable on the books of the seller, and to reduce an account receivable requires a credit.

From this discussion it can be seen that a debit or a credit memorandum may originate with either party to a transaction. The memorandum gets its name from the action of the originator. If the originator debits, the originator sends a debit memorandum. If the originator credits, a credit memorandum is sent.

Trade discounts

A *trade discount* is a deduction (often as much as 40% or more) from a *list* (or catalog) *price* that is used in determining the actual price of the goods to which it applies. Trade discounts are commonly used by manufacturers and wholesalers to avoid republication of catalogs when selling prices change. If selling prices change, catalog prices can be adjusted by merely issuing a new list of discounts to be applied to the catalog prices. Such discounts are discussed here primarily to distinguish them from the cash discounts described earlier in this chapter.

Trade discounts are not entered in the accounts by either party to a sale. For example, if a manufacturer sells on credit an item listed in its catalog at $100, less a 40% trade discount, it will record the sale as follows:

Dec.	10	Accounts Receivable	60.00	
		Sales		60.00
		Sold merchandise on credit.		

The buyer will also enter the purchase in the records at $60. Also, if a cash discount is involved, it applies only to the amount of the purchase, $60.

Code numbers as a means of identifying accounts

The account numbering scheme used in the chapters before this has been a simple one in which the accounts have been numbered consecutively. Such a scheme is satisfactory in a small business. However, in a larger more complicated accounting system, account numbers commonly become code numbers. The *account code numbers* not only identify accounts but also tell their statement classifications. For example, in one numbering system three-digit numbers with each digit having a significant meaning are used. In this system the first digit in each account number tells the major balance sheet or income statement classification of the account to which it is assigned. For example, account numbers with first digits of 1, numbers 111 to 199, are assigned to asset accounts. Liability accounts are then assigned numbers with the first digits of 2, numbers 211 to 299. When this system is used, main balance sheet and income statement account classifications may be assigned the following numbers:

111 to 199 are assigned to asset accounts.
211 to 299 are assigned to liability accounts.

311 to 399 are assigned to owner's equity accounts.
411 to 499 are assigned to sales or revenue accounts.
511 to 599 are assigned to cost of goods sold accounts.
611 to 699 are assigned to operating expense accounts.
711 to 799 are assigned to other revenue and expense accounts.

In the system under discussion, the second and third digits further classify an account. For example, the second digits under each of the following main classifications indicate the subclassification shown:

111 to 199. Asset accounts
    111 to 119. Current asset accounts (second digits of 1)
    121 to 129. Long-term investment accounts (second digits of 2)
    131 to 139. Plant asset accounts (second digits of 3)
    141 to 149. Intangible asset accounts (second digits of 4)

211 to 299. Liability accounts
    211 to 219. Current liability accounts (second digits of 1)
    221 to 229. Long-term liability accounts (second digits of 2)

611 to 699. Operating expense accounts
    611 to 629. Selling expense accounts (second digits of 1 and 2)
    631 to 649. Delivery expense accounts (second digits of 3 and 4)
    651 to 669. General administrative expense accounts (second digits of 5 and 6)

The third digit in each number further classifies the account. For example, in the system under discussion, all selling expense accounts, which have account numbers with first digits of 6 and second digits of 1 and 2, are further classified as follows:

611 to 699. Operating expense accounts
    611 to 629. Selling expense accounts
        611. Sales salaries expense (third digit of 1)
        613. Advertising expense (third digit of 3)
        615. Depreciation expense, store equipment (third digit of 5)

GLOSSARY

Account code number. An identifying number assigned to an account and used as the account's posting reference number.

Cash discount. A deduction from the invoice price of goods allowed if payment is made within a specified period of time.

Credit memorandum. A memorandum sent to notify its recipient that the business sending the memorandum has in its records credited the account of the recipient.

Credit period. The agreed period of time for which credit is granted and at the end of which payment is expected.

Credit terms. The agreed terms upon which credit is granted in the sale of goods or services.

Debit memorandum. A memorandum sent to notify its recipient that the business sending the memorandum has in its records debited the account of the recipient.

Discount period. The period of time in which a cash discount may be taken.

EOM. An abbreviation meaning "end of month."

Freight-in. Transportation charges on merchandise purchased for resale.

FOB. The abbreviation for "free on board," which is used to denote that goods purchased are placed on board the means of transportation at a specified geographic point free of any loading and transportation charges to that point.

General and administrative expenses. The general office, accounting, personnel, and credit and collection expenses.

Gross profit from sales. Net sales minus cost of goods sold.

Inventory ticket. A form attached to counted items in the process of taking an inventory.

List price. The catalog or other listed price from which a trade discount is deducted in arriving at the invoice price for goods.

Merchandise inventory. The unsold merchandise on hand at a given time.

Multiple-step income statement. An income statement on which cost of goods sold and the expenses are subtracted in steps to arrive at net income.

Periodic inventory system. An inventory system in which periodically, at the end of each accounting period, the cost of the unsold goods on hand is determined by counting units of each product on hand, multiplying the count for each product by its cost, and adding costs of the various products.

Perpetual inventory system. An inventory system in which an individual record is kept for each product of the units on hand at the beginning, the units purchased, the units sold, and the new balance after each purchase or sale.

Purchases discounts. Discounts taken on merchandise purchased for resale.

Retained earnings statement. A statement which reports changes in a corporation's retained earnings during an accounting period.

Sales discounts. Discounts given on sales of merchandise.

Selling expenses. The expenses of preparing and storing goods for sale, promoting sales, making sales, and if a separate delivery department is not maintained, the expenses of delivering goods to customers.

Single-step income statement. An income statement on which cost of goods sold and the expenses are added together and subtracted in one step from revenue to arrive at net income.

Trade discount. The discount that may be deducted from a catalog list price to determine the invoice price of goods.

QUESTIONS FOR CLASS DISCUSSION

1. What is gross profit from sales?
2. May a concern earn a gross profit on its sales and still suffer a loss? How?
3. Why should a concern be interested in the amount of its sales returns and allowances?
4. Since sales returns and allowances are subtracted from sales on the income statement, why not save the effort of this subtraction by debiting all such returns and allowances directly to the Sales account?
5. What is a cash discount? If terms are 2/10, n/60, what is the length of the credit period? What is the length of the discount period?
6. How and when is cost of goods sold determined in a store using a periodic inventory system?
7. Which of the following are debited to the Purchases account of a grocery store: *(a)* the purchase of a cash register, *(b)* the purchase of a refrigerated display case, *(c)* the purchase of advertising space in a newspaper, and *(d)* the purchase of a case of tomato soup?
8. If a concern may return for full credit all unsatisfactory merchandise purchased, why should it be interested in controlling the amount of its returns?
9. When applied to transportation terms, what do the letters FOB mean? What does FOB destination mean?
10. At the end of an accounting period, which inventory, the beginning inventory or the ending, appears on the trial balance?
11. What is shown on a retained earnings statement? What is the purpose of the statement?
12. How does a single-step income statement differ from a multiple-step income statement?
13. What is gained by using inventory tickets in taking a physical inventory?
14. During a year a company purchased merchandise costing $220,000. What was the company's cost of goods sold if there were *(a)* no beginning or ending inventories? *(b)* a beginning inventory of $28,000 and no ending inventory? *(c)* a $25,000 beginning inventory and a $30,000 ending inventory? and *(d)* no beginning inventory and a $15,000 ending inventory?
15. In counting the merchandise on hand at the end of an accounting period, a clerk failed to count, and consequently omitted from the inventory, all the merchandise on one shelf. If the cost of the merchandise on the shelf was $100, what was the effect of the omission on *(a)* the balance sheet and *(b)* the income statement?
16. Suppose that the omission of the $100 from the inventory (Question 15) was not discovered. What would be the effect on the balance sheet and income statement prepared at the end of the next accounting period?

17. Distinguish between cash discounts and trade discounts. Is the amount of a trade discount on merchandise purchased credited to the Purchases Discounts account?
18. When a debit memorandum is issued, who debits, the originator of the memorandum or the company receiving it?
19. When a three-digit account numbering system like the one described in this chapter is in use, which digit of an account's number is the most significant?

CLASS EXERCISES

Exercise 5–1

Rock Shop purchased merchandise having a $1,000 invoice price, terms 2/10, n/60, from Hill Company and paid for the merchandise within the discount period. *(a)* Give without dates the journal entry made by Rock Shop to record the purchase and payment and *(b)* give without dates the entries made by Hill Company to record the sale and collection. *(c)* If Rock Shop borrowed sufficient money at 9% interest on the last day of the discount period in order to pay the invoice, how much did it save by borrowing to take advantage of the discount?

Exercise 5–2

The following items, with expenses condensed to conserve space, appeared in the Income Statement columns of a work sheet prepared for Campus Shop, Incorporated, as of December 31, 198B, the end of its annual accounting period. From the information prepare a 198B income statement for the shop.

	Income Statement	
	Debit	*Credit*
Income summary	18,000	20,000
Sales		100,000
Sales returns and allowances	500	
Sales discounts	800	
Purchases	60,000	
Purchases returns and allowances		300
Purchases discounts		1,200
Freight-in	200	
Selling expenses	15,000	
General and administrative expenses	7,000	
Income taxes expense	4,000	
	105,500	121,500
Net income.........................	16,000	
	121,500	121,500

Exercise 5–3

Rule a balance-column Merchandise inventory account on note paper, and under the date, December 31, 198A, enter the $18,000 beginning inventory of Exercise 5–2 as its balance. Then prepare *(a)* the adjusting entry that removes the beginning inventory from the inventory account and charges it to Income Summary and *(b)* the adjusting entry that enters the ending inventory in the inventory account. Post the entries to the Merchandise Inventory account.

Exercise 5–4

Prepare entries to close the revenue, expense, and Income Summary accounts of Campus Shop, Incorporated, as they appear in Exercise 5–2.

Exercise 5–5

Copy the following tabulation and fill in the missing amounts. Indicate a loss by placing a minus sign before the amount. Each horizontal row of figures is a separate problem situation.

Sales	Beginning Inventory	Purchases	Ending Inventory	Cost of Goods Sold	Gross Profit	Expenses	Net Income or Loss
80,000	50,000	40,000	?	65,000	?	20,000	?
95,000	35,000	?	45,000	50,000	?	25,000	20,000
120,000	50,000	?	40,000	?	55,000	35,000	20,000
?	40,000	70,000	35,000	?	40,000	35,000	?
110,000	40,000	65,000	?	60,000	?	25,000	?
70,000	30,000	?	35,000	40,000	?	?	10,000
?	40,000	50,000	30,000	?	40,000	?	−5,000
80,000	?	50,000	35,000	?	30,000	?	10,000

Exercise 5–6

The following trial balance was taken from the ledger of Alpha, Incorporated, at the end of its annual accounting period. (To simplify the problem and to save time, the account balances are in numbers of not more than two digits.)

Required:

Prepare a work sheet form having no Adjusted Trial Balance columns on note paper and copy the trial balance on the work sheet. Then complete the work sheet using the following information:

a. Ending merchandise inventory, $6.
b. Ending store supplies inventory, $1.
c. Estimated depreciation of store equipment, $1.
d. Accrued sales salaries payable, $2.

ALPHA, INCORPORATED
Trial Balance, December 31, 19—

Cash	$ 3	
Accounts receivable	2	
Merchandise inventory	5	
Store supplies	4	
Store equipment	9	
Accumulated depreciation, store equipment		$ 2
Accounts payable		2
Salaries payable		—
Common stock, $1 par value		10
Retained earnings		6
Income summary	—	—
Sales		31
Sales returns	1	
Purchases	12	
Purchases discounts		1
Freight-in	1	
Salaries expense	6	
Rent expense	7	
Advertising expense	2	
Depreciation expense, store equipment	—	
Store supplies expense	—	—
Totals	$52	$52

PROBLEMS

Problem 5–1

Prepare general journal entries to record the following transactions:

Nov. 1 Purchased merchandise on credit, terms 2/10, n/30, $800.
  1 Paid $35 cash for freight charges on the merchandise shipment of the previous transaction.
  4 Sold merchandise on credit, terms 2/10, 1/15, n/60, $500.
  7 Purchased on credit a new typewriter for office use, $550.
  9 Purchased merchandise on credit, terms 2/10, n/60, $580.
  11 Received a $30 credit memorandum for merchandise purchased on November 9 and returned for credit.
  13 Sold merchandise for cash, $65.
  15 Purchased office supplies on credit, $75.
  16 Received a credit memorandum for unsatisfactory office supplies purchased on November 15 and returned for credit, $15.
  17 Sold merchandise on credit, terms 2/10, 1/15, n/60, $540.
  18 Issued a $40 credit memorandum to the customer of November 17 who returned a portion of the merchandise purchased.
  19 Paid for the merchandise purchased on November 9, less the return and the discount.

Nov. 19 The customer who purchased merchandise on November 4 paid for the purchase of that date less the applicable discount.

27 Received payment for the merchandise sold on November 17, less the return and applicable discount.

30 Paid for the merchandise purchased on November 1.

Problem 5–2

Valley Sales, Inc., began the year with $23,450 of retained earnings, and during the year it declared and paid $20,000 of dividends on its outstanding common stock. At the year-end the Income Statement columns of its work sheet carried the following amounts:

	Income Statement	
	Debit	Credit
Income summary	21,310	22,460
Sales....................................		215,280
Sales returns and allowances	1,120	
Purchases	144,530	
Purchases returns and allowances		470
Purchases discounts		2,280
Freight-in	890	
Sales salaries expense	18,780	
Rent expense, selling space	10,800	
Advertising expense......................	880	
Store supplies expense	550	
Depreciation expense, store equipment	1,410	
Office salaries expense	10,200	
Rent expense, office space	1,200	
Telephone expense	435	
Office supplies expense	115	
Insurance expense	850	
Depreciation expense, office equipment....	420	
Income taxes expense	4,500	
	217,990	240,490
Net income	22,500	
	240,490	240,490

Required:

1. Under the assumption that the annual accounting period of Valley Sales, Inc., ends on December 31, prepare a classified, multiple-step income statement for the concern, showing the expenses and the items entering into cost of goods sold in detail.
2. Prepare a retained earnings statement for the concern.
3. Prepare for the concern a single-step, combined income and retained earnings statement with the items condensed as is commonly done on published financial statements.

Problem 5–3

Hobby Shop, Inc., began the current year with $16,585 of retained earnings, declared and paid $12,000 of dividends, and at the year-end the following trial balance was taken from its ledger.

HOBBY SHOP, INC.

Trial Balance, December 31, 19—

Cash	$ 3,350	
Merchandise inventory	20,760	
Store supplies	575	
Office supplies	180	
Prepaid insurance	935	
Store equipment	22,410	
Accumulated depreciation, store equipment		$ 3,120
Office equipment	5,210	
Accumulated depreciation, office equipment		1,130
Accounts payable		895
Income taxes payable		—
Common stock, $10 par value		20,000
Retained earnings		4,585
Income summary	—	—
Sales		181,240
Sales returns and allowances	510	
Purchases	112,650	
Purchases discounts		1,830
Freight-in	670	
Sales salaries expense	19,410	
Rent expense, selling space	8,100	
Store supplies expense	—	
Depreciation expense, store equipment	—	
Office salaries expense	12,540	
Rent expense, office space	900	
Office supplies expense	—	
Insurance expense	—	
Depreciation expense, office equipment	—	
Income taxes expense	4,600	
Totals	$212,800	$212,800

Required:

1. Copy the trial balance on an eight-column work sheet form and complete the work sheet using the following information:

   a. Ending merchandise inventory, $21,115.
   b. Store supplies inventory, $135; and office supplies inventory, $50.
   c. Expired insurance, $780.
   d. Estimated depreciation on store equipment, $1,515; and on office equipment, $510.
   e. Additional federal income taxes expense, $320.

2. Prepare a multiple-step classified income statement showing expenses and the items entering into the calculation of cost of goods sold in detail.

3. Prepare a retained earnings statement.
4. In addition to the foregoing, prepare a single-step combined income and retained earnings statement with the items condensed as is commonly done in published statements.

Problem 5–4

(If the working papers that accompany this text are not being used, omit this problem)

The unfinished eight-column work sheet of Eastgate Shop, Incorporated, is reproduced in the booklet of working papers.

Required:

1. Complete the work sheet by combining the trial balance amounts with the adjustments and sorting the items to the proper Income Statement and Balance Sheet columns.
2. Prepare an income statement for the company showing the details of cost of goods sold and the expenses. Also prepare a balance sheet and a retained earnings statement. The company began the year with $19,425 of retained earnings, and it declared and paid $16,000 of dividends during the year.
3. In addition to the foregoing statements, prepare a combined income and retained earnings statement with the items condensed as is common in published statements.
4. Prepare adjusting and closing entries for Eastgate Shop, Incorporated.

Problem 5–5

The following trial balance was taken from the ledger of Western Sales, Inc., at the end of its annual accounting period.

Required:

1. Enter the trial balance on an eight-column work sheet form and complete the work sheet using the following information:
   a. Ending merchandise inventory, $25,115.
   b. Store supplies inventory, $180; and office supplies inventory, $110.
   c. Expired insurance, $1,020.
   d. Estimated depreciation of store equipment, $3,240; and of office equipment, $730.
   e. Accrued sales salaries payable, $210; and accrued office salaries payable, $160.
   f. Additional income taxes expense, $325.
2. From the work sheet prepare a multiple-step income statement showing the details of cost of goods sold and the expenses. Also prepare a balance sheet and a retained earnings statement. The company began the year with $17,565 of retained earnings, and it declared and paid $12,000 of dividends during the year.
3. In addition to the foregoing statements, prepare a combined income and retained earnings statement on which the items are condensed and the expenses are subtracted in a single step.
4. Prepare adjusting and closing entries for the company.

WESTERN SALES, INC.
Trial Balance, December 31, 19—

Cash	$ 5,120	
Accounts receivable	6,985	
Merchandise inventory	23,980	
Store supplies	695	
Office supplies	325	
Prepaid insurance	1,410	
Store equipment	27,770	
Accumulated depreciation, store equipment		$ 3,165
Office equipment	5,980	
Accumulated depreciation, office equipment		690
Accounts payable		1,395
Salaries payable		—
Income taxes payable		
Common stock, $10 par value		30,000
Retained earnings		5,565
Income summary	—	—
Sales		320,255
Sales returns and allowances	2,910	
Purchases	223,675	
Purchases returns and allowances		875
Purchases discounts		3,140
Freight-in	3,270	
Sales salaries expense	27,210	
Rent expense, selling space	9,720	
Advertising expense	3,190	
Store supplies expense	—	
Depreciation expense, store equipment	—	
Office salaries expense	14,820	
Rent expense, office space	1,080	
Telephone expense	545	
Insurance expense	—	
Office supplies expense	—	
Depreciation expense, office equipment	—	
Income taxes expense	6,400	
Totals	$365,085	$365,085

ALTERNATE PROBLEMS

Problem 5–1A

Prepare general journal entries to record the following transactions:

Nov. 1 Purchased merchandise on credit, terms 1/10, n/30, $700.
    4 Sold merchandise for cash, $55.
    7 Purchased office equipment on credit, $300.
    8 Purchased merchandise on credit, terms 2/10, n/60, $645.
    8 Paid $30 cash for freight charges on the merchandise shipment of

the previous transaction.

Nov. 11   Received a $45 credit memorandum for merchandise purchased on November 8 and returned for credit.

12   Sold merchandise on credit, terms 2/10, 1/15, n/60, $500.

15   Purchased office supplies on credit, $85.

16   Sold merchandise on credit, terms 2/10, 1/15, n/60, $675.

17   Received a credit memorandum for unsatisfactory office supplies purchased on November 15 and returned, $20.

18   Issued a $25 credit memorandum to the customer who purchased merchandise on November 16 and returned a portion for credit.

18   Paid for the merchandise purchased on November 8, less the return and the discount.

26   Received payment for the merchandise sold on November 16, less the return and applicable discount.

27   The customer of November 12 paid for the purchase of that date, less the applicable discount.

30   Paid for the merchandise purchased on November 1.

Problem 5–2A

Red Rock Sales, Inc., began the year with $41,235 of retained earnings, and during the year declared and paid $20,000 of dividends on its outstanding common stock. At the year-end the following items appeared in the Income Statement columns of a work sheet covering its annual accounting period:

	Income Statement	
	Debit	*Credit*
Income summary	31,445	29,340
Sales		393,750
Sales returns and allowances	1,550	
Sales discounts	4,310	
Purchases	279,125	
Purchases returns and allowances		1,175
Purchases discounts		4,580
Freight-in	2,335	
Sales salaries expense	31,315	
Rent expense, selling space	12,960	
Advertising expense	2,915	
Store supplies expense	610	
Depreciation expense, store equipment	3,560	
Office salaries expense	15,340	
Rent expense, office space	1,440	
Telephone expense	645	
Insurance expense	1,215	
Office supplies expense	280	
Depreciation expense, office equipment	965	
Income tax expense	8,045	
	398,055	428,845
Net income	30,790	
	428,845	428,845

Required:

1. Prepare a classified, multiple-step income statement for the company, showing the expenses and the items entering into cost of goods sold in detail.
2. Prepare a retained earnings statement for the company.
3. Prepare for the company a single-step, combined income and retained earnings statement with the items condensed as is commonly done in published financial statements.

Problem 5–3A

Universal Sales, Inc., began the current year with $24,045 of retained earnings, declared and paid $20,000 of dividends during the year, and prepared the following trial balance of its ledger at the year-end.

UNIVERSAL SALES, INC.
Trial Balance, December 31, 19—

Cash	$ 4,345	
Merchandise inventory	26,560	
Store supplies	915	
Office supplies	310	
Prepaid insurance	1,295	
Store equipment	28,950	
Accumulated depreciation, store equipment		$ 3,170
Office equipment	7,440	
Accumulated depreciation, office equipment		985
Accounts payable		2,135
Income taxes payable	—	
Common stock, $10 par value		25,000
Retained earnings		4,045
Income summary	—	—
Sales		295,310
Sales returns and allowances	615	
Purchases	198,285	
Purchases discounts		1,820
Freight-in	2,610	
Sales salaries expense	27,560	
Rent expense, selling space	11,200	
Store supplies expense	—	
Depreciation expense, store equipment	—	
Office salaries expense	15,380	
Rent expense, office space	1,200	
Office supplies expense	—	
Insurance expense	—	
Depreciation expense, office equipment	—	
Income taxes expense	5,800	
Totals	$332,465	$332,465

Required:

1. Copy the trial balance on an eight-column work sheet form and complete the work sheet using the following information:
   a. Ending merchandise inventory, $24,745.
   b. Store supplies inventory, $175; and office supplies inventory, $115.
   c. Expired insurance, $965.
   d. Estimated depreciation on store equipment, $2,965; and on office equipment, $825.
   e. Additional federal income taxes expense, $810.
2. Prepare a multiple-step classified income statement showing in detail the items entering into cost of goods sold and the expenses.
3. Prepare a retained earnings statement.
4. In addition to the foregoing statements, prepare a combined income and retained earnings statement in single-step form with the items condensed as is commonly done in published statements.

Problem 5–5A

Apex Sales, Inc., began the current year with $13,855 of retained earnings, declared and paid $10,000 of dividends during the year, and prepared the following trial balance of its ledger at the year-end:

APEX SALES, INC.
Trial Balance, December 31, 19—

Cash	$ 6,345	
Accounts receivable	10,220	
Merchandise inventory	31,315	
Store supplies	885	
Office supplies	340	
Prepaid insurance	1,570	
Store equipment	32,320	
Accumulated depreciation, store equipment		$ 4,215
Office equipment	7,980	
Accumulated depreciation, office equipment		1,035
Accounts payable		1,240
Salaries payable		—
Income taxes payable		—
Common stock, $10 par value		50,000
Retained earnings		3,855
Income summary	—	—
Sales		347,885
Sales returns and allowances	2,610	
Purchases	242,450	
Purchases returns and allowances		1,095
Purchases discounts		3,535
Freight-in	3,920	
Sales salaries expense	31,315	
Rent expense, selling space	10,500	
Totals carried forward	$381,770	$412,860

Totals brought forward	$381,770	$412,860
Advertising expense.........................	4,310	
Store supplies expense	—	
Depreciation expense, store equipment	—	
Office salaries expense	18,635	
Rent expense, office space	1,500	
Telephone expense	645	
Office supplies expense	—	
Insurance expense	—	
Depreciation expense, office equipment........	—	
Income taxes expense	6,000	
Totals	$412,860	$412,860

Required:

1. Enter the trial balance on an eight-column work sheet form and complete the work sheet using the following information:
    a. Ending merchandise inventory, $33,110.
    b. Store supplies inventory, $220; and office supplies inventory, $130.
    c. Expired insurance, $1,150.
    d. Estimated depreciation on store equipment, $3,840; and on office equipment, $885.
    e. Accrued sales salaries payable, $265; and accrued office salaries payable, $180.
    f. Additional income taxes expense, $590.
2. From the work sheet prepare a multiple-step income statement showing the details of cost of goods sold and the expenses. Also prepare a balance sheet and a retained earnings statement.
3. In addition to the foregoing statements, prepare a combined income and retained earnings statement in single-step form with the items condensed as is commonly done on published statements.
4. Prepare adjusting and closing entries for the company.

PROVOCATIVE PROBLEMS

Provocative problem 5–1
Larkin Paint Store

Elmer Larkin retired from farming last year, sold his equipment, paid off his debts, and placed the remaining cash in a savings account. However, he soon became restless, and six months ago he opened a retail paint store in his small rural community. At that time there was no such store in the community, and it appeared that the venture would be profitable.

He began business by transferring $35,000 from his savings account to a checking account opened in the store's name. He immediately bought for cash store equipment costing $6,000, which he expected to use ten years, after which it would be worn out and valueless, and a stock of merchandise costing $20,000. He paid six months' rent in advance on the store building, $2,400.

He estimated that like stores in neighboring communities marked their goods for sale at prices 35% above cost. In other words, an item costing $10 was marked for sale at $13.50. In order to get his store off to a good start, he decided to mark his goods for sale at 30% above cost, and because of his low overhead, he thought this would still leave a net income of 10% on sales.

Since he was in a rural farming community, Mr. Larkin granted liberal credit terms, telling his credit-worthy customers to pay "when the crops are in." His suppliers granted Mr. Larkin the normal 30-day credit period on his purchases.

Today, October 1, six months after opening the store, Mr. Larkin has come to you for advice. He thinks business has been excellent. He has paid his suppliers for all purchases when due and owes only for purchases, $9,000, made during the last 30 days and for which payment is not due. He has replaced his original inventory three times during the last six months, and an income statement he has prepared shows $85,500 of sales, a $25,500 gross profit, and an $8,900 net income, which is a little better than he anticipated. He says he has a full stock of merchandise which cost $20,000 and his customers owe him $26,200. In addition to the rent paid in advance, he has paid all of his other expenses, $14,200, with cash.

Nevertheless, Mr. Larkin doubts the validity of his gross profit and net income figures, since he started business with $35,000 in cash and now has only $700 in the bank and owes $9,000 for merchandise purchased on credit.

Did Mr. Larkin actually meet his profit expectations? If so, explain to him the apparent paradox of adequate income and a declining cash balance. Back your explanation with a statement accounting for the October 1 cash balance, a six months' income statement, and a September 30 balance sheet.

Provocative problem 5–2
Jed's Feed Store

Jed Reed opened a feed store, Jed's Feed Store, on January 4 of the current year by investing $2,500 in cash and a $7,500 inventory of merchandise. During the year he paid out in cash $28,000 to purchase additional merchandise and $9,600 for operating expenses. He also withdrew $12,000 in cash from the business for personal use, and at the year-end he prepared the following balance sheet:

JED'S FEED STORE
Balance Sheet, December 31, 19—

Cash	$ 2,000	Accounts payable (for	
Accounts receivable	6,200	merchandise)	$ 6,500
Merchandise inventory ...	9,000	Jed Reed, capital	10,700
Total assets	$17,200	Total equities	$17,200

Based on the information given, prepare an income statement showing the results of the first year's operations of the business. Support your income statement with schedules showing your calculations of net income, cost of goods sold, and sales.

part three
Accounting for assets

CHAPTER 6 Accounting for cash and marketable securities. CHAPTER 7 Accounts and notes receivable. CHAPTER 8 Inventories and cost of goods sold. CHAPTER 9 Plant and equipment, natural resources, and intangible assets.

6

Accounting for cash and marketable securities

**After studying Chapter 6,
you should be able to:**

- Explain why internal control procedures are needed in a large concern and state the broad principles of internal control.

- Describe internal control procedures to protect cash received from cash sales, cash received through the mail, and cash disbursements.

- Tell how a petty cash fund operates and be able to make entries to establish a petty cash fund and reimburse it.

- Explain why the bank balance and the book balance of cash are reconciled and be able to prepare such a reconciliation.

- Tell how recording invoices at net amounts helps gain control over cash discounts taken and be able to account for invoices recorded at net amounts.

- Be able to identify and account for marketable securities.

- Define or explain the words and phrases listed in the chapter Glossary.

Cash has universal usefulness, small bulk for high value, and no convenient identification marks by which ownership may be established. Consequently, in accounting for cash, the procedures for protecting it from fraud and theft are very important. They are called *internal control procedures* and apply to all assets owned by a business and to all phases of its operations.

INTERNAL CONTROL

In a small business the owner-manager commonly controls the entire operation through personal supervision and direct participation in the activities of the business. For example, he or she commonly buys all the assets, goods, and services bought by the business. Such a manager also hires and closely supervises all employees, negotiates all contracts, and signs all checks. As a result, in signing checks, for example, he or she knows from personal contact and observation that the assets, goods, and services for which the checks are in payment were received by the business. However, as a business grows it becomes increasingly difficult to maintain this personal contact. Therefore, at some point it becomes necessary for the manager to delegate responsibilities and rely on internal control procedures rather than personal contact in controlling the operations of the business. In a properly designed system the procedures encourage adherence to prescribed managerial policies. They also promote operational efficiencies; protect the business assets from waste, fraud, and theft; and ensure accurate and reliable accounting data.

Internal control procedures vary from company to company, depending on such factors as the nature of the business and its size. However, some broad principles of internal control are discussed below.[1]

Responsibilities should be clearly established

Good internal control necessitates that responsibilities be clearly established and for a given task, one person be made responsible. When

---

[1] For a discussion that continues to offer an unusually balanced analysis of the principles of internal control, see AICPA, *Internal Control* (New York, 1949).

responsibility is shared and something goes wrong, it is difficult to determine who was at fault. For example, when two salesclerks share the same cash drawer and there is a shortage, it is normally impossible to tell which clerk is at fault. Each will tend to blame the other. Neither can prove that he or she is not responsible. In such a situation each clerk should be assigned a separate cash drawer or one of the clerks should be given responsibility for making all change.

Adequate records should be maintained

Good records provide a means of control by placing responsibility for the care and protection of assets. Poor records invite laxity and often theft. When a company has poor accounting control over its assets, dishonest employees soon become aware of this and are quick to take advantage.

Assets should be insured and employees bonded

Assets should be covered by adequate casualty insurance, and employees who handle cash and negotiable assets should be bonded. Bonding provides a means for recovery if a loss occurs. It also tends to prevent losses, since a bonded employee is less apt to take assets if the employee knows a bonding company must be dealt with when the shortage is revealed.

Record keeping and custody should be separated

A fundamental principle of internal control requires that the person who has access to or is responsible for an asset should not maintain the accounting record for that asset. When this principle is observed, the custodian of an asset, knowing that a record of the asset is being kept by another person, is not apt to either misappropriate the asset or waste it; and the record keeper, who does not have access to the asset, has no reason to falsify the record. Furthermore, if the asset is to be misappropriated and the theft concealed in the records, collusion is necessary.

Responsibility for related transactions should be divided

Responsibility for a divisible transaction or a series of related transactions should be divided between individuals or departments in such a manner that the work of one acts as a check on that of another. This does not mean there should be duplication of work. Each employee or department should perform an unduplicated portion. For example, responsibility for placing orders, receiving the merchandise, and paying the vendors should not be given to one individual or department. To do so is to invite laxity in checking the quality and quantity of goods received, and carelessness in verifying the validity and accuracy of invoices. It also invites the purchase of goods for an employee's personal use and the payment of fictitious invoices.

Mechanical devices should be used whenever practicable

Cash registers, check protectors, time clocks, and mechanical counters are examples of control devices that should be used whenever practicable. A cash register with a lock-in tape makes a record of each cash sale. A check protector by perforating the amount of a check into its face makes it very difficult to change the amount. A time clock registers the exact time an employee arrived on the job and when the employee departed.

INTERNAL CONTROL FOR CASH

A good system of internal control for cash should provide adequate procedures for protecting both cash receipts and cash disbursements. In the procedures three basic principles should always be observed. First, there should be a separation of duties so that the people responsible for handling cash and for its custody are not the same people who keep the cash records. Second, all cash receipts should be deposited in the bank, intact, each day. Third, all payments should be made by check. The one exception to the last principle is that small disbursements may be made in cash from a petty cash fund. Petty cash funds are discussed later in this chapter.

The reason for the first principle is that a division of duties necessitates collusion between two or more people if cash is to be embezzled and the theft concealed in the accounting records. The second, requiring that all receipts be deposited intact each day, prevents an employee from making personal use of the money for a few days before depositing it. And, requiring that all receipts be deposited intact and all payments be made by check provides in the records of the bank a separate and external record of all cash transactions that may be used to prove the company's own records.

The exact procedures used to achieve control over cash vary from company to company. They depend upon such things as company size, number of employees, cash sources, and so on. Consequently, the following procedures are only illustrative of some that are in use.

Cash from cash sales

Cash sales should be rung up on a cash register at the time of each sale. To help ensure that correct amounts are rung up, each register should be so placed that customers can see the amounts rung up. Also, the clerks should be required to ring up each sale before wrapping the merchandise. Finally, each cash register should have a locked-in tape on which the amount of each sale and total sales are printed by the register.

Good cash control, as previously stated, requires a separation of custody for cash from record keeping for cash. For cash sales this separation begins with the cash register. The salesclerk who has access to the cash in the register should not have access to its locked-in tape. At the end of each day the salesclerk is usually required to count the cash in the register and to turn the cash and its count over to an employee in the cashier's office. The employee in the cashier's office, like the salesclerk, has access to the cash and should not have access to the register tape or other accounting records. A third employee, commonly from the accounting department, removes the tape from the register. He or she compares its total with the cash turned over to the cashier's office and uses the tape's information as a basis for the entry recording cash sales. This employee who has access to the register tape does not have access to the cash and therefore cannot take any. Likewise, since the salesclerk and the employee from the cashier's office do not have access to the cash register tape, they cannot take cash without the shortage being revealed.

Cash received through the mail

Control of cash coming in through the mail begins with a mail clerk who opens the mail and makes a list in triplicate of the money received. The list should give each sender's name, the purpose for which the money was sent, and the amount. One copy of the list is sent to the cashier with the money. The second copy goes to the bookkeeper. The third copy is kept by the mail clerk. The cashier deposits the money in the bank, and the bookkeeper records the amounts received in the accounting records. Then, if the bank balance is reconciled (discussed later) by a fourth person, errors or fraud by the mail clerk, the cashier, or bookkeeper will be detected. They will be detected because the cash deposited and the records of three people must agree. Furthermore, fraud is impossible, unless there is collusion. The mail clerk must report all receipts or customers will question their account balances. The cashier must deposit all receipts because the bank balance must agree with the bookkeeper's cash balance. The bookkeeper and the person reconciling the bank balance do not have access to cash and, therefore, have no opportunity to withhold any.

Cash disbursements

It is important to gain control over cash from sales and cash received through the mail. However, most large embezzlements have not involved cash receipts but have been accomplished through the payment of fictitious invoices. Consequently, procedures for controlling cash disbursements are equally as important and sometimes more important than those for cash receipts.

To gain control over cash disbursements, all disbursements should be made by check, excepting those from petty cash. If authority to sign checks is delegated to some person other than the business owner, that person should not have access to the accounting records. This helps prevent a fraudulent disbursement being made and concealed in the accounting records.

In a small business the owner manager usually signs checks and normally knows from personal contact that the items for which the checks pay were received by the business. However, this is impossible in a large business. In a large business internal control procedures must be substituted for personal contact. The procedures tell the person who signs checks that the obligations for which the checks pay are proper obligations, properly incurred, and should be paid. Often these procedures take the form of a *voucher system.*

THE VOUCHER SYSTEM AND CONTROL

A voucher system helps gain control over cash disbursements as follows: (1) It permits only designated departments and individuals to incur obligations that will result in cash disbursements. (2) It establishes procedures for incurring such obligations and for their verification, approval, and recording. (3) It permits checks to be issued only in payment of properly verified, approved, and recorded obligations. Finally (4), it requires that every obligation be recorded at the time it is incurred and every purchase be treated as an independent transaction, complete in itself. It requires this even though a number of purchases may be made from the same company during a month or other billing period.

When a voucher system is in use, control over cash disbursements begins with the incurrence of obligations that will result in cash disbursements. Only specified departments and individuals are authorized to incur such obligations, and the kind each may incur is limited. For example, in a large store only the purchasing department may incur obligations by purchasing merchandise. However, to gain control, the purchasing-receiving-and-paying procedures are divided among several departments. They are the departments requesting that merchandise be purchased, the purchasing department, the receiving department, and the accounting department. To coordinate and control the responsibilities of these departments, business papers are used. A list of the papers follows, and an explanation of each will show how a large concern may gain control over cash disbursements resulting from the purchase of merchandise.

Business paper	Prepared by the—	Sent to the—
1. Purchase requisition	Selling department manager desiring that merchandise be purchased	Purchasing department, with a copy to the accounting department
2. Purchase order	Purchasing department	Vendor, with a copy to the accounting department
3. Invoice	Company selling the merchandise	Accounting department
4. Receiving report	Receiving department	Accounting department, with a copy to the purchasing and requisitioning departments
5. Invoice approval form	Accounting department	Attached to invoice in the accounting department
6. Voucher	Accounting department	Cashier's department with other business papers attached

Purchase requisition

The department managers in a large store cannot be permitted to place orders directly with supply sources. If each manager were permitted to deal directly with wholesalers and manufacturers, the amount of merchandise purchased and the resulting liabilities could not be controlled. Therefore, to gain control over purchases and resulting liabilities, department managers are commonly required to place all orders through the purchasing department. In such cases the function of the several department managers in the purchasing procedure is to inform the purchasing department of their needs. Each manager performs this function by preparing in triplicate and signing a business paper called a *purchase requisition*. On the requisition the manager lists the merchandise needs of his or her department. The original and a duplicate copy of the purchase requisition are sent to the purchasing department. The third copy is retained by the requisitioning department as a check on the purchasing department.

Purchase order

A *purchase order* is a business form used by the purchasing department in placing an order with a manufacturer or wholesaler. It authorizes the supplier to ship the merchandise ordered and takes the place of a typewritten letter placing the order. On receipt of a purchase requisition from a selling department, the purchasing department prepares four or more copies of the purchase order. The copies are distributed as follows:

Copy 1, the original copy, is sent to the supplier as a request to purchase and as authority to ship the merchandise listed.

Copy 2, with a copy of the purchase requisition attached, is sent to the accounting department where it will ultimately be used in approving the invoice of the purchase for payment.

Copy 3 is sent to the department issuing the requisition to acknowledge the requisition and tell the action taken.

Copy 4 is retained on file by the purchasing department.

Invoice

An *invoice* is an itemized statement of goods bought and sold. It is prepared by the seller or *vendor,* and to the seller it is a sales invoice. However, when the same invoice is received by the buyer or *vendee,* it becomes a purchase invoice to the buyer. Upon receipt of a purchase order, the manufacturer or wholesaler receiving the order ships the ordered merchandise to the buyer and mails a copy of the invoice covering the shipment. The goods are delivered to the buyer's receiving department. The invoice is sent directly to the buyer's accounting department.

Receiving report

Most large companies maintain a special department assigned the duty of receiving all merchandise or other assets purchased. As each shipment is received, counted, and checked, the receiving department prepares four or more copies of a *receiving report.* On this report are listed the quantity, description, and condition of the items received. The original copy is sent to the accounting department. The second copy is sent to the department that requisitioned the merchandise. The third copy is sent to the purchasing department. The fourth copy is retained on file in the receiving department. The copies sent to the purchasing and requisitioning departments act as notification of the arrival of the goods.

Invoice approval form

When the receiving report arrives in the accounting department, it has in its possession copies of the—

1. Requisition listing the items that were to be ordered.
2. Purchase order that lists the merchandise actually ordered.
3. Invoice showing quantity, description, unit price, and total of the goods shipped by the seller.

4. Receiving report that lists quantity and condition of the items received.

With the information of these papers, the accounting department is in position to approve the invoice for entry on the books and ultimate payment. In approving the invoice, the accounting department checks and compares the information on all the papers. To facilitate the checking procedure and to ensure that no step is omitted, an *invoice approval form* is commonly used. This may be a separate business paper that is attached to the invoice, or the information shown in Illustration 6–1 may be stamped directly on the invoice with a rubber stamp.

INVOICE APPROVAL FORM

Purchase Order Number _____

Requisition Check _____

Purchase Order Check _____

Receiving Report Check _____

Invoice Check

 Price Approval _____

 Calculations _____

 Terms _____

Approved for Payment:

_____

Illustration 6–1

As each step in the checking procedure is completed, the clerk making the check initials the invoice approval form. Initials in each space on the form indicate:

1. Requisition Check .... The items on the invoice agree with the requisition and were requisitioned.

2. Purchase Order Check ... The items on the invoice agree with the purchase order and were ordered.

3. Receiving Report Check The items on the invoice agree with the receiving report and were received.

4. Invoice Check:
 Price Approval .... The invoice prices are the agreed prices.

Calculations . . . .   The invoice has no mathematical er-
                                   rors.

Terms . . . .   The terms are the agreed terms.

The voucher

When a voucher system is in use, after the invoice is checked and
approved, a *voucher* is prepared. A voucher is a business paper on
which a transaction is summarized, its correctness certified, and its
recording and payment approved. Vouchers vary somewhat from company to company. However, in general they are so designed that the
invoice, bill, or other documents from which they are prepared are
attached to and folded inside the voucher. This makes for ease in
filing. The inside of a voucher is shown in Illustration 6–2, and the
outside in Illustration 6–3. The preparation of a voucher is a simple
task requiring only that a clerk enter the required information in the
proper blank spaces on a voucher form. The information is taken from
the invoice and its supporting documents. After the voucher is com-

Voucher No. ___767___

VALLEY SUPPLY COMPANY
Eugene, Oregon

Date ___Oct. 1, 19--___
Pay to ___A.B. Seay Wholesale Company___
City ___Salem___   State ___Oregon___

For the following: (attach all invoices and supporting papers)

Date of Invoice	Terms	Invoice Number and Other Details,	Amount
Sept. 30,19--	2/10,n/60	Invoice No. C-11756	800.00
		Less Discount	16.00
		Net Amount Payable	784.00

Payment Approved

___M. O. Neal___
Auditor

Illustration 6–2
Inside of a voucher

Voucher No. _767_

ACCOUNTING DISTRIBUTION

Account Debited	Amount
Purchases	800.00
Freight-In	
Store Supplies	
Office Supplies	
Sales Salaries	

Due Date _____ October 6, 19-- _____

Pay to __ A.B. Seay Wholesale Co. __
City ____ Salem ____
State ____ Oregon ____

Total Vouch. Pay.Cr.	800.00

Summary of Charges:
Total Charges _____ 800.00
Discount _____ 16.00
Net Payment _____ 784.00

Record of Payment:
Paid _____
Check No. _____

Illustration 6–3
Outside of a voucher

pleted, the invoice and its supporting documents are attached to and folded inside the voucher. The voucher is then sent to the desk of the chief clerk or auditor who makes an additional check, approves the accounting distribution (the accounts to be debited), and approves the voucher for recording.

After being approved and recorded, a voucher is filed until its due date, when it is sent to the office of the company cashier or other disbursing officer for payment. Here the person responsible for issuing checks depends upon the approved voucher and its signed supporting documents to verify that the obligation is a proper obligation, properly incurred, and should be paid. For example, the purchase requisition and purchase order attached to the voucher confirm that the purchase was authorized. The receiving report shows that the items were received, and the invoice approval form verifies that the invoice was checked for errors. As a result, there is little chance for fraud, unless all the documents were stolen and the signatures forged, or there was collusion.

THE VOUCHER SYSTEM AND EXPENSES

Under a voucher system, to gain control over disbursements, every obligation that will result in a cash disbursement must be approved for payment and recorded as a liability at the time it is incurred. This includes all expenses. As a result, for example, when the monthly telephone bill is received, it is verified and any long-distance calls are approved. A voucher is then prepared, and the telephone bill is attached to and folded inside the voucher. The voucher is then recorded, and a check is issued in its payment, or the voucher is filed for payment at a later date.

Requiring that an expense be approved for payment and recorded as an expense and a liability at the time it is incurred helps ensure that every expense payment is approved when information for its approval is available. Often invoices, bills, and statements for such things as equipment repairs are received weeks after the work is done. If no record of the repairs exists, it is difficult at that time to determine whether the invoice or bill is a correct statement of the amount owed. Also, if no records exist, it is possible for a dishonest employee to arrange with an outsider for more than one payment of an obligation, for payment of excessive amounts, and for payment for goods and services not received, all with kickbacks to the dishonest employee.

RECORDING VOUCHERS

Normally a company large enough to use a voucher system will use bookkeeping machines or punched cards, magnetic tape, and a computer in recording its transactions. Consequently, for this reason and also because the primary purpose of this discussion is to describe the control techniques of a voucher system, a pen-and-ink system of recording vouchers is not described here.

THE PETTY CASH FUND

A basic principle in controlling cash disbursements is that all such disbursements be made by check. However, an exception to this rule is made for petty cash disbursements. Every business must make many small payments for items such as postage, express charges, telegrams, and small items of supplies. If each such payment is made by check, many checks for immaterial amounts are written. This is both time consuming and expensive. Therefore, to avoid writing checks for small amounts, a petty cash fund is established, and such payments are made from this fund.

When a petty cash fund is established, an estimate is made of the total small payments likely to be disbursed during a short period, usually not more than a month. A check is drawn and debited to the

Petty Cash account for an amount slightly in excess of this estimate. The check is cashed, and the money is turned over to a member of the office staff who is designated *petty cashier* and who is responsible for the petty cash and for making payments therefrom.

The petty cashier usually keeps the petty cash in a locked box in the office safe. As each disbursement is made, a *petty cash receipt,* Illustration 6–4, is signed by the person receiving payment and is placed with the remaining money in the petty cashbox. Under this system, the petty cashbox should always contain paid petty cash receipts and money equal to the amount of the fund.

Each disbursement reduces the money and increases the sum of the receipts in the petty cashbox. When the money is nearly exhausted, the fund is reimbursed. To reimburse the fund, the petty cashier presents the receipts for petty cash payments to the company cashier.

No. __-1-__ $ __5.00__

RECEIVED OF PETTY CASH

DATE __Nov. 3__   19 __--__

FOR __Washing windows__

CHARGE TO __Miscellaneous General Expenses__
ACCOUNT

APPROVED BY __CaB.__   RECEIVED BY __Bob Tone__

TOPS—FORM 3008

Illustration 6–4

The company cashier stamps each receipt "paid" so that it may not be reused, retains the receipts, and gives the petty cashier a check for their sum. When this check is cashed and the proceeds returned to the petty cashbox, the money in the box is restored to its original amount and the fund is ready to begin anew the cycle of its operations.

In making petty cash payments, some companies have the petty cashier enter each payment in a Petty Cash Record. This is a book in which the various petty cash payments are entered in columns according to the expense or other accounts to be debited when the fund is reimbursed. The columns have such headings as Postage, Freight-In, Miscellaneous General Expenses, Office Supplies, and so forth. The Petty Cash Record is not a book of original entry. It is only a supplementary record, the column totals of which provide information as to the amounts to be debited to the various accounts when the petty cash fund is reimbursed.

Although many companies use a Petty Cash Record, other companies are of the opinion that such a record is unnecessary. In the latter companies, when the petty cash fund is to be reimbursed, the petty cashier sorts the paid petty cash receipts into groups according to the expense or other accounts to be debited in recording payments from the fund. Each group is then totaled, and the totals are used in making the reimbursing entry. This method is assumed in the illustration that follows.

PETTY CASH FUND ILLUSTRATED

To avoid writing numerous checks for small amounts, a company established a petty cash fund on November 1, designating one of its office clerks, Ned Fox, petty cashier. A $25 check was drawn, cashed, and the proceeds turned over to the clerk. The following entry in general journal form was used to record the check:

Nov.	1	Petty Cash	25.00	
		Cash		25.00
		Established a petty cash fund.		

Observe that the entry transfers $25 from the regular Cash account to the Petty Cash account. Also remember that the Petty Cash account is debited when the fund is established but is not debited or credited again unless the size of the fund is changed. If the fund is exhausted and reimbursements occur too often, the fund should be increased. This results in an additional debit to the Petty Cash account and a credit to the regular Cash account for the amount of the increase. If the fund is too large, part of its cash should be returned to general cash.

During November the petty cashier of this illustration made several payments from the petty cash fund, each time taking a receipt from the person receiving payment. Then on November 27 the petty cashier made a $6.50 payment for repairs to an office typewriter and realized there was not sufficient cash in the fund for another payment. Consequently, the paid petty cash receipts were separated into groups by the petty cashier and totaled with the results shown in Illustration 6–5. Next, the paid petty cash receipts and a summary of the payments were given to the company cashier in exchange for a $24.25 check to reimburse the fund. The petty cashier then cashed the check, put the $24.25 proceeds in the petty cashbox, and was ready to begin again to make payments from the fund.

Summary of Petty Cash Payments

Explanation of Payments	Freight-In	Misc. Gen. Expenses	Delivery Expense	Office Supplies
Washing windows		$ 5.00		
Delivery of merchandise purchased	$4.25			
Purchased paper clips				$2.00
Delivery of customer's package			$3.00	
Delivery of merchandise purchased	3.50			
Typewriter repairs		6.50		
Totals........................	$7.75	$11.50	$3.00	$2.00

Illustration 6–5

The reimbursing check is recorded with an entry having these debits:

Nov.	27	Freight-In	7.75	
		Miscellaneous General Expenses	11.50	
		Delivery Expense	3.00	
		Office Supplies	2.00	
		Cash		24.25
		Reimbursed the petty cash fund.		

Information for the entry came from the petty cashier's payments summary. Note that its debits record the petty cash payments. Such an entry is necessary to get the debits into the accounts. Consequently, petty cash must be reimbursed at the end of each accounting period, as well as at any time the money in the fund is low. If the fund is not reimbursed at the end of each accounting period, the asset petty cash is overstated and the expenses and assets of the petty cash payments are understated on the financial statements.

Occasionally, at the time of a petty cash expenditure a petty cashier will forget to secure a receipt, and by the time the fund is reimbursed, will have forgotten the expenditure. This causes the fund to be short. If at reimbursement time the petty cash fund is short because the petty cashier forgot to secure a receipt for a payment or from other cause, the shortage is recorded as an expense in the reimbursing entry with a debit to the *Cash Over and Short account* discussed in the next section.

CASH OVER AND SHORT

Regardless of care exercised in making change, customers are sometimes given too much change or are shortchanged. As a result, at the end of a day the actual cash from a cash register is commonly not equal to the cash sales "rung up" on the register. When this occurs and, for example, actual cash as counted is $557 but the register shows cash sales of $556, the entry in general journal form to record sales and the overage is:

Nov.	23	Cash	557.00	
		Cash Over and Short		1.00
		Sales		556.00
		Day's cash sales and overage.		

If, on the other hand, cash is short, the entry in general journal form to record sales and the shortage is:

Nov.	24	Cash	621.00	
		Cash Over and Short	4.00	
		Sales		625.00
		Day's cash sales and shortage.		

Over a period of time cash overages should about equal cash short-ages. However, customers are more prone to report instances in which they are given too little change. Therefore, amounts of cash short are apt to be greater than amounts of cash over. Consequently, the Cash Over and Short account normally reaches the end of the accounting period with a debit balance. When it does so, the balance represents an expense. The expense may appear on the income statement as a separate item in the general and administrative expense section. Or if the amount is small, it may be combined with other miscellaneous expenses and appear as part of the item, miscellaneous expenses. When Cash Over and Short reaches the end of the period with a credit bal-ance, the balance represents revenue and normally appears on the income statement as part of the item, miscellaneous revenues.

RECONCILING THE BANK BALANCE

Once each month banks furnish each commercial depositor a bank statement which shows (1) the balance of the depositor's account at the beginning of the month; (2) checks and any other amounts deducted from the account; (3) deposits and any other amounts added to the account; and (4) the account balance at the end of the month, according to the records of the bank. A bank statement is shown in Illustration 6–6.

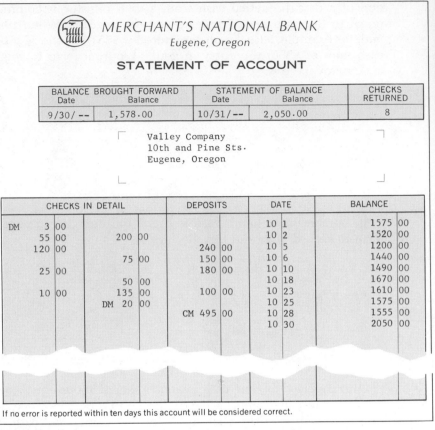

MERCHANT'S NATIONAL BANK
Eugene, Oregon

STATEMENT OF ACCOUNT

BALANCE BROUGHT FORWARD		STATEMENT OF BALANCE		CHECKS RETURNED
Date	Balance	Date	Balance	
9/30/--	1,578.00	10/31/--	2,050.00	8

```
        Valley Company
        10th and Pine Sts.
        Eugene, Oregon
```

CHECKS IN DETAIL						DEPOSITS		DATE		BALANCE	
DM	3	00						10	1	1575	00
	55	00	200	00				10	2	1520	00
	120	00				240	00	10	5	1200	00
			75	00		150	00	10	6	1440	00
	25	00				180	00	10	10	1490	00
			50	00				10	18	1670	00
	10	00	135	00		100	00	10	23	1610	00
			DM 20	00				10	25	1575	00
						CM 495	00	10	28	1555	00
								10	30	2050	00

If no error is reported within ten days this account will be considered correct.

Illustration 6–6

Banks commonly mail a depositor's bank statement. Included in the envelope with the statement are the depositor's *canceled checks* and any debit or credit memoranda that have affected the account. The checks returned are the ones the bank has paid during the month. They are called canceled checks because they are canceled by stamping or punching to show that they have been paid. During any month, in addition to the checks the depositor has drawn, the bank may deduct from the depositor's account amounts for service charges, items deposited that are uncollectible, and for errors. The bank notifies the depositor of each such deduction with a debit memorandum. A copy of the memorandum is always included with the monthly statement. The bank may also add amounts to the depositor's account for errors and for amounts collected for the depositor. A credit memorandum is used to notify of any additions.

If all receipts are deposited intact and all payments, other than petty cash payments, are made by check, the bank statement becomes a device for proving the depositor's cash records. The proof normally begins with the preparation of a *reconciliation of the bank balance.*

Need for reconciling the bank balance

Normally, when the bank statement arrives, the balance of cash as shown by the statement does not agree with the balance shown by the depositor's accounting records. Consequently, in order to prove the accuracy of both the depositor's records and those of the bank, it is necessary to *reconcile* and account for any differences between the two balances.

Numerous things may cause the bank statement balance to differ from the depositor's book balance of cash. Some are:

1. *Outstanding checks.* These are checks that have been drawn by the depositor and deducted on the depositor's records but have not reached the bank for payment and deduction.
2. *Unrecorded deposits.* Concerns often make deposits at the end of each business day, after the bank has closed. These deposits are made in the bank's night depository and are not recorded by the bank until the next business day. Consequently, if a deposit is placed in the night depository the last day of the month, it does not appear on the bank statement for that month.
3. *Charges for service and uncollectible items.* A bank often deducts amounts from a depositor's account for services rendered and for items deposited that it is unable to collect. Insufficient funds checks are the most common of the latter. The bank notifies the depositor of each such deduction with a debit memorandum. If the item is material in amount, the memorandum is mailed to the depositor on the day of the deduction. Furthermore, in a well-managed company, each such deduction is recorded on the day the memorandum is received. However, occasionally there are unrecorded amounts near the end of the month.
4. *Collections.* Banks often act as collecting agents for their depositors, collecting for a small fee promissory notes and other items. When an item such as a promissory note is collected, the bank usually adds the proceeds to the depositor's account. It then sends a credit memorandum as notification of the transaction. As soon as the memorandum is received, it should be recorded. Occasionally, there are unrecorded amounts near the end of the month.
5. *Errors.* Regardless of care and systems of internal control for automatic error detection, both the bank and the depositor make errors that affect the bank balance. Occasionally, these errors are not discovered until the balance is reconciled.

Steps in reconciling the bank balance

The steps in reconciling the bank balance are the following:

1. Compare the deposits listed on the bank statement with deposits shown in the accounting records. Note any discrepancies and discover which is correct. List any errors or unrecorded items.
2. When canceled checks are returned by the bank, they are in a stack in the order of their listing on the bank statement. While the checks are in this order, compare each with its bank statement listing. Note any discrepancies or errors.
3. Rearrange the returned checks in numerical order, the order in which they were written. Secure the previous month's reconciliation and determine if any checks outstanding at the end of the previous month are still outstanding. If there are any, list them. Also, see that any deposits that were unrecorded by the bank at the end of the previous month have been recorded.
4. Insert among the canceled checks any bank memoranda according to their dates. Compare each check with its entry in the accounting records. Note for correction any discrepancies, and list any unpaid checks or unrecorded memoranda.
5. Prepare a reconciliation of the bank statement balance with the book balance of cash. Such a reconciliation is shown in Illustration 6–7.
6. Determine if any debits or credits appearing on the bank statement are unrecorded in the books of account. Make journal entries to record them.

ILLUSTRATION OF A BANK RECONCILIATION

To illustrate a bank reconciliation, assume that Valley Company found the following when it attempted to reconcile its bank balance of October 31. The bank balance as shown by the bank statement was $2,050, and the cash balance according to the accounting records was $1,373. Check No. 124 for $150 and Check No. 126 for $200 were outstanding and unpaid by the bank. A $145 deposit, placed in the bank's night depository after banking hours on October 31, was unrecorded by the bank. Among the returned checks was a credit memorandum showing the bank had collected a note receivable for the company on October 30, crediting the proceeds, $500 less a $5 collection fee, to the company account. Also returned with the bank statement was a $3 debit memorandum for checks printed by the bank and an NSF (not sufficient funds) check for $20. This check had been received from a customer, Frank Jones, on October 25, and had been included in that day's deposit. The collection of the note, the

Valley Company
Bank Reconciliation as of October 31, 19—

Book balance of cash		$1,373	Bank statement balance			$2,050
Add:			Add:			
Proceeds of note less			Deposit of 10/31			145
collection fee		495				$2,195
		$1,868				
Deduct:			Deduct:			
NSF check of Frank Jones	$20		Outstanding checks:			
Check printing charge	3	23	No. 124	$150		
			No. 126	200		350
Reconciled balance		$1,845	Reconciled balance			$1,845

ustration 6–7

return of the NSF check, and the check printing charge were unrecorded on the company books. The statement reconciling these amounts is shown in Illustration 6–7.

A bank reconciliation helps locate any errors made by either the bank or the depositor. It discloses any items which have been entered on the company books but have not come to the bank's attention. Also, it discloses items that should be recorded on the company books but are unrecorded on the date of the reconciliation. For example, in the reconciliation illustrated, the reconciled cash balance, $1,845, is the true cash balance. However, at the time the reconciliation is completed, Valley Company's accounting records show a $1,373 book balance. Consequently, entries must be made to adjust the book balance, increasing it to the true cash balance. This requires three entries. The first in general journal form is:

Nov.	2	Cash	495.00	
		Collection Expense	5.00	
		Notes Receivable		500.00
		To record the proceeds and collection charge of a note collected by the bank.		

This entry is self-explanatory. The bank collected a note receivable, deducted a collection fee, and deposited the difference to the Valley Company account. The entry increases the amount of cash on the books, records the collection expense, and reduces notes receivable.

The second entry is:

Nov.	2	Accounts Receivable—Frank Jones	20.00	
		Cash		20.00
		To charge back the NSF check received from Frank Jones.		

This entry records the NSF check returned as uncollectible. The check was received from Jones in payment of his account and was deposited as cash. The bank, unable to collect the check, deducted $20 from the Valley Company account. This made it necessary for the company to reverse the entry made when the check was received. After recording the returned check, the company will endeavor to collect the $20 from Jones. If after all legal means of collection have been exhausted and the company is still unable to collect, the amount will be written off as a bad debt. (Bad debts are discussed in the next chapter. Also, the reason the name, Frank Jones, appears in the debit of the entry is explained there.)

The third entry debits the check printing charge to Miscellaneous General Expenses and in general journal form is:

Nov.	2	Miscellaneous General Expenses	3.00	
		Cash		3.00
		Check printing charge.		

MARKETABLE SECURITIES

When readily marketable stocks and bonds are bought and held as "an investment of cash available for current operations,"[2] the investment is classified as a *temporary investment,* a current asset. Such investments commonly appear on a balance sheet under the caption, "Marketable securities,"[3] which is normally the next item after "Cash" in the current asset section. To appear in this classification, the securities must be readily marketable, for example, stocks and bonds of the kinds traded on a major stock exchange. Also, the securities must be salable without interfering with the normal operations of the business.

When such securities are purchased, the investment must be recorded at cost, which includes any commissions paid. For example,

---

[2] Committee on Accounting Procedure, "Accounting Research Bulletin No. 43," *Accounting Research and Terminology Bulletins, Final Edition* (New York: AICPA, 1961), chap. 3, sec. A, par. 4.

[3] Financial Accounting Standards Board, "Accounting for Certain Marketable Securities," *Statement of Financial Accounting Standards No. 12* (New York, 1975), par. 7.

if 1,000 shares of Atlas, Inc., stock are purchased as a temporary investment at 60⅛ ($60.125 per share)[4] plus a $600 broker's commission,
the entry to record the transaction appears as follows:

Oct.	12	Investment in Atlas, Inc., Stock	60,725.00	
		Cash		60,725.00
		Bought 1,000 shares of stock for $60,125 plus a $600 broker's commission.		

When a cash dividend is received on stock held as a temporary
investment, the dividend is recorded with an entry like this:

Dec.	10	Cash	1,000.00	
		Dividends Earned		1,000.00
		Received a $1 per share dividend on the Atlas, Inc., stock.		

Marketable securities are reported on the balance sheet at the lower
of cost or market, but both cost and market are shown. For example,
if the market value of the previously purchased Atlas, Inc., stock is
$63,500 on the balance sheet date, the investment is reported as fol-
lows:

Current assets:
  Cash $72,100
  Marketable securities at cost (present
    market value $63,500) 60,725

However, if on the balance sheet date market value is below cost,
say a market value of $58,525 for the Atlas, Inc., stock, an entry like
this is made:

Dec.	31	Loss on Marketable Security Investments	2,200.00	
		Investment in Atlas, Inc., Stock		2,200.00
		To reduce the carrying amount of the invest-ment to the lower of cost or market.		

---

[4] Stocks are quoted on stock exchanges on the basis of dollars and ⅛ dollars per
share. For example, a stock quoted at 23⅛ sold for $23.125 per share and one quoted
at 36½ sold for $36.50 per share.

And the investment is shown on the balance sheet like this:

Current assets:
Cash $72,100
Marketable securities at market (cost
$60,725) 58,525

After temporary investments in marketable securities are valued below cost, later recoveries of value up to cost are reported as income. But, unrealized increases above cost are not recorded. If several kinds of marketable securities are owned as temporary investments, their reported balance sheet amount is calculated on the basis of the lower of cost or market for the entire portfolio rather than on a security by security basis.

When marketable securities are sold, normally a gain or loss is incurred. If the selling price, less any commission and other costs in making the sale, is greater than the carrying amount of the investment, there is a gain. For example, if the Atlas, Inc., stock carried in the accounts at the reduced $58,525 amount is sold for $60,500, less a $600 commission, the transaction is recorded:

Apr.	15	Cash	59,900.00	
		Gain on Sale of Investments		1,375.00
		Investment in Atlas, Inc., Stock		58,525.00
		Sold marketable securities.		

Investments not intended as a ready source of cash in case of need are classified as *long-term investments*. Such investments include stocks bought to influence or control the operations of other companies and funds earmarked for special purposes, such as funds to repay bondholders at maturity. Long-term investments appear on the balance sheet in the long-term investments section, which immediately follows the current asset section. Long-term investments are discussed in Chapters 11 and 13.

OTHER INTERNAL CONTROL PROCEDURES

Internal control procedures apply to every phase of a company's operations from purchases through sales, cash receipts, cash disbursements, and the control of plant assets. Many of these procedures are discussed in later chapters. However, the way in which a company can gain control over purchases discounts can be discussed here where there is time and space for problems illustrating the technique.

Recall that thus far the following entries in general journal form have been used in recording the receipt and payment of an invoice for merchandise purchased.

Oct.	2	Purchases	1,000.00	
		Accounts Payable		1,000.00
		Purchased merchandise, terms 2/10, n/60.		
	12	Accounts Payable	1,000.00	
		Purchases Discounts		20.00
		Cash		980.00
		Paid the invoice of October 2.		

The invoice of these entries was recorded at its *gross*, $1,000, amount. This is the way in which invoices are recorded in many companies. However, well-managed companies follow the practice of taking all offered cash discounts. In many of these companies invoices are recorded at their *net*, after discount amounts. To illustrate, a company that records invoices at net amounts purchased merchandise having a $1,000 invoice price, terms 2/10, n/60. On receipt of the goods, it deducted the offered $20 discount from the gross invoice amount and recorded the purchase with these debits and credits:

Oct.	2	Purchases	980.00	
		Accounts Payable		980.00
		Purchased merchandise on credit.		

If the invoice for this purchase is paid within the discount period (all invoices should be so paid), the cash disbursements entry to record the payment has a debit to Accounts Payable and a credit to Cash for $980. However, if payment is not made within the discount period and the discount is *lost*, an entry like the following must be made in the General Journal either before or when the invoice is paid:

Dec.	1	Discounts Lost	20.00	
		Accounts Payable		20.00
		To record the discount lost.		

A check for the full $1,000 invoice amount is then drawn, recorded, and mailed to the creditor.

Advantage of the net method

When invoices are recorded at gross amounts, the amount of discounts taken is deducted from the balance of the Purchases account on the income statement to arrive at the cost of merchandise purchased. However, when invoices are recorded at gross amounts, if through oversight or carelessness discounts are lost, the amount of discounts lost does not appear in any account or on the income statement and may not come to the attention of management. On the other hand, when purchases are recorded at net amounts, the amount of discounts taken does not appear on the income statement. However, the amount of discounts lost is called to management's attention through the appearance on the income statement of the expense account, Discounts Lost, as in the condensed income statement of Illustration 6–8.

XYZ Company
Income Statement for Year Ended December 31, 19—

Sales	$100,000
Cost of goods sold	60,000
Gross profit from sales	$ 40,000
Operating expenses	28,000
Income from operations	$ 12,000
Other revenues and expenses:	
Discounts lost	(150)
Net income	$ 11,850

Illustration 6–8

Of the two methods, recording invoices at their net amounts probably supplies management with the more valuable information, the amount of discounts lost through oversight, carelessness, or other cause. It also gives management better control over the work of the people responsible for taking cash discounts. If discounts are lost, someone must explain why. As a result, few discounts are lost through carelessness.

GLOSSARY

Bank reconciliation. An analysis explaining the difference between an enterprise's book balance of cash and its bank statement balance.

Cash Over and Short account. An account in which are recorded cash overages and cash shortages arising from making change.

Canceled checks. Checks paid by the bank and canceled by punching or stamping.

Discounts lost. Cash discounts offered but not taken.

Gross method of recording invoices. Recording invoices at the full amount of the sale price without deducting offered cash discounts.

Internal controls system. The methods and procedures adopted by a business to control its operations and protect its assets from waste, fraud, and theft.

Invoice. A document listing items sold, together with prices, the customer's name, and the terms of sale.

Invoice approval form. A document used in checking an invoice and approving it for recording and payment.

Marketable securities. Readily salable stocks and bonds held as an investment of cash available for use in current operations.

Net method of recording invoices. Recording invoices at the full amount of the sale price less offered cash discounts.

Outstanding checks. Checks that have been written, recorded, and sent or given to payees but have not been received by the bank, paid, and returned.

Purchase order. A business form used in placing an order for the purchase of goods from a vendor.

Purchase requisition. A business form used within a business to ask the purchasing department of the business to buy needed items.

Receiving report. A form used within a business to notify the proper persons of the receipt of goods ordered and of the quantities and condition of the goods.

Reconcile. To account for the difference between two amounts.

Vendee. The purchaser of something.

Vendor. The individual or enterprise selling something.

Voucher. A business paper used in summarizing a transaction and approving it for recording and payment.

Voucher system. An accounting system used to control the incurrence and payment of obligations requiring the disbursement of cash.

QUESTIONS FOR CLASS DISCUSSION

1. Internal control procedures are important in every business, but at what stage in the development of a business do they become critical?
2. Name some of the broad principles of internal control.
3. Why should the person who keeps the record of an asset be a different person from the one responsible for custody of the asset?
4. Why should responsibility for a sequence of related transactions be divided among different departments or individuals?
5. In a small business it is sometimes impossible to separate the functions of record keeping and asset custody, and it is sometimes impossible to divide responsibilities for related transactions. What should be substituted for these control procedures?

6. What is meant by the phrase "all receipts should be deposited intact"? Why should all receipts be deposited intact on the day of receipt?

7. Why should a company's bookkeeper not be given responsibility for receiving cash for the company nor the responsibility for signing checks or making cash disbursements in any other way?

8. In purchasing merchandise in a large store, why are the department managers not permitted to deal directly with the sources of supply?

9. What are the duties of the selling department managers in the purchasing procedures of a large store?

10. Tell *(a)* who prepares, *(b)* who receives, and *(c)* the purpose of each of the following business papers:

    a. Purchase requisition.   *d.* Receiving report.
    b. Purchase order.   *e.* Invoice approval form.
    c. Invoice.   *f.* Voucher.

11. Do all companies need a voucher system? At what approximate point in a company's growth would you recommend the installation of such a system?

12. When a disbursing officer issues a check in a large business, he or she usually cannot know from personal contact that the assets, goods, or services for which the check pays were received by the business or that the purchase was properly authorized. However, if the company has an internal control system, the officer can depend on the system. Exactly what documents does the officer depend on to tell that the purchase was authorized and properly made and the goods were actually received?

13. Why are some cash payments made from a petty cash fund? Why are not all payments made by check?

14. What is a petty cash receipt? When a petty cash receipt is prepared, who signs it?

15. Explain how a petty cash fund operates.

16. Why must a petty cash fund be reimbursed at the end of each accounting period?

17. What are two results of reimbursing the petty cash fund?

18. What is a bank statement? What kind of information appears on a bank statement?

19. What is the meaning of the phrase "to reconcile"?

20. Why are the bank statement balance of cash and the depositor's book balance of cash reconciled?

21. What valuable information becomes readily available to management when invoices are recorded at net amounts? Is this information readily available when invoices are recorded at gross amounts?

CLASS EXERCISES

Exercise 6–1

A company established a $25 petty cash fund on July 5. Two weeks later, on July 19, there were in the fund $1.75 in cash and receipts for these expenditures: postage, $7.50; freight-in, $6.75; miscellaneous general expenses, $4;

and office supplies, $5. Give in general journal form *(a)* the entry to establish the fund and *(b)* the entry to reimburse it. *(c)* Make the alternate assumption that since the fund was exhausted so quickly, it was not only reimbursed on July 19 but increased in size to $50, and give the entry to reimburse and increase the fund size.

Exercise 6–2

A company established a $50 petty cash fund on October 2, and on November 30 there were in the fund $22 in cash and receipts for the following expenditures: freight-in, $11; miscellaneous general expenses, $8; and office supplies, $6.50. The petty cashier could not account for the $2.50 shortage in the fund. Give in general journal form *(a)* the entry to establish the fund and *(b)* the November 30 entry to reimburse the fund and reduce it to $25.

Exercise 6–3

Western Shop deposits all receipts intact each day and makes all payments by check; and on November 30, after all posting was completed, its Cash account had a $1,420 debit balance; but its November 30 bank statement showed only $1,295 on deposit in the bank on that day. Prepare a bank reconciliation for Western Shop, using the following information:

a. Outstanding checks, $150.
b. The November 30 cash receipts, $315, were placed in the bank's night depository after banking hours on that date and were unrecorded by the bank.
c. Included with the November canceled checks returned by the bank was an unrecorded $5 debit memorandum for bank services.
d. Check No. 815 for store supplies was correctly drawn for $127 and paid by the bank, but it was erroneously recorded as though it were for $172.

Exercise 6–4

Prepare in general journal form any entries that Western Shop should make as a result of preparing the bank reconciliation of Exercise 6–3.

Exercise 6–5

Olive Company incurred $14,000 of operating expenses in August, a month in which it had $50,000 of sales. The company began August with a $26,000 merchandise inventory and ended the month with a $28,000 inventory. During the month it purchased merchandise having a $32,000 invoice price, all of which was subject to a 2% discount for prompt payment. The company took advantage of the discounts on $27,000 of purchases; but through an error in filing, it did not earn and could not take the discount on a $5,000 invoice paid on August 29.

Required:

1. Prepare an August income statement for the company under the assumption it records invoices at gross amounts.
2. Prepare a second income statement for the company under the assumption it records invoices at net amounts.

Exercise 6–6

On March 24, 198A, 1,000 shares of Dow Chemical stock were purchased at 34¼ plus a $350 broker's commission. On December 31, at the year-end, the stock had a $29,500 market value; and on April 12, 198B, the stock was sold at 32½ less a $325 broker's commission.

Required:

1. Prepare general journal entries to record *(a)* the stock's purchase, *(b)* the reduction in its carrying amount to market value on December 31, and *(c)* its sale.
2. Under the assumption that this was the only stock the company owned, show how it should appear on the company's December 31, 198A, balance sheet.

PROBLEMS

Problem 6–1

A concern completed the following petty cash transactions during November of the current year:

Nov. 1 Drew a $35 check, cashed it, and turned the proceeds and the petty cashbox over to Ted Hall, an office clerk who had been appointed petty cashier.

5 Ted paid $6.50 from petty cash for COD delivery charges on merchandise purchased for resale.

7 Paid $7.50 from petty cash for minor repairs to an office typewriter.

10 Gave Mrs. Walter Nash, wife of the owner of the business, $5 from petty cash for cab fare.

17 Paid Merchants Delivery $2.50 to deliver merchandise to a customer.

19 Purchased a new typewriter ribbon for the office typewriter from petty cash, $2.

23 Paid $5.75 from petty cash for COD delivery charges on merchandise purchased for resale.

26 Purchased office supplies with petty cash, $3.50.

26 Ted Hall exchanged his paid petty cash receipts for a check to reimburse the fund for expenditures and a $1 shortage of cash in the fund.

Required:

Prepare in general journal form the entry to establish the petty cash fund and the entry to reimburse it on November 26.

Problem 6-2

A company completed these petty cash transactions:

Oct. 4 Drew a $25 check to establish a petty cash fund, cashed it, and turned the proceeds and the petty cashbox over to June Cole, an office secretary who had been appointed petty cashier.

5 Paid $5 to have the office windows washed.

8 Paid $3.50 to have merchandise delivered to a customer.

10 Paid $8.50 COD delivery charges on merchandise purchased for resale.

11 Purchased paper clips and carbon paper with petty cash, $6.25.

11 The petty cashier sorted her petty cash receipts by accounts affected and exchanged them for a check to reimburse the petty cash fund. However, since the fund had been exhausted so quickly, the check was made sufficiently large to increase the size of the fund to $50.

12 Joe Keller, the owner of the business, signed a petty cash receipt and took $1 from petty cash for coffee money.

14 Paid $6.50 for minor repairs to an office typewriter.

17 Paid $7.75 COD delivery charges on merchandise purchased for resale.

23 Paid $10.50 to Quick Printer for advertising circulars.

24 Paid a high school boy $10 from petty cash to deliver the advertising circulars to prospective customers.

Nov. 3 Paid $4.50 to have merchandise delivered to a customer.

7 Paid $6 COD delivery charges on merchandise purchased for resale.

7 The petty cashier sorted the paid petty cash receipts by accounts affected and exchanged them for a check to reimburse the petty cash fund for expenditures and, since there was only $2.50 in cash in the fund, for the shortage which the petty cashier could not explain.

Required:

Prepare entries in general journal form to establish the petty cash fund, reimburse and increase its size on October 11, and reimburse it on November 7.

Problem 6-3

Hillside Shop follows the practice of depositing all receipts intact and making payments by check. After all posting was completed, the balance of its Cash account on October 31 was $2,104.75. However, its bank statement of that date showed a $2,220.25 ending balance. The following information was available to reconcile the two amounts:

a. The September bank reconciliation showed two checks outstanding on September 30, No. 761 for $76.25 and No. 763 for $89.65. Check No. 763 was returned with the October bank statement, but Check No. 761 was not.

b. In comparing the October canceled checks with the entries in the accounting records, it was found that Check No. 799 was correctly drawn for

$547 in payment for a new cash register. However, in recording this check the amount was transposed and it was recorded as though it were for $574.

c. It was also found that Checks No. 842 for $35.75 and No. 847 for $103.25, both written and recorded on October 28, were not among the canceled checks returned.

d. Two debit memoranda and a credit memorandum were included with the returned checks. None of the memoranda had been recorded at the time of the reconciliation. The first debit memorandum had a $65 NSF check written by a customer, Jay Neal, attached and had been used by the customer in paying his account. The second debit memorandum was a $3.25 memorandum for service charges. The credit memorandum was for $247 and represented the proceeds less a $3 collection fee from a $250 noninterest-bearing note collected for Hillside Shop by the bank.

e. The October 31 cash receipts, $305.50, had been placed in the bank's night depository after banking hours on that date; and, consequently, did not appear on the bank statement as a deposit.

Required:

1. Prepare an October 31 bank reconciliation for Hillside Shop.
2. Prepare general journal entries to record the information of the reconciliation.

Problem 6–4

Bluelake Company reconciled its bank balance on October 31 with two checks, No. 818 for $136 and No. 820 for $210, outstanding. The following information was available for the November 30 reconciliation:

Bluelake Company 12 West 1st Street			Statement of account with FIRST NATIONAL BANK	
Date	Checks and Other Debits		Deposits	Balance
Nov. 1	Balance brought forward			2,215.00
2	210.00		295.00	2,300.00
3	175.00		244.00	2,369.00
5	240.00		178.00	2,307.00
9	562.00		270.00	2,015.00
12	84.00	97.00		1,834.00
14	42.00		127.00	1,919.00
18	135.00		255.00	2,039.00
21			365.00	2,404.00
28	334.00		125.00	2,195.00
29			245.00	2,440.00
30	125.00 NSF	4.00 SC	497.00 CM	2,808.00
Code: CM Credit memorandum DM Debit memorandum			NSF Not sufficient funds check SC Service charge	

Cash Receipts

Date			Cash Debit
Nov. 1			295.00
2			244.00
4			178.00
7			270.00
12			127.00
17			255.00
20			365.00
26			125.00
28			245.00
30			285.00
			2,389.00

Cash Disbursements

Check No.			Cash Credit
821			175.00
822			240.00
823			84.00
824			42.00
825			562.00
826			97.00
827			124.00
828			185.00
829			334.00
830			105.00
			1,948.00

From the General Ledger
Cash

Date	Explanation	P R	Debit	Credit	Balance
Oct. 31	Balance	✓			1,869.00
Nov. 30		R8	2,389.00		4,258.00
30		D9		1,948.00	2,310.00

Check No. 828 was correctly drawn for $135 in payment for store equipment; however, the bookkeeper misread its amount and recorded it as though it were for $185. The bank paid and deducted the correct $135 amount.

The NSF check was received from a customer, Roy Hall, in payment of his account. The credit memorandum resulted from a $500 noninterest-bearing note collected for Bluelake Company by the bank. The bank deducted a $3 fee for collecting the note. None of the memoranda, including the $4 for bank services, had been recorded.

Required:

1. Prepare a November 30 bank reconciliation for Bluelake Company.
2. Prepare in general journal form the entries required to bring the company's book balance for cash into agreement with the reconciled balance.

Problem 6–5

On November 30 the credit balance in the Sales account of Hurron Company showed it had sold $41,300 of merchandise during the month. The company had begun November with a $50,000 merchandise inventory and it ended the month with a $40,000 inventory, and it had $14,250 of operating expenses during the month. It had also recorded these transactions:

Nov. 1 Received merchandise purchased at a $3,000 invoice price, invoice dated October 29, terms 2/10, n/30.

Nov. 5 Received merchandise purchased at a $5,000 invoice price, invoice dated November 3, terms 2/10, n/30.
      7 Received a $500 credit memorandum (invoice price) for merchandise received on November 1 and returned for credit.
     13 Paid the $5,000 invoice received on November 5, less the discount.
     15 Received merchandise purchased at a $7,500 invoice price, invoice dated November 12, terms 2/10, n/30.
     22 Paid the $7,500 invoice received on November 15, less the discount.
     28 Paid the invoice received on November 1 and to which a $500 credit memorandum was attached. The invoice had been refiled in error, after the credit memorandum was attached on November 7, for payment on this date, the last day of its credit period.

Required:

1. Assume that Hurron Company records invoices at gross amounts and *(a)* prepare general journal entries to record the transactions. *(b)* Prepare a November income statement for the company.
2. Assume that the company records invoices at net amounts and *(a)* prepare a second set of journal entries to record the transactions. *(b)* Prepare a second income statement for the company under this assumption.

ALTERNATE PROBLEMS

Problem 6–1A

A company completed these petty cash transactions during October:

Oct. 2 Drew a $50 check, cashed it, and gave the proceeds and the petty cashbox to Joe Marsh, an office clerk who was to act as petty cashier.
      5 Paid $7.25 COD delivery charges on merchandise purchased for resale.
      7 Gave Mrs. West, wife of Robert West the business owner, $10 from petty cash for cab fare and other personal expenses.
     10 Purchased carbon paper with petty cash, $5.50.
     11 Paid $5 for delivery charges on merchandise delivered to a customer.
     13 Paid a service station attendant $4.50 upon the delivery to the office of the personal car of the business owner, which the attendant had washed.
     15 Paid $6.50 COD delivery charges on merchandise purchased for resale.
     21 Paid $5 for minor repairs to an office typewriter.
     28 Paid $2.50 delivery charges on merchandise delivered to a customer.
     28 The petty cashier sorted the paid petty cash receipts by accounts affected and exchanged them for a check to reimburse the fund for expenditures and, since there was only $2.50 in cash in the fund, for the shortage which the petty cashier could not explain.

Required:

Prepare entries in general journal form to establish the petty cash fund and to reimburse it on October 28.

Problem 6–2A

A business completed these petty cash transactions:

Nov. 25 Drew a $25 check to establish a petty cash fund, cashed it, and delivered the proceeds and the petty cashbox to Jane Cory, an office secretary who was to act as petty cashier.

27 Paid $6.25 COD delivery charges on merchandise purchased for resale.

28 Paid $5 from petty cash to have the windows washed.

29 Purchased office supplies with petty cash, $7.25.

30 Paid Cycle Delivery $3 to deliver merchandise to a customer.

Dec. 3 Dale Mohr, the owner of the business, signed a petty cash receipt and took $1 from petty cash for coffee money.

3 The petty cashier sorted the paid petty cash receipts by accounts affected and exchanged them for a check to reimburse the petty cash fund; but since the fund had been so rapidly exhausted, the check was made for an amount sufficiently large enough to increase the size of the fund to $50.

6 Paid Cycle Delivery $3.50 to deliver merchandise to a customer.

9 Paid the driver of Delux Cleaner's delivery truck $5.50 upon delivery to the office of cleaning Mr. Mohr had dropped off at the cleaners.

14 Paid $7 COD delivery charges on merchandise purchased for resale.

19 Gave Mrs. Mohr, wife of the business owner, $10 from petty cash for cab fare and other personal expenditures.

22 Paid Cycle Delivery $3.50 to deliver merchandise to a customer.

27 Paid $8 for minor repairs to an office typewriter.

30 Paid $5.75 COD delivery charges on merchandise purchased for resale.

31 The petty cashier sorted the petty cash receipts by accounts affected and exchanged them for a check to reimburse the petty cash fund for expenditures and, since there was only $6 in cash in the fund, for the shortage which the petty cashier could not explain.

Required:

Prepare general journal entries to establish the petty cash fund, reimburse and increase its size on December 3, and reimburse it on December 31.

Problem 6–3A

Western Store's October 31 bank statement showed $1,735.75 on deposit on the last day of the month. The store follows the practice of depositing all receipts intact and paying all obligations with checks; and after posting was completed on the last day of October, its Cash account showed a $1,577 balance. The following information was available to reconcile the two amounts:

a. Checks No. 810 for $102.50 and No. 812 for $87.25 were outstanding on the September 30 bank reconciliation. Check No. 812 was returned with the October checks, but Check No. 810 was not.

b. In comparing the October canceled checks with the entries in the accounting records it was found that Check No. 848 was correctly drawn for

$142 in payment for several items of office supplies but had been recorded as though it were for $124. Also, Check No. 885 for $71.25 and Check No. 886 for $32.50, both drawn on October 31, were not among the canceled checks returned.

c.   A debit memorandum with a $105.50 NSF check received from a customer, Dale Green, on October 27 and deposited was among the canceled checks returned.

d.   Also among the canceled checks was a $4.75 debit memorandum for bank services.

e.   A credit memorandum enclosed with the bank statement indicated the bank had collected a $500 noninterest-bearing note for Western Store, deducted a $3.50 collection fee, and credited the remainder to the store's account. None of the memoranda enclosed with the canceled checks had been recorded.

f.   The October 31 cash receipts of the store, $415.75, were placed in the bank's night depository after banking hours on October 31 and, consequently, did not appear on the bank statement as a deposit.

Required:

1.   Prepare an October 31 bank reconciliation for Western Store.
2.   Prepare in general journal form the entries the store would have to make to adjust its book balance of cash to the reconciled balance.

Problem 6–4A

South Company reconciled its bank balance on September 30 with two checks. No. 710 for $165 and No. 711 for $240, outstanding. The following information was available for the company's October 31 bank reconciliation:

Date	South Company 10 East 1st Street		Statement of account with THE SECURITY BANK	
	Checks and Other Debits		Deposits	Balance
Oct. 1	Balance brought forward			2,143.00
2	240.00			1,903.00
3	205.00		315.00	2,013.00
5	175.00		295.00	2,133.00
6	310.00			1,823.00
12	190.00		425.00	2,058.00
15	135.00	255.00	235.00	1,903.00
22	260.00		535.00	2,178.00
28	210.00	280.00	115.00	1,803.00
30			550.00	2,353.00
31	115.00 NSF	3.00 SC	396.00 CM	2,631.00
Code:	CM Credit memorandum		NSF Not sufficient funds check	
	DM Debit Memorandum		SC Service charge	

Cash Receipts

Date			Cash Debit
Oct. 2			315.00
4			295.00
11			425.00
14			235.00
20			535.00
27			115.00
29			550.00
31			220.00
			2,690.00

Cash Disbursements

Check No.			Cash Credit
712			205.00
713			310.00
714			100.00
715			175.00
716			85.00
717			135.00
718			260.00
719			280.00
720			255.00
721			210.00
722			105.00
			2,120.00

From the General Ledger
Cash

Date	Explanation	P R	Debit	Credit	Balance
Sept. 30	Balance	√			1,738.00
Oct. 31		R9	2,690.00		4,428.00
31		D8		2,120.00	2,308.00

The NSF check returned was received from Earl Black in payment of his account. The credit memorandum resulted from a $400 noninterest-bearing note, less a $4 collection fee, which the bank had collected for South Company. None of the memoranda enclosed with the bank statement had been recorded.

Check No. 714 was correctly drawn for $190 in payment for office equipment. The bookkeeper had carelessly read the amount and had recorded the check as though it were for $100. The bank had paid and deducted the correct $190 amount.

Required:

1. Prepare an October 31 bank reconciliation for South Company.
2. Prepare in general journal form the entries required to bring the company's book balance of cash into agreement with the reconciled balance.

Problem 6–5A

The October 31 credit balance in the Sales account of Northern Company showed it had sold $46,800 of merchandise during the month. The company began October with a $55,000 merchandise inventory and ended the month with a $43,000 inventory, and it had incurred $17,000 of operating expenses during the month. It had also recorded these transactions:

Oct. 2 Received merchandise purchased at a $6,500 invoice price, invoice dated September 30, terms 2/10, n/30.

6 Received a $1,000 credit memorandum (invoice price) for merchandise received on October 2 and returned for credit.

10 Received merchandise purchased at a $2,500 invoice price, invoice dated October 7, terms 2/10, n/30.

14 Received merchandise purchased at a $7,500 invoice price, invoice dated October 12, terms 2/10, n/30.

17 Paid for the merchandise received on October 10, less the discount.

22 Paid for the merchandise received on October 14, less the discount.

30 The invoice received on October 2 had been refiled in error, after the credit memorandum was attached, for payment on this, the last day of its credit period, causing the discount to be lost. Paid the invoice.

Required:

1. Assume the company records invoices at gross amounts and *(a)* prepare general journal entries to record the transactions. *(b)* Prepare an October income statement for the company.
2. Assume the company records invoices at net amounts and *(a)* prepare a second set of journal entries to record the transactions. *(b)* Prepare a second income statement for the company under this assumption.

PROVOCATIVE PROBLEMS

Provocative problem 6–1
Vagabond Trailer Company

Vagabond Trailer Company, a manufacturer of travel trailers, began operations in a very small way 15 years ago and has since grown rapidly in size. Last year its sales were in excess of five million dollars. However, its purchasing procedures have not kept pace with its growth. When a plant supervisor or department head needs raw materials, plant assets, or supplies, he or she tells the purchasing department manager by phone or in person. The purchasing department manager prepares a purchase order in duplicate, sends one copy to the company selling the goods, and keeps the other copy in the files. When the invoice arrives, it is sent directly to the purchasing department; and when the goods arrive, receiving department personnel count and inspect the items and prepare one copy of a receiving report which is sent to the purchasing department. The purchasing department manager attaches the receiving report and the retained copy of the purchase order to the invoice; and if all is in order, stamps the invoice "approved for payment" and signs his name. The invoice and its attached documents are then sent to the accounting department where a voucher is prepared, the invoice and its supporting documents are attached, and the voucher is recorded. On its due date the voucher and its supporting documents are sent to the office of the company treasurer where a check in payment of the voucher is prepared and mailed. The voucher is then stamped "paid," the number of the paying check is entered on it, and the paid voucher is returned to the accounting department for an entry to record its payment.

Do the present procedures of Vagabond Trailer Company make it fairly easy for someone in the company to institute the payment of fictitious invoices by the company? If so, who is this person and what would the person have to do to receive payment for a fictitious invoice. What changes should be made in the company's purchasing procedures, and why should each change be made?

Provocative problem 6–2
Cinema East

Ted Gage owns and operates Cinema East, acting as both manager and projectionist. The theater has not been too profitable of late; and this morning at breakfast, while discussing ways to cut costs, his wife suggested that he discharge the theater's doorman whose job is to collect and destroy the tickets sold by the cashier, and that he permit the cashier to collect an admission from each patron without issuing a ticket. This, Mrs. Gage pointed out, would result in a double savings, the wages of the doorman and, also, since there would be no one to take up tickets, rolls of prenumbered tickets would not have to be purchased. Mr. Gage said he could not do this unless Mrs. Gage would take over the cashier's job.

Discuss the wife's suggestion and her husband's counter proposal from an internal control point of view. You may assume the cashier is a college student and that cashiers change frequently, since the job interferes with dating.

Provocative problem 6–3
Old bookkeeper

The bookkeeper at Todd's Department Store will retire next week after more than 40 years with the store, having been hired by the father of the store's present owner. He has always been a very dependable employee, and as a result has been given more and more responsibilities over the years. Actually, for the past 15 years he has "run" the store's office, keeping books, verifying invoices, and issuing checks in their payment, which in the absence of the store's owner, Jack Todd, he could sign. In addition, at the end of each day the store's salesclerks turn over their daily cash receipts to the old bookkeeper, who after counting the money and comparing the amounts with the cash register tapes, which he is responsible for removing from the cash registers, makes the journal entry to record cash sales and then deposits the money in the bank. He also reconciles the bank balance each month with his book balance of cash.

Mr. Todd, the store's owner, realizes he cannot expect a new bookkeeper to accomplish as much in a day as the old bookkeeper; and since the store is not large enough to warrant more than one office employee, he recognizes he must take over some of the old bookkeeper's duties when he retires. Mr. Todd already places all orders for merchandise and supplies and closely supervises all employees and does not want to add more to his duties than necessary.

Discuss the situation described here from an internal control point of view, setting forth which of the old bookkeeper's tasks should be taken over by Mr. Todd and which can be assigned to the new bookkeeper with safety.

7

Accounts and notes receivable

**After studying Chapter 7,
you should be able to:**

- Explain how a controlling account and its subsidiary ledger operate and give the rule for posting to a subsidiary ledger and its controlling account.
- Prepare entries accounting for bad debts both by the allowance method and the direct write-off method.
- Explain the materiality principle and the full-disclosure principle.
- Calculate the interest on promissory notes and the discount on notes receivable discounted.
- Prepare entries to record the receipt of promissory notes and their payment or dishonor.
- Prepare entries to record the discounting of notes receivable and if dishonored, their dishonor.
- Define or explain the words and phrases listed in the chapter Glossary.

Most of the problems encountered in recording transactions with customers have been discussed. However, two very important topics remain: (1) accounting for how much each individual customer bought and paid for and (2) accounting for bad debts.

CUSTOMER ACCOUNTS

Thus far credit sales and accounts receivable collections have been recorded by debiting Accounts Receivable for the amount of each sale and crediting Accounts Receivable for collections. This simplified the recording. However, after posting was completed, the Accounts Receivable account did not readily tell how much each customer had bought and paid for or how much each customer owed. To supply this information, additional accounts receivable, one for each customer, are required.

The additional accounts receivable do not replace the Accounts Receivable account used thus far but are in addition to it. They are normally kept in a book or tray, called a *subsidiary ledger,* that is separate and distinct from the book or tray containing the financial statement accounts. The book or tray containing the customer accounts is called the *Accounts Receivable Ledger.* The book or tray containing the financial statement accounts, including the Accounts Receivable account, is known as the *General Ledger.*

RECORDING CREDIT SALES

In a manual accounting system, sales to customers on credit are commonly recorded in a Sales Journal like the one shown at the top of Illustration 7–1. Such a journal is used because it saves posting labor. Labor is saved by entering the amount of each credit sale in the journal's last column and posting the total to the debit of Accounts Receivable and the credit of Sales at the end of the month.

The journal of Illustration 7–1 is called a *columnar journal* because it has columns for recording the date, the customer's name, invoice

Sales Journal

Date		Account Debited	Invoice Number	Post. Ref.	Amount
Feb.	2	James Henry	307	✓	450.00
	7	Albert Smith....................................	308	✓	500.00
	13	Sam Moore	309	✓	350.00
	15	Paul Roth	310	✓	200.00
	22	James Henry	311	✓	225.00
	25	Frank Booth	312	✓	175.00
	28	Albert Smith....................................	313	✓	250.00
	28	Total—Accounts Receivable, Dr.; Sales, Cr.			2,150.00

(113/411)

Individual amounts are posted daily to the subsidiary ledger.

Total is posted at the end of the month to the general ledger accounts.

Accounts Receivable Ledger

Frank Booth

Date		Debit	Credit	Balance
Feb.	25	175.00		175.00

James Henry

Date		Debit	Credit	Balance
Feb.	2	450.00		450.00
	22	225.00		675.00

Sam Moore

Date		Debit	Credit	Balance
Feb.	13	350.00		350.00

Paul Roth

Date		Debit	Credit	Balance
Feb.	15	200.00		200.00

Albert Smith

Date		Debit	Credit	Balance
Feb.	7	500.00		500.00
	28	250.00		750.00

General Ledger

Accounts Receivable　　113

Date		Debit	Credit	Balance
Feb.	28	2,150.00		2,150.00

Sales　　411

Date		Debit	Credit	Balance
Feb.	28		2,150.00	2,150.00

The double ruled lines around the accounts are meant to convey the idea that the customer accounts are in one ledger and the financial statement accounts are in a different ledger, kept in a different book or file tray.

Illustration 7–1

number, and the amount of each credit sale. Only credit sales can be recorded in it, and they are recorded daily. The information about each sale is taken from a copy of the sales ticket or sales invoice prepared at the time of the sale. Observe that the information about each sale is placed on a separate line.

Posting the Sales Journal

The individual sales recorded in the Sales journal are posted each day to the proper customer accounts in the Accounts Receivable Ledger, as shown in Illustration 7–1. These daily postings keep the customer accounts up to date. This is important in granting credit, because the person responsible for granting credit should know in each case the amount currently owed by the credit seeking customer. The source of this information is the customer's account. If the account is not up to date, an incorrect decision may be made.

Note the check marks in the Sales Journal's Posting Reference column. They indicate that the sales recorded in the journal were individually posted to the customer accounts in the Accounts Receivable Ledger. Check marks rather than account numbers are used because the customer accounts commonly do not have numbers. Rather, as an aid in locating individual accounts, they are alphabetically arranged in the Accounts Receivable Ledger, with new accounts being added in their proper alphabetical positions as required. Consequently, numbering the accounts is impractical, since many numbers would have to be changed each time new accounts are added.

In addition to the daily postings to customer accounts, at the end of the month the Sales Journal's Amount column is totaled and the total is debited to Accounts Receivable and credited to Sales. The credit records the month's revenue from charge sales. The debit records the resulting increase in accounts receivable.

Before going on, note again in Illustration 7–1 that the individual customer accounts in the subsidiary Accounts Receivable Ledger do not replace the Accounts Receivable account described in previous chapters but are in addition to it. The Accounts Receivable account of previous chapters must still be maintained in the General Ledger where it serves three functions: (1) It shows the total amount owed by all customers. (2) It helps keep the General Ledger a balancing ledger in which debits equal credits. (3) It offers a means of proving the accuracy of the customer accounts in the subsidiary Accounts Receivable Ledger. The proof is that after all posting is completed, if no errors were made, the balance of the Accounts Receivable account will equal the sum of the balances of the customer accounts in the subsidiary ledger. The proof is made by preparing an adding machine list of the account balances in the subsidiary ledger and comparing its total with the balance of the Accounts Receivable account. Because of this proof, the Accounts Receivable account is said to control the subsidiary ledger accounts and is called a *controlling account.*

CASH RECEIPTS JOURNAL

When cash is received from charge customers, as well as from other sources, posting labor can be saved by recording the receipts in a Cash Receipts Journal like the one in Illustration 7–2. A store commonly receives cash from customers in payment of their accounts, from cash sales, and from miscellaneous sources. Note how the illustrated journal has a special column for entering the credits when cash is received from each of these sources.

Cash from charge customers

When cash received from a charge customer in payment of his or her account is recorded in a columnar Cash Receipts Journal like Illustration 7–2, the customer's name is entered in the Account Credited column. The amount credited to the customer's account is entered in the Accounts Receivable credit column; and the debits to Sales Discounts and Cash are entered in the journal's last two columns.

Give close attention to the Accounts Receivable credit column. Observe that (1) only credits to customer accounts are entered in this column. (2) The individual credits are posted daily to the customer accounts in the subsidiary Accounts Receivable. (3) The column total is posted at the month end to the credit of the Accounts Receivable controlling account.

Cash sales

Cash sales are normally "rung up" each day on one or more cash registers, and their total is recorded each day with an entry having a debit to Cash and a credit to Sales. When such sales are recorded in a Cash Receipts Journal like that of Illustration 7–2, the debits to Cash are entered in the Cash debit column and a special column headed "Sales credit" is provided for the credits to Sales. By entering each day's cash sales in this column, the cash sales of a month may be posted at the month's end in a single amount, the column total. (Although cash sales are normally recorded daily from the cash register reading, the cash sales of Illustration 7–2 are recorded only once each week in order to shorten the illustration.)

At the time daily cash sales are recorded in the Cash Receipts Journal, some bookkeepers, as in Illustration 7–2, place a check mark in the Posting Reference column to indicate that no amount is individually posted from that line of the journal. Other bookkeepers use a double

Cash Receipts Journal

Date		Account Credited	Explanation	Post. Ref.	Other Accounts Credit	Accts. Rec. Credit	Sales Credit	Sales Dis. Debit	Cash Debit
Feb.	7	Sales	Cash sales	✓			4,450.00		4,450.00
	12	James Henry ...	Invoice, 2/2 ...	✓		450.00		9.00	441.00
	14	Sales	Cash sales	✓			3,925.00		3,925.00
	17	Albert Smith	Invoice, 2/7 ...	✓		500.00		10.00	490.00
	20	Notes Payable ..	Note to bank ..	211	1,000.00				1,000.00
	21	Sales	Cash sales	✓			4,700.00		4,700.00
	23	Sam Moore	Invoice, 2/13 ..	✓		350.00		7.00	343.00
	25	Paul Roth	Invoice, 2/15 ..	✓		200.00		4.00	196.00
	28	Sales	Cash sales	✓			4,225.00		4,225.00
	28	Totals ...	....		1,000.00	1,500.00	17,300.00	30.00	19,770.00
					(✓)	(113)	(411)	(413)	(111)

Individual amounts in the Other Accounts credit and Accounts Receivable credit columns are posted daily.

Total is not posted.

Totals posted at the end of the month.

Accounts Receivable Ledger

Frank Booth

Date		Debit	Credit	Balance
Feb.	25	175.00		175.00

James Henry

Date		Debit	Credit	Balance
Feb.	2	450.00		450.00
	12		450.00	–0–
	22	225.00		225.00

Sam Moore

Date		Debit	Credit	Balance
Feb.	13	350.00		350.00
	23		350.00	–0–

Paul Roth

Date		Debit	Credit	Balance
Feb.	15	200.00		200.00
	25		200.00	–0–

Albert Smith

Date		Debit	Credit	Balance
Feb.	7	500.00		500.00
	17		500.00	–0–
	28	250.00		250.00

General Ledger

Cash   111

Date		Debit	Credit	Balance
Feb.	28	19,770.00		19,770.00

Accounts Receivable   113

Date		Debit	Credit	Balance
Feb.	28	2,150.00		2,150.00
	28		1,500.00	650.00

Notes Payable   211

Date		Debit	Credit	Balance
Feb.	20		1,000.00	1,000.00

Sales   411

Date		Debit	Credit	Balance
Feb.	28		2,150.00	2,150.00
	28		17,300.00	19,450.00

Sales Discounts   413

Date		Debit	Credit	Balance
Feb.	28	30.00		30.00

Illustration 7–2

check (√) to distinguish amounts not posted from amounts posted to customer accounts.

Miscellaneous receipts of cash

Most cash receipts come from customer collections and cash sales. However, cash is occasionally received from other sources such as, for example, the sale for cash of an unneeded asset, or a promissory note is given to a bank in order to borrow money. For miscellaneous receipts such as these the Other Accounts credit column is provided. The items entered in the Other Accounts column are few in number and are commonly posted daily.

Month-end posting

The amounts in the Accounts Receivable, Sales, Sales Discounts, and Cash columns of the Cash Receipts Journal are posted as column totals at the end of the month. However, the transactions recorded in any journal must result in equal debits and credits to general ledger accounts. Consequently, the debit and credit equality in a columnar journal such as the Cash Receipts Journal is proved by *crossfooting* or cross adding the column totals before they are posted. To *foot* a column of figures is to add it. To crossfoot the Cash Receipts Journal the debit column totals are added together, the credit column totals are added together, and the two sums are compared for equality. For Illustration 7–2 the two sums appear as follows:

Debit columns		Credit columns	
Sales discounts debit	$ 30	Other accounts credit	$ 1,000
Cash debit	19,770	Accounts receivable credit ..	1,500
		Sales credit	17,300
Total...............	$19,800	Total...............	$19,800

And since the sums are equal, the debits in the journal are assumed to equal the credits.

After the debit and credit equality is proved by crossfooting, the totals of the last four columns are posted as indicated in each column heading. As for the Other Accounts column, since the individual items in this column are posted daily, the column total is not posted. Note in Illustration 7–2 the check mark below the Other Accounts column. The check mark indicates that the column total was not posted. The account numbers of the accounts to which the remaining column totals were posted are indicated in parentheses below each column.

SALES RETURNS

When columnar journals are used, a Sales Returns and Allowances Journal may be designed and used in recording returned sales. However, when such returns are not too numerous, they are recorded in the General Journal with an entry like this:

Oct.	17	Sales Returns and Allowances	412	17.50	
		Accounts Receivable—George Ball	113/√		17.50
		Returned defective merchandise.			

The debit of the entry is posted to the Sales Returns and Allowances account. The credit is posted to both the Accounts Receivable controlling account and to the customer's account. Note the account number and the check, 113/√, in the Posting Reference column. This indicates that both the Accounts Receivable controlling account in the General Ledger and the George Ball account in the Accounts Receivable Ledger were credited for $17.50. Both were credited because the balance of the controlling account in the General Ledger will not equal the sum of the customer account balances in the subsidiary ledger unless both are credited.

OTHER CONTROLLING ACCOUNTS

The mechanics of controlling accounts and subsidiary ledgers as described here with accounts receivable apply to accounts payable (discussed in the Appendix at the end of this chapter) and in accounting for plant assets (discussed in Chapter 9). Consequently, care should be taken to understand the basic ideas involved. They are as follows: (1) The equality of a controlling account balance to the sum of the account balances in its subsidiary ledger is a proof of the accuracy of the accounts in the subsidiary ledger. (2) The controlling account balance will equal the sum of the balances in its subsidiary ledger if the controlling account is debited periodically for an amount or amounts equal to the sum of the debits to the subsidiary accounts and credited periodically for an amount or amounts equal to the sum of the credits to the subsidiary ledger accounts.

BAD DEBTS

When goods and services are sold on credit, there are almost always a few customers who do not pay. The accounts of such customers are called *bad debts* and are a loss and an expense of selling on credit. It might be asked: Why do merchants sell on credit if bad debts result? The answer is, of course, that they sell on credit in order to increase sales and profits. They are willing to take a reasonable loss from bad debts in order to increase sales and profits. Therefore, bad debt losses are an expense of selling on credit, an expense incurred in order to increase sales. Consequently, if the requirements of the *matching principle* are met, bad debt losses must be matched against the sales they helped produce.

MATCHING BAD DEBT LOSSES WITH SALES

A bad debt loss results from an error in judgment, an error in granting credit and making a sale to a customer who will not pay. Therefore, a bad debt loss is incurred at the moment credit is granted and a sale is made to such a customer. Of course the merchant making such a sale does not know at the time of the sale that a loss has been incurred. Actually, the merchant normally will not be sure of the loss for as much as a year or more, after every means of collecting has been exhausted. Nevertheless, final recognition a year or so later does not change the time of the loss. The loss occurred at the moment of the sale.

It is recognized that a bad debt loss occurs at the moment of a sale to a customer who will not pay. It is also recognized that a merchant cannot be sure the customer will not pay until a year or more after the sale. Consequently, if bad debt losses are matched with the sales they helped produce, they must be matched on an estimated basis. The *allowance method of accounting for bad debts* does just that.

ALLOWANCE METHOD OF ACCOUNTING FOR BAD DEBTS

Under the allowance method of accounting for bad debts, an estimate is made at the end of each accounting period of the total bad debts that are expected to result from the period's sales. An allowance is then provided for the loss. This has two advantages: (1) the estimated loss is charged to the period in which the revenue is recognized; and (2) the accounts receivable appear on the balance sheet at their estimated realizable value, a more informative balance sheet amount.

Estimating bad debts

In making the year-end estimate of bad debts that are expected to result from the year's sales, companies commonly assume that "history will repeat." For example, over the past several years Alpha Company has experienced bad debt losses equal to one half of 1% of its charge sales. During the past year its charge sales were $300,000. Consequently, if history repeats, Alpha Company can expect $1,500 of bad debt losses to result from the year's sales ($300,000 × 0.005 = $1,500).

Recording the estimated bad debts loss

Under the allowance method of accounting for bad debts, the estimated bad debts loss is recorded at the end of each accounting period with a work sheet adjustment and an adjusting entry. For example, Alpha Company will record its $1,500 estimated bad debts loss with a work sheet adjustment and an adjusting entry like the following:

Dec.	31	Bad debts Expense	1,500.00	
		Allowance for Doubtful Accounts		1,500.00
		To record the estimated bad debts.		

The debit of this entry causes the estimated bad debts loss to appear on the income statement of the year in which the sales were made. As a result, the estimated $1,500 expense of selling on credit is matched with the $300,000 of revenue it helped to produce.

Bad debt losses normally appear on the income statement as an administrative expense rather than as a selling expense because granting credit is usually not a responsibility of the sales department. Therefore, since the sales department is not responsible for granting credit, it should not be held responsible for bad debt losses. The sales department is usually not given responsibility for granting credit because it is feared the sales department would at times be swayed in its judgment of a credit risk by its desire to make a sale.

Bad debts in the accounts

If at the time its bad debts adjusting entry is posted, Alpha Company has $20,000 of accounts receivable, its Accounts Receivable and Allowance for Doubtful Accounts accounts will show these balances:

Accounts Receivable		Allowance for Doubtful Accounts	
Dec. 31 20,000			Dec. 31 1,500

The bad debts adjusting entry reduces the accounts receivable to their estimated realizable value. However, note that the credit of the entry is to the contra account, Allowance for Doubtful Accounts. It is necessary to credit the contra account because at the time of the adjusting entry it is not known for certain which customers will fail to pay. (The total loss from bad debts can be estimated from past experience. However, the exact customers who will not pay cannot be known until every means of collecting from each has been exhausted.) Consequently, since the bad accounts are not identifiable at the time of the adjusting entry, they cannot be removed from the subsidiary Accounts Receivable Ledger. As a result, the Allowance for Doubtful Accounts account must be credited instead of the controlling account. The allowance account must be credited because to credit the controlling account without removing the bad accounts from the subsidiary ledger would cause the controlling account balance to differ from the sum of the balances in the subsidiary ledger.

Allowance for doubtful accounts on the balance sheet

When the balance sheet is prepared, the *allowance for doubtful accounts* is subtracted thereon from the accounts receivable to show the amount that is expected to be realized from the accounts, as follows:

Current assets:		
Cash		$11,300
Accounts receivable	$20,000	
Less allowance for doubtful accounts....	(1,500)	18,500
Merchandise inventory		67,200
Prepaid expenses		1,100
Total current assets		$98,100

Writing off a bad debt

When an allowance for doubtful accounts is provided, accounts deemed uncollectible are written off against this allowance. For example, after spending a year trying to collect, Alpha Company finally concluded the $100 account of George Vale was uncollectible and made the following entry to write it off:

Jan.	23	Allowance for Doubtful Accounts	100.00	
		Accounts Receivable—George Vale		100.00
		To write off an uncollectible account.		

Posting the credit of the entry to the Accounts Receivable account removes the amount of the bad debt from the controlling account. Posting it to the George Vale account removes the amount of the bad debt from the subsidiary ledger. Posting the entry has this effect on the general ledger accounts:

Accounts Receivable				Allowance for Doubtful Accounts			
Dec. 31	20,000	Jan. 23	100	Jan. 23	100	Dec. 31	1,500

Two points should be observed in the entry and accounts. First, although bad debts are an expense of selling on credit, the allowance account rather than an expense account is debited in the write-off. The allowance account is debited because the expense was recorded at the end of the period in which the sale occurred. At that time, the loss was foreseen, and the expense was recorded in the estimated bad debts adjusting entry.

Second, although the write-off removed the amount of the account receivable from the ledgers, it did not affect the estimated realizable amount of Alpha Company's accounts receivable, as the following tabulation shows:

	Before write-off	After write-off
Accounts receivable	$20,000	$19,900
Less allowance for doubtful accounts	1,500	1,400
Estimated realizable accounts receivable ..	$18,500	$18,500

Bad debts written off seldom equal the allowance provided

The uncollectible accounts from a given year's sales seldom, if ever, exactly equal the allowance provided for their loss. If accounts written off are less than the allowance provided, the allowance account reaches the end of the year with a credit balance. On the other hand, if accounts written off exceed the allowance provided, the allowance account reaches the period end with a debit balance, which is then eliminated with the new bad debts adjusting entry. In either case no harm is done if the allowance provided is approximately equal to the bad debts written off and is neither continually excessive nor insufficient.

Often when the addition to the allowance for doubtful accounts is based on a percentage of sales, the passage of several accounting periods is required before it becomes apparent the percentage is either too large or too small. In such cases when it becomes apparent the percentage is incorrect, a change in the percentage should be made.

BAD DEBT RECOVERIES

Frequently an error in judgment is made and accounts written off as uncollectible are later sometimes collected in full or in part. If an account is written off as uncollectible and later the customer pays part or all of the amount previously written off, the payment should be shown in the customer's account for future credit action. It should be shown because when a customer fails to pay and his or her account is written off, the customer's credit standing is impaired. Later when the customer pays, the payment helps restore the credit standing.

When an account previously written off as a bad debt is collected, two entries are made. The first reinstates the customer's account and has the effect of reversing the original write-off. The second entry records the collection of the reinstated account.

For example, assume that George Vale, whose account was previously written off, pays in full on August 15. The entries in general journal form to record the bad debt recovery are:

Aug.	15	Accounts Receivable—George Vale	100.00	
		Allowance for Doubtful Accounts		100.00
		To reinstate the account of George Vale written off on January 23.		
	15	Cash	100.00	
		Accounts Receivable—George Vale		100.00
		In full of account.		

In this case George Vale paid the entire amount previously written off. Sometimes after an account is written off the customer will pay a portion of the amount owed. The question then arises, should the entire balance of the account be returned to accounts receivable or just the amount paid? The answer is a matter of judgment. If it is thought the customer will pay in full, the entire amount owed should be returned. However, only the amount paid should be returned if it is thought that no more will be collected.

AGING ACCOUNTS RECEIVABLE

In estimating bad debt losses, many companies age their accounts receivable. This consists of preparing a schedule of accounts receivable with their balances entered in columns according to age, as in Illustration 7–3. After such a schedule is prepared, executives of the sales and credit departments examine each account listed and by judgment decide which are probably uncollectible. Normally, most of the accounts on the schedule are current and not past due. These are examined for possible losses but receive less scrutiny than past-due accounts. The older accounts are more apt to prove uncollectible. These receive the greatest attention. After decisions are made as to which accounts are probably uncollectible, the allowance account is adjusted to provide for them.

To illustrate this adjustment, assume that a company ages its accounts receivable and estimates that accounts totaling $1,950 are probably uncollectible. Assume further that the company has a $250 credit balance in its allowance account. Under these assumptions the company

Schedule of Accounts Receivable by Age					
Customer's Name	Not Due	1 to 30 Days Past Due	31 to 60 Days Past Due	61 to 90 Days Past Due	Over 90 Days Past Due
Charles Abbot	45.00				
Frank Allen	53.00				
George Arden			14.00		
Paul Baum					27.00

Illustration 7–3

will make the following adjusting entry to increase the balance of the allowance account to the amount needed to provide for the estimated uncollectible accounts:

Dec.	31	Bad Debts Expense	1,700.00	
		Allowance for Doubtful Accounts		1,700.00
		To increase the allowance for doubtful accounts to $1,950.		

The $1,700 credit of the entry increases the balance of the allowance account to the $1,950 needed to provide for the estimated bad debts. If it had been assumed that the allowance account had a $150 debit balance before adjustment, rather than the assumed $250 credit balance, it would have been necessary to increase the entry amounts to $2,100 ($150 + $1,950) in order to bring the account balance up to the required amount.

Aging accounts receivable and increasing the allowance for doubtful accounts to an amount sufficient to provide for the accounts deemed uncollectible normally provides a better balance sheet figure than does the percent of sales method, a figure closer to realizable value. However, the aging method may not as closely match revenues and expenses as the percent of sales method.

DIRECT WRITE-OFF OF BAD DEBTS

The allowance method of accounting for bad debts better fulfills the requirements of the *matching principle.* Consequently, it is the method that should be used in most cases. However, under certain circumstances another method, called the *direct write-off method,* may be used. Under this method, when it is decided that an account is uncollectible, it is written off directly to Bad Debts Expense with an entry like this:

Nov.	23	Bad Debts Expense	52.50	
		Accounts Receivable—Dale Hall		52.50
		To write off the uncollectible account.		

The debit of the entry charges the bad debt loss directly to the current year's Bad Debts Expense account. The credit removes the balance of the account from the subsidiary ledger and controlling account.

If an account previously written off directly to Bad Debts Expense is later collected in full, the following entries are used to record the recovery:

Mar.	11	Accounts Receivable—Dale Hall	52.50	
		Bad Debts Expense		52.50
		To reinstate the account of Dale Hall previously written off.		
	11	Cash	52.50	
		Accounts Receivable—Dale Hall		52.50
		In full of account.		

Sometimes a bad debt previously written off directly to the Bad Debts Expense account is recovered in the year following the write-off. If at that time the Bad Debts Expense account has no balance from other write-offs and no write-offs are expected, the credit of the entry recording the recovery can be to a revenue account called Bad Debt Recoveries.

Direct write-off mismatches revenues and expenses

The direct write-off method commonly mismatches revenues and expenses. The mismatch results because the revenue from a bad debt sale appears on the income statement of one year while the expense of the loss is deducted on the income statement of the following or a later year. Nevertheless, it may still be used in situations where its use does not materially affect reported net income. For example, it may be used in a concern where bad debt losses are immaterial in relation to total sales and net income. In such a concern, the use of direct write-off comes under the accounting *principle of materiality.*

The principle of materiality

Under the *principle of materiality* it is held that a strict adherence to any accounting principle, in this case the *matching principle*, is not required when adherence is relatively difficult or expensive and the lack of adherence does not materially affect reported net income. Or in other words, failure to adhere is permissible when the failure does not produce an error or misstatement sufficiently large as to influence a financial statement reader's judgment of a given situation.

NOTES RECEIVABLE

Companies selling merchandise on the installment plan commonly take promissory notes from their customers. Likewise when the credit period is long, as in the sale of farm machinery, promissory notes are often required. Also, creditors frequently ask for promissory notes from customers who are granted additional time in which to pay their past-due accounts. In these situations creditors prefer notes to accounts receivable because the notes may be readily turned into cash before becoming due by discounting (selling) them to a bank. Likewise, notes are preferred because if a lawsuit is needed to collect, a note represents written acknowledgment by the debtor of both the debt and its amount. Also, notes are preferred because they generally earn interest.

PROMISSORY NOTES

A promissory note is an unconditional promise in writing to pay on demand or at a fixed or determinable future date a definite sum of money. In the note shown in Illustration 7–4, Hugo Brown promises

$ 1,000.00	Eugene, Oregon	March 9, 19--

Thirty days _____after date_____ I _____promise to pay to

the order of_____ Frank Black

One thousand and no/100--dollars

for value received with interest at____ 8%

payable at_ First National Bank of Eugene, Oregon

Hugo Brown

Illustration 7–4

to pay Frank Black or his order a definite sum of money at a fixed future date. Hugo Brown is the *maker* of the note. Frank Black is the *payee*. To Hugo Brown the illustrated note is a *note payable,* a liability. To Frank Black the same note is a *note receivable,* an asset.

The illustrated Hugo Brown note bears interest at 8%. Interest is a charge for the use of money. To a borrower, interest is an expense. To a lender, it is a revenue. A note may be interest bearing or it may be noninterest bearing. If a note bears interest, the rate or the amount of interest must be stated on the note.

CALCULATING INTEREST

Unless otherwise stated, the rate of interest on a note is the rate charged for the use of the principal for one year. The formula for calculating interest is:

$$\text{Principal of the note} \times \text{Annual rate of interest} \times \text{Time of the note expressed in years} = \text{Interest}$$

For example, interest on a $1,000, 8%, one-year note is calculated:

$$\$1,000 \times \frac{8}{100} \times 1 = \$80$$

Most note transactions involve a period less than a full year, and this period is usually expressed in days. When the time of a note is expressed in days, the actual number of days elapsing, not including the day of the note's date but including the day on which it falls due, are counted. For example, a 90-day note, dated July 10, is due on October 8. This October 8 due date, called the *maturity date*, is calculated as follows:

Number of days in July	31
Minus the date of the note	10
Gives the number of days the note runs in July	21
Add the number of days in August	31
Add the number of days in September	30
Total through September 30	82
Days in October needed to equal the time of the note, 90 days, also the maturity date of the note—October	8
Total time the note runs in days	90

Occasionally, the time of a note is expressed in months. In such cases, the note matures and is payable in the month of its maturity on the same day of the month as its date. For example, a note dated July 10 and payable three months after date is payable on October 10.

In calculating interest, it was once almost the universal practice to treat a year as having just 360 days. This simplified most interest calculations. However, the practice is no longer so common. Nevertheless, to simplify the calculation of interest in assigned problems and to be consistent in the illustrations and problems, the practice is continued in this text. It makes the interest calculation on a 90-day, 8%, $1,000 note as follows:

$$\text{Principal} \times \text{Rate} \times \frac{\text{Exact days}}{360} = \text{Interest}$$

or

$$\$1,000 \times \frac{8}{100} \times \frac{90}{360} = \text{Interest}$$

or

$$\overset{10}{\cancel{\$1,000}} \times \frac{\overset{2}{\cancel{8}}}{\cancel{100}} \times \frac{\cancel{90}}{\cancel{360}} = \$20$$

RECORDING THE RECEIPT OF A NOTE

Notes receivable are recorded in a single Notes Receivable account. Each note may be identified in the account by writing the name of the maker in the Explanation column on the line of the entry recording its receipt or payment. Only one account is needed because the individual notes are on hand. Consequently, the maker, rate of interest, due date, and other information may be learned by examining each note.

A note received at the time of a sale is recorded as follows:

Dec.	5	Notes Receivable	650.00	
		Sales		650.00
		Sold merchandise, terms six-month, 9% note.		

When a note is taken in granting a time extension on a past-due account receivable, the creditor usually attempts to collect part of the past-due account in cash. This reduces the debt and requires the acceptance of a note for a smaller amount. For example, Symplex Company agrees to accept $232 in cash and a $500, 60-day, 9% note from Joseph Cook in settlement of his $732 past-due account. When Symplex receives the cash and note, the following entry in general journal form is made:

Oct.	5	Cash	232.00	
		Notes Receivable	500.00	
		Accounts Receivable—Joseph Cook		732.00
		Received cash and a note in settlement of an account.		

Observe that this entry changes the form of $500 of the debt from an account receivable to a note receivable.

When Cook pays the note, this entry in general journal form is made:

Dec.	4	Cash	507.50	
		Notes Receivable		500.00
		Interest Earned		7.50
		Collected the Joseph Cook note.		

Look again at the last two entries. If Symplex Company uses columnar journals, the entry of December 4 would be recorded in its Cash Receipts Journal. Two lines would be required, one for the credit to Interest Earned and a second for the credit to Notes Receivable. Likewise, the October 5 transaction would be recorded with two entries, one on the Cash Receipts Journal for the money received and a second entry in the General Journal for the note. Nevertheless, to simplify the illustrations, general journal entries are shown here and will be used through the remainder of this text. However, the student should realize that the entries would be made in a Cash Receipts Journal or other appropriate journal if in use.

DISHONORED NOTES RECEIVABLE

Occasionally, the maker of a note either cannot or will not pay the note at maturity. When a note's maker refuses to pay at maturity, the note is said to be *dishonored*. Dishonor does not relieve the maker of the obligation to pay. Furthermore, every legal means should be made to collect. However, collection may require lengthy legal proceedings.

The balance of the Notes Receivable account should show only the amount of notes that have not matured. Consequently, when a note is dishonored, its amount should be removed from the Notes Receivable account and charged back to the account of its maker. To illustrate, Simplex Company holds an $800, 9%, 60-day note of George Jones. At maturity, Jones dishonors the note. To remove the dishonored note from its Notes Receivable account, the company makes the following entry:

Oct.	14	Accounts Receivable—George Jones	812.00	
		Interest Earned		12.00
		Notes Receivable		800.00
		To charge the account of George Jones for his dishonored note.		

Charging a dishonored note back to the account of its maker serves two purposes. It removes the amount of the note from the Notes Receivable account, leaving in the account only notes that have not matured. It also records the dishonored note in the maker's account. The second purpose is important. If in the future the maker of the dishonored note again applies for credit, his or her account will show all past dealings, including the dishonored note.

Observe in the entry that the Interest Earned account is credited for interest earned even though it was not collected. The reason for this is that Jones owes both the principal and the interest. Consequently, his account should reflect the full amount owed on the date of the entry.

DISCOUNTING NOTES RECEIVABLE

As previously stated, a note receivable is preferred to an account receivable because the note can be turned into cash before maturity by discounting (selling) it to a bank. In *discounting a note receivable,* the owner endorses and delivers the note to the bank in exchange for cash. The bank holds the note to maturity and then collects its maturity value from the maker. To illustrate, assume that on May 28 Symplex Company received a $1,200, 60-day, 8% note dated May 27 from John Owen. It held the note until June 2 and then discounted it at its bank at 9%. Since the maturity date of this note is July 26, the bank must wait 54 days after discounting the note to collect from Owen. These 54 days are called the *discount period* and are calculated as follows:

Time of the note in days		60
Less time held by Symplex Company:		
Number of days in May	31	
Less the date of the note	27	
Days held in May	4	
Days held in June	2	
Total days held		6
Discount period in days		54

At the end of the discount period the bank expects to collect the *maturity value* of this note from Owen. Therefore, as is customary, it bases its discount on the maturity value of the note, which is calculated as follows:

Principal of the note	$1,200
Interest on $1,200 for 60 days at 8%	16
Maturity value	$1,216

In this case the bank's discount rate, or the rate of interest it charges for lending money, is 9%. Consequently, in discounting the note, it will deduct 54 days' interest at 9% from the note's maturity value and will give Symplex Company the remainder. The remainder is called the *proceeds of the note*. The amount of interest deducted is known as *bank discount*. The bank discount and the proceeds are calculated as follows:

Maturity value of the note......................	$1,216.00
Less interest on $1,216 for 54 days at 9%......	16.42
Proceeds	$1,199.58

Observe in this case that the proceeds, $1,199.58, are $0.42 less than the $1,200 principal amount of the note. Consequently, Symplex will make this entry in recording the discount transaction:

June	2	Cash	1,199.58	
		Interest Expense	.42	
		Notes Receivable		1,200.00
		Discounted the John Owen note for 54 days at 9%.		

In recording the transaction, Symplex in effect offsets the $16 of interest it would have earned by holding the note to maturity against the $16.42 discount charged by the bank and records only the difference, the $0.42 excess of expense.

In the situation just described the principal of the discounted note exceeded the proceeds. However, in many cases the proceeds exceed the principal. When this happens, the difference is credited to Interest Earned. For example, suppose that instead of discounting the John Owen note on June 2, Symplex held the note and discounted it on June 26. If the note is discounted on June 26 at 9%, the discount period is 30 days, the discount is $9.12, and the proceeds of the note are $1,206.88, calculated as follows:

Maturity value of the note......................	$1,216.00
Less interest on $1,216 at 9% for 30 days......	9.12
Proceeds	$1,206.88

And since the proceeds exceed the principal, the transaction is recorded as follows:

June	26	Cash	1,206.88	
		Interest Earned		6.88
		Notes Receivable		1,200.00
		Discounted the John Owen note for 30 days at 9%.		

Contingent liability

A person or company discounting a note is ordinarily required to endorse the note because an endorsement, unless it is restricted,[1] makes the endorser contingently liable for payment of the note. The *contingent liability* depends upon the note's dishonor by its maker. If the maker pays, the endorser has no liability. However, if the maker defaults, the endorser's contingent liability becomes an actual liability and the endorser must pay the note for the maker.

A contingent liability, since it can become an actual liability, may affect the credit standing of the person or concern contingently liable. Consequently, a discounted note should be shown as such in the Notes Receivable account. Also, if a balance sheet is prepared before the discounted note's maturity date, the contingent liability should be indicated on the balance sheet. For example, if in addition to the John Owen note, Symplex Company holds $500 of other notes receivable, the record of the discounted John Owen note may appear in its Notes Receivable account as follows:

Notes Receivable

Date		Explanation	Post. Ref.	Debit	Credit	Balance
May	28	John Owen note	G6	1,200.00		1,200.00
June	7	Earl Hill note	G6	500.00		1,700.00
	26	Discounted the J. Owen note	G7		1,200.00	500.00

The contingent liability resulting from discounted notes receivable is commonly shown on a balance sheet by means of a footnote. If Symplex Company follows this practice, it will show the $500 of notes it has not discounted and the contingent liability resulting from discounting the John Owen note on its June 30 balance sheet as follows:

---

[1] A restricted endorsement is one in which the endorser states in writing that he or she will not be liable for payment.

Current assets:
Cash .... $ 5,315
Notes receivable (Footnote 2) 500
Accounts receivable 21,475

Footnote 2: Symplex Company is contingently liable for $1,200 of notes receivable discounted.

Full-disclosure principle

The balance sheet disclosure of contingent liabilities is required under the *full-disclosure principle.* Under this principle it is held that financial statements and their accompanying footnotes should disclose fully and completely all relevant data of a material nature relating to the financial position of the company for which they are prepared. This does not necessarily mean that the information should be detailed, for details can at times obscure. It simply means that all information necessary to an appreciation of the company's position be reported in a readily understandable manner and that nothing of a significant nature be withheld. For example, any of the following would be considered relevant and should be disclosed.

Contingent liabilities   In addition to discounted notes, a company that is contingently liable due to possible additional tax assessments, pending lawsuits, or product guarantees should disclose this on its statements.

Long-term commitments under a contract   If the company has signed a long-term lease requiring a material annual payment, this should be disclosed even though the liability does not appear in the accounts. Also, if the company has pledged certain of its assets as security for a loan, this should be revealed.

Accounting methods used   Whenever there are several acceptable accounting methods that may be followed, a company should report in each case the method used, especially when a choice of methods can materially affect reported net income. For example, a company should report by means of footnotes accompanying its statements the inventory method or methods used, depreciation methods, method of recognizing revenue under long-term construction contracts, and the like.[2]

DISHONOR OF A DISCOUNTED NOTE

A bank always tries to collect a discounted note directly from the maker. If it is able to do so, the one who discounted it will not hear

[2] APB, "Disclosure of Accounting Policies," *APB Opinion No. 22* (New York: AICPA, April 1972), pars. 12 and 13.

from the bank and will need to do nothing more in regard to the note. However, according to law, if a discounted note is dishonored, the bank must before the end of the next business day notify each endorser of the note if it is to hold the endorsers liable on the note. To notify the endorsers, the bank will normally protest the dishonored note. To protest a note, the bank prepares and mails before the end of the next business day a *notice of protest* to each endorser. A notice of protest is a statement, usually attested by a notary public, that says the note was duly presented to the maker for payment and payment was refused. The cost of protesting a note is called a *protest fee*, and the bank will look to the one who discounted the note for payment of both the note's maturity value and the protest fee.

For example, suppose that instead of paying the $1,200 note previously illustrated, John Owen dishonored it. In such a situation the bank would notify Symplex Company immediately of the dishonor by mailing a notice of protest and a letter asking payment of the note's maturity value plus the protest fee. If the protest fee is, say $5, Symplex must pay the bank $1,221; and in recording the payment, Symplex will charge the $1,221 to the account of John Owen, as follows:

July	27	Accounts Receivable—John Owen	1,221.00	
		Cash		1,221.00
		To charge the account of Owen for the maturity value of his dishonored note plus the protest fee.		

Of course, upon receipt of the $1,221, the bank will deliver to Symplex the dishonored note. Symplex Company will then make every legal effort to collect from Owen, not only the maturity value of the note and protest fee but also interest on both from the date of dishonor until the date of final settlement. However, it may not be able to collect, and after exhausting every legal means to do so, it may have to write the account off as a bad debt. Normally in such cases no additional interest is taken onto the books before the write-off.

Although dishonored notes commonly have to be written off as bad debts, some are also eventually paid by their makers. For example, if 30 days after dishonor, John Owen pays the maturity value of his dishonored note, the protest fee, and interest at 8% on both for 30 days beyond maturity, he will pay the following:

Maturity value	$1,216.00
Protest fee	5.00
Interest on $1,221 at 8% for 30 days	8.14
Total	$1,229.14

And Symplex will record receipt of his money as follows:

Aug.	25	Cash	1,229.14	
		Interest Earned		8.14
		Accounts receivable—John Owen		1,221.00
		Dishonored note and protest fee collected with interest.		

END-OF-THE-PERIOD ADJUSTMENTS

If any notes receivable are outstanding at the accounting period end, their accrued interest should be calculated and recorded. For example, on December 11 a company accepted a $3,000, 60-day, 9% note from a customer in granting an extension on a past-due account. If the company's accounting period ends on December 31, by then $15 interest has accrued on this note and should be recorded with this adjusting entry:

Dec.	31	Interest Receivable	15.00	
		Interest Earned		15.00
		To record accrued interest on a note receivable.		

The adjusting entry causes the interest earned to appear on the income statement of the period in which it was earned. It also causes the interest receivable to appear on the balance sheet as a current asset.

Collecting interest previously accrued

When the note is collected, the transaction may be recorded as follows:

Feb.	9	Cash	3,045.00	
		Interest Earned		30.00
		Interest Receivable		15.00
		Notes Receivable		3,000.00
		Received payment of a note and its interest.		

The entry's credit to Interest Receivable records collection of the interest accrued at the end of the previous period.

APPENDIX: SUBSIDIARY LEDGERS AND COLUMNAR JOURNALS FOR ACCOUNTS PAYABLE

As with accounts receivable, the one Accounts Payable account used thus far does not show how much is owed each creditor. One way to secure this information is to maintain an individual account for each creditor in a susidiary Accounts Payable Ledger controlled by an Accounts Payable controlling account in the General Ledger. If maintained, the controlling account, subsidiary ledger, and columnar journal techniques demonstrated with accounts receivable apply to accounts payable. The only difference is that a Purchases Journal and a Cash Disbursements Journal are used in recording most of the transactions affecting the accounts.

PURCHASES JOURNAL

A one-money column Purchases Journal similar to the Sales Journal previously described may be used to record purchases of merchandise on credit. However, a multicolumn journal in which purchases of both merchandise and supplies can be recorded is commonly preferred. Such a journal may have the columns shown in Illustration 7A–1. In the illustrated journal, the invoice date and terms together indicate the date on which payment for each purchase is due. The Accounts Payable credit column is used to record the amounts credited to each creditor's account. The amounts are posted daily to the individual creditor accounts in the Accounts Payable Ledger. The column total is posted to the Accounts Payable controlling account at the month end. The items purchased are recorded in debit columns and are posted in the column totals.

THE CASH DISBURSEMENTS JOURNAL

A Cash Disbursements Journal, like the Cash Receipts Journal, has columns that make it possible to post repetitive debits and credits in column totals. The repetitive debits and credits of cash payments are debits to the Accounts Payable controlling account and credits to both Purchases Discounts and Cash. In most companies the purchase of merchandise for cash is not common; therefore, a Purchases column is not needed and a cash purchase is recorded as on line 2 of Illustration 7A–2.

Observe that the illustrated journal has a column headed "Check No." In order to gain control over cash disbursements, all such disbursements, except petty cash disbursements, should be made by check. The checks should be prenumbered by the printer, and should be entered in the journal in numerical order with each check's number in the column headed "Check No." This makes it possible to scan

Purchases Journal

Date	Account Credited	Date of Invoice	Terms	P R	Accounts Payable Credit	Purchases Debit	Store Supplies Debit	Office Supplies Debit
Feb. 3	Horn Supply Co.	2/2	n/30	✓	350.00	275.00	50.00	25.00
5	Acme Mfg. Co.	2/5	2/10, n/30	✓	200.00	200.00		
13	Wycoff & Co.	2/10	2/10, n/30	✓	150.00	150.00		
20	Smith and Co.	2/18	2/10, n/30	✓	300.00	300.00		
25	Acme Mfg. Co.	2/24	2/10, n/30	✓	100.00	100.00		
28	H. A. Green Co.	2/28	n/30	✓	225.00	125.00	75.00	25.00
28	Totals				1,325.00	1,150.00	125.00	50.00
					(212)	(511)	(115)	(116)

Individual amounts are posted daily.	Totals are posted at the end of the month.

Accounts Payable Ledger

Acme Mfg. Company

Date	Debit	Credit	Balance
Feb. 5		200.00	200.00
15	200.00		–0–
25		100.00	100.00

H. A. Green Company

Date	Debit	Credit	Balance
Feb. 28		225.00	225.00

Horn Supply Company

Date	Debit	Credit	Balance
Feb. 3		350.00	350.00

Smith and Company

Date	Debit	Credit	Balance
Feb. 20		300.00	300.00

Wycoff & Company

Date	Debit	Credit	Balance
Feb. 13		150.00	150.00

General Ledger

Store Supplies 115

Date	Debit	Credit	Balance
Feb. 28	125.00		125.00

Office Supplies 116

Date	Debit	Credit	Balance
Feb. 28	50.00		50.00

Accounts Payable 212

Date	Debit	Credit	Balance
Feb. 28		1,325.00	1,325.00

Purchases 511

Date	Debit	Credit	Balance
Feb. 12	25.00		25.00
28	1,150.00		1,175.00

Illustration 7A–1

Cash Disbursements Journal

Date	Ch. No.	Payee	Account Debited	P R	Other Accounts Debit	Accts. Pay. Debit	Pur. Disc. Credit	Cash Credit
Feb. 3	105	L. & N. Railroad ...	Freight in	514	15.00			15.00
12	106	East Sales Co......	Purchases	511	25.00			25.00
15	107	Acme Mfg. Co.	Acme Mfg. Co......	✓		200.00	4.00	196.00
15	108	Jerry Hale	Salaries Expense ...	611	250.00			250.00
20	109	Wycoff & Co.	Wycoff & Co.	✓		150.00	3.00	147.00
28	110	Smith and Co.	Smith and Co.	✓		300.00	6.00	294.00
28		Totals			290.00	650.00	13.00	927.00
					(✓)	(212)	(513)	(111)

Individual amounts in the Other Accounts debit column and Accounts Payable debit column are posted daily.

Totals posted at the end of the month.

Accounts Payable Ledger

Acme Mfg. Company

Date	Debit	Credit	Balance
Feb. 5		200.00	200.00
15	200.00		–0–
25		100.00	100.00

H. A. Green Company

Date	Debit	Credit	Balance
Feb. 28		225.00	225.00

Horn Supply Company

Date	Debit	Credit	Balance
Feb. 3		350.00	350.00

Smith and Company

Date	Debit	Credit	Balance
Feb. 20		300.00	300.00
28	300.00		–0–

Wycoff & Company

Date	Debit	Credit	Balance
Feb. 13		150.00	150.00
20	150.00		–0–

General Ledger

Cash 111

Date	Debit	Credit	Balance
Feb. 28	19,770.00		19,770.00
28		927.00	18,843.00

Accounts Payable 212

Date	Debit	Credit	Balance
Feb. 28		1,325.00	1,325.00
28	650.00		675.00

Purchases 511

Date	Debit	Credit	Balance
Feb. 12	25.00		25.00
28	1,150.00		1,175.00

Purchases Discounts 513

Date	Debit	Credit	Balance
Feb. 28		13.00	13.00

Freight-In 514

Date	Debit	Credit	Balance
Feb. 3	15.00		15.00

Salaries Expense 611

Date	Debit	Credit	Balance
Feb. 15	250.00		250.00

Illustration 7A–2

the numbers in the column for omitted checks. When a Cash Disbursements Journal has a column for check numbers, it is often called a Check Register.

A Cash Disbursements Journal or Check Register like Illustration 7A–2 is posted as follows. The individual amounts in the Other Accounts column are posted daily to the debit of the general ledger accounts named. The individual amounts in the Accounts Payable column are posted daily to the subsidiary Accounts Payable Ledger to the debit of the creditors named. At the end of the month, after the column totals are crossfooted to prove their equality, the Accounts Payable column total, the Purchases Discounts column total, and the Cash column total are posted as indicated in the column headings. Since the items in the Other Accounts column are posted individually, this column total is not posted.

GENERAL JOURNAL ENTRIES

When columnar journals like the ones described in this chapter are used, a General Journal must be provided for adjusting, closing, and correcting entries and for a few transactions that cannot be recorded in any of the columnar journals, such as purchases returns and plant asset purchases. Illustrative entries for purchases returns and plant asset purchases appear as follows:

Oct.	8	Accounts Payable—Medford Company	212/√	32.00	
		Purchases Returns and Allowances	512		32.00
		Returned defective merchandise.			
	29	Office Equipment	133	685.00	
		Accounts Payable—Ace Supply Co.	212/√		685.00
		Purchased a typewriter.			

Note the 212/√ in the Posting Reference column for the two entries. In both cases this indicates that the entries were posted to both the Accounts Payable controlling account and the proper account in the subsidiary Accounts Payable Ledger.

IDENTIFYING POSTED AMOUNTS

When several journals are posted to ledger accounts, it is necessary to indicate in the Posting Reference column before each posted amount the journal as well as the page number of the journal from which the amount was posted. The journal is indicated by using its initial. Thus items posted from the Cash Disbursements Journal carry the initial "D" before their journal page numbers in the Posting Reference columns. Likewise, items from the Cash Receipts Journal carry the letter "R," those from the Sales Journal carry the initial "S," items from the Purchases Journal carry the initial "P," and from the General Journal, the letter "G."

PROVING THE LEDGERS

When subsidiary ledgers are used, periodically, after all posting is completed, the General Ledger and the subsidiary ledgers are proved. The General Ledger is proved first by preparing a trial balance. If the trial balance balances, the accounts in the General Ledger, including the controlling accounts, are assumed to be correct. The subsidiary ledgers are then proved, commonly by preparing schedules of accounts receivable and accounts payable. A schedule of accounts payable, for example, is prepared by listing with their balances the accounts in the Accounts Payable Ledger having balances. The balances are totaled; and if the total is equal to the balance of the Accounts Payable controlling account, the accounts in the Accounts Payable Ledger are assumed to be correct. Illustration 7A–3 shows a schedule of the creditor accounts having balances in the Accounts Payable Ledger of Illustration 7A–2. Note that the schedule total is equal to the balance of the Accounts Payable controlling account in the General Ledger of Illustration 7A–2. A schedule of accounts receivable is prepared in the same way as a schedule of accounts payable. Also, if its total is equal to the balance of the Accounts Receivable controlling account, the accounts in the Account Receivable Ledger are also assumed to be correct.

Hawaiian Sales Company
Schedule of Accounts Payable, December 31, 19—

Acme Mfg. Company	$100
H. A. Green Company	225
Horn Supply Company	350
Total accounts payable	$675

Illustration 7A–3

Instead of a formal schedule to prove the accounts in a subsidiary ledger, an adding machine list may also be used. For example, the balances of the accounts in the Accounts Payable Ledger may be proved by listing on an adding machine the balance of each account in the ledger, totaling the list, and comparing the total with the balance of the Accounts Payable controlling account. A similar list may be used to prove the accounts in the Accounts Receivable Ledger.

GLOSSARY

Accounts receivable ledger. A subsidiary ledger having an account for each customer.

Aging accounts receivable. Preparing a schedule listing accounts receivable by the number of days each account has been unpaid.

Allowance for doubtful accounts. The estimated amount of accounts receivable that will prove uncollectible.

Allowance method of accounting for bad debts. The accounting procedure whereby an estimate is made at the end of each accounting period of the portion of the period's credit sales that will prove uncollectible, and an entry is made to charge this estimated amount to an expense account and to an allowance account against which actual uncollectible accounts can be written off.

Bad debt. An uncollectible account receivable.

Bank discount. The amount of interest a bank deducts in lending money.

Contingent liability. A potential liability that may become an actual liability if certain events occur.

Columnar journal. A book of original entry having columns for entering specific data about each transaction of a group of like transactions.

Controlling account. A general ledger account that controls the accounts in a subsidiary ledger.

Crossfoot. To add the column totals of a journal or a report.

Direct write-off method of accounting for bad debts. The accounting procedure whereby uncollectible accounts are written off directly to an expense account.

Discount period of a note. The number of days for which a note is discounted.

Discounting a note receivable. Selling a note receivable to a bank or other concern.

Dishonoring a note. Refusing to pay a promissory note on its due date.

Foot. To add a column of figures.

Full-disclosure principle. The accounting rule requiring that financial statements and their accompanying notes disclose all information of a material nature relating to the financial position and operating results of the company for which they were prepared.

General Ledger. A ledger containing the financial statement accounts of a business.

Maker of a note. One who signs a note and promises to pay it at maturity.

Materiality principle. The accounting rule that a strict adherence to any accounting principle is not required when adherence is relatively difficult or expensive and lack of adherence will not materially affect reported net income.

Maturity date of a note. The date on which a note and any interest are due and payable.

Maturity value of a note. Principal of the note plus any interest due on the note's maturity date.

Notes receivable discounted. The amount of notes receivable that have been discounted or sold.

Notice of protest. A document that gives notice that a promissory note was presented for payment on its due date and payment was refused.

Payee of a note. The one to whom a promissory note is made payable.

Proceeds of a discounted note. The maturity value of a note minus any interest deducted because of its being discounted before maturity.

Protest fee. The fee charged for preparing and issuing a notice of protest.

Subsidiary ledger. A group of accounts other than general ledger accounts which show the details underlying the balance of a controlling account in the General Ledger.

QUESTIONS FOR CLASS DISCUSSION

1. How do columnar journals save posting labor?
2. How do columnar journals take advantage of the fact that for any single class of transactions either the debit or the credit of each transaction is always to the same account?
3. What functions are served by the Accounts Receivable controlling account?
4. Why should sales to charge customers and receipts of cash from charge customers be recorded and posted daily?
5. How is the equality of a controlling account and its subsidiary ledger maintained?
6. At what point in the selling-collecting procedures of a company does a bad debt loss occur?
7. In estimating bad debt losses it is commonly assumed that "history will repeat." How is this assumption used in estimating bad debt losses?
8. A company had $484,000 of charge sales in a year. How many dollars of bad debt losses may the company expect to experience from these sales if its past bad debt losses have averaged one fourth of 1% of charge sales.
9. What is a contra account? Why are estimated bad debt losses credited to a contra account rather than to the Accounts Receivable controlling account?

10. Classify the following accounts: (a) Accounts Receivable, (b) Allowance for Doubtful Accounts, and (c) Bad Debts Expense.
11. Explain why writing off a bad debt against the allowance account does not reduce the estimated realizable amount of a company's accounts receivable.
12. Why does the direct write-off method of accounting for bad debts commonly fail in matching revenues and expenses?
13. What is the essence of the accounting principle of materiality?
14. Why does a business prefer a note receivable to an account receivable?
15. Define:

    a. Promissory note.   f. Discount period of a note.
    b. Payee of a note.   g. Maker of a note.
    c. Maturity date.   h. Principal of a note.
    d. Dishonored note.   i. Maturity value.
    e. Notice of protest.   j. Contingent liability.

16. What are the due dates of the following notes: (a) a 90-day note dated June 10, (b) a 60-day note dated May 13, and (c) a 90-day note dated November 12?
17. Distinguish between bank discount and cash discount.
18. What does the full-disclosure principle require in a company's accounting statements?

EXERCISES

Exercise 7–1

At the end of November Rex Company's Sales Journal showed the following credit sales:

SALES JOURNAL

Date		Account Debited	Invoice Number	P R	Amount
Nov.	3	Dale Hall	123		250.00
	8	John Mohr.............................	124		100.00
	19	Gary Roth	125		225.00
	26	Dale Hall	126		300.00
	30	Total			875.00

The company's General Journal carried this entry:

Nov.	22	Sales Returns and Allowances	25.00	
		Accounts Receivable—Gary Roth		25.00
		Customer returned merchandise.		

Required:

1. On a sheet of notebook paper open a subsidiary Accounts Receivable Ledger having a T-account for each of Dale Hall, John Mohr, and Gary

Roth. Post the sales journal entries to the customer accounts and also post the portion of the general journal entry that affects a customer's account.

2. Open a General Ledger having an Accounts Receivable controlling account, a Sales account, and a Sales Returns and Allowances account. Post the portions of the sales journal and general journal entries that affect these accounts.

3. Prove the subsidiary ledger accounts by listing the balances of the accounts in the subsidiary ledger, totaling the balances, and comparing the total with balance of the Accounts Receivable controlling account.

Exercise 7–2

On December 31, 198A, a company estimated it would lose as bad debts an amount equal to one fourth of 1% of its $724,000 of 198A charge sales, and it provided an addition to its allowance for doubtful accounts equal to that amount. On the following March 27 it decided the $285 account of Arno Fall was uncollectible and wrote it off as a bad debt. On July 7 Arno Fall unexpectedly paid the amount previously written off. Give the required entries in general journal form to record these transactions.

Exercise 7–3

At the end of each year a company ages its accounts receivable and increases its allowance for doubtful accounts by an amount sufficient to provide for the estimated uncollectible accounts. At the end of last year it estimated it would not be able to collect $2,450 of its total accounts receivable. (a) Give the entry to increase the allowance account under the assumption it had a $125 credit balance before the adjustment. (b) Give the entry under the assumption the allowance account had a $150 debit balance before the adjustment.

Exercise 7–4

Prepare general journal entries to record these transactions:

Mar. 11   Accepted a $900, 60-day, 8% note dated this day from Carl Lee in granting a time extension on his past-due account.

May 10   Carl Lee dishonored his note when presented for payment.

Dec. 31   After exhausting all legal means of collecting, wrote off the account of Carl Lee against the allowance for doubtful accounts.

Exercise 7–5

Prepare general journal entries to record these transactions:

June 3   Sold merchandise to Fred Gage, $1,500, terms 2/10, n/60.

Aug. 15   Received $300 in cash and a $1,200, 60-day, 8% note dated August 12 in granting a time extension on the amount due from Fred Gage.

18   Discounted the Fred Gage note at the bank at 9%.

Oct. 16   Since notice protesting the Fred Gage note had not been received, assumed that Fred Gage had paid the note.

Exercise 7–6

Prepare general journal entries to record these transactions:

Aug. 5 Accepted a $1,000, 60-day, 9% note dated August 3 from Earl Ball in granting a time extension on his past-due account.

27 Discounted the Earl Ball note at the bank at 10%.

Oct. 3 Received notice protesting the Earl Ball note. Paid the bank the maturity value of the note plus a $5 protest fee.

Nov. 1 Received payment from Earl Ball of the maturity value of his dishonored note, the protest fee, and interest at 9% on both for 30 days beyond maturity.

Exercise 7–7

On August 2 Mesa Sales sold Ted Hall merchandise having a $2,000 catalog list price, less a 25% trade discount, 2/10, n/60. Hall was unable to pay and was granted a time extension on receipt of his 60-day, 8% note for the amount of the debt, dated October 10. Mesa Sales held the note until November 9, when it discounted it at its bank at 9%. The note was not protested. Answer these questions:

a. How many dollars of trade discount were granted on the sale?
b. How many dollars of cash discount could Hall have earned?
c. What was the maturity date of the note?
d. How many days were in the discount period?
e. How much bank discount was deducted by the bank?
f. What were the proceeds of the discounted note?

Exercise 7–8

Northland Sales accepted a $3,000, 9%, 60-day note dated December 11, 20 days before the end of its annual accounting period, in granting a time extension on the past-due account of Lee Best. Give in general journal form the entries made by Northland Sales to record (a) receipt of the note, (b) the accrued interest on the note on December 31, and (c) payment of the note by Lee Best.

PROBLEMS

Problem 7–1

Lake Company completed these transactions during February:

Feb. 2 Sold merchandise on credit to Paul Eddy, Invoice No. 933, $700. The terms of all credit sales are 2/10, n/60.

5 Borrowed $5,000 from Guaranty Bank by giving a 60-day, 9% note payable.

7 Cash sales for the week ended February 7 were $6,275. (Cash sales are usually recorded daily from the cash register readings; however, they are recorded weekly in this problem in order to reduce the repetitive transactions.)

Feb. 7 *Post the amounts that are posted as individual amounts from the journals. (Normally such amounts are posted daily; but since they are few in number in this problem, you are to post them weekly.)*

11 Sold merchandise on credit to David Case, Invoice No. 934, $785.

12 Received payment from Paul Eddy for the February 2 sale, less the discount.

14 Cash sales for the week ended February 14 were $5,150.

14 *Post the amounts that are individually posted from the journals.*

16 Issued a $35 credit memorandum to David Case for defective merchandise sold on February 11 and returned for credit.

18 Sold merchandise on credit to Paul Eddy, Invoice No. 935, $650.

20 Sold store supplies to the merchant next door for cash at cost, $25.

21 Received payment from David Case for the February 11 sale, less the return and the discount.

21 Cash sales for the week ended February 21, $6,225.

21 *Post the amounts that are individually posted from the journals.*

25 Sold merchandise on credit to David Case, Invoice No. 936, $750.

26 Sold merchandise on credit to A. J. Allen, Invoice No. 937, $825.

28 Received payment from Paul Eddy for the sale of February 18, less the discount.

28 Cash sales for the week ended February 28, $6,200.

28 *Post the amounts that are individually posted from the journals.*

28 *Foot the Sales Journal and foot and crossfoot the Cash Receipts Journal and make the month-end postings.*

Required:

1. Open the following general ledger accounts: Cash, Accounts Receivable, Store Supplies, Notes Payable, Sales, Sales Returns and Allowances, and Sales Discounts.
2. Open the following accounts receivable ledger accounts: A. J. Allen, David Case, and Paul Eddy.
3. Enter the transactions in the journals and post when instructed to do so.
4. Prove the general ledger accounts by preparing a trial balance, and prove the subsidiary ledger accounts by totaling their balances and comparing the total with the balance of the Accounts Receivable controlling account.

Problem 7–2

A company completed these transactions during a 15-month period:

Oct.   8 Sold merchandise to Fred Best, $1,445, terms, 2/10, n/60.

Dec. 16 Accepted $245 in cash and a $1,200, 60-day, 8% note dated this day in granting Fred Best a time extension on his past-due account.

31 Made an adjusting entry to record the accrued interest on the Fred Best note.

31 An examination showed a $135 credit balance in the Allowance for Doubtful Accounts account. Provided an addition to the allowance equal to one fourth of 1% of the year's $976,000 of charge sales.

31 Closed the Interest Earned and Bad Debts Expense accounts.

Feb. 14 Received payment of the maturity value of the Fred Best note.

15 Learned of the bankruptcy of Joe Nash and made a claim on his

receiver in bankruptcy for the $460 owed by Mr. Nash for merchandise purchased.

Apr. 14   After making every effort to collect, decided the $375 account of Lee Wolf was uncollectible and wrote it off as a bad debt.

July 17   Lee Wolf walked into the store and paid $150 of the amount written off on April 14. He said his financial position had improved and he expected to pay the balance of his account within a short period.

Oct. 15   Received $185 from Joe Nash's receiver in bankruptcy. A letter accompanying the payment stated that no more would be paid. Made an entry to record receipt of the cash and to write off the balance of Nash's account.

Dec. 18   Made a compound entry to write off the accounts off Earl Barker, $640; Jerry Davis, $585; and Lee Hall, $890.

31   Provided an addition to the allowance for doubtful accounts equal to one fourth of 1% of the year's $964,000 of charge sales.

31   Closed the Bad Debts Expense and Interest Earned accounts.

Required:

1. Open Interest Receivable, Allowance for Doubtful Accounts, Interest Earned, and Bad Debts Expense accounts. Enter the $135 credit balance in the Allowance for Doubtful Accounts account and prepare general journal entries to record the transactions. Post those portions of the entries that affect the four accounts opened.

2. Prepare an alternate bad debts adjusting entry for the second December 31 of the problem under the assumption that rather than providing an addition to the allowance account equal to one fourth of 1% of charge sales, the company aged its accounts, estimated that $2,100 of accounts were probably uncollectible, and increased its allowance to provide for them.

Problem 7–3

Prepare entries in general journal form to record these transactions:

Jan.   4   Sold merchandise to Ted Fall, terms $445 in cash and an $800, 60-day, 9% note dated this day.

Mar.   5   Received payment from Ted Fall of the maturity value of his $800 note.

12   Accepted a $1,500, 60-day, 8% note dated March 10 in granting a time extension on the past-due account of Allen Moss.

16   Discounted the Allen Moss note at the bank at 9%.

May 10   Received notice protesting the Allen Moss note. Paid the bank the maturity value of the note plus a $5 protest fee.

July   8   Received payment from Allen Moss of the maturity value of his dishonored note plus the protest fee and interest on both for 60 days beyond maturity at 8%.

14   Accepted $350 in cash and a $1,200, 90-day, 8% note dated July 13 in granting a time extension on the past-due account of Joel Nash.

Sept. 11   Discounted the Joel Nash note at the bank at 9%.

Oct. 15   Since notice protesting the Joel Nash note had not been received, assumed it paid.

Oct. 16 Accepted an $800, 60-day, 9% note dated October 15 from Ned Green in granting a time extension on his past-due account.

Nov. 8 Discounted the Ned Green note at the bank at 10%.

Dec. 14 Received notice protesting the Ned Green note. Paid the bank the maturity value of the note plus a $4 protest fee.

31 Wrote off as uncollectible the account of Ned Green against the allowance for doubtful accounts.

Problem 7–4

Prepare general journal entries to record these transactions:

Dec. 16 Accepted a $1,200, 60-day, 8% note dated this day in granting a time extension on the past-due account of Paul Roth.

31 Made an adjusting entry to record the accrued interest on the Paul Roth note.

31 Made an adjusting entry to increase the allowance for doubtful accounts by an amount equal to one third of 1% of the year's $828,000 of charge sales.

Feb. 14 Received payment from Paul Roth of the maturity value of his note.

Mar. 3 Accepted a $900, 8%, 60-day note dated March 2 in granting a time extension on the past-due account of Dale Parr.

Apr. 1 Discounted the Dale Parr note at the bank at 9%.

May 2 Received notice protesting the Dale Parr note. Paid the bank the maturity value of the note plus a $5 protest fee.

5 Accepted $225 in cash and a $1,500, 60-day, 8% note dated May 3 in granting a time extension on the past-due account of Carl Lane.

18 Discounted the Carl Lane note at the bank at 10%.

July 3 Received notice protesting the Carl Lane note. Paid the bank the maturity value of the note and a $5 protest fee.

Aug. 7 Received payment from Carl Lane of the maturity value of his dishonored note plus the protest fee and interest on both for 36 days beyond maturity at 8%.

10 Accepted an $800, 60-day, 9% note dated this day in granting a time extension on the past-due account of Fred Hall.

Oct. 9 Fred Hall dishonored his note when presented for payment.

Dec. 28 Decided the accounts of Dale Parr and Fred Hall were uncollectible and wrote them off as bad debts.

Problem 7–5

Prepare general journal entries to record these transactions:

Dec. 21 Accepted an $1,800, 60-day, 8% note dated this day in granting a time extension on the past-due account of Lee Byrd.

31 Made an adjusting entry to record the accrued interest on the Lee Byrd note.

Jan. 30 Discounted the Lee Byrd note at the bank at 9%.

Feb. 20 Received notice protesting the Lee Byrd note. Paid the bank the maturity value of the note plus a $5 protest fee.

Mar. 3 Accepted a $1,400, 9%, 60-day note dated this day from Walter Dent in granting a time extension on his past-due account.

27 Discounted the Walter Dent note at the bank at 10%.

May   5   Since notice protesting the Walter Dent note had not been received, assumed it paid.

June   8   Accepted a $1,600, 9%, 60-day note dated this day from Ned Fox in granting a time extension on his past-due account.

Aug.   7   Received payment in full of the maturity value of the Ned Fox note.

       10 Accepted a $2,400, 8%, 60-day note dated August 9 from Ted Bush in granting a time extension on his past-due account.

Sept. 11   Discounted the Ted Bush note at the bank at 10%.

Oct.   9   Received notice protesting the Ted Bush note. Paid the bank the maturity value of the note plus a $4 protest fee.

Nov.   7   Received payment from Ted Bush of the maturity value of his dishonored note, the protest fee, and interest at 8% on both for 30 days beyond maturity.

Dec. 27   Wrote off the Lee Byrd account against the allowance for doubtful accounts.

Problem 7–6
(A portion of this problem is based on information in the chapter's Appendix)

Hilltop Sales completed these transactions during February of the current year:

Feb.   1   Sold merchandise on credit to Tom Moss, Invoice No. 617, $750. (The terms of all credit sales are 2/10, n/60.)

       2   Received merchandise and an invoice dated January 30, terms 2/10, n/60, from Case Company, $1,685.

       3   Purchased office equipment from Office Outfitters, invoice dated February 3, terms n/10 EOM, $585.

       4   Sold merchandise on credit to John Rice, Invoice No. 618, $1,350.

       5   Received merchandise, $1,595, store supplies, $65, office supplies, $30, and an invoice dated February 4, terms n/10 EOM, from New Company.

       6   Received a credit memorandum from Case Company for unsatisfactory merchandise received on February 2 and returned for credit, $135.

       7   Received a credit memorandum from Office Outfitters for office equipment received on February 3 and returned for credit, $60.

       7   Cash sales for the first week of February, $1,445.

       7   *Post to the customer and creditor accounts and also post any amounts that should be posted as individual amounts to the general ledger accounts. (Normally such items are posted daily; but to shorten the problem, you are asked to post them only once each week.)*

       9   Sent Case Company Check No. 312 in payment of its invoice of January 30, less the return and discount.

       11 Sold merchandise on credit to Fred Able, Invoice No. 619, $1,710.

       11 Received a check from Tom Moss in payment of the sale of February 1, less the discount.

       13 Received a check from John Rice in payment of the sale of February 4, less the discount.

Feb. 14 Received merchandise and an invoice dated February 11, terms 2/ 10, n/60, from Taylor Company, $1,700.

14 Issued Check No. 313, payable to Payroll, in payment of the sales salaries for the first half of the month, $815. Cashed the check and paid the employees.

14 Cash sales for the week ended February 14, $1,395.

14 *Post to the customer and creditor accounts and also post any amounts that should be posted as individual amounts to the general ledger accounts.*

16 Issued a $160 credit memorandum to Fred Able for defective merchandise sold on February 11 and returned.

17 Received merchandise and an invoice dated February 14, terms 2/ 10, n/60, from Taylor Company, $1,450.

18 Received merchandise, $370, store supplies, $45, office supplies, $20, and an invoice dated February 17, terms n/10 EOM, from New Company.

18 Sold merchandise on credit to Tom Moss, Invoice No. 620, $650.

21 Received a check from Fred Able in payment of the sale of February 11, less the return and discount.

21 Sent Taylor Company Check No. 314 in payment of its invoice of February 11, less the discount.

21 Cash sales for the week ended February 21, $1,425.

21 *Post to the customer and creditor accounts and also post any amounts that should be posted as individual amounts to the general ledger accounts.*

24 Sent Taylor Company Check No. 315 in payment of its invoice of February 14, less the discount.

25 Borrowed $4,000 by giving Valley National Bank a 60-day, 9% promissory note payable.

26 Sold merchandise on credit to Fred Able, Invoice No. 621, $915.

27 Sold merchandise on credit to John Rice, Invoice No. 622, $1,085.

28 Issued Check No. 316 to *The Gazette* for advertising expense, $375.

28 Issued Check No. 317 payable to Payroll for sales salaries, $815. Cashed the check and paid the employees.

28 Received a check from Tom Moss in payment of the February 18 sale, less the discount.

28 Cash sales for the last week of the month, $1,345.

28 *Post to the customer and creditor accounts and also post any amounts that should be posted as individual amounts to the general ledger accounts.*

28 *Make the month-end postings from the journals.*

Required:

1. Open the following general ledger accounts: Cash, Accounts Receivable, Store Supplies, Office Supplies, Office Equipment, Notes Payable, Accounts Payable, Sales, Sales Returns and Allowances, Sales Discounts, Purchases, Purchases Returns and Allowances, Purchases Discounts, Advertising Expense, and Sales Salaries Expense.
2. Open the following accounts receivable ledger accounts: Fred Able, Tom Moss, and John Rice.

3. Open the following accounts payable ledger accounts: Case Company, New Company, Office Outfitters, and Taylor Company.
4. Prepare a Sales Journal, a Purchases Journal, a Cash Receipts Journal, a Cash Disbursements Journal, and a General Journal similar to the ones illustrated in this chapter.
5. Enter the transactions in the journals and post when instructed to do so.
6. Prepare a trial balance and prove the subsidiary ledgers with schedules of accounts receivable and payable.

ALTERNATE PROBLEMS

Problem 7–1A

Island Sales completed these transactions during February:

Feb. 3 Sold merchandise on credit to David Case, Invoice No. 812, $495. Terms of all credit sales are 2/10, n/60.

    6 Sold merchandise on credit to A. J. Allen, Invoice No. 813, $600.

    6 Issued a $45 credit memorandum to David Case for defective merchandise sold on February 3 and returned for credit.

    7 Cash sales for the week ended February 7 were $6,215. (Cash sales are usually recorded daily from the cash register readings; however, they are recorded weekly in this problem in order to reduce the number of repetitive transactions.)

    7 *Post the amounts that are posted as individual amounts from the journals. Normally such amounts are posted daily; but since they are few in number in this problem, you are to post them weekly.*

  10 Borrowed $2,500 from Valley Bank by giving a 60-day, 9% note payable.

  12 Sold merchandise on credit to Paul Eddy, Invoice No. 814, $550.

  13 Received payment from David Case for the February 3 sale, less the return and the discount.

  14 Cash sales for the week ended February 14 were $5,980.

  14 *Post the amounts that are individually posted from the journals.*

  16 Received payment from A. J. Allen for the February 6 sale, less the discount.

  17 Sold merchandise on credit to Paul Eddy, Invoice No. 815, $350.

  19 Sold store supplies to the merchant next door for cash at cost, $30.

  21 Cash sales for the week ended February 21, $6,210.

  21 *Post the amounts that are individually posted from the journals.*

  22 Received payment from Paul Eddy for the February 12 sale, less the discount.

  23 Sold merchandise on credit to A. J. Allen, Invoice No. 816, $475.

  24 Sold merchandise on credit to David Case, Invoice No. 817, $520.

  27 Received payment from Paul Eddy for the February 17 sale, less the discount.

  28 Cash sales for the week ended February 28 were $6,460.

  28 *Post the amounts that are individually posted from the journals.*

  28 *Foot the Sales Journal and foot and crossfoot the Cash Receipts Journal and make the month-end postings.*

Required:

1. Open the following general ledger accounts: Cash, Accounts Receivable, Store Supplies, Notes Payable, Sales, Sales Returns and Allowances, and Sales Discounts.
2. Open the following accounts receivable ledger accounts: A. J. Allen, David Case, and Paul Eddy.
3. Enter the transactions in the journals and post when instructed to do so.
4. Prove the general ledger accounts by preparing a trial balance, and prove the subsidiary ledger accounts by totaling their balances and comparing the total with the balance of the Accounts Receivable controlling account.

Problem 7–2A

A company completed these transactions:

Dec. 7 Accepted a $2,800, 9%, 60-day note dated this day and $475 in cash in granting a time extension of the past-due account of Larry Vale.

 31 Aged the accounts receivable and estimated that $2,110 would prove uncollectible. Examined the Allowance for Doubtful Accounts account and determined that it had a $140 debit balance. Made an adjusting entry to provide for the estimated bad debts.

 31 Made an adjusting entry to record the accrued interest on the Larry Vale note.

 31 Closed the Bad Debts Expense and Interest Earned accounts.

Feb. 5 Received payment of the maturity value of the Larry Vale note.

 11 Learned that Earl Hill had gone out of business, leaving no assets to attach. Wrote off his $285 account as a bad debt.

Mar. 10 Learned of the bankruptcy of Joel Kane and made a claim on his receiver in bankruptcy for the $410 owed by Mr. Kane for merchandise purchased on credit.

May 15 Accepted $265 in cash and a $1,200, 9%, 60-day note dated this day in granting a time extension on the past-due account of Ted Rust.

June 14 Discounted the Ted Rust note at the bank at 10%.

July 15 Received notice protesting the Ted Rust note. Paid the bank the maturity value of the note plus a $5 protest fee.

Aug. 12 Earl Hill paid $100 of the amount written off on February 11. In a letter accompanying the payment he stated that his finances had improved and he expected to pay the balance owed within a short time.

Oct. 3 Received $85 from the receiver in bankruptcy of Joel Kane. A letter accompanying the payment said that no more would be paid. Recorded receipt of the $85 and wrote off the balance owed as a bad debt.

 3 Decided the account of Ted Rust was uncollectible and wrote it off as a bad debt.

Dec. 22 Made a compound entry to write off the accounts of James Wells, $215, and Robert Neal, $185, as uncollectible.

 31 Aged the accounts receivable and estimated that $2,300 would prove

uncollectible. Made an adjusting entry to provide for the estimated bad debts.

Dec. 31   Closed the Bad Debts Expense and Interest Earned accounts.

Required:

1.   Open Interest Receivable, Allowance for Doubtful Accounts, Interest Earned, and Interest Expense accounts. Enter the $140 debit balance in the Allowance for Doubtful Accounts account.
2.   Prepare general journal entries to record the transactions and post those portions of the entries that affect the accounts opened.

Problem 7–3A

Prepare general journal entries to record these transactions:

Dec. 13   Accepted an $1,800, 60-day, 8% note dated this day in granting Earl Larr a time extension on his past-due account.

31   Made an adjusting entry to record the accrued interest on the Earl Larr note.

31   Closed the Interest Earned account.

Feb. 11   Received payment of the maturity value of the Earl Larr note.

14   Accepted a $1,400, 30-day, 9% note dated this day in granting a time extension on the past-due account of Ted Hall.

Mar. 16   Ted Hall dishonored his 30-day note when presented for payment.

Apr. 5   Accepted a $1,200, 90-day, 9% note dated April 3 in granting Carl Jacks a time extension on his past-due account.

9   Discounted the Carl Jacks note at the bank at 10%.

July 5   Since notice protesting the Carl Jacks note had not been received assumed it paid.

7   Accepted an $800, 60-day, 9% note dated this day from Larry Moss in granting a time extension on his past-due account.

31   Discounted the Larry Moss note at the bank at 10%.

Sept. 6   Received notice protesting the Larry Moss note. Paid the bank the maturity value of the note plus a $4 protest fee.

Oct. 5   Received payment from Larry Moss of the maturity value of his dishonored note, the protest fee, and interest on both for 30 days beyond maturity at 9%.

Dec. 28   Decided the account of Ted Hall was uncollectible and wrote it off against the allowance for doubtful accounts.

Problem 7–4A

Prepare general journal entries to record these transactions:

Dec. 7   Accepted $225 in cash and a $2,400, 60-day, 8% note dated this day in granting Ned Ross a time extension on his past-due account.

31   Made an adjusting entry to record the accrued interest on the Ned Ross note.

31   Made an adjusting entry to increase the allowance for doubtful accounts by an amount equal to one third of 1% of the year's $858,000 of charge sales.

Jan. 18   Discounted the Ned Ross note at the bank at 10%.
Feb. 9   Since notice protesting the Ned Ross note had not been received, assumed it paid.
     12   Accepted a $2,000, 60-day, 9% note from John Ellis in granting a time extension on his past-due account. The note was dated February 10.
Apr. 11   Received payment of the maturity value of the John Ellis note.
     15   Decided the $435 account of Walter Sears was uncollectible and wrote it off against the allowance for doubtful accounts.
     22   Accepted an $1,800, 60-day, 9% note dated this day in granting Harold Jones an extension on his past-due account.
May   4   Discounted the Harold Jones note at the bank at 10%.
June 22   Received notice protesting the Harold Jones note. Paid the bank the note's maturity value plus a $5 protest fee.
July 6   Walter Sears paid $135 of the amount written off on April 15. In a letter accompanying the payment he said his finances had improved and he expected to pay the balance owed within a short time.
     21   Received payment from Harold Jones of the maturity value of his dishonored note, the protest fee, and interest on both for 30 days beyond maturity at 9%.

Problem 7–5A

Prepare general journal entries to record these transactions:

Dec. 21   Accepted $365 in cash and a $2,800, 60-day, 9% note dated this day in granting Jerry Neal a time extension on his past-due account.
     31   Made an adjusting entry to record the accrued interest on the Jerry Neal note.
     31   Made an adjusting entry to increase the allowance for doubtful accounts by an amount equal to one fourth of 1% of the year's $840,000 of charge sales.
     31   Closed the Bad Debts Expense and Interest Earned accounts.
Feb. 1   Discounted the Jerry Neal note at the bank at 10%.
     20   Received notice protesting the Jerry Neal note. Paid the bank the note's maturity value plus a $6 protest fee.
Mar. 21   Received payment from Jerry Neal of the maturity value of his dishonored note, the protest fee, and interest on both for 30 days beyond maturity at 9%.
     24   Accepted a $2,400, 90-day, 9% note dated this day in granting a time extension on the past-due account of Fred Ball.
     30   Discounted the Fred Ball note at the bank at 10%.
June 27   Since notice protesting the Fred Ball note had not been received, assumed it paid.
Aug. 7   Accepted an $1,800, 8%, 60-day note dated this day in granting a time extension on the past-due account of Joel Kane.
     31   Discounted the Joel Kane note at the bank at 10%.
Oct. 7   Received notice protesting the Joel Kane note. Paid the bank the maturity value of the note plus a $5 protest fee.
Dec. 28   Decided the Joel Kane account was uncollectible and wrote it off against the allowance for doubtful accounts.

PROVOCATIVE PROBLEMS

Provocative problem 7–1
Red Rock Sales

When his auditor arrived early in January to begin the annual audit, Robert Hamilton, the owner of Red Rock Sales, asked that special attention be given the accounts receivable. Two things caused this request: (1) During the previous week Mr. Hamilton had encountered Ed Barr, a former customer, on the street, and had asked him about his account which had recently been written off as uncollectible. Mr. Barr had indignantly replied that he had paid his $305 account in full, and he later produced canceled checks endorsed by Red Rock Sales to prove it. (2) The income statement prepared for the quarter ended the previous December 31 showed an unusually large volume of sales returns. The bookkeeper who had prepared the statement had resigned at the end of the first week in January. He had worked for Red Rock Sales only since October 1, after having been hired on the basis of out-of-town letters of reference. While on the job, in addition to doing all the record keeping, he had acted as cashier, receiving and depositing the cash from both cash sales and that received through the mail.

In the course of her investigation, the auditor prepared from the company's records the following analysis of the accounts receivable for the period October 1 through December 31:

	Ames	Barr	Cole	Doak	Eble	Finn	Glen
Balance, October 1	$ 315	$ 140	$ 285	$ 260	$ 140	$ 510	$ 445
Sales	580	165	560	–0–	725	385	520
Totals	$ 895	$ 305	$ 845	$ 260	$ 865	$ 895	$ 965
Collections	(480)	–0–	(525)	–0–	(445)	(385)	(585)
Returns	(95)	(65)	(30)	–0–	(110)	(80)	(15)
Bad debts written off ..	–0–	(240)	–0–	(260)	–0–	–0–	–0–
Balance, December 31 .	$ 320	–0–	$ 290	–0–	$ 310	$ 430	$ 365

The auditor communicated with all charge customers and learned that although their account balances as of December 31 agreed with the amounts shown in Red Rock Company's records, the individual transactions did not. They reported credit purchases totaling $3,410 during the three-month period and $95 of returns for which credit had been granted. Correspondence with Mr. Doak, the customer whose $260 account had been written off, revealed that he had become bankrupt and his creditor claims had been settled by his receiver in bankruptcy at $0.25 on the dollar. The checks had been mailed by the receiver on November 8, and all had been paid and returned by the bank, properly endorsed by the recipients.

Under the assumption the late bookkeeper had embezzled cash from the company, determine the total amount he took and attempted to conceal with false accounts receivable entries. Account for the deficiency by listing the concealment methods used and the amount he attempted to conceal with each method. Also outline an internal control system that will help protect the company's cash from future embezzlement. Assume the company is small and can have only one office employee who must do all the bookkeeping.

Provocative problem 7–2
Jewels Unlimited

Jewels Unlimited, a jewelry store, has been in operation for five years. Three years ago Ted Hall, the store's owner, liberalized the store's credit policy in an effort to increase sales. Sales have increased, but Ted is now concerned with the effects of the more liberal credit policy. Bad debts written off, (the store used the direct write-off method) have increased materially during the past two years, and now Ted wonders if the sales increase justifies the substantial bad debt losses which he is certain have resulted from the more liberal credit policy.

The following tabulation shows the store's operating results and bad debt losses. On the tabulation's last line bad debt losses are reclassified by years in which the sales that resulted in the losses were made. Consequently, the $2,790 of fifth-year losses includes $1,710 of estimated bad debts in present accounts receivable.

	1st year	2d year	3d year	4th year	5th year
Credit sales....................	$100,000	$110,000	$150,000	$180,000	$200,000
Cost of goods sold..............	49,900	55,100	75,300	89,800	99,700
Gross profit on credit sales......	$ 50,100	$ 54,900	$ 74,700	$ 90,200	$100,300
Expenses other than bad debts ..	30,300	33,100	44,900	54,400	59,800
Income before bad debts	$ 19,800	$ 21,800	$ 29,800	$ 35,800	$ 40,500
Bad debts written off...........	100	520	700	2,350	2,300
Net income from credit sales....	$ 19,700	$ 21,280	$ 29,100	$ 33,450	$ 38,200
Bad debts by year of sales	$ 360	$ 410	$ 1,960	$ 2,160	$ 2,790

Prepare a schedule showing in columns by years: income before bad debts, bad debts incurred, and net income from credit sales. Then below the net income figures show for each year bad debts written off as a percentage of sales followed on the next line by bad debts incurred as a percentage of sales. Also prepare a report to Mr. Hall answering his concern about the new credit policy and recommending any changes you consider desirable in his accounting for bad debts.

8

Inventories and cost of goods sold

After studying Chapter 8 you should be able to

- Calculate the cost of an inventory based on *(a)* specific invoice prices, *(b)* weighted-average cost, *(c)* Fifo, and *(d)* Lifo.
- Explain the income tax effect of the use of Lifo.
- Tell what is required by the accounting principle of consistency and why the application of this principle is important.
- Tell what is required of a concern when it changes its accounting procedures.
- Tell what is required by the accounting principle of conservatism.
- Explain the effect of an inventory error on the income statements of the current and succeeding years.
- Tell how a perpetual inventory system operates.
- Estimate an inventory by the retail method and by the gross profit method.
- Define or explain the words and phrases listed in the chapter Glossary.

A merchandising business earns revenue by selling merchandise. For such a concern the phrase *merchandise inventory* is used to describe the aggregate of the items of tangible personal property it holds for sale. As a rule the items are sold within a year or one cycle. Consequently, the inventory is a current asset, usually the largest current asset on a merchandising concern's balance sheet.

MATCHING MERCHANDISE COSTS WITH REVENUES

An AICPA committee said: "A major objective of accounting for inventories is the proper determination of income through the process of matching appropriate costs against revenues."[1] The matching process referred to is one with which the student is already familiar. For inventories, it consists of determining how much of the cost of the goods that were for sale during a period should be deducted from the period's revenue and how much should be carried forward as inventory to be matched against a future period's revenue.

In separating cost of goods available for sale into its components of cost of goods sold and cost of goods not sold, the key problem is that of assigning a cost to the goods not sold or to the ending inventory. However, it should be borne in mind that the procedures for assigning a cost to the ending inventory are also the means of determining cost of goods sold. For whatever portion of the cost of goods for sale is assigned to the ending inventory, the remainder goes into cost of goods sold.

ASSIGNING A COST TO THE ENDING INVENTORY

Assigning a cost to the ending inventory normally involves two problems: (1) determining the quantity of each product on hand and (2) pricing the products.

The quantity of unsold merchandise on hand at the end of an accounting period is usually determined by a physical inventory. Physical

---

[1] Committee on Accounting Procedures, "Accounting Research Bulletin No. 43," *Accounting Research and Terminology Bulletins, Final Edition* (New York: AICPA, 1961), p. 28.

inventories and the way in which such inventories are taken were discussed in Chapter 5. Consequently, it is only necessary to repeat that in a physical inventory the unsold merchandise is counted to determine the units of each product on hand.

After an inventory is counted, the units are priced. Generally, inventories are priced at cost. However, a departure from cost is sometimes necessary when goods have been damaged or have deteriorated. Likewise, a departure from cost is sometimes necessary when replacement costs are less than the amounts paid for the items when they were purchased.[2] These points are discussed later in this chapter.

ACCOUNTING FOR AN INVENTORY AT COST

Pricing an inventory at cost is not difficult when costs remain fixed. However, when identical items were purchased during a period at different costs, a problem arises as to which costs apply to the ending inventory and which apply to the goods sold. There are four commonly used ways of assigning costs to goods in the ending inventory and to goods sold. They are (1) specific invoice prices; (2) weighted-average cost; (3) first-in, first-out; and (4) last-in, first-out. Each is a *generally accepted accounting procedure.*

To illustrate the four, assume that a company has on hand at the end of an accounting period 12 units of Article X. Also, assume that the company began the year and purchased Article X during the year as follows:

Jan. 1	Beginning inventory	10 units @ $100 =	$1,000
Mar. 13	Purchased	15 units @ $108 =	1,620
Aug. 17	Purchased	20 units @ $120 =	2,400
Nov. 10	Purchased	10 units @ $125 =	1,250
	Total	55 units	$6,270

Specific invoice prices

When it is possible to identify each item in an inventory with a specific purchase and its invoice, *specific invoice prices* may be used to assign costs. For example, assume that 6 of the 12 unsold units of Article X were from the November purchase and 6 were from the August purchase. Under this assumption, costs are assigned to the inventory and goods sold by means of specific invoice prices as follows:

---

[2] APB, "Basic Concepts and Accounting Principles Underlying Financial Statements of Business Enterprises," *APB Statement No. 4* (New York: AICPA, October 1970), par. 183.

Total cost of 55 units available for sale		$6,270
Less ending inventory priced by means of specific invoices:		
6 units from the November purchase at $125 each	$750	
6 units from the August purchase at $120 each	720	
12 units in ending inventory		1,470
Cost of goods sold		$4,800

Weighted average

Under this method prices for the units in the beginning inventory and in each purchase are weighted by the number of units in the beginning inventory and in each purchase and are averaged to find the *weighted-average cost* per unit as follows:

10 units @ $100	=	$1,000
15 units @ $108	=	1,620
20 units @ $120	=	2,400
10 units @ $125	=	1,250
55		$6,270

$6,270 ÷ 55 = $114, weighted-average cost per unit

After the weighted-average cost per unit is determined, this average is used to assign costs to the inventory and the units sold as follows:

Total cost of 55 units available for sale	$6,270
Less ending inventory priced on a weighted-average	
cost basis: 12 units at $114 each	1,368
Cost of goods sold	$4,902

First-in, first-out

In a merchandising business clerks are instructed to sell the oldest merchandise first. Consequently, when this instruction is followed, merchandise tends to flow out on a first-in, first-out basis. When first-in, first-out is applied in pricing an inventory, it is assumed that costs follow this pattern. As a result, the cost of the last items received are assigned to the ending inventory and the remaining costs are assigned to goods sold. When first-in, first-out, or *Fifo* as it is often called from its first letters, is used, costs are assigned to the inventory and goods sold as follows:

Total cost of 55 units available for sale		$6,270
Less ending inventory priced on a basis of Fifo:		
10 units from the November purchase at $125 each	$1,250	
2 units from the August purchase at $120 each	240	
12 units in the ending inventory		1,490
Cost of goods sold		$4,780

Last-in, first-out

Under this method of inventory pricing, commonly called *Lifo*, the costs of the last goods received are matched with revenue from sales. The theoretical justification for this is that a going concern must at all times keep a certain amount of goods in stock. Consequently, when goods are sold, replacements are purchased. Thus it is a sale that causes the replacement of goods. If costs and revenues are then matched, replacement costs should be matched with the sales that induced the acquisitions.

Under Lifo, costs are assigned to the 12 remaining units of Article X and to the goods sold as follows:

Total cost of 55 units available for sale		$6,270
Less ending inventory priced on a basis of Lifo:		
10 units in the beginning inventory at $100 each	$1,000	
2 units from the first purchase at $108 each	216	
12 units in the ending inventory		1,216
Cost of goods sold		$5,054

Notice that this method of matching costs and revenue results in the final inventory being priced at the cost of the oldest 12 units.

Tax effect of Lifo

During periods of rising prices Lifo offers a tax advantage to its users. This advantage arises because when compared with other methods the application of Lifo results in assigning greatest amounts of costs to goods sold. This in turn results in the smallest reported net incomes and income taxes.

The use of Lifo is not limited to concerns in which goods are actually sold on a last-in, first-out basis. A concern may choose Lifo even though it actually sells goods on a first-in, first-out basis, or on an average basis.

Comparison of methods

In a stable market where prices remain unchanged, the inventory pricing method is of little importance. For when prices are unchanged over a period of time, all methods give the same cost figures. However, in a changing market where prices are rising or falling, each method may give a different result. This may be seen by comparing the costs of the units in the ending inventory and the units of Article X sold as calculated by the several methods discussed. These costs are as follows:

	Ending inventory	Cost of units sold
Based on specific invoice prices	$1,470	$4,800
Based on weighted average	1,368	4,902
Based on Fifo	1,490	4,780
Based on Lifo	1,216	5,054

Each of the four pricing methods is recognized as a generally accepted accounting procedure, and arguments can be advanced for the use of each. Specific invoice prices exactly match costs and revenues. However, this method is of practical use only for relatively high-priced items of which only a few units are kept in stock and sold. Weighted-average costs tend to smooth out price fluctuations. Fifo causes the last costs incurred to be assigned to the ending inventory. It thus provides an inventory valuation for the balance sheet that most closely approximates the current replacement costs. Lifo causes last costs incurred to be assigned to cost of goods sold. Therefore, it results in a better matching of current costs with revenues. However, the method used commonly affects the amounts of reported ending inventory, cost of goods sold, and net income. Consequently, the *full-disclosure principle* requires that a company show in its statements by means of footnotes or other manner the pricing method used.[3]

THE PRINCIPLE OF CONSISTENCY

Look again at the table of costs for Article X. Note that a company can change its reported net income for an accounting period simply by changing its inventory pricing method. However, the change would violate the accounting *principle of consistency*. Furthermore, it would make a comparison of the company's inventory and income with previous periods more or less meaningless.

As with inventory pricing, more than one generally accepted

---

[3] APB, "Disclosure of Accounting Policies," *APB Opinion No. 22* (New York: AICPA, April 1972), pars. 12 and 13.

method or procedure has been derived in accounting practice to account for an item or an activity. In each case one method may be considered better for one enterprise, while another may be considered more satisfactory for a concern operating under different circumstances. Nevertheless, the *principle of consistency* requires a persistent application by a company of any selected accounting method or procedure, period after period. As a result, a reader of a company's financial statements may assume that in keeping its records and in preparing its statements the company used the same procedures used in previous years. Only on the basis of this assumption can meaningful comparisons be made of the data in a company's statements year after year.

CHANGING ACCOUNTING PROCEDURES

In achieving comparability, the *principle of consistency* does not require that a method or procedure once chosen can never be changed. Rather, if a company decides that a different acceptable method or procedure from the one in use will better serve its needs, a change may be made. However, when such a change is made, the *full-disclosure principle* requires that the nature of the change, justification for the change, and the effect of the change on net income be disclosed in notes accompanying the statements.[4]

ITEMS INCLUDED ON AN INVENTORY

A concern's inventory should include all goods owned by the business and held for sale, regardless of where the goods may be located at the time of the inventory. In the application of this rule, there are generally no problems with respect to most items. For most items all that is required is to see that they are counted, that nothing is omitted, and that nothing is counted more than once. However, goods in transit, goods sold but not delivered, goods on consignment, and obsolete and damaged goods do require special attention.

When goods are in transit on the inventory date, the purchase should be recorded and the goods should appear on the purchaser's inventory if ownership has passed to the purchaser. Generally, if the buyer is responsible for paying the freight charges, ownership passes as soon as the goods are loaded aboard the means of transportation. Likewise, if the seller is to pay the freight charges, ownership passes when the goods arrive at their destination.

Goods on consignment are goods shipped by their owner (known as the *consignor*) to another person or firm (called the *consignee*) who

---

[4] APB, "Accounting Changes," *APB Opinion No. 20* (New York: AICPA, July 1971), par. 17.

is to sell the goods for the owner. Consigned goods belong to the consignor and should appear on the consignor's inventory.

Damaged goods and goods that have deteriorated or become obsolete should not be placed on the inventory if they are not salable. If such goods are salable but at a reduced price, they should be placed on the inventory at a conservative estimate of their realizable value (sale price less the cost of making the sale). This causes the accounting period in which the goods were damaged, deteriorated, or became obsolete to suffer the resultant loss.

ELEMENTS OF INVENTORY COST

As applied to inventories, cost means the sum of the applicable expenditures and charges directly or indirectly incurred in bringing an article to its existing condition and location.[5] Therefore, the cost of an inventory item includes the invoice price, less the discount, plus any additional incidental costs necessary to put the goods into place and condition for sale. The additional incidental costs include import duties, transportation, storage, insurance, and any other applicable costs, such as those incurred during an aging process.

If incurred, any of the foregoing enter into the cost of an inventory. However, in pricing an inventory, most concerns do not take into consideration the incidental costs of acquiring merchandise. They price the inventory on the basis of invoice prices only, and treat all incidental costs as expenses of the period in which incurred.

Although not correct in theory, treating incidental costs as expenses of the period in which incurred is commonly permissible and often best. In theory a share of each incidental cost should be assigned to every unit purchased. This causes a portion of each to be carried forward in the inventory to be matched against the revenue of the period in which the inventory is sold. However, the expense of computing costs on such a precise basis usually outweighs any benefit from the extra accuracy. Consequently, when possible, most concerns take advantage of the principle of materiality and treat such costs as expenses of the period in which incurred.

COST OR MARKET, THE LOWER

Over the years the traditional rule for pricing inventory items has been *the lower of cost or market*. "Cost" is the price that was paid for an item when it was purchased. "Market" is the price that would have to be paid to purchase or replace the item on the inventory date. The use of this rule gained its wide acceptance because it placed an inventory on the balance sheet at a conservative figure, the lower

---

[5] *Accounting Research and Terminology Bulletins, Final Edition*, p. 28.

of what the inventory cost or its replacement cost on the balance sheet date.

The argument advanced to support the use of lower of cost or market was that if the replacement cost of an inventory item had declined, then its selling price would probably have to be reduced. Since this might result in a loss, the loss should be anticipated and taken in the year of the price decline. It was a good argument. However, selling prices do not always exactly and quickly follow cost prices. As a result, the application of the rule often resulted in misstating net income in the year of a price decline and again in the succeeding year. For example, suppose that a firm purchased merchandise costing $1,000; marked it up to a $1,500 selling price; and sold one half of the goods. The gross profit on the goods sold would be calculated as follows:

Sales	$750
Cost of goods sold	500
Gross profit on sales....	$250

However, if the $500 replacement cost of the unsold goods declined to $450 on the inventory date, an income statement based upon the traditional application of cost or market would show the following:

Sales		$750
Cost of goods sold:		
Purchases	$1,000	
Less ending inventory....	450	550
Gross profit on sales		$200

The $450 would be a conservative balance sheet figure for the unsold goods. However, if these goods were sold at their full price early in the following year, the $450 inventory figure would have the erroneous effect of deferring $50 of income to the second year's income statement as follows:

Sales	$750
Cost of goods sold:	
Beginning inventory....	450
Gross profit on sales	$300

Merchants are prone to be slow in marking down goods; they normally try to sell merchandise at its full price if possible. Consequently, the illustrated situation is not uncommon. For this reason the lower of cost or market rule has been modified as follows for situations in which replacement costs are below actual costs.[6]

1. Goods should be placed on an inventory at cost, even though replacement cost is lower, if there has not been and there is not expected to be a decline in selling price.
2. Goods should at times be placed on an inventory at a price below cost but above replacement cost. For example, suppose the cost of an item that is normally bought for $20 and sold for $30 declines from $20 to $16, and its selling price declines from $30 to $27. The normal profit margin on this item is one third of its selling price. If this normal margin is applied to $27, the item should be placed on the inventory at two thirds of $27, or at $18. This is below cost but above replacement cost.
3. At times, goods should be placed on an inventory at a price below replacement cost. For example, assume that the goods described in the preceding paragraph can only be sold for $18.50 and that the disposal costs are estimated at $3. In this case the goods should be placed on the inventory at $15.50, a price below their replacement cost of $16.

PRINCIPLE OF CONSERVATISM

Decisions based on estimates and opinions as to future events affect financial statements. Financial statements are also affected by the selection of accounting procedures. The *principle of conservatism* holds that accountants should be conservative in their estimates and opinions and in their selection of procedures, choosing those that neither unduly understate nor overstate the situation.

Something called balance sheet conservatism was once considered the "first" principle of accounting. Its objective was to place every item on the balance sheet at a conservative figure. This in itself was commendable. However, it was often carried too far and resulted not only in the misstatement of asset values but also in unconservative income statements. For example, when prices are falling, the blind application of the lower of cost or market to inventories may result in a conservative balance sheet figure for inventories. It may also result in an improper deferring of net income and in inaccurate income statements. Consequently, accountants recognize that balance sheet conservatism does not outweigh other factors. They favor practices that result in a fair statement of net income period after period.

INVENTORY ERRORS

An error in determining the end-of-the-period inventory will cause misstatements in cost of goods sold, gross profit, net income, current

---

[6] Ibid., pp. 30 and 31.

assets, and owner's equity. Also, the ending inventory of one period is the beginning inventory of the next. Therefore, the error will carry forward and cause misstatements in the succeeding period's cost of goods sold, gross profit, and net income. Furthermore, since the amount involved in an inventory is often large, the misstatements can be material without being readily apparent.

To illustrate the effects of an inventory error, assume that in each of the years 198A, 198B, and 198C a company had $100,000 in sales. If the company maintained a $20,000 inventory throughout the period and made $60,000 in purchases in each of the years, its cost of goods sold each year was $60,000 and its annual gross profits were $40,000. However, assume the company incorrectly calculated its December 31, 198A, inventory at $18,000 rather than $20,000. The error would have the effects shown in Illustration 8–1.

Observe in Illustration 8–1 that the $2,000 understatement of the December 31, 198A, inventory caused a $2,000 overstatement in 198A cost of goods sold and a $2,000 understatement in gross profit and net income. Also, since the ending inventory of 198A became the beginning inventory of 198B, the error caused an understatement in the 198B cost of goods sold and a $2,000 overstatement in gross profit and net income. However, by 198C the error had no effect.

In Illustration 8–1 the December 31, 198A, inventory is understated. Had it been overstated, it would have caused opposite results—the 198A net income would have been overstated and the 198B income understated.

	198A		198B		198C	
Sales		$100,000		$100,000		$100,000
Cost of goods sold:						
Beginning inventory	$20,000		$18,000*		$20,000	
Purchases	60,000		60,000		60,000	
Goods for sale	$80,000		$78,000		$80,000	
Ending inventory	18,000*		20,000		20,000	
Cost of goods sold......		62,000		58,000		60,000
Gross profit		$ 38,000		$ 42,000		$ 40,000
* Should have been $20,000.						

Illustration 8–1

It has been argued that an inventory mistake is not too serious, since the error it causes in reported net income the first year is exactly offset by an opposite error in the second. However, such reasoning is unsound. It fails to consider that management, creditors, and owners base many important decisions on fluctuations in reported net income. Consequently, such mistakes should be avoided.

PERPETUAL INVENTORIES

Concerns selling a limited number of products of relatively high value often keep perpetual or book inventories. Also, concerns that use computers in processing their accounting data commonly keep such records. Furthermore, the essential information provided is the same whether accumulated by computer or with pen and ink.

A perpetual or book inventory based on pen and ink makes use of a subsidiary record card for each product in stock. On these individual cards, the number of units received is recorded as units are received and the number of units sold is recorded as units are sold. Then, after each receipt or sale, the balance remaining is recorded. (An inventory record card for Product Z is shown in Illustration 8–2.) At any time, each perpetual inventory card tells the balance on hand of any one product; and the total of all cards is the amount of the inventory.

Item	Product Z						Location in stock room	Bin 8	
Maximum	25						Minimum	5	

Date	Received			Sold			Balance		
	Units	Cost	Total	Units	Cost	Total	Units	Cost	Balance
1/1							10	10.00	100.00
1/5				5	10.00	50.00	5	10.00	50.00
1/8	20	10.50	210.00				5	10.00	
							20	10.50	260.00
1/10				3	10.00	30.00	2	10.00	
							20	10.50	230.00

Illustration 8–2

The January 10 sale on the card of Illustration 8–2 indicates that the inventory of this card is kept on a first-in, first-out basis, since the sale is recorded as being from the oldest units in stock. Perpetual inventories may also be kept on a last-in, first-out basis. When this is done, each sale is recorded as being from the last units received, until these are exhausted, then sales are from the next to last, and so on.

When a concern keeps perpetual inventory records, it normally also makes a once-a-year physical count of each kind of goods in stock in order to check the accuracy of its book inventory records.

Perpetual inventories not only tell the amount of inventory on hand at any time but they also aid in controlling the total amount invested in inventory. Each perpetual inventory card may have on it the maximum and minimum amounts of that item that should be kept in stock. By keeping the amount of each item within these limits, an oversupply or an undersupply of inventory is avoided.

PERPETUAL INVENTORY SYSTEMS

Under a *perpetual inventory system*, cost of goods sold during a period, as well as the ending inventory, may be determined from the accounting records. Under such a system an account called Merchandise is used in the place of the Purchases and Merchandise Inventory accounts. It is a controlling account that controls the numerous perpetual inventory cards described in previous paragraphs.

When merchandise is purchased by a concern using a perpetual inventory system, the acquisition is recorded as follows:

Jan.	8	Merchandise	210.00	
		Accounts Payable—Blue Company		210.00
		Purchased merchandise on credit.		

In addition to the entry debiting the purchase to the Merchandise account, entries are also made on the proper perpetual inventory cards in the Received columns to show the kinds of merchandise bought. (See Illustration 8–2.)

When a sale is made, since the inventory cards show the cost of each item sold, it is possible to record both the sale and the cost of the goods sold. For example, if goods that according to the inventory cards cost $30 are sold for $50, cost of goods sold and the sale may be recorded as follows:

Jan.	10	Accounts Receivable—George Black	50.00	
		Cost of Goods Sold	30.00	
		Sales		50.00
		Merchandise		30.00
		Sold merchandise on credit.		

In addition to the credit in this entry to the Merchandise account for the cost of the goods sold, the costs of the items sold are also deducted in the Sold columns of the proper inventory cards.

Note the debit to the Cost of Goods Sold account in the entry just given. If this account is debited at the time of each sale for the cost of the goods sold, the debit balance of the account will show at the end of the accounting period the cost of all goods sold during the period.

Note also the debit and the credit to the Merchandise account as they appear in the two entries just given. If this account is debited for the cost of merchandise purchased and credited for the cost of merchandise sold, at the end of an accounting period its debit balance will show the cost of the unsold goods on hand, the ending inventory.

ESTIMATED INVENTORIES

Retail method

Good management requires that income statements be prepared more often than once each year, and inventory information is necessary in their preparation. However, taking a physical inventory in a retail store is both time consuming and expensive. Consequently, many retailers use the so-called *retail inventory method* to estimate inventories for monthly or quarterly statements. These monthly or quarterly statements are called *interim statements,* since they are prepared in between the regular year-end statements.

Estimating an ending inventory by the retail method   When the retail method is used to estimate an inventory, a store's records must show the amount of inventory it had at the beginning of the period both *at cost* and *at retail.* At cost for an inventory means just that, while "at retail" means the dollar amount of the inventory at the marked selling prices of the inventory items.

In addition to the beginning inventory, the records must also show the amount of goods purchased during the period both at cost and at retail plus the net sales at retail. The last item is easy; it is the balance of the Sales account less returns and discounts. Then, with this information the interim inventory is estimated as follows: (Step 1) The amount of goods that were for sale during the period both at cost and at retail is first computed. Next (Step 2), "at cost" is divided by "at retail" to obtain a cost ratio. Then (Step 3), sales (at retail) are deducted from goods for sale (at retail) to arrive at the ending inventory (at retail). And finally (Step 4), the ending inventory at retail is multiplied by the cost ratio to reduce it to a cost basis. These calculations are shown in Illustration 8–3 on the next page.

This is the essence of Illustration 8–3: (1) The store had $100,000 of goods (at marked selling prices) for sale during the period. (2) These goods cost 60% of the $100,000 total amount at which they were marked for sale. (3) The store's records (its Sales account) showed that $70,000 of these goods were sold, leaving $30,000 of merchandise un-

	At cost	At retail
(Step 1) Goods available for sale:		
Beginning inventory	$20,500	$ 34,500
Net purchases	39,500	65,500
Goods available for sale	$60,000	$100,000
(Step 2) Cost ratio: $60,000 ÷ $100,000 = 60%		
(Step 3) Deduct sales at retail		70,000
Ending inventory at retail		$ 30,000
(Step 4) Ending inventory at cost ($30,000 × 60%)....	$18,000	

Illustration 8–3

sold and presumably in the ending inventory. Therefore, (4) since cost in this store is 60% of retail, the estimated cost of this ending inventory is $18,000.

An ending inventory calculated as in Illustration 8–3 is an estimate arrived at by deducting sales (goods sold) from goods for sale. Inventories estimated in this manner are satisfactory for interim statements, but for year-end statements, or at least once each year, a store should take a physical inventory.

Using the retail method to reduce a physical inventory to cost   Items for sale in a store normally have price tickets attached that show selling prices. Consequently, when a store takes a physical inventory, it commonly takes the inventory at the marked selling prices of the inventoried items. It then reduces the dollar total of this inventory to a cost basis by applying its cost ratio. It does this because the selling prices are readily available and the application of the cost ratio eliminates the need to look up the invoice price of each inventoried item.

For example, assume that the store of Illustration 8–3, in addition to estimating its inventory by the retail method, also takes a physical inventory at the marked selling prices of the inventoried goods. Assume further that the total of this physical inventory is $29,600. Under these assumptions the store may arrive at a cost basis for this inventory, without having to look up the cost of each inventoried item, simply by applying its cost ratio to the $29,600 inventory total as follows:

$$\$29,600 \times 60\% = \$17,760$$

The $17,760 cost figure for this store's ending physical inventory is a satisfactory figure for year-end statement purposes. It is also acceptable to the Internal Revenue Service for tax purposes.

Inventory shortage   An inventory determined as in Illustration 8–3 is an estimate of the amount of goods that should be on hand. However, since it is arrived at by deducting sales from goods for sale, it does not reveal any actual shortages due to breakage, loss, or theft. Nevertheless, the amount of such shortages may be determined by first estimating an inventory as in Illustration 8–3 and then taking a physical inventory at marked selling prices.

For example, by means of the Illustration 8–3 calculations, it was estimated the store of this discussion had a $30,000 ending inventory at retail. However, in the previous section it was assumed that this same store took a physical inventory and had only $29,600 of merchandise on hand. Therefore, if this store should have had $30,000 of goods in its ending inventory as determined in Illustration 8–3, but had only $29,600 when it took a physical inventory, it must have had a $400 inventory shortage at retail or a $240 shortage at cost ($400 × 60% = $240).

Markups and markdowns The calculation of a cost ratio is often not as simple as that shown in Illustration 8–3. It is not simple because many stores not only have a *normal markup* (often called a *markon*) that they apply to items purchased for sale but also make *additional markups* and *markdowns*. A normal markup or markon is the normal amount or percentage that is applied to the cost of an item to arrive at its selling price. For example, if a store's normal markup is 50% on cost and it applies this markup to an item that cost $10, it will mark the item for sale at $15. Normal markups appear in the calculation of a store's cost ratio as the difference between net purchases at cost and at retail.

Additional markups are markups made in addition to normal markups. Stores commonly give goods of outstanding style or quality such additional markups because they can get a higher than normal price for such goods. They also commonly mark down for a clearance sale any slow-moving merchandise.

When a store using the retail inventory method makes additional markups and markdowns, it must keep a record of them. It then uses the information in calculating its cost ratio and in estimating an interim inventory as in Illustration 8–4.

	At cost	At retail
Goods available for sale:		
Beginning inventory	$18,000	$27,800
Net purchases	34,000	50,700
Additional markups		1,500
Goods available for sale	$52,000	$80,000
Cost ratio: $52,000 ÷ $80,000 = 65%		
Sales at retail................................		$54,000
Markdowns.....................................		2,000
Total sales and markdowns		$56,000
Ending inventory at retail ($80,000 less $56,000)....		$24,000
Ending inventory at cost ($24,000 × 65%)........	$15,600	

Illustration 8–4

Observe in Illustration 8–4 that the store's $80,000 of goods for sale at retail were reduced $54,000 by sales and $2,000 by markdowns, a total of $56,000. (To understand the markdowns, visualize this effect of a markdown. The store had an item for sale during the period at $25. The item did not sell, and to move it the manager marked its price down from $25 to $20. By this act the amount of goods for sale in the store at retail was reduced by $5. Likewise, by a number of such markdowns during the year goods for sale at retail in the store of Illustration 8–4 were reduced $2,000.) Now back to the calculations of Illustration 8–4. The store's $80,000 of goods for sale were reduced $54,000 by sales and $2,000 by markdowns, leaving an estimated $24,000 ending inventory at retail. Therefore, since "cost" is 65% of "retail," the ending inventory at "cost" is $15,600.

Observe in Illustration 8–4 that markups enter into the calculation of the cost ratio but markdowns do not. It has long been customary in using the retail inventory method to add additional markups but to ignore markdowns in computing the percentage relation between goods for sale at cost and at retail. The justification for this was and is that a more conservative figure for the ending inventory results, a figure that approaches "cost or market, the lower." A further discussion of this phase of the retail inventory method is reserved for a more advanced text.

Gross profit method

Often retail price information about beginning inventory, purchases, and markups is not kept. In such cases the retail inventory method cannot be used. However, if a company knows its normal gross profit margin or rate; has information at cost in regard to its beginning inventory, net purchases, and freight-in; and knows the amount of its sales and sales returns, the company can estimate its ending inventory by the *gross profit method*.

For example, on March 27, the inventory of a company was totally destroyed by a fire. The company's average gross profit rate during the past five years has been 30% of net sales. And on the date of the fire the company's accounts showed the following balances:

Sales	$31,500
Sales returns	1,500
Inventory, January 1, 19—	12,000
Net purchases	20,000
Freight-in	500

With this information the gross profit method may be used to estimate the company's inventory loss for insurance purposes. The first step in applying the method is to recognize that whatever portion of each dollar of net sales was gross profit, the remaining portion was cost of goods sold. Consequently, if the company's gross profit rate averaged 30%, then 30% of each dollar of net sales was gross profit and 70% was cost of goods sold. The 70% is used in estimating the inventory and inventory loss as in Illustration 8–5.

Goods available for sale:		
Inventory, January 1, 19—		$12,000
Net purchases	$20,000	
Add freight-in	500	20,500
Goods available for sale		$32,500
Less estimated cost of goods sold:		
Sales	$31,500	
Less sales returns	(1,500)	
Net sales	$30,000	
Estimated cost of goods sold (70% × $30,000)		(21,000)
Estimated March 27 inventory and inventory loss		$11,500

Illustration 8–5

To understand Illustration 8–5, recall that in a normal situation an ending inventory is subtracted from goods for sale to determine cost of goods sold. Then observe in Illustration 8–5 that the opposite subtraction is made. Estimated cost of goods sold is subtracted from goods for sale to arrive at the estimated ending inventory.

In addition to its use in insurance cases, as in this illustration, the gross profit method is also commonly used by accountants in checking on the probable accuracy of a physical inventory taken and priced in the normal way.

GLOSSARY

Conservatism principle. The rule that accountants should be conservative in their estimates and opinions and in their selection of procedures.

Consignee. One to whom something is consigned or shipped.

Consignor. One who consigns or ships something to another person or enterprise.

Consistency principle. The accounting rule requiring a persistent application of a selected accounting method or procedure, period after period.

Fifo inventory pricing. The pricing of an inventory under the assumption that the first items received were the first items sold.

Gross profit inventory method. A procedure for estimating an ending inventory in which an estimated cost of goods sold based on past gross profit rates is subtracted from the cost of goods available for sale to arrive at an estimated ending inventory.

Interim statements. Financial statements prepared in between the regular annual statements.

Inventory cost ratio. The ratio of goods available for sale at cost to goods available for sale at retail prices.

Lifo inventory pricing. The pricing of an inventory under the assumption that the last items received were the first items sold.

Lower-of-cost-or-market pricing of an inventory. The pricing of inventory at the lower of what each item actually cost or what it would cost to replace each item on the inventory date.

Markdown. A reduction in the marked selling price of an item.

Markon. The normal percentage of its cost that is added to the cost of an item to arrive at its selling price.

Markup. An addition to the normal markon given to an item.

Normal markup. A phrase meaning the same as markon.

Periodic inventory system. An inventory system in which inventories and cost of goods sold are based on periodic physical inventories.

Perpetual inventory system. An inventory system in which inventories and cost of goods sold are based on book inventory records.

Retail inventory method. A method for estimating an ending inventory based on the ratio of the cost of goods for sale at cost and cost of goods for sale at marked selling prices.

Specific invoice inventory pricing. The pricing of an inventory where each inventory item can be associated with a specific invoice and be priced accordingly.

Weighted-average cost inventory pricing. An inventory pricing system in which the units in the beginning inventory of a product and in each purchase of the product are weighted by the number of units in the beginning inventory and in each purchase to determine a weighted-average cost per unit of the product, and after which this weighted-average cost is used to price the ending inventory of the product.

QUESTIONS FOR CLASS DISCUSSION

1. It has been said that cost of goods sold and ending inventory are opposite sides of the same coin? What is meant by this?
2. Give the meanings of the following when applied to inventory:

   a. First-in, first-out.   *c.* Last-in, first-out.
   b. Fifo.   *d.* Lifo.

  e. Cost.
  f. Market.
  g. Cost or market, the lower.
  h. Perpetual inventory.
  i. Physical inventory.
  j. Book inventory.

3. If prices are rising, will the Lifo or the Fifo method of inventory valuation result in the higher gross profit?
4. May a company change its inventory pricing method at will?
5. What is required by the accounting principle of consistency?
6. If a company changes one of its accounting procedures, what is required of it under the full-disclosure principle?
7. Of what does the cost of an inventory item consist?
8. Why are incidental costs commonly ignored in pricing an inventory? Under what accounting principle is this permitted?
9. What is meant when it is said that inventory errors "correct themselves"?
10. If inventory errors "correct themselves," why be concerned when such errors are made?
11. What is required of an accountant under the principle of conservatism?
12. Give the meanings of the following when applied in the retail method of estimating an inventory: *(a)* at cost, *(b)* at retail, *(c)* cost ratio, *(d)* normal markup, *(e)* markon, *(f)* additional markup, and *(g)* markdown.

CLASS EXERCISES

Exercise 8–1

A company began a year and purchased Article A as follows:

Jan. 1	Beginning inventory	100 units @ 53¢	=	$ 53
Jan. 5	Purchased	300 units @ 51¢	=	153
May 21	Purchased	200 units @ 55¢	=	110
Oct. 3	Purchased	200 units @ 56¢	=	112
Dec. 7	Purchased	200 units @ 61¢	=	122
	Total	1,000		$550

Required:

Under the assumption the ending inventory of Article A consisted of 100 units from each of the last three purchases, a total of 300 units, determine the share of the cost of the units for sale that should be assigned to the ending inventory and the share that should be assigned to goods sold under each of the following additional assumptions: *(a)* costs are assigned on the basis of specific invoice prices, *(b)* costs are assigned on a weighted-average cost basis, *(c)* costs are assigned on the basis of Fifo, and *(d)* costs are assigned on the basis of Lifo.

Exercise 8–2

A company had $500,000 of sales during each of three consecutive years, and it purchased merchandise costing $300,000 during each of the years. It also maintained a $40,000 inventory throughout the three-year period. However, it made an error that caused the December 31, end-of-year-one, inventory to appear on its statements at $42,000, rather than the correct $40,000.

Required:
1. State the actual amount of the company's gross profit in each of the years.
2. Prepare a comparative income statement like the one illustrated in this chapter to show the effect of the error on the company's cost of goods sold and gross profit for each of Year 1, Year 2, and Year 3.

Exercise 8–3

During an accounting period a company sold $153,000 of merchandise at marked retail prices. At the period end the following information was available from its records:

	At cost	At retail
Beginning inventory	$30,000	$ 49,000
Net purchases	90,000	147,000
Additional markups		4,000
Markdowns		2,000

Use the retail method to estimate the store's ending inventory.

Exercise 8–4

Assume that in addition to estimating its ending inventory by the retail method, the store of Exercise 8–3 also took a physical inventory at marked selling prices that totaled $44,000. Determine the store's inventory shrinkage from breakage, theft, or other cause at retail and at cost.

Exercise 8–5

A company had a $25,000 inventory at cost on January 1 of the current year. During the year's first three months it bought merchandise costing $68,000, returned $1,000 of the merchandise, and paid freight charges on purchases totaling $3,000. During the past several years the company's gross profit rate has averaged 35%. Assume the company had $100,000 of sales during the three months and use the gross profit method to estimate its March 31 inventory.

PROBLEMS

Problem 8–1

Zeal Company began last year and purchased Article Z as follows:

January 1 inventory	1,000 units @ $6.10 per unit
Purchases:	
February 5	2,000 units @ $6.00 per unit
June 3	3,000 units @ $6.30 per unit
September 14	3,000 units @ $6.40 per unit
December 3	1,000 units @ $6.60 per unit

Required:

Under the assumption the company incurred $20,000 of selling and administrative expenses last year in selling 8,500 units of the product at $10 per unit, prepare a comparative income statement for the company showing in adjacent columns the net income earned from the sale of the product under the assumptions the company priced its ending inventory on the basis of *(a)* Fifo, *(b)* Lifo, and *(c)* weighted-average cost.

Problem 8–2

A company began an accounting period and made successive purchases of one of its products as follows:

Jan.   1   Beginning inventory . . . . .   200 units @ $75 per unit
Feb. 12   Purchased . . . .   300 units @ $90 per unit
Apr. 21   Purchased . . . .   400 units @ $100 per unit
June 14   Purchased . . . .   400 units @ $95 per unit
Aug. 30   Purchased . . . .   400 units @ $95 per unit
Nov. 27   Purchased . . . .   300 units @ $105 per unit

Required:

1.   Prepare a calculation to show the number and total cost of the units for sale during the period.
2.   Under the assumption the company had 400 units of the product in its end-of-the-year inventory, prepare calculations to show the portions of the total cost of the units for sale during the period that should be assigned to the ending inventory and to the units sold *(a)* first on a Fifo basis, *(b)* then on a Lifo basis, and *(c)* finally on a weighted-average cost basis.

Problem 8–3

A company that keeps perpetual inventory records completed the following transactions involving one of its products:

Dec.   1   Beginning inventory: 12 units costing $6.25 each.
         3   Received ten units costing $6.50 each.
         8   Sold five units.
       12   Sold eight units.
       18   Received ten units costing $7 each.
       22   Sold six units.
       30   Sold eight units.

Required:

1.   Under the assumption the company keeps its records on a first-in, first-out basis, record the transactions on a perpetual inventory record card. Use two or more lines to show units on hand at each price or units sold when units costing different amounts are on hand or sold.
2.   Record the transactions on a second card under the assumption the company keeps its records on a last-in, first-out basis.
3.   Under the assumption that the last sale was to Carl Berg at $11 per unit,

prepare a general journal entry to record the sale and cost of goods sold on a last-in, first-out basis.

Problem 8–4

Sport Shop takes a year-end physical inventory at marked selling prices and reduces the total to a cost basis for year-end statement purposes. It also uses the retail method to estimate the dollar amount of inventory it should have at the end of a year, and by comparison determines any inventory shortages due to shoplifting or other cause. At the end of the current year the following information was available to make the calculations:

	At cost	At retail
Sales		$220,960
Sales returns		1,745
January 1 inventory	$ 21,630	32,950
Purchases	146,400	219,735
Purchases returns	980	1,470
Additional markups		5,785
Markdowns		1,285
December 31 year-end physical inventory		35,800

Required:
1. Prepare a calculation to estimate the dollar amount of the store's year-end inventory, using the retail method.
2. Prepare a calculation showing the amount of inventory shortage at cost and at retail.

Problem 8–5

Rockhill Company's records provide the following December 31, year-end information:

	At cost	At retail
January 1, beginning inventory	$ 24,510	$ 39,215
Purchases	194,460	310,340
Purchases returns	1,970	3,100
Additional markups		3,545
Markdowns		1,450
Sales		308,270
Sales returns		1,220
Year-end physical inventory		39,750

Required:
1. Use the retail method to estimate the company's year-end inventory at cost.
2. Prepare a schedule showing the company's inventory shortage at retail and at cost.

Problem 8–6

On May 20 of the current year Country Store burned and everything excepting the accounting records, which were kept in a fireproof vault, was destroyed. The store's owner has asked you to prepare an estimate of the dollar amount of inventory in the store on the night of the fire, so an insurance claim can be filed. The following information is available:

1. The store's accounts were closed on the previous December 31.
2. The store has earned an average 32% gross profit on sales for a number of years.
3. After all posting was completed, the store's accounts showed these May 20 balances:

Merchandise inventory (January 1 balance) .... $ 42,850
Sales 188,950
Sales returns 2,450
Purchases 123,900
Purchases returns 1,250
Freight-in 2,730

Required:

Prepare an estimate of the store's inventory at the time of the fire.

Problem 8–7

Olive Company wants a June 30, midyear estimate of its inventory. During the past five years its gross profit rate has averaged 34%. The following information is available from its records for the first half of the year:

January 1, beginning inventory ... $ 48,450
Purchases 198,370
Purchases returns 1,150
Freight-in 2,710
Sales 308,900
Sales returns 2,400

Required:

Use the gross profit method to prepare an estimate of the company's June 30 inventory.

ALTERNATE PROBLEMS

Problem 8–1A

Glendon Company sold 880 units of its Product X last year at $50 per unit. It began the year and purchased the product as follows:

January 1, inventory .... 100 units at $28 per unit
Purchases:
   February 12 .... 100 units at $30 per unit
   April 30 .... 400 units at $32 per unit
   August 3 .... 300 units at $33 per unit
   December 15 .... 100 units at $35 per unit

Required:

Under the assumption the company's selling and administrative expenses were $10 per unit sold, prepare a comparative income statement for the company showing in adjacent columns the net income earned from the sale of the product with the ending inventory priced on the basis of *(a)* Fifo, *(b)* Lifo, and *(c)* weighted-average cost.

Problem 8–2A

A concern began an accounting period with 200 units of a product that cost $40 each, and it made successive purchases of the product as follows:

Jan. 10 500 units @ $50 each
Apr. 27 600 units @ $55 each
Aug. 22 300 units @ $60 each
Oct. 15 400 units @ $55 each

Required:

1. Prepare a calculation showing the number and total cost of the units for sale during the period.
2. Under the assumption the company had 500 units of the product in its December 31 end of the period periodic inventory, prepare calculations to show the portions of the total cost of the units for sale during the period that should be assigned to the ending inventory and to the units sold *(a)* first on a Fifo basis, *(b)* then on a Lifo basis, and *(c)* finally on a weighted-average cost basis.

Problem 8–3A

A company's inventory records for one of its products showed the following transactions:

Jan. 1 Beginning inventory: 15 units costing $35 each.
  10 Purchased 10 units at $40 each.
  16 Sold five units.
  18 Sold eight units.
  20 Purchased 10 units at $45 each.
  25 Sold 14 units.

Required:

1. Assume the company keeps its records on a Fifo basis and enter the transactions on a perpetual inventory record card. Use two or more lines to show units on hand at each price or units sold when units costing different amounts are on hand or sold.

2. Assume the company keeps its records on a Lifo basis and record the transactions on a second record card.

3. Assume the last sale was on credit to Lee Barr for $900 and prepare an entry in general journal form to record the sale and cost of goods sold on a Fifo basis.

Problem 8–4A

A specialty shop has the following information from its records and from a year-end physical inventory at marked selling prices:

	At cost	At retail
January 1, beginning inventory	$ 23,980	$ 33,440
Purchases	166,290	232,920
Purchases returns	2,110	3,190
Additional markups		5,630
Markdowns.......................		2,180
Sales		235,450
Sales returns		1,230

The shop reduces its year-end physical inventory taken at marked selling prices to a cost basis by an application of the retail inventory method. However, the shop always estimates its year-end inventory by the retail method and by comparison determines the amount of inventory shortage, if any.

Required:

1. Prepare a calculation to estimate the shop's year-end inventory at cost.
2. Under the assumption the shop's year-end physical inventory at marked selling prices totaled $31,300, prepare a calculation showing the amount of its inventory shortage at cost and at retail.

Problem 8–5A

Berg Company's records provide the following information for the year ended last December 31:

	At cost	At retail
Sales		$321,250
Sales returns		2,440
January 1 inventory	$ 31,940	46,290
Purchases........................	218,240	316,420
Purchases returns	2,320	3,390
Additional markups		5,180
Markdowns		3,940
December 31 physical inventory		40,250

Required:

1. Use the retail method to prepare a calculation estimating Berg Company's year-end inventory at cost.
2. Prepare a calculation showing the amount of its inventory shortage at cost and at retail.

Problem 8–6A

Valley Auto Parts suffered a disastrous fire during the night of April 5, and everything excepting the accounting records, which were in a fireproof vault, was destroyed. As an insurance adjuster, you have been called upon to determine the store's inventory loss. The following information is available from the store's accounting records.

Merchandise inventory on January 1	$ 33,150
Purchases, January 1 through April 5	92,215
Purchases returns for the same period	410
Freight on purchases for the period	1,285
Sales, January 1 through April 5	138,975
Sales returns and allowances	475
Average gross profit margin past five years ..	34%

Required:

Use the gross profit method to prepare a statement estimating the store's inventory loss.

Problem 8–7A

Cornelia, the owner and manager of Cornelia's Fur Salon, opened her shop on Monday morning, April 9, and discovered that thieves had broken in over the weekend and made off with the shop's entire inventory. Fortunately it was near the end of the season and the inventory was low. Nevertheless, as an insurance adjuster, you have been called upon to determine the loss. The following information is available from the shop's accounting records, which were closed the previous December 31.

Merchandise inventory, January 1	$ 75,410
Purchases	92,850
Purchases returns	1,730
Freight-in	880
Sales	178,480
Sales returns	2,230
Average gross profit rate for past four years ..	38%

Required:

Prepare a calculation estimating the shop's inventory loss.

PROVOCATIVE PROBLEMS

Provocative Problem 8–1
Fashion Footwear, Ltd.

Fashion Footwear, Ltd., suffered extensive damage from water and smoke and a small amount of fire damage on the night of October 12. The store carried adequate insurance, and next morning the insurance company's claims agent arrived to inspect the damage. After completing a survey, the agent agreed with Dale Eble, the store's owner, that the inventory could be sold to a company specializing in fire sales for about one fifth of its cost. The agent offered Mr. Eble $20,000 in full settlement for the damage to the inventory. He suggested that Mr. Eble accept the offer and said he had authority to deliver at once a check for the amount of the damage. He pointed out that a prompt settlement would provide funds to replace the inventory in time for the store to participate in the Christmas shopping season.

Mr. Eble felt the loss might exceed $20,000 but he recognized that a time-consuming physical count and inspection of each item in the inventory would be necessary to establish the loss more precisely; and he was reluctant to take the time for the inventory, since he was anxious to get back into business before the Christmas rush, the season making the largest contribution to his annual profit. Yet he was also unwilling to take a substantial loss on the insurance settlement; so he asked for and received a 24-hour period in which to consider the insurance company offer, and he immediately went to his records for the following information:

		At cost	At retail
a.	January 1 inventory	$ 23,480	$ 37,100
	Purchases, January 1 through October 12 .	181,900	288,700
	Net sales, January 1 through October 12 ..		282,200

b. On March 1 the remaining inventory of winter footwear was marked down from $12,000 to $9,600, and placed on sale in the annual end-of-the-winter-season sale. Three fourths of the shoes were sold; the markdown on the remainder was canceled, and the shoes were returned to their regular retail price. (A markdown cancellation is subtracted from a markdown, and a markup cancellation is subtracted from a markup.)

c. In June a special line of imported Italian shoes proved popular, and 60 high-styled pairs were marked up from their normal $40 retail price to $45 per pair. Forty pairs were sold at this higher price, and on August 1 the markup on the remaining 20 pairs was canceled and they were returned to their regular $40 per pair price.

d. Between January 1 and October 12 markdowns totaling $1,500 were taken on several odd lots of shoes.

Recommend whether or not you think Mr. Eble should accept the insurance company's offer. Back your recommendation with figures.

Provocative problem 8–2
Barr's Home Store

Barr's Home Store has been in business for five years, during which it has earned a 35% average annual gross profit on sales. However, night before last, on May 5, it suffered a disastrous fire that destroyed its entire inventory; and Ed Barr, the store's owner, has filed a $56,000 inventory loss claim with the store's insurance company. When asked on what he based his claim, he replied that during the day before the fire he had marked every item in the store down 20% in preparation for the annual summer clearance sale, and during the marking-down process he had also taken an inventory of the merchandise in the store. Furthermore, he said, "It's a big loss, but every cloud has a silver lining because I am giving you fellows (the insurance company) the benefit of the 20% markdown in filing this claim."

When it was explained to Mr. Barr that he had to back his loss claim with more than his word as to the amount of the loss, he produced the following information from his pre-sale inventory and his accounting records, which fortunately were in a fireproof vault and were not destroyed in the fire.

a.   The store's accounts were closed on December 31, of last year.

b.   After all posting was completed, the accounts showed these May 5 balances:

Sales	$189,860
Sales returns	4,760
Purchases.......................................	119,800
Purchases returns	1,450
Freight-in	3,140
Merchandise inventory (January 1, balance)	44,370

c.   Mr. Barr's pre-fire inventory totaled $70,000 at pre-markdown prices.

Required:

1.   Prepare a calculation showing the estimated amount of Mr. Barr's inventory loss.
2.   Present figures showing how Mr. Barr arrived at the amount of his loss claim.
3.   Present figures based on the amount of Mr. Barr's pre-fire inventory figure, $70,000, to substantiate the inventory estimate arrived at in Part 1 above.

9

Plant and equipment, natural resources, and intangible assets

After studying Chapter 9, you should be able to:

- Tell what is included in the cost of a plant asset.
- Calculate depreciation by the *(a)* straight-line, *(b)* units-of-production, *(c)* declining-balance, and *(d)* sum-of-the-years'-digits methods.
- Make the calculations and prepare the entries to account for revisions in depreciation rates.
- Make the calculations and prepare the entries to account for plant asset repairs and betterments.
- Prepare entries to record the purchase and disposal of plant assets.
- Prepare entries to record the exchange of plant assets under accounting rules and under income tax rules and tell which rules should be applied in any given exchange.
- Prepare entries to account for wasting assets and for intangible assets.
- Define or explain the words and phrases listed in the chapter Glossary.

Assets used in the production or sale of other assets or services and that have a useful life longer than one accounting period are called *plant and equipment* or *fixed assets*. The phrase "fixed assets" has been used in accounting literature for many years in referring to items of plant and equipment. It was once commonly used as a balance sheet caption. However, as a caption it is rapidly disappearing from published balance sheets.

Use in the production or sale of other assets or services is the characteristic that distinguishes a plant asset from an item of merchandise or an investment. An office machine or a factory machine held for sale by a dealer is merchandise to the dealer. Likewise, land purchased and held for future expansion but presently unused is classified as a long-term investment. Neither is a plant asset until put to use in the production or sale of other assets or services. However, standby equipment for use in case of a breakdown or for use during peak periods of production is a plant asset.

COST OF A PLANT ASSET

The cost of a plant asset consists of all normal, necessary, and reasonable costs incurred in getting the asset in place and ready to produce. For example, the cost of a factory machine includes its invoice price, less any discount for cash, plus freight, unpacking, and assembling costs. For a secondhand machine that must be repaired, reconditioned, or remodeled, the expenditures for repairing, reconditioning, and remodeling are part of its cost. Likewise, in the case of land purchased as a building site and having an old building that must be removed, cost consists of the entire purchase price, including the cost of the to-be-removed building, plus the cost of removing the building, but less any amount recovered through the sale of salvaged material from the building.

A cost must be normal and reasonable as well as necessary if it is to be properly included in the cost of a plant asset. For example, if a machine is damaged by being dropped in unpacking, repairs should not be added to its cost. They should be charged to an expense account. Likewise, a fine paid for moving a heavy machine on city streets without proper permits is not part of the cost of the machine. However, if secured, the cost of the permits would be.

Often land, buildings, and equipment are purchased together for one lump sum. When this occurs, the purchase price must be apportioned among the assets on some fair basis, since some of the assets depreciate and some do not. A fair basis may be tax-assessed values or appraised values. For example, assume that land independently appraised at $30,000 and a building appraised at $70,000 are purchased together for $90,000. The cost may be apportioned on the basis of appraised values as follows:

	Appraised value	Percent of total	Apportioned cost
Land	$ 30,000	30%	$27,000
Building	70,000	70	63,000
Totals	$100,000	100%	$90,000

NATURE OF DEPRECIATION

When a plant asset is purchased, in effect a quantity of usefulness that will contribute to production throughout the service life of the asset is acquired. However, since the life of any plant asset (other than land) is limited, this quantity of usefulness is also limited and will in effect be consumed by the end of the asset's service life. Consequently, depreciation, as the term is used in accounting, is nothing more than the expiration of a plant asset's quantity of usefulness. Also, the recording of depreciation is a process of allocating and charging the cost of this usefulness to the accounting periods that benefit from the asset's use.

For example, when a company purchases an automobile to be used by one of its salespeople, it in effect purchases a quantity of usefulness, a quantity of transportation for the salesperson. The cost of this quantity of usefulness is the cost of the car less whatever will be received for it when sold or traded in at the end of its service life. And, recording depreciation on the car is a process of allocating the cost of this usefulness to the accounting periods that benefit from the car's use. Note that it is not the recording of physical deterioration nor recording the decline in the car's market value.

SERVICE LIFE OF A PLANT ASSET

The *service life* of a plant asset is the period of time it will be used in producing or selling other assets or services. This may not be the same as the asset's potential life. For example, typewriters have a potential six- or eight-year life. However, if a company finds from a production-cost view that it is wise to trade its old typewriters on new ones every three years, in this company typewriters have a three-year service life. Furthermore, in this business the cost of new typewriters less their trade-in value should be charged to depreciation expense over this three-year period.

Predicting the service life of an asset is sometimes difficult because several factors are often involved. Wear and tear and the action of the elements determine the useful life of some assets. However, two additional factors, *inadequacy* and *obsolescence,* often need be considered. When a business acquires plant assets, it should acquire assets of sufficient capacity to take care of its foreseeable needs. However, a business often grows more rapidly than anticipated. In such cases plant asset capacity may become too small for the productive demands of the business long before the assets wear out. When this happens, inadequacy is said to have taken place. Inadequacy cannot easily be predicted. Obsolescence is also difficult to foretell because the exact occurrence of new inventions and improvements normally cannot be predicted. Yet, new inventions and improvements often cause an asset to become obsolete and make it wise to discard the obsolete asset long before it wears out.

A company that has previously used a particular type of asset may estimate the service life of a new asset of like kind from past experience. A company without previous experience must depend upon the experience of others or upon engineering studies and judgment. The Internal Revenue Service publishes information giving estimated service lives for hundreds of assets. Many concerns refer to this information in estimating the life of a new asset.

SALVAGE VALUE

The total amount an asset may be depreciated over its service life is its cost minus its *salvage value.* Some assets such as typewriters, trucks, and some machines are traded in on similar new assets at the ends of their service lives. The salvage value of each such asset is its trade-in value. Other assets are sold at the ends of their service lives. In each such case the net amount realized is the asset's salvage value. Often in the case of a machine the cost to remove the machine will equal the amount that can be realized from its sale. In such a case the machine has no salvage value.

ALLOCATING DEPRECIATION

Many methods of allocating a plant asset's total depreciation to the several accounting periods in its service life have been suggested and are used. Four of the more common are the *straight-line method,* the *units-of-production method*, the *declining-balance method*, and the *sum-of-the-years'-digits method*. Each is acceptable and falls within the realm of *generally accepted accounting principles*.

Straight-line method

When the straight-line method is used, the cost of the asset minus its estimated salvage value is divided by the estimated number of accounting periods in the asset's service life. The result is the estimated amount the asset depreciates each period. For example, if a machine costs $550, has an estimated service life of five years, and an estimated $50 salvage value, its depreciation per year by the straight-line method is $100 and is calculated as follows:

$$\frac{\text{Cost} - \text{Salvage}}{\text{Service life in years}} = \frac{\$550 - \$50}{5} = \$100$$

Note that the straight-line method allocates an equal share of an asset's total depreciation to each accounting period in its life.

Units-of-production method

The purpose of recording depreciation is to charge each accounting period in which an asset is used with a fair share of its depreciation. The straight-line method charges an equal share to each period; and when plant assets are used about the same amount in each accounting period, this method rather fairly allocates total depreciation. However, in some lines of business the use of certain plant assets varies greatly from accounting period to accounting period. For example, a contractor may use a particular piece of construction equipment for a month and then not use it again for many months. For such an asset, since use and contribution to revenue may not be uniform from period to period, it is argued that the units-of-production method better meets the requirements of the *matching principle* than does the straight-line method.

When the units-of-production method is used in allocating depreciation, the cost of an asset minus its estimated salvage value is divided by the estimated units of product it will produce during its entire service life. This division gives depreciation per unit of product. Then the amount the asset is depreciated in any one accounting period is determined by multiplying the units of product produced in that period by depreciation per unit. Units of product may be expressed as units of product or in any other unit of measure such as hours of use or miles driven. For example, a truck costing $6,000 is estimated to have a $2,000 salvage value. If it is also estimated that during the truck's service life it will be driven 50,000 miles, the depreciation per mile, or the depreciation per unit of product, is $0.08 and is calculated as follows:

$$\frac{\text{Cost} - \text{Salvage value}}{\text{Estimated units of production}} = \frac{\text{Depreciation per}}{\text{unit of product}}$$

or

$$\frac{\$6,000 - \$2,000}{50,000 \text{ miles}} = \$0.08 \text{ per mile}$$

If these estimates are used and the truck is driven 20,000 miles during its first year, depreciation for the first year is $1,600. This is 20,000 miles at $0.08 per mile. If the truck is driven 15,000 miles in the second year, depreciation for the second year is 15,000 times $0.08, or $1,200.

Declining-balance method

The *Internal Revenue Code* permits depreciation methods for tax purposes which result in higher depreciation charges during the early years of a plant asset's life. These methods are also used in preparing financial reports to investors. The declining-balance method is one of these. Under this method, depreciation of up to twice the straight-line rate, without considering salvage value, may be applied each year to the declining book value of a new plant asset having an estimated life of three years or more. If this method is followed and twice the straight-line rate is used, depreciation on an asset is determined by (1) calculating a straight-line depreciation rate for the asset. Next, (2) double this rate. Then, (3) at the end of each year in the asset's life, this doubled rate is applied to the asset's remaining *book value*. (The book value of a plant asset is its cost less accumulated depreciation; it is the value shown for the asset on the books.)

If this method is used to charge depreciation on a $10,000 new asset that has an estimated five-year life and no salvage value, these steps are followed: (Step 1) A straight-line depreciation rate is calculated by dividing 100% by five (years) to determine the straight-line annual depreciation rate of 20%. Next (Step 2) this rate is doubled; and then (Step 3) annual depreciation charges are calculated as in the following table:

Year	Annual depreciation calculation	Annual depreciation expense	Remaining book value
1st year	40% of $10,000	$4,000.00	$6,000.00
2d year	40% of 6,000	2,400.00	3,600.00
3d year	40% of 3,600	1,440.00	2,160.00
4th year	40% of 2,160	864.00	1,296.00
5th year	40% of 1,296	518.40	777.60

Under the declining-balance method the book value of a plant asset never reaches zero. Consequently, when the asset is sold, exchanged, or scrapped, any remaining book value is used in determining the gain or loss on the disposal. However, if an asset has a salvage value, the asset may not be depreciated beyond its salvage value. For example, if instead of no salvage value the foregoing $10,000 asset has an estimated $1,000 salvage value, depreciation for its fifth year is limited to $296. This is the amount required to reduce the asset's book value to its salvage value.

Declining-balance depreciation results in what is called *accelerated depreciation* or higher depreciation charges in the early years of a plant asset's life. The sum-of-the-years'-digits method has a like result.

Sum-of-the-years'-digits method

Under the sum-of-the-years'-digits method the years in an asset's service life are added. Then their sum becomes the denominator of a series of fractions used in allocating total depreciation to the periods in the asset's service life. The numerators of the fractions are the years in the asset's life in their reverse order. For example, assume this method is used in allocating depreciation on a machine costing $7,000, having an estimated five-year life and an estimated $1,000 salvage value. The sum of the years' digits in the asset's life are:

$$1 + 2 + 3 + 4 + 5 = 15$$

and annual depreciation charges are calculated as follows:

Year	Annual depreciation calculation	Annual depreciation expense
1st year	$5/15$ of $6,000	$2,000
2d year	$4/15$ of 6,000	1,600
3d year	$3/15$ of 6,000	1,200
4th year	$2/15$ of 6,000	800
5th year	$1/15$ of 6,000	400
Total depreciation		$6,000

When a plant asset has a long life, the sum of the years' digits in its life may be calculated by using the formula: $SYD = n[(n + 1)/2]$. For example, sum of the years' digits for a five-year life is: $5\left(\dfrac{5 + 1}{2}\right) = 15$.

ACCELERATED DEPRECIATION AND TAXES

The use of declining-balance and sum-of-the-years'-digits depreciation has significantly increased in recent years because both offer a tax advantage. The tax advantage is that both *defer the payment of income taxes* from the early years of a plant asset's life until its later years. Taxes are deferred because accelerated depreciation causes larger amounts of depreciation to be charged to the early years. This results in smaller amounts of income and income taxes in these years. However, the taxes are only deferred because offsetting smaller amounts of depreciation are charged in later years, which results in larger amounts of income and taxes in these years. Nevertheless, through accelerated depreciation a company does have the "interest-free" use of the deferred tax dollars until the later years of a plant asset's life.

PLANT ASSETS ON THE BALANCE SHEET

From the discussion thus far it should be recognized that the recording of depreciation is not primarily a valuing process. Rather it is a process of allocating the costs of plant assets to the several accounting periods that benefit from their use. Also, since the recording of depreciation is an allocating process rather than a valuing process, balance sheets show for plant assets unallocated costs or undepreciated costs rather than market values.

In presenting information about plant assets, the *full-disclosure principle* requires and the APB ruled that both the cost of such assets and their accumulated depreciation be shown in the statements by major plant asset classes. In addition, a general description of the depreciation method or methods used must be given in a balance sheet footnote or other manner.[1] When such information is given, a much better understanding can be gained by a balance sheet reader than if only net undepreciated costs are given. For example, $50,000 of assets with $40,000 of accumulated depreciation are quite different from $10,000 of new assets, although they both have the same book value. Likewise, the picture is different if the $40,000 of accumulated depreciation resulted from accelerated depreciation rather than straight-line depreciation.

DEPRECIATION FOR PARTIAL YEARS

Plant assets are normally bought when needed and disposed of when they are no longer usable or needed. Consequently, when an asset is

---

[1] APB, "Omnibus Opinion—1967," *APB Opinion No. 12* (New York: AICPA, December 1967), par. 5.

acquired at other than the beginning of an accounting period or disposed of at other than the end of a period, depreciation must be recorded for part of a year. Otherwise neither the year of purchase nor the year of disposal is charged with its share of the asset's depreciation. For example, if a machine costing $4,600 and having an estimated five-year service life and a $600 salvage value is purchased on October 8 and the annual accounting period ends on December 31, three months' depreciation on the machine must be recorded on the latter date. Three months are three twelfths of a year. Consequently, if straight-line depreciation is in use, the three months' depreciation is calculated as follows:

$$\frac{\$4,600 - \$600}{5} \times \frac{3}{12} = \$200$$

Note that depreciation was calculated for a full three months, even though the asset was purchased on October 8. Depreciation is an estimate; therefore, calculation to the nearest full month is usually sufficiently accurate. This means that depreciation is usually calculated for a full month on assets purchased before the 15th of the month. Likewise, depreciation for the month of purchase is normally disregarded if the asset is purchased after the middle of the month.

When units-of-production depreciation is in use, calculating depreciation for part of a year presents no problem. It simply depends upon the number of units produced during the period. However, more complicated calculations are necessary for sum-of-the-years'-digits and declining-balance depreciation. To illustrate, assume that the machine for which sum-of-the-years'-digits depreciation was calculated on page 314 is placed in use on April 1 and the annual accounting periods of the company owning the machine end on December 31. Under these assumptions the machine will be in use three fourths of a year during the first accounting period in its life. As a result, this period should be charged with $1,500 depreciation ($2,000 × ¾ = $1,500). Likewise, the second accounting period should be charged with $1,700 depreciation [(¼ × $2,000) + (¾ × $1,600) = $1,700]. And like calculations should be used for the remaining periods in the asset's life.

REVISING DEPRECIATION RATES

An occasional error in estimating the useful life of a plant asset is to be expected. Furthermore, when such an error is discovered, it is corrected by spreading the remaining amount the asset is to be depreciated over its remaining useful life.[2] For example, seven years ago a machine was purchased at a cost of $10,500. At that time the machine

---

[2] APB, "Accounting Changes," *APB Opinion No. 20* (New York: AICPA, July 1971), par. 31.

was estimated to have a ten-year life with a $500 salvage value. There-fore, it was depreciated at the rate of $1,000 per year [($10,-500 − $500) ÷ 10 = $1,000]; and it began its eighth year with a $3,500 book value, calculated as follows:

Cost	$10,500
Less seven years' accumulated depreciation	7,000
Book value	$ 3,500

Assume that at the beginning of its eighth year the estimated num-ber of years remaining in this machine's useful life is changed from three to five years with no change in salvage value. Under this assump-tion, depreciation for each of the machine's remaining years should be recalculated as follows:

$$\frac{\text{Book value} - \text{Salvage value}}{\text{Remaining useful life}} = \frac{\$3,500 - \$500}{5 \text{ years}} = \$600 \text{ per year}$$

And $600 of depreciation should be recorded on the machine at the end of the eighth and each succeeding year in its life.

If depreciation is charged at the rate of $1,000 per year for the first seven years of this machine's life and $600 per year for the next five, depreciation expense is overstated during the first seven years and understated during the next five. However, if a concern has many plant assets, the lives of some will be underestimated and the lives of others will be overestimated at the time of purchase. Consequently, such errors will tend to cancel each other out with little or no effect on the income statement.

CONTROL OF PLANT ASSETS

Good internal control for plant assets requires specific identification of each plant asset and formal records. It also requires periodic invento-ries in which each plant asset carried in the records is identified and its continued existence and use are verified. For identification purposes, each plant asset is commonly assigned a serial number at the time it is acquired. The number is stamped, etched, or affixed to the plant asset with a small decal not easily removed or altered. The exact kind of records kept depends upon the size of the business and the number of its plant assets. They range from handwritten records to punched cards and computer tapes. However, regardless of their nature, all provide the same basic information contained in the handwritten re-cords which follow.

In keeping plant asset records, concerns normally divide their plant assets into functional groups and provide in their General Ledger sepa-

Office Equipment   ACCOUNT NO. 132

DATE	EXPLANATION	POST. REF.	DEBIT	CREDIT	BALANCE
198A July 2	Desk and chair	G1	5 3 3 00		5 3 3 00

Accumulated Depreciation, Office Equipment   ACCOUNT NO. 132A

DATE	EXPLANATION	POST. REF.	DEBIT	CREDIT	BALANCE
198A Dec. 31		G23		2 1 00	2 1 00
198B Dec. 31		G42		4 2 00	6 3 00
198C Dec. 31		G65		4 2 00	1 0 5 00

Plant Asset
No. *132-1*

SUBSIDIARY PLANT ASSET AND DEPRECIATION RECORD

Item _Office chair_   General Ledger Account _Office Equipment_

Description _Office chair_

Mfg. Serial No. _____   Purchased from _Office Equipment Co._

Where Located _Office_

Person Responsible for the Asset _Office Manager_

Estimated Life _12 years_ Estimated Salvage Value _$4.00_

Depreciation per Year _$6.00_ per Month _$0.50_

Date	Explanation	P R	Asset Record			Depreciation Record		
			Dr.	Cr.	Bal.	Dr.	Cr.	Bal.
July 2, 198A		G1	76.00		76.00			
Dec. 31, 198A		G23					3.00	3.00
Dec. 31, 198B		G42					6.00	9.00
Dec. 31, 198C		G65					6.00	15.00

Final Disposition of the Asset _____

Illustration 9-1

Plant Asset
No. *132-2*

SUBSIDIARY PLANT ASSET AND DEPRECIATION RECORD
General Ledger
Item *Desk*   Account *Office Equipment*
Description *Office desk*

Purchased
Mfg. Serial No. _____   from *Office Equipment Co.*
Where Located *Office*
Person Responsible for the Asset *Office Manager*
Estimated Life *12 years*   Estimated Salvage Value *$25.00*
Depreciation per Year *$36.00* per Month *$3.00*

Date	Explanation	P R	Asset Record			Depreciation Record		
			Dr.	Cr.	Bal.	Dr.	Cr.	Bal.
July 2, 198A		G1	457.00		457.00			
Dec. 31, 198A		G23					18.00	18.00
Dec. 31, 198B		G42					36.00	54.00
Dec. 31, 198C		G65					36.00	90.00

Final Disposition of the Asset _____

Illustration 9–1 *(continued)*

rate asset and accumulated depreciation accounts for each group. Furthermore, each plant asset account and its related accumulated depreciation account is normally a controlling account controlling detailed subsidiary records. For example, in a store the Store Equipment account and the Accumulated Depreciation, Store Equipment account control a subsidiary ledger having a separate record for each individual item of store equipment. Likewise, the same holds true for the Office Equipment account and the Accumulated Depreciation, Office Equipment account.

In a handwritten system the subsidiary records are kept on plant asset record cards. To illustrate these cards and the controlling accounts, assume that a concern's office equipment consists of just one desk and a chair. The general ledger record for these assets is maintained in the Office Equipment account and the Accumulated Depreciation, Office Equipment account. Both are controlling accounts controlling sections of the subsidiary record cards for the desk and chair. The general ledger and subsidiary ledger records of these assets are shown in Illustration 9–1.

Observe at the top of the cards the plant asset numbers assigned to these two items of office equipment. In each case the assigned number consists of the number of the Office Equipment account, 132, followed by the asset's number. As previously said, these numbers are stenciled on or otherwise attached to the items of office equipment as a means of identification. The remaining information on the cards is more or less self-evident. Note how the balance of the general ledger account, Office Equipment, is equal to the sum of the balances in the asset record section of the two subsidiary ledger cards. The general ledger account controls this section of the subsidiary ledger. Observe also how the Accumulated Depreciation, Office Equipment account controls the depreciation record section of the cards. The disposition section at the bottom of the card is used to record the final disposal of the asset. When the asset is discarded, sold, or exchanged, a notation telling of the final disposition is entered here. The card is then removed from the subsidiary ledger and filed for future reference.

PLANT ASSETS OF LOW COST

Because individual plant asset records are expensive to keep, many concerns establish a minimum, say $50 or $100, and do not keep such records for assets costing less than the minimum. Rather, they charge the cost of such plant assets directly to an expense account at the time of purchase. Furthermore, if about the same amount is expended for such assets each year, this is acceptable under the *materiality principle.*

ORDINARY AND EXTRAORDINARY REPAIRS

Repairs made to keep an asset in its normal good state of repair are classified as *ordinary repairs.* A building must be repainted and its roof repaired. A machine must be cleaned, oiled, adjusted, and have any worn small parts replaced. Such repairs and maintenance are necessary, and their costs should appear on the current income statement as an expense.

Extraordinary repairs are major repairs made, not to keep an asset in its normal good state of repair but to extend its service life beyond that originally estimated. As a rule, the cost of such repairs should be debited to the repaired asset's accumulated depreciation account under the assumption they make good past depreciation, add to the asset's useful life, and benefit future periods. For example, a machine was purchased for $8,000 and depreciated under the assumption it would last eight years and have no salvage value. As a result, at the end of the machine's sixth year its book value is $2,000, calculated as follows:

Cost of machine	$8,000
Less six years' accumulated depreciation	6,000
Book value	$2,000

If at the beginning of the machine's seventh year a major overhaul extends its estimated useful life three years beyond the eight originally estimated, the $2,100 cost should be recorded as follows:

Jan.	12	Accumulated Depreciation, Machinery	2,100.00	
		Cash (or Accounts Payable)		2,100.00
		To record extraordinary repairs.		

In addition, depreciation for each of the five years remaining in the machine's life should be calculated as follows:

Book value before extraordinary repairs	$2,000
Extraordinary repairs	2,100
Total	$4,100
Annual depreciation expense for remaining years ($4,100 ÷ 5 years)	$ 820

And, if the machine remains in use for five years after the major overhaul, the five annual $820 depreciation charges will exactly write off its new book value, including the cost of the extraordinary repairs.

BETTERMENTS

A *betterment* may be defined as the replacement of an existing plant asset portion with an improved or superior portion, usually at a cost materially in excess of the replaced item. Replacing the manual controls on a machine with automatic controls is an example. Usually a betterment results in a better, more efficient, or more productive asset, but not necessarily one having a longer life. When a betterment is made, its cost should be debited to the improved asset's account, say, the Machinery account, and depreciated over the remaining service life of the asset. Also, the cost and applicable depreciation of the replaced asset portion should be removed from the accounts.

CAPITAL AND REVENUE EXPENDITURES

A *revenue expenditure* is one that should appear on the current income statement as an expense and a deduction from the period's revenues. Expenditures for ordinary repairs, rent, and salaries are examples. Expenditures for betterments and for extraordinary repairs, on the other hand, are examples of what are called *capital expenditures* or *balance sheet expenditures*. They should appear on the balance sheet as asset increases.

Obviously, care must be exercised to distinguish between capital and revenue expenditures when transactions are recorded. For if errors are made, such errors often affect a number of accounting periods. For instance, an expenditure for a betterment initially recorded in error as an expense overstates expenses in the year of the error and understates net income. Also, since the cost of a betterment should be depreciated over the remaining useful life of the bettered asset, depreciation expense of future periods is understated and net income is overstated.

PLANT ASSET DISPOSALS

Sooner or later a plant asset wears out, becomes obsolete, or becomes inadequate. When this occurs, the asset is discarded, sold, or traded in on a new asset. The entry to record the disposal will vary with its nature.

Discarding a plant asset

When an asset's accumulated depreciation is equal to its cost, the asset is said to be fully depreciated; and if a fully depreciated asset is discarded, the entry to record the disposal is:

Jan.	7	Accumulated Depreciation, Machinery	1,500.00	
		Machinery		1,500.00
		Discarded a fully depreciated machine.		

Although often discarded, sometimes a fully depreciated asset is kept in use. In such situations the asset's cost and accumulated depreciation should not be removed from the accounts but should remain on the books until the asset is sold, traded, or discarded. Otherwise the accounts do not show its continued existence. However, no additional depreciation should be recorded, since the reason for recording depreciation is to charge an asset's cost to depreciation expense. In no case should the expense exceed the asset's cost.

Sometimes an asset is discarded before being fully depreciated. For example, suppose an error was made in estimating the service life of a $1,000 machine and it becomes worthless and is discarded after having only $800 of depreciation recorded against it. In such a situation there is a loss and the entry to record the disposal is:

Jan.	10	Loss on Disposal of Machinery	200.00	
		Accumulated Depreciation, Machinery	800.00	
		Machinery.............................		1,000.00
		Discarded a worthless machine.		

Discarding a damaged plant asset

Occasionally, before the end of its service life, a plant asset is wrecked in an accident or destroyed by fire. For example, a machine that cost $900 and which had been depreciated $400 was totally destroyed in a fire. If the loss was partially covered by insurance and the insurance company paid $350 to settle the loss claim, the entry to record the machine's destruction is:

Jan.	12	Cash	350.00	
		Loss from Fire.............................	150.00	
		Accumulated Depreciation, Machinery	400.00	
		Machinery.............................		900.00
		To record the destruction of machinery and the receipt of insurance compensation.		

If the machine were uninsured, the entry to record its destruction would not have a debit to Cash and the loss from fire would be greater.

Selling a plant asset

When a plant asset is sold, if the selling price exceeds the asset's book value, there is a gain. If the price is less than book value, there is a loss. For example, assume that a machine which cost $5,000 and had been depreciated $4,000 is sold for a price in excess of its book value, say for $1,200. If the machine is sold for $1,200, there is a gain and the entry to record the sale is:

Jan.	4	Cash	1,200.00	
		Accumulated Depreciation, Machinery	4,000.00	
		Machinery.............................		5,000.00
		Gain on the Sale of Plant Assets		200.00
		Sold a machine at a price in excess of book value.		

However, if the machine is sold for $750, there is a $250 loss and the entry to record the sale is:

Jan.	4	Cash	750.00	
		Loss on the Sale of Plant Assets	250.00	
		Accumulated Depreciation, Machinery	4,000.00	
		Machinery		5,000.00
		Sold a machine at a price below book value.		

EXCHANGING PLANT ASSETS

Some plant assets are sold at the ends of their useful lives. Others, such as machinery, automobiles, and office equipment, are commonly exchanged for new up-to-date assets of like purpose. In such exchanges a trade-in allowance is normally received on the old asset, with the balance being paid in cash. The APB ruled that in recording the exchanges a material book loss should be recognized in the accounts but a book gain should not.[3] A book loss is experienced when the trade-in allowance is less than the book value of the traded asset. A book gain results from a trade-in allowance that exceeds the book value of the traded asset.

Recognizing a material book loss

To illustrate recognition of a material book loss on an exchange of plant assets, assume that a machine which cost $18,000 and had been depreciated $15,000 was traded in on a new machine having a $21,000 cash price. A $1,000 trade-in allowance was received, and the $20,000 balance was paid in cash. Under these assumptions the book value of the old machine is $3,000, calculated as follows:

Cost of old machine	$18,000
Less accumulated depreciation	15,000
Book value	$ 3,000

And since the $1,000 trade-in allowance resulted in a $2,000 loss on the exchange, the transaction should be recorded as follows:

---

[3] APB, "Accounting for Nonmonetary Transactions," *APB Opinion No. 29* (New York: AICPA, May 1973), par. 22.

Jan.	5	Machinery...............................	21,000.00	
		Loss on Exchange of Machinery	2,000.00	
		Accumulated Depreciation, Machinery	15,000.00	
		Machinery.............................		18,000.00
		Cash		20,000.00
		Exchanged old machine and cash for a new machine of like purpose.		

The $21,000 debit to Machinery puts the new machine in the accounts at its cash price. The debit to Loss on Exchange of Machinery records the loss. The old machine is removed from the accounts with the $15,000 debit to accumulated depreciation and the $18,000 credit to Machinery.

Nonrecognition of a book gain

When there is a book gain on an exchange of plant assets, the APB ruled that the new asset should be taken into the accounts at an amount equal to the book value of the traded-in asset plus the cash given. This results in the nonrecognition of the gain. For example, assume that in acquiring the $21,000 machine of the previous section a $4,500 trade-in allowance, rather than a $1,000 trade-in allowance, was received, and the $16,500 balance was paid in cash. A $4,500 trade-in allowance would result in a $1,500 gain on the exchange. However, in recording the exchange, the book gain should not be recognized in the accounts. Rather, it should be absorbed into the cost of the new machine by taking the new machine into the accounts at an amount equal to the sum of the book value of the old machine plus the cash given. This is $19,500 and is calculated as follows:

Book value of old machine	$ 3,000
Cash given in the exchange	16,500
Cost basis for the new machine....	$19,500

And the transaction should be recorded as follows:

Jan.	5	Machinery...............................	19,500.00	
		Accumulated Depreciation, Machinery	15,000.00	
		Machinery.............................		18,000.00
		Cash		16,500.00
		Exchanged old machine and cash for a new machine of like purpose.		

Observe that the $19,500 recorded amount for the new machine is equal to its cash price less the $1,500 book gain on the exchange ($21,000 − $1,500 = $19,500). In other words, the $1,500 book gain was absorbed into the amount at which the new machine was recorded. The $19,500 is called the *cost basis* of the new machine and is the amount used in recording depreciation on the machine or any gain or loss on its sale.

The APB based its ruling that gains on plant asset exchanges should not be recognized on the opinion that ". . . revenue should not be recognized merely because one productive asset is substituted for a similar productive asset but rather should be considered to flow from the production and sale of the goods or services to which the substituted productive asset is committed."[4] In other words, the APB's opinion was that any gain from a plant asset exchange should be taken in the form of increased net income resulting from smaller depreciation charges on the asset acquired. In this case depreciation calculated on the recorded $19,500 cost basis of the new machine is less than if calculated on the machine's $21,000 cash price.

Tax rules and plant asset exchanges

Income tax rules and accounting principles are in agreement on the treatment of gains on plant asset exchanges but do not agree on the treatment of losses. According to the Internal Revenue Service, when an old asset is traded in on a new asset of like purpose, either a gain or a loss on the exchange must be absorbed into the cost of the new machine. This cost basis then becomes for tax purposes the amount that must be used in calculating depreciation on the new asset or any gain or loss on its sale or exchange. Consequently, for tax purposes the cost basis of an asset acquired in an exchange is the sum of the book value of the old asset plus the cash given, and it makes no difference whether there is a gain or a loss on the exchange.

As a result of the difference between accounting principles and tax rules, if a loss on a plant asset exchange is recorded as such, two sets of depreciation records must be kept throughout the life of the new asset. One set must be kept for determining net income for accounting purposes, and the other for determining the depreciation deduction for tax purposes. Keeping two sets of records is obviously more costly than keeping one. Yet, when an exchange results in a material loss, the loss should be recorded and the two sets of records kept. On the other hand, when an exchange results in an immaterial loss, it is permissible under the *principle of materiality* to avoid the two sets of records by putting the new asset on the books at its cost basis for tax purposes.

---

[4] Ibid., par. 16.

For example, an old typewriter that cost $500 and upon which $420 of depreciation had been recorded was traded in at $50 on a new $600 typewriter, with the $550 difference being paid in cash. In this case the old typewriter's book value is $80; and if it was traded at $50, there was a $30 book loss on the exchange. However, the $30 loss is an immaterial amount, and the following method, called the income tax method, may be used in recording the exchange.

Jan.	7	Office Equipment	630.00	
		Accumulated Depreciation, Office Equipment ...	420.00	
		Office Equipment.......................		500.00
		Cash		550.00
		Traded an old typewriter and cash for a new typewriter.		

The $630 at which the new typewriter is taken into the accounts by the income tax method is its cost basis for tax purposes and is calculated as follows:

Book value of old typewriter ($500 less $420)	$ 80
Cash paid ($600 less the $50 trade-in allowance)	550
Income tax basis of the new typewriter	$630

Not recording the loss on this exchange and taking the new typewriter into the accounts at its cost basis for income tax purposes violates the ruling of the APB that a loss on a plant asset exchange should be recorded. However, when there is an immaterial loss on an exchange, as in this case, the violation is permissible under the *principle of materiality*. Under this principle an adherence to any accounting principle, including rulings of the APB and the FASB, is not required when the cost to adhere is proportionally great and the lack of adherence does not materially affect reported periodic net income. In this case failing to record the $30 loss on the exchange would not materially affect the average company's statements. On the other hand, recording the loss and thereafter keeping two sets of depreciation records would be costly.

NATURAL RESOURCES

Natural resources such as standing timber, mineral deposits, and oil reserves are known as wasting assets. In their natural state they represent inventories that will be converted into a product by cutting, mining, or pumping. However, until cut, mined, or pumped they are noncurrent assets and commonly appear on a balance sheet under such captions as "Timberlands," "Mineral deposits," or "Oil reserves."

Natural resources are accounted for at cost, and appear on the balance sheet at cost less accumulated *depletion*. The amount such assets are depleted each year by cutting, mining, or pumping is commonly calculated on a "units-of-production" basis. For example, if a mineral deposit having an estimated 500,000 tons of available ore is purchased for $500,000, the depletion charge per ton of ore mined is $1. Furthermore, if 85,000 tons are mined during the first year, the depletion charge for the year is $85,000 and is recorded as follows:

Dec.	31	Depletion of Mineral Deposit	85,000.00	
		Accumulated Depletion, Mineral Deposit ...		85,000.00
		To record depletion of the mineral deposit.		

On the balance sheet prepared at the end of the first year the mineral deposit should appear at its $500,000 cost less $85,000 accumulated depletion. If the 85,000 tons of ore are sold by the end of the first year, the entire $85,000 depletion charge reaches the income statement as the depletion cost of the ore mined and sold. However, if a portion remains unsold at the year-end, the depletion cost of the unsold ore is carried forward on the balance sheet as part of the cost of the unsold ore inventory, a current asset.

Often machinery must be installed or a building constructed in order to exploit a natural resource. The costs of such assets should be depreciated over the life of the natural resource with annual depreciation charges that are in proportion to the annual depletion charges. For example, if a machine is installed in a mine and one eighth of the mine's ore is removed during a year, one eighth of the amount the machine is to be depreciated should be recorded as a cost of the ore mined.

INTANGIBLE ASSETS

Intangible assets have no physical existence; rather, they represent certain legal rights and economic relationships which are beneficial to the owner. Patents, copyrights, leaseholds, goodwill, and trademarks are examples. Intangible assets are accounted for at cost. They should appear on the balance sheet in the intangible asset section at cost or at that portion of cost not previously *amortized* (written off).

Patents

Patents are granted by the federal government to encourage the invention of new machines and mechanical devices. A patent gives its owner the exclusive right to manufacture and sell a patented machine or device for a period of 17 years. However, its cost should be amortized over a shorter period if its useful or economic life is estimated to be less than 17 years. For example, if a patent costing $25,000 has an estimated useful life of only ten years, the following adjusting entry is made at the end of each year in the patent's life.

Dec.	31	Patents Written Off	2,500.00	
		Patents		2,500.00
		To amortize one tenth of patent costs.		

The entry's debit causes $2,500 of patent costs to appear on the annual income statement as one of the costs of the patented product manufactured. The credit directly reduces the balance of the Patents account. Normally, patents are written off directly to the Patents account as in this entry.

Copyrights

A *copyright* is granted by the federal government and in most cases gives its owner the exclusive right to publish and sell a musical, literary, or artistic work during the life of the composer, author, or artist and for 50 years thereafter. Many copyrights have value for a much shorter time, and their costs should be amortized over the shorter period. Often the only cost of a copyright is the fee paid the Copyright Office. Since this is nominal, it is commonly charged directly to an expense account.

Leaseholds

Property is rented under a contract called a *lease*. The person or company owning the property and granting the lease is called the *lessor*. The person or company securing the right to possess and use the property is called the *lessee*. The rights granted the lessee under the lease are called a *leasehold*.

Some leases require no advance payment from the lessee but do require monthly rent payments. In such cases a Leasehold account is not needed and the monthly payments are debited to a Rent Expense account. Sometimes a long-term lease is so drawn that the last year's rent must be paid in advance at the time the lease is signed. When this occurs, the last year's advance payment is debited to the Leasehold account. It remains there until the last year of the lease, at which time it is transferred to Rent Expense.

Often a long-term lease, one running 20 or 25 years, becomes very valuable after a few years because its required rent payments are much less than current rentals for identical property. In such cases the increase in value of the lease should not be entered on the books since no extra cost was incurred in acquiring it. However, if the property is subleased and a cash payment is made for the rights under the old lease, the new tenant should debit the payment to a Leasehold account and write it off as additional rent expense over the remaining life of the lease.

Leasehold improvements

Long-term leases often require the lessee to pay for any alterations or improvements to the leased property, such as new partitions and store fronts. Normally the costs of *leasehold improvements* are debited to an account called Leasehold Improvements. Also, since the improvements become part of the property and revert to the lessor at the end of the lease, their cost should be amortized over the life of the lease or the life of the improvements, whichever is shorter. The amortization entry commonly has a debit to Rent Expense and a credit to Leasehold Improvements.

Goodwill

The term *goodwill* has a special meaning in accounting. In accounting, *a business is said to have goodwill when its rate of expected future earnings is greater than the rate of earnings normally realized in its industry.* Above-average earnings and the existence of goodwill may be demonstrated as follows with Companies A and B, both of which are in the same industry:

	Company A	Company B
Net assets (other than goodwill)	$100,000	$100,000
Normal rate of return in this industry	10%	10%
Normal return on net assets	$ 10,000	$ 10,000
Actual net income earned	10,000	15,000
Earnings above average	$ 0	$ 5,000

Company B has an above-average earnings rate for its industry and is said to have goodwill. Its goodwill may be the result of excellent customer relations, the location of the business, monopolistic privileges, superior management, or a combination of factors. Furthermore, a prospective investor would normally be willing to pay more for Company B than for Company A if the investor felt the extra earnings rate would continue. Thus, goodwill is an asset having value, and it can be sold.

Accountants are in general agreement that goodwill should not be recorded unless it is bought or sold. This normally occurs only when a business is purchased and sold in its entirety. When this occurs, the goodwill of the business may be valued in several ways. If the business is expected to have $5,000 each year in above-average earnings, its goodwill may be valued at, say, four times its above-average earnings or at $20,000. Or the buyer and seller may simply agree that the goodwill should be valued at, say, $25,000. There are other ways to value goodwill, but in a final analysis goodwill is always valued at an amount a seller is willing to take and a buyer is willing to pay.

Trademarks and trade names

Proof of prior use of a trademark or trade name is sufficient under common law to prove ownership and right of use. However, both may be registered at the Patent Office at a nominal cost for the same purpose. The cost of developing a trademark or trade name through, say, advertising should be charged to an expense account in the period or periods incurred. However, if a trademark or trade name is purchased, its cost should be amortized as explained in the next section.

Amortization of intangibles

Some intangibles, such as patents, copyrights, and leaseholds, have determinable lives based on a law, contract, or the nature of the asset; and the costs of such assets should be amortized over the shorter of the term of their existence or the period expected to be benefited by their use. Other intangibles, such as goodwill, trademarks, and trade names, have indeterminable lives. However, the APB ruled that the value of any intangible will eventually disappear; that a reasonable estimate of the period of usefulness of such assets should be made; and that their costs should be amortized over the periods estimated to be benefited by their use, which in no case should exceed 40 years.[5]

GLOSSARY

Accelerated depreciation. Any depreciation method resulting in greater amounts of depreciation expense in the early years of a plant asset's life and lesser amounts in later years.

Amortize. To periodically write off as an expense a share of the cost of an asset, usually an intangible asset.

---

[5] APB, "Intangible Assets," *APB Opinion No. 17* (New York: AICPA, August 1970), par. 29.

Balance sheet expenditure. Another name for *capital expenditure.*

Betterment. The replacement of an existing asset portion with an improved or superior asset portion.

Book value. The carrying amount for an item in the accounting records. When applied to a plant asset, it is the cost of the asset minus its accumulated depreciation.

Capital expenditure. An expenditure that increases net assets. Also called *balance sheet expenditure.*

Copyright. An exclusive right granted by the federal government to publish and sell a musical, literary, or artistic work for a period of years.

Declining-balance depreciation. A depreciation method in which up to twice the straight-line rate of depreciation, without considering salvage value, is applied to the remaining book value of a plant asset to arrive at the asset's annual depreciation charge.

Deferred income tax. Amounts of income tax the incurrence of which is delayed or put off until later years due to accelerated depreciation or other cause.

Depletion. The amount a wasting asset is reduced through cutting, mining, or pumping.

Extraordinary repairs. Major repairs that extend the life of a plant asset beyond the number of years originally estimated.

Fixed asset. A plant asset.

Goodwill. That portion of the value of a business due to its ability to earn a rate of return greater than the average in its industry.

Inadequacy. The situation where a plant asset does not produce enough product to meet current needs.

Intangible asset. An asset having no physical existence but having value due to the rights resulting from its ownership and possession.

Internal Revenue Code. The codification of the numerous revenue acts passed by Congress.

Lease. The contractural right to possess and use property under the terms of a lease contract.

Leasehold. Property held under the terms of a lease contract.

Leasehold improvements. Improvements to leased property made by the lessee.

Lessee. An individual granted possession of property under the terms of a lease contract.

Lessor. The individual or enterprise that has granted possession and use of property under the terms of a lease contract.

Obsolescence. The situation where because of new inventions and improvements, an old plant asset can no longer produce its product on a competitive basis.

Office Equipment Ledger. A subsidiary ledger having a record card for each item of office equipment owned.

Ordinary repairs. Repairs made to keep a plant asset in its normal good operating condition.

Patent. An exclusive right granted by the federal government to manufacture and sell a machine or mechanical device for a period of years.

Revenue expenditure. An expenditure that should be deducted from current revenue on the income statement.

Salvage value. The share of a plant asset's cost recovered at the end of its service life through a sale or as a trade-in allowance on a new asset.

Service life. The period of time a plant asset is used in the production and sale of other assets or services.

Store Equipment Ledger. A subsidiary ledger having a record card for each item of store equipment owned.

Straight-line depreciation. A depreciation method that allocates an equal share of the total estimated amount a plant asset will be depreciated during its service life to each accounting period in that life.

Sum-of-the-years'-digits depreciation. A depreciation method that allocates depreciation to each year in a plant asset's life on a fractional basis. The denominator of the fractions used is the sum-of-the-years' digits in the estimated service life of the asset, and the numerators are the years' digits in reverse order.

QUESTIONS FOR CLASS DISCUSSION

1. What are the characteristics of an asset classified as a plant asset?
2. What is the balance sheet classification of land held for future expansion? Why is such land not classified as a plant asset?
3. What in general is included in the cost of a plant asset?
4. A company has just purchased a machine that has a potential life of 15 years. However, the company's management believes that the development of a more efficient machine will make it necessary to replace the machine in eight years. What period of useful life should be used in calculating depreciation on this machine?
5. A building estimated to have a useful life of 30 years was completed at a cost of $85,000. It was estimated that at the end of the building's life it would be wrecked at a cost of $1,000 and that materials salvaged from the wrecking operation would be sold for $2,000. How much straightline depreciation should be charged on the building each year?
6. Define the following terms as used in accounting for plant assets:

a. Trade-in value.	*c.* Book value.	*e.* Inadequacy.
b. Market value.	*d.* Salvage value.	*f.* Obsolescence.

7. What is the sum-of-the-years' digits in the life of a plant asset that will be used for 12 years?

8. Does the recording of depreciation cause a plant asset to appear on the balance sheet at market value? What is accomplished by recording depreciation?

9. Does the balance of the account, Accumulated Depreciation, Machinery, represent funds accumulated to replace the machinery as it wears out? Tell in your own words what the balance of such an account represents.

10. If at the end of four years it is discovered that a machine that was expected to have a five-year life will actually have an eight-year life, how is the error corrected?

11. Distinguish between ordinary repairs and replacements and extraordinary repairs and replacements.

12. How should ordinary repairs to a machine be recorded? How should extraordinary repairs be recorded?

13. What is a betterment? How should a betterment to a machine be recorded?

14. Distinguish between revenue expenditures and capital expenditures.

15. When should a loss on the exchange of a plant asset be recorded? When is it permissible to absorb a loss into the cost basis of the new plant asset? Should a gain on a plant asset exchange be recorded as such?

16. When plant assets of like purpose are exchanged, what determines the cost basis of the newly acquired asset for federal income tax purposes?

17. When the loss on an exchange of plant assets is immaterial in amount, what advantage results from taking the newly acquired asset into the records at the amount of its cost basis for tax purposes?

18. When an old plant asset is traded in at a book loss on a new asset of like purpose, the loss is not recognized for tax purposes. In the end this normally does not work a financial hardship on the taxpayer. Why?

19. What are the characteristics of an intangible asset?

20. In general, how are intangible assets accounted for?

21. Define (a) lease, (b) lessor, (c) leasehold, and (d) leasehold improvement.

22. In accounting, when is a business said to have goodwill?

CLASS EXERCISES

Exercise 9–1

A machine was purchased for $3,000, terms 2/10, n/60, FOB shipping point. The invoice was paid within the discount period along with $140 of freight charges. The machine required a special concrete base and power connections costing $345. In moving the machine onto its new concrete base, it was dropped and damaged. The damage cost $65 to repair. After being repaired, $40 of raw materials were consumed in adjusting the machine so that it would produce a satisfactory product. The adjustments were normal for this type of machine and were not the result of its having been damaged. The product produced while the adjustments were being made was not salable. Prepare a calculation to show the cost of the machine for accounting purposes.

Exercise 9–2

Three machines were acquired in a lump-sum purchase for $5,490. The purchaser paid $200 to transport the machines to his factory. Machine No. 1 was twice as big and weighed twice as much as Machine No. 2, and Machines 2 and 3 were approximately equal in size and weight. The machines had the following appraised values and installation costs:

	Machine No.1	Machine No. 2	Machine No.3
Appraised values	$2,000	$4,000	$3,000
Installation costs	150	350	200

Determine the cost of each machine for accounting purposes.

Exercise 9–3

A machine was installed at a $3,600 cost. Its useful life was estimated at five years or 5,000 units of product with a $600 trade-in value. During its second year it produced 1,100 units of product. Determine the machine's second-year depreciation under each of the following assumptions. Depreciation was calculated on a *(a)* straight-line basis, *(b)* units-of-production basis, *(c)* declining-balance basis at twice the straight-line rate, and *(d)* sum-of-the-year's-digits basis.

Exercise 9–4

A machine cost $1,600 installed and was estimated to have a four-year life and a $150 trade-in value. Use declining-balance depreciation at twice the straight-line rate to determine the amount of depreciation to be charged against the machine in each of the four years in its life.

Exercise 9–5

A machine was installed on January 4, 19—, at a $3,600 total cost. A full year's depreciation on a straight-line basis was charged against the machine on December 31, at the end of each of the first three years in its life, under the assumption the machine would have a four-year life and no salvage value. The machine was sold at its book value on May 1, during its fourth year. *(a)* Give the entry to record the partial year's depreciation on May 1, and *(b)* give the entry to record the sale.

Exercise 9–6

A machine that cost $4,000 and that had $2,800 of accumulated depreciation recorded against it was traded in on a new machine of like purpose having a $4,500 cash price. A $1,000 trade-in allowance was received, and the balance was paid in cash. Determine *(a)* the book value of the old machine, *(b)* the cash given in making the exchange, *(c)* the book loss on the exchange, *(d)* the cost basis of the new machine for income tax purposes, and (e) the annual straight-line depreciation on the new machine for income tax purposes under the assumption it will have an estimated six-year life and a $500 trade-in value.

Exercise 9–7

A machine that cost $3,500 and on which $2,000 of depreciation had been recorded was disposed of on January 2 of the current year. Give without explanations the entries to record the disposal under each of the following unrelated assumptions:

a.   The machine was sold for $1,600 cash.
b.   The machine was sold for $400 cash.
c.   The machine was traded in on a new machine of like purpose having a $4,000 cash price. A $1,600 trade-in allowance was received, and the balance was paid in cash.
d.   A $400 trade-in allowance was received for the machine on a new machine of like purpose having a $4,000 cash price. The balance was paid in cash, and the loss was considered material in amount.
e.   Transaction (d) was recorded by the income tax method because the loss was considered immaterial.

Exercise 9–8

A machine that cost $8,000 was depreciated on a straight-line basis for 10 years under the assumption it would have a 12-year life and an $800 trade-in value. At that point it was recognized that the machine had four years of remaining useful life, after which it would still have an $800 trade-in value.

a.   Determine the machine's book value at the end of its tenth year.
b.   Determine the total depreciation to be charged against the machine during its remaining years of life.
c.   Give the entry to record depreciation on the machine for its 11th year.

Exercise 9–9

On January 3, 198A, a company paid $180,000 for an ore body containing an estimated 900,000 tons of ore and it installed machinery costing $240,000, having a 12-year life and capable of removing the entire ore body in 10 years. The company began operations on May 25, and it mined 45,000 tons of ore during the remainder of 198A. Give the entries to record depletion of the ore body and depreciation on the machinery as of December 31, 198A.

PROBLEMS

Problem 9–1

Part 1. A machine costing $20,000 was installed in a factory. Its useful life was estimated at four years, after which it would have a $2,000 trade-in value. It was estimated the machine would produce 60,000 units of product during its life. It actually produced 12,000 units during its first year, 18,000 during the second, 20,000 during the third, and 10,000 during its fourth year.

Required:

1. Prepare a calculation to show the number of dollars of this machine's cost that should be charged to depreciation over its four-year life.
2. Prepare a form with the following column headings:

Year	Straight Line	Units of Production	Declining Balance	Sum-of-the-Years' Digits

Then enter on the form the depreciation for each year and the total depreciation on the machine under each depreciation method. Use twice the straight-line rate for declining-balance depreciation.

Part 2. A secondhand machine was purchased on January 3, 198A, for $1,650. During the next six days it was repaired and repainted at a cost of $265 and was placed in operation on a new specially built concrete base that cost $135. It was estimated the machine would have a three-year life and a $250 salvage value. Depreciation on a straight-line basis was charged against the machine on December 31, 198A; and on August 28, 198B, the machine was sold for its book value.

Required:

Prepare the necessary entries to record these transactions under the assumption the costs of repairing and repainting the machine and its new concrete base were paid for on January 10, 198A.

Problem 9–2

A company purchased four machines during 198A and 198B, and it used four ways to allocate depreciation on them. Information about the machines follows:

Machine number	Placed in use on—	Cost	Estimated life	Salvage value	Depreciation method
1	Oct. 29, 198A	$5,400	8 years	$600	Straight line
2	Nov. 27, 198A	3,650	4 years	650	Sum-of-the-years' digits
3	Mar. 15, 198B	8,310	15,000 units	810	Units of production
4	Aug. 30, 198B	?	8 years	700	Declining balance

Machine No. 3 produced 2,500 units of product during 198B and 3,000 units in 198C. Machine No. 4 had a $5,600 invoice price, 2/10, n/60, FOB shipping point. The invoice was paid on the last day of its discount period, August 31, but the company had to borrow $5,000 in order to do so (90-day, 8% note). The loan was repaid on November 29. Freight charges on Machine No. 4 were $122, and the machine was placed on a special concrete base that cost $190. It was assembled and installed by the company's own employees. Their wages during the installation period were $200. Payment for the freight charges, the concrete base, and the employees' wages were made on August 31.

Required:

1. Prepare a form with the following columnary headings:

Machine Number	Amount to Be Charged to Depreciation	198A Depreciation	198B Depreciation	198C Depreciation

Enter the machine numbers in the first column and complete the information opposite each machine's number. Use twice the straight-line rate in depreciating Machine No. 4. Total all columns.

2. Prepare entries to record all transactions involving the purchase of Machine No. 4, including the note transactions.
3. Prepare an entry to record the 198C depreciation on the machines.

Problem 9–3

Essex Company completed these store equipment transactions:

198A
Jan.   4   Purchased on credit from Alpha Equipment Company a Fair scale, serial number 00–123, $200. The scale's service life was estimated at ten years with a $20 trade-in value. It was assigned plant asset number 131–1.

6   Purchased on credit from Alpha Equipment Company an Accurate cash register, serial number XX–1212, $320. The register's life was estimated at eight years with an $80 trade-in value. It was assigned plant asset number 131–2.

Feb. 28   Purchased on credit from Gamma Equipment Sales an Iceair refrigerated display case, serial number MM–777, $2,000. The asset's service life was estimated at 12 years with a $200 trade-in value. It was assigned plant asset number 131–3.

Dec. 31   Recorded the 198A depreciation on the store equipment.

198B
Aug. 24   Sold the Fair scale to Corner Market for its book value.

26   Purchased a new Apex scale from Alpha Equipment Company on credit for $265. Its serial number was BB–321, and it was assigned plant asset number 131–4. The scale's service life was estimated at ten years with a $25 trade-in value.

Dec. 31   Record the 198B depreciation on the store equipment.

Required:

1. Open a Store Equipment account and an Accumulated Depreciation, Store Equipment account plus subsidiary plant asset record cards as needed.
2. Prepare general journal entries to record the transactions. Post to the general ledger accounts and to the plant asset record cards.
3. Prove the December 31, 198B, balances of the Store Equipment and Accumulated Depreciation, Store Equipment accounts by preparing with totals a schedule showing the cost and accumulated depreciation on each plant asset owned on that date.

Problem 9–4

Prepare general journal entries to record the following transactions involving the purchase and operation of a secondhand truck:

198A
Jan.   5   Purchased for $4,640 cash a secondhand delivery truck with an estimated three-year remaining useful life and a $1,330 trade-in value.
        6   Paid Service Garage for the following:

Repairs to truck's motor	$ 44
New tires	246
Gas and oil	10
Total	$300

Dec. 31   Recorded straight-line depreciation on the truck.
198B
Jan. 10   Installed a hydraulic loader on the truck at a cost of $570. The loader increased the truck's estimated salvage value to $1,400.
May 25   Paid Service Garage for the following:

Minor repairs to the truck's motor	$35
New battery for the truck	45
Gas and oil	8
Total	$88

Nov.   4   Paid $45 for repairs to the hydraulic loader damaged when the driver backed into a loading dock.
Dec. 31   Recorded straight-line depreciation on the truck.
198C
Jan.   7   Paid Service Garage $400 to overhaul the truck's motor, replacing bearings and rings and extending the truck's life one year beyond the original three-year estimate. However, it was also estimated that the extra year's operation would reduce the truck's trade-in value to $1,050.
Dec. 31   Recorded straight-line depreciation on the truck.
198D
June 29   Traded the old truck on a new one having a $6,100 cash price. Received a $1,700 trade-in allowance and paid cash for the balance. It was estimated the new truck would have a four-year service life and a $1,200 trade-in value.
Dec. 31   Recorded declining-balance depreciation on the new truck at twice the straight-line rate.

Problem 9–5

A company purchased, traded, and sold the following machines:
Machine No. 133–1 was purchased on April 21, 1975, for $5,050. Its useful life was estimated at five years with a $550 trade-in value. Straight-line depreciation was recorded on the machine at the ends of 1975 and 1976; and on

January 7, 1977, it was traded in on Machine No. 133–8. A $2,800 trade-in allowance was received.

Machine No. 133–8 was purchased on January 7, 1977, at an installed cost of $6,450 less the trade-in allowance received on Machine No. 133–1. Its life was estimated at five years with a $600 trade-in value. Sum-of-the-years'-digits depreciation was recorded against the machine at the end of each of the five years in its life; and on January 10, 1982, it was sold for $900.

Machine No. 133–9 was purchased on January 11, 1977, at a total cost of $3,200. Its useful life was estimated at four years with a $300 trade-in value. Declining-balance depreciation at twice the straight-line rate was recorded against the machine at the end of each of the four years in its life; and it was traded in on Machine No. 133–15 on January 5, 1981. A $150 trade-in allowance was received.

Machine No. 133–15 was purchased on January 5, 1981, at an installed cost of $3,100 less the trade-in allowance received on Machine No. 133–9. It was estimated the machine would produce 60,000 units of product during its useful life and would then have a $250 trade-in value. It produced 10,200 units in 1981 and an additional 4,000 units before it was sold on March 8, 1982, for $2,500.

Required:

Assume the company's accounting periods end on December 31 and prepare general journal entries to record (1) the purchase of each machine, (2) the depreciation recorded on the first December 31 of each machine's life, and (3) the disposal of each machine. Use the income tax method to record exchanges and treat the entries of the first two machines as one series of transactions and those of the second two machines as an unrelated second series. The exchange of one machine for another should be recorded one time only.

Problem 9–6

Prepare general journal entries to record these transactions:

1977
Jan.   5   Purchased and placed in operation Machine No. 133–52 which was estimated to have an eight-year life and no salvage value. The machine and its special power connections cost $16,000.
Dec. 31   Recorded straight-line depreciation on the machine.

1978
Mar. 17   After a little over a year's operation Machine No. 133–52 was cleaned, oiled, and adjusted by a factory mechanic at a $195 cost.
Dec. 31   Recorded 1978 depreciation on the machine.

1979
July   6   Added a new device to Machine No. 133–52 at a $1,100 cost. The device materially increased the machine's output but did not change its expected life and zero salvage value.
Dec. 31   Recorded depreciation on the machine.

1980
Dec. 31   Recorded depreciation on the machine.

1981

Jan. 10   Completely overhauled Machine No. 133–52 at a $3,000 cost, of which $400 was for ordinary repairs and $2,600 was for extraordinary repairs that extended the service life of the machine an estimated two years beyond the eight originally expected.

Dec. 31   Recorded depreciation on the machine.

1982

June 28   Machine No. 133–52 was destroyed in a fire, and the insurance company settled the loss claim for $7,500.

ALTERNATE PROBLEMS

Problem 9–1A

Part 1. A machine costing $13,000 was installed in a factory. Its useful life was estimated at four years, after which it would have a $1,000 trade-in value; and it was estimated the machine would produce 30,000 units of product during its life. It actually produced 6,000 units during its first year, 9,000 during the second, 8,000 during the third, and 7,000 during its last year.

Required:

1.   Prepare a calculation to show the number of dollars of this machine's cost that should be charged to depreciation over its four-year life.
2.   Prepare a form with the following column headings:

Year	Straight Line	Units of Production	Declining Balance	Sum-of-the-Years' Digits

Then show the depreciation for each year and the total depreciation for the machine under each depreciation method. Use twice the straight-line rate for the declining-balance method.

Part 2. A secondhand delivery truck was purchased for $4,470 on March 5, 198A. The next day it was repainted and the company's name and business were lettered on its sides at a cost of $150. Also, $210 was paid for a new set of tires. The tires were priced at $224, but a $14 trade-in allowance was received on the truck's old tires. Cash was paid in each instance.

At the time of purchase it was estimated the truck would be driven 30,000 miles, after which it would have a $1,830 trade-in value. The truck was driven 12,000 miles in 198A; and between January 1 and November 3, 198B, it was driven an additional 15,000 miles. On the latter date it was sold for its book value.

Required:

Prepare general journal entries to record the transactions.

Problem 9–2A

A company purchased four machines during 198A and 198B. Machine No. 1 was placed in use on September 2, 198A. It cost $13,150, had an estimated eight-year life and a $1,150 salvage value, and was depreciated on a straight-line basis. Machine No. 2 was placed in use on September 29, 198A, and was depreciated on a units-of-production basis. It cost $12,200, and it was estimated that it would produce 50,000 units of product during its five-year life, after which it would have a $2,200 salvage value. It produced 3,000 units during 198A, 11,500 during 198B, and 12,000 during 198C. Machines 3 and 4 were purchased from a bankrupt firm at auction for $17,100 cash on May 17, 198B, and were placed in service on June 25 of that year. Additional information about the machines follow:

Machine number	Appraised value	Salvage value	Estimated life	Installation cost	Depreciation method
3	$ 8,000	$500	6 years	$250	Sum-of-the-years' digits
4	10,000	800	10 years	500	Declining balance

Required:

1. Prepare a form with the following columnar headings:

Machine Number	Amount to Be Charged to Depreciation	198A Depreciation	198B Depreciation	198C Depreciation

Enter the machine numbers in the first column, complete the information opposite each machine number, and total the columns. Assume that twice the straight-line rate was used for the declining-balance depreciation.

2. Prepare entries to record payment for Machines 3 and 4 and for their installation. Assume cash was paid for the installation on the day the machines were placed in use.

3. Prepare an entry to record the 198C depreciation on the four machines.

Problem 9–3A

ABC Company completed these plant asset transactions:

198A
Dec. 28   Purchased on credit from Office Suppliers a Clear copier, serial number WM178, $870. The copier's service life was estimated at eight years with a $150 trade-in value. Assigned plant asset number 131–1 to the machine.

198B
Jan. 3   Purchased on credit from Speedy Typewriter Sales a Speedy typewriter, serial number M0778, $300. The machine's service life was estimated at five years with a $45 trade-in value. Assigned plant asset number 131–2 to the typewriter.

July 7   Purchased on credit from Zippo, Inc., a Zippo calculator, serial number 2X345, $290. The machine's service life was estimated at eight years with a $50 trade-in value. Assigned plant asset number 131–3 to the machine.

Dec. 31   Recorded the 198B straight-line depreciation on the office equipment.

198C

Aug. 23   Sold the Speedy Typewriter to Ted Orr at its book value.

25   Purchased on credit from Office Suppliers an Accurate typewriter, serial number MMM–123, $425. The typewriter's service life was estimated at five years with a $125 trade-in value. Assigned plant asset number 131–4 to the typewriter.

Dec. 31   Recorded the 198C depreciation on the office equipment.

Required:

1.   Open Office Equipment and Accumulated Depreciation, Office Equipment accounts plus plant asset record cards as needed.
2.   Prepare general journal entries to record the transactions and post to the general ledger accounts and plant asset record cards.
3.   Prove the December 31, 198C, balances of the Office Equipment and Accumulated Depreciation, Office Equipment accounts by preparing a schedule showing the cost and accumulated depreciation on each plant asset owned on that date.

Problem 9–4A

A company completed these transactions involving the purchase and operation of a delivery truck.

198A

June 28   Paid cash for a new truck, $6,500 plus $325 state and city sales taxes. The truck's service life was estimated at four years with an $1,800 trade-in value.

30   Paid $375 for special racks and shelves installed in the truck. The racks and shelves did not increase the truck's estimated trade-in value.

Dec. 31   Recorded straight-line depreciation on the truck.

198B

July   2   Paid $440 cash to install an air-conditioning unit in the truck. The unit increased the truck's estimated trade-in value $50.

Oct. 11   Paid $60 for repairs to the truck's rear bumper damaged when the driver backed into a loading dock.

Dec. 31   Recorded straight-line depreciation on the truck.

198C

Dec. 31   Recorded straight-line depreciation on the truck.

198D

Dec. 31   Recorded straight-line depreciation on the truck.

198E

Jan. 11   Paid Apex Garage $410 to overhaul the truck's motor, replacing bearings and rings and extending the truck's service life one and one-half years beyond the four originally estimated. However, it was estimated that the extra year and one half of operation would reduce the truck's trade-in value to $1,000.

Oct.   1   Traded the old truck and $5,040 in cash for a new truck. The new truck was estimated to have a three-year life and a $2,790 trade-in value, and the invoice on the exchange showed these items:

Price of the new truck	$6,800
Trade-in allowances granted	2,000
Balance	$4,800
State and city sales taxes	240
Balance paid in cash	$5,040

The loss on the exchange was considered immaterial, and the income tax method was used to record the exchange.

Dec. 31   Recorded straight-line depreciation on the new truck.

Required:

Prepare general journal entries to record the transactions.

Problem 9–5A

A company that has accounting periods which end each December 31 purchased, traded, and sold the following machines:

Machine No. 133–45 was installed on January 5, 1976, at a $9,000 cost. It was estimated the machine would produce 90,000 units of product, after which it would have a $450 salvage value. During its first year it produced 20,000 units; and on July 2, 1979, after producing a total of 80,000 units it was traded on Machine No. 133–81. A $1,200 trade-in allowance was received, and the loss was considered immaterial.

Machine No. 133–81 was purchased on July 2, 1979, at an installed cost of $10,450, less the trade-in allowance received on Machine No. 133–45. It was estimated Machine No. 133–81 would have a four-year life and a $650 salvage value. Straight-line depreciation was recorded on each December 31 of the machine's life; and on January 5, 1983, it was sold for $1,500.

Machine No. 133–58 was purchased on January 7, 1977, for $8,000. Its useful life was estimated at five years, after which it would have a $2,000 trade-in value. Declining-balance depreciation at twice the straight-line rate was used in recording depreciation on this machine at the ends of 1977, 1978, and 1979, after which it was traded on Machine No. 133–87. A $2,400 trade-in allowance was received.

Machine No. 133–87 was purchased on January 5, 1980, at an installed cost of $8,500, less the trade-in allowance received on Machine No. 133–58. It was estimated that Machine No. 133–87 would have a five-year life and a $600 trade-in value. Sum-of-the-years'-digits depreciation was recorded on this machine at the ends of 1980, 1981, and 1982; and on January 11, 1983, it was sold for $2,500.

Required:

Prepare general journal entries to record (1) the purchase of each machine, (2) the depreciation recorded on the first December 31 of each machine's life, and (3) the disposal of each machine. Treat the entries for the first two machines as one series of transactions and those of the next two machines as an unrelated second series. The exchange of machines should be recorded one time only.

Problem 9-6A

On May 4, 1976, a company purchased and placed in operation a machine costing $12,000 and having an estimated eight-year life and no salvage value. The machine was cleaned and inspected; and minor adjustments were made on October 10, 1977, by a factory expert called in for that purpose. This cost $180. On April 27, 1979, a $750 device that increased its hourly output by one fourth was added to the machine. The device did not change the machine's zero salvage value. During the first week in January 1981, the machine was completely overhauled at a $2,900 cost (completed and paid for on January 12). The overhaul increased the machine's remaining useful life to a total of six years beyond the overhaul date but did not change its zero salvage value. On June 25, 1982, the machine was completely destroyed in a fire and the insurance company settled the loss claim for $5,000.

Required:

Under the assumption the machine was depreciated on a straight-line basis, prepare general journal entries to record the purchase, operation, and destruction of the machine.

PROVOCATIVE PROBLEMS

Provocative problem 9-1
Second audit

You have graduated from college, taken a job with a public accounting firm, and are working on your second audit; and in helping to verify the records of the firm being audited, you find the following:

1981					
July	12	Cash	10,000.00	
		Loss from Fire	6,000.00	
		Accumulated Depreciation, Machinery ..	12,000.00	
		Machinery		28,000.00
		Received payment of fire loss claim.		
Aug.	15	Cash	18,000.00	
		Factory Land.....................		18,000.00
		Sold unneeded factory land.		

An investigation revealed that the first entry resulted from recording a $10,000 check received from an insurance company in full settlement of a loss claim resulting from the destruction of a machine in a small plant fire on June 30, 1981. The machine had originally cost $24,000, was put in operation on January 7, 1976, and had been depreciated on a straight-line basis at the ends of each of the first five years in its life under the assumption it would have a ten-year life and no salvage value. During the first week in January 1981, the machine had been overhauled at a $4,000 cost. The overhaul did not increase the machine's capacity nor change its zero salvage value. However, it was expected the overhaul would lengthen the machine's service life three years beyond the ten originally estimated.

The second entry resulted from recording a check received from selling a portion of a tract of land. The tract was adjacent to the company's plant and had been purchased on February 22, 1981. It cost $22,000, and $3,000 was paid for clearing and grading it. Both amounts were debited to the Factory Land account. The land was to be used for storing raw materials. However, after the grading was completed, it was obvious the company did not need the entire tract, and it was pleased when it received an offer from a purchaser who was willing to pay $12,000 for the east half or $18,000 for the west half. The company decided to sell the west half, and it recorded the receipt of the purchaser's check with the entry previously given.

Were any errors made in recording the transactions discussed here? If so, describe the errors and in each case give an entry or entries that will correct the account balances under the assumption the 1981 revenue and expense accounts have not been closed.

Provocative problem 9–2
Bitton Company

Bitton Company, a manufacturer, is about to invest $120,000 in new machinery to add a new product to its line. The new machinery is expected to have a four-year life and an $8,000 salvage value; and you, the concern's accountant, have prepared the following statement showing the expected results from the sale of the product under the assumption the new machinery will be depreciated on a straight-line basis and that 50% of the income earned will have to be paid out in state and federal income taxes.

BITTON COMPANY
Expected Results from Sale of New Product

	1st year	2d year	3d year	4th year	Total
Sales	$200,000	$200,000	$200,000	$200,000	$800,000
All costs other than depreciation and income taxes	120,000	120,000	120,000	120,000	480,000
Income before depreciation and income taxes	$ 80,000	$ 80,000	$ 80,000	$ 80,000	$320,000
Depreciation of machinery	28,000	28,000	28,000	28,000	112,000
Income before taxes	$ 52,000	$ 52,000	$ 52,000	52,000	$208,000
Income taxes	26,000	26,000	26,000	26,000	104,000
Net income	$ 26,000	$ 26,000	$ 26,000	$ 26,000	$104,000

When the company president examined your statement, he said that he knew that regardless of how calculated, the company could charge off no more than $112,000 of depreciation on the new machinery during its four-year life. Furthermore, he said, as he could see, this would result in $208,000 of income before taxes for the four years, $104,000 of income taxes, and $104,000 of net income for the period, regardless of how depreciation was calculated. Nevertheless, he continued that he had been talking with a friend on the golf course a few days back and the friend had tried to explain the tax advantage of using declining-balance depreciation. He said he did not understand all the friend had tried to tell him; and as a result he would like for you to prepare an additional statement like the one already prepared, but based on the assumption that declining-balance depreciation at twice the straight-line rate would be used in depreciating the new machinery. He said he would also like a written explanation of the tax advantage gained through the use of declining-balance depreciation, with a dollar estimate of the amount the company would gain in this case. Prepare the information for the president. (In making your estimate, assume the company can invest any deferred tax moneys in its operations and can earn an 8% after-tax return compounded annually on the amounts invested. Also, to simplify the problem, assume that the taxes must be paid on the first day of January in the year following their incurrence.)

part four
Accounting for liabilities

10

Current and long-term liabilities

After studying Chapter 10,
you should be able to:

- Prepare entries to record transactions involving short-term notes payable.
- Explain the concept of present value.
- Calculate the present value of a sum of money to be received a number of periods in the future.
- Calculate the present value of a sum of money to be received periodically for a number of periods in the future.
- Account for a plant asset purchased with a long-term noninterest-bearing note payable.
- Account for a plant asset acquired through leasing.
- Account for payroll liabilities.
- Define or explain the words and phrases listed in the chapter Glossary.

A liability is a legal obligation requiring the future payment of an asset, the future performance of a service, or the creation of another liability. In accounting for liabilities the *cost principle* applies and each liability is accounted for at the cost of the asset or service received in exchange for the liability.

A business normally has several kinds of liabilities, which are classified as either current or long-term liabilities. Current liabilities are debts or other obligations the liquidation of which is reasonably expected to require the use of existing current assets or the creation of other current liabilities.[1] Accounts payable, short-term notes payable, wages payable, payroll and other taxes payable, and unearned revenues are common examples of current liabilities. Long-term liabilities are obligations that will not require the use of existing current assets in their liquidation, generally because they are not to be paid or liquidated within one year or one operating cycle.

Accounts payable, wages payable, and unearned revenues and the accounting procedures applicable to these liabilities were discussed in previous chapters. Consequently, this chapter is devoted to notes payable and liabilities arising from payrolls and from leasing. Mortgages payable and bonds payable are discussed in the next chapter.

SHORT-TERM NOTES PAYABLE

Short-term notes payable often arise in gaining an extension of time in which to pay an account payable. They frequently arise in borrowing from a bank.

Note given to secure a time extension on an account

A note payable may be given to secure an extension of time in which to pay an account payable. For example, Brock Company cannot pay its past-due, $600 account with Ajax Company, and Ajax Company has agreed to accept Brock Company's 60-day, 8%, $600 note in grant-

---

[1] APB, "Basic Concepts and Accounting Principles Underlying Financial Statements of Business Enterprises," *APB Statement No. 4* (New York: AICPA, October 1970), par. 198.

ing an extension on the due date of the debt. Brock Company will record the issuance of the note as follows:

Aug.	23	Accounts Payable—Ajax Company	600.00	
		Notes Payable		600.00
		Gave a 60-day, 8% note to extend the due date on the amount owed.		

Observe that the note does not pay the debt. It merely changes it from an account payable to a note payable. Ajax Company should prefer the note to the account because in case of default and a lawsuit to collect, the note improves its legal position, since the note is written evidence of the debt and its amount.

When the note becomes due, Brock Company will give Ajax Company a check for $608 and record the payment of the note and its interest with an entry like this:

Oct.	22	Notes Payable	600.00	
		Interest Expense	8.00	
		Cash		608.00
		Paid our note with interest.		

Borrowing from a bank

In lending money, banks distinguish between *loans* and *discounts*. In case of a loan, the bank collects interest when the loan is repaid. In a discount, it deducts interest at the time the loan is made. To illustrate loans and discounts, assume that H. A. Green wishes to borrow approximately $2,000 for 60 days at the prevailing 9% rate of interest.

A loan   In a loan transaction the bank will lend Green $2,000 in exchange for a signed promissory note. The note will read: "Sixty days after date I promise to pay $2,000 with interest at 9%." Green will record the transaction as follows:

Sept.	10	Cash	2,000.00	
		Notes Payable		2,000.00
		Gave the bank a 60-day, 9% note.		

When the note and interest are paid, Green makes this entry:

Nov.	9	Notes Payable	2,000.00	
		Interest Expense	30.00	
		Cash		2,030.00
		Paid our 60-day, 9% note.		

Observe that in a loan transaction the interest is paid at the time the loan is repaid.

A discount If it is the practice of Green's bank to deduct interest at the time a loan is made, the bank will discount Green's $2,000 note. If it discounts the note at 9% for 60 days, it will deduct from the face amount of the note 60 days' interest at 9%, which is $30, and will give Green the difference, $1,970. The $30 of deducted interest is called *bank discount,* and the $1,970 are the *proceeds* of the discounted note. Green will record the transaction as follows:

Sept.	10	Cash	1,970.00	
		Interest Expense	30.00	
		Notes Payable		2,000.00
		Discounted our $2,000 note payable at 9%.		

When the note matures, Green is required to pay the bank just the face amount of the note, $2,000, and Green will record the transaction like this:

Nov.	9	Notes Payable	2,000.00	
		Cash		2,000.00
		Paid our discounted note payable.		

Since interest is deducted in a discount transaction at the time the loan is made, the note used in such a transaction must state that only the principal amount is to be repaid at maturity. Such a note may read: "Sixty days after date I promise to pay $2,000 with no interest," and is commonly called a noninterest-bearing note. However, banks are not in business to lend money interest free. Interest is paid in a discount transaction. However, since it is deducted at the time the loan is made, the note used must state that no additional interest is to be collected at maturity. Nevertheless, interest is collected in a discount transaction and at a rate slightly higher than in a loan transaction at the same stated interest rate. For example, in this instance

Green paid $30 for the use of $1,970 for 60 days, which was at an effective interest rate just a little in excess of 9% on the $1,970 received.

END-OF-THE-PERIOD ADJUSTMENTS

Accrued interest expense

Interest accrues daily on all interest-bearing notes. Consequently, if any notes payable are outstanding at the end of an accounting period, their accrued interest should be recorded. For example, a company gave its bank a $4,000, 60-day, 9% note on December 16 to borrow that amount of money. If the company's accounting period ends on December 31, by then 15 days' or $15 interest has accrued on this note. It may be recorded with this adjusting entry:

Dec.	31	Interest Expense	15.00	
		Interest Payable.........................		15.00
		To record accrued interest on a note payable.		

The adjusting entry causes the $15 accrued interest to appear on the income statement as an expense of the period benefiting from 15 days' use of the money. It also causes the interest payable to appear on the balance sheet as a current liability.

When the note matures in the next accounting period, its payment may be recorded as follows:

Feb.	14	Notes Payable	4,000.00	
		Interest Payable............................	15.00	
		Interest Expense	45.00	
		Cash		4,060.00
		Paid a $4,000 note and its interest.		

Interest on this note for 60 days is $60. In the illustrated entry the $60 is divided between the interest accrued at the end of the previous period, $15, and interest applicable to the current period, $45. Some accountants avoid the necessity of making this division by reversing the accrued interest adjusting entry as a last step in their end-of-the-period work.

Discount on notes payable

When a note payable is discounted at a bank, interest based on the principal of the note is deducted and the interest is normally recorded as interest expense. Furthermore, since most such notes run for 30, 60, or 90 days, the interest is usually an expense of the period in which it is deducted. However, when the time of a note extends beyond a single accounting period, an adjusting entry is required. For example, on December 11, 198A, a company discounted at 9% its own $6,000, 60-day, noninterest-bearing note payable. It recorded the transaction as follows:

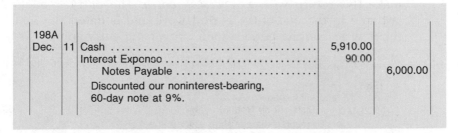

198A				
Dec.	11	Cash	5,910.00	
		Interest Expense	90.00	
		Notes Payable		6,000.00
		Discounted our noninterest-bearing, 60-day note at 9%.		

If this company operates with accounting periods that end each December 31, 20 days' interest on this note, or $30 of the $90 of discount, is an expense of the 198A accounting period and 40 days' interest or $60 is an expense of 198B. Consequently, if revenues and expenses are matched, the company must make the following December 31, 198A, adjusting entry:

198A				
Dec.	31	Discount on Notes Payable	60.00	
		Interest Expense		60.00
		To set up as a contra liability the interest applicable to 198B.		

The adjusting entry removes from the Interest Expense account the $60 of interest that is applicable to 198B. It leaves in the account the $30 that is an expense of 198A. The $30 then appears on the 198A income statement as an expense, and the $60 appears on the 198A balance sheet. If this is the only note the company has outstanding, the $60 is deducted on the balance sheet as follows:

Current liabilities:		
Notes payable	$6,000	
Less discount on notes payable	60	$5,940

Putting discount on notes payable on the balance sheet as a contra liability results in showing as a liability on the balance sheet date the amount received in discounting the note plus the accrued interest on the note to the balance sheet date. In this example $5,910 was received in discounting the note and accrued interest on the note is $30. Together they total $5,940, which is the amount actually owed the bank on December 31.

The $60 interest set out as discount on notes payable in the previous paragraphs becomes an expense early in 198B. Consequently, sooner or later it must be taken from the Discount on Notes Payable account and returned to the Interest Expense account. Accountants commonly make this return with a *reversing entry.* The entry is made as the last step in the end-of-the-period work and is dated the first day of the new accounting period. Such a reversing entry appears as follows:

198B				
Jan.	1	Interest Expense	60.00	
		Discount on Notes Payable		60.00
		To reverse the adjusting entry that set out discount on notes payable.		

Observe that the reversing entry is debit for credit and credit for debit the reverse of the adjusting entry it reverses. That is where it gets its name. Also, observe that it returns the $60 interest to the expense account so that it will appear on the 198B income statement as an expense without further ado.

THE CONCEPT OF PRESENT VALUE

The concept of present value enters into many financing and investing decisions and any resulting liabilities. Consequently, an understanding of it is important. The concept is based on the idea that the right to receive, say, $1 a year from today is worth somewhat less than $1 today. Or stated another way, $1 to be received a year hence has a *present value* of somewhat less than $1. How much less depends on how much can be earned on invested funds. If, say, a 10% annual return can be earned, the expectation of receiving $1 a year hence has a present value of $0.909. This can be verified as follows: $0.909 invested today to earn 10% annually will earn $0.0909 in one year, and when the $0.0909 earned is added to the $0.909 invested—

Investment	$0.909
Earnings	0.0909
Total	$0.9999

the investment plus the earnings equal $0.9999, which rounds to the $1 expected.

Likewise, the present value of $1 to be received two years hence is $0.826 if a 10% compound annual return is expected. This also can be verified as follows: $0.826 invested to earn 10% compounded annually will earn $0.0826 the first year it is invested, and when the $0.0826 earned is added to the $0.826 invested—

Investment	$0.826
First year earnings	0.0826
End-of-year-one amount	$0.9086

the investment plus the first year's earnings total $0.9086. And during the second year this $0.9086 will earn $0.09086, which when added to the end-of-the-first-year amount—

End-of-year-one amount	$0.9086
Second year earnings	0.09086
End-of-year-two amount	$0.99946

equals $0.99946, which rounds to the $1 expected at the end of the second year.

Present value tables

The present value of $1 to be received any number of years in the future can be calculated by using the formula, $1/(1 + i)^n$. The i is the interest rate, and n is the number of years to the expected receipt. However, the formula need not be used, since tables showing present values computed with the formula at various interest rates are readily available. Table 10–1, with its amounts rounded to either three or four decimal places, is such a table. (Three or four decimal places would not be sufficiently accurate for some uses but will suffice here.)

Observe in Table 10–1 that the first amount in the 10% column is the 0.909 used in the previous section to introduce the concept of present value. The 0.909 in the 10% column means that the expectation of receiving $1 a year hence when discounted for one period, in this case one year, at 10%, has a present value of $0.909. Then note that the second amount in the 10% column is the 0.826 previously used, which means that the expectation of receiving $1 two years hence, discounted at 10%, has a present value of $0.826.

Using a present value table

To demonstrate the use of the present value table, Table 10–1, assume that a company has an opportunity to invest $20,000 in a project,

Present Value of $1 at Compound Interest

Periods hence	3½%	4%	4½%	6%	7%	8%	10%	12%	14%	15%
1	0.9662	0.9615	0.9569	0.943	0.935	0.926	0.909	0.893	0.877	0.870
2	0.9335	0.9246	0.9157	0.890	0.873	0.857	0.826	0.797	0.769	0.756
3	0.9019	0.8890	0.8763	0.840	0.816	0.794	0.751	0.712	0.675	0.658
4	0.8714	0.8548	0.8386	0.792	0.763	0.735	0.683	0.636	0.592	0.572
5	0.8420	0.8219	0.8025	0.747	0.713	0.681	0.621	0.567	0.519	0.497
6	0.8135	0.7903	0.7679	0.705	0.666	0.630	0.565	0.507	0.456	0.432
7	0.7860	0.7599	0.7348	0.665	0.623	0.584	0.513	0.452	0.400	0.376
8	0.7594	0.7307	0.7032	0.627	0.582	0.540	0.467	0.404	0.351	0.327
9	0.7337	0.7026	0.6729	0.592	0.544	0.500	0.424	0.361	0.308	0.284
10	0.7089	0.6756	0.6439	0.558	0.508	0.463	0.386	0.322	0.270	0.247
11	0.6849	0.6496	0.6162	0.527	0.475	0.429	0.351	0.287	0.237	0.215
12	0.6618	0.6246	0.5897	0.497	0.444	0.397	0.319	0.257	0.208	0.187
13	0.6394	0.6006	0.5643	0.469	0.415	0.368	0.290	0.229	0.182	0.163
14	0.6178	0.5775	0.5400	0.442	0.388	0.341	0.263	0.205	0.160	0.141
15	0.5969	0.5553	0.5167	0.417	0.362	0.315	0.239	0.183	0.140	0.123
16	0.5767	0.5339	0.4945	0.394	0.339	0.292	0.218	0.163	0.123	0.107
17	0.5572	0.5134	0.4732	0.371	0.317	0.270	0.198	0.146	0.108	0.093
18	0.5384	0.4936	0.4528	0.350	0.296	0.250	0.180	0.130	0.095	0.081
19	0.5202	0.4746	0.4333	0.331	0.277	0.232	0.164	0.116	0.083	0.070
20	0.5026	0.4564	0.4146	0.312	0.258	0.215	0.149	0.104	0.073	0.061

Table 10–1

the risks of which it feels justify a 12% compound return. The investment will return $10,000 at the end of the first year, $9,000 at the end of the second year, $8,000 at the end of the third year, and nothing thereafter. Will the project return the original investment plus the 12% demanded? The calculations of Illustration 10–1, which use the first three amounts in the 12% column of the Table 10–1, indicate that it will. In Illustration 10–1 the expected returns in the second

Years hence	Expected returns	Present value of $1 at 12%	Present value of expected returns
1	$10,000	0.893	$ 8,930
2	9,000	0.797	7,173
3	8,000	0.712	5,696
Total present value of the returns			$21,799
Less investment required			20,000
Excess over 12% demanded			$ 1,799

Illustration 10–1

column are multiplied by the present value amounts in the third column to determine the present values in the last column. Since the total of the present values exceeds the required investment by $1,799, the project will return the $20,000 investment, plus a 12% return thereon, and $1,799 extra.

In Illustration 10–1 the present value of each year's return was separately calculated, after which the present values were added to determine their total. Separately calculating the present value of each of several returns from an investment is necessary when the returns are unequal, as in this example. However, in cases where the periodic returns are equal, there are shorter ways of calculating the sum of their present values. For instance, suppose a $3,500 investment will return $1,000 at the end of each year in its five-year life and an investor wants to know the present value of these returns discounted at 12%. In this case the periodic returns are equal, and a short way to determine their total present value at 12% is to add the present values of $1 at 12% for periods one through five (from Table 10–1), as follows—

```
0.893
0.797
0.712
0.636
0.567
3.605
```

and then to multiply $1,000 by the total. The $3,605 result ($1,000 × 3.605 = $3,605) is the same as would be obtained by calculating the present value of each year's return and adding the present values. However, although the result is the same either way, the method demonstrated here requires four fewer multiplications.

Present value of $1 received periodically for a number of periods

Table 10–2 is based on the idea demonstrated in the previous paragraph, the idea that the present value of a series of equal returns to be received at periodic intervals is nothing more than the sum of the present values of the individual returns. Note the amount on the table's fifth line in the 12% column. It is the same 3.605 amount arrived at in the previous section by adding the first five present values of $1 at 12%. All the amounts shown in Table 10–2 could be arrived at by adding amounts found in Table 10–1. However, there would be some slight variations due to rounding.

When available, Table 10–2 is used to determine the present value of a series of equal amounts to be received at periodic intervals. For

Present Value of $1 Received Periodically for a Number of Periods

Periods hence	3½%	4%	4½%	6%	7%	8%	10%	12%	14%	15%
1	0.966	0.962	0.957	0.943	0.935	0.926	0.909	0.893	0.877	0.870
2	1.900	1.886	1.873	1.833	1.808	1.783	1.736	1.690	1.647	1.626
3	2.802	2.775	2.749	2.673	2.624	2.577	2.487	2.402	2.322	2.283
4	3.672	3.630	3.588	3.465	3.387	3.312	3.170	3.037	2.914	2.855
5	4.515	4.452	4.390	4.212	4.100	3.993	3.791	3.605	3.433	3.352
6	5.329	5.242	5.158	4.917	4.767	4.623	4.355	4.111	3.889	3.784
7	6.115	6.002	5.893	5.582	5.389	5.206	4.868	4.564	4.288	4.160
8	6.874	6.733	6.596	6.210	5.971	5.747	5.335	4.968	4.639	4.487
9	7.608	7.435	7.269	6.802	6.515	6.247	5.759	5.328	4.946	4.772
10	8.317	8.111	7.913	7.360	7.024	6.710	6.145	5.650	5.216	5.019
11	9.002	8.761	8.529	7.887	7.499	7.139	6.495	5.988	5.453	5.234
12	9.663	9.385	9.119	8.384	7.943	7.536	6.814	6.194	5.660	5.421
13	10.303	9.986	9.683	8.853	8.358	7.904	7.103	6.424	5.842	5.583
14	10.921	10.563	10.223	9.295	8.746	8.244	7.367	6.628	6.002	5.724
15	11.517	11.118	10.740	9.712	9.108	8.560	7.606	6.811	6.142	5.847
16	12.094	11.652	11.234	10.106	9.447	8.851	7.824	6.974	6.265	5.954
17	12.651	12.166	11.707	10.477	9.763	9.122	8.022	7.120	6.373	6.047
18	13.190	12.659	12.160	10.828	10.059	9.372	8.201	7.250	6.467	6.128
19	13.710	13.134	12.593	11.158	10.336	9.604	8.365	7.366	6.550	6.198
20	14.212	13.590	13.008	11.470	10.594	9.818	8.514	7.469	6.623	6.259

Table 10–2

example, what is the present value of a series of ten $1,000 amounts, with one $1,000 amount to be received at the end of each of ten successive years, discounted at 8%? To determine the answer, go down the 8% column to the amount opposite ten periods (years in this case). It is 6.710, and $6.71 is the present value of $1 to be received annually at the ends of each of ten years, discounted at 8%. Therefore, the present value of the ten $1,000 amounts is 1,000 times $6.71 or is $6,710.

Discount periods less than a year in length

In the examples thus far the discount periods have been measured in intervals one year in length. Often discount periods are based on intervals shorter than a year. For instance, although interest rates on corporation bonds are usually quoted on an annual basis, the interest on such bonds is normally paid semiannually. As a result, the present value of the interest to be received on such bonds must be based on interest periods six months in length.

To illustrate a calculation based on six-month interest periods, assume an investor wants to know the present value of the interest that will be received over a period of five years on some corporation bonds. The bonds have a $10,000 par value, and interest is paid on them every six months at an 8% annual rate. Interest at an 8% annual rate is at the rate of 4% per six-month interest period. Consequently, the investor will receive $10,000 times 4% or $400 in interest on these bonds at the end of each six-month interest period. In five years there are ten such periods. Therefore, if these ten receipts of $400 each are to be discounted at the interest rate of the bonds, to determine their present value, go down the 4% column of Table 10–2 to the amount opposite ten periods. It is 8.111, and the present value of the ten $400 semiannual receipts is 8.111 times $400 or is $3,244.40.

EXCHANGING A NOTE FOR A PLANT ASSET

When a relatively high-cost plant asset is purchased, particularly if the credit period is long, a note is sometimes given in making the purchase. If the amount of the note is approximately equal to the cash price for the asset and the interest on the note is at approximately the prevailing rate, the transaction is recorded as follows:

Feb.	12	Store Equipment	4,500.00	
		Notes Payable		4,500.00
		Exchanged a $4,500, one-year, 8½% note payable for a refrigerated display case.		

A note given in exchange for a plant asset has two elements, which may or may not be stipulated in the note. They are (1) a dollar amount equivalent to the bargained cash price of the asset and (2) an interest factor to compensate the supplier for the use of the funds that otherwise would have been received in a cash sale. Consequently, when a note is exchanged for a plant asset and the face amount of the note approximately equals the cash price of the asset and the note's interest rate is at or near the prevailing rate, the asset may be recorded at the face amount of the note as in the previous illustration. However, if no interest rate is stated, or the interest rate is unreasonable, or the face amount of the note materially differs from the cash price for the asset, the asset should be recorded at its cash price or at the present value of the note, whichever is more clearly determinable.[2] In such a situation to record the asset at the face amount of the note would cause the asset, the liability, and interest expense to be misstated. Furthermore, the misstatements could be material in case of a long-term note.

---

[2] APB, "Interest on Receivables and Payables," *APB Opinion No. 21* (New York: AICPA, August 1971), pars. 8 and 12.

To illustrate a situation in which a note having no interest rate stated is exchanged for a plant asset, assume that on January 2, 198A, a noninterest-bearing, five-year, $10,000 note payable is exchanged for a factory machine, the cash price of which is not readily determinable. If the prevailing rate for interest on the day of the exchange is 8%, the present value of the note on that day is $6,810 [based on the fifth amount in the 8% column of Table 10–1 ($10,000 × 0.681 = $6,810)], and the exchange should be recorded as follows:

198A Jan.	2	Factory Machinery	6,810.00	
		Discount on Notes Payable	3,190.00	
		Long-Term Notes Payable		10,000.00
		Exchanged a five-year, noninterest-bearing note for a machine.		

The $6,810 debit amount in the entry is the present value of the note on the day of the exchange. It is also the cost of the machine and is the amount to be used in calculating depreciation and any future loss or gain on the machine's sale or exchange. The entry's notes payable and discount amounts together measure the liability resulting from the transaction. They should appear on a balance sheet prepared immediately after the exchange as follows:

Long-term liabilities:
 Long-term notes payable $10,000
  Less unamortized discount based on the 8% interest
   rate prevailing on the date of issue 3,190 $6,810

The $3,190 discount is a contra liability and also the interest element of the transaction. Column 3 of Illustration 10–2 shows the portions

Year	Beginning-of-the-year carrying amount	Discount to be amortized each year	Unamortized discount at the end of the year	End-of-the-year carrying amount
198A	$6,810	$545	$2,645	$ 7,355
198B	7,355	588	2,057	7,943
198C	7,943	635	1,422	8,578
198D	8,578	686	736	9,264
198E	9,264	736*	–0–	10,000

* Adjusted for rounding.

Illustration 10–2

of the $3,190 that should be amortized and charged to interest expense at the ends of each of the five years in the life of the note. The first year's amortization entry is:

198A Dec.	31	Interest Expense .... Discount on Notes Payable .... To amortize a portion of the discount on our long-term note.	545.00	545.00

The $545 amortized is interest at 8% on the note's $6,810 value on the day it was exchanged for the machine. [The $545 is rounded to the nearest full dollar, as are all the Column 3 amounts ($6,810 × 8% = $544.80).]

Posting the amortization entry causes the note to appear on the December 31, 198A, balance sheet as follows:

Long-term liabilities:		
Long-term notes payable	$10,000	
Less unamortized discount based on the 8% interest rate prevailing on the date of issue	2,645	$7,355

Compare the net amount at which the note is carried on the December 31, 198A, balance sheet with the net amount shown for the note on the balance sheet prepared on its date of issue. Observe that the *carrying amount* increased $545 between the two dates. The $545 is the amount of discount amortized and charged to interest expense at the end of 198A.

At the end of 198B and each succeeding year the remaining amounts of discount shown in Column 3 of Illustration 10–2 should be amortized and charged to interest expense. This will cause the carrying amount of the note to increase each year by the amount of discount amortized that year and to reach $10,000, the note's maturity value, at the end of the fifth year. Payment of the note may then be recorded as follows:

198F Jan.	2	Long-Term Notes Payable .... Cash .... Paid our long-term noninterest-bearing note.	10,000.00	10,000.00

Now return to Illustration 10–2. Each end-of-the-year carrying amount in the last column is determined by subtracting the end-of-the-year unamortized discount from the $10,000 face amount of the note. For example, $10,000 − $2,645 = $7,355. Each beginning-of-the-year carrying amount is the same as the previous year's end-of-the-year amount. The amount of discount to be amortized each year is determined by multiplying the beginning-of-the-year carrying amount by the 8% interest rate prevailing at the time of the exchange. For example, $7,355 × 8% = $588 (rounded). Each end-of-the-year amount of unamortized discount is the discount remaining after subtracting the discount amortized that year. For example, $3,190 − $545 = $2,645.

LIABILITIES FROM LEASING

The leasing of plant assets, rather than purchasing them, has increased tremendously in recent years, primarily because leasing does not require a large cash outflow at the time the assets are acquired. Leasing has been called "off balance sheet financing" because assets leased under certain conditions do not appear on the balance sheet of the lessee. However, some leases have essentially the same economic consequences as if the lessee secured a loan and purchased the leased asset. Such leases are called *capital leases* or *financing leases*. The FASB ruled that a lease meeting any one of the following criteria is a capital lease.[3]
1. Ownership of the leased asset is transferred to the lessee at the end of the lease period.
2. The lease gives the lessee the option of purchasing the leased asset at less than fair value at some point during or at the end of the lease period.
3. The period of the lease is 75% or more of the estimated service life of the leased asset.
4. The present value of the minimum lease payments is 90% or more of the fair value of the leased asset.

A lease that does not meet any one of the four criteria is classified as an *operating lease.*

To illustrate accounting for leases, assume that Alpha Company plans to produce a product requiring the use of a new machine costing approximately $40,000 and having an estimated ten-year life and no salvage value. It does not have $40,000 in available cash and is planning to lease the machine as of December 31, 198A. It will lease the machine under one of the following contracts, each of which requires Alpha Company to pay maintenance, taxes, and insurance on the machine: (1) Lease the machine for five years, annual payments of $7,500 payable at the end of each of the five years, the machine to be returned to the lessor at the end of the lease period. (2) Lease the machine for

---

[3] FASB, "Accounting for Leases," *FASB Statement No. 13* (Stamford, Conn., 1976), par. 7.

five years, annual payments of $10,000 payable at the end of each of the five years, the machine to become the property of Alpha Company at the end of the lease period.

If the prevailing interest rate is 8%, the first lease contract does not meet any of the four criteria of the FASB. Therefore, it is an operating lease. If Alpha Company chooses this contract, it should make no entry to record the lease contract. However, each annual rental payment should be recorded as follows:

198B Dec.	31	Machinery Rentals Expense	7,500.00	
		Cash		7,500.00
		Paid the annual rent on a leased machine.		

Alpha Company should also expense the payments for taxes, insurance, and any repairs to the machine, but it should not record depreciation on it. It should also append a footnote to its income statement giving a general description of the leasing arrangements.

The second lease contract meets the first and fourth criteria of the FASB and is a capital lease. It is in effect a purchase transaction with the lessor company financing the purchase of the machine for Alpha Company. To charge each of the $10,000 lease payments to an expense account would overstate expenses during the first five years of the machine's life and understate expenses during the last five. It would also understate the company's assets and liabilities. Consequently, the FASB ruled that such a lease should be treated as a purchase transaction and be recorded on the lease date at the present value of the lease payments.

If Alpha Company chooses the second lease contract and the prevailing interest rate on such contracts is 8% annually, it should (based on the fifth amount in the 8% column of Table 10–2) multiply $10,000 by 3.993 to arrive at a $39,930 present value for the five lease payments. It should then make this entry:

198A Dec.	31	Machinery	39,930.00	
		Discount on Lease Financing	10,070.00	
		Long-Term Lease Liability		50,000.00
		Purchased a machine through a long- term lease contract.		

The $39,930 is the cost of the machine. As with any plant asset, it should be charged off to depreciation expense over the machine's expected service life. The $10,070 discount is the interest factor in the transaction. The long-term lease liability less the amount of the discount measures the net liability resulting from the purchase. The two items should appear on a balance sheet prepared immediately after the transaction as follows:

Long-term liabilities:		
Long-term lease liability[4]	$50,000	
Less unamortized discount based on the 8% interest		
rate prevailing on the date of the contract	10,070	$39,930

If Alpha Company plans to depreciate the machine on a straight-line basis over its ten-year life, it should make the following entries at the end of the first year in the life of the lease:

198B				
Dec.	31	Depreciation Expense, Machinery	3,993.00	
		Accumulated Depreciation, Machinery		3,993.00
		To record depreciation on the machine.		
	31	Long-Term Lease Liability	10,000.00	
		Cash		10,000.00
		Made the annual payment on the lease.		
	31	Interest Expense	3,194.00	
		Discount on Lease Financing		3,194.00
		Amortized a portion of the discount on the lease financing		

The first two entries need no comment. The $3,194 amortized in the third entry is interest at 8% for one year on the $39,930 beginning-of-the-year carrying amount of the lease liability ($39,930 × 8% = $3,194). The $3,194 is rounded to the nearest full dollar, as are all amounts in Column 5 of Illustration 10–3.

Posting the entries recording the $10,000 payment and the amortization of the discount causes the lease liability to appear on the December 31, 198B, balance sheet as follows:

Long-term liabilities:		
Long-term lease liability	$40,000	
Less unamortized discount based on the 8% interest		
rate prevailing on the date of the contract	6,876	$33,124

---

[4] To simplify the illustration, the fact that the first installment on the lease should probably be classified as a current liability is ignored here and should be ignored in the problems at the end of the chapter.

Year	Beginning-of-year lease liability	Beginning-of-year unamortized discount	Beginning-of-year carrying amount	Discount to be amortized	Unamortized discount at the end of the year	End-of-the-year lease liability	End-of-the-year carrying amount
198B	$50,000	$10,070	$39,930	$3,194	$6,876	$40,000	$33,124
198C	40,000	6,876	33,124	2,650	4,226	30,000	25,774
198D	30,000	4,226	25,774	2,062	2,164	20,000	17,836
198E	20,000	2,164	17,836	1,427	737	10,000	9,263
198F	10,000	737	9,263	737*	–0–	–0–	–0–

* Adjusted for rounding.

Illustration 10–3

At the end of 198C and each succeeding year thereafter the remaining amounts in column 5 of Illustration 10–3 should be amortized. This together with the $10,000 annual payments will reduce the carrying amount of the lease liability to zero by the end of the fifth year.

Return again to Illustration 10–3, Column 5. Each year's amount of discount to be amortized is determined by multiplying the beginning of the year carrying amount of the lease liability by 8%. For example, the 198C amount to be amortized is $2,650 ($33,124 × 8% = $2,650 rounded). Likewise each end-of-the-year carrying amount is determined by subtracting the end-of-the-year unamortized discount from the remaining end-of-the-year lease liability. For example, the December 31, 198C, carrying amount is $30,000 − $4,226 = $25,774.

PAYROLL LIABILITIES

Amounts withheld from employees' wages plus payroll taxes levied on the employer can create a significant share of the current liabilities appearing on a balance sheet. Discussions of these withholdings, taxes, and the resulting liabilities follow.

FICA taxes

The federal Social Security Act provides that a qualified worker who reaches the age of 62 and retires shall receive monthly retirement benefits for the remainder of his or her life plus certain medical benefits after reaching 65. It also provides benefits for the family of a qualified deceased worker. Funds for the payment of these benefits are obtained from taxes levied under a law called the Federal Insurance Contributions Act. They are called *FICA taxes* or simply "social security taxes."

The Federal Insurance Contributions Act requires, among other things, that an employer (1) withhold from the wages of each employee each payday an amount of FICA tax equal, at this writing, to 6.13% of the wages earned, with the withholding to cease each year as soon as the employee has earned $22,900. (2) Pay a payroll tax equal to the amount withheld from the wages of all employees. (3) Periodically remit the amounts withheld and the employer's tax to the Internal Revenue Service. The amounts of employees' FICA taxes withheld and the employer's FICA tax are a current liability until remitted to the Internal Revenue Service.

Employees' federal income taxes

Employers of one or more employees, with a few exceptions, are required to withhold from the wages of each employee each payday an amount of federal income tax. The amount withheld is determined from a tax table furnished by the Internal Revenue Service. In each case the amount withheld depends on the employee's earnings and the number of exemptions (also called withholding allowances). Each exemption or allowance exempts $1,000 of the employee's yearly earnings from the tax. An employee is allowed one exemption for himself or herself, additional exemptions if either the employee or the employee's spouse is blind or over 65, and additional exemptions for each dependent. The amount of employees' income taxes withheld is a current liability until remitted to the Internal Revenue Service.

Other deductions from wages

In addition to compulsory deductions for FICA and federal income taxes, employees may voluntarily authorize an employer to deduct from wages, among other things, charitable contributions and amounts to pay health and hospital insurance premiums, to purchase U.S. savings bonds, and to pay union dues. The latter may not be voluntary, but required by a union contract. The amounts deducted are current liabilities until remitted to the proper organization.

PAYROLL RECORDS AND PROCEDURES

Payroll records and procedures vary from company to company, depending upon the number of employees and the extent computers and other machines are used in processing the payroll data. However, a basic procedure in any system is the preparation of a *payroll record* showing the name, hours worked, pay rate, earnings, deductions, and net amount owed each employee. In a manual system this information is entered on the record in columns with each employee's data on a separate line. Columns are also provided for sorting the employees' wages into proper expense accounts. After the data are entered, the columns are totaled and the totals become the bases of an entry like the following to record the payroll.

Jan.	7	Sales Salaries Expense	1,500.00	
		Office Salaries Expense	500.00	
		FICA Taxes Payable		122.60
		Employees' Income Taxes Payable		212.40
		Employees' Health Insurance Payable		85.00
		Employees' Union Dues Payable		25.00
		Accrued Payroll Payable		1,555.00
		To record the payroll for the pay period ended January 7, 19—.		

The debits of the entry indicate that the employees earned $1,500 of sales salaries and $500 of office salaries. However, they will receive only $1,555 of the $2,000 earned. The remainder was deducted from their pay and is represented by the first four credits in the entry. To pay the employees, another entry or series of entries, one for each check written, must be made in the Cash Disbursements Journal. The entry or entries have a debit or debits to Accrued Payroll Payable and a credit or credits to Cash.

In addition to the payroll record previously described, an employer must maintain an *individual earnings record* for each employee. The employer must also give each employee within one month after the year-end a W-2 Form. The form tells the employee the amount he or she earned during the year, the wages subject to FICA and federal income taxes, and the amounts of these taxes withheld. Copies of the employees' W-2 Forms must also be sent to the Internal Revenue Service.

EMPLOYER'S PAYROLL TAXES

Employer's FICA tax

As previously stated, in addition to withholding FICA taxes from the wages of its employees, an employer must pay an FICA tax equal to the sum of the FICA taxes withheld from the wages of all its employees. The employer's tax is credited to the same FICA Taxes Payable account as are the withheld FICA taxes of its employees and is a current liability until remitted to the Internal Revenue Service.

State unemployment tax

All states maintain unemployment insurance programs, and while the programs differ in some respects, all have three common objectives:

1. To pay unemployment compensation for limited periods to unemployed individuals.

2. To stabilize employment. In all states this is accomplished by a so-called merit-rating plan. Under a merit-rating plan an employer who provides steady employment for its employees gains a *merit rating* that substantially reduces its state unemployment tax rate.
3. To establish and operate employment facilities that assist unemployed individuals in finding suitable employment and assist employers in finding employees.

All states support their unemployment insurance programs by placing a payroll tax on employers. A few states place an additional tax on employees. The basic rate in most states is 2.7% of the first $6,000 paid each employee, and an employer can gain a merit rating that will reduce this basic rate to as little as 0.5% in some states and to zero in others. An employer gains a merit rating by not laying employees off during a slack season to draw unemployment benefits. To most employers such a rating offers an important tax savings. For example, an employer with just ten employees who each earn $6,000 or more per year can save $1,320 of state unemployment taxes each year by gaining a merit rating that reduces its state unemployment tax rate to 0.5%.

Federal unemployment tax

The federal government levies a payroll tax on employers of one or more persons equal to 0.7% of the first $6,000 paid each employee. Primarily the funds raised by the tax are distributed to the states to help pay the administrative expenses of the various state unemployment programs. Note that the federal tax is levied on employers only; employees are not taxed.

Recording the employer's payroll taxes

The payroll taxes of an employer are an expense and are recorded each pay period with a general journal entry. The entry to record the employer's taxes on the $2,000 payroll previously described is:

Jan.	7	Payroll Taxes Expense	190.60	
		FICA Taxes Payable		122.60
		State Unemployment Taxes Payable		54.00
		Federal Unemployment Taxes Payable		14.00
		To record the employer's payroll taxes.		

TAX RETURNS AND PAYING THE TAXES

Within one month after the end of each calendar quarter an employer must file a special payroll tax return reporting the amount of income taxes withheld from the wages of its employees and the amount of employer's and employees' FICA taxes for the quarter. Times for remitting the taxes to the Internal Revenue Service depend on the amounts involved. If the taxes do not exceed $200 during the quarter, they may be paid quarterly. However, for quarterly taxes totaling more than $200, payments must be made more often, as often as weekly for taxes totaling $2,000 or more per week.

Federal unemployment taxes must be paid as often as quarterly, depending on the amount; and a special federal unemployment tax return must be filed each year within one month after the end of the year. Most states require a tax return and the payment of state unemployment taxes on a quarterly basis.

GLOSSARY

Bank discount. Interest charged and deducted by a bank in discounting a note.

Capital lease. A lease having essentially the same economic consequences as if the lessee had secured a loan and purchased the leased asset.

Carrying amount of a note. The face amount of a note minus the unamortized discount on the note.

Carrying amount of a lease. The remaining lease liability minus the unamortized discount on the lease financing.

Federal unemployment tax. A federal tax levied on employers, the proceeds of which are used primarily to finance the unemployment programs of the states.

FICA taxes. Federal Insurance Contributions Act taxes, otherwise known as social security taxes.

Financing lease. Another name for a capital lease.

Individual earnings record. A record of an employee's hours worked, gross pay, deductions, net pay, and certain personal information about the employee.

Merit rating. A rating granted an employer by a state, which is based on whether or not the employer's employees have experienced periods of unemployment. A good rating reduces the employer's unemployment tax rate.

Operating lease. A lease not meeting any one of the criteria of the FASB that would make it a capital lease.

Payroll tax. A tax levied on the amount of a payroll or the amount of an employee's gross pay.

Present value. The estimated worth today of an amount of money to be received at a future date.

Present value table. A table showing the present value of one amount to be received at various future dates when discounted at various interest rates.

State unemployment tax. A tax levied by a state, the proceeds from which are used to pay benefits to unemployed workers.

QUESTIONS FOR CLASS DISCUSSION

1. Define *(a)* a current liability and *(b)* a long-term liability.
2. The legal position of a company is improved by its acceptance of a promissory note in exchange for granting a time extension on the due date of a customer's debt. Why?
3. What distinction do banks make between loans and discounts?
4. Which is to the advantage of a bank *(a)* making a loan to a customer in exchange for the customer's $1,000, 60-day, 9% note or *(b)* making a loan to the customer by discounting the customer's $1,000 noninterest-bearing note for 60 days at 9%? Why?
5. Distinguish between bank discount and cash discount.
6. What determines the present value of $1,000 to be received at some future date?
7. If a $5,000, noninterest-bearing, five-year note is exchanged for a machine, what two elements of the transaction are represented in the $5,000 face amount of the note?
8. If the Machinery account is debited for $5,000 and Notes Payable is credited for $5,000 in recording the machine of Question 7, what effects will this have on the financial statements?
9. What is the advantage of leasing a plant asset instead of purchasing it?
10. Distinguish between a capital lease and an operating lease. Which causes an asset and a liability to appear on the balance sheet?
11. At what amount is a machine acquired through a capital lease recorded?
12. What are FICA taxes? Who pays these taxes and for what purposes are funds from FICA taxes used?
13. Who pays federal unemployment insurance taxes? What is the tax rate?
14. What are the objectives of state unemployment insurance programs? Who pays state unemployment insurance taxes?
15. What is a state unemployment merit rating? Why are such merit ratings granted?

CLASS EXERCISES

Exercise 10–1

A company borrowed $10,000 from its bank by giving a 9%, 60-day note dated December 11, 198A. Prepare entries to record *(a)* issuance of the note, *(b)* the December 31 accrued interest on the note, and *(c)* the payment of the note under the assumption the company does not make reversing entries.

Exercise 10–2

A company borrowed from its bank on December 11, 198A, by discounting its $10,000, noninterest-bearing note for 60 days at 9%. Prepare entries to record (a) the issuance of the note, (b) the December 31 adjusting entry to remove from the Interest Expense account the interest applicable to 198B, (c) the reversing entry, and (d) the payment of the note.

Exercise 10–3

Present calculations to show the following: (a) The present value of $5,000 to be received five years hence, discounted at 8%. (b) The total present value of three payments consisting of $8,000 to be received one year hence, $6,000 to be received two years hence, and $4,000 to be received three years hence, all discounted at 10%. (c) The present value of five payments of $2,000 each, with a payment to be received at the end of each of the next five years, discounted at 8%.

Exercise 10–4

On January 1, 198A, a day when the prevailing interest rate was 8%, a company exchanged a $5,000, noninterest bearing, four-year note for a machine the cash price of which was not readily determinable. (a) Prepare the entry to record the purchase of the machine. (b) Show how the liability will appear on a balance sheet prepared on the day of the purchase. (c) Prepare the entry to amortize a portion of the discount on the note at the end of its first year.

Exercise 10–5

On January 1, 198A, a day when the prevailing interest rate was 8%, a company had an opportunity to either buy a machine for $16,500 cash or lease it for four years under a contract calling for a $5,000 annual lease payment at the end of each of the next four years, with the machine becoming the property of the lessee company at the end of that period. The company decided to lease the machine. Prepare entries to record (a) the leasing of the machine, (b) the amortization of the discount of the lease financing at the end of the first year, and (c) the first annual payment under the lease.

PROBLEMS

Problem 10–1

Prepare general journal entries to record these transactions:

Mar. 3   Purchased machinery on credit from Litton Company, invoice dated March 1, terms 2/10, n/60, $5,500.

May 4   Borrowed money from Security Bank by discounting our own $6,000 note payable for 60 days at 8%.

May 6   Gave Litton Company $1,000 in cash and a $4,500, 60-day, 8% note to secure a time extension on the balance owed on our past-due account.

July 3   Paid the note discounted at Security Bank on May 4.

      5   Paid the note given Litton Company on May 6.

Nov. 1   Borrowed money at Security Bank by discounting our own $8,000 note payable for 90 days at 9%.

Dec. 16   Borrowed money at Guaranty Bank by giving a $6,000, 60-day, 8% note payable.

    31   Made an adjusting entry to remove from the Interest Expense account the interest applicable to next year on the note discounted at Security Bank on November 1.

    31   Made an adjusting entry to record the accrued interest on the note given Guaranty Bank on December 16.

    31   Reversed the adjusting entry applicable to the note given Security Bank on November 1. Dated the entry January 1.

Jan. 30   Paid the note discounted at Security Bank on November 1.

Feb. 13   Paid the note given to Guaranty Bank on December 16.

Problem 10–2

A company completed these transactions involving a factory machine.

198A

Dec. 31   Exchanged an $8,000, three-year, noninterest-bearing note payable for a machine, the cash price of which was not readily determinable. The prevailing interest rate on the day of the exchange was 8%. The machine's service life was estimated at eight years with no salvage value.

198B

Dec. 31   Amortized a portion of the discount on the note payable. (Round all amounts to the nearest full dollar.)

    31   Recorded straight-line depreciation on the machine.

198C

Dec. 31   Amortized a portion of the discount on the note payable.

    31   Recorded straight-line depreciation on the machine.

198D

Jan. 5   Added device onto the machine at a $600 cost. The device increased the machine's output by 25% but did not change its estimated service life or zero salvage value.

Dec. 31   Amortized the remaining amount of discount on the note payable.

    31   Paid the noninterest-bearing note payable.

    31   Recorded straight-line depreciation on the machine.

198E

Dec. 31   Recorded straight-line depreciation on the machine.

198F

June 28   Traded the old machine on a new machine of like purpose but capable of double the output and having a $10,000 cash price. A $3,500 trade-in allowance was received, and the balance was paid in cash.

Required:

1. Prepare general journal entries to record the transactions, rounding all amounts to the nearest full dollar.
2. Under the assumption that the machine and the note payable were the only machine and note payable of the company on December 31, 198B, show how they would appear on the balance sheet of that date.

Problem 10–3

A company exchanged a $12,000, five-year, noninterest-bearing note payable for a machine, the cash price of which was not readily determinable The prevailing interest rate on the day of the exchange, January 1, 198A, was 8%. The machine's service life was estimated at nine years with no salvage value, and it was to be depreciated on a straight-line basis.

Required:

1. Prepare a general journal entry to record acquisition of the machine.
2. Prepare a schedule with the columnar headings of Illustration 10–2. Enter the years 198A through 198E in the schedule's first column and complete the schedule by filling in the proper amounts. (Round all amounts to the nearest full dollar and adjust the last year's discount to be amortized for rounding.)
3. Show how the machine and the note should appear on the December 31, 198B, balance sheet.
4. Show how the machine and the note should appear on the December 31, 198C, balance sheet.
5. Prepare entries to record (a) the 198D discount to be amortized and (b) the 198D depreciation expense. Also, (c) prepare the entry to record the payment of the note on January 1, 198F.

Problem 10–4

A company required the use of two machines in its operations. The life of each machine was estimated at ten years with no salvage value. Machine No. 1 would have cost $50,000 and Machine No. 2 $51,750 if purchased for cash. However, the company did not have the required funds, and it leased the machines on December 31, 198A, a day when the prevailing interest rate was 8%. Machine No. 1 leased for five years under a contract calling for $9,000 annual lease payments and the return of the machine to the lessor at the end of the lease period. Machine No. 2 was leased for eight years under a contract calling for $9,000 annual lease payments, with the machine becoming the property of the lessee company at the end of the lease period. In both cases the payments were to be made at the end of each year in the lives of the leases.

Required:

1. Prepare any required entries to record the lease of (a) Machine No. 1 and (b) Machine No. 2.

2. Prepare the required entries as of the end of the first year in (a) the life of Machine No. 1 and (b) the life of Machine No. 2. (Round all amounts to the nearest full dollar and use straight-line depreciation.)
3. Machine No. 1 was returned to the lessor on December 31, 198F, the end of the fifth year. Prepare the required entries as of the end of the fifth year in (a) the life of Machine No. 1 and (b) the life of Machine No. 2.
4. Show how Machine No. 2 and the lease liability for the machine should appear on the balance sheet as of the end of the fifth year in the life of the lease.

Problem 10–5

A company needed a new machine in its operations. The machine could be purchased for $33,000 cash or it could be leased for four years under a contract calling for annual payments of $10,000 at the end of each of the four years in the life of the lease, with the machine becoming the property of the lessee after the last lease payment. The machine's service life was estimated at six years with no salvage value. The company decided to lease the machine; and on December 31, 198A, a day when the prevailing interest rate was 8%, it signed the lease contract. The machine was delivered two days later and was placed in operation on January 12, 198B. On April 3, during the sixth year in the life of the machine, it was traded in on a new machine of like purpose having a $40,000 cash price. A $2,000 trade-in allowance was received, and the balance was paid in cash.

Required:

1. Prepare a schedule with the columnar headings of Illustration 10–3. Enter the years 198B through 198E in the first column and complete the schedule by filling in the proper amounts. Round all amounts to the nearest full dollar.
2. Prepare the entry to record the leasing of the machine.
3. Using straight-line depreciation, prepare the required entries as of the end of the first year in the life of the machine and the lease. Show how the machine and the lease liability should appear on the December 31, 198B, balance sheet.
4. Prepare the required entries as of the end of the third year in the life of the lease and the machine. Show how the machine and the lease liability should appear on the December 31, 198D, balance sheet.
5. Prepare the April 3, 198G, entry to record the exchange of the old and new machines, using the income tax method.

ALTERNATE PROBLEMS

Problem 10–1A

Prepare general journal entries to record these transactions:

Mar. 29   Gave $1,200 in cash and a $6,000, 8%, 120-day note to purchase store equipment.

Apr. 12 Borrowed money at the bank by discounting our $5,000 note payable for 60 days at 9%.

June 11 Paid the note discounted at the bank on April 12.

July 27 Paid the $6,000 note of the March 29 transaction and the interest.

Aug. 31 Purchased merchandise on credit from Otto Company, invoice date August 29, terms 2/10, n/60, $4,800.

Nov. 1 Gave Otto Company $300 in cash and a $4,500, 90-day, 8% note dated this day to gain a time extension on the balance owed.

Dec. 1 Borrowed money at Security Bank by discounting our $8,000 note payable for 90 days at 9%.

   31 Made an adjusting entry to record the accrued interest on the note given Otto Company on November 1.

   31 Made an adjusting entry to remove from the Interest Expense account the interest applicable to the next year on the note discounted on December 1.

   31 Reversed the adjusting entry applicable to the note given Security Bank on December 1. Dated the entry January 1.

Jan. 30 Paid the note given Otto Company on November 1.

Mar. 1 Paid the note discounted at Security Bank on December 1.

Problem 10–2A

A company completed these transactions:

198A

Dec. 31 Exchanged a $7,500, three-year, noninterest-bearing note payable for a machine, the cash price of which was not readily determinable. The machine's service life was estimated at five years with no salvage value. The prevailing interest rate on the day of the exchange was 8%.

198B

Dec. 31 Amortized a portion of the discount on the note payable.

   31 Recorded straight-line depreciation on the machine.

198C

Dec. 31 Amortized a portion of the discount on the note payable.

   31 Recorded straight-line depreciation on the machine.

198D

Jan. 10 Added a $756 device onto the machine, which increased the machine's hourly output by one third but did not change its estimated service life or its zero salvage value.

Dec. 31 Amortized the remaining amount of discount on the note payable.

   31 Paid the noninterest-bearing note payable.

   31 Recorded straight-line depreciation on the machine.

198E

Dec. 31 Recorded straight-line depreciation on the machine.

198F

Apr. 27 Traded the old machine on a new machine having twice the hourly output. The new machine had a $9,000 cash price and a $1,000 trade-in allowance was received. The balance was paid in cash.

Required:

1. Prepare general journal entries to record the transactions, rounding all amounts to the nearest full dollar.
2. Show how the machine and the note payable should appear on the December 31, 198B, balance sheet.

Problem 10–3A

A company exchanged a $14,000 four-year, noninterest-bearing note payable for a machine, the cash price of which was not readily determinable. The prevailing interest rate on the day of the exchange, January 1, 198A, was 8%. The machine's service life was estimated at six years with no salvage value, and it was to be depreciated on a straight-line basis.

Required:

1. Prepare a general journal entry to record acquisition of the machine.
2. Prepare a schedule with columnar headings like Illustration 10–2. Enter the years 198A through 198D in the schedule's first column and complete the schedule by filling in the proper amounts. (Round all amounts to the nearest full dollar and adjust the last year's discount for rounding.)
3. Show how the machine and the note should appear on the December 31, 198A, balance sheet.
4. Show how the machine and the note should appear on the December 31, 198B, balance sheet.
5. Prepare entries to record *(a)* the 198C discount to be amortized and *(b)* the 198C depreciation expense. Also, *(c)* prepare the entry to record the payment of the note on January 1, 198E.

Problem 10–4A

On December 31, 198A, a day when the prevailing interest rate was 8%, a company leased two machines. Machine No. 1 was leased for six years under a contract calling for an $8,000 lease payment at the end of each year in the life of the lease, with the machine becoming the property of the lessee company after the sixth lease payment. Machine No. 2 was leased for four years under a contract calling for an $8,000 annual lease payment at the end of each year in the life of the lease and the machine to be returned to the lessor at the end of the fourth year. Each machine could have been purchased for $36,950 cash, and each machine was estimated to have no salvage value at the end of an estimated ten-year life.

Required:

1. Prepare any required entries to record the lease of *(a)* Machine No. 1 and *(b)* Machine No. 2.
2. Prepare the required entries as of the end of the first year in *(a)* the life of Machine No. 1 and *(b)* the life of Machine No. 2. (Round all amounts to the nearest full dollar and use straight-line depreciation.)
3. Machine No. 2 was returned to the lessor on December 31, 198E, the end of the fourth year. Prepare the required entries as of the end of the

fourth year in *(a)* the life of Machine No. 1 and *(b)* the life of Machine No. 2.

4. Show how Machine No. 1 and the lease liability for the machine should appear on the balance sheet prepared at the end of the fourth year in the life of the lease.

Problem 10–5A

A company leased a machine on December 31, 198A, under a contract calling for annual payments of $12,000 at the end of each of four years, with the machine becoming the property of the lessee company after the fourth $12,000 lease payment. The machine was estimated to have an eight-year life and no salvage value, and the prevailing interest rate on the day the lease was signed was 8%. The machine was delivered on January 3, 198B, and was placed in operation eight days later. During the first week in January, at the beginning of the eighth year in the machine's life, it was overhauled at a $1,200 total cost. The overhaul was paid for on January 10, and it did not increase the machine's efficiency but it did add an additional year to its expected service life. On March 28, during the ninth year in the machine's life, it was traded in on a new machine of like purpose having a $45,000 cash price. A $2,000 trade-in allowance was received and the balance was paid in cash.

Required:

1. Prepare a schedule with the columnar headings of Illustration 10–3. Enter the years 198B through 198E in the first column and complete the schedule by filling in the proper amounts. (Round all amounts to the nearest full dollar.)
2. Prepare the entry to record the leasing of the machine.
3. Using straight-line depreciation, prepare the required entries as of the end of the second year in the life of the lease. Also show how the machine and the lease liability should appear on the December 31, 198C, balance sheet.
4. Prepare the entries to record the machine's overhaul and the depreciation on the machine at the end of its eighth year.
5. Prepare the March 28, 198J, entries to record the exchange of the machines.

11

Mortgages and bonds payable

After studying Chapter 11 you should be able to:

- Account for the issuance and payment of a mortgage.
- Explain the difference between a share of stock and a bond.
- State the advantages and disadvantages of securing capital by issuing bonds.
- Explain how bond interest rates are established.
- Use present value tables to calculate the premium or discount on a bond issue.
- Prepare entries to account for bonds issued between interest dates at par.
- Prepare entries to account for bonds sold on their date of issue at par, at a discount, and at a premium.
- Explain the purpose and operation of a bond sinking fund and prepare entries to account for the operation of such a fund.
- Define or explain the words and phrases listed in the chapter Glossary.

When a business borrows money that is not to be repaid for a relatively long period of time, 10, 20, or more years, it may borrow by means of a mortgage or by issuing bonds.

ISSUING A MORTGAGE TO BORROW MONEY

When a business needs long-term money, it may obtain the money by placing a mortgage on some or all of its plant assets. A mortgage actually involves two legal documents. The first is a kind of promissory note called a *mortgage note*, which is secured by a second legal document called a *mortgage* or a *mortgage contract*. In the mortgage note the mortgagor, the one who mortgages property, promises to repay the money borrowed. The mortgage or mortgage contract commonly requires the mortgagor to keep the mortgaged property in a good state of repair, carry adequate insurance, and pay the interest on the mortgage note. In addition it normally grants the mortgage holder the right to foreclose in case the mortgagor fails in any of the required duties. In a foreclosure a court takes possession of the mortgaged property for the mortgage holder and may order its sale. If the property is sold, the proceeds go first to pay court costs and the claims of the mortgage holder. Any money remaining is then paid to the former owner of the property.

A loan secured by a mortgage is recorded as follows:

Feb.	1	Cash	40,000.00	
		Mortgage Payable		40,000.00
		Borrowed by placing a 20-year, 8½% mortgage on the building.		

In addition to paying interest, a mortgage contract commonly requires the mortgagor to make periodic payments to reduce the mortgage debt. For example, if the foregoing mortgage requires semiannual interest payments plus semiannual $1,000 payments to reduce the mortgage debt, the following entry is used to record the first semiannual payments:

381

Aug.	1	Mortgage Payable...........................	1,000.00	
		Interest Expense............................	1,700.00	
		Cash		2,700.00
		Paid the interest and the first semiannual payment on the mortgage principal.		

On a mortgage such as this the balance of the mortgage debt at the beginning of each interest period is normally used in calculating the period's mortgage interest. Likewise, at the end of each year the portion of the mortgage debt to be paid with current assets during the next year becomes a current liability for statement purposes.

DIFFERENCE BETWEEN STOCKS AND BONDS

The phrase "stocks and bonds" commonly appears on the financial pages of newspapers and is often heard in conversations. However, before beginning a study of bonds, the difference between a share of stock and a bond should be clearly understood. A share of stock represents an equity or ownership right in a corporation. For example, if a person owns 1,000 of the 10,000 shares of common stock a corporation has outstanding, the person has an equity in the corporation measured at $\frac{1}{10}$ of the corporation's total stockholders' equity and has a right to $\frac{1}{10}$ of the corporation's earnings. If on the other hand a person owns a $1,000, 8%, 20-year bond issued by a corporation,[1] the *bond* represents a debt or a liability of the corporation. Its owner has two rights: (1) the right to receive 8% or $80 interest each year the bond is outstanding and (2) the right to be paid $1,000 when the bond matures 20 years after its date of issue.

WHY BONDS ARE ISSUED

A corporation in need of long-term funds may secure the funds by issuing additional shares of stock or by selling bonds. Each has its advantages and disadvantages. Stockholders are owners, and issuing additional stock spreads ownership, control of management, and earnings over more shares. Bondholders, on the other hand, are creditors and do not share in either management or earnings. However, bond interest must be paid whether there are any earnings or not. Otherwise the bondholders may foreclose and take the assets pledged for their security.

Nevertheless, issuing bonds, rather than additional stock, will com-

---

[1] The federal government and other governmental units, such as cities, states, and school districts also issue bonds. However, the discussions in this chapter are limited to the bonds of corporations.

monly result in increased earnings for the owners (the common stock-holders) of the issuing corporation. For example, assume a corporation with 200,000 shares of common stock outstanding needs $1,000,000 to expand its operations. The corporation's management estimates that after the expansion the company can earn $600,000 annually before bond interest, if any, and corporation income taxes; and it has proposed two plans for securing the needed funds. Plan No. 1 calls for issuing 100,000 additional shares of the corporation's common stock at $10 per share. This will increase the total outstanding shares to 300,000. Plan No. 2 calls for the sale at par of $1,000,000 of 8% bonds. Illustration 11–1 shows how the plans will affect the corporation's earnings.

	Plan 1	Plan 2
Earnings before bond interest and income taxes	$600,000	$600,000
Deduct bond interest expense		(80,000)
Income before corporation income taxes	$600,000	$520,000
Deduct income taxes (assumed 50% rate)	(300,000)	(260,000)
Net income	$300,000	$260,000
Plan 1 income per share (300,000 shares)	$1.00	
Plan 2 income per share (200,000 shares)		$1.30

Illustration 11–1

Corporations are subject to state and federal income taxes, which together may take as much as 50% of the corporation's before-tax income. However bond interest expense is a deductible expense in arriving at income subject to taxes. Consequently, when the combined state and federal tax rate is 50%, as in Illustration 11–1, the tax reduction from issuing bonds equals one half the annual interest on the bonds. In other words, the tax savings in effect pays one half the interest cost of the bonds.

BORROWING BY ISSUING BONDS

When a large corporation wishes to borrow several millions of dollars, it will normally borrow by issuing bonds. Bonds are issued because few banks or insurance companies are able or willing to make a loan of such size. Also, bonds enable the corporation to divide the loan among many lenders.

Borrowing by issuing bonds is in many ways similar to borrowing by giving a mortgage. Actually, the real difference is that a number of bonds, often in denominations of $1,000, are issued in the place of a single mortgage note. For all practical purposes each bond is a promissory note, promising to pay a definite sum of money to its holder, or owner of record, at a fixed future date. Like promissory notes, bonds bear interest; and like a mortgage note, they are often secured by a mortgage. However, since bonds may be owned and transferred during their lives by a number of people, they differ from promissory notes in that they do not namc the lender.

When a company issues bonds secured by a mortgage, it normally sells the bonds to an investment firm, known as the *underwriter*. The underwriter in turn resells the bonds to the public. In addition to the underwriter, the company issuing bonds selects a trustee to represent the bondholders. In most cases the trustee is a large bank or trust company to which the company issuing the bonds executes and delivers the mortgage contract that acts as security for the bonds. It is the duty of the trustee to see that the company fulfills all the pledged responsibilities of the mortgage contract, or as it is often called the *deed of trust*. It is also the duty of the trustee to foreclose if any pledges are not fulfilled.

CHARACTERISTICS OF BONDS

Over the years corporation lawyers and financiers have created a wide variety of bonds, each with different combinations of characteristics. For example, bonds may be *serial bonds* or *sinking fund bonds*. When serial or term bonds are issued, portions of the issue become due and are paid in installments over a period of years. Sinking fund bonds differ in that they are paid at maturity in one lump sum from a sinking fund created for that purpose. Sinking funds are discussed later in this chapter.

Bonds may also be either *registered bonds* or *coupon bonds*. Ownership of registered bonds is registered or recorded with the issuing corporation. This offers some protection from loss or theft. Interest payments on such bonds are usually made by checks mailed to the registered owners. Coupon bonds secure their name from the interest coupons attached to each bond. Each coupon calls for payment on the interest payment date of the interest due on the bond to which it is attached. The coupons are detached as they become due and are deposited with a bank for collection. Often ownership of a coupon bond is not registered. Such unregistered bonds are payable to bearer or are bearer paper, and ownership is transferred by delivery. Sometimes bonds are registered as to principal with interest payments by coupons.

Bonds also may be secured or unsecured. Unsecured bonds are called *debentures* and depend upon the general credit standing of their issuing corporation for security. Only financially strong companies are able to sell unsecured bonds or bonds that are not secured by a mortgage.

ISSUING BONDS

When a corporation issues bonds, the bonds are printed and the deed of trust is drawn and deposited with the trustee of the bondholders. At that point a memorandum describing the bond issue is commonly entered in the Bonds Payable account. Such a memorandum might read, "Authorized to issue $8,000,000 of 9%, 20-year bonds dated January 1, 19—, and with interest payable semiannually on each July 1 and January 1." As in this case, bond interest is usually payable semiannually.

After the deed of trust is deposited with the trustee of the bondholders, all or a portion of the bonds may be sold. If all are sold at their *par value*, also called their *face amount*, an entry like this is made to record the sale:

Jan.	1	Cash	8,000,000.00	
		Bonds Payable		8,000,000.00
		Sold bonds at par on their interest date.		

When the semiannual interest is paid on these bonds, the transaction is recorded as follows:

July	1	Bond Interest Expense	360,000.00	
		Cash		360,000.00
		Paid the semiannual interest on the bonds.		

And when the bonds are paid at maturity, an entry like this is made:

Jan.	1	Bonds Payable	8,000,000.00	
		Cash		8,000,000.00
		Paid bonds at maturity.		

BONDS SOLD BETWEEN INTEREST DATES

Sometimes bonds are sold on their date of issue, which is also their interest date, as in the previous illustration. More often they are sold after their date of issue and between interest dates. In such cases, it is customary to charge and collect from the purchasers the interest that has accrued on the bonds since the previous interest payment and to return this accrued interest to the purchasers on the next interest date. For example, assume that on March 1, a corporation sold at par $100,000 of 9% bonds on which interest is payable semiannually on each January 1 and July 1. (Small dollar amounts are used in order to conserve space.) The entry to record the sale between interest dates is:

Mar.	1	Cash	101,500.00	
		Bond Interest Expense		1,500.00
		Bonds Payable		100,000.00
		Sold $100,000 of bonds on which two months' interest has accrued.		

At the end of four months, on the July 1 semiannual interest date, the purchasers of these bonds are paid a full six months' interest. This payment includes four months' interest earned by the bondholders after March 1 and the two months' accrued interest collected from them at the time the bonds were sold. The entry to record the payment is:

July	1	Bond Interest Expense	4,500.00	
		Cash		4,500.00
		Paid the semiannual interest on the bonds.		

After both of these entries are posted, the Bond Interest Expense account has a $3,000 debit balance and appears as follows:

Bond Interest Expense			
July 1 (Payment)	4,500.00	Mar. 1 (Accrued interest)	1,500.00

The $3,000 debit balance is the interest on the $100,000 of bonds at 9% for the four months from March 1 to July 1.

Students often think it strange to charge bond purchasers for accrued interest when bonds are sold between interest dates, and to return this accrued interest in the next interest payment. However, this is the custom, all bond transactions are "plus accrued interest"; and there is a good reason for the practice. For instance, if a corporation sells portions of a bond issue on different dates during an interest period without collecting the accrued interest, it must keep records of the purchasers and the dates on which they bought bonds. Otherwise it cannot pay the correct amount of interest to each. However, if it charges each buyer for accrued interest at the time of the purchase, it need not keep records of the purchasers and their purchase dates. It can pay a full period's interest to all purchasers for the period in which they bought their bonds and each receives the interest he or she has earned and gets back the accrued interest paid at the time of the purchase.

BOND INTEREST RATES

At this point students who are not sure of their understanding of the concept of present value should turn back to Chapter 10 and review this concept before going further into this chapter.

A corporation issuing bonds specifies in the deed of trust and on each bond the interest rate it will pay. This rate is called the *contract rate*. It is usually stated on an annual basis, although bond interest is normally paid semiannually. Also, it is applied to the par value of the bonds to determine the dollars of interest the corporation will pay. For example, a corporation will pay $80 each year in two semiannual installments of $40 each on a $1,000, 8% bond on which interest is paid semiannually.

Although the contract rate establishes the interest a corporation will pay, it is not necessarily the interest the corporation will incur in issuing bonds. The interest it will incur depends upon what lenders consider their risks to be in lending to the corporation and upon the current *market rate for bond interest.* The market rate for bond interest is the rate borrowers are willing to pay and lenders are willing to take for the use of money at the level of risk involved. It fluctuates from day to day at any level of risk as the supply and demand for loanable funds fluctuate. It goes up when the demand for bond money increases and the supply decreases, and it goes down when the supply increases and the demand decreases.

A corporation issuing bonds usually offers a contract rate of interest equal to what it estimates the market will demand on the day the bonds are to be issued. If its estimate is correct, and the contract rate and market rate coincide on the day the bonds are issued, the bonds will sell at par, their face amount. However, when bonds are sold, their contract rate seldom coincides with the market rate. As a result, bonds usually sell either at a premium or at a discount.

BONDS SOLD AT A DISCOUNT

When a corporation offers to sell bonds carrying a contract rate below the prevailing market rate, the bonds will sell at a *discount.* Investors can get the market rate of interest elsewhere for the use of their money, so they will buy the bonds only at a price that will yield the prevailing market rate on the investment. What price will they pay and how is it determined? The price they will pay is the *present value* of the expected returns from the investment. It is determined by discounting the returns at the current market rate for bond interest.

To illustrate how bond prices are determined, assume that on a day when the market rate for bond interest is 9%, a corporation offers to sell and issue bonds having a $100,000 par value, a ten-year life, and on which interest is to be paid semiannually at an 8% annual rate.[2] In exchange for current dollars a buyer of these bonds will gain two monetary rights.

1. The right to receive $100,000 at the end of the bond issue's ten-year life.
2. The right to receive $4,000 in interest at the end of each six-month interest period throughout the ten-year life of the bonds.

Since both are rights to receive money in the future, to determine their present value, the amounts to be received are discounted at the prevailing market rate of interest. If the prevailing market rate is 9% annually, it is 4½% semiannually; and in ten years there are 20 semiannual periods. Consequently, using the last number in the 4½% column of Table 10–1, page 358, to discount the first amount and the last number in the 4½% column of Table 10–2, page 360, to discount the series of $4,000 amounts, the present value of the rights and the price an informed buyer will offer for the bonds is:

Present value of $100,000 to be received 20 periods hence, discounted at 4½% per period ($100,000 × 0.4146)	$41,460
Present value of $4,000 to be received periodically for 20 periods, discounted at 4½% ($4,000 × 13.008)	52,032
Present value of the bonds	$93,492

If the corporation accepts the $93,492 offer for its bonds and sells them on their date of issue, it will record the sale with an entry like this:

Jan.	1	Cash	93,492.00	
		Discount on Bonds Payable	6,508.00	
		Bonds Payable		100,000.00
		Sold bonds at a discount on their date of issue.		

---

[2] The spread between the contract rate and the market rate of interest on a new bond issue is seldom more than a fraction of a percent. However, a spread of a full percent is used here to simplify the illustrations.

If the corporation prepares a balance sheet on the day the bonds are sold, it may show the bonds in the long-term liability section as follows:

Long-term liabilities:
  First mortgage, 8% bonds payable, due January 1,
    199A $100,000
  Less unamortized discount based on the 9%
    market rate for bond interest prevailing on the
    date of issue.....................................   6,508 $93,492

On a balance sheet any unamortized discount on a bond issue is deducted from the par value of the bonds to show the amount at which the bonds are carried on the books, called the *carrying amount.*

Amortizing the discount

The corporation of this discussion received $93,492 for its bonds, but in ten years it must pay the bondholders $100,000. The difference, the $6,508 discount, is a cost of using the $93,492 that was incurred because the contract rate of interest on the bonds was below the prevailing market rate. It is a cost that must be paid when the bonds mature. However, each semiannual interest period in the life of the bond issue benefits from the use of the $93,492. Consequently, it is only fair that each should bear a fair share of this cost.

The procedure for dividing a discount and charging a share to each period in the life of the applicable bond issue is called *amortizing* a discount. A simple method of amortizing a discount is the *straight-line method,* a method in which an equal portion of the discount is amortized each interest period. If this method is used to amortize the $6,508 discount of this discussion, the $6,508 is divided by 20, the number of interest periods in the life of the bond issue, and $325.40 ($6,508 ÷ 20 = $325.40) of discount is amortized at the end of each interest period with an entry like this:

July	1	Bond Interest Expense	4,325.40	
		Discount on Bonds Payable		325.40
		Cash		4,000.00
		To record payment of six months' interest and amortization of ¹⁄₂₀ of the discount.		

The amortization of $325.40 of discount each six months will completely write off the $6,508 of discount by the end of the issue's ten-year life. It also increases the amount of bond interest expense recorded each six months to the sum of the $4,000 paid the bondholders plus the discount amortized.

Straight-line amortization is easy to understand and once was commonly used. However, the APB ruled that it may now be used only in situations where the results do not materially differ from those obtained through use of the so-called interest method.[3] The APB favored the interest method because it results in a constant rate of interest on the carrying amount of a bond issue. The straight-line method results in a decreasing rate when a discount is amortized and an increasing rate when a premium is amortized.

When the interest method is used, the interest expense to be recorded each period is determined by applying a constant rate of interest to the beginning-of-the-period carrying amount of the bonds. The constant rate applied is the market rate prevailing at the time the bonds were issued. The discount amortized each period is then determined by subtracting the interest to be paid the bondholders from the interest expense to be recorded. Illustration 11–2, with amounts rounded to full dollars, shows the interest expense to be recorded, the discount to be amortized, and so forth, when the interest method

Period	Beginning of-period carrying amount	Interest expense to be recorded	Interest to be paid the bondholders	Discount to be amortized	Unamortized discount at end of period	End-of-period carrying amount
1	93,492	4,207	4,000	207	6,301	93,699
2	93,699	4,216	4,000	216	6,085	93,915
3	93,915	4,226	4,000	226	5,859	94,141
4	94,141	4,236	4,000	236	5,623	94,377
5	94,377	4,247	4,000	247	5,376	94,624
6	94,624	4,258	4,000	258	5,118	94,882
7	94,882	4,270	4,000	270	4,848	95,152
8	95,152	4,282	4,000	282	4,566	95,434
9	95,434	4,295	4,000	295	4,271	95,729
10	95,729	4,308	4,000	308	3,963	96,037
11	96,037	4,322	4,000	322	3,641	96,359
12	96,359	4,336	4,000	336	3,305	96,695
13	96,695	4,351	4,000	351	2,954	97,046
14	97,046	4,367	4,000	367	2,587	97,413
15	97,413	4,384	4,000	384	2,203	97,797
16	97,797	4,401	4,000	401	1,802	98,198
17	98,198	4,419	4,000	419	1,383	98,617
18	98,617	4,438	4,000	438	945	99,055
19	99,055	4,457	4,000	457	488	99,512
20	99,512	4,488*	4,000	488	–0–	100,000

* Adjusted to compensate for accumulated rounding of amounts.

Illustration 11–2

[3] APB, "Interest on Receivables and Payables," *APB Opinion No. 21* (New York: AICPA, August 1971), par. 15.

of amortizing a discount is applied to the bond issue of this discussion. In examining Illustration 11–2, note these points:

1. The bonds were sold at a $6,508 discount, which when subtracted from their face amount gives a beginning of Period 1 carrying amount of $93,492.
2. The interest expense amounts result from multiplying each beginning-of-the-period carrying amount by the 4½% semiannual market rate prevailing when the bonds were issued. For example, $93,492 × 4½% = $4,207 and $93,699 × 4½% = $4,216.
3. Interest to be paid bondholders each period is determined by multiplying the par value of the bonds by the contract rate of interest.
4. The discount to be amortized each period is determined by subtracting the amount of interest to be paid the bondholders from the amount of interest expense.
5. The unamortized discount at the end of each period is determined by subtracting the discount amortized that period from the unamortized discount at the beginning of the period.
6. The end-of-the-period carrying amount for the bonds is determined by subtracting the end-of-the-period amount of unamortized discount from the face amount of the bonds. For example, at the end of Period 1: $100,000 − $6,301 = $93,699.

When the interest method is used in amortizing a discount, the periodic amortizing entries are like the entries used with the straight-line method, excepting as to the amounts. For example, the entry to pay the bondholders and amortize a portion of the discount at the end of the first semiannual interest period of the issue of Illustration 11–2 is:

July	1	Bond Interest Expense	4,207.00	
		Discount on Bonds Payable		207.00
		Cash		4,000.00
		To record payment of the bondholders and amortization of a portion of the discount.		

Similar entries, differing only in the amounts of interest expense recorded and discount amortized, are made at the end of each semiannual interest period in the life of the bond issue.

BONDS SOLD AT A PREMIUM

When a corporation offers to sell bonds carrying a contract rate of interest above the prevailing market rate for the risks involved, the bonds will sell at a premium. Buyers will bid up the price of the bonds, going as high, but no higher than a price that will return the current market rate of interest on the investment. What price will they pay? They will pay the present value of the expected returns from the investment, determined by discounting these returns at the prevailing market rate for bond interest. For example, assume that on a day the current market rate for bond interest is 7%, a corporation offers to sell bonds having a $100,000 par value and a ten-year life with interest to be paid semiannually at an 8% annual rate. An informed buyer of these bonds will discount the expectation of receiving $100,000 in ten years and the expectation of receiving $4,000 semiannually for 20 periods at the current 7% market rate as follows:

Present value of $100,000 to be received 20 periods hence, discounted at 3½% per period ($100,000 × 0.5026)	$ 50,260
Present value of $4,000 to be received periodically for 20 periods, discounted at 3½% ($4,000 × 14.212)	56,848
Present value of the bonds	$107,108

And the informed investor will offer the corporation $107,108 for its bonds. If the corporation accepts and sells the bonds on their date of issue, say, May 1, 198A, it will record the sale as follows:

198A					
May	1	Cash		107,108.00	
		Premium on Bonds Payable			7,108.00
		Bonds Payable			100,000.00
		Sold bonds at a premium on their date of issue.			

It may then show the bonds on a balance sheet prepared on the day of the sale as follows:

Long-term liabilities:		
First mortgage, 8% bonds payable, due May 1, 199A	$100,000	
Add unamortized premium based on the 7% market rate for bond interest prevailing on the date of issue	7,108	$107,108

On a balance sheet any unamortized premium on bonds payable is added to the par value of the bonds to show the carrying amount of the bonds, as illustrated.

Amortizing the premium

Although the corporation discussed here received $107,108 for its bonds, it will have to repay only $100,000 to the bondholders at maturity. The difference, the $7,108 premium, represents a reduction in the cost of using the $107,108. It should be amortized over the life of the bond issue in such a manner as to lower the recorded bond interest expense. If the $7,108 premium is amortized by the interest method, Illustration 11–3 shows the amounts of interest expense to be recorded each period, the premium to be amortized, and so forth.

Observe in Illustration 11–3 that the premium to be amortized each period is determined by subtracting the interest to be recorded from the interest to be paid the bondholders.

Period	Beginning-of-period carrying amount	Interest expense to be recorded	Interest to be paid the bondholders	Premium to be amortized	Unamortized premium at end of period	End-of-period carrying amount
1	107,108	3,749	4,000	251	6,857	106,857
2	106,857	3,740	4,000	260	6,597	106,597
3	106,597	3,731	4,000	269	6,328	106,328
4	106,328	3,721	4,000	279	6,049	106,049
5	106,049	3,712	4,000	288	5,761	105,761
6	105,761	3,702	4,000	298	5,463	105,463
7	105,463	3,691	4,000	309	5,154	105,154
8	105,154	3,680	4,000	320	4,834	104,834
9	104,834	3,669	4,000	331	4,503	104,503
10	104,503	3,658	4,000	342	4,161	104,161
11	104,161	3,646	4,000	354	3,807	103,807
12	103,807	3,633	4,000	367	3,440	103,440
13	103,440	3,620	4,000	380	3,060	103,060
14	103,060	3,607	4,000	393	2,667	102,667
15	102,667	3,593	4,000	407	2,260	102,260
16	102,260	3,579	4,000	421	1,839	101,839
17	101,839	3,564	4,000	436	1,403	101,403
18	101,403	3,549	4,000	451	952	100,952
19	100,952	3,533	4,000	467	485	100,485
20	100,485	3,515*	4,000	485	–0–	100,000

* Adjusted to compensate for accumulated rounding of amounts.

Illustration 11–3

Based on Illustration 11–3 the entry to record the first semiannual interest payment and premium amortization is:

198A Nov.	1	Bond Interest Expense	3,749.00	
		Premium on Bonds Payable	251.00	
		Cash		4,000.00
		To record payment of the bondholders and amortization of a portion of the premium.		

Note how the amortization of the premium results in a reduction in the amount of interest expense recorded. Similar entries having decreasing amounts of interest expense and increasing amounts of premium amortized are made at the ends of the remaining periods in the life of the bond issue.

ACCRUED BOND INTEREST EXPENSE

Often when bonds are sold the bond interest periods do not coincide with the issuing company's accounting periods. In such cases it is necessary at the end of each accounting period to make an adjustment for accrued interest. For example, it was assumed that the bonds of Illustration 11–3 were issued on May 1, 198A, and interest was paid on these bonds on November 1 of that year. If the accounting periods of the corporation end each December 31, on December 31, 198A, two months' interest has accrued on these bonds, and the following adjusting entry is required:

198A				
Dec.	31	Bond Interest Expense	1,246.67	
		Premium on Bonds Payable	86.66	
		Bond Interest Payable		1,333.33
		To record two months' accrued interest and amortize one third of the premium applicable to the interest period.		

Two months are one third of a semiannual interest period. Consequently, the amounts in the entry are one third of the amounts applicable to the second interest period in the life of the bond issue. Similar entries will be made on each December 31 throughout the life of the issue. However, the amounts will differ, since in each case they will apply to a different interest period.

When the interest is paid on these bonds on May 1, 198B, an entry like this is required:

198B				
May	1	Bond Interest Expense	2,493.33	
		Bond Interest Payable	1,333.33	
		Premium on Bonds Payable	173.34	
		Cash		4,000.00
		Paid the interest on the bonds, a portion of which was previously accrued, and amortized four months' premium.		

SALE OF BONDS BY INVESTORS

A purchaser of a bond may not hold it to maturity but may sell it after a period of months or years to a new investor at a price determined by the market rate for bond interest on the day of the sale. The market rate for bond interest on the day of the sale determines the price because the new investor can get this current rate elsewhere. Therefore, the investor will discount the right to receive the bond's face amount at maturity and the right to receive its interest for the remaining periods in its life at the current market rate to determine the price to pay for the bond. As a result, since bond interest rates may vary greatly over a period of months or years, a bond that originally sold at a premium may later sell at a discount, and vice versa.

REDEMPTION OF BONDS

Bonds are commonly issued with the provision that they may be redeemed at the issuing corporation's option, usually upon the payment of a redemption premium. Such bonds are known as *callable bonds*. Corporations commonly insert redemption clauses in deeds of trust because if interest rates decline, it may be advantageous to call and redeem outstanding bonds and issue in their place new bonds paying a lower interest rate.

Not all bonds have a provision giving their issuing company the right to call. However, even though the right is not provided, a company may secure the same effect by purchasing its bonds on the open market and retiring them. Often such action is wise when a company has funds available and its bonds are selling at a price below their carrying amount. For example, a company has outstanding on their interest date $1,000,000 of bonds on which there is $12,000 unamortized premium. The bonds are selling at 98½ (98½% of par value), and the company decides to buy and retire one tenth of the issue. The entry to record the purchase and retirement is:

Apr.	1	Bonds Payable	100,000.00	
		Premium on Bonds Payable	1,200.00	
		Gain on the Retirement of Bonds		2,700.00
		Cash		98,500.00
		To record the retirement of bonds.		

The retirement resulted in a $2,700 gain in this instance because the bonds were purchased at a price $2,700 below their carrying amount.

A paragraph back the statement was made that the bonds were selling at 98½. Bond quotations are commonly made in this manner. For example, a bond may be quoted for sale at 101¼. This means the bond is for sale at 101¼% of its par value, plus accrued interest, of course, if applicable.

CONVERTIBLE BONDS

To make an issue more attractive, bond owners may be given the right to exchange their bonds for a fixed number of shares of the issuing company's common stock. Such bonds are known as *convertible bonds*. They offer investors initial investment security, and if the issuing company prospers and the market value of its stock goes up, an opportunity to share in the prosperity by converting their bonds to stock. Conversion is always at the bondholders' option and is not exercised except when to do so is to their advantage. Converting bonds to shares of stock is discussed further in Chapter 13.

BOND SINKING FUND

Because of their fixed return and greater security, bonds appeal to a portion of the investing public. A corporation issuing bonds may offer investors a measure of security by placing a mortgage on certain of its assets. Often it will give additional security by agreeing in its deed of trust to create a *bond sinking fund*. This is a fund of assets accumulated to pay the bondholders at maturity.

When a corporation issuing bonds agrees to create a bond sinking fund, it normally agrees to create the fund by making periodic cash deposits with a sinking fund trustee. It is the duty of the trustee to safeguard the cash, to invest it in good sound securities, and to add the interest or dividends earned to the sinking fund. Generally, when the bonds become due, it is also the duty of the sinking fund trustee to sell the sinking fund securities and to use the proceeds to pay the bondholders.

When a sinking fund is created, the amount that must be deposited periodically in order to provide enough money to retire a bond issue at maturity will depend upon the net rate of compound interest that can be earned on the invested funds. The rate is a compound rate because earnings are continually reinvested by the sinking fund trustee to earn an additional return. It is a net rate because the trustee commonly deducts the fee for its services from the earnings.

To illustrate the operation of a sinking fund, assume a corporation issues $1,000,000 of ten-year bonds and agrees to deposit with a sinking fund trustee at the end of each year in the issue's life sufficient cash to create a fund large enough to retire the bonds at maturity. If the trustee is able to invest the funds in such a manner as to earn a 7% net return, $72,378 must be deposited each year and the fund will grow to maturity (in rounded dollars) as shown in Illustration 11–4.

End of year	Amount deposited	Interest earned on fund balance	Balance in fund after deposit and interest
1	$72,378	-0-	$ 72,378
2	72,378	$ 5,066	149,822
3	72,378	10,488	232,688
4	72,378	16,288	321,354
5	72,378	22,495	416,227
6	72,378	29,136	517,741
7	72,378	36,242	626,361
8	72,378	43,845	742,584
9	72,378	51,981	866,943
10	72,378	60,679*	1,000,000

* Adjusted for rounding.

Illustration 11–4

When a sinking fund is created by periodic deposits, the entry to record the amount deposited each year appears as follows:

Dec.	31	Bond Sinking Fund	72,378.00	
		Cash		72,378.00
		To record the annual sinking fund deposit.		

Each year the sinking fund trustee invests the amount deposited, and each year it collects and reports the earnings on the investments. The earnings report results in an entry to record the sinking fund income. For example, if $72,378 is deposited at the end of the first year in the sinking fund, the accumulation of which is shown in Illustration 11–4, and 7% is earned, the entry to record the sinking fund earnings of the second year is:

Dec.	31	Bond Sinking Fund	5,066.00	
		Sinking Fund Earnings		5,066.00
		To record the sinking fund earnings.		

Sinking fund earnings appear on the income statement as financial revenue in a section titled "Other revenues and expenses." A sinking fund is the property of the company creating the fund and should appear on its balance sheet in the long-term investments section.

When bonds mature, it is usually the duty of the sinking fund trustee to convert the fund's investments into cash and pay the bondholders. Normally the sinking fund securities, when sold, produce either a little more or a little less cash than is needed to pay the bondholders. If more cash than is needed is produced, the extra cash is returned to the corporation; and if less cash is produced than is needed, the corporation must make up the deficiency. For example, if the securities in the sinking fund of a $1,000,000 bond issue produce $1,001,325 when converted to cash, the trustee will use $1,000,000 to pay the bondholders and will return the extra $1,325 to the corporation. The corporation will then record the payment of its bonds and the return of the extra cash with an entry like this:

Jan.	3	Cash	1,325.00	
		Bonds Payable	1,000,000.00	
		Bond Sinking Fund		1,001,325.00
		To record payment of our bonds and the return of extra cash from the sinking fund.		

RESTRICTION ON DIVIDENDS DUE TO OUTSTANDING BONDS

To protect a corporation's financial position and the interests of its bondholders, a deed of trust may restrict the dividends the corporation may pay while its bonds are outstanding. Commonly the restriction provides that the corporation may pay dividends in any year only to the extent that the year's earnings exceed sinking fund requirements.

LONG-TERM NOTES

When bond interest rates are temporarily unfavorable and funds are available from several large banks or insurance companies, often long-term notes maturing in two, three, or more years are issued with the intention of refinancing the debt at maturity by issuing bonds. Also, in some instances, in order to avoid the costs of issuing bonds and dealing with several thousand bondholders, long-term notes maturing in 10, 20, or more years are issued instead of bonds.

Long-term notes are often secured by mortgages, and those maturing in ten or more years may provide for periodic payments to reduce the amounts owed. Consequently, long-term notes take on the characteristics of both mortgages and bonds. Ordinarily they differ only in that they may be placed with several lenders, normally at the current market rate of interest. This causes their present value at issuance to equal their maturity value. As a result, they are normally issued at par and receive the same accounting treatment as mortgages or bonds issued at par.

GLOSSARY

Bond. A type of long-term note payable issued by a corporation or a political subdivision.

Bond discount. The difference between the par value of a bond and the price at which it is issued when issued at a price below par.

Bond premium. The difference between the par value of a bond and the price at which it is issued when issued at a price above par.

Bond sinking fund. A fund of assets accumulated to pay a bond issue at maturity.

Callable bond. A bond that may be called in and redeemed at the option of the corporation or political subdivision that issued it.

Carrying amount of a bond issue. The par value of a bond issue less any unamortized discount or plus any unamortized premium.

Contract rate of bond interest. The rate of interest to be paid the bondholders.

Convertible bond. A bond that may be converted into shares of its issuing corporation's stock at the option of the bondholder.

Coupon bond. A bond having coupons that are detached by the bond-holder to collect interest on the bond.

Debenture bond. An unsecured bond.

Deed of trust. The contract between a corporation and its bondholders governing the duties of the corporation in relation to the bonds.

Face amount of a bond. The bond's par value.

Market rate of bond interest. The current bond interest rate that borrowers are willing to pay and lenders are willing to take for the use of their money.

Mortgage. A lien or prior claim to an asset or assets given by a borrower to a lender as security for a loan.

Mortgage contract. A document setting forth the terms under which a mortgage loan is made.

Par value of a bond. The face amount of the bond, which is the amount the borrower agrees to repay at maturity and the amount on which interest is based.

Registered bond. A bond the ownership of which is registered with the issuing corporation or political subdivision.

Serial bonds. An issue of bonds that will be repaid in installments over a period of years.

Sinking fund. A fund of assets accumulated for some purpose.

Sinking fund bonds. Bonds which are to be paid at maturity from funds accumulated in a sinking fund.

QUESTIONS FOR CLASS DISCUSSION

1. What two legal documents are involved when a company borrows by giving a mortgage? What is the purpose of each?
2. What is the primary difference between a share of stock and a bond?
3. What is a deed of trust? What are some of the provisions commonly contained in a deed of trust?
4. Define or describe: (a) registered bonds, (b) coupon bonds, (c) serial bonds, (d) sinking fund bonds, (e) callable bonds, (f) convertible bonds, and (g) debenture bonds.
5. Why does a corporation issuing bonds between interest dates charge and collect accrued interest from the purchasers of the bonds?
6. As it relates to a bond issue, what is the meaning of "contract rate of interest"? What is the meaning of "market rate for bond interest"?
7. What determines bond interest rates?
8. Convertible bonds are very popular with investors. Why?
9. If a $1,000 bond is sold at 98¼, at what price is it sold? If a $1,000 bond is sold at 101½, at what price is it sold?
10. If the quoted price for a bond is 97¾, does this include accrued interest?
11. What purpose is served by creating a bond sinking fund?
12. How are bond sinking funds classified for balance sheet purposes?

CLASS EXERCISES

Exercise 11-1

On May 1 of the current year a corporation sold at par plus accrued interest $1,000,000 of its 8.4% bonds. The bonds were dated January 1 of the current year, with interest payable on each July 1 and January 1. (a) Give the entry to record the sale. (b) Give the entry to record the first interest payment. (c) Set up a T-account for Bond Interest Expense and post the portions of the entries that affect the account. Answer these questions: (d) How many months' interest were accrued on these bonds when they were sold? (e) How many months' interest were paid on July 1? (f) What is the balance of the Bond Interest Expense account after the entry recording the first interest payment is posted? (g) How many months' interest does this balance represent? (h) How many months' interest did the bondholders earn during the first interest period?

Exercise 11-2

On December 31, 198A, a corporation sold $100,000 of its own 7.8%, eight-year bonds. The bonds were dated December 31, 198A, with interest payable on each June 30 and December 31, and were sold to yield the buyers an

8% annual return. *(a)* Prepare a calculation to show the price at which the bonds sold and *(b)* prepare an entry in general journal form to record the sale. (Use the present value tables, Tables 10–1 and 10–2, pages 358 and 360.)

Exercise 11–3

Prepare a form with the columnar headings of Illustration 11–2, and under the assumption the corporation of Exercise 11–2 sold its bonds for $98,833, determine and fill in the amounts for the first two interest periods on the form. Round all amounts to the nearest full dollar.

Exercise 11–4

Prepare entries in general journal form to record the first and second annual payments of interest to the bondholders of Exercise 11–3.

Exercise 11–5

On October 1, 198A, a corporation sold $100,000 of its own 8.2%, ten-year bonds. The bonds were dated October 1, 198A, with interest payable on each April 1 and October 1 and were sold to yield the buyers an 8% annual return. *(a)* Prepare a calculation to show the price at which the bonds sold and *(b)* prepare an entry in general journal form to record the sale. (Use the present value tables, Tables 10–1 and 10–2, pages 358 and 360.)

Exercise 11–6

Assume the bonds of Exercise 11–5 sold for $101,350 and that the annual accounting periods of the corporation selling the bonds end on December 31. Then prepare entries to record *(a)* the accrued interest on the bonds on the first December 31 they were outstanding and *(b)* the payment of the bondholders on the following April 1.

Exercise 11–7

A corporation sold $1,000,000 of its 8½%, ten-year bonds for $1,055,000 on their date of issue, March 1, 19—. Five years later, on March 1, after bond interest for the period had been paid and 40% of the total premium on the issue had been amortized, the corporation purchased $100,000 par value of the bonds on the open market at 98½ and retired them. Give the entry to record the retirement.

PROBLEMS

Problem 11–1

A corporation sold $1,000,000 of its own 8.8%, ten-year bonds on their date of issue, January 1, 198A. Interest was payable on the bonds on each

June 30 and December 31, and they were sold at a price to yield the buyers a 9% annual return.

Required:

1. Prepare a calculation to show the price at which the bonds were sold. (Use the present value tables, Tables 10–1 and 10–2, pages 358 and 360.)
2. Prepare a form with the columnar headings of Illustration 11–2 and fill in the amounts for the first two interest periods of the bond issue. Round all amounts to the nearest full dollar.
3. Prepare entries in general journal form to record the sale of the bonds and the payment of interest at the ends of the first two interest periods.

Problem 11–2

On January 1, 198A, a corporation sold $1,000,000 of its own 9.2%, ten-year bonds. The bonds were dated January 1, 198A, with interest payable on each June 30 and December 31, and were sold to yield the buyers a 9% annual return.

Required:

1. Prepare a calculation to show the price at which the bonds were sold. (Use the present value tables, Tables 10–1 and 10–2, pages 358 and 360.)
2. Prepare a form with the columnar headings of Illustration 11–3 and fill in the amounts for the first two interest periods of the bond issue. Round all amounts to the nearest full dollar.
3. Prepare entries in general journal form to record the sale of the bonds and the payment of interest at the ends of the first two interest periods.

Problem 11–3

Part 1. A corporation completed these bond transactions:

198A
Jan. 1 Sold $1,000,000 of its own 8.7%, ten-year bonds dated January 1, 198A, with interest payable each June 30 and December 31. The bonds sold for $980,448, a price to yield the buyers a 9% annual return on their investment.

June 30 Paid the semiannual interest on the bonds and amortized a portion of the discount calculated by the interest method.

Dec. 31 Paid the semiannual interest on the bonds and amortized a portion of the discount calculated by the interest method.

Required:

Prepare general journal entries to record the transactions. Round the amounts of discount amortized each period to the nearest full dollar.

Part 2. A corporation completed these bond transactions:

198A
May 1 Sold $1,000,000 of its own 9.3%, ten-year bonds dated May 1, 198A, with interest payable each November 1 and May 1. The bonds were sold for $1,019,472, a price to yield the buyers a 9% annual return.

Nov. 1   Paid the semiannual interest on the bonds and amortized a portion of the premium calculated by the interest method.

Dec. 31   Made an adjusting entry to record the accrued interest on the bonds and amortize one third of the amount of premium applicable to the second interest period of the bond issue.

198B

May 1   Paid the semiannual interest on the bonds and amortized the remainder of the premium applicable to the second interest period of the issue.

Required:

Prepare general journal entries to record the transactions. Round all amounts of premium amortized to the nearest whole dollar.

Problem 11-4

Part 1. A corporation completed these transactions:

198A

Jan. 1   Sold $1,000,000 par value of its own 8.9%, ten-year bonds at a price to yield the buyers a 9% annual return. The bonds were dated January 1, 198A, with interest payable each June 30 and December 31.

June 30   Paid the semiannual interest on the bonds and amortized a portion of the discount calculated by the interest method.

Dec. 31   Paid the semiannual interest on the bonds and amortized a portion of the discount calculated by the interest method.

Required:

Prepare general journal entries to record the transactions. Round all dollar amounts to the nearest whole dollar.

Part 2. A corporation completed these transactions:

198A

Apr. 1   Sold $1,000,000 par value of its 9.1%, ten-year bonds at a price to yield the buyers a 9% annual return. The bonds were dated April 1, 198A, with interest payable each October 1, and April 1.

Oct. 1   Paid the semiannual interest on the bonds and amortized a portion of the premium calculated by the interest method.

Dec. 31   Made an adjusting entry to record the accrued interest on the bonds and to amortize one half of the premium applicable to the second interest period of the bond issue.

198B

Apr. 1   Paid the semiannual interest on the bonds and amortized the remainder of the premium applicable to the second interest period of the issue.

Required:

Prepare general journal entries to record the transactions. Round the amounts of premium amortized each period to the nearest full dollar.

Problem 11-5

Prepare general journal entries to record the following bond transactions of a corporation. Round all dollar amounts to the nearest full dollar.

198A
Nov. 1   Sold $2,000,000 par value of its own 9.2%, ten-year bonds at a price to yield the buyers a 9% annual return. The bonds were dated November 1, 198A, with interest payable on each May 1 and November 1.

Dec. 31   Made an adjusting entry to record the accrued interest on the bonds and amortize one third of the premium applicable to the first interest period of the issue. (Use the interest method in calculating the premium to be amortized.)

198B
May 1   Paid the semiannual interest on the bonds and amortized the remainder of the premium applicable to the first interest period.

Nov. 1   Paid the semiannual interest on the bonds and amortized the premium applicable to the second interest period of the issue.

198F
Nov. 1   After recording the semiannual interest payment and amortizing the applicable premium, the carrying amount of the bonds on the corporation's books was $2,015,500, and the corporation purchased one tenth of the bonds at 99¼ and retired them.

ALTERNATE PROBLEMS

Problem 11-1A

A corporation sold $1,000,000 of its own 8.6%, ten-year bonds on their date of issue, January 1, 198A. Interest was payable on the bonds on each June 30 and December 31, and they were sold at a price to yield the buyers a 9% annual return.

Required:

1. Prepare a calculation to show the price at which the bonds were sold. (Use the present value tables, Tables 10–1 and 10–2, pages 358 and 360.)
2. Prepare a form with the columnar headings of Illustration 11–2 and fill in the amounts for the first two interest periods of the bond issue. Round amounts to the nearest full dollar.
3. Prepare general journal entries to record the sale of the bonds and the payment of interest at the ends of the first two interest periods.

Problem 11-2A

On January 1, 198A, a corporation sold $1,000,000 of its own 9.4%, ten-year bonds. The bonds were dated January 1, 198A, with interest payable on each June 30 and December 31, and were sold to yield the buyers a 9% annual return.

Required:

1. Prepare a calculation to show the price at which the bonds were sold. (Use the present value tables, Tables 10–1 and 10–2, pages 358 and 360.)
2. Prepare a form with the columnar headings of Illustration 11–3 and fill in the amounts for the first two interest periods of the bond issue. Round all amounts to the nearest full dollar.
3. Prepare entries in general journal form to record the sale of the bonds and the payment of interest at the ends of the first two interest periods.

Problem 11–3A

Part 1. A corporation completed these bond transactions:

198A

Jan.   1   Sold $2,000,000 of its own 8.9%, ten-year bonds dated January 1, 198A, with interest payable each June 30 and December 31. The bonds sold for $1,986,912, a price to yield the buyers a 9% annual return on their investment.

June 30   Paid the semiannual interest on the bonds and amortized a portion of the discount calculated by the interest method.

Dec. 31   Paid the semiannual interest on the bonds and amortized a portion of the discount calculated by the interest method.

Required:

Prepare general journal entries to record the transactions. Round the amounts of discount amortized each period to the nearest full dollar.

Part 2. A corporation completed these bond transactions:

198A

Nov.   1   Sold $2,000,000 of its own 9.1%, ten-year bonds dated November 1, 198A, with interest payable each May 1 and November 1. The bonds were sold for $2,012,928, a price to yield the buyers a 9% annual return.

Dec. 31   Made an adjusting entry to record the accrued interest on the bonds and to amortize one third of the premium applicable to the first interest period of the issue calculated by the interest method.

198B

May   1   Paid the semiannual interest on the bonds and amortized the remainder of the premium applicable to the first interest period of the issue.

Nov.   1   Paid the semiannual interest on the bonds and amortized the premium applicable to the second interest period of the issue.

Required:

Prepare general journal entries to record the transactions. Round all amounts of premium amortized to the nearest full dollar.

Problem 11–4A

Part 1. Prepare general journal entries to record the following transactions of a corporation. Round dollar amounts of interest expense and discount amortized to the nearest full dollar.

198A
Jan.   1   Sold $2,000,000 par value of its own 8.8%, ten-year bonds at a price to yield the buyers a 9% annual return. The bonds were dated January 1, 198A, with interest payable each June 30 and December 31.

June 30   Paid the semiannual interest on the bonds and amortized a portion of the discount calculated by the interest method.

Dec. 31   Paid the semiannual interest on the bonds and amortized a portion of the discount calculated by the interest method.

Part 2. Prepare general journal entries to record the following bond transactions of a corporation. Round all dollar amounts to the nearest full dollar.

198A
Sept.   1   Sold $2,000,000 par value of its 9.3%, ten-year bonds at a price to yield the buyers a 9% annual return. The bonds were dated September 1, 198A, with interest payable each March 1 and September 1.

Dec. 31   Made an adjusting entry to record the accrued interest on the bonds, calculated by the interest method, and to amortize two thirds of the premium applicable to the first interest period of the issue.

198B
Mar.   1   Paid the semiannual interest on the bonds and amortized the remainder of the premium applicable to the first interest period of the issue.

Sept.   1   Paid the semiannual interest on the bonds and amortized the premium applicable to the second interest period.

Problem 11–5A

Prepare general journal entries to record the following bond transactions of a corporation. Round the interest expense of each interest period to the nearest whole dollar.

198A
Oct.   1   Sold $2,000,000 par value of its own 8.7%, ten-year bonds at a price to yield the buyers a 9% annual return. The bonds were dated October 1, 198A, with interest payable each April 1 and October 1.

Dec. 31   Made an adjusting entry to record the accrued interest on the bonds, calculated by the interest method, and to amortize one half the discount applicable to the first interest period of the issue.

198B
Apr.   1   Paid the semiannual interest on the bonds and amortized the remainder of the discount applicable to the first interest period.

Oct.   1   Paid the semiannual interest on the bonds and amortized the discount applicable to the second interest period.

198F

Oct. 1 After recording the semiannual interest payment and amortizing the applicable amount of discount, the carrying amount of the bonds on the corporation's books was $1,975,000, and the corporation bought one tenth of the issue at 97½ and retired the bonds.

PROVOCATIVE PROBLEM

Provocative problem 11–1
Rockhill, Inc.

Stockholders' equity in Rockhill, Inc., is represented by 200,000 shares of outstanding common stock on which the corporation has earned an unsatisfactory average of $0.60 per share during each of the last three years. And, as a result of the unsatisfactory earnings, management of the corporation is planning an expansion that will require the investment of an additional $1,000,000 in the business. The $1,000,000 is to be acquired either by selling an additional 100,000 shares of the company's common stock at $10 per share or selling at par $1,000,000 of 9%, 20-year bonds. Management estimates that the expansion will double the company's before-tax earnings in the years following completion of the expansion.

The company's management wants to finance the expansion in the manner that will best serve the interests of present stockholders, and they have asked you to determine this. In your report express an opinion as to the relative merits and disadvantages of each proposed way of securing the funds needed for the expansion. Attach to your report a schedule showing expected earnings per common share under each method of financing. Assume the company presently pays out in state and federal income taxes 50% of its before-tax earnings and that it will continue to pay out the same share after the expansion.

part five
Accounting for owners' equity

CHAPTER 12 Partnerships and corporations.   CHAPTER 13 Corporations, additional transactions.

12

Partnerships and corporations

After studying Chapter 12, you should be able to:

- Explain the importance of an understanding of mutual agency and unlimited liability to a person about to become a partner.

- Explain the nature of partnership earnings and be able to calculate and divide partnership earnings on a stated fractional basis and through the use of salary and interest allowances.

- State the advantages and disadvantages of the corporate form of business organization and explain how a corporation is organized and managed.

- Record the issuance of par value stock at par or at a premium in exchange for cash or other assets.

- Record the issuance of no-par stock with or without a stated value.

- Record transactions involving stock subscriptions and explain the effects of subscribed stock on corporation assets and stockholders' equity.

- Explain the concept of minimum legal capital and explain why corporation laws governing minimum legal capital were written.

- State the differences between common and preferred stocks and explain why preferred stock is issued.

- Define or explain the words and phrases listed in the chapter Glossary.

Partnerships, corporations, and some of their transactions were discussed in the early chapters of this text. However, it is now time to add to an understanding of these forms of business organizations.

FORMING A PARTNERSHIP

An advantage of the *partnership* type of business organization is the ease with which a partnership may be formed. All that is required is for two or more people to agree to be partners. Their agreement is a contract and should be in writing, with all anticipated points of future disagreement covered. However, it is just as binding if only orally expressed.

Although easy to form, anyone forming a partnership should fully understand two important characteristics of a partnership, namely *mutual agency* and *unlimited liability*.

Mutual agency

Normally there is *mutual agency* in a partnership. This means that under normal circumstances every partner is an agent of his or her partnership and can enter into and bind the partnership to any contract within the apparent scope of its business. For example, a partner in a merchandising business can bind the partnership to contracts to buy merchandise, lease a store building, borrow money, or hire employees. These are all within the scope of a trading firm. On the other hand, a partner in a law firm, acting alone, cannot bind his or her partners to a contract to buy merchandise for resale or rent a store building. These are not within the normal scope of a law firm's business.

Partners among themselves may agree to limit the right of any of the partners to negotiate certain contracts for the partnership. However, although such an agreement is binding on the partners and on outsiders who know of the agreement, it is not binding on outsiders who are unaware of its existence. Outsiders who are unaware of anything to the contrary have a right to assume that each partner has the normal agency rights of a partner.

Mutual agency offers an important reason for care in the selection of partners. Good partners benefit all; but a poor partner can do great

411

damage. Mutual agency plus unlimited liability are the reasons most partnerships have only a few members.

Unlimited liability

When a partnership business is unable to pay its debts, the creditors may satisfy their claims from the personal assets of the partners. Furthermore, if the property of a partner is insufficient to meet his or her share, the creditors may turn to the assets of the remaining partners who are able to pay. Thus, a partner may be called on to pay all the debts of a partnership, both the partner's own share and the shares of any partners who are unable to pay. Consequently, a partner is said to have *unlimited liability* for the debts of his or her partnership.

PARTNERSHIP ACCOUNTING

Partnership accounting is exactly like that of a single proprietorship except for transactions directly affecting the partners' equities. Here, because ownership rights are divided between two or more partners, there must be—

1. A capital account for each partner.
2. A withdrawals account for each partner.
3. An accurate measurement and division of earnings among the partners.

As for the separate capital and withdrawals accounts, each partner's capital account is credited in recording the investment of the partner. Likewise, a partner's withdrawals are debited to his or her withdrawals account, and in the end-of-the-period closing procedure the capital account is credited for a partner's share of the net income. Obviously, these procedures are not new, only the added accounts are new, and they need no further consideration here. However, the matter of dividing earnings among partners does need additional discussion.

NATURE OF PARTNERSHIP EARNINGS

Partners cannot enter into legally binding contracts to hire themselves and pay themselves a salary. Consequently, partners have no legal right to salaries in payment for their partnership services or interest on their partnership investments. Law and custom recognize this. Nevertheless, if partnership earnings are to be fairly shared, it is often necessary to recognize that the earnings do include compensation for services and a return on investments. For example, if earnings are to be fairly shared and one partner contributes five times as much capital as another, it is only fair that this be taken into consideration in sharing earnings. Likewise, if the services of one partner are much more valuable than those of another, it is only fair that some provision be made for the unequal service contributions.

SHARING EARNINGS

The law provides that in the absence of a contrary agreement, partnership earnings are shared equally between or among the partners. Partners may agree to share earnings in any way they think is fair; and if they agree as to how earnings are to be shared but say nothing of losses, losses are shared in the same way as earnings.

Earnings shared on a fractional basis

The easiest way to divide partnership earnings is to give each partner a stated fraction of the total. A division on a fractional basis may provide for an equal sharing if service and capital contributions are equal. An equal sharing may also be provided when the greater capital contribution of one partner is offset by a greater service contribution of another. Or, if the service and capital contributions are unequal, a fractional basis may easily provide for an unequal sharing. All that is necessary in any case is for the partners to agree as to the fractional share to be given each.

To illustrate sharing on a fractional basis, assume the partnership agreement of Morse and North provides that Morse is to receive two thirds of their partnership earnings and North is to receive one third. Under this agreement, if earnings are, say, $30,000, after all revenue and expense accounts are closed, the partnership's Income Summary account is closed and the earnings are allocated to the partners with an entry like the following:

Dec.	31	Income Summary	30,000.00	
		A. P. Morse, Capital		20,000.00
		R. G. North, Capital		10,000.00
		To close the Income Summary account and allocate the earnings to the partners.		

Sometimes partners share earnings in the ratio of their investments. When they do, this is nothing more than sharing on a fractional basis. For example, Albert invested $50,000 and Bates invested $30,000 in a partnership in which the partners agreed to share earnings in their investment ratio. Their investments total $80,000. Therefore, Albert should receive $50,000/$80,000 or ⅝ of the earnings and Bates should receive $30,000/$80,000 or ⅜.

Salary and interest allowances in sharing

Sometimes partners' capital and service contributions are unequal. If capital contributions are unequal, to share earnings fairly the partners may allocate a portion of their net income to themselves in the form of interest. Or if service contributions are unequal, they may use salary allowances as a means of compensating for unequal service contributions. Or if investment and service contributions are both unequal, they may use a combination of interest and salary allowances in an effort to share earnings fairly.

For example, Hill and Dale began a partnership business of a kind in which Hill has had experience and could command an $18,000 annual salary working for another firm of like nature. Dale is new to the business and could expect to earn not more than $12,000 working elsewhere. Furthermore, Hill invested $15,000 in the business and Dale invested $5,000. Consequently, the partners agreed that in order to compensate for the unequal service and capital contributions, they will share losses and gains as follows:

1. A share of the profits equal to interest at 8% is to be allowed on the partner's initial investments.
2. Annual salary allowances of $18,000 per year to Hill and $12,000 per year to Dale are to be allowed.
3. The remaining balance of income or loss is to be shared equally.

Under this agreement a first year $32,700 net income would be shared as in Illustration 12–1.

	Share to Hill	Share to Dale	Income allocated
Total net income			$32,700
Allocated as interest:			
Hill (8% on $15,000)	$ 1,200		
Dale (8% on $5,000)		$ 400	
Total allocated as interest			1,600
Balance of income after interest allowances			$31,100
Allocated as salary allowances:			
Hill	18,000		
Dale		12,000	
Total allocated as salary allowances			30,000
Balance of income after interest and salary allowances			$ 1,100
Balance allocated equally:			
Hill	550		
Dale		550	
Total allocated equally			1,100
Balance of income			-0-
Shares of the partners	$19,750	$12,950	

Illustration 12–1

Give close attention to the word "allowances" as it appears in the phrase "salary allowances" in preceding paragraphs. Then remember that in a legal sense partners do not work for salaries, nor do they invest in a partnership to earn interest. They invest and work for earnings. Consequently, when a partnership agreement provides for salary and interest allowances, it should be clearly understood that the allowances are not really salaries and interest but are only a means of sharing losses and gains.

In the illustration just completed, the net income exceeded the salary and interest allowances of the partners. However, Hill and Dale would use the same method to share a net income smaller than their salary and interest allowances, or to share a loss. For example, assume that Hill and Dale earned only $9,600 in a year. A $9,600 net income would be shared by the partners as in Illustration 12–2, where the items enclosed in parentheses are negative amounts.

	Share to Hill	Share to Dale	Income allocated
Total net income			$ 9,600
Allocated as interest:			
Hill (8% on $15,000)	$ 1,200		
Dale (8% on $5,000)		$ 400	
Total allocated as interest			1,600
Balance of income after interest allowances			$ 8,000
Allocated as salary allowances:			
Hill	18,000		
Dale		12,000	
Total allocated as salary allowances			30,000
Balance of income after interest and salary allowances (a negative amount)			$(22,000)
Balance allocated equally:			
Hill	(11,000)		
Dale		(11,000)	
Total allocated equally			(22,000)
Balance of income			-0-
Shares of the partners	$ 8,200	$ 1,400	

Illustration 12–2

A net loss would be shared by Hill and Dale in the same manner as the foregoing $9,600 net income. The only difference being that the loss-and-gain-sharing procedure would begin with a negative amount of income, in other words a net loss. The amount allocated equally would then be a larger negative amount.

Time and space do not permit further consideration of partnership accounting. Consequently, discussions of the admission of a new partner into an existing partnership, the withdrawal of a partner from a partnership, and the liquidation of a partnership must be deferred to an advanced text.

CORPORATIONS

ADVANTAGES OF THE CORPORATE FORM

Corporations have become the dominant type of business in our country because of the advantages offered by this form of business organization. Among the advantages are the following:

Separate legal entity

A corporation is a separate legal entity, separate and distinct from its stockholders who are its owners. Because it is a separate legal entity, a corporation, through its agents, may conduct its affairs with the rights, duties, and responsibilities of a person.

Lack of stockholders' liability

As a separate legal entity a corporation is responsible for its own acts and its own debts, and its shareholders have no liability for either. From the viewpoint of an investor, this is perhaps the most important advantage of the corporate form.

Ease of transferring ownership rights

Ownership rights in a corporation are represented by shares of stock that generally can be transferred and disposed of any time the owner wishes. Furthermore, the transfer has no effect on the corporation and its operations.

Continuity of life

A corporation's life may continue for the time stated in its charter, which may be of any length permitted by the laws of the state of its incorporation. Furthermore, at the expiration of the stated time, the charter may normally be renewed and the period extended. Thus a perpetual life is possible for a successful corporation.

No mutual agency

Mutual agency does not exist in a corporation. A corporation stockholder, acting as a stockholder, has no power to bind the corporation to contracts. Stockholders' participation in the affairs of the corporation is limited to the right to vote in the stockholders' meetings. Consequently, stockholders need not exercise the care of partners in selecting people with whom they associate themselves in the ownership of a corporation.

Ease of capital assembly

Lack of stockholders' liability, lack of mutual agency, and the ease with which an interest may be transferred make it possible for a corporation to assemble large amounts of capital from the combined investments of many stockholders. Actually, a corporation's capital-raising ability is as a rule limited only by the profitableness with which it can employ the funds. This is very different from a partnership. In a partnership, capital-raising ability is always limited by the number of partners and their individual wealth. The number of partners is in turn usually limited because of mutual agency and unlimited liability.

DISADVANTAGES OF THE CORPORATE FORM

Governmental regulation

Corporations are created by fulfilling the requirements of a state's corporation laws, and the laws subject a corporation to considerable state regulation and control. Single proprietorships and partnerships escape this regulation and also many governmental reports required of corporations.

Taxation

Corporations as business units are subject to all the taxes of single proprietorships and partnerships. In addition, corporations are subject to several taxes not levied on either of the other two. The most burdensome of these are state and federal income taxes which together may take 50% of a corporation's pretax income. However, for the stockholders of a corporation, the burden does not end there. The income of a corporation is taxed twice, first as corporation income and again as personal income when distributed to the stockholders as dividends. This differs from single proprietorships and partnerships, which as business units are not subject to income taxes. Their income is normally taxed only as the personal income of their owners.

ORGANIZING A CORPORATION

As previously stated, a corporation is created by securing a charter from one of the states. The requirements that must be met to secure a charter vary with the states. In general, however, a charter application must be signed by three or more subscribers to the prospective corporation's stock (who are called the incorporators). It must then be filed with the proper state official. If the application complies with the law and all fees are paid, the charter is issued and the corporation comes into existence. The subscribers then purchase the corporation's stock and become stockholders. After this they meet and elect a board of directors who are made responsible for directing the corporation's affairs.

ORGANIZATION COSTS

The *costs* of organizing a corporation, such as legal fees, promoters' fees, and amounts paid the state to secure a charter, are called organization costs and are debited on incurrence to an account called Organization Costs. Theoretically, the sum of these costs represents an intangible asset from which the corporation will benefit throughout its life. However, this is an indeterminable period. Therefore, a corporation should make a reasonable estimate of the benefit period, which in no case should exceed 40 years, and write off its organization costs over the estimated period.[1] Although not necessarily related to the benefit period, income tax rules permit a corporation to write off organization costs as a tax-deductible expense over a period of not less than five years. Consequently, many corporations adopt five years as the period over which to write off such costs. There is no theoretical justification for this, but it is generally accepted in practice. Organization costs are usually immaterial in amount and under the *principle of materiality* the write-off eliminates an unnecessary balance sheet item.

MANAGEMENT OF A CORPORATION

Although ultimate control of a corporation rests with its stockholders, this control is exercised indirectly through the election of the board of directors. The individual stockholder's right to participate in management begins and ends with a vote in the stockholders' meeting, where each stockholder has one vote for each share of stock owned.

Normally a corporation's stockholders meet once each year to elect directors and transact such other business as is provided in the corporation's bylaws. Theoretically, stockholders owning or controlling the votes of 50% plus one share of a corporation's stock can elect the board and control the corporation. Actually, because many stockholders do not attend the annual meeting, a much smaller percentage is frequently sufficient for control. Commonly, stockholders who do not attend the annual meeting delegate to an agent their voting rights. This is done by signing a legal document called a *proxy*, which gives the agent the right to vote the stock.

---

[1] APB, "Intangible Assets," *APB Opinion No. 17* (New York: AICPA, August 1970), par. 29.

A corporation's board of directors is responsible and has final authority for the direction of corporation affairs. However, it may act only as a collective body. An individual director, as a director, has no power to transact corporation business. And, as a rule, although it has final authority, a board will limit itself to establishing policy. It will then delegate the day-by-day direction of corporation business to the corporation's administrative officers whom it selects and elects.

A corporation's administrative officers are commonly headed by a president who is directly responsible to the board for supervising the corporation's business. To aid the president, many corporations have one or more vice presidents who are vested with specific managerial powers and duties. In addition, the corporation secretary keeps the minutes of the meetings of the stockholders and directors. In a small corporation the secretary may also be responsible for keeping a record of the stockholders and the changing amounts of their stock interests.

STOCK CERTIFICATES AND THE TRANSFER OF STOCK

When a person invests in a corporation by buying its stock, the person receives a stock certificate as evidence of the shares purchased. Usually in a small corporation only one certificate is issued for each block of stock purchased. The one certificate may be for any number of shares. For example, the certificate of Illustration 12–3 is for 50

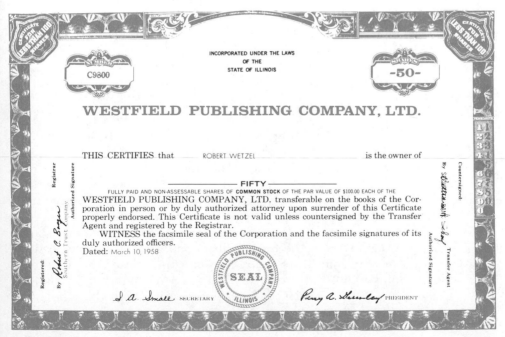

Illustration 12–3

shares. Large corporations commonly use preprinted 100-share denomination certificates in addition to blank certificates that may be made out for any number of shares.

An owner of stock may transfer at will either part or all the shares represented by a stock certificate. To do so the owner fills in and signs the transfer endorsement on the reverse side of the certificate and sends the certificate to the corporation secretary in a small corporation or to the corporation's transfer agent in a large one. The old certificate is canceled and retained, and a new certificate is issued to the new stockholder.

Transfer agent and registrar

A large corporation, one whose stock is sold on a major stock exchange, must have a registrar and a transfer agent who are assigned the responsibilities of transferring the corporation's stock. Also, the registrar is assigned the duty of keeping its stockholder records and preparing the official lists of stockholders for stockholders' meetings and for payment of dividends. Usually registrars and transfer agents are large banks or trust companies.

When the owner of stock in a corporation having a registrar and a transfer agent wishes to transfer the stock to a new owner, he or she completes the transfer endorsement on the back of the stock certificate and, usually through a stockbroker, sends the certificate to the transfer agent. The transfer agent cancels the old certificate and issues one or more new certificates which the agent sends to the registrar. The registrar enters the transfer in the stockholder records and sends the new certificate or certificates to the proper owners.

AUTHORIZATION AND ISSUANCE OF STOCK

When a corporation is organized, it is authorized in its charter to issue a certain amount of stock. The stock may be of one kind, *common stock*, or both common and preferred stock may be authorized. (Preferred stock is discussed later in this chapter.) However, regardless of whether one or two kinds of stock are authorized, the corporation may issue no more of each than the amount authorized by its charter.

Often a corporation will secure an authorization to issue more stock than it plans to sell at the time of its organization. This enables it to expand at any time in its future through the sale of the additional stock, and without the need of applying to the state for the right to issue more. When a balance sheet is prepared, both the amount of stock authorized and the amount issued are commonly shown in its equity section as on page 423.

Sale of stock for cash

When stock is sold for cash and immediately issued, an entry in general journal form like the following may be used to record the sale and issuance:

June	5	Cash	300,000.00	
		Common Stock		300,000.00
		Sold and issued 30,000 shares of $10 par value common stock.		

Exchanging stock for noncash assets

A corporation may accept assets other than cash in exchange for its stock. When it does so, the transactions may be recorded like this:

Apr.	3	Machinery	10,000.00	
		Buildings	25,000.00	
		Land	5,000.00	
		Common Stock		40,000.00
		Exchanged 4,000 shares of $10 par value common stock for machinery, buildings, and land.		

A corporation may also give shares of its stock to its promoters in exchange for their services in getting the corporation organized. In such a case the corporation receives the intangible asset of being organized in exchange for its stock. The transaction is recorded as follows:

Apr.	5	Organization Costs........................	5,000.00	
		Common Stock		5,000.00
		Gave the promoters 500 shares of $10 par value common stock in exchange for their services in getting the corporation organized.		

PAR VALUE AND MINIMUM LEGAL CAPITAL

Many stocks have a *par value.* The par value of a stock is an arbitrary value the issuing corporation chose for the stock at the time it sought authorization of the stock. A corporation may choose to issue stock having a par value of any amount, but par values of $100, $25, $10, $5, and $1 are common.

When a corporation issues par value stock, the par value is printed on each certificate and is used in accounting for the stock. Also, in many states when a corporation issues par value stock, it establishes for itself a *minimum legal capital* equal to the par value of the issued stock. For example, if a corporation issues 1,000 shares of $100 par value stock, it establishes for itself a minimum legal capital of $100,000.

Laws establishing minimum legal capital normally require stockholders in a corporation to invest assets equal in value to minimum legal capital or be liable to the corporation's creditors for the deficiency. In other words, these laws require stockholders to give a corporation par value for its stock or be liable for the deficiency. Minimum legal capital requirements also make illegal any payments to stockholders for dividends or their equivalent when these payments reduce stockholders' equity below minimum legal capital.

Corporation laws governing minimum legal capital were written in an effort to protect corporation creditors. The authors of these laws reasoned as follows: A corporation's creditors may look only to the assets of the corporation for satisfaction of their claims. Consequently, when a corporation is organized, its stockholders should provide it with a fund of assets equal to its minimum legal capital. Thereafter, this fund of assets should remain with the corporation and should not be returned to the stockholders in any form until all creditor claims are paid.

Par value helps establish minimum legal capital and is used in accounting for par value stock. However, it does not establish a stock's worth nor the price at which a corporation must issue the stock. If purchasers are willing to pay more than par, a corporation may sell and issue its stock at a price above par. Likewise, in some states, if purchasers will not pay par, a corporation may issue its stock at a price below par.

STOCK PREMIUMS AND DISCOUNTS

Premiums

When a corporation sells and issues stock at a price above the stock's par value, the stock is said to be issued at a *premium*. For example, if a corporation sells and issues its $10 par value common stock at $12 per share, the stock is sold at a $2 per share premium. Although a premium is an amount in excess of par paid by purchasers of newly issued stock, it is not considered a profit to the issuing corporation. Rather a premium is part of the investment of stockholders who pay more than par for their stock.

In accounting for stock sold at a premium, the premium is recorded separately from the par value of the stock to which it applies. For example, if a corporation sells and issues 10,000 shares of its $10 par value common stock for cash at $12 per share, the sale is recorded as follows:

Dec.	1	Cash	120,000.00	
		Premium on Common Stock		20,000.00
		Common Stock		100,000.00
		Sold and issued 10,000 shares of $10 par value common stock at $12 per share.		

When stock is issued in exchange for assets other than cash and the fair value of the assets exceeds the par value of the stock, a premium is recorded. If fair value for the assets cannot be determined within reasonable limits, a price established by recent sales of the stock may be used in recording the exchange. This too may require that a premium be recorded.

When a balance sheet is prepared, stock premium is added in the equity section to the par value of the stock to which it applies, as follows:

Stockholders' Equity

Common stock, $10 par value, 25,000 shares authorized, 20,000 shares issued	$200,000	
Add premium on common stock	30,000	
Total contributed capital		$230,000
Retained earnings		82,400
Total stockholders' equity		$312,400

Discounts

Stock issued at a price below par is said to be issued at a *discount.* Many states prohibit the issuance of stock at a discount because the stockholders invest less than minimum legal capital. Also, in those states in which stock may be issued at a discount, purchasers of the stock usually become contingently liable to the issuing corporation's creditors for the amount of the discount. Consequently, stock is seldom issued at a discount, and a discussion of stock discounts is of little practical importance. However, if stock is issued at less than par, the discount is debited to a discount account and is subtracted on the balance sheet from the par value of the stock to which it applies.

NO-PAR STOCK

At one time all stocks were required to have a par value. Today all jurisdictions permit the issuance of *no-par stocks* or stocks without a par value. The primary advantage claimed for no-par stock is that since it does not have a par value, it may be issued at any price without a *discount liability* attaching. Also, printing a par value, say $100, on a stock certificate may cause a person lacking in knowledge to believe a share of the stock to be worth $100, when it actually may be worthless. Therefore, eliminating the par value helps force such a person to examine the factors which give a stock value, which are earnings, dividends, and future prospects.

In some states the entire proceeds from the sale of no-par stock becomes minimum legal capital and must be credited to a no-par stock account. In these states, if a corporation issues 1,000 shares of no-par stock at $42 per share, the transaction is recorded like this:

Oct.	20	Cash	42,000.00	
		No-Par Common Stock		42,000.00
		Sold and issued 1,000 shares of no-par common stock at $42 per share.		

In other states a corporation may place a *stated value* on its no-par stock. The stated value then becomes minimum legal capital and is credited to the no-par stock account. If the stock is issued at an amount in excess of stated value, the excess is credited to a contributed capital account called, for instance, "Contributed Capital in Excess of Stated Value of No-Par Stock." In these states if a corporation issues at $42 per share 1,000 shares of no-par common stock on which it has placed a $25 per share stated value, the transaction is recorded as follows:

Oct.	20	Cash	42,000.00	
		No-Par Common Stock		25,000.00
		Contributed Capital in Excess of Stated		
		Value, No-Par Common Stock		17,000.00
		Sold at $42 per share 1,000 shares of no-par stock having a $25 per share stated value.		

In still other states a corporation may place a stated value on its no-par stock and record the transaction as in the preceding entry, but the entire proceeds from the sale of the stock becomes minimum legal capital.

SALE OF STOCK THROUGH SUBSCRIPTIONS

Often stock is sold for cash and immediately issued. Often, too, especially in organizing a new corporation, stock is sold by means of *subscriptions.* In the latter instance a person wishing to become a stockholder signs a subscription blank or a subscription list, agreeing to buy a certain number of the shares. When the subscription is accepted by the corporation, it becomes a contract; and the corporation acquires an asset, the right to receive payment from the subscriber. At the same time the subscriber gains an equity in the corporation equal to the amount the subscriber agrees to pay. Payment may be in one amount or in installments.

To illustrate the sale of stock through subscriptions, assume that on June 6 Northgate Corporation accepted subscriptions to 5,000 shares of its $10 par value common stock at $12 per share. The subscription contracts called for a 10% down payment to accompany the subscriptions and the balance in two equal installments due in 30 and 60 days.

The subscriptions were recorded with the following entry:

June	6	Subscriptions Receivable, Common Stock	60,000.00	
		Premium on Common Stock		10,000.00
		Common Stock Subscribed		50,000.00
		Accepted subscriptions to 5,000 shares of		
		$10 par value common stock at $12		
		per share.		

Notice that the subscriptions receivable account is debited at the time the subscriptions are accepted for the sum of the stock's par value and premium. This is the amount the subscribers agree to pay. Notice, too, that the stock subscribed account is credited for par value and that the premium is credited to a premium account at the time the subscriptions are accepted. The subscriptions receivable and stock subscribed accounts are of temporary nature. The subscriptions receivable will be turned into cash when the subscribers pay for their stock. Likewise, when payment is completed, the subscribed stock will be issued and will become outstanding stock. Normally subscribed stock is not issued until paid for.

Receipt of the down payments and the two installment payments may be recorded with these entries:

June	6	Cash	6,000.00	
		Subscriptions Receivable, Common Stock		6,000.00
		Collected 10% down payments on the		
		common stock subscribed.		

July	6	Cash	27,000.00	
		Subscriptions Receivable, Common Stock .		27,000.00
		Collected the first installment payments		
		on the common stock subscribed.		
Aug.	5	Cash	27,000.00	
		Subscriptions Receivable, Common Stock		27,000.00
		Collected the second installment payments		
		on the common stock subscribed.		

In this case, the down payments accompanied the subscriptions. Consequently, the entry to record the receipt of the subscriptions and the entry to record the down payments may be combined.

When stock is sold through subscriptions, the stock is usually not issued until the subscriptions are paid in full. However, as soon as the subscriptions are paid, the stock is issued. The entry to record the issuance of the Northgate common stock appears as follows:

Aug.	5	Common Stock Subscribed	50,000.00	
		Common Stock		50,000.00
		Issued 5,000 shares of common stock sold		
		through subscriptions.		

Most subscriptions are collected in full, although not always. Sometimes a subscriber fails to pay; and when this happens, the subscription contract must be canceled. In such a case, if the subscriber has made a partial payment on the contract, the amount paid may be returned. Or, a smaller amount of stock than that subscribed, an amount equal to the partial payment, may be issued. Or, in some states the subscriber's partial payment may be kept by the corporation to compensate for any damages suffered.

Subscriptions receivable and stock subscribed on the balance sheet

Subscriptions receivable are normally to be collected within a relatively short time. Consequently, they appear on the balance sheet as a current asset. Also, if a corporation prepares a balance sheet after accepting subscriptions to its stock but before the stock is issued, it should show both its issued stock and its subscribed stock on the balance sheet as follows:

Common stock, $10 par value, 25,000 shares authorized,
   20,000 shares issued $200,000
Unissued common stock subscribed, 5,000 shares   50,000
    Total common stock issued and subscribed $250,000
Add premium on common stock   40,000
   Amount contributed and subscribed by the common
    stockholders $290,000

RIGHTS OF COMMON STOCKHOLDERS

When investors buy a corporation's common stock, they acquire all the specific rights granted by the corporation's charter to its common stockholders. They also acquire the general rights granted stockholders by the laws of the state in which the corporation is organized. The laws vary, but in general all common stockholders have the following rights:

1. The right to vote in the stockholders' meetings.
2. The right to sell or otherwise dispose of their stock.
3. The right of first opportunity to purchase any additional shares of common stock issued by the corporation. (This is called the common stockholders' *preemptive right*. It gives common stockholders the opportunity to protect their proportionate interest in the corporation. For example, a stockholder who owns one fourth of a corporation's common stock has the first opportunity to buy one fourth of any new common stock issued. This enables the stockholder to maintain a one-fourth interest.)
4. The right to share pro rata with other common stockholders in any dividends distributed to common stockholders.
5. The right to share in any assets remaining after creditors are paid if the corporation is liquidated.

PREFERRED STOCK

A corporation may issue more than one kind or class of stock. If two classes are issued, one is generally known as common stock and the other as *preferred stock*. Preferred stock is so called because of the preferences granted its owners. These commonly include a preference as to payment of *dividends,* and may include a preference in the distribution of assets in a liquidation.

A preference as to dividends does not give an absolute right to dividends. Rather if dividends are declared, it gives the preferred stockholders the right to receive their preferred dividend before the common stockholders are paid a dividend. In other words, if dividends are declared, a dividend must be paid the preferred stockholders before a dividend may be paid to the common stockholders. However, if the directors are of the opinion that no dividends should be paid, then neither the preferred nor the common stockholders receive a dividend.

Dividends on the majority of preferred stocks are limited to a fixed maximum amount. For example, a share of $100 par value, 7%, nonparticipating preferred stock has a preference each year to a dividend equal to 7% of its par value, or $7. However, the dividend is limited to that amount. On the other hand, dividends on a corporation's common stock are unlimited, except by the earning power of the corporation and the judgment of its board of directors.

While dividends on most preferred stocks are limited to a fixed basic percentage or amount, some preferred stocks have the right under certain circumstances to dividends in excess of a fixed basic percentage or amount. Such preferred stocks are called *participating preferred stocks*. Participating preferred stocks may be fully participating, or participation may be limited to a fixed amount. If a corporation issues fully participating, 6%, $100 par value, preferred stock and $50 par value common stock, the owners of the preferred stock have a preference to a 6% or $6 per share dividend each year. Then, each year, after the common stockholders have received a 6% or $3 per share dividend, the preferred stockholders have a right to participate with the common stockholders in any additional dividends declared. The participation is usually on the basis of the same additional percent-on-par-value-per-share dividend to each kind of stock. For instance, if in this case the common stockholders are paid an additional 2% or $1 per share dividend, the preferred stockholders should receive an additional 2% or $2 per share dividend.

Often when preferred stock is participating, participation is limited. For example, a $100 par value, 7%, preferred stock may be issued with the right to participate in dividends to 10% of its par value. Such a stock has a preference to dividends of 7% each year. It also has a right after the common stockholders receive a 7% dividend to participate in additional dividends until it has received 10%, or $10, per share. Its participation rights end at this point.

In addition to being participating or nonparticipating, preferred stocks are either *cumulative* or *noncumulative*. A cumulative preferred stock is one on which any undeclared dividends accumulate each year until paid. A noncumulative preferred stock is one on which the right to receive dividends is forfeited in any year in which dividends are not declared.

The accumulation of dividends on cumulative preferred stocks does not guarantee payment. Dividends cannot be guaranteed because earnings from which they are paid cannot be guaranteed. However, when a corporation issues cumulative preferred stock, it does agree to pay its cumulative preferred stockholders both their current dividends and any unpaid back dividends, called *dividends in arrears,* before it pays a dividend to its common stockholders.

In addition to the preferences it receives, preferred stock carries with it all the rights of common stock, unless such rights are specifically denied in the corporation charter. Commonly, preferred stock is denied the right to vote in the stockholders' meetings.

Preferred dividends in arrears on the balance sheet date

A liability for a dividend does not come into existence until the dividend is declared by the board of directors; and unlike interest, dividends do not accrue. Consequently, if on the dividend date a corporation's board fails to declare a dividend on its cumulative preferred stock, the dividend in arrears is not a liability and does not appear on the balance sheet as such. However, if there are preferred dividends in arrears, the *full-disclosure principle* requires that this information appear on the balance sheet, and normally such information is given in a balance sheet footnote. When a balance sheet does not carry such a footnote, a balance sheet reader has the right to assume that there are no dividends in arrears.

WHY PREFERRED STOCK IS ISSUED

Two common reasons why preferred stock is issued can best be shown by means of an example. Suppose that three persons with a total of $100,000 to invest wish to organize a corporation requiring $200,000 capital. If they sell and issue $200,000 of common stock, they will have to share control with other stockholders. However, if they sell and issue $100,000 of common stock to themselves and sell to outsiders $100,000 of 8%, cumulative preferred stock having no voting rights, they can retain control of the corporation for themselves.

Also, suppose the three promoters expect their new corporation to earn an annual after-tax return of $24,000. If they sell and issue $200,000 of common stock, this will mean a 12% return. However, if they sell and issue $100,000 of each kind of stock, retaining the common for themselves, they can increase their own return to 16%, as follows:

Net after-tax income	$24,000
Less preferred dividends at 8%	(8,000)
Balance to common stockholders (equal to 16% on their $100,000 investment)	$16,000

In this case the common stockholders earn 16% because the dividends on the preferred stock are less than the amount that can be earned on the preferred stockholders' investment.

STOCK VALUES

In addition to a par value, stocks may have a redemption value, a market value, and a book value.

Redemption value

Redemption values apply to preferred stocks. Often corporations issuing preferred stock reserve the right to redeem the stock by paying the preferred stockholders the par value of their stock plus a premium. The amount a corporation agrees to pay to redeem a share of its preferred stock is called the redemption value of the stock. Normally, a corporation reserves the right to either redeem or permit the stock to remain outstanding, as it chooses.

Market value

The market value of a share of stock is the price at which a share can be bought or sold. Market values are influenced by earnings, dividends, future prospects, and general market conditions.

Book value

The *book value of a share of stock* measures the equity of the owner of one share of the stock in the assets of its issuing corporation. If a corporation has issued only common stock, its book value per share is determined by dividing total stockholders' equity by the number of shares outstanding. For example, if total stockholders' equity is $285,000 and there are 10,000 shares outstanding, the book value per share is $28.50 ($285,000 ÷ 10,000 = $28.50).

To compute book values when both common and preferred stock are outstanding, the preferred stock is assigned a portion of the total stockholders' equity equal to its redemption value plus any cumulative dividends in arrears. The remaining stockholders' equity is then assigned to the common shares outstanding. After this the book value of each class is determined by dividing its share of stockholders' equity by the number of shares of that class outstanding. For instance, assume a corporation has the stockholders' equity showing in Illustration 12–4.

Stockholders' Equity

Preferred stock, $100 par value, 7% cumulative and nonparticipating, 2,000 shares authorized, 1,000 shares issued and outstanding	$100,000	
Premium on preferred stock	5,000	
Total capital contributed by preferred stockholders		$105,000
Common stock, $25 par value, 12,000 shares authorized, 10,000 shares issued and outstanding.....................	$250,000	
Premium on common stock	10,000	
Total capital contributed by common stockholders		260,000
Total contributed capital		$365,000
Retained earnings		82,000
Total stockholders' equity...............................		$447,000

stration 12–4

If the preferred stock is redeemable at $103 per share and two years' of cumulative preferred dividends are in arrears, the book values of the corporation's shares are calculated as follows:

Total stockholders' equity		$447,000	
Less equity applicable to preferred shares:			
Redemption value	$103,000		
Cumulative dividends in arrears	14,000	(117,000)	
Equity applicable to common shares			$330,000
Book value of preferred shares ($117,000 ÷ 1,000)		$117	
Book value of common shares ($330,000 ÷ 10,000)		$ 33	

Corporations in their annual reports to their shareholders often point out the increase that has occurred in the book value of the corporation's shares during a year. Book value may also be of significance in a contract. For example, a stockholder may enter into a contract to sell shares at their book value at some future date. However, book value should not be confused with *liquidation value* because if a corporation is liquidated, its assets will probably sell at prices quite different from the amounts at which they are carried on the books. Also, book value generally has little bearing upon the market value of stock. Dividends, earning capacity, and future prospects are usually of much more importance. For instance a common stock having a $11 book value may sell for $25 per share if its earnings, dividends, and prospects are good. However, it may sell for $5 per share if these factors are unfavorable.

GLOSSARY

Book value of a share of stock. The equity represented by one share of stock in the issuing corporation's net assets.

Common stock. Stock of a corporation that has only one class of stock; if there is more than one class, the class that has no preferences relative to the corporation's other classes of stock.

Common stock subscribed. Unissued common stock for which the issuing corporation has a subscription contract to issue.

Cumulative preferred stock. Preferred stock on which any undeclared dividends accumulate each year until paid.

Discount on stock. The difference between the par value of stock and the amount below par value contributed by stockholders.

Dividend. A distribution made by a corporation to its stockholders of cash, other assets, or additional shares of the corporation's own stock.

Dividends in arrears. Unpaid back dividends on preferred stock which must be paid before dividends are paid to common stockholders.

Minimum legal capital. An amount that stockholders must invest in a corporation or be contingently liable to its creditors.

Mutual agency. The legal situation in a partnership whereby each partner is an agent of the partnership and is able to bind the partnership to contracts within the normal scope of the partnership business.

Noncumulative preferred stock. A stock for which the right to receive dividends is forfeited in any year in which dividends are not declared.

No-par stock. A class of stock having no par value.

Organization costs. Cost of bringing a corporation into existence, such as legal fees, promoters' fees, and amounts paid the state to secure a charter.

Participating preferred stock. Preferred stock that has the right to share in dividends above the fixed basic amount or percentage which is preferred.

Partnership. An association of two or more persons to carry on a business as co-owners for profit.

Partnership contract. The document setting forth the agreed terms under which the members of a partnership will conduct the partnership business.

Par value. An arbitrary value placed on a share of stock at the time the corporation seeks authorization of the stock.

Preemptive right. The right of a common stockholder to have the first opportunity to purchase additional shares of common stock issued by the corporation.

Preferred stock. Stock other than common stock the owners of which are granted certain preferences such as a preference to payment of dividends or in the distribution of assets in a liquidation.

Premium on stock. The amount of capital contributed by stockholders above the stock's par value.

Proxy. A legal document which gives an agent of a stockholder the right to vote the stockholder's shares.

Redemption value of stock. The amount a corporation must pay for the return of a share of preferred stock previously issued by the corporation.

Stated value of no-par stock. An amount, established by a corporation's board of directors, that is credited to the no-par stock account at the time the stock is issued.

Stock subscription. A contractual commitment to purchase unissued shares of stock and become a stockholder.

Unlimited liability. The legal situation in a partnership which makes each partner responsible for paying all the debts of the partnership if his or her partners are unable to pay a share.

QUESTIONS FOR CLASS DISCUSSION

1. What is the meaning of the term "mutual agency" as applied to a partnership?
2. Jack and Jill are partners in the operation of a store. Jack without consulting Jill enters into a contract for the purchase of merchandise for resale by the store. Jill contends that she did not authorize the order and refuses to take delivery. The vendor sues the partners for the contract price of the merchandise. Will the firm have to pay? Why?
3. Would your answer to Question 2 differ if Jack and Jill were partners in a public accounting firm?
4. May partners limit the right of a member of their firm to bind their partnership to contracts? Is such an agreement binding *(a)* on the partners and *(b)* on outsiders?
5. What is the meaning of the term "unlimited liability" when it is applied to members of a partnership?
6. Kennedy, Porter, and Foulke have been partners for three years. The partnership is dissolving, Kennedy is leaving the firm, and Porter and Foulke plan to carry on the business. In the final settlement Kennedy places a $45,000 salary claim against the partnership. His contention is that since he devoted all of his time for three years to the affairs of the partnership, he has a claim for a salary of $15,000 for each year. Is his claim valid? Why?
7. The partnership agreement of Martin and Tritt provides for a two-thirds, one-third sharing of income but says nothing of losses. The operations for a year result in a loss. Martin claims the loss should be shared equally since the partnership agreement said nothing of sharing losses. Do you agree?
8. What are the advantages and disadvantages of the corporate form of business organization?
9. What is a proxy?
10. What are organization costs? List several.

11. What are the duties and responsibilities of a corporation's registrar and transfer agent?

12. Why is a corporation the stock of which is sold on a stock exchange required to have a registrar and transfer agent? Why is such a corporation required to have both a registrar and a transfer agent?

13. List the general rights of common stockholders.

14. What is the preemptive right of common stockholders?

15. Laws place no limit on the amounts partners may withdraw from a partnership. On the other hand, laws regulating corporations place definite limits on the amounts corporation owners may withdraw from a corporation in dividends. Why is there a difference?

16. What is a stock premium? What is a stock discount?

17. Does a corporation earn a profit by selling its stock at a premium? Does it incur a loss by selling its stock at a discount?

18. Why do corporation laws make purchasers of stock at a discount contingently liable for the discount? To whom are such purchasers contingently liable?

19. What is the main advantage of no-par stock?

20. What are the meanings of the following when applied to preferred stock: (a) preferred, (b) participating, (c) nonparticipating, (d) cumulative, and (e) noncumulative?

21. What are the meanings of the following terms when applied to stock: (a) par value, (b) book value, (c) market value, and (d) redemption value?

CLASS EXERCISES

Exercise 12–1

Able and Best began a partnership by investing $18,000 and $12,000, respectively, and during its first year the partnership earned $33,000.

Required:

1. Prepare a schedule with the following columnar headings:

Ways of Sharing	Able's Share	Best's Share

2. List the following ways of sharing income by letter on separate lines in the first column and then opposite each letter show the share of each partner in the $33,000 net income.

   a. The partners could not agree on a method of sharing income.
   b. The partners agreed to share income in their investment ratio.
   c. The partners agreed to share income by granting a $12,000 per year salary allowance to Able, a $15,000 per year salary allowance to Best, 10% interest on their investments, and the balance equally.

Exercise 12–2

Assume the partners of Exercise 12–1 agreed to share losses and gains by allowing salary allowances of $12,000 per year to Able and $15,000 per year to Best, 10% interest on investments, and the balance equally. Determine the partners' shares in (a) a $12,000 net income and (b) a $6,000 net loss.

Exercise 12–3

A corporation has outstanding 1,000 shares of $100 par value, 7% cumulative and nonparticipating preferred stock and 8,000 shares of $25 par value common stock. During the first four years in its life it paid out the following amounts in dividends: first year, nothing; second year, $8,000; third year, $24,000; and fourth year, $30,000. Determine the total dividends paid to each class of stockholders each year.

Exercise 12–4

Determine the total dividends paid each class of stockholders of the previous exercise under the assumption that rather than being cumulative and nonparticipating, the preferred stock is noncumulative and nonparticipating.

Exercise 12–5

A corporation has outstanding 1,000 shares of $100 par value, 7% cumulative and fully participating preferred stock and 20,000 shares of $10 par value common stock. It has regularly paid all dividends on the preferred stock. This year the board of directors voted to pay out a total of $28,500 in dividends to the two classes of stockholders. Determine the percent on par to be paid each class of stockholders and the dividend per share to be paid each class.

Exercise 12–6

The stockholders' equity section of a corporation's balance sheet appeared as follows:

Stockholders' Equity

Preferred stock, $100 par value, 7% cumulative and nonparticipating, 1,000 shares authorized and outstanding	$100,000	
Premium on preferred stock	6,000	
Total capital contributed by preferred stockholders		$106,000
Common stock, $10 par value, 25,000 shares authorized, 20,000 shares issued and outstanding	$200,000	
Premium on common stock	10,000	
Total capital contributed by common stockholders..............		210,000
Total contributed capital		$316,000
Retained earnings		64,500
Total stockholders' equity		$380,500

Under the assumption the preferred stock is redeemable at $103.50 per share and there is one year's dividends in arrears on the stock, determine the book value per share of each class of stock.

Exercise 12–7

On March 3 a corporation accepted subscriptions to 10,000 shares of its $5 par value common stock at $5.50 per share. The subscription contracts called for one fifth of the subscription price to accompany each contract as a down payment and the balance to be paid on April 2. Give the entries to record (a) the subscriptions, (b) the down payments, (c) receipt of the remaining amounts due on the subscriptions on April 2, and (d) issuance of the stock.

Exercise 12–8

A corporation sold and issued 2,000 shares of its no-par common stock for $27,500 on March 6. (a) Give the entry to record the sale under the assumption the board of directors did not place a stated value on the stock. (b) Give the entry to record the sale under the assumption the board placed a $10 per share stated value on the stock.

PROBLEMS

Problem 12–1

Ted Allen, John Bell, and Gary Cole invested $16,000, $12,000, and $8,000, respectively, in a partnership. During its first year the partnership earned $41,400.

Required:

Prepare entries dated December 31 to close the Income Summary account and allocate the net income to the partners under each of the following assumptions:

a. The partners could not agree on the method of sharing.
b. The partners agreed to share earnings in the ratio of their beginning investments.
c. The partners agreed to share income by allowing annual salary allowances of $12,000 each to Allen and Bell and $18,000 to Cole, allowing a share of the income equal to 10% interest on partners' investments, and sharing any remainder equally.

Problem 12–2

Mary Clay and Joan Dent are in the process of forming a partnership to which Mary Clay will devote one third of her time and Joan Dent will devote full time. They have discussed the following plans for sharing gains and losses:

a. In the ratio of their investments which they have agreed to maintain at $18,000 for Clay and $12,000 for Dent.

b. In proportion to the time devoted to the business.
c. Salary allowance of $5,000 per year to Clay and $15,000 per year to Dent and the balance in their investment ratio.
d. Salary allowances of $5,000 per year to Clay and $15,000 per year to Dent, 10% interest on their investments, and the balance equally.

Required:

1. Prepare a schedule with the following columnar headings:

Income Sharing Plan	$32,000 Net Income		$18,000 Net Income		$6,000 Net Loss	
	Clay	Dent	Clay	Dent	Clay	Dent

2. List the plans by letter in the first column and show opposite each letter the shares of the partners in a $32,000 net income, an $18,000 net income, and a $6,000 net loss.

Problem 12–3

A corporation received a charter granting it the right to issue 2,000 shares of $100 par value, 8% cumulative and nonparticipating, preferred stock and 100,000 shares of $10 par value common stock. It then completed these transactions:

Jan. 27 Accepted subscriptions to 50,000 shares of common stock at $11.50 per share. Down payments equal to 20% of the subscription price accompanied each subscription.

31 Gave the corporation's promoters 1,000 shares of common stock for their services in getting the corporation organized. The board valued the services at $11,500.

Feb. 3 Accepted subscriptions to 1,500 shares of preferred stock at $110 per share. The subscriptions were accompanied by 50% down payments.

26 Collected the balance due on the January 27 common stock subscriptions and issued the stock.

28 Accepted subscriptions to 500 shares of preferred stock at $108 per share. The subscriptions were accompanied by 50% down payments.

Mar. 5 Collected the balance due on the February 3 preferred stock subscriptions and issued the stock.

Required:

1. Prepare general journal entries to record the transactions.
2. Prepare the stockholders' equity section of the corporation's balance sheet as of the close of business on March 5.

Problem 12–4

A corporation received a charter granting the right to issue 50,000 shares of $10 par value common stock. It then completed these transactions:

198A

Feb. 17   Sold and issued 15,000 shares of common stock for cash at $11 per share.

17   Gave the corporation's promoters 1,000 shares of common stock for their services in getting the corporation organized. The board of directors valued the promoters' services at $11,000.

17   Exchanged 25,000 shares of common stock for the following assets at fair values: land, $30,000; buildings, $100,000; and machinery, $145,000.

Dec. 10   Accepted subscriptions to 2,000 shares of common stock at par. Ten percent down payments accompanied the subscriptions.

31   Closed the Income Summary account. A $17,500 loss was incurred.

198B

Jan. 10   Received payment of the balance due on the December 10 subscriptions and issued the stock.

Dec. 31   Closed the Income Summary account. A $34,800 net income was earned.

198C

Jan.   8   The board of directors declared a $0.20 per share dividend on the outstanding common stock, payable on February 10 to the January 31 stockholders of record.

Feb. 10   Paid the previously declared dividend.

Required:

1.   Prepare general journal entries to record the transactions.
2.   Prepare the stockholders' equity section of the corporation's December 31, 198A, balance sheet.

Problem 12–5

A corporation has outstanding 25,000 shares of $10 par value common stock, all owned by five men who are the corporation's board of directors. The corporation is in a position to expand; but to do so it needs $250,000 additional capital which the owners are unable to supply. Consequently, they are considering the issuance at par of 2,500 shares of $100 par value, 8%, cumulative and nonparticipating preferred stock to gain the needed capital, and they have asked you to prepare a report showing the return to the two classes of stockholders from the following amounts of anticipated after-tax earnings: 198A, $25,000; 198B, $35,000; 198C, $55,000; and 198D, $60,000.

Required:

1.   Prepare a form with columnar headings as follows:

Year	After-Tax Earnings		Preferred Dividends		Common Dividends	
	Amount	Percent Return on Investment	Total Paid to Preferred	Percent Return on Investment	Total Paid to Common	Percent Return on Investment

2. Enter the years in the first column, each year's anticipated after-tax earnings in the second column, and each year's rate of return on the total $500,000 investment in the third column. Then complete the form under the assumption that all after-tax earnings are to be paid out in dividends.
3. Explain why at the after-tax levels of $55,000 and $60,000 the after-tax rate of return of the common stockholders will be greater than the after-tax rate earned by the corporation as a whole.
4. Prepare a calculation to account for the difference between the rate of return to the corporation as a whole at the $60,000 level and the rate of return to the common stockholders at that level.

ALTERNATE PROBLEMS

Problem 12–1A

During its first year, ended December 31, the partnership of More, Neal, and Orr earned a $42,600 net income.

Required:

Prepare entries to close the Income Summary account and to allocate the net income to the partners under each of the following assumptions:

a. The partners could not agree on a method of sharing earnings.
b. The partners agreed to share earnings in the ratio of their investments, which were Ted More, $12,000; Roy Neal, $16,000; and Ned Orr, $20,000.
c. The partners agreed to share earnings by allowing annual salary allowances of $14,000 to More, $16,000 to Neal, and $12,000 to Orr, plus interest at 10% on investments, and any remainder equally.

Problem 12–2A

June Clay and Ann Dent are forming a partnership to which Ms. Clay will devote full time and Ms. Dent will devote one third of her time. They have discussed the following plans for sharing losses and gains.

a. In the ratio of their investments which they have agreed to maintain at $10,000 for Ms. Clay and $20,000 for Ms. Dent.
b. In proportion to the time devoted to the business.
c. Salary allowances of $18,000 per year to Clay and $6,000 per year to Dent and any balance in their investment ratio.
d. Salary allowances of $18,000 per year to Clay and $6,000 per year to Dent, 8% interest on investments, and the balance equally.

Required:

1. Prepare a schedule with the following columnar headings:

Income Sharing Plan	$30,600 Net Income		$20,400 Net Income		$8,400 Net Loss	
	Clay	Dent	Clay	Dent	Clay	Dent

2. List the plans by letter in the first column and show opposite each letter the shares of the partners in a $30,600 net income, a $20,400 net income, and an $8,400 net loss.

Problem 12–3A

A corporation received a charter which granted it the right to issue 2,000 shares of $100 par value, 8% cumulative and nonparticipating preferred stock and 200,000 shares of $5 par value common stock. It then completed these transactions:

Feb. 3 Exchanged 100,000 shares of common stock for the following assets at fair values: land, $50,000; buildings, $150,000; and machinery, $325,000.

  3 Accepted subscriptions to 50,000 shares of common stock at $5.25 per share. The subscription contracts were accompanied by 10% down payments.

  5 Accepted subscriptions and $21,000 in down payments on 1,000 shares of preferred stock at $105 per share.

  7 Gave the corporation's attorneys $1,000 in cash and 400 shares of common stock for their services in securing the corporation charter. The services were valued by the board of directors at $3,100.

Mar. 5 Collected the balance due on the February 3 common stock subscriptions and issued the stock.

  7 Collected the balance due on the preferred stock subscriptions and issued the stock.

  31 Accepted subscriptions accompanied by 10% down payments to 10,000 shares of common stock at $5.50 per share.

Required:

1. Prepare general journal entries to record the transactions.
2. Prepare the stockholders' equity section of the corporation's balance sheet as of the close of business on March 31.

Problem 12–4A

A corporation received a charter granting it the right to issue 200,000 shares of $5 par value common stock. It then completed these transactions:

198A
Mar. 7 Sold and issued 10,000 shares of common stock at $5.50 per share for cash.

  7 Issued 1,000 shares of common stock to the corporation's attorney for services in getting the corporation organized. The board of directors placed a $5,500 value on the services.

  8 Exchanged 100,000 shares of common stock for the following assets at fair values: land, $50,000; buildings, $200,000; and machinery, $300,000.

Dec. 20 Accepted subscriptions to 50,000 shares of common stock at $5.25 per share. Down payments of 20% accompanied the subscription contracts.

Dec. 31   Closed the Income Summary account. There was a $11,400 net loss.

198B

Jan. 19   Collected the balance due on the December 20 subscriptions and issued the stock.

Dec. 31   Closed the Income Summary account. There was a $45,800 net income.

198C

Jan. 10   The board of directors declared a $0.10 per share dividend on the outstanding common stock, payable February 10 to the January 31 stockholders of record.

Feb. 10   Paid the dividend previously declared.

Required:

1. Prepare general journal entries to record the transactions.
2. Prepare the stockholders' equity section of the corporation's December 31, 198A, balance sheet.

Problem 12–5A

A corporation has outstanding 10,000 shares of $10 par value, 8%, preferred stock and 20,000 shares of $10 par value common stock. During a five-year period it paid out the following amounts in dividends: 198A, nothing; 198B, $22,000; 198C, $20,000; 198D, $30,000; and 198E, $36,000.

Required:

1. Prepare three schedules with columnar headings as follows:

Year	Amount Distributed in Dividends	Total to Preferred	Balance Due Preferred	Total to Common	Dividend per Share Preferred	Dividend per Share Common

2. Complete a schedule under each of the following assumptions, showing for each year the total dollars paid the preferred stockholders, balance due the preferred stockholders, and so forth. There were no dividends in arrears for the years prior to 198A.
   a. The preferred stock is noncumulative and nonparticipating.
   b. The preferred stock is cumulative and nonparticipating.
   c. The preferred stock is cumulative and fully participating.

PROVOCATIVE PROBLEMS

Provocative problem 12–1
Bill and Bob

Bill Larkin recently received a patent on a gadget on which he had spent his spare time for several years. He is certain the gadget has tremendous market potential, but as a school teacher he has never been able to save much money and does not have the capital to manufacture and sell it. Consequently, last night he approached Bob Walker, a long-time friend who recently inherited several hundred thousand dollars from his father, for a $10,000 loan. Before asking for the loan, Bill demonstrated the gadget to Bob. Bob immediately became excited about its possibilities and agreed to make the loan. However, Bob pointed out that $10,000 would hardly get the item into production, and it would take much more for a marketing campaign.

After discussing production and marketing needs for some time, Bob suggested that instead of a loan he should go into business with Bill. He suggested that he furnish the capital for the business and that Bill transfer his patent rights to the business. Bill accepted the offer, and after more discussion it was agreed that Bill would resign his teaching job at the end of the school year, a month away, and devote full time to organizing and managing the new business. Both men agreed that the marketing campaign should be turned over to professionals, but they did not agree as to the form of business organization for their new business.

Write a report to Bill and Bob outlining the factors they should consider in choosing between a partnership form of organization or a corporate form for their business.

Provocative problem 12–2
Loose Knot Lumber Company

Ed Loose and Ted Knot have operated a building supply firm for a number of years as partners sharing losses and gains in a 3 to 2 ratio. However, they need to increase the inventory of the business but do not have the necessary funds. Consequently, they have entered into an agreement with Lee Nail to reorganize their firm into a corporation, to be called Loose Knot Lumber Company, and they have just received a charter granting their corporation the right to issue 15,000 shares of $10 par value common stock.

On the date of the reorganization, June 8 of the current year, a trial balance of the partnership ledger appears as follows:

LOOSE AND KNOT

Trial Balance, June 8, 19—

Cash	$ 2,800	
Accounts receivable	8,250	
Allowance for doubtful accounts		$ 350
Merchandise inventory	62,700	
Store equipment	16,800	
Accumulated depreciation, store equipment		5,300
Buildings	80,000	
Accumulated depreciation, building		15,000
Land	17,250	
Accounts payable		13,150
Mortgage payable		60,000
Ed Loose, capital		55,000
Ted Knot, capital		39,000
Totals	$187,800	$187,800

The agreement between the partners and Lee Nail carries these provisions:

1. The partnership assets are to be revalued as follows:
    a. The $250 account of Valley Builders is known to be uncollectible and is to be written off as a bad debt, after which *(b)* the allowance for doubtful accounts is to be increased to 5% of the remaining accounts receivable.
    c. The merchandise inventory is to be written down to $60,000 to provide for damaged and shopworn goods.
    d. Insufficient depreciation has been taken on the store equipment; consequently, its book value is to be decreased to $10,000 by increasing the balance of the accumulated depreciation account.
    e. The building is to be written up to its replacement cost, $100,000, and the balance of the accumulated depreciation account is to be increased to show the building one-fifth depreciated.
2. After the partnership assets are revalued, the assets and liabilities are to be transferred to the corporation in exchange for its stock, with each partner accepting stock at par value for his equity in the partnership.
3. Lee Nail is to buy the remaining stock for cash at par.

After reaching the agreement outlined, the three men hired you as accountant for the new corporation. Your first task is to determine the amount of stock each partner should receive, and to prepare the entry on the corporation's books to record the issuance of stock in exchange for the partnership assets and liabilities. You are then to prepare the entry recording the sale of the remainder of the stock to Lee Nail for cash.

13

Corporations, additional transactions

After studying Chapter 13, you should be able to:

- Record purchases and sales of treasury stock, and describe their effects on stockholders' equity.
- Record stock dividends, and describe their effects on stockholders' equity.
- Explain the financial statement effects of converting bonds to common stock.
- Describe the reasons for appropriations of retained earnings and the disclosure of such appropriations in the financial statements.
- Prepare consolidated financial statements which include such matters as excess of investment cost over book value and minority interests.
- Account for the earnings and dividends of a subsidiary by the equity method.
- Explain the differences between the pooling of interests and purchase methods of accounting for corporate combinations.
- Define or explain the words and phrases listed in the chapter Glossary.

When a corporation earns a net income, more assets flow into the business from revenues than flow out for expenses. As a result, the net income increases both assets and stockholders' equity. The increase in stockholders' equity appears on the corporation's balance sheet as retained earnings. Once retained earnings were commonly called *earned surplus.* However, since the word "surplus" is subject to misinterpretation, the AICPA's Committee on Terminology recommended that its use be discontinued. Consequently, the term "surplus" has all but disappeared from published balance sheets.

RETAINED EARNINGS AND DIVIDENDS

In most states a corporation must have retained earnings in order to pay a cash dividend. However, the payment of a cash dividend reduces in equal amounts both cash and stockholders' equity. Consequently, in order to pay a cash dividend, a corporation must have not only a credit balance in its Retained Earnings account but also cash with which to pay the dividend. If cash or assets that will shortly become cash are not available, a board may think it wise to forgo the declaration of a dividend, even though retained earnings exist. Often the directors of a corporation having a large amount of retained earnings will not declare a dividend because all current assets are needed in the operation of the business.

In considering the wisdom of a dividend, a board must recognize that earnings are a source of assets. Some assets from earnings should probably be paid out in dividends, but some should be retained for emergencies and for distribution as dividends in years in which earnings are not sufficient to pay normal dividends. Also, some assets from earnings should be retained for use in expanding operations. The last reason is an important one. If a corporation is to expand and grow, it may sell additional stock to secure the assets needed in expansion. However, it may also expand by using assets acquired through earnings.

Entries for the declaration and distribution of a cash dividend were given on page 132 and need not be repeated here.

DISTRIBUTIONS FROM CONTRIBUTED CAPITAL

Some states permit the payment of a "dividend" from amounts received as stock premiums, but others make such distributions illegal. Nevertheless, and regardless of legality, accountants are opposed to calling such a distribution a dividend. It is obviously a return of invested capital and should be labeled clearly as such. Calling it a dividend might lead an uninformed person to believe the payment was from earnings. As to the legality of a dividend, state laws governing the payment of dividends commonly make directors personally liable for repayment to the corporation and its creditors of an illegal dividend.

STOCK DIVIDENDS

A *stock dividend* is a distribution by a corporation of shares of its own common stock to its common stockholders without any consideration being given in return therefor. Usually the distribution is prompted by a desire to give the stockholders some evidence of their interest in retained earnings without distributing cash or other assets which the board of directors thinks it wise to retain in the business. A clear distinction should be made between a cash dividend and a stock dividend. A cash dividend reduces both assets and stockholders' equity. A stock dividend differs in that shares of the corporation's own stock rather than cash are distributed. Such a dividend has no effect on assets, total capital, or the amount of a stockholder's equity.

A stock dividend has no effect on corporation assets, total capital, and the amount of a stockholder's equity because it involves nothing more than a transfer of retained earnings to contributed capital. To illustrate this assume that Northwest Corporation has the following stockholders' equity:

Stockholders' Equity		
Common stock, $10 par value, authorized 15,000 shares, issued and outstanding 10,000 shares	$100,000	
Premium on common stock	8,000	
Total contributed capital	$108,000	
Retained earnings	35,000	
Total stockholders' equity		$143,000

Assume further that on December 28 the directors of Northwest Corporation declared a 10% or 1,000-share stock dividend distributable on January 20 to the January 15 stockholders of record.

If the market value of Northwest Corporation's stock on December 28 is $15 per share, the following entries may be made to record the dividend declaration and distribution:

Dec.	28	Retained Earnings	15,000.00	
		Common Stock Dividend Distributable		10,000.00
		Premium on Common Stock		5,000.00
		To record the declaration of a 1,000-share		
		common stock dividend.		
Jan.	20	Common Stock Dividend Distributable	10,000.00	
		Common Stock		10,000.00
		To record the distribution of a 1,000-share		
		common stock dividend.		

Note that the entries change $15,000 of the stockholders' equity from retained earnings to contributed capital, or as it is said, $15,000 of retained earnings are *capitalized*. Note also that the retained earnings capitalized are equal to the market value of the 1,000 shares issued ($15 × 1,000 shares = $15,000).

As previously pointed out, a stock dividend does not distribute funds from earnings to the stockholders, nor does it affect in any way the corporation assets. Likewise, it has no effect on total capital and on the individual equities of the stockholders. To illustrate these last points, assume that Johnson owned 100 shares of Northwest Corporation's stock prior to the dividend. The corporation's total contributed and retained capital before the dividend and the book value of Johnson's 100 shares were as follows:

Common stock (10,000 shares)	$100,000
Premium on common stock	8,000
Retained earnings	35,000
Total contributed and retained capital	$143,000

$143,000 ÷ 10,000 shares outstanding = $14.30 per share book value
$14.30 × 100 = $1,430 for the book value of Johnson's 100 shares

A 10% stock dividend gives a stockholder one new share for each ten shares previously held. Consequently, Johnson received ten new shares; and after the dividend, the contributed and retained capital of the corporation and the book value of Johnson's holdings are as follows:

Common stock (11,000 shares)	$110,000
Premium on common stock	13,000
Retained earnings	20,000
Total contributed and retained capital	$143,000

$143,000 ÷ 11,000 shares outstanding = $13 per share book value
$13 × 110 = $1,430 for the book value of Johnson's 110 shares

Before the stock dividend, Johnson owned 100/10,000 or 1/100 of the Northwest Corporation stock and his holdings had a $1,430 book value. After the dividend, he owned 110/11,000 or 1/100 of the corporation and his holdings still had a $1,430 book value. In other words, there was no effect on his equity other than that it was repackaged from 100 units into 110. Likewise, the only effect on corporation capital was a permanent transfer to contributed capital of $15,000 of retained earnings. Consequently, insofar as both the corporation and Johnson are concerned, there was no shift in equities or corporation assets.

Why stock dividends are distributed

If a stock dividend has no effect on corporation assets and stockholders' equities other than to repackage the equities into more units, why are such dividends declared and distributed? Insofar as a corporation is concerned, a stock dividend enables it to give its shareholders some evidence of their interest in retained earnings without the necessity of distributing corporation cash or other assets to them. Consequently, stock dividends are often declared by corporations that have used funds from earnings in expanding and, as a result, do not feel they have sufficient cash with which to pay a cash dividend. Also, if a profitable corporation grows by retaining earnings, the price of its common stock also tends to grow. Eventually, the price of a share may become high enough to prevent some investors from considering purchase of the stock. Thus, corporations may declare stock dividends to keep the price of their shares from growing too high. For this reason, some corporations declare small stock dividends each year.

Stockholders may benefit from a stock dividend in another way. Often corporations declaring stock dividends continue to pay the same cash dividend per share after a stock dividend as before, with the result that stockholders receive more cash from each cash dividend.

Amount of retained earnings capitalized

The AICPA Committee on Accounting Procedure recognized that some stockholders incorrectly believe that earnings are distributed in a stock dividend. Consequently, it ruled that the amount of retained earnings capitalized in a small stock dividend and made unavailable for future dividends should equal the market value of the shares to be distributed.[1] A *small stock dividend* was defined as one of 25% or less of the previously outstanding shares.

A small stock dividend is likely to have only a small impact on the price of the stock. On the other hand, a large stock dividend normally

---

[1] Committee on Accounting Procedure, "Accounting Research Bulletin No. 43," *Accounting Research and Terminology Bulletins, Final Edition* (New York: AICPA, 1961), chap. 7, sec. B, pars. 10, 13.

has a pronounced impact, and for this reason is not apt to be perceived as a distribution of earnings. Consequently, in recording a large stock dividend (over 25%), the committee ruled that it is only necessary to capitalize retained earnings to the extent required by law. As a result, in most states a corporation may record a large stock dividend by debiting Retained Earnings and crediting the stock account for the par value of the shares issued.[2]

Stock dividends on the balance sheet

Since a stock dividend is "payable" in stock rather than in assets, it is not a liability of its issuing corporation. Therefore, if a balance sheet is prepared between the declaration and distribution dates of a stock dividend, the amount of the dividend distributable should appear on the balance sheet in the stockholders' equity section as follows:

Common stock, $10 par value, 50,000 shares authorized, 20,000 shares issued	$200,000
Common stock subscribed, 5,000 shares	50,000
Common stock dividend distributable, 1,900 shares	19,000
Total common stock issued and to be issued	$269,000
Capital contributed by common stockholders in excess of the par value of their shares	46,000
Total capital contributed and subscribed by common stockholders	$315,000

In addition to the stock dividend distributable, note in the equity section the item "Capital contributed by common stockholders in excess of the par value of their shares." The item resulted from common stock premiums and is probably carried in the ledger in the Premium on Common Stock account. However, as in this case items are commonly shown on the balance sheet under more descriptive captions than the name of the account in which they are recorded.

STOCK SPLITS

Sometimes, when a corporation's stock is selling at a high price, the corporation will call it in and issue two, three, four, five, or more new shares in the place of each old share previously outstanding. For example, a corporation having outstanding $100 par value stock selling for $375 a share may call in the old shares and issue to the stockholders four shares of $25 par, or ten shares of $10 par, or any number of shares of no-par stock in exchange for each $100 share formerly held. This is known as a *stock split* or a *stock split-up,* and its usual purpose

---

[2] Ibid., chap. 7, sec. B, par. 11.

is to cause a reduction in the market price of the stock and, consequently, to facilitate trading in the stock.

A stock split has no effect on total stockholders' equity, the equities of the individual stockholders, or on the balances of any of the contributed or retained capital accounts. Consequently, all that is required in recording a stock split is a memorandum entry in the stock account reciting the facts of the split. For example, such a memorandum might read, "Called in the outstanding $100 par value common stock and issued ten shares of $10 par value common stock for each old share previously outstanding." Also, there would be a change in the description of the stock on the balance sheet.

CONVERTING BONDS TO STOCK

It was pointed out in Chapter 11 that to make a bond issue more attractive, bondholders may be given the right to exchange their bonds for a fixed number of shares of the issuing company's common stock. Such convertible bonds offer investors initial investment security, and if the issuing company prospers and its stock increases in price, an opportunity to share in the prosperity by converting their bonds to the more valuable stock. Conversion is always at the bondholders' option and therefore does not take place unless it is to their advantage.

When bonds are converted into stock, the conversion changes creditor equity into ownership equity. The generally accepted rule for measuring the contribution for the issued shares is that the carrying amount of the converted bonds becomes the book value of the capital contributed for the new shares. For example, assume the following: (1) A company has outstanding $1,000,000 of bonds upon which there is $8,000 unamortized discount. (2) The bonds are convertible at the rate of a $1,000 bond for 90 shares of the company's $10 par value common stock. And (3) $100,000 in bonds have been presented on their interest date for conversion. The entry to record the conversion is:

May	1	Bonds Payable	100,000.00	
		Discount on Bonds Payable		800.00
		Common Stock		90,000.00
		Premium on Common Stock		9,200.00
		To record the conversion of bonds.		

Note in this entry that the bonds' $99,200 carrying amount sets the accounting value for the capital contributed. Usually when bonds have a conversion privilege, it is not exercised until the stock's market value and normal dividend payments are sufficiently high to make the conversion profitable to the bondholders.

TREASURY STOCK

Corporations often reacquire shares of their own stock. Sometimes a corporation will purchase its own stock on the open market to be given to employees as a bonus or to be used in acquiring other corporations. Sometimes shares are bought in order to maintain a favorable market for the stock. Regardless, if a corporation reacquires shares of its own stock, such stock is known as *treasury stock*. Treasury stock is a corporation's own stock that has been issued and then reacquired either by purchase or gift. Notice that the stock must be the corporation's own stock. The acquisition of stock of another corporation does not create treasury stock. Furthermore, the stock must have been issued and then reacquired. The last point distinguishes treasury stock from unissued stock. The distinction is important because stock once issued at par or above and then reacquired as treasury stock may be legally reissued at a discount without discount liability. Although treasury stock differs from unissued stock in that it may be sold at a discount without discount liability, in other respects it has the same status as unissued stock. Both are equity items rather than assets. Both are subtracted from authorized stock to determine outstanding stock when such things as book values are calculated. Neither receives cash dividends nor has a vote in the stockholders' meetings.

PURCHASE OF TREASURY STOCK[3]

When a corporation purchases its own stock, it reduces in equal amounts both its assets and its stockholders' equity. To illustrate this, assume that on May 1 of the current year the condensed balance sheet of Curry Corporation appears as in Illustration 13–1.

Curry Corporation			
Balance Sheet, May 1, 19—			
Assets		*Capital*	
Cash	$ 30,000	Common stock, $10 par	
Other assets	95,000	value, authorized and	
		issued 10,000 shares	$100,000
		Retained earnings	25,000
Total assets	$125,000	Total capital	$125,000

Illustration 13–1

If on May 1 Curry Corporation purchases 1,000 shares of its outstanding stock at $11.50 per share, the transaction is recorded as follows:

[3] There are several ways of accounting for treasury stock transactions. This text will discuss the so-called cost basis, which seems to be the most widely used, and it will leave a discussion of other methods to a more advanced text.

May	1	Treasury Stock, Common	11,500.00	
		Cash		11,500.00
		Purchased 1,000 shares of treasury stock at $11.50 per share.		

The debit of the entry records a reduction in the equity of the stockholders. The credit records a reduction in assets. Both are equal to the cost of the treasury stock. After the entry is posted, a new balance sheet will show the reductions as in Illustration 13–2.

Curry Corporation
Balance Sheet, May 1, 19—

Assets		*Capital*	
Cash	$ 18,500	Common stock, $10 par value, authorized and issued 10,000 shares of which 1,000 are in the treasury	$100,000
Other assets	95,000		
		Retained earnings of which $11,500 is restricted by the purchase of treasury stock	25,000
		Total	$125,000
		Less cost of treasury stock ..	11,500
Total assets	$113,500	Total capital	$113,500

Illustration 13–2

Notice in the second balance sheet that the cost of the treasury stock appears in the stockholders' equity section as a deduction from common stock and retained earnings. In comparing the two balance sheets, notice that the treasury stock purchase reduces both assets and stockholders' equity by the $11,500 cost of the stock. Also, observe that the dollar amount of issued stock remains at $100,000 and is unchanged from the first balance sheet. The amount of *issued stock* is not changed by the purchase of treasury stock. However, the purchase does reduce *outstanding stock*. In Curry Corporation, the purchase reduced the outstanding stock from 10,000 to 9,000 shares.

There is a distinction between issued stock and outstanding stock. Issued stock may or may not be outstanding. Outstanding stock is stock that has been issued and is currently outstanding. Only outstanding stock is effective stock, receives cash dividends, and is given a vote in the meetings of stockholders.

Restricting retained earnings by the purchase of treasury stock

The purchase of treasury stock by a corporation has the same effect on its assets and stockholders' equity as the payment of a cash dividend. Both transfer corporation assets to stockholders and thereby reduce assets and stockholders' equity. Consequently, in most states a corporation may purchase treasury stock or it may pay cash dividends, but the sum of both cannot exceed the amount of its retained earnings available for dividends.

Unlike the payment of a cash dividend, the purchase of treasury stock does not reduce the balance of the Retained Earnings account. However, the purchase does place a restriction on the amount of retained earnings available for dividends. Note how the restriction is shown in Illustration 13–2. It is also commonly shown by means of a balance sheet footnote. The restriction was once shown in the accounts by transferring an amount of retained earnings from the Retained Earnings account to an account titled Retained Earnings Restricted by the Purchase of Treasury Stock. However, this is seldom done today.

REISSUING TREASURY STOCK

When treasury stock is reissued, it may be reissued at cost, above cost, or below cost. If reissued at cost, the entry to record the transaction is the reverse of the entry used to record the purchase.

Although treasury stock may be sold at cost, it is commonly sold at a price either above or below cost. When sold above cost, the amount received in excess of cost is credited to a contributed capital account called "Contributed Capital, Treasury Stock Transactions." For example, if Curry Corporation sells for $12 per share 500 of the treasury shares purchased at $11.50 per share, the entry to record the transaction appears as follows:

June	3	Cash	6,000.00	
		Contributed Capital, Treasury Stock		
		Transactions		250.00
		Treasury Stock		5,750.00
		Sold at $12 per share 500 treasury shares that cost $11.50 per share.		

When treasury stock is reissued at a price below cost, the entry to record the sale depends upon whether or not there is contributed capital from previous treasury stock transactions. If there is no such contributed capital, the "loss" is debited to Retained Earnings. However, if there is such contributed capital, the "loss" is debited to the account of this contributed capital to the extent of its balance. Any remainder is then debited to Retained Earnings. For example, if Curry Corporation sells its remaining 500 shares of treasury stock at $10 per share, the entry to record the sale is:

July	10	Cash	5,000.00	
		Contributed Capital, Treasury Stock		
		Transactions	250.00	
		Retained Earnings	500.00	
		Treasury Stock		5,750.00
		Sold at $10 per share 500 treasury shares that cost $11.50 per share.		

RETIREMENT OF STOCK

A corporation may purchase shares of its own stock which are not to be held as treasury stock but for immediate retirement, with the shares being permanently canceled upon receipt. Such action is permissible if the interests of creditors and other stockholders are not jeopardized.

When stock is purchased for retirement, all capital items related to the shares being retired are removed from the accounts. If there is a "gain" on the transaction, it should be credited to contributed capital. On the other hand, a loss should be debited to Retained Earnings.

For example, assume a corporation originally issued its $10 par value common stock at $12 per share, with the premium being credited to Premium on Common Stock. If the corporation later purchased for retirement 1,000 shares of this stock at the price for which it was issued, the entry to record the retirement is:

Apr.	12	Common Stock	10,000.00	
		Premium on Common Stock	2,000.00	
		Cash		12,000.00
		Purchased and retired 1,000 shares of common stock at $12 per share.		

If on the other hand the corporation paid $11 per share instead of $12, the entry for the retirement is:

Apr.	12	Common Stock	10,000.00	
		Premium on Common Stock	2,000.00	
		Cash		11,000.00
		Contributed Capital from the Retirement of		
		Common Stock		1,000.00
		Purchased and retired 1,000 shares of		
		common stock at $11 per share.		

Or if the corporation paid $15 per share, the entry for the purchase and retirement is:

Apr.	12	Common stock	10,000.00	
		Premium on Common Stock	2,000.00	
		Retained Earnings	3,000.00	
		Cash		15,000.00
		Purchased and retired 1,000 shares of		
		common stock at $15 per share.		

CONTRIBUTED CAPITAL AND DIVIDENDS

Generally contributed capital may not be returned to stockholders as dividends. However, in some states dividends may be debited or charged to certain contributed capital accounts. Seldom may dividends be charged against the par or stated value of the outstanding stock. However, the exact contributed capital accounts to which a corporation may charge dividends depend upon the laws of the state of its incorporation. For this reason it is usually wise for a board of directors to secure competent legal advice before voting to charge dividends to any contributed capital account.

APPROPRIATIONS OF RETAINED EARNINGS

A corporation may *appropriate retained earnings* for some special purpose or purposes and show the amounts appropriated as separate items in the equity section of its balance sheet. The appropriations may be voluntarily made by the board of directors or required by a contract. Such appropriations may be recorded by transferring portions of retained earnings from the Retained Earnings account to accounts such as "Retained Earnings Appropriated for Contingencies" or "Retained Earnings Appropriated for Plant Expansion."

The appropriations do not reduce total retained earnings. Rather, their purpose is to inform balance sheet readers that portions of retained earnings are not available for the declaration of cash dividends. When the contingency or other reason for an appropriation has passed, the appropriation account is eliminated by returning its balance to the Retained Earnings account.

Appropriations of retained earnings were once common, but such appropriations are seldom seen on balance sheets today. Today, the same information is conveyed with less chance of misunderstanding by means of footnotes accompanying the financial statements.

PARENT AND SUBSIDIARY CORPORATIONS

Corporations commonly own and control other corporations. For example, if Corporation A owns more than 50% of the voting stock of Corporation B, Corporation A can elect Corporation B's board of directors and thus control its activities and resources. In such a situation the controlling corporation, Corporation A, is known as the *parent company* and Corporation B is called a *subsidiary*.

When a corporation owns all the outstanding stock of a subsidiary, it can take over the subsidiary's assets, cancel its stock, and fuse the subsidiary into the parent company. However, there are often financial, legal, and tax advantages in operating a large business as a parent company controlling one or more subsidiaries rather than as a single corporation. Actually, most large companies are parent corporations owning one or more subsidiaries.

When a business is operated as a parent company with subsidiaries, separate accounting records are kept for each corporation. Also, from a legal viewpoint the parent and each subsidiary is a separate entity with all the rights, duties, and responsibilities of a separate corporation. However, investors in the parent company depend on the parent to present a set of *consolidated statements* which show the results of all operations under the parent's control, including those of any subsidiaries. In these statements the assets and liabilities of all affiliated companies are combined on a single balance sheet and their revenues and expenses are combined on a single income statement, as though the business were in fact a single company.

CONSOLIDATED BALANCE SHEETS

When parent and subsidiary balance sheets are consolidated, duplications in items are eliminated so that the combined figures do not show more assets and equities than actually exist. For example, a parent's investment in a subsidiary is evidenced by shares of stock which are carried as an asset in the parent company's records. However, these shares actually represent an equity in the subsidiary's assets. Consequently, if the parent's investment in a subsidiary and the subsidiary's assets were both shown on the consolidated balance sheet, the same resources would be counted twice. To prevent this, the parent's investment and the subsidiary's capital accounts are offset and eliminated in preparing a consolidated balance sheet.

Likewise, a single enterprise cannot owe a debt to itself. This would be analogous to a student borrowing $20 for a date from funds saved for next semester's expenses and then preparing a balance sheet showing the $20 as both receivable from himself and payable to himself. To prevent such a double showing, intercompany debts and receivables are also eliminated in preparing a consolidated balance sheet.

Balance sheets consolidated at time of acquisition

When a parent's and a subsidiary's assets are combined in the preparation of a consolidated balance sheet, a work sheet is normally used to effect the consolidation. Illustration 13–3 shows such a work sheet. It was prepared to consolidate the accounts of Parent Company and its subsidiary, called Subsidiary Company, on January 1, 198A, the day Parent Company acquired Subsidiary Company through the purchase for cash of all its outstanding $10 par value common stock. The stock had a book value of $115,000, or $11.50 per share, which in this first illustration is the amount Parent Company is assumed to have paid for it. Explanation of the work sheet's two eliminating entries follow.

Parent Company and Subsidiary Company
Work Sheet for a Consolidated Balance Sheet, January 1, 198A

	Parent Company	Subsidiary Company	Eliminations Debit	Eliminations Credit	Consolidated Amounts
Assets					
Cash......................	5,000	15,000			20,000
Notes receivable	10,000			(a) 10,000	
Accounts receivable, net ...	20,000	13,000			33,000
Inventories	45,000	22,000			67,000
Investment in Subsidiary Company	115,000			(b) 115,000	
Buildings and equipment, net	100,000	74,000			174,000
Land	25,000	8,000			33,000
	320,000	132,000			327,000
Equities					
Accounts payable	15,000	7,000			22,000
Notes payable		10,000	(a) 10,000		
Common stock	250,000	100,000	(b) 100,000		250,000
Retained earnings	55,000	15,000	(b) 15,000		55,000
	320,000	132,000	125,000	125,000	327,000

Entry (a)   On the day it acquired Subsidiary Company, Parent Company lent Subsidiary Company $10,000 for use in the subsidiary's operations. It took the subsidiary's note as evidence of the transaction. This intercompany debt was in reality a transfer of funds within the organization. Consequently, since it did not increase the total assets and total liabilities of the affiliated companies, it is eliminated by means of Entry *(a)*. To understand this entry, recall that the subsidiary's promissory note is represented by a $10,000 debit in Parent Company's Notes Receivable account. Then observe that the first credit in the Eliminations column exactly offsets and eliminates this item. Next, recall that the subsidiary's note appears as a credit in its Notes Payable account. Then observe that the $10,000 debit in the Eliminations column completes the elimination of this intercompany debt.

Entry (b)   When a parent company buys a subsidiary's stock, the investment appears on the parent's balance sheet as an asset, "Investment in Subsidiary." The investment represents an equity in the subsidiary's assets. Consequently, to show both the subsidiary's assets and the investment in the assets on a consolidated balance sheet would be to show more resources than exist. As a result, on the work sheet the amount of the parent's investment (an equity in the subsidiary's assets) is offset against the subsidiary's stockholder equity accounts, which also represent an equity in the assets, and both are eliminated.

After the intercompany items are eliminated on a work sheet like Illustration 13–3, the assets of the parent and the subsidiary and the remaining equities in these assets are combined and carried into the work sheet's last column. The combined amounts are then used to prepare a consolidated balance sheet showing all the assets and equities of the parent and its subsidiary.

Parent company does not buy all of subsidiary's stock and does not pay book value

In the situation just described, Parent Company purchased all of its subsidiary's stock, paying book value for it. Often a parent company purchases less than 100% of a subsidiary's stock, and commonly pays a price either above or below book value. To illustrate such a situation, assume Parent Company purchased for cash only 80% of its subsidiary's stock rather than 100%, and that it paid $13 per share, a price $1.50 above the stock's book value.

These new assumptions result in a more complicated work sheet entry to eliminate the parent's investment and the subsidiary's stockholders' equity accounts. The entry is complicated by (1) the minority interest in the subsidiary and (2) the excess over book value paid by the parent company for the subsidiary's stock.

Minority interest   When a parent buys a controlling interest in a subsidiary, the parent company is the subsidiary's majority stockholder. However, when the parent owns less than 100% of the subsidiary's stock, the subsidiary has other stockholders who own a *minority interest* in its assets and share its earnings. Consequently, when there is a minority interest, the minority interest must be set out as on the last line of Illustration 13–4 in making the work sheet entry to eliminate the stockholders' equity accounts of the subsidiary. In this case the minority stockholders have a 20% interest in the subsidiary. Consequently, 20% of the subsidiary's common stock and retained earnings accounts [($100,000 + $15,000) × 20% = $23,000] is set out on the work sheet as the minority interest.

Parent Company and Subsidiary Company
Work Sheet for a Consolidated Balance Sheet, January 1, 198A

	Parent Company	Subsidiary Company	Eliminations Debit	Eliminations Credit	Consolidated Amounts
Assets					
Cash......................	16,000	15,000			31,000
Notes receivable	10,000			(a) 10,000	
Accounts receivable, net ...	20,000	13,000			33,000
Inventories	45,000	22,000			67,000
Investment in Subsidiary					
Company	104,000			(b) 104,000	
Buildings and					
equipment, net	100,000	74,000			174,000
Land	25,000	8,000			33,000
Excess of cost					
over book value			(b) 12,000		12,000
	320,000	132,000			350,000
Equities					
Accounts payable	15,000	7,000			22,000
Notes payable		10,000	(a) 10,000		
Common stock	250,000	100,000	(b) 100,000		250,000
Retained earnings	55,000	15,000	(b) 15,000		55,000
Minority interest				(b) 23,000	23,000
	320,000	132,000	137,000	137,000	350,000

Illustration 13–4

Excess of investment cost over book value Parent Company paid $13 per share for its 8,000 shares of Subsidiary Company's stock. Consequently, the cost of these shares exceeded their book value by $12,000, calculated as follows:

Cost of stock (8,000 shares at $13 per share)	$104,000
Book value (8,000 shares at $11.50 per share)	92,000
Excess of cost over book value	$ 12,000

Now observe how this excess of cost over book value is set out on the work sheet in eliminating the parent's investment in the subsidiary and how it is carried into the Consolidated Amounts column as an asset.

After its completion, the consolidated amounts in the last column of the work sheet of Illustration 13–4 were used to prepare the consolidated balance sheet of Illustration 13–5. Note the treatment of the minority interest in the balance sheet. The minority stockholders have a $23,000 equity in the consolidated assets of the affiliated companies. Many have argued that this item should be disclosed in the stockholders' equity section. Others believe it should be shown in the long-term liabilities section. Both alternatives can be found in published financial statements. However, a more common alternative is to disclose minority interest as a separate item between the liabilities and stockholders' equity sections, as is shown in Illustration 13–5.

Next observe that the $12,000 excess over book value paid by the parent company for the subsidiary's stock appears on the consolidated balance sheet as the asset, "Goodwill from consolidation." When a parent company purchases an interest in a subsidiary, it may pay more than book value for its equity because (1) certain of the subsidiary's assets are carried on the subsidiary's books at less than fair value. It also may pay more because (2) certain of the subsidiary's liabilities

Parent Company and Subsidiary
Consolidated Balance Sheet, January 1, 198A

Assets

Current assets:

Cash	$ 31,000	
Accounts receivable, net	33,000	
Inventories	67,000	
Total current assets		$131,000
Plant and equipment:		
Buildings and equipment, net	$174,000	
Land	33,000	
Total plant and equipment		207,000
Goodwill from consolidation		12,000
Total assets		$350,000

Liabilities and Stockholders' Equity

Liabilities:		
Accounts payable		$ 22,000
Minority interest		23,000
Stockholders' equity:		
Common stock	$250,000	
Retained earnings	55,000	
Total stockholders' equity		305,000
Total liabilities and stockholders' equity		$350,000

Illustration 13–5

are carried at book values which are greater than fair values, or (3) the subsidiary's earnings prospects are good enough to justify paying more than the net fair (market) value of its assets and liabilities. In this illustration, it is assumed that the book values of Subsidiary Company's assets and liabilities are their fair values. However, Subsidiary Company's expected earnings justified paying $104,000 for an 80% equity in the subsidiary's net assets (assets less liabilities).

The APB ruled that where a company pays more than book value because the subsidiary's assets are undervalued or its liabilities are overvalued, the cost in excess of book value should be allocated to those assets and liabilities so that they are restated at fair values. After the subsidiary's assets and liabilities have been restated to reflect fair values, any remaining cost in excess of book value should be reported on the consolidated balance sheet as "Goodwill from consolidation."[4]

Occasionally a parent company pays less than book value for its interest in a subsidiary. In such a case, since a "bargain" purchase is very unlikely, the logical reason for a price below book value is that certain of the subsidiary's assets are carried on its books at amounts in excess of fair value. In such a situation the APB ruled that the amounts at which the overvalued assets are placed on the consolidated balance sheet should be reduced accordingly.[5]

EARNINGS AND DIVIDENDS OF A SUBSIDIARY

In the years following acquisition, if a subsidiary's operations are profitable, its net assets and retained earnings increase. Also, if it pays dividends, the dividends are paid to the parent company and any minority stockholders in proportion to the stockholdings of each. Furthermore, the subsidiary records the transactions that result in earnings, closes its Income Summary account, and records the declaration and payment of dividends just like any other corporation.

In accounting for its share of a subsidiary's earnings and dividends, the APB ruled that a parent company should use the *equity method.*[6] Under this method it is recognized that a subsidiary's earnings not only increase the subsidiary's net assets but also increase the parent company's equity in the assets. Consequently, under this method, when the subsidiary reports the amount of its earnings, the parent company takes up its share in its account, Investment in Subsidiary Company. For example, if the subsidiary of these discussions earned $12,500 during the first year in which 80% of its stock was owned by Parent Company, Parent Company records its share as follows:

---

[4] APB, "Business Combinations," *APB Opinion No. 16* (New York: AICPA, 1970), par. 87.

[5] Ibid., par. 91.

[6] APB, "The Equity Method of Accounting for Investments in Common Stock," *APB Opinion No. 18* (New York: AICPA, 1971), par. 17.

Dec.	31	Investment in Subsidiary Company	10,000.00	
		Earnings from Investment in Subsidiary		10,000.00
		To take up 80% of the net income reported by Subsidiary Company.		

The debit of the entry records the increase in Parent Company's equity in the subsidiary. The credit causes 80% of the subsidiary's net income to appear on Parent Company's income statement as earnings from the investment. Parent Company closes the earnings to its Income Summary account and on to its Retained Earnings account just as with earnings from any investment.

In case of a loss the Parent Company debits the loss to an account called Loss from Investment in Subsidiary and credits and reduces the balance of its Investment in Subsidiary account. It then carries the loss to its Income Summary account and on to its Retained Earnings account.

Dividends paid by a subsidiary decrease its net assets and, as a result, also decrease the amount of the parent's equity in the subsidiary. For example, if the subsidiary of this discussion paid a $7,500 cash dividend at the end of its first year as a subsidiary, the dividend reduced the parent company's equity in the subsidiary by 80% of the $7,500 or by $6,000. Parent Company records receipt of its share of the cash and the reduction in its equity with an entry like this:

Dec.	31	Cash	6,000.00	
		Investment in Subsidiary Company		6,000.00
		To record the receipt of 80% of the $7,500 dividend paid by Subsidiary Company.		

From this discussion it can be seen that a subsidiary's earnings and dividends not only affect the balance of its Retained Earnings account but also result in changes in the parent company's account, Investment in Subsidiary Company. As a result, in the years following acquisition, when consolidated balance sheets are prepared, the amounts eliminated from these accounts change as the account balances change.

CONSOLIDATED BALANCE SHEETS AT A DATE AFTER ACQUISITION

If Subsidiary Company earned $12,500 during its first year as a subsidiary and paid out $7,500 in dividends, the balance of its Retained Earnings account increased from $15,000 at the beginning of the year to $20,000 at the year-end. Consequently, $20,000 of retained earnings are eliminated on the year-end work sheet, Illustration 13–6, to consoli-

Parent Company and Subsidiary Company
Work Sheet for a Consolidated Balance Sheet, December 31, 198A

	Parent Company	Subsidiary Company	Eliminations		Consolidated Amounts
			Debit	Credit	
Assets					
Cash....................	14,000	10,000			24,000
Notes receivable	10,000			(a) 10,000	
Accounts receivable, net ...	27,000	14,000			41,000
Inventories	50,000	29,000			79,000
Investment in Subsidiary					
Company	108,000			(b) 108,000	
Buildings and					
equipment, net	95,000	76,000			171,000
Land	25,000	8,000			33,000
Excess of cost					
over book value			(b) 12,000		12,000
	329,000	137,000			360,000
Equities					
Accounts payable	15,000	7,000			22,000
Notes payable		10,000	(a) 10,000		
Common stock	250,000	100,000	(b) 100,000		250,000
Retained earnings	64,000	20,000	(b) 20,000		64,000
Minority interest				(b) 24,000	24,000
	329,000	137,000	142,000	142,000	360,000

stration 13–6

date the balance sheets of the companies. (To simplify the illustration, it is assumed that the liabilities of both companies are unchanged and that the subsidiary has not paid the note given parent company.)

To continue the explanation, Parent Company paid $104,000 for 80% of Subsidiary Company's stock and debited that amount to its Investment in Subsidiary Company account. During the year Parent Company increased this account $10,000 by taking up 80% of the subsidiary's earnings and decreased it $6,000 upon receipt of its share of the subsidiary's dividend. As a result, the account had a $108,000 year-end balance, which is the amount eliminated on the work sheet.

Two additional items in Illustration 13–6 require explanations. First, the minority interest set out on the year-end work sheet is greater than on the beginning-of-the-year work sheet (Illustration 13–4). The minority stockholders have a 20% equity in Subsidiary Company, and the $24,000 shown on the year-end work sheet is 20% of the year-end balances of the Subsidiary's Common Stock and Retained Earnings accounts. This $24,000 is $1,000 greater than the beginning-of-the-year minority interest because the subsidiary's retained earnings increased $5,000 during the year and the minority stockholder's share of the increase is 20% or $1,000. Second, the $12,000 amount set out as the excess cost of Parent Company's investment over its book value is, in this illustration, the same on the end-of-the-year work sheet as on the work sheet at the beginning. The APB ruled that such excess cost or "goodwill" should be amortized by systematic charges to income over the accounting periods estimated to be benefited.[7] An explanation of the amortization entries is left to a more advanced text.

OTHER CONSOLIDATED STATEMENTS

Consolidated income statements and consolidated retained earnings statements are also prepared for affiliated companies. However, preparation of these require procedures a discussion of which must be deferred to an advanced accounting course. Knowledge of the procedures is not necessary to a general understanding of such statements. The reader should recognize that all duplications in items and all profit arising from intercompany transactions are eliminated in their preparation. Also, the amounts of net income and retained earnings which are reported in consolidated statements are equal to the amounts recorded by the parent under the equity method.

PURCHASE VERSUS A POOLING OF INTERESTS

The method of consolidation described thus far is called the *purchase method*. Where a parent company acquired its interest in a subsidiary by paying cash, as here, or by issuing bonds or preferred stock, it is assumed that the subsidiary's shareholders sold their interest in the subsidiary and consolidated statements are prepared by the purchase method.

If a parent company issues common stock to acquire a subsidiary, the transaction may still be regarded as a purchase requiring the preparation of consolidated statements by the purchase method. However, if common stock is issued and certain other criteria are met,[8] consolidated statements are prepared in accordance with the *pooling-of-interests method*. Under this method it is assumed that a sale did not occur and that the stockholders of the parent and subsidiary companies combined or pooled their interests to form the consolidated company.

Time and space do not permit a discussion of pooling-of-interests consolidations. Such a discussion must be deferred to an advanced accounting or finance course.

THE CORPORATION BALANCE SHEET

A number of balance sheet sections have been illustrated in this and previous chapters. To bring together as much of the information

---

[7] APB, "Intangible Assets," *APB Opinion No. 17* (New York: AICPA, 1970), pars. 27–31.

[8] *APB Opinion No. 16,* pars. 45–49.

Betco Corporation
Consolidated Balance Sheet, December 31, 198A

Assets

Current assets:

Cash			$ 15,000
Marketable securities			5,000
Accounts receivable		$ 50,000	
Less allowance for doubtful accounts		1,000	49,000
Merchandise inventory			115,000
Subscriptions receivable, common stock			15,000
Prepaid expenses			1,000
Total current assets				$200,000

Long-term investments:

Bond sinking fund	$ 15,000	
Toledo Corporation common stock	5,000	
Total long-term investments		20,000

Plant assets:

Land		50,000
Buildings	$285,000	
Less accumulated depreciation	30,000	255,000
Store equipment	$ 85,000	
Less accumulated depreciation	20,000	65,000
Total plant assets		370,000

Intangible assets:

Goodwill from consolidation	10,000
Total assets	$600,000

Liabilities

Current liabilities:

Notes payable	$ 10,000	
Accounts payable	14,000	
State and federal income taxes payable	16,000	
Total current liabilities		$ 40,000

Long-term liabilities:

First 8% real estate mortgage bonds, due in 199E	$100,000	
Less unamortized discount based on the 8¼% market rate for bond interest prevailing on the date of issue	2,000	98,000
Total liabilities		$138,000
Minority interest		15,000

Stockholders' Equity

Contributed capital:

Common stock, $10 par value, authorized 50,000 shares, issued 30,000 shares of which 1,000 are in the treasury	$300,000	
Unissued common stock subscribed, 2,500 shares	25,000	
Capital contributed by the stockholders in excess of the par value of their shares	33,000	
Total contributed capital		358,000
Retained earnings (Note 1)		105,000
Total contributed and retained capital		$463,000
Less cost of treasury stock		16,000
Total stockholders' equity		447,000
Total liabilities and stockholder's equity		$600,000

Note 1: Retained earnings in the amount of $31,000 is restricted under an agreement with the corporations bondholders and because of the purchase of treasury stock, leaving $74,000 of retained earnings not so restricted.

from all these sections as space allows, the balance sheet of Betco Corporation is shown in Illustration 13–7.

Betco Corporation's balance sheet is a consolidated balance sheet, as indicated in the title and by the items "Goodwill from consolidation" and "Minority interest." In preparing the balance sheet, Betco Corporation's investment in its subsidiary was eliminated. Consequently, the Toledo Corporation stock shown on the consolidated balance sheet represents an investment in an unconsolidated (outside) company that is not a subsidiary of either Betco or Betco's subsidiary.

GLOSSARY

Appropriated retained earnings. Retained earnings earmarked for a special use as a means of informing stockholders that assets from earnings equal to the appropriations are unavailable for dividends.

Earned surplus. A synonym for retained earnings, no longer in use.

Equity method of accounting for stock investments. The investment is recorded at total cost, investor's equity in subsequent earnings of the investee increases the investment account, and subsequent dividends of the investee reduce the investment account.

Minority interest. Stockholders' equity in a subsidiary not owned by the parent corporation.

Parent company. A corporation that owns a controlling interest (more than 50% of the voting stock is required) in another corporation.

Pooling of interests. A combination between two corporations in which the stockholders of the two companies combine their interests to form the consolidated company without either stockholder group selling its interest.

Purchase method of acquiring a subsidiary. A combination between two corporations where the shareholders of one company sell their interest, taking cash, bonds, and sometimes shares of the parent company's stock in payment.

Small stock dividend. A stock dividend 25% or less of a corporation's previously outstanding shares.

Stock dividend. A distribution by a corporation of shares of its own common stock to its common stockholders without any consideration being received in return therefor.

Stock split. The act of a corporation of calling in its stock and issuing more than one new share in the place of each old share previously outstanding.

Subsidiary. A corporation that is controlled by another (parent) corporation because the parent owns more than 50% of the subsidiary's voting stock.

Treasury stock: Issued stock that has been reacquired by the issuing corporation.

QUESTIONS FOR CLASS DISCUSSION

1. What are the effects in terms of assets and stockholders' equity of the declaration and distribution of *(a)* a cash dividend and *(b)* a stock dividend?
2. What is the difference between a stock dividend and a stock split?
3. Courts have held that a dividend in the stock of the distributing corporation is not taxable income to its recipients. Why?
4. If a balance sheet is prepared between the date of declaration and the date of distribution of a dividend, how should the dividend be shown if it is to be distributed in *(a)* cash and *(b)* stock?
5. What is treasury stock? How is it like unissued stock? How does it differ from unissued stock? What is the legal significance of this difference?
6. General Plastics Corporation bought 1,000 shares of Capital Steel Corporation stock and turned it over to its treasurer for safekeeping. Is this treasury stock? Why or why not?
7. What is the effect of a treasury stock purchase in terms of assets and stockholders' equity?
8. Distinguish between issued stock and outstanding stock.
9. Why do state laws place limitations on the purchase of treasury stock?
10. What are consolidated financial statements?
11. What account balances must be eliminated in preparing a consolidated balance sheet? Why are they eliminated?
12. Why would a parent corporation pay more than book value for the stock of a subsidiary?
13. When a parent pays more than book value for the stock of a subsidiary, how should this additional cost be allocated in the consolidated balance sheet?
14. What is meant by "minority interest?" Where is this item disclosed on a consolidated balance sheet?
15. When a parent corporation uses the equity method to account for its investment in a subsidiary, what recognition is given by the parent corporation to the income or loss reported by the subsidiary? What recognition is given to dividends declared by the subsidiary?

CLASS EXERCISES

Exercise 13-1

The stockholders' equity section of a corporation's balance sheet appeared as follows on April 1:

Stockholders' Equity

Common stock, $5 par value, 250,000 shares authorized, 200,000 shares issued..............	$1,000,000	
Premium on common stock.....................	200,000	
Total contributed capital	$1,200,000	
Retained earnings	270,000	
Total stockholders' equity.............		$1,470,000

On that date, when the stock was selling for $7.50 per share, the corporation's directors voted a 5% stock dividend distributable on May 15 to the May 1 stockholders of record. The dividend's declaration and distribution had no apparent effect on the market price of the shares, since they were still selling at $7.50 per share as of the close of business on May 15.

Required:
1. Give the entries to record the declaration and distribution of the dividend.
2. Under the assumption that Jessie Bork owned 1,000 shares of the stock on April 1 and received the proper number of dividend shares on May 15, prepare a schedule showing the numbers of shares held by this stockholder on April 1 and May 15, with their total book values and total market values.

Exercise 13–2

A corporation has outstanding $1,000,000 of 9%, 20-year bonds on which there is $25,000 of unamortized bond premium. The bonds are convertible into the corporation's $10 par value common stock at the rate of one $1,000 bond for 95 shares of the stock, and $100,000 of the bonds have been presented for conversion. Give the entry to record the conversion as of May 1.

Exercise 13–3

On February 5 the stockholders' equity section of a corporation's balance sheet appeared as follows:

Stockholders' Equity

Common stock, $10 par value, 25,000 shares authorized and issued	$250,000	
Retained earnings	65,000	
Total stockholders' equity		$315,000

On the date of the equity section the corporation purchased 1,000 shares of treasury stock at $13.50 per share. Give the entry to record the purchase and prepare a stockholders' equity section as it would appear immediately after the purchase.

Exercise 13–4

On February 15 the corporation of Exercise 13–3 sold 400 shares of its treasury stock at $14 per share, and on March 10 it sold the remaining treasury shares at $12.75 per share. Give the entries to record the sales.

Exercise 13–5

On January 2 Company B had the following stockholders' equity:

Common stock, $10 par value, 10,000 shares authorized and outstanding	$100,000	
Retained earnings	20,000	
Total stockholders' equity		$120,000

a. Under the assumption that Company A purchased all of Company B's stock on January 2, paying $12 per share, and that a work sheet to consolidate the two companies' balance sheets was prepared, given the entry made on this work sheet to eliminate Company A's investment and Company B's stockholders' equity accounts.

b. Make the contrary assumption that Company A purchased only 90% of Company B's stock, paying $14 per share, and give the entry to eliminate Company A's investment and Company B's stockholders' equity accounts.

Exercise 13–6

Assume again that Company A of Exercise 13–5 purchased for cash 90% of Company B's stock, paying $14 per share. Also assume that Company B earned $10,000 during the year following its acquisition, paid out $8,000 of these earnings in dividends, and retained the balance for use in its operations. (a) Give the entry made by Company A to take up its share of Company B's earnings. (b) Give the entry made by Company A to record its share of the $8,000 in dividends paid by Company B. (c) Give the work sheet entry made to eliminate Company A's investment and Company B's stockholders' equity accounts at the end of the year following acquisition.

PROBLEMS

Problem 13–1

On January 1, 198A, stockholders' equity in Hilltop Corporation consisted of the following items:

Common stock, $10 par value, 50,000 shares authorized, 40,000 shares issued and outstanding	$400,000	
Premium on common stock	60,000	
Retained earnings	120,000	
Total stockholders' equity		$580,000

During the year the corporation completed these transactions affecting stockholders' equity:

Apr. 4 Purchased 1,000 shares of treasury stock at $14 per share.

June 20 The board of directors voted a $0.25 per share cash dividend payable on July 15 to the July 10 stockholders of record.

July 15 Paid the dividend declared in June.

22 Sold 500 of the treasury shares at $17 per share.

Oct. 12 Sold the remaining treasury shares at $13 per share.

Dec. 18 The board of directors voted a $0.25 per share cash dividend and a 5% stock dividend payable on January 15 to the January 10 stockholders of record. The stock was selling at $12.50 per share.

31 Closed the Income Summary account and carried the company's $28,000 net income to Retained Earnings.

Required:

1. Prepare general journal entries to record the transactions.
2. Prepare a retained earnings statement for the year and the stockholders' equity section of the company's year-end balance sheet.

Problem 13–2

On October 31, 198A, stockholders' equity in a corporation consisted of the following:

Common stock, $25 par value, 10,000 shares
   authorized, 8,000 shares issued $200,000
Premium on common stock 20,000
      Total contributed capital $220,000
Retained earnings 132,000
        Total stockholders' equity $352,000

During the succeeding three months the corporation completed these transactions:

Nov. 1 Declared a $0.25 per share dividend on the common stock, payable on November 28 to the November 20 stockholders of record.

     28 Paid the dividend declared on November 1.

Dec. 3 Declared a 25% stock dividend, distributable on December 29 to the December 21 stockholders of record. The stock was selling for $45 per share, and the directors voted to use that amount in recording the dividend.

     29 Distributed the stock dividend previously declared.

     31 Closed the Income Summary account on a $30,000 after-tax income for the year.

Jan. 5 The board of directors voted to split the corporation's stock 2½ for 1 by calling in the old stock and issuing 25 shares of $10 par value common stock for each 10 of the old $25 par value shares held. The stockholders voted approval of the split and authorization of the required 25,000 new shares; all legal requirements were met; and the split was completed on February 1.

Required:

1. Prepare general journal entries to record the transactions and to close the Income summary account at the year-end.

2. Under the assumption Ted Hall owned 200 of the $25 par value shares on October 31 and neither bought nor sold any shares during the three-month period, prepare a schedule showing in one column the book value per share of the corporations stock and in a second column the book value of Hall's shares at the close of business on each of October 31, November 1, November 28, December 2, December 29, December 31, and February 1.

3. Prepare the stockholders' equity section of the corporation's balance sheet as of December 31, 198A, and prepare a second stockholders' equity section as of February 1, 198B.

Problem 13–3

A corporation received a charter granting it the right to issue 25,000 shares of $10 par value common stock and 1,000 shares of $100 par value, 7% cumulative and nonparticipating, preferred stock which is redeemable at par and on which a $3.50 dividend is payable semiannually. On May 31 of the year in which the charter was granted, 20,000 shares of the common stock were subscribed at $12 per share. One fourth of that amount accompanied the subscription contracts, and all subscribers paid their remaining balances 30 days thereafter, on which date the stock was issued. The preferred stock was issued at par for cash on the same day. The company prospered from the beginning and paid all dividends on its preferred stock plus dividends on its common stock.

On October 10 of its fourth year when the corporation had a $43,500 balance in its Retained Earnings account and its common stock was selling at $16 per share, the board of directors voted a 5% common stock dividend which was distributed on November 20 to the November 15 stockholders of record.

One year later, on November 20, when the corporation had a $52,000 balance in its Retained Earnings account, the common stock was split two for one by calling in the old $10 par value shares and issuing two $5 par value shares for each old share held.

Near the end of the fifth year, on November 27, the corporation declared the regular $3.50 per share semiannual dividend on its preferred stock and a $0.10 per share dividend on its common stock, payable on December 31 to the December 20 stockholders of record.

Required:

1. Prepare general journal entries to record:
   a. The sale and issuance of the original common stock through subscriptions.
   b. The sale and issuance of the preferred stock.
   c. The declaration and distribution of the common stock dividend.
   d. The declaration and distribution of the fifth-year cash dividends.
2. Dale Nash owned 100 shares of the corporation's common stock on the record date of the fourth-year common stock dividend. Under the assumption the market value of the stock was not affected by the stock dividend and was still $16 per share on the day the dividend was distributed and that Nash neither bought nor sold any shares during the year, prepare a schedule showing the shares held by Nash, their total book value, and their total market value on the day the dividend was declared and on the day it was distributed. (Remember preferred dividends do not accrue.)
3. Prepare the stockholders' equity section of the corporation's balance sheet as of the close of business on the day the $5 par value shares were distributed. (Assume that 50,000 of these shares were authorized.)

Problem 13–4

On May 10 of the current year Alpha Company gained control of Beta Company through the purchase of 85% of Beta Company's outstanding $5 par value common stock at $6.50 per share. On that date Beta Company owed Alpha Company $4,000 for merchandise purchased on credit and $10,000 it had borrowed by giving a promissory note. The condensed May 10 balance sheets of the two companies carried these items:

ALPHA AND BETA COMPANIES
Balance Sheets, May 10, 19—

Assets	Alpha Company	Beta Company
Cash..	$ 6,500	$ 10,500
Note receivable, Beta Company	10,000	
Accounts receivable, net	29,000	24,500
Inventories...................................	42,000	35,000
Investment in Beta Company	110,500	
Equipment, net	80,000	70,000
Buildings, net	85,000	
Land	20,000	
Total assets............................	$383,000	$140,000

Equities		
Note payable, Alpha Company		$ 10,000
Accounts payable	$ 20,000	10,000
Common stock	250,000	100,000
Retained earnings	113,000	20,000
Total equities..........................	$383,000	$140,000

Prepare a consolidated balance sheet for Alpha Company and its subsidiary, and write a short explanation of why consolidated statements are prepared and explain the principles of consolidation.

Problem 13–5

The following items appeared in the first two columns of a work sheet prepared to consolidate the balance sheets of Company X and Company Y on the day Company X gained control of Company Y by purchasing for cash 8,000 shares of its $10 par value common stock at $12 per share.

Assets	Company X	Company Y
Cash	$ 7,000	$ 12,000
Note receivable, Company Y	5,000	
Accounts receivable, net	32,000	28,000
Inventories	45,000	30,000
Investment in Company Y	96,000	
Equipment, net	75,000	60,000
Buildings, net................................	80,000	
Land	20,000	
Total assets	$360,000	$130,000

Equities		
Accounts payable	$ 28,000	$ 10,000
Note payable, Company X		5,000
Common stock	250,000	100,000
Retained earnings	82,000	15,000
Total equities	$360,000	$130,000

At the time Company X acquired control of Company Y it took Company Y's note in exchange for $5,000 in cash and it sold and delivered to it $3,000 of equipment at cost on open account (account receivable). Both transactions are reflected in the foregoing accounts. Management of Company X believed that Company Y's earnings prospects justified the $12 per share paid for its stock.

Required:

1. Prepare a work sheet for consolidating the balance sheets of the two companies and prepare a consolidated balance sheet.
2. Under the assumption Company Y earned $11,000 during the first year after it was acquired by Company X, paid out $6,000 of the earnings in dividends, and retained the balance in its operations, give in general journal form the entries made by Company X *(a)* to take up its share of Company Y's earnings and *(b)* to record the receipt of its share of the dividends paid by Company Y. Also *(c)* give the entry to eliminate Company X's investment in Company Y and Company Y's stockholders' equity accounts on the end-of-the-first-year work sheet to consolidate the balance sheets of the two companies.

ALTERNATE PROBLEMS

Problem 13–1A

The stockholders' equity in Phoenix Corporation consisted of the following items on January 1, 198A:

Common stock, $25 par value, 10,000 shares authorized, 8,000 shares issued and outstanding.........	$200,000	
Premium on common stock	40,000	
Retained earnings	85,000	
Total stockholders' equity		$325,000

During 198A the company completed these transactions affecting its stockholders' equity:

Apr. 10   The directors voted a $0.50 per share cash dividend payable on May 15 to its May 10 stockholders of record.

May 15   Paid the previously declared cash dividend.

Aug. 21   Purchased 500 shares of treasury stock at $40 per share.

Oct. 11   The directors voted a $0.50 per share cash dividend payable on November 15 to the November 10 stockholders of record.

Nov. 15   Paid the previously declared cash dividend.

   25   Sold the 500 treasury shares at $45 per share.

Dec. 12   The directors voted a 5% stock dividend distributable on January 15 to the January 10 stockholders of record. The stock was selling at $45 per share.

   31   Closed the Income Summary account and carried the company's $32,000 net income to Retained Earnings.

Required:

1. Prepare general journal entries to record the transactions.

2. Prepare a retained earnings statement for the year and the stockholders' equity section of the corporation's year-end balance sheet.

Problem 13-2A

On September 30, 198A, stockholders' equity in a corporation consisted of the following:

Common stock, $10 par value, 50,000 shares authorized, 40,000 shares issued	$400,000	
Premium on common stock	20,000	
Total contributed capital	$420,000	
Retained earnings	192,000	
Total stockholders' equity		$612,000

On October 1, 198A, the corporation's board of directors declared a $0.10 per share cash dividend payable on October 25 to the October 20 stockholders of record. On November 1 the board declared a 25% stock dividend distributable on November 25 to the November 20 stockholders of record. The stock was selling at $16 per share on the day of the declaration, and the board voted to use that price in recording the dividend. The corporation earned $40,000, after taxes, during 198A; and on January 2, 198B, the board voted to split the stock two for one by calling in the old shares and issuing each stockholder two shares of $5 par value common stock for each $10 share previously held. The stockholders voted to approve the split and the authorization of the necessary 100,000 new shares; all legal requirements were fulfilled; and the split was completed on January 30.

Required:

1. Prepare general journal entries to record the transactions and to close the Income Summary account.
2. Under the assumption that Ted Gage owned 400 shares of the corporation's stock on September 30 and neither bought nor sold any shares during the next six months, prepare a schedule showing the book value per share of the corporation's stock in one column and the book value of all of Gage's shares in a second column at the close of business on September 30, October 1, October 25, October 31, November 25, January 1, and January 30.
3. Prepare the stockholders' equity section of the corporation's balance sheet as of the close of business on December 31, and prepare another equity section as of the close of business on January 30.

Problem 13-3A

Stockholders' equity in Potter Corporation on October 25 consisted of the following:

Common stock, $5 par value, 500,000 shares authorized, 400,000 shares issued	$2,000,000	
Premium on common stock	200,000	
Retained earnings	2,024,000	
Total stockholders' equity		$4,224,000

On the equity section date, when the stock was selling at $12 per share, the corporation's directors voted a 20% stock dividend, distributable on November 30 to the November 20 stockholders of record. The directors also voted a $0.45 per share annual cash dividend payable on December 15 to the December 1 stockholders of record. The amount of the latter dividend was a disappointment to some stockholders, since the company had paid a $0.50 per share annual cash dividend for a number of years.

Walter Nash owned 1,000 shares of the corporation's stock on October 25, which he had purchased a number of years previously, and as a result he received his dividend shares. He continued to hold all of his shares until after he received the December 15 cash dividend. However, he did note that his stock had a $12 per share market value on October 25, a market value it held until the close of business on November 20, when the market value declined to $10.50 per share.

Give the entries to record the declaration and payment of the dividends involved here, and answer these questions:

a. What was the book value of Nash's total shares on October 25, and what was the book value on November 30, after he received his dividend shares?
b. What fraction of the corporation did Nash own on October 25, and what fraction did he own on November 30?
c. What was the market value of Nash's total shares on October 25, and what was the market value at the close of business on November 20?
d. What did Nash gain from the stock dividend?

Problem 13–4A

The following items appeared in the first two columns of a work sheet prepared to consolidate the balance sheets of Company S and Company T on the day Company S gained control of Company T by purchasing 3,600 shares of its $25 par value common stock at $35 per share.

Assets	Company S	Company T
Cash	$ 8,000	$ 12,000
Note receivable, Company T	5,000	
Accounts receivable, net	37,000	22,000
Inventories	35,000	32,000
Investment in Company T	126,000	
Equipment, net	75,000	70,000
Buildings, net	100,000	
Land	25,000	
Total assets	$411,000	$136,000

Equities	Company S	Company T
Note payable, Company S		$ 5,000
Accounts payable	$ 24,000	11,000
Common stock	300,000	100,000
Premium on common stock	30,000	5,000
Retained earnings	57,000	15,000
Total equities	$411,000	$136,000

At the time Company S gained control of Company T it took Company T's note in exchange for equipment that cost Company S $5,000 and it also sold and delivered $2,000 of inventory at cost to Company T on credit. Both transactions are reflected in the foregoing accounts.

Required:

Prepare a consolidated balance sheet for Company S and its subsidiary. Then write a short explanation of why consolidated statements are prepared and the principles of consolidation.

Problem 13–5A

The following assets and equities appeared on the balance sheets of Company A and Company B on the day Company A acquired control of Company B by purchasing 8,500 shares of its $10 par value common stock for cash at $13 per share.

Assets	*Company A*	*Company B*
Cash	$ 9,500	$ 9,000
Accounts receivable	39,000	21,000
Allowance for doubtful accounts	(3,000)	(2,000)
Inventories	40,000	32,000
Investment in Company B	110,500	
Equipment	85,000	80,000
Accumulated depreciation, equipment	(14,000)	(5,000)
Buildings	90,000	
Accumulated depreciation, buildings	(12,000)	
Land	15,000	
Total assets	$360,000	$135,000

Equities		
Accounts payable	$ 27,000	$ 15,000
Note payable	10,000	
Common stock	250,000	100,000
Retained earnings	73,000	20,000
Total equities	$360,000	$135,000

Included in the items is a $5,000 debt of Company B to Company A for the sale and delivery of some equipment at cost on the day Company A acquired control of Company B. The sale was an open account (account receivable). Management of Company A believed Company B's earnings prospects justified the $13 per share paid for its stock.

Required:

1. Enter the items on a work sheet and consolidate them for preparation of a consolidated balance sheet.
2. Prepare a consolidated balance sheet for Company A and its subsidiary.
3. Under the assumption that Company B earned $10,000 during the first

year after it was acquired by Company A, paid out $6,000 of the earnings in dividends, and retained the balance in its operations, give in general journal form the entries made by Company A *(a)* to take up its share of Company B's earnings and *(b)* to record receipt of its share of the dividends paid by Company B. Also *(c)* give the entry to eliminate Company A's investment in Company B and Company B's stockholders' equity accounts on the end-of-the-first-year work sheet to consolidate the balance sheets of the two companies.

PROVOCATIVE PROBLEMS

Provocative problems 13–1
Holloway Corporation

The equity sections of Holloway Corporation's 198A and 198B balance sheets carried the following shareholders' equity items:

Shareholders' Equity
As of December 31, 198A

Common stock, $10 par value, 150,000 shares authorized, 100,000 shares issued	$1,000,000	
Premium on common stock	150,000	
Total contributed capital	$1,150,000	
Retained earnings	655,500	
Total shareholders' equity		$1,805,500

Shareholders' Equity
As of December 31, 198B

Common stock, $10 par value, 150,000 shares authorized, 104,900 shares issued of which 2,000 are in the treasury	$1,049,000	
Premium on common stock	203,900	
Total contributed capital	$1,252,900	
Retained earnings of which $41,000 is restricted by the purchase of treasury stock	665,820	
Total	$1,918,720	
Less cost of treasury stock	41,000	
Total shareholders' equity		$1,877,720

On March 15, June 12, September 17, and again on December 14, 198B, the corporation's board of directors declared $0.20 per share dividends on the outstanding stock. The treasury stock was purchased on July 20. On September 17, when the stock was selling at $21 per share, the corporation declared a 5% stock dividend on its outstanding shares. The new shares were issued on October 20.

Under the assumption there were no transactions affecting retained earnings other than the ones given, determine the corporation's net income. Present calculations to prove your net income figure.

Provocative problem 13–2
Detrick Stores, Inc.

Detrick Stores, Inc., operates six hardware stores in a western city and its suburbs. Stockholders' equity in the corporation consists of 50,000 shares of $10 par value common stock, all owned by Carlos Detrick, his wife, and only son, and approximately $800,000 of retained earnings. Mr. Detrick began the business 32 years ago with one store, and the business has grown to its present size primarily from the retention of assets from earnings. The company has no long-term debt and only normal amounts of accounts payable, short-term bank loans, and accrued payables. It has an excellent reputation with its creditors and has always paid its debts on time.

An opportunity to expand the number of the company's stores from six to eight has recently arisen, but the expansion will make it necessary to borrow $300,000 by issuing a ten-year mortgage note. The company has never before borrowed to an extent that made the issuance of financial statements to outsiders necessary. Actually, since all the company's stock is owned by the three members of the Detrick family and Carlos Detrick has always been most secretive about his business affairs, the only people who have ever seen the company's financial statements are the family members, a very few employees, and some internal revenue service people. Consequently, when Carlos Detrick was told by the company's bank that it could not consider the loan unless it was provided with detailed financial statements for the past five years and audited statements for the most recent year, he was ready to call off the expansion. However, after additional consideration he changed his position to a willingness to have the audit and to provide the balance sheets for the most recent five years, but he was unwilling to provide income statements or retained earnings statements.

If the balance sheets are detailed and the last one is audited, what information will they give the bank? Will this information be sufficient to justify the loan? If you were the bank's loan officer and sought to compromise with Mr. Detrick in order to secure more financial information without receiving summarized or complete income statements and retained earnings statements, what information would you seek?

part six
Financial statements, interpretation and modifications

14

Statement of changes in financial position

After studying Chapter 14, you should be able to:

- Tell of what working capital consists and explain why an adequate amount of working capital is important in the operation of a business.
- List a number of sources and uses of working capital.
- Explain why the net income reported on an income statement is not the amount of working capital generated by operations.
- Tell the adjustments that must be made to the reported net income figure in order to determine the amount of working capital generated by operations.
- Prepare a statement of changes in financial position.
- Prepare an analysis of changes in working capital items.
- Explain why cash generated by operations differs from net income from operations.
- Prepare a simple cash flow statement.
- Define or explain the words and phrases listed in the chapter glossary.

When financial statements are prepared for a business, the income statement shows the income earned or the loss incurred during the accounting period. The retained earnings statement summarizes the changes in retained earnings, and the balance sheet shows the end-of-the-period financial position. However, for a better understanding of the financing and investing activities of the business, more information is needed. This information is supplied by a *statement of changes in financial position*. Such a statement summarizes the changes that occurred in the financial position of the business by showing where it acquired resources during the period and where it applied or used resources. Usually the statement is also designed to emphasize and account for the change in the *working capital* of the business.

WORKING CAPITAL

The working capital of a business is the excess of its current assets over its current liabilities. The more important of a concern's current assets are usually its cash, accounts receivable, and merchandise. The merchandise is normally acquired through the use of short-term credit, primarily accounts payable. It is sold and turned into accounts receivable, which are collected and turned into cash. The cash is then used to pay bills so that short-term credit can be used again to buy more merchandise. As a result, it can be said that a concern's current assets and current liabilities circulate. Furthermore, in the circulation it is important for the current assets to exceed the current liabilities by an adequate amount.

An adequate excess of current assets over current liabilities, in other words, an adequate amount of working capital, enables a business to meet current debts, carry sufficient inventory, take advantage of cash discounts, and offer favorable credit terms to customers. A company that is deficient in working capital and unable to do these things is in a poor competitive position. Its survival may even be threatened, unless its working capital position can be improved. Inadequacy of working capital has ended the business lives of many companies in which the assets far exceeded the liabilities.

483

Funds

The general public uses the word *funds* to mean cash, but business people apply a broader meaning. They commonly use the word as a synonym for working capital. This is understandable. Since working capital items circulate, it is only normal to think of that portion of the current assets not immediately needed to pay current debts as liquid resources or available funds. However, business people recognize that only a portion of the funds can be drawn off at any one time to pay dividends, buy plant assets, pay long-term debt, or for other like purposes. Only a portion can be used because a large share must remain in circulation.

SOURCES AND USES OF WORKING CAPITAL

Transactions that increase working capital are called *sources of working capital,* and transactions that decrease working capital are called *uses of working capital.* If the working capital of a business increased during an accounting period, more working capital was generated by its transactions than was used. On the other hand, if working capital decreased, more working capital was used than was generated.

Sources of working capital

Some of the more common sources of working capital are as follows:

Current operations   Funds in the form of cash and accounts receivable flow into a business from sales; and most expenses and goods sold result in outflows of funds. Consequently, working capital is increased by normal operations if the inflow of funds from sales exceeds the outflows for goods sold and expenses. However, the net income figure appearing on an income statement generally does not represent the amount of working capital generated by operations, because some expenses listed on the income statement do not cause working capital outflows in the period of the statement.

For example, Rexel Sales Company of Illustration 14–1 experienced a $50,000 funds inflow from sales during the year. It also experienced outflows of $30,000 for goods sold, $8,000 for salaries, and $1,200 for rent. However, there was no outflow of working capital for depreciation expense. Consequently, during the period the company gained working capital from operations equal to the sum of its reported net income plus the recorded depreciation, or it gained $9,800 plus $1,000 or $10,800 of working capital from operations.

Business executives often speak of depreciation as a source of funds, but it is not. Look again at Illustration 14–1. Sales are the source of working capital on this statement. No funds flowed into this company from recording depreciation. In this case, as with every business, the

Rexel Sales Company
Income Statement for Year Ended December 31, 19—

Sales		$50,000
Cost of goods sold		30,000
Gross profit from sales		$20,000
Operating expenses:		
Sales salaries expense	$8,000	
Rent expense	1,200	
Depreciation expense, equipment....	1,000	10,200
Net income		$ 9,800

Illustration 14–1

revenues are the source of working capital from operations. However, since depreciation, unlike most expenses, did not and does not cause a funds outflow in the current period, it must be added to the net income to determine working capital from operations.

Long-term liabilities   Transactions that increase long-term liabilities increase working capital or are so treated. Therefore, they are sources of working capital regardless of whether long-term notes, mortgages, or bonds are involved. On the other hand, short-term credit, whether obtained from banks or other creditors, is not a source of working capital because short-term credit does not increase working capital. For example, if $10,000 is borrowed for, say, six months, both current assets and current liabilities are increased. However, since both are increased the same amount, total working capital is unchanged.

Sale of noncurrent assets   When a plant asset, long-term investment, or other noncurrent asset is sold for cash or receivables, working capital is increased by the amount of the sale. Therefore, such sales are sources of working capital.

Sale of capital stock   The issuance of stock for cash or current receivables increases current assets; and as a result, such sales are sources of funds. Likewise, an additional investment of current assets by a single proprietor or partner is also a source of working capital.

Uses of working capital

Common uses of working capital are the following:

Purchase of noncurrent assets   When noncurrent assets such as plant and equipment or long-term investments are purchased, working capital is reduced. Consequently, such purchases are uses of working capital.

Payment of noncurrent liabilities   Payment of a long-term debt such as a mortgage reduces working capital and is a use of working capital.

Likewise, a contribution to a debt retirement fund, bond sinking fund, or other special noncurrent fund is also a use of working capital.

Capital reductions The withdrawals of cash or other current assets by a proprietor, the purchase of treasury stock, or the purchase of stock for retirement reduce working capital and are uses of working capital.

Declaration of a dividend The declaration of a dividend which is to be paid in cash or other current assets reduces working capital and is a use of working capital. Note that it is the declaration that is the use. The declaration creates a current liability, dividends payable, and therefore reduces working capital as soon as it is voted by the board of directors. The final payment of a dividend previously declared does not affect working capital because it reduces current assets and current liabilities in equal amounts.

STATEMENT OF CHANGES IN FINANCIAL POSITION

As previously stated, a statement of changes in financial position summarizes and discloses the financing and investing activities of the business for which it was prepared. The statement covers a period of time and is commonly designed to account for the change in the concern's working capital during the period. Such a statement is shown in Illustration 14–2.

Delta Company
Statement of Changes in Financial Position
For Year Ended December 31, 198B

Sources of working capital:		
Current operations:		
Net income	$12,200	
Add expenses not requiring outlays of working capital in the current period:		
Depreciation of buildings and equipment	4,500	
Working capital provided by operations	$16,700	
Other sources:		
Sale of common stock	12,500	
Total sources of working capital		$29,200
Uses of working capital:		
Purchase of office equipment	$ 500	
Purchase of store equipment	6,000	
Addition to building	15,000	
Reduction of mortgage debt	2,500	
Declaration of dividends	3,100	
Total uses of working capital		27,100
Net increase in working capital		$ 2,100

Illustration 14–2

The ability of an enterprise to generate working capital in its operations is an important factor in evaluating its ability to pay dividends, to finance new investment opportunities, and to grow. Consequently, the amount of working capital generated by operations is commonly summarized first on a statement of changes in fianancial position. Normally the summary begins with the amount of the net income reported on the income statement. To this are added any expenses deducted on the income statement that did not decrease working capital, such as depreciation, depletion, and bond discount. (Bond premium is deducted from the income figure on the statement.) The resulting amount is then described as, for example, "Working capital provided by operations." (If the summary begins with a net loss, rather than a net income, and the net loss exceeds the expenses that did not decrease working capital, the resulting amount may be described as "Working capital used in operations.")

Working capital is commonly secured from sources other than operations. These are shown next on the statement of changes in financial position. The uses of working capital are then listed, after which the net increase or decrease in working capital is shown.

PREPARING A STATEMENT OF CHANGES IN FINANCIAL POSITION

A statement of changes in financial position could be prepared by searching through a concern's current asset and current liability accounts for the transactions that increased or decreased its working capital. However, this would be time consuming because almost every transaction completed by a concern affected these accounts and only a very few of the transactions either increased or decreased its working capital. Therefore, in preparing a statement of changes in financial position, it is not the current asset and current liability accounts that are examined for working capital changes but rather the *noncurrent accounts*. (The noncurrent accounts are the accounts other than the current asset and current liability accounts.) The noncurrent accounts are examined because (1) only a few transactions affected these accounts and (2) almost every one either increased or decreased working capital.

Normally, in making an audit of a company's noncurrent accounts, the auditor makes a list of the transactions that affected these accounts during the period under review. This list is then used along with the company's balance sheets as of the beginning and end of the period to prepare the statement of changes in financial position. The comparative balance sheet of Illustration 14–3 and the following list of transactions that affected the noncurrent accounts of Delta Company were used in preparing the Illustration 14–2 statement of changes in financial position.

Delta Company
Comparative Balance Sheet
December 31, 198B, and December 31, 198A

Assets

	198B	198A
Current assets:		
Cash...	$ 7,500	$ 4,800
Accounts receivable, net	8,000	9,500
Merchandise inventory	31,500	32,000
Prepaid expenses	1,000	1,200
Total current assets	$ 48,000	$ 47,500
Plant and equipment:		
Office equipment	$ 3,500	$ 3,000
Accumulated depreciation, office equipment	(900)	(600)
Store equipment	26,200	21,000
Accumulated depreciation, store equipment	(5,200)	(4,200)
Buildings	95,000	80,000
Accumulated depreciation, buildings	(10,600)	(8,200)
Land...	25,000	25,000
Total plant and equipment	$133,000	$116,000
Total assets	$181,000	$163,500

Liabilities

Current liabilities:		
Notes payable	$ 2,500	$ 1,500
Accounts payable	16,700	19,600
Dividends payable	1,000	700
Total current liabilities.........................	$ 20,200	$ 21,800
Long-term liabilities:		
Mortgage payable	$ 17,500	$ 20,000
Total liabilities.............................	$ 37,700	$ 41,800

Stockholders' Equity

Common stock, $10 par value	$115,000	$100,000
Premium on common stock	8,500	5,000
Retained earnings	19,800	16,700
Total stockholders' equity	$143,300	$121,700
Total liabilities and stockholders' equity	$181,000	$163,500

Illustration 14–3

a. Purchased office equipment costing $500 during the year.
b. Purchased store equipment that cost $6,000.
c. Discarded and junked fully depreciated store equipment that cost $800 when new.
d. Added a new addition to the building that cost $15,000.
e. Earned a $12,200 net income during the year.
f. Delta Company deducted on its 198B income statement $300 of depreciation on office equipment, *(g)* $1,800 on its store equipment, and *(h)* $2,400 on its building.
i. Made a $2,500 payment on the mortgage.

j. Declared a 5% stock dividend at a time when the company's stock was selling for $12 per share.

k. Sold and issued 1,000 shares of common stock at $12.50 per share.

l. Declared cash dividends totaling $3,100 during the year.

Steps in preparing a statement of changes in financial position

Three steps are involved in preparing a statement of changes in financial position. They are the following:

1. Determine the increase or decrease in working capital for the period of the statement.
2. Prepare a working paper to account for the changes in the company's noncurrent accounts and in the process set out on the working paper the period's sources and uses of working capital.
3. Use the working paper to prepare the formal statement of changes in financial position.

DETERMINING THE CHANGE IN WORKING CAPITAL

The 198B change in Delta Company's working capital is calculated in Illustration 14–4. The calculation is a simple one requiring nothing more than a determination of the amounts of working capital at the beginning and at the end of the period and a subtraction to arrive at the increase or decrease in working capital.

Working capital, December 31, 198B:		
Current assets	$ 48,000	
Current liabilities	(20,200)	
Working capital		$ 27,800
Working capital, December 31, 198A:		
Current assets	$ 47,500	
Current liabilities	(21,800)	
Working capital		(25,700)
Increase in working capital		$ 2,100

Illustration 14–4

PREPARING THE WORKING PAPER

Delta Company's sources and uses of working capital resulted from simple transactions, and a statement of changes in financial position could be prepared for the company without a working paper. However, the working paper helps to organize the information needed for the statement and also offers a proof of the accuracy of the work.

The working paper for Delta Company's statement of changes in financial position is shown in Illustration 14–5. Such a working paper is prepared as follows:

1. First the amount of working capital at the beginning of the period under review is entered on the first line in the first money column and the amount of working capital at the end is entered in the last column.

2. Next, the noncurrent balance sheet amounts are entered on the

Delta Company
Working Paper for Statement of Changes in Financial Position
For Year Ended December 31, 198B

	Account Balances 12/31/8A	Analyzing Entries Debit	Analyzing Entries Credit	Account Balances 12/31/8B
Debits				
Working capital	25,700			27,800
Office equipment	3,000	(a) 500		3,500
Store equipment	21,000	(b) 6,000	(c) 800	26,200
Buildings	80,000	(d) 15,000		95,000
Land	25,000			25,000
Totals	154,700			177,500
Credits				
Accumulated depreciation, office equipment .	600		(f) 300	900
Accumulated depreciation, store equipment .	4,200	(c) 800	(g) 1,800	5,200
Accumulated depreciation, buildings	8,200		(h) 2,400	10,600
Mortgage payable	20,000	(i) 2,500		17,500
Common stock	100,000		(j) 5,000 (k) 10,000	115,000
Premium on common stock	5,000		(j) 1,000 (k) 2,500	8,500
Retained earnings	16,700	(j) 6,000 (l) 3,100	(e) 12,200	19,800
Totals	154,700			177,500
Sources of working capital:				
Current operations:				
Net income		(e) 12,200		
Depreciation of office equipment		(f) 300		
Depreciation of store equipment		(g) 1,800		
Depreciation of buildings		(h) 2,400		
Other sources:				
Sale of stock		(k) 12,500		
Uses of working capital:				
Purchase of office equipment			(a) 500	
Purchase of store equipment			(b) 6,000	
Addition to building			(d) 15,000	
Reduction of mortgage			(i) 2,500	
Declaration of dividends			(l) 3,100	
Totals		63,100	63,100	

Illustration 14–5

working paper. The amounts or account balances as of the beginning of the period are entered in the first money column and those of the end in the last. Observe that debit items are listed first and are followed by credit items. This is a convenience that places the accumulated depreciation items with the liability and capital amounts.

3. After the noncurrent account balances are entered, the working capital amount and debit items in each column are added. Next, the credit items are added to be certain that debits equal credits.

4. After the items are added to see that debits equal credits, the phrase "Sources of working capital:" is written on the line following the total of the credit items. Sufficient lines are then skipped to allow for listing all possible sources and then the phrase "Uses of working capital:" is written.

5. Next, analyzing entries are entered in the second and third money columns. These entries do two things: (1) they account for or explain the amount of change in each noncurrent account, and (2) they set out the sources and uses of working capital. (The analyzing entries on the illustrated working paper are discussed later in this chapter.)

6. After the last analyzing entry is entered, the working paper is completed by adding the Analyzing Entries columns to determine their equality. The information on the paper as to sources and uses of working capital is then used to prepare the formal statement of changes in financial position.

In passing it should be observed that the working paper is prepared solely for the purpose of bringing together information as to sources and uses of working capital. Its analyzing entries are never entered in the accounts.

Analyzing entries

As previously stated, in addition to setting out sources and uses of working capital, the analyzing entries on the working paper also account for or explain the amount of change in each noncurrent account. The change in each noncurrent account is explained with one or more analyzing entries because every transaction that caused an increase or decrease in working capital also increased or decreased a noncurrent account. Consequently, when all increases and decreases in noncurrent accounts are explained by means of analyzing entries, all sources and uses of working capital are set out on the working paper.

The analyzing entries on the working paper of Illustration 14–5 account for the changes in Delta Company's noncurrent accounts and set out its sources and uses of working capital. Explanations of the entries follow:

a. During the year Delta Company purchased new office equipment that cost $500. This required the use of working capital and also caused a $500 increase in the balance of its Office Equipment account. Consequently, analyzing entry (a) has a $500 debit to Office Equipment and a like credit to "Uses of working capital: Purchase of office equipment." The debit accounts for the change in the Office Equipment account, and the credit sets out the use of working capital.

b. Delta Company purchased $6,000 of new store equipment during the period. This required the use of $6,000 of working capital, and the use is set out with analyzing entry (b). However, the $6,000 debit of the entry does not fully account for the change in the balance of the Store Equipment account. Analyzing entry (c) is also needed.

c. During the period under review Delta Company discarded and junked fully depreciated store equipment. The equipment when new had cost $800, and the entry made to record the disposal decreased the company's Store Equipment and related accumulated depreciation accounts by $800. However, the disposal had no effect on the company's working capital. Nevertheless, analyzing entry (c) must be made to account for the changes in the accounts. Otherwise all changes in the company's noncurrent accounts will not be explained. Unless all changes are explained, the person preparing the working paper cannot be certain that all sources and uses of working capital have been set out on the working paper.

d. Delta Company used $15,000 to increase the size of its building. The cost of the addition was debited to the Buildings account, and analyzing entry (d) sets out this use of working capital.

e. Delta Company reported a $12,200 net income for 198B, and the income was a source of working capital. In the end-of-the-year closing procedures the amount of this net income was transferred from the company's Income Summary account to its Retained Earnings account. It helped change the balance of the latter account from $16,700 at the beginning of the year to $19,800 at the year-end. Observe the analyzing entry that sets out this source of working capital. The entry's debit sets out the net income as a source of working capital, and the credit helps explain the change in the Retained Earnings account.

f. (g), and (h). On its 198B income statement Delta Company deducted $300 of depreciation expense on its office equipment, $1,800 on its store equipment, and $2,400 on its building. As previously explained, although depreciation is a rightful deduction from revenues in arriving at net income, any depreciation so deducted must be added to net income in determining working capital from operations. The debits of entries (f), (g), and (h) show the depreciation taken by the company as part of the working capital generated by operations. The credits of the entries either account for or help account for the changes in the accumulated depreciation accounts.

i. On June 10 Delta Company made a $2,500 payment on the mortgage on its plant and equipment. The payment required the use of working capital, and it reduced the balance of the Mortgage Payable account by $2,500. Entry (i) sets out this use of working capital and accounts for the change in the Mortgage Payable account.

j. At the September board meeting the directors of the company declared a 5% or 500-share stock dividend on a day the company's stock was selling at $12 per share. The declaration and later distribution of this dividend had no effect on the company's working capital. However, it did decrease Retained Earnings $6,000 and increase the Common Stock account $5,000 and Premium on Common Stock $1,000. Entry (j) accounts for the changes in the accounts resulting from the dividend.

k. In October the company sold and issued 1,000 shares of its common stock for cash at $12.50 per share. The sale was a source of working capital that increased the balance of the company's Common Stock account $10,000 and the balance of its Premium on Common Stock account $2,500. Entry (k) sets out this source of working capital and completes the explanation of the changes in the stock and premium accounts.

l. At the end of each of the first three quarters in the year the company declared a $700 quarterly cash dividend. Then, on December 22 it declared a $1,000 dividend, payable on the following January 15. The fourth dividend brought the total cash dividends declared during the year to $3,100. Each declaration required the use of working capital, and each reduced the balance of the Retained Earnings account. On the working paper the four dividends are combined and one analyzing entry is made for the $3,100 use of working capital. The entry's debit helps account for the change in the balance of the Retained Earnings account, and its credit sets out the use of working capital.

After the last analyzing entry is entered on the working paper, an examination is made to be certain that all changes in the noncurrent accounts listed on the paper have been explained with analyzing entries. To make this examination, the debits and credits in the Analyzing Entries columns opposite each beginning account balance are added to or are subtracted from the beginning balance. The result must equal the ending balance. For example, the $3,000 beginning debit balance of office equipment plus the $500 debit of analyzing entry (a) equals the $3,500 ending amount of office equipment. Likewise, the $21,000 beginning balance of store equipment plus the $6,000 debit and minus the $800 credit equals the $26,200 ending balance for this asset, and so on down the working paper until all changes are accounted for. Then if in every case the debits and credits opposite each beginning balance explain the change in the balance, all sources and uses of working capital have been set out on the working paper and the working paper is completed by adding the amounts in its Analyzing Entries columns.

Preparing the statement of changes in financial position from the working paper

After the working paper is completed, the sources and uses of working capital set out on the bottom of the paper are used to prepare the formal statement of changes in financial position. This is a simple task that requires little more than a relisting of the sources and uses of working capital on the formal statement. A comparison of the items appearing on the statement of Illustration 14–2 with the items at the bottom of the working paper of Illustration 14–5 will show this.

A net loss on the working paper

When a concern incurs a net loss, the amount of the loss is debited to its Retained Earnings account in the end-of-the-period closing procedures. Then, when the working paper for a statement of changes in financial position is prepared, the words "Net loss" are substituted for "Net income" in its sources of working capital section. The amount of the loss is then debited to Retained Earnings and credited to "Net loss" on the working paper. After this the loss is placed on the formal statement of changes in financial position as the first monetary item and the expenses not requiring outlays of working capital are deducted therefrom. If the net loss is less than these expenses, the resulting amount is working capital provided by operations. If the net loss exceeds these expenses, the result is working capital used in operations.

BROAD CONCEPT OF FINANCING AND INVESTING ACTIVITIES

The APB held that a statement of changes in financial position should be based on a broad concept of the financing and investing activities of a business. Also, it should disclose all important aspects of such activities even though elements of working capital are not directly affected.[1] For example, the acquisition of a building in exchange for a mortgage or the conversion of bonds to stock are transactions that do not directly affect elements of working capital. However, the Board has held that

---

[1] APB, "Reporting Changes in Financial Position," *APB Opinion No. 19* (New York: AICPA, 1971), par. 8.

such transactions should be disclosed on the statement of changes in financial position even though working capital is not directly involved. For example, if a building is acquired by issuing a mortgage, the issuance of the mortgage should be disclosed on the statement as a source of working capital, "Mortgage issued to acquire building." Likewise the acquisition of the building should appear as a use of working capital, "Building acquired by issuing a mortgage."

ANALYSIS OF WORKING CAPITAL CHANGES

The APB ruled that where a statement of changes in financial position accounts for the change in working capital, the usefulness of the statement is enhanced if it is accompanied by a report on which the changes in the various elements of working capital are analyzed in appropriate detail.[2] Such a report for Delta Company is shown in Illustration 14–6. Note how the report's final figure ties back to the final figure in Illustration 14–2.

Delta Company
Analysis of Changes in Working Capital Items
For Year Ended December 31, 198B

	Dec. 31, 198B	Dec. 31, 198A	Working Capital	
			Increases	Decreases
Current assets:				
Cash	$ 7,500	$ 4,800	$2,700	
Accounts receivable, net	8,000	9,500		$1,500
Merchandise inventory	31,500	32,000		500
Prepaid expenses	1,000	1,200		200
Total current assets	$48,000	$47,500		
Current liabilities:				
Notes payable	$ 2,500	$ 1,500		1,000
Accounts payable	16,700	19,600	2,900	
Dividends payable	1,000	700		300
Total current liabilities	$20,200	$21,800		
Working capital	$27,800	$25,700		
			$5,600	$3,500
Net increase in working capital				2,100
			$5,600	$5,600

Illustration 14–6

Information for preparing the analysis of changes in working capital is taken from balance sheets as of the beginning and end of the period under review. (Compare the information in Illustration 14–6 with that

[2] Ibid., par. 12.

in Illustration 14–3.) The current asset and current liability items in the analysis and the preparation of the analysis need little discussion. However, students sometimes have difficulty understanding how, for example, an increase in a current liability results in a decrease in working capital. They should not, for when a current liability increases, a larger amount is subtracted from current assets in determining working capital.

STATEMENT OF CHANGES IN FINANCIAL POSITION, CASH BASIS

The primary purpose of a statement of changes in financial position is to show where a company acquired resources and where it applied or used resources. Most such statements are also designed to account for the change in working capital. However, the statement may instead be designed to account for the change in cash. If it is, the terminology used should clearly indicate this. For example, terminology such as "Cash provided by operations" should be used rather than "Working capital provided by operations."

The procedures for preparing a statement of changes in financial position that show the change in cash are similar to the ones used when the statement is to show change in working capital. However, a discussion of these procedures and the APB requirements that must be met if the statement is to be published are left to a more advanced book.

CASH FLOW STATEMENT

An important phase of management's work is the management of cash so that adequate cash is available to meet current debts, pay dividends, and so on, with any temporarily unneeded cash being invested to earn interest or dividends. To assist management in planning and controlling cash, a statement called a *cash flow statement* is commonly prepared. Such a statement is prepared for internal use, is not to be published, and commonly does not meet the APB requirements for a published statement of changes in financial position, cash basis.

A cash flow statement covers a period of time and accounts for the increase or decrease in a company's cash by showing where the company got cash and the uses it made of cash during the period. For example, Royal Supply Company of Illustration 14–7 began the period of the statement with $2,200 of cash. This beginning balance was increased $22,000 by cash from operations and $4,500 by cash from the sale of investments. It was decreased $12,000 by the withdrawals of the business owner and $6,500 by the purchase of plant assets. All of this resulted in an $8,000 net increase in cash during the period.

Royal Supply Company
Cash Flow Statement
For Year Ended December 31, 19—

Cash balance, January 1, 19—		$ 2,200
Sources of cash:		
Cash generated by operations......	$22,000	
Sale of investments	4,500	
Total sources of cash		$26,500
Uses of cash:		
Withdrawals of owner	$12,000	
Purchase of plant assets	6,500	
Total uses of cash		18,500
Increase in cash		8,000
Cash balance, December 31, 19—....		$10,200

Illustration 14–7

A work sheet is commonly used to bring together the data needed to prepare a cash flow statement. A discussion of this work sheet is deferred to a more advanced text, and a simple analysis based on the difference between the cash basis and the accrual basis of accounting is used here to introduce the subject of cash flow. However, before beginning the analysis a review of the difference between the cash and the accrual bases of accounting is in order.

Under the cash basis of accounting a revenue appears on the income statement of the period in which it is collected in cash, regardless of when earned. For example, if a sale of merchandise is made in November 198A but the customer does not pay for the goods until January 198B, under the cash basis of accounting the revenue from the sale appears on the 198B income statement. Likewise, under the cash basis an expense appears on the income statement of the period in which cash is disbursed in its payment, regardless of which accounting period benefited from its incurrence. Consequently, under the cash basis the gain or loss reported for an accounting period is the difference between cash received from revenues and cash disbursed for expenses. The difference is also the amount of cash generated by operations during the period.

Under the accrual basis of accounting all of this differs. Under the accrual basis revenues are credited to the period in which they are earned regardless of when cash is received and expenses are matched with revenues regardless of when cash is disbursed. As a result, under the accrual basis the profit or loss of an accounting period is the difference between revenues earned and the expenses incurred in earning the revenues. Most enterprises use the accrual basis of accounting, and all accounting demonstrated thus far in this text has been accrual basis accounting.

PREPARING A CASH FLOW STATEMENT

Reexamine the cash flow statement of Illustration 14–7. The cash inflow shown thereon from the sale of investments and the outflow for withdrawals and to buy plant assets need no explanations. However, the inflow of cash from operations does.

Cash flows into a company from sales, and it flows out for goods sold and expenses. However, although cost of goods sold and expenses are deducted from sales on an accrual basis income statement, the resulting net income figure does not show the amount of cash generated by operations. To determine cash from operations, it is necessary to convert the item amounts on a company's income statement from an accrual basis to a cash basis.

Royal Supply Company's accrual basis income statement appears in Illustration 14–8, and its amounts are converted from an accrual

Royal Supply Company
Income Statement for Year Ended December 31, 19—

Sales, net		$90,000
Cost of goods sold:		
Inventory, January 1, 19—.......	$10,000	
Purchases, net	55,000	
Goods for sale	$65,000	
Inventory, December 31, 19— ...	11,000	
Cost of goods sold		54,000
Gross profit from sales		$36,000
Operating expenses:		
Depreciation expense	$ 3,400	
Bad debts expense	300	
Salaries and wages expense	12,500	
Other expenses	3,300	
Total operating expenses		19,500
Net income		$16,500

Illustration 14–8

basis to a cash basis in Illustration 14–10. The conversion is based on the information in the company's condensed Cash account which is shown in Illustration 14–9. Explanations of the conversion follow.

a. Cash flowed into Royal Supply Company from sales. However, the $90,000 sales figure on the company's income statement was not the amount. Rather, cash from goods sold consisted of cash sales, $40,000, plus collections from customers, $50,500, a total of $90,500, as shown in the condensed Cash account of Illustration 14–9. Consequently, since cash from goods sold was $500 greater

Condensation of Royal Supply Company's Cash Account

(Debits)		(Credits)	
Balance, January 1	2,200	Cash purchases of	
Cash sales	40,000	merchandise	200
Accounts receivable		Payments to creditors for	
collections	50,500	merchandise purchased	52,800
Sale of investments	4,500	Salary and wage payments ...	12,100
		Payments for other expenses .	3,400
		Plant asset purchases	6,500
		Withdrawals by owner	12,000
		Balance, December 31	10,200
Total	97,200	Total	97,200

Illustration 14–9

Royal Supply Company

Conversion of Income Statement Amounts from an Accrual to a Cash Basis for Year Ended December 31, 19—

	Accrual basis amounts	Add (deduct)	Cash basis amounts
Sales, net	$90,000	$ 500	$90,500
Cost of goods sold	54,000	(1,000)	53,000
Gross profit from sales	$36,000		$37,500
Operating expenses:			
Depreciation expense	$ 3,400	(3,400)	$ –0–
Bad debts expense	300	(300)	–0–
Salaries and wages expense	12,500	(400)	12,100
Other expenses	3,300	100	3,400
Total operating expenses	$19,500		$15,500
Net income	$16,500		
Cash generated by operations			$22,000

Illustration 14–10

than the income statement sales figure, $500 is added to convert the sales figure from an accrual basis to a cash basis.

b. Likewise, the $54,000 cost of goods sold figure on the income statement is not the amount of money that flowed out to pay for goods sold. Rather, the actual cash outflow for merchandise amounted to $53,000, $200 for cash purchases plus $52,800 paid to creditors for merchandise, as shown in the condensed Cash account. Since the cash outflow for the purchase of merchandise was $1,000 less than the accrual basis cost of goods sold figure, $1,000 is subtracted in converting cost of goods sold from an accrual to a cash basis.

c. Since depreciation and bad debts expense did not take cash, the amounts for these items are deducted in converting the income statement amounts to a cash basis.

d. And since the cash paid by Royal Supply Company for salaries and wages was $400 less than the accrual basis income statement amount for this expense and cash disbursed for "other expenses" was $100 more, $400 is deducted and $100 is added in converting these expenses to a cash basis.

The last figure in Illustration 14–10, the $22,000 of cash generated by operations, is the amount Royal Supply Company would have reported as net income had it kept its books on a cash basis rather than an accrual basis. The $22,000 is also the amount of cash the company got from its operations and the amount that appears on its Illustration 14–7 cash flow statement as cash from this source.

GLOSSARY

Cash flow statement. A financial statement that accounts for the increase or decrease in a company's cash during a period by showing where the company got cash and the uses it made of cash.

Funds. Cash to the general public; working capital to business people.

Net working capital. A synonym for working capital.

Source of working capital. A transaction that increases working capital.

Statement of changes in financial position. A statement that reports the financing and investing activities of a business during a period, generally indicating their effects on working capital.

Use of working capital. A transaction that decreased working capital.

Working capital. The excess of a company's current assets over its current liabilities.

QUESTIONS FOR CLASS DISCUSSION

1. Tell two different meanings of the word "funds."
2. List several sources of working capital and several uses of working capital.
3. Explain why such expenses as depreciation, amortization of patents, and amortization of bond discount are added to the net income in order to determine working capital provided by operations?
4. Some people speak of depreciation as a source of funds. Is depreciation a source of funds?
5. On May 14 a company borrowed $30,000 by giving its bank a 60-day, interest-bearing note. Was this transaction a source of working capital?
6. A company began an accounting period with a $90,000 merchandise inven-

tory and ended it with a $50,000 inventory. Was the decrease in inventory a source of working capital?

7. What is shown on a statement of changes in financial position?
8. Why are the noncurrent accounts examined to discover changes in working capital?
9. When a working paper for the preparation of a statement of changes in financial position is prepared, all changes in noncurrent balance sheet accounts are accounted for on the working paper. Why?
10. A company discarded and wrote off fully depreciated store equipment. What account balances appearing on the statement of changes in financial position working paper were affected by the write-off? What analyzing entry was made on the working paper to account for the write-off? If the write-off did not affect working capital, why was the analyzing entry made on the working paper?
11. Explain why a decrease in a current liability represents an increase in working capital.
12. How is the amount of cash generated by a company's operations determined?

CLASS EXERCISES

Exercise 14–1

From the following income statement, list and total the amounts of working capital the company gained from current operations.

ROCKHILL, INC.
Income Statement for Year Ended December 31, 19—

Sales		$750,000
Cost of goods sold		525,000
Gross profit from sales		$225,000
Operating expenses:		
Salaries and wages	$115,000	
Depreciation expense	20,000	
Advertising expense	5,000	
Patent costs written off	2,000	
Bad debts expense	3,000	145,000
Operating income		$ 80,000
Bond interest expense (including $6,000 accrued interest and $500 of bond discount amortized)		12,500
Net income		$ 67,500

Exercise 14–2

The 198A and 198B balance sheets of Blue Haze, Inc., carried these debit and credit amounts:

Debits	198B	198A
Cash	$ 4,000	$ 3,000
Accounts receivable, net	8,000	10,000
Merchandise inventory	22,000	20,000
Equipment	19,000	15,000
Totals	$53,000	$48,000

Credits		
Accumulated depreciation, equipment	$ 5,000	$ 4,000
Accounts payable	4,000	6,000
Taxes payable	2,000	1,000
Common stock, $10 par value	27,000	25,000
Premium on common stock	1,000	
Retained earnings	14,000	12,000
Totals	$53,000	$48,000

Required:

Prepare a working paper for a 198B statement of changes in financial position, using the following information from the company's 198B income statement and accounts:

a. The company's income statement showed an $8,000 net income for 198B.
b. The company's equipment was depreciated $2,000 during the year.
c. Equipment costing $5,000 was purchased.
d. Fully depreciated equipment that cost $1,000 was discarded, and its cost and accumulated depreciation were removed from the accounts.
e. Two hundred shares of the company's common stock were sold and issued at $15 per share.
f. Dividends totaling $6,000 were declared and paid during the year.

Exercise 14–3

From the working paper prepared for Exercise 14–2 prepare a statement of changes in financial position for Blue Haze, Inc.

Exercise 14–4

From the information supplied in Exercise 14–2 prepare an analysis of changes in the corporation's working capital items for the year ended December 31, 198B.

Exercise 14–5

Following is the 198A income statement of Olive Company and an analysis of the items in its Cash account.

OLIVE COMPANY

Income Statement for Year Ended December 31, 198A

Sales, net		$80,000
Cost of goods sold:		
Merchandise inventory, January 1, 198A	$10,000	
Purchases, net	52,000	
Goods for sale	$62,000	
Merchandise inventory, December 31, 198A.........	12,000	
Cost of goods sold		50,000
Gross profit on sales		$30,000
Operating expenses:		
Salaries and wages expense	$10,000	
Rent expense	6,000	
Depreciation expense, equipment	3,000	
Bad debts expense	1,000	20,000
Net income.......................................		$10,000

Cash Account Analysis

Cash balance, January 1, 198A		$ 5,000
Debits:		
Cash sales	$25,000	
Accounts receivable collections	50,000	
Bank loan	3,000	78,000
Total		$83,000
Credits:		
Payments to creditors for merchandise	$51,000	
Salary and wage payments	9,700	
Rent payments	6,000	
Payment for new equipment purchased	3,800	
Personal withdrawals of proprietor	8,000	78,500
Cash balance, December 31, 198A....................		$ 4,500

Required:

1. Prepare a statement converting the company's income statement amounts from an accrual basis to a cash basis.
2. Prepare a cash flow statement for the company.

PROBLEMS

Problem 14–1

The December 31, 198A, and 198B, balance sheets of Mesa, Inc., carried the following items:

Assets	198B	198A
Cash	$ 7,000	$ 4,800
Accounts receivable, net	8,500	9,500
Merchandise inventory	31,500	32,000
Prepaid expenses	1,000	1,200
Equipment	30,100	24,000
Accumulated depreciation, equipment	(6,100)	(4,800)
Total assets	$72,000	$66,700

Equities	198B	198A
Notes payable	$ 2,500	$ 1,500
Accounts payable	14,300	17,900
Mortgage payable	6,000	10,000
Common stock, $10 par value	30,000	25,000
Premium on common stock	2,500	
Retained earnings	16,700	12,300
Total equities	$72,000	$66,700

The company's 198B income statement and accounts revealed the following:

a. Net income for the year, $7,400.
b. The equipment depreciated $2,100 during the year.
c. Fully depreciated equipment that cost $800 was discarded, and its cost and accumulated depreciation were removed from the accounts.
d. Equipment costing $6,900 was purchased.
e. The mortgage was reduced by a $4,000 payment.
f. Five hundred shares of common stock were issued at $15 per share.
g. Cash dividends totaling $3,000 were declared and paid.

Required:

Prepare a working paper for a statement of changes in financial position, a statement of changes in financial position, and an analysis of changes in working capital items.

Problem 14–2

Ed Mills operates Racquet Shop as a single proprietorship, and the shop's 198A and 198B balance sheets carried these items:

Assets	198B	198A
Cash	$ 5,200	$ 4,400
Accounts receivable, net	15,100	15,600
Merchandise inventory	30,300	31,200
Prepaid expenses	1,100	900
Office equipment	2,800	2,600
Accumulated depreciation, office equipment	(900)	(800)
Store equipment	14,900	12,500
Accumulated depreciation, store equipment	(4,700)	(3,800)
Total assets	$63,800	$62,600

Liabilities and Owner's Equity	*198B*	*198A*
Notes payable	$ 4,000	$ 5,000
Accounts payable	16,000	14,500
Ed Mills, capital	43,800	43,100
Total liabilities and owner's equity...........	$63,800	$62,600

The store's 198B balance sheet summarized the change in owner's equity as follows:

Ed Mills, capital, January 1, 198B		$43,100
Net income for the year	$10,300	
Less withdrawals	9,600	
Excess of income over withdrawals		700
Ed Mills, capital, December 31, 198B		$43,800

The accounts showed that the following occurred during 198B: (1) Office equipment that cost $400 and had been depreciated $200 was traded on office equipment having a $500 cash price. A $100 trade-in allowance was received, and the income tax method was used to record the transaction. (2) Store equipment costing $3,000 was purchased. (3) Fully depreciated store equipment that cost $600 when new was discarded. (4) The 198B income statement showed depreciation expense on office equipment, $300; and on store equipment, $1,500.

Required:

Prepare a working paper for a statement of changes in financial position, a statement of changes in financial position, and an analysis of changes in working capital items.

Problem 14–3

Greentree Corporation's December 31, 198A, and 198B balance sheets carried the following items:

Assets	*198B*	*198A*
Cash	$ 19,100	$ 22,300
Accounts receivable, net	16,200	15,600
Merchandise inventory	50,200	51,400
Prepaid expenses	1,300	1,100
Investment in bonds	–0–	15,000
Office equipment	4,400	4,200
Accumulated depreciation, office equipment	(1,400)	(1,300)
Store equipment	26,000	24,300
Accumulated depreciation, store equipment	(5,200)	(3,600)
Store building	100,000	–0–
Accumulated depreciation, store building	(1,200)	–0–
Land	20,000	–0–
Total assets	$229,400	$129,000

Equities	198B	198A
Accounts payable	$ 20,300	$ 21,700
Income taxes payable	1,400	1,100
Mortgage payable	65,000	–0–
Common stock, $10 par value	100,000	80,000
Premium on common stock	4,000	–0–
Retained earnings	38,700	26,200
Total equities	$229,400	$129,000

The company's 198B income statement and accounting records showed:

a. The company had earned a $18,500 net income during the year.
b. It sold a long-term investment in bonds for cash at cost.
c. It then purchased for $120,000 the land and building it had occupied as a rental for a number of years, giving $55,000 in cash and issuing a mortgage for the balance.
d. Office equipment that cost $500 and had been depreciated $300 was traded in on new office equipment priced at $800. A $300 trade-in allowance was received.
e. Store equipment that cost $2,500 was purchased during the year.
f. Fully depreciated store equipment that cost $800 was discarded, and its cost and accumulated depreciation were removed from the accounts.
g. The office equipment was depreciated $400, the store equipment $2,400, and the building $1,200 during the year.
h. Two thousand shares of common stock were sold and issued at $12 per share.
i. Cash dividends totaling $6,000 were declared and paid during the year.

Required:

Prepare a working paper for a statement of changes in financial position, a statement of changes in financial position, and an analysis of changes in the company's working capital items.

Problem 14–4

The December 31, 198A, and 198B balance sheets of Hardrock, Inc., carried the following items:

Assets	198B	198A
Cash	$ 20,200	$ 15,400
Accounts receivable, net	33,200	32,100
Inventories	60,700	56,400
Prepaid expenses	2,000	1,700
Bond sinking fund	8,000	–0–
Long-term investment, bonds	–0–	10,000
Machinery	126,600	92,800
Accumulated depreciation, machinery	(39,700)	(33,700)
Buildings	194,500	112,500
Accumulated depreciation, buildings	(25,000)	(20,200)
Factory land	30,000	30,000
Total assets	$410,500	$297,000

Equities	198B	198A
Accounts payable	$ 24,400	$ 26,600
Wages payable	2,900	2,800
Federal income taxes payable	2,100	1,200
Bonds payable	100,000	–0–
Discount on bonds payable	(1,800)	–0–
Common stock, $10 par value....................	210,000	200,000
Premium on common stock	22,500	20,000
Retained earnings...............................	50,400	46,400
Total equities	$410,500	$297,000

At the end of 198B the company's noncurrent accounts showed these amounts:

Bond Sinking Fund

Date		Explanation	Debit	Credit	Balance
198B					
Dec.	31	First annual deposit	8,000		8,000

Long-Term Investment, Bonds

Date		Explanation	Debit	Credit	Balance
198B					
Jan.	1	Balance			10,000
May	7	Sold		10,000	–0–

Machinery

Date		Explanation	Debit	Credit	Balance
198B					
Jan.	1	Balance			92,800
	23	Purchase	38,100		130,900
July	8	Discarded machinery		4,300	126,600

Accumulated Depreciation, Machinery

Date		Explanation	Debit	Credit	Balance
198B					
Jan.	1	Balance			33,700
July	8	Discarded machinery	4,300		29,400
Dec.	31	Year's depreciation		10,300	39,700

Buildings

Date		Explanation	Debit	Credit	Balance
198B					
Jan.	1	Balance			112,500
	8	Building addition	82,000		194,500

Accumulated Depreciation, Buildings

Date		Explanation	Debit	Credit	Balance
198B					
Jan.	1	Balance			20,200
Dec.	31	Year's depreciation		4,800	25,000

Factory Land

Date		Explanation	Debit	Credit	Balance
198B					
Jan.	1	Balance			30,000

Bonds Payable

Date		Explanation	Debit	Credit	Balance
198B					
Jan.	1	Issued 8½%, 10-year bonds		100,000	100,000

Bond Discount

Date		Explanation	Debit	Credit	Balance
198B					
Jan.	1	Discount on issuance	2,000		2,000
June	30	Amortization		100	1,900
Dec.	31	Amortization		100	1,800

Common Stock, $10 Par Value

Date		Explanation	Debit	Credit	Balance
198B					
Jan.	1	Balance			200,000
Dec.	1	Stock dividend		10,000	210,000

Premium on Common Stock

Date		Explanation	Debit	Credit	Balance
198B					
Jan.	1	Balance			20,000
Dec.	1	Stock dividend		2,500	22,500

Retained Earnings

Date		Explanation	Debit	Credit	Balance
198B					
Jan.	1	Balance			46,400
June	9	Cash dividend	16,000		30,400
Dec.	1	Stock dividend	12,500		17,900
	31	Net income		32,500	50,400

The bonds held as a long-term investment were sold for cash at cost, and the proceeds were used to help finance the plant expansion. The company reported a 198B net income of $32,500.

Required:

Use the information supplied to prepare a working paper for a statement of changes in financial position, a statement of changes in financial position, and an analysis of changes in working capital items.

Problem 14–5

The income statement of Pro Shop and an analysis of the entries in its Cash account for the year of the income statement follow:

PRO SHOP

Income Statement for Year Ended December 31, 19—

Sales, net		$121,400
Cost of goods sold:		
Merchandise inventory, January 1, 19—	$22,400	
Purchases, net.................................	77,100	
Goods for sale	$99,500	
Merchandise inventory, December 31, 19—	21,300	
Cost of goods sold		78,200
Gross profit on sales		$ 43,200
Operating expenses:		
Salaries and wages expense	$30,300	
Rent expense	9,000	
Depreciation expense	2,400	
Bad debts expense	600	
Store supplies expense	1,200	
Total operating expenses		43,500
Operating loss...................................		$ (300)
Interest expense		200
Net loss..		$ (500)

Analysis of Cash Account

Cash balance, January 1, 19—		$ 6,200
Debits:		
Cash sales	$26,400	
Accounts receivable collections	97,100	
Sale of unneeded equipment at book value	200	
Bank loan	5,000	128,700
Total		$134,900
Credits:		
Payments to creditors for merchandise	$78,400	
Payments for store supplies	1,400	
Salary and wage payments	30,200	
Rent payments	8,250	
Purchase of equipment	1,500	
Personal withdrawals of proprietor	7,200	126,950
Cash balance, December 31, 19—		$ 7,950

Required:

Prepare a statement converting the shop's income statement amounts from an accrual basis to a cash basis and prepare a cash flow statement for the shop.

ALTERNATE PROBLEMS

Problem 14–1A

The 198A and 198B balance sheets of Hilltop, Inc., carried these items:

Assets	198B	198A
Current assets:		
Cash	$ 12,700	$ 11,800
Accounts receivable, net	34,900	33,400
Merchandise inventory	85,900	86,700
Prepaid expenses	2,000	1,800
Total current assets	$135,500	$133,700
Plant and equipment:		
Office equipment	$ 5,400	$ 6,100
Accumulated depreciation, office equipment	(2,500)	(2,400)
Store equipment	31,700	27,800
Accumulated depreciation, store equipment	(7,400)	(6,500)
Total plant and equipment	$ 27,200	$ 25,000
Total assets	$162,700	$158,700

Equities	198B	198A
Current liabilities:		
Accounts payable	$ 22,500	$ 23,200
Notes payable	4,500	5,000
Income taxes payable	500	300
Total liabilities	$ 27,500	$ 28,500
Stockholders' equity:		
Common stock, $5 par value	$105,000	$100,000
Premium on common stock	8,500	5,500
Retained earnings	21,700	24,700
Total stockholders' equity	$135,200	$130,200
Total equities	$162,700	$158,700

An examination of the company's 198B income statement and accounting records revealed this additional information:

a. A $15,000 net income was earned in 198B.
b. Depreciation charged on office equipment, $600; and on store equipment, $1,500.
c. Office equipment that cost $700 and had been depreciated $500 was sold to an employee for its book value.
d. Store equipment that cost $4,500 was purchased during 198B.
e. Fully depreciated store equipment that cost $600 was discarded, and its cost and accumulated depreciation were removed from the accounts.
f. Cash dividends totaling $10,000 were declared during the year.
g. A 5% stock dividend was declared and distributed during the year at a time when the company's stock was selling at $8 per share.

Required:

Prepare a working paper for a statement of changes in financial position, a statement of changes in financial position, and an analysis of the changes in working capital items.

Problem 14–2A

The December 31, 198A, and 198B, balance sheets of Seaside, Inc. carried these items:

Assets	198B	198A
Cash	$ 10,400	$ 11,500
Accounts receivable, net	26,600	27,300
Merchandise inventory	68,700	64,200
Prepaid expenses................................	1,100	800
Office equipment	6,100	6,200
Accumulated depreciation, office equipment	(2,100)	(1,900)
Store equipment	39,900	39,800
Accumulated depreciation, store equipment	(10,900)	(7,600)
Total assets	$139,800	$140,300

Liabilities and Stockholders' Equity	198B	198A
Notes payable	$ 5,000	$ 2,500
Accounts payable	17,300	17,600
Common stock, $5 par value	105,000	100,000
Premium on common stock	5,500	4,000
Retained earnings	7,000	16,200
Total liabilities and stockholders' equity	$139,800	$140,300

The company's 198B income statement and accounting records revealed the following:

a. A $700 net loss was incurred in 198B.
b. Depreciation on office equipment, $600; and on store equipment, $3,800.
c. Office equipment costing $300 was purchased during the year.
d. Fully depreciated office equipment that cost $400 was discarded, and its cost and accumulated depreciation were removed from the accounts.
e. Store equipment that cost $800 and had been depreciated $500 was traded in on new equipment having a $1,000 cash price. A $400 trade-in allowance was received.
f. A 1,000-share stock dividend was declared and distributed while the stock was selling at $6.50 per share.
g. Cash dividends totaling $2,000 were declared and paid during the year.

Required:

Prepare a working paper for a statement of changes in financial position, a statement of changes in financial position, and an analysis of changes in working capital items.

Problem 14–3A

Dale Corporation's 198A and 198B balance sheets carried these items:

	December 31,	
Assets	*198B*	*198A*
Cash	$ 14,800	$ 18,600
Accounts receivable, net	15,800	16,200
Merchandise inventory	73,500	72,400
Other current assets	1,100	1,400
Office equipment	4,500	4,700
Accumulated depreciation, office equipment	(1,900)	(1,600)
Store equipment	22,000	15,500
Accumulated depreciation, store equipment	(4,600)	(4,200)
Building	85,000	–0–
Accumulated depreciation, building	(2,000)	–0–
Land	20,000	–0–
Total assets	$228,200	$123,000

	December 31,	
Equities	*198B*	*198A*
Notes payable	$ 7,500	–0–
Accounts payable	29,200	28,400
Other current liabilities	1,800	2,100
Mortgage payable	60,000	–0–
Common stock, $25 par value	100,000	75,000
Premium on common stock	5,000	–0–
Retained earnings	24,700	17,500
Total equities	$228,200	$123,000

The company's 198B income statement and accounting records showed the following:

a. A 198B net income of $13,200.
b. Depreciation on office equipment, $500; on store equipment, $1,600; and on the building, $2,000.
c. Fully depreciated office equipment that cost $200 was discarded, and its cost and accumulated depreciation were removed from the accounts.
d. Store equipment that cost $8,000 was purchased during the year.
e. Store equipment that cost $1,500 and had been depreciated $1,200 was sold to an employee for its book value.
f. The mortgage was incurred in purchasing for $105,000 the land and building previously rented by the company.
g. One thousand shares of common stock were sold and issued at $30 per share.
h. Cash dividends totaling $6,000 were declared and paid during the year.

Required:

Prepare a working paper for a statement of changes in financial position and a statement of changes in financial position. Also prepare an analysis of changes in working capital items.

Problem 14–5A

The income statement of Westgate Shop and an analysis of its Cash account for the year of the income statement follow:

WESTGATE SHOP

Income Statement for Year Ended December 31, 19—

Sales, net		$258,400
Cost of goods sold:		
Merchandise inventory, January 1, 19—	$ 52,200	
Purchases, net	174,500	
Goods for sale	$226,700	
Merchandise inventory, December 31, 19—	53,800	
Cost of goods sold		172,900
Gross profit on sales		$ 85,500
Operating expenses:		
Salaries and wages expense	$ 48,600	
Rent expense	15,000	
Depreciation expense	3,200	
Bad debts expense	1,200	
Store supplies expense	1,000	
Other operating expenses	1,800	
Total operating expenses		70,800
Operating income		$ 14,700
Interest expense		100
Net income		$ 14,600

Analysis of Cash Account

Cash balance, January 1, 19—		$ 10,200
Debits:		
Cash sales	$ 62,500	
Accounts receivable collections	196,500	
Bank loan	5,000	
Sale of unneeded equipment at book value	300	264,300
Total		$274,500
Credits:		
Creditor payments for merchandise purchased	$175,300	
Rent payments	16,250	
Creditor payments for store supplies bought	800	
Salary and wage payments	48,100	
Other operating expense payments	1,700	
New equipment purchased	10,000	
Personal withdrawals by proprietor	12,000	264,150
Cash balance, December 31, 19—		$ 10,350

Required:

Prepare a statement converting the shop's income statement amounts from an accrual basis to a cash basis and prepare a cash flow statement for the shop.

PROVOCATIVE PROBLEMS

Provocative problem 14–1
Alpha Company

The presidents of Alpha Company and Beta Company are goods friends and often play golf together. Today on the golf course the president of Alpha Company bragged that his company had purchased $2,500,000 of new plant and equipment during the past two years without incurring any long-term debt or issuing any additional stock. The president of Beta Company wondered how this was done, but he did not ask. However, on returning to his office he got out the published year-end financial statements of Alpha Company, which provided the following information:

	In thousands of dollars		
Assets	*198C*	*198B*	*198A*
Cash	$ 790	$ 660	$ 510
Temporary investments	–0–	1,150	1,550
Accounts receivable, net	840	790	820
Inventories	960	1,020	930
Plant and equipment	7,000	5,300	4,500
Accumulated depreciation, plant and equipment...........................	(1,990)	(1,570)	(1,210)
Total assets	$ 7,600	$ 7,350	$ 7,100
Equities			
Accounts payable........................	$ 960	$ 970	$ 940
Other short-term payables	830	810	800
Common stock	3,000	3,000	3,000
Premium on common stock	500	500	500
Retained earnings	2,310	2,070	1,860
Total equities	$ 7,600	$ 7,350	$ 7,100
Net income after taxes...................	$ 390	$ 360	$ 320
Depreciation expense, plant and equipment	420	360	300
Dividends declared and paid	150	150	150

Explain how Alpha Company was able to purchase $2,500,000 of new plant and equipment during 198B and 198C. Back your explanation with figures and a statement of changes in financial position.

Provocative problem 14–2
Sports Center

Ed Mann owns Sports Center, a sporting goods store. During 198B he remodeled and replaced $18,000 of the store's fully depreciated equipment with new equipment costing $22,000. However, by the year-end he was having trouble meeting the store's current expenses and had to borrow $5,000 from the bank on a short-term note payable. As a result, he asked his accountant to prepare some sort of a report showing what had happened to the store's funds during the year. The accountant analyzed the changes in the store's accounts and produced the following statement of changes in financial position, which he called a statement of sources and uses of funds.

SPORTS CENTER
Statement of Sources and Uses of Funds
Year Ended December 31, 198B

Sources of funds:		
Current operations:		
Net income earned in 198B	$17,200	
Add expenses not requiring the use of funds:		
Depreciation of store equipment	4,500	
Total funds from operations	$21,700	
Other sources:		
Mortgage on new store equipment	15,000	
Total new funds		$36,700
Uses of funds:		
Purchase of new equipment	$22,000	
Personal withdrawals of proprietor	12,000	
Total uses of funds		34,000
Net increase in funds................................		$ 2,700

On reading the report, Mr. Mann was dumbfounded by the $2,700 increase in funds in a year he knew his store's bank balance had decreased by $8,500. Also, he could not understand how depreciation was a source of funds, but the $5,000 bank loan was not. Explain these points to Mr. Mann, and use the following post-closing trial balances from the store's ledger to prepare a different statement from that prepared by the accountant that you think helps make your explanation clear.

SPORTS CENTER
Post-Closing Trial Balances

	Dec. 31, 198B		*Dec. 31, 198A*	
Cash	$ 2,900		$11,400	
Accounts receivable	17,900		13,900	
Allowance for doubtful accounts ...		$ 500		$ 400
Merchandise inventory	27,400		17,200	
Prepaid expenses	800		500	
Store equipment	39,000		35,000	
Accumulated depr., store				
equipment		10,500		24,000
Notes payable		5,000		
Accounts payable		8,800		10,400
Accrued payables		500		700
Mortgage payable		15,000		
Ed Mann, capital		47,700		42,500
Totals	$88,000	$88,000	$78,000	$78,000

15

Analyzing financial statements

After studying Chapter 15, you should be able to:

- Describe comparative financial statements, how they are prepared, and the limitations associated with interpreting them.
- Prepare common-size comparative statements and interpret them.
- Explain the importance of working capital in the analysis of financial statements and list the typical ratios used to analyze working capital.
- Calculate the common ratios used in analyzing the balance sheet and income statement and state what each ratio purports to measure.
- State the limitations associated with using financial statement ratios and the sources from which standards for comparison may be obtained.
- Define or explain the words and phrases listed in the chapter Glossary.

The financial statements of a business are analyzed to determine its overall position and to find out about certain aspects of that position, such as earnings prospects and debt-paying ability. In making the analysis, individual statement items are in themselves generally not too significant. However, relationships between items and groups of items plus changes that have occurred are significant. As a result, financial statement analysis requires that relationships between items and groups of items and changes in items and groups be seen.

COMPARATIVE STATEMENTS

Changes in statement items can usually best be seen when item amounts for two or more successive years are placed side by side in columns on a single statement. Such a statement is called a *comparative statement*. Each of the financial statements, or portions thereof, may be presented in the form of a comparative statement.

In its most simple form a comparative balance sheet consists of the item amounts from two or more of a company's successive balance sheets arranged side by side, so that changes in amounts may be seen. However, such a statement can be improved by also showing in both dollar amounts and in percentages the changes that have occurred. When this is done, as in Illustration 15–1, large dollar and large percentage changes become more readily apparent.

A comparative income statement is prepared in the same manner as a comparative balance sheet. Income statement amounts for two or more successive periods are placed side by side, with dollar and percentage changes in additional columns. Such a statement is shown in Illustration 15–2.

Analyzing and interpreting comparative statements

In analyzing and interpreting comparative data, it is necessary for the analyst to select for study any items showing significant dollar or percentage changes. The analyst then trys to determine the reasons for each change and if possible whether they are favorable or unfavorable. For example, in Illustration 15–1, the first item, "Cash," shows a large decrease. At first glance this appears unfavorable. However, when the decrease in "Cash" is considered with the decrease in "Investments" and the increases in "Store equipment," "Buildings," and "Land," plus the increase in "Mortgage payable," it becomes apparent the company has materially increased its plant assets between the two balance sheet dates. Further study reveals the company has apparently

Anchor Supply Company
Comparative Balance Sheet
December 31, 198A, and December 31, 198B

	Years Ended December 31		Amount of Increase or (Decrease) during 198B	Percent of Increase or (Decrease) during 198B
	198B	198A		
Assets				
Current assets:				
Cash	$ 18,000	$ 90,500	$ (72,500)	(80.1)
Accounts receivable, net	68,000	64,000	4,000	6.3
Merchandise inventory	90,000	84,000	6,000	7.1
Prepaid expenses	5,800	6,000	(200)	(3.3)
Total current assets	$181,800	$244,500	$ (62,700)	(25.6)
Long-term investments:				
Real estate	$ –0–	$ 30,000	$ (30,000)	(100.0)
Apex Company common stock	–0–	50,000	(50,000)	(100.0)
Total long-term investments	$ –0–	$ 80,000	$ (80,000)	(100.0)
Plant and equipment:				
Office equipment, net	$ 3,500	$ 3,700	$ (200)	(5.4)
Store equipment, net	17,900	6,800	11,100	163.2
Buildings, net	176,800	28,000	148,800	531.4
Land	50,000	20,000	30,000	150.0
Total plant and equipment	$248,200	$ 58,500	$189,700	324.3
Total assets	$430,000	$383,000	$ 47,000	12.3
Liabilities				
Current liabilities:				
Notes payable	$ 5,000	$ –0–	$ 5,000	
Accounts payable	43,600	55,000	(11,400)	(20.7)
Taxes payable	4,800	5,000	(200)	(4.0)
Wages payable	800	1,200	(400)	(33.3)
Total current liabilities	$ 54,200	$ 61,200	$ (7,000)	(11.4)
Long-term liabilities:				
Mortgage payable	$ 60,000	$ 10,000	$ 50,000	500.0
Total liabilities	$114,200	$ 71,200	$ 43,000	60.4
Capital				
Common stock, $10 par value	$250,000	$250,000	$ –0–	–0–
Retained earnings	65,800	61,800	4,000	6.5
Total capital	$315,800	$311,800	$ 4,000	1.3
Total liabilities and capital	$430,000	$383,000	$ 47,000	12.3

Illustration 15–1

Anchor Supply Company
Comparative Income Statement
Years Ended December 31, 198A, and 198B

	Years Ended December 31		Amount of Increase or (Decrease) during 198B	Percent of Increase or (Decrease) during 198B
	198B	198A		
Gross sales	$973,500	$853,000	$120,500	14.1
Sales returns and allowances	13,500	10,200	3,300	32.4
Net sales	$960,000	$842,800	$117,200	13.9
Cost of goods sold	715,000	622,500	92,500	14.9
Gross profit from sales	$245,000	$220,300	$ 24,700	11.2
Operating expenses:				
Selling expenses:				
Advertising expense	$ 7,500	$ 5,000	$ 2,500	50.0
Sales salaries expense	113,500	98,000	15,500	15.8
Store supplies expense	3,200	2,800	400	14.3
Depreciation expense, store equipment	2,400	1,700	700	41.2
Delivery expense	14,800	14,000	800	5.7
Total selling expenses	$141,400	$121,500	$ 19,900	16.4
General and administrative expenses:				
Office salaries expense	$ 41,000	$ 40,050	$ 950	2.4
Office supplies expense	1,300	1,250	50	4.0
Insurance expense	1,600	1,200	400	33.3
Depreciation expense, office equipment	300	300	–0–	–0–
Depreciation expense, buildings	2,850	1,500	1,350	90.0
Bad debts expense	2,250	2,200	50	2.3
Total general and admin. expenses	$ 49,300	$ 46,500	$ 2,800	6.0
Total operating expenses	$190,700	$168,000	$ 22,700	13.5
Operating income	$ 54,300	$ 52,300	$ 2,000	3.8
Less interest expense	2,300	1,000	1,300	130.0
Income before taxes	$ 52,000	$ 51,300	$ 700	1.4
Income taxes	19,000	18,700	300	1.6
Net income	$ 33,000	$ 32,600	$ 400	1.2

Illustration 15–2

constructed a new building on land it has held as an investment until needed in this expansion. Also, it seems the company paid for its new plant assets by reducing cash, selling its Apex Company common stock, and issuing a $50,000 mortgage.

As an aid in controlling operations, a comparative income statement is usually more valuable than a comparative balance sheet. For example, in Illustration 15–2, "Gross sales" increased 14.1% and "Net sales" increased 13.9%. At the same time, "Sales returns" increased 32.4%, or at a rate more than twice that of gross sales. Returned sales represent wasted sales effort and indicate dissatisfied customers. Consequently, such an increase in returns should be investigated, and the reason therefor determined if at all possible. Also, in addition to the large increase in the "Sales returns," it is significant that the rate of increase in "Cost of goods sold" is greater than that of "Net sales." This is an unfavorable trend and should be remedied if at all possible.

In attempting to account for Anchor Supply Company's increase in sales, the increases in advertising and in plant assets merit attention. It is reasonable to expect an increase in advertising to increase sales. It is also reasonable to expect an increase in plant assets to result in a sales increase.

Calculating percentage increases and decreases

When percentage increases and decreases are calculated for comparative statements, the increase or decrease in an item is divided by the amount shown for the item in the base year. No problems arise in these calculations when positive amounts are shown in the base year. However, when no amount is shown or a negative amount is shown in the base year, a percentage increase or decrease cannot be calculated. For example, in Illustration 15–1 there were no notes payable at the end of 198A and a percentage change for this item cannot be calculated.

In this text, percentages and ratios are typically rounded to one or two decimal places. However, there is no uniform agreement on this matter. In general, percentages should be carried out to the point of assuring that meaningful information is conveyed. However, they should not be carried so far that the significance of relationships tend to become "lost" in the length of the numbers.

Trend percentages

Trend percentages or index numbers are useful in comparing data covering a number of years, since they emphasize changes that have occurred during the period. They are calculated as follows:

1. A base year is selected, and each item amount on the base year statement is assigned a weight of 100%.
2. Then each item from the statements for the years after the base year is expressed as a percentage of its base year amount. To determine these percentages, the item amounts in the years after the base year are divided by the amount of the item in the base year.

For example, if 198A is made the base year for the following data, the trend percentages for "Sales" are calculated by dividing by $210,000, the amount shown for "Sales" in each year after the first. The trend percentages for "Cost of goods sold" are found by dividing by $145,000 the amount shown for "Cost of goods sold" in each year after the first. And, the trend percentages for "Gross profit" are found by dividing the amounts shown for "Gross profit" by $65,000.

	198A	198B	198C	198D	198E	198F
Sales	$210,000	$204,000	$292,000	$284,000	$310,000	$324,000
Cost of goods sold	145,000	139,000	204,000	198,000	218,000	229,000
Gross profit	$ 65,000	$ 65,000	$ 88,000	$ 86,000	$ 92,000	$ 95,000

When these divisions are made, the trends for these three items appear as follows:

	198A	198B	198C	198D	198E	198F
Sales	100	97	139	135	148	154
Cost of goods sold	100	96	141	137	150	158
Gross profit	100	100	135	132	142	146

It is interesting to note in the illustrated trends that while after the second year the sales trend is upward, the cost of goods sold trend is upward at a slightly more rapid rate. This indicates a contracting gross profit rate and should receive attention.

It should be pointed out in a discussion of trends that the trend for a single balance sheet or income statement item is seldom very informative. However, a comparison of trends for related items often tells the analyst a great deal. For example, a downward sales trend with an upward trend for merchandise inventory, accounts receivable, and loss on bad debts would generally indicate an unfavorable situation. On the other hand, an upward sales trend with a downward trend or a slower upward trend for accounts receivable, merchandise inventory, and selling expenses would indicate an increase in operating efficiency.

Common-size comparative statements

The comparative statements illustrated thus far do not show proportional changes in items except in a general way. Changes in proportions are often shown and emphasized by *common-size comparative statements.*

A common-size statement is so called because its items are shown in common-size figures, figures that are fractions of 100%. For example, on a common-size balance sheet (1) the asset total is assigned a value of 100%. (2) The total of the liabilities and owners' equity is also assigned a value of 100%. Then (3), each asset, liability, and owners' equity item is shown as a fraction of one of the 100% totals. When a company's successive balance sheets are shown in this manner (see Illustration 15–3), proportional changes are emphasized.

A common-size income statement is prepared by assigning net sales a 100% value and then expressing each statement item as a percent of net sales. Such a statement is an informative and useful tool. If the 100% sales amount on the statement is assumed to represent one

Anchor Supply Company
Common-Size Comparative Balance Sheet
December 31, 198A, and December 31, 198B

	Years Ended December 31		Common-Size Percentages	
	198B	198A	198B	198A
Assets				
Current assets:				
Cash....................................	$ 18,000	$ 90,500	4.19	23.63
Accounts receivable, net	68,000	64,000	15.81	16.71
Merchandise inventory	90,000	84,000	20.93	21.93
Prepaid expenses	5,800	6,000	1.35	1.57
Total current assets	$181,800	$244,500	42.28	63.84
Long-term investments:				
Real estate	$ –0–	$ 30,000		7.83
Apex Company common stock	–0–	50,000		13.05
Total long-term investments	$ –0–	$ 80,000		20.88
Plant and equipment:				
Office equipment, net	$ 3,500	$ 3,700	0.81	0.97
Store equipment, net	17,900	6,800	4.16	1.78
Buildings, net	176,800	28,000	41.12	7.31
Land....................................	50,000	20,000	11.63	5.22
Total plant and equipment	$248,200	$ 58,500	57.72	15.28
Total assets	$430,000	$383,000	100.00	100.00
Liabilities				
Current liabilities:				
Notes payable	$ 5,000	$ –0–	1.16	
Accounts payable	43,600	55,000	10.14	14.36
Taxes payable	4,800	5,000	1.12	1.31
Wages payable	800	1,200	0.19	0.31
Total current liabilities	$ 54,200	$ 61,200	12.61	15.98
Long-term liabilities:				
Mortgage payable	$ 60,000	$ 10,000	13.95	2.61
Total liabilities....................	$114,200	$ 71,200	26.56	18.59
Capital				
Common stock, $10 par value	$250,000	$250,000	58.14	65.27
Retained earnings	65,800	61,800	15.30	16.14
Total capital	$315,800	$311,800	73.44	81.44
Total liabilities and capital	$430,000	$383,000	100.00	100.00

Illustration 15–3

sales dollar, then the remaining items show how each sales dollar was distributed to costs, expenses, and profit. For example, on the comparative income statement shown in Illustration 15–4, the 198A cost of goods sold consumed 73.86 cents of each sales dollar. In 198B cost of goods sold consumed 74.48 cents of each sales dollar. While this increase is small, if in 198B the proportion of cost of goods sold had remained at the 198A level, almost $6,000 additional net income would have been earned.

' Common-size percentages point out efficiencies and inefficiencies that are otherwise difficult to see. For this reason they are a valuable management tool. To illustrate, sales salaries of Anchor Supply Company took a higher percentage of each sales dollar in 198B than in

Anchor Supply Company
Common-Size Comparative Income Statement
Year Ended December 31, 198A, and 198B

	Years Ended December 31		Common-Size Percentages	
	198B	198A	198B	198A
Gross sales	$973,500	$853,000	101.41	101.21
Sales returns and allowances	13,500	10,200	1.41	1.21
Net sales	$960,000	$842,800	100.00	100.00
Cost of goods sold	715,000	622,500	74.48	73.86
Gross profit from sales	$245,000	$220,300	25.52	26.14
Operating expenses:				
Selling expenses:				
Advertising expense	$ 7,500	$ 5,000	0.78	0.59
Sales salaries expense	113,500	98,000	11.82	11.63
Store supplies expense	3,200	2,800	0.33	0.33
Depreciation expense, store equipment	2,400	1,700	0.25	0.20
Delivery expense	14,800	14,000	1.54	1.66
Total selling expenses	$141,400	$121,500	14.72	14.41
General and administrative expenses:				
Office salaries expense	$ 41,000	$ 40,050	4.27	4.75
Office supplies expense	1,300	1,250	0.14	0.15
Insurance expense	1,600	1,200	0.17	0.14
Depreciation expense, office equipment	300	300	0.03	0.04
Depreciation expense, buildings	2,850	1,500	0.30	0.18
Bad debts expense	2,250	2,200	0.23	0.26
Total general and administrative expenses	$ 49,300	$ 46,500	5.14	5.52
Total operating expenses	$190,700	$168,000	19.86	19.93
Operating income	$ 54,300	$ 52,300	5.66	6.21
Less interest expense	2,300	1,000	0.24	0.12
Income before taxes	$ 52,000	$ 51,300	5.42	6.09
Income taxes	19,000	18,700	1.98	2.22
Net income	$ 33,000	$ 32,600	3.44	3.87

Illustration 15–4

198A. On the other hand, office salaries took a smaller percentage. Furthermore, although the loss from bad debts was greater in 198B than in 198A, loss from bad debts took a smaller proportion of each sales dollar in 198B than in 198A.

ANALYSIS OF WORKING CAPITAL

When balance sheets are analyzed, working capital always receives close attention because an adequate amount of working capital enables a company to meet current debts, carry sufficient inventories, and take advantage of cash discounts. However, the amount of working capital a company has is not a measure of these abilities. This may be demonstrated as follows with Companies A and B:

	Company A	Company B
Current assets	$100,000	$20,000
Current liabilities	90,000	10,000
Working capital	$ 10,000	$10,000

Companies A and B have the same amounts of working capital. However, Company A's current liabilities are nine times its working capital, while Company B's current liabilities and working capital are equal. As a result, if liabilities are to be paid on time, Company A must experience much less shrinkage and delay in converting its current assets to cash than Company B. Thus, the amount of a company's working capital is not a measure of its working capital position. However, the relation of its current assets to its current liabilities is such a measure.

Current ratio

The relation of a company's current assets to its current liabilities is known as its *current ratio*. A current ratio is calculated by dividing current assets by current liabilities. The current ratio of the foregoing Company B is calculated as follows:

$$\frac{\text{Current assets, \$20,000}}{\text{Current liabilities, \$10,000}} = 2$$

After the division is made, the relation is expressed as, for example, Company B's current assets are two times its current liabilities or simply Company B's current ratio is 2 to 1.

The current ratio is the relation of current assets and current liabilities expressed mathematically. A high current ratio indicates a large proportion of current assets to current liabilities. The higher the ratio, the better is a company's current position, and normally the better it can meet current obligations.

For years bankers and other credit grantors measured a credit-seeking company's debt-paying ability by whether or not it had a 2 to 1 current ratio. Today, most credit grantors realize that the 2 to 1 rule of thumb is not an adequate test of debt-paying ability. They realize that whether or not a company's current ratio is good or bad depends upon at least three factors:

1. The nature of the company's business.
2. The composition of its current assets.
3. The turnover of certain of its current assets.

The nature of a company's business has much to do with whether or not its current ratio is adequate. A public utility which has no inventories other than supplies and grants little or no credit can operate on a current ratio less than 1 to 1. On the other hand, because a misjudgment of style can make an inventory of goods for sale almost worthless, a company in which style is the important sales factor may find a current ratio of much more than 2 to 1 to be inadequate. Consequently, when the adequacy of working capital is studied, consideration must be given to the type of business under review.

Also, in an analysis of a company's working capital, the composition of its current assets should be considered. Normally a company with a high proportion of cash to accounts receivable and merchandise is in a better position to meet quickly its current obligations than is a company with most of its current assets tied up in accounts receivable and merchandise. The company with cash can pay its current debts at once. The company with accounts receivable and merchandise must often turn these items into cash before it can pay.

Acid-test ratio

An easily calculated check on current asset composition is the *acid-test ratio,* also called the *quick ratio* because it is the ratio of "quick assets" to current liabilities. "Quick assets" are cash, notes receivable, accounts receivable, and marketable securities. They are the current assets that can quickly be turned into cash. An acid-test ratio of 1 to 1 is normally considered satisfactory. However, this is a rule of thumb and should be applied with care. The acid-test ratio of Anchor Supply Company as of the end of 198B is calculated as follows:

Quick assets:		Current liabilities:	
Cash	$18,000	Notes payable	$ 5,000
Accounts receivable	68,000	Accounts payable	43,600
		Taxes payable	4,800
		Wages payable	800
Total	$86,000	Total	$54,200

Acid-test ratio is $86,000 ÷ $54,200 = 1.59 or is 1.6 to 1

Certain current asset turnovers affect working capital requirements. For example, assume Companies A and B sell the same amounts of merchandise on credit each month. However, Company A grants 30-day terms to its customers, while Company B grants 60 days. Both collect their accounts at the end of the credit periods granted. But as a result of the difference in terms, Company A turns over or collects its accounts twice as rapidly as does Company B. Also, as a result of the more rapid turnover, Company A requires only one half the investment in accounts receivable that is required of Company B and can operate with a smaller current ratio.

Accounts receivable turnover is calculated by dividing net sales for a year by the year-end accounts receivable. Anchor Supply Company's turnovers for 198A and 198B are calculated as follows:

		198B	198A
a.	Net sales for year	$960,000	$842,800
b.	Year-end accounts receivable	68,000	64,000
	Times accounts receivable were		
	turned over *(a ÷ b)*	14.1	13.2

The turnover of 14.1 times in 198B in comparison to 13.2 in 198A indicates the company's accounts receivable were collected more rapidly in 198B.

The year-end amount of accounts receivable is commonly used in calculating accounts receivable turnover. However, if year-end accounts receivable are not representative, an average of the year's accounts receivable by months should be used. Also, credit sales rather than the sum of cash and credit sales, and accounts receivable before subtracting the allowance for doubtful accounts should be used. However, information as to credit sales is seldom available in a published balance sheet. Likewise, many published balance sheets report accounts receivable at their net amount. Consequently, total sales and net accounts receivable must often be used.

Days' sales uncollected

Accounts receivable turnover is one indication of the speed with which a company collects its accounts. *Days' sales uncollected* is another indication of the same thing. To illustrate the calculation of days' sales uncollected, assume a company had charge sales during a year of $250,000, and that it has $25,000 of accounts receivable at the year-end. In other words, one tenth of its charge sales, or the charge sales made during one tenth of a year, or the charge sales of 36.5 days ($\frac{1}{10}$ × 365 days in a year = 36.5 days) are uncollected. This calculation of days' sales uncollected in equation form appears as follows:

$$\frac{\text{Accounts receivable, \$25,000}}{\text{Charge sales, \$250,000}} \times 365 = 36.5 \text{ days' sales uncollected}$$

Days' sales uncollected takes on more meaning when credit terms are known. According to a rule of thumb, a company's days' sales uncollected should not exceed one and one-third times the days in its credit period when it does not offer discounts and one and one-third times the days in its discount period when it does. If the company, whose days' sales uncollected is calculated in the illustration just given, offers 30-day terms, then 36.5 days is within the rule-of-thumb amount. However, if its terms are 2/10, n/30, its days' sales uncollected seem excessive.

Turnover of merchandise inventory

A company's *merchandise turnover* is the number of times its average inventory is sold during an accounting period. A high turnover is considered an indication of good merchandising. Also, from a working capital point of view, a company with a high turnover requires a smaller investment in inventory than one producing the same sales with a low turnover. Merchandise turnover is calculated by dividing cost of goods sold by average inventory. Cost of goods sold is the amount of merchandise at cost that was sold during an accounting period. Average inventory is the average amount of merchandise, at cost on hand during the period. The 198B merchandise turnover of Anchor Supply Company is calculated as follows:

$$\frac{\text{Cost of goods sold, \$715,000}}{\text{Average merchandise inventory, \$87,000}} = \text{Merchandise turnover of 8.2 times}$$

The cost of goods sold is taken from the company's 198B income statement. The average inventory is found by dividing by two the sum of the $84,000, January 1, 198B, inventory and the $90,000, December 31, 198B, inventory. In a company in which beginning and ending inventories are not representative of the inventory normally on hand, a more accurate turnover may be secured by using the average of all the 12 month-end inventories.

STANDARDS OF COMPARISON

When financial statements are analyzed by computing ratios and turnovers, the analyst must determine whether the ratios and turnovers obtained are good, bad, or just average. Furthermore, in making the decision the analyst must have some basis for comparison. The following are available:

1. A trained analyst may compare the ratios and turnovers of the company under review with mental standards acquired from past experiences.

2. An analyst may calculate for purposes of comparison the ratios and turnovers of a selected group of competitive companies in the same industry as the one whose statements are under review.
3. Published ratios and turnovers such as those put out by Dun & Bradstreet may be secured for comparison.
4. Some local and national trade associations gather data from their members and publish standard or average ratios for their trade or industry. These offer the analyst a very good basis of comparison when available.
5. Rule-of-thumb standards may be used as a basis for comparison.

Of these five standards, the ratios and turnovers of a selected group of competitive companies normally offer the best basis for comparison. Rule-of-thumb standards should be applied with care if erroneous conclusions are to be avoided.

OTHER BALANCE SHEET AND INCOME STATEMENT RELATIONS

Several balance sheet and income statement relations in addition to those having to do with working capital are important to the analyst. Some of the more important are discussed below.

Capital contributions of owners and creditors

The share of a company's assets contributed by its owners and the share contributed by creditors are always of interest to the analyst. The owners' and creditors' contributions of Anchor Supply Company are calculated as follows:

		198B	198A
a.	Total liabilities	$114,200	$ 71,200
b.	Total owners' equity	315,800	311,800
c.	Total liabilities and owners' equity	$430,000	$383,000
	Creditors' equity (a ÷ c)	26.6%	18.6%
	Owners' equity (b ÷ c)	73.4%	81.4%

Creditors like to see a high proportion of owners' equity because owners' equity acts as a cushion in absorbing losses. The greater the equity of the owners in relation to liabilities, the greater the losses that can be absorbed by the owners before the creditors begin to lose.

From the creditors' standpoint a high percentage of owners' equity is desirable. However, if an enterprise can earn a return on borrowed capital that is in excess of the capital's cost, then a reasonable amount of creditors' equity is desirable from the owners' viewpoint.

Pledged plant assets to long-term liabilities

Companies commonly borrow by issuing a note or bonds secured by a mortgage on certain of their plant assets. The ratio of pledged plant assets to long-term debt is often calculated to measure the security granted to mortgage or bondholders by the pledged assets. This ratio is calculated by dividing the pledged assets' book value by the liabilities for which the assets are pledged. It is calculated for Anchor Supply Company as of the ends of 198A and 198B as follows:

		198B	198A
	Buildings, net	$176,800	$28,000
	Land...................................	50,000	20,000
a.	Book value of pledged plant assets	$226,800	$48,000
b.	Mortgage payable	$ 60,000	$10,000
	Ratio of pledged assets to secured liabilities *(a ÷ b)*	3.8 to 1	4.8 to 1

The usual rule-of-thumb minimum for this ratio is 2 to 1. However, the ratio needs careful interpretation because it is based on the *book value* of the pledged assets. Often book values bear little or no relation to the amount that would be received for the assets in a foreclosure or a liquidation. As a result, estimated liquidation values or foreclosure values are normally a better measure of the protection offered bond or mortgage holders by pledged assets. Also, the long-term earning ability of the company whose assets are pledged is usually more important to long-term creditors than the pledged assets' book value.

Times fixed interest charges earned

The number of times fixed interest charges were earned is often calculated to measure the security of the return offered to bondholders or a mortgage holder. The amount of income before the deduction of fixed interest charges and income taxes is available to pay the fixed interest charges. Consequently, the calculation is made by dividing income before fixed interest charges and income taxes by fixed interest charges. The result is the number of times fixed interest charges were earned. Often fixed interest charges are considered secure if the company consistently earns its fixed interest charges two or more times each year.

Rate of return on total assets employed

The return earned on total assets employed is a measure of management's performance. Assets are used to earn a profit, and management is responsible for the way in which they are used. Consequently, the return on assets employed is a measure of management's performance.

The return figure used in this calculation should be after-tax income plus interest expense. Interest expense is included because it is a return paid creditors for assets they have supplied. Likewise, if the amount of assets has fluctuated during the year, an average of the beginning- and end-of-the-year assets employed should be used.

The rates of return earned on the average total assets employed by Anchor Supply Company during 198A and 198B are calculated as follows:

		198B	198A
	Net income after taxes	$ 33,000	$ 32,600
	Add interest expense	2,300	1,000
a.	Net income plus interest expense	$ 35,300	$ 33,600
b.	Average total assets employed	$406,500	$380,000
	Rate of return on total assets employed (a ÷ b)	8.7%	8.8%

In the case of Anchor Supply Company the change in the rates is not too significant. It is also impossible to tell whether the returns are good or bad without some basis of comparison. The best comparison would be the returns earned by similar-size companies engaged in the same kind of business. A comparison could also be made with the returns earned by this company in previous years. Neither of these is available in this case.

Rate of return on common stockholders' equity

A primary reason for the operation of a corporation is to earn a net income for its common stockholders. The rate of return on the common stockholders' equity is a measure of the success achieved in this area. Usually an average of the beginning- and end-of-the-year equities is used in calculating the return. For Anchor Supply Company the 198A and 198B calculations are as follows:

		198B	198A
a.	Net income after taxes	$ 33,000	$ 32,600
b.	Average stockholders' equity	313,800	309,000
	Rate of return on stockholders' equity (a ÷ b)	10.5%	10.6%

Compare Anchor Supply Company's returns on stockholders' equity with its returns on total assets employed and note that the return on the stockholders' equity is greater in both years. The greater returns resulted from using borrowed money.

When there is preferred stock outstanding, the preferred dividend requirements must be subtracted from net income to arrive at the common stockholders' share of income to be used in this calculation.

Earnings per common share

Earnings per common share data are among the most commonly quoted figures on the financial pages of daily newspapers. Such data are used by investors in evaluating the past performance of a business, in projecting its future earnings, and in weighing investment opportunities. Because of the significance attached to earnings per share data by investors and others, the APB concluded that earnings per common share or net loss per common share data should be shown on the face of a published income statement.[1]

For corporations having only common stock outstanding, the amount of earnings per share is determined by dividing net income by the number of common shares outstanding. For example, Anchor Supply Company of previous illustrations earned $33,000 in 198B and it had 25,000 common shares outstanding. Consequently, the amount of its earnings per common share is calculated:

$$\frac{\text{Net income, \$33,000}}{\text{25,000 common shares}} = \text{\$1.32 per share}$$

Where there are also nonconvertible preferred shares outstanding, the year's preferred dividend requirement must be deducted from net income before dividing by the number of outstanding common shares. Also, if the number of common shares changed during the year, a weighted-average number of shares (weighted by the length of time each number of shares was outstanding) is used in the calculation.

Many corporations, like Anchor Supply Company, have simple capital structures consisting only of common stock and, perhaps, preferred stock that is not convertible into common stock. Other corporations have more complex capital structures which include preferred stocks and bonds that are convertible into common stock at the option of the owners. In the latter corporations, if conversion should occur, earnings per share would undoubtedly change due solely to the conversion. Recognizing this, the APB provided specific requirements in *Opinion No. 15* for calculating and reporting earnings per share for corporations

---

[1] APB, "Earnings per Share," *APB Opinion No. 15* (New York: AICPA, 1969), par. 12.

with complex capital structures. However, these requirements are so lengthy and involved that a discussion must be left to an advanced course.

Price-earnings ratio

Price-earnings ratios are commonly used in comparing investment opportunities. A price-earnings ratio is calculated by dividing market price per share by earnings per share. For example, if Anchor Supply Company's common stock sold at $12 per share at the end of 198B, the stock's end-of-the-year price-earnings ratio is calculated:

$$\frac{\text{Market price per share, \$12}}{\text{Earnings per share, \$1.32}} = 9.09$$

After the calculation is made, it may be said that the stock had a 9.1 price-earnings ratio at the end of 198B, or it may be said that approximately $9.10 was required at that time to buy $1 of the company's 198B earnings.

In comparing price-earnings ratios it must be remembered that such ratios vary from industry to industry. For example, in the steel industry a 9 or 10 price-earnings ratio is normal, while in a growth industry, such as electronics, 20 or 25 price-earnings ratios are common.

GLOSSARY

Accounts receivable turnover. An indication of how long it takes a company to collect its accounts, calculated by dividing net sales or credit sales by ending or average accounts receivable.

Acid-test ratio. The relation of quick assets, such as cash, notes receivable, accounts receivable, and marketable securities to current liabilities, calculated as quick assets divided by current liabilities.

Common-size comparative statements. Comparative financial statements in which each amount is expressed as a percentage of a base amount. In the balance sheet, total assets is usually selected as the base amount and is expressed as 100%. In the income statement, net sales is usually selected as the base amount.

Comparative statement. A financial statement with data for two or more successive years placed in columns side by side in order to better illustrate changes in the data.

Current ratio. The relation of a company's current assets to its current liabilities, that is, current assets divided by current liabilities.

Merchandise turnover. The number of times a company's average inventory is sold during an accounting period, calculated by dividing cost of goods sold by average merchandise inventory.

Price-earnings ratio. Market price per share of common stock divided by earnings per share.

Quick ratio. A synonym for acid-test ratio.

Rate of return on common stockholders' equity. Net income after taxes and dividends on preferred stock divided by average common stockholders' equity.

Rate of return on total assets employed. Net income after taxes, plus interest expense, expressed as a percentage of total assets employed during the period.

Times fixed charges earned. An indicator of a company's ability to satisfy fixed charges, calculated as net income before fixed charges and income taxes divided by fixed charges (e.g., interest).

QUESTIONS FOR CLASS DISCUSSION

1. Comparative balance sheets often have columns showing increases and decreases in both dollar amounts and percentages. Why is this so?
2. When trends are calculated and compared, what item trends should be compared with the trend of sales?
3. What is meant by "common-size" financial statements?
4. What items are assigned a value of 100% *(a)* on a common-size balance sheet and *(b)* on a common-size income statement?
5. Why is working capital given special attention in the process of analyzing balance sheets?
6. For the following transactions tell which increase working capital, which decrease working capital, and which have no effect on working capital:
   a. Collected accounts receivable.
   b. Borrowed money by giving a 90-day interest-bearing note.
   c. Declared a cash dividend.
   d. Paid a cash dividend previously declared.
   e. Sold plant assets at their book value.
   f. Sold merchandise at a profit.
7. List several factors that have an effect on working capital requirements.
8. A company has a 2 to 1 current ratio. List several reasons why this ratio may not be adequate.
9. State the significance of each of the following ratios and turnovers and tell how each is calculated:
   a. Current ratio.
   b. Acid-test ratio.
   c. Turnover of accounts receivable.
   d. Turnover of merchandise inventory.
   e. Rate of return on common stockholders' equity.
   f. Ratio of pledged plant assets to long-term liabilities.
10. How are days' sales uncollected calculated? What is the significance of the number of days' sales uncollected?
11. Why do creditors like to see a high proportion of owner equity?

12. What is the ratio of pledged plant assets to long-term liabilities supposed to measure? Why must this ratio be interpreted with care?
13. What does the rate of return on assets employed tell about management?
14. How are earnings per share calculated in a corporation having outstanding only common stock and preferred stock not convertible into common stock?
15. How is a price-earnings ratio calculated?

CLASS EXERCISES

Exercise 15–1

Where possible calculate percentages of increase and decrease for the following unrelated items. The parentheses indicate deficit items.

	198B	198A
Buildings, net	$75,000	$60,000
Investments	–0–	20,000
Notes payable	5,000	–0–
Retained earnings	(4,500)	15,000
Cash	12,000	(1,500)

Exercise 15–2

Calculate trend percentages for the following items and tell whether the situation shown by the trends is favorable or unfavorable.

	198A	198B	198C
Sales	$150,000	$169,500	$178,500
Merchandise inventory	30,000	36,000	39,600
Accounts receivable	18,000	23,040	24,300

Exercise 15–3

Express the following income statement information in common-size percentages and tell whether the situation shown is favorable or unfavorable.

MAPLE SALES, INC.
Comparative Income Statement
Years Ended June 30, 198A, and 198B

	198B	198A
Sales	$100,000	$90,000
Cost of goods sold	67,500	60,390
Gross profit from sales	$ 32,500	$29,610
Operating expenses	25,300	22,860
Net income	$ 7,200	$ 6,750

Exercise 15–4

The 198A statements of Agate, Inc., follow:

AGATE, INC.
Income Statement for Year Ended December 31, 198A

Sales		$365,000
Cost of goods sold:		
Merchandise inventory, January 1, 198A	$ 29,400	
Purchases	241,200	
Goods for sale	$270,600	
Merchandise inventory, December 31, 198A	30,600	
Cost of goods sold		240,000
Gross profit on sales		$125,000
Operating expenses		106,200
Operating income		$ 18,800
Interest expense		3,000
Income before taxes		$ 15,800
Income taxes		3,300
Net income		$ 12,500

AGATE, INC.
Balance Sheet, December 31, 198A

Cash	$ 6,500	Accounts payable	$ 20,000
Accounts receivable, net	22,500	Mortgate payable secured by	
Merchandise inventory	30,600	a lien on the plant assets ..	50,000
Prepaid expenses	400	Common stock $10 par value	100,000
Plant assets, net	140,000	Retained earnings	30,000
Total assets	$200,000	Total equities	$200,000

Required:

Calculate the following: *(a)* current ratio, *(b)* acid-test ratio, *(c)* days' sales uncollected, *(d)* merchandise turnover, *(e)* capital contribution of the owners expressed as a percent, *(f)* ratio of pledged plant assets to long-term liabilities, *(g)* return on total assets employed, *(h)* return on stockholders' equity, and *(i)* earnings per share. (Assume all sales were on credit, the stockholders' equity was $120,000 on January 1, 198A, and total assets has not fluctuated during the year.)

Exercise 15–5

Common-size and trend percentages for a company's sales, cost of goods sold, and expenses follow:

COMMON-SIZE PERCENTAGES				TREND PERCENTAGES			
	198A	198B	198C		198A	198B	198C
Sales	100	100	100	Sales	100	110	120
Cost of goods sold ..	68	67	65	Cost of goods sold ..	100	108	115
Expenses	22	24	27	Expenses	100	120	147

Required:

Present statistics to prove whether the company's net income increased, decreased, or remained unchanged during the three-year period.

PROBLEMS

Problem 15–1

The condensed statements of Apple Corporation follow. Calculate the following ratios and turnovers for 198B: (1) current ratio, (2) acid-test ratio, (3) days' sales uncollected, (4) accounts receivable turnover, (5) merchandise turnover, (6) earnings per share, (7) rate of return on total assets employed, (8) rate of return on stockholders' equity, (9) percent of capital contributed by owners, and (10) ratio of pledged plant assets to long-term liabilities (assume both building and equipment are mortgaged).

APPLE CORPORATION
Comparative Balance Sheets
December 31, 198A, and 198B

	198B	198A
Assets		
Cash	$ 6,000	$ 8,000
Accounts receivable, net	16,000	14,000
Merchandise inventory	32,000	28,000
Building and equipment, net	186,000	180,000
Total assets	$240,000	$230,000
Equities		
Current liabilities	$ 20,000	$ 15,000
Mortgage payable	80,000	85,000
Common stock, $10 par value	100,000	100,000
Retained earnings	40,000	30,000
Total equities	$240,000	$230,000

APPLE CORPORATION
Comparative Income Statements
Years Ended December 31, 198A and 198B

	198B	198A
Sales, all on credit	$200,000	$180,000
Cost of goods sold	120,000	109,000
Gross profit on sales	$ 80,000	$ 71,000
Operating expenses	49,000	45,000
Operating income	$ 31,000	$ 26,000
Interest expense	5,000	5,500
Income before taxes	$ 26,000	$ 20,500
Income taxes	6,000	5,500
Net income	$ 20,000	$ 15,000

Problem 15–2

The 198B and 198C statements of Oxbow Corporation follow:

OXBOW CORPORATION
Comparative Income Statements
Years Ended December 31, 198B, and 198C

	198C	198B
Sales	$900,000	$800,000
Cost of goods sold	559,200	488,500
Gross profit from sales	$340,800	$311,500
Operating expenses....................	$247,000	$226,000
Income before taxes	$ 93,800	$ 85,500
Income taxes.........................	46,900	42,750
Net income	$ 46,900	$ 42,750

OXBOW CORPORATION
Comparative Balance Sheets
December 31, 198B, and 198C

Assets	198C	198B
Cash	$ 24,000	$ 24,000
Accounts receivable	50,000	56,000
Merchandise inventory	84,000	64,000
Plant assets, net	167,000	168,000
Total assets	$325,000	$312,000

Liabilities and Capital		
Current liabilities.....................	$ 50,000	$ 50,000
Long-term liabilities	60,000	60,000
Common stock	150,000	150,000
Retained earnings	65,000	52,000
Total liabilities and capital	$325,000	$312,000

Required:

1. Express the income statement data in common-size percentages and calculate the current ratio, acid-test ratio, merchandise turnover, and days' sales uncollected for each year. Assume the January 1, 198A, inventory was $58,000.
2. Comment on the situation shown by your calculations.

Problem 15–3

The condensed 198A, 198B, and 198C statements of Doric, Inc., follow:

DORIC, INC.
Comparative Income Statements
Years Ended December 31, 198A, 198B, and 198C
(in thousands of dollars)

	198C	198B	198A
Sales	$13,000	$12,000	$10,000
Cost of goods sold	8,995	8,260	6,800
Gross profit on sales	$ 4,005	$ 3,740	$ 3,200
Selling expenses	$ 2,120	$ 1,970	$ 1,600
Administrative expenses	1,120	1,110	1,000
Interest expense	25		
Total expenses	$ 3,265	$ 3,080	$ 2,600
Income before taxes	$ 740	$ 660	$ 600
Income taxes	370	330	300
Net income	$ 370	$ 330	$ 300

DORIC, INC.
Comparative Balance Sheets
December 31, 198A, 198B, and 198C
(in thousands of dollars)

Assets	198C	198B	198A
Current assets	$ 750	$ 600	$ 800
Plant assets, net	4,000	3,520	3,200
Total assets	$4,750	$4,120	$4,000
Liabilities and Capital			
Current liabilities	$ 250	$ 295	$ 250
Long-term liabilities	500		
Common stock, $10 par value	2,500	2,500	2,500
Retained earnings	1,500	1,325	1,250
Total liabilities and capital	$4,750	$4,120	$4,000

Required:

1. Express the income statement items in common-size percentages.
2. Express the balance sheet items in trend percentages, using 198A as the base year.
3. Comment on the trends and relations shown by your calculations.

Problem 15–4

The condensed comparative statements of Zoom Corporation follow:

ZOOM CORPORATION
Comparative Income Statements
Years Ended December 31, 198A–8F
(in thousands of dollars)

	198A	198B	198C	198D	198E	198F
Sales	$500	$625	$735	$890	$930	$975
Cost of goods sold	350	441	511	637	672	714
Gross profit from sales	$150	$184	$224	$253	$258	$261
Operating expenses	100	124	146	181	190	202
Income before taxes	$ 50	$ 60	$ 78	$ 72	$ 68	$ 59

ZOOM CORPORATION
Comparative Balance Sheets
December 31, 198A–8F
(in thousands of dollars)

Assets	198A	198B	198C	198D	198E	198F
Cash	$ 20	$ 21	$ 19	$ 13	$ 11	$ 9
Accounts receivable, net	50	58	56	92	97	99
Merchandise inventory	100	106	112	186	194	204
Long-term investments	30	30	30			
Plant and equipment, net	300	297	306	465	468	462
Total assets	$500	$512	$523	$756	$770	$774

Liabilities and Capital	198A	198B	198C	198D	198E	198F
Current liabilities	$ 50	$ 53	$ 58	$ 96	$107	$114
Long-term liabilities	60	60	60	165	165	165
Common stock	250	250	250	300	300	300
Premium on common stock	20	20	20	45	45	45
Retained earnings	120	129	135	150	153	150
Total liabilities and capital . .	$500	$512	$523	$756	$770	$774

Required:

1. Express the data of the statements in trend percentages.
2. Analyze and comment on any situation shown in the statements.

Problem 15–5

A company had $250,000 of current assets, a 2½ to 1 current ratio, and a 1¼ to 1 acid-test ratio. It then completed these transactions:

a. Collected a $1,500 account receivable.
b. Sold for $35,000 a short-term investment carried on the books at its $25,000 cost.
c. Wrote off a $500 bad debt against the allowance for doubtful accounts.
d. Declared a $0.10 per share cash dividend on the 100,000 shares of $10 par value common stock.
e. Paid the cash dividend declared in transaction (d).
f. Borrowed $10,000 by issuing a 60-day, 6% note payable.

g. Declared a 5,000-share stock dividend. The stock was selling for $12 per share on the day of the declaration.
h. Distributed the stock dividend of transaction *(g)*.
i. Sold for $15,000 merchandise that cost $10,000.
j. Purchased $10,000 of merchandise on credit. The company uses a perpetual inventory system.

Required:

Prepare a three-column schedule showing the company's current ratio, acid-test ratio, and working capital after each transaction.

ALTERNATE PROBLEMS

Problem 15–1A

The condensed 198A financial statements of Castle, Inc., follow:

CASTLE, INC.
Balance Sheet, December 31, 198A

Assets		*Equities*	
Cash	$ 7,750	Accounts payable	$ 17,500
Accounts receivable, net ...	18,250	Federal income taxes payable ..	2,500
Merchandise inventory	38,500	Mortgage payable, secured by	
Prepaid expenses	1,500	a lien on land and building ..	40,000
Equipment, net	78,000	Common stock, $10 par value .	125,000
Building, net	84,000	Retained earnings	55,000
Land	12,000		
Total assets	$240,000	Total equities	$240,000

CASTLE, INC.
Income Statement for Year Ended December 31, 198A

Sales		$365,000
Cost of goods sold:		
Merchandise inventory, January 1, 198A	$ 41,500	
Purchases, net	257,000	
Goods for sale	$298,500	
Merchandise inventory, December 31, 198A	38,500	
Cost of goods sold		260,000
Gross profit on sales		$105,000
Operating expenses		75,500
Operating income..............................		$ 29,500
Interest expense		2,500
Income before taxes		$ 27,000
Federal income taxes		6,000
Net income.....................................		$ 21,000

Required:

Under the assumption the previous year's balance sheet showed total assets at $230,000 and stockholders' equity at $170,000, calculate the following: (1) current ratio, (2) acid-test ratio, (3) days' sales uncollected, (4) accounts receivable turnover, (5) merchandise turnover, (6) earnings per share, (7) rate of return on total assets employed, (8) rate of return on stockholders' equity, (9) percent of capital contributed by the owners, and (10) pledged plant assets to long-term liabilities.

Problem 15–2A

Following are data from the statements of two competing companies:

Data from the Current December 31 Balance Sheets

Assets	Company A	Company B
Cash	$ 8,000	$ 10,000
Notes receivable	3,500	4,000
Accounts receivable, net	32,000	44,000
Merchandise inventory	28,500	40,500
Prepaid expenses	1,500	1,000
Plant assets, net	139,500	165,500
Total assets	$213,000	$265,000

Liabilities and Capital		
Current liabilities	$ 30,000	$ 40,000
Long-term liabilities	50,000	50,000
Common stock, $10 par value	100,000	100,000
Retained carnings	33,000	75,000
Total liabilities and capital	$213,000	$265,000

Data from the Current Yearly Income Statements

	Company A	Company B
Sales	$288,000	$380,000
Cost of goods sold	191,700	254,600
Interest expense	3,000	3,000
Net Income	13,200	16,900

Beginning-of-the-Year Data

	Company A	Company B
Merchandise inventory	$ 25,500	$ 37,500
Total assets	207,000	255,000
Stockholders' equity	127,000	169,000

Required:

1. Calculate current ratios, acid-test ratios, merchandise turnovers, and days' sales uncollected for the two companies. Then state which company you think is the better short-term credit risk and why.
2. Calculate earnings per share, rate of return on total assets employed, and rate of return on stockholders' equity. Then under the assumption that each company's stock could be purchased at book value, state which company's stock you think is the better investment and why.

Problem 15–3A

The 198A, 198B, and 198C income statements of Webster Corporation carried the following information (in thousands of dollars):

	198C	198B	198A
Sales	$14,000	$12,000	$10,000
Cost of goods sold	10,150	8,580	7,000
Gross profit from sales	$ 3,850	$ 3,420	$ 3,000
Operating expenses	3,190	2,810	2,450
Income before taxes	$ 660	$ 610	$ 550
Income taxes	330	305	275
Net income	$ 330	$ 305	$ 275

Its balance sheets for the same period carried this information (in thousands of dollars):

Assets	198C	198B	198A
Current assets	$ 900	$ 700	$1,000
Plant and equipment	4,600	4,400	4,000
Total assets	$5,500	$5,100	$5,000

Liabilities and Capital			
Current liabilities	$ 360	$ 410	$ 400
Long-term liabilities	1,000	1,000	1,000
Common stock, $25 par value	2,800	2,500	2,500
Other contributed capital	260	200	200
Retained earnings	1,080	990	900
Total liabilities and capital	$5,500	$5,100	$5,000

Required:

1. Express the income statement items in common-size percentages.
2. Express the balance sheet items in trend percentages, using 198A as the base year.
3. Comment on the trends and relations shown by your calculations.

Problem 15–5A

A company had $120,000 of current assets, a 2.4 to 1 current ratio, and a 1.2 to 1 acid-test ratio before completing the following transactions:

a. Wrote off against the allowance for doubtful accounts an $800 uncollectible account receivable.
b. Sold for $5,000 a plant asset having a $6,000 book value.
c. Sold for $10,000 temporary investments that cost $15,000.
d. Sold for $15,000 merchandise that cost $10,000.
e. Borrowed $10,000 by giving the bank a 60-day note payable.
f. Declared a $0.50 per share dividend on the 10,000 outstanding shares of $10 par value common stock.
g. Paid the dividend declared in transaction (f).

h. Borrowed $20,000 by placing a 6%, 20-year mortgage on the plant.
i. Declared a 1,000-share common stock dividend on a day when the stock was selling at $12.50 per share.
j. Distributed the stock of the dividend declared in transaction (i).

Required:

Prepare a three-column schedule showing in columns the company's current ratio, acid-test ratio, and working capital after each of the transactions.

PROVOCATIVE PROBLEMS

Provocative problem 15–1
Companies A and B

Company A and Company B are competitors; both were organized ten years ago; and both have seen their sales increase tenfold during the ten-year period. However, the tenfold increase is not as good as it sounds because both companies' costs and selling prices have doubled during the same period. Nevertheless, the sales of both companies have and are increasing. Both offer the same credit terms; age their accounts receivable to allow for bad debts; and collect their accounts in about the same length of time. Actually about the only real difference in their accounting procedures is that Company A since its organization has used Fifo in costing its goods sold and Company B has used Lifo.

The current ratios of the two companies for the past four years were as follows:

	Company A	Company B
December 31, 198A	5.2 to 1	3.3 to 1
December 31, 198B	5.6 to 1	3.1 to 1
December 31, 198C	5.9 to 1	2.8 to 1
December 31, 198D	6.0 to 1	3.0 to 1

You are the loan officer of a bank, and both companies have come to your bank for 90-day loans. In addition to the current ratios, you note that Company B has turned its inventory more than two and one half times as fast as Company A in each of the last four years. You also discover that for each $10,000 of current liabilities the companies have the following amounts of inventory:

	Company A	Company B
December 31, 198A	$41,000	$21,000
December 31, 198B	47,000	20,000
December 31, 198C	50,000	18,000
December 31, 198D	52,000	18,000

Which company do you think is the better short-term credit risk? Back your opinion with computations showing why. Are the inventory turnovers of the two companies comparable? Explain. Which company seems to have the better inventory turnover?

Provocative problem 15–2
Jane Howe

Jane Howe is considering an investment in either Company O or Company P. Either company's stock can be purchased at book value, and she is undecided as to which is the better managed company and the better investment. Following are data from the financial statements of the two companies:

Data from the Current Year-End Balance Sheets

Assets	Company O	Company P
Cash	$ 12,000	$ 14,500
Accounts receivable, net	30,000	40,000
Merchandise inventory	44,000	54,800
Prepaid expenses	1,200	1,200
Plant and equipment, net	165,800	174,500
Total assets	$253,000	$285,000

Liabilities and Capital		
Current liabilities	$ 40,000	$ 50,000
Mortgage payable	50,000	50,000
Common stock, $10 par value	100,000	100,000
Retained earnings	63,000	85,000
Total liabilities and capital	$253,000	$285,000

Data from the Current Year's Income Statements

	Company O	Company P
Sales	$597,000	$696,000
Cost of goods sold	430,500	502,200
Gross profit on sales	$166,500	$193,800
Operating expenses	142,000	167,000
Operating income	$ 24,500	$ 26,800
Interest expense	3,000	3,500
Income before taxes	$ 21,500	$ 23,300
Income taxes	4,700	5,200
Net income	$ 16,800	$ 18,100

Beginning-of-the-Year Data

	Company O	Company P
Merchandise inventory	$ 38,000	$ 53,200
Total assets	247,000	277,000
Stockholders' equity	157,000	177,000

Prepare a report to Jane Howe stating which company you think is the better managed and which company's stock you think is the better investment. Back your report with any ratios, turnovers, and other analyses you think pertinent.

16

Accounting for price-level changes

After studying Chapter 16, you should be able to:

- Describe the effects of inflation on historical financial statements.
- Explain how price-level changes are measured.
- Tell how to construct both general and specific price-level indexes.
- Describe the use of price indexes in constant dollar accounting.
- Restate unit-of-money financial statements for general price-level changes.
- Explain how purchasing power gains and losses arise and how they are computed and integrated into constant dollar financial statements.
- State the differences between general price-level-adjusted costs and current values such as exit prices and current costs.
- Explain what current costs measure and the use of recoverable amounts in current cost accounting.
- Describe the reporting requirements of *FASB Statement No. 33.*
- Define or explain the words and phrases listed in the chapter Glossary.

Perhaps all accountants agree that conventional financial statements provide useful information for making economic decisions. However, many accountants also agree that conventional financial statements fail to adequately account for the impact of price-level changes. Usually, this means a failure to adequately account for the impact of inflation. Indeed, this failure of conventional financial statements may sometimes even make the statements misleading. That is, the statements may imply certain facts that are inconsistent with the real state of affairs. As a result, decision makers may be inclined to make decisions that are inconsistent with their objectives.

In what ways do conventional financial statements fail to account for inflation? The general problem is that transactions are recorded in terms of the historical number of dollars received or paid. These amounts are not adjusted even though subsequent price changes may dramatically change the purchasing power of the dollars received or paid. For example, Old Company purchased ten acres of land for $25,000. At the end of each accounting period thereafter, Old Company presented a balance sheet showing "Land, $25,000." Six years later, after inflation of 97% (12% per year, compounded for six years), New Company purchased ten acres of land that was adjacent and nearly identical to Old Company's land. New Company paid $49,250 for the land. In comparing the conventional balance sheets of the two companies, which own identical pieces of property, the following balances are observed:

	Balance Sheets	
	Old Company	New Company
Land......	$25,000	$49,250

Without knowing the details that underlie these balances, a statement reader is likely to conclude that New Company either has more land than does Old Company or that New Company's land is more valuable than is Old Company's. But, both companies own ten acres, which are identical in value. The entire difference between the prices paid by the two companies is explained by the 97% inflation between the two purchase dates. That is, $25,000 × 1.97 = $49,250.

The failure of conventional financial statements to adequately account for inflation also shows up in the income statement. For example, assume that in the previous example, machinery was purchased instead of land. Also, assume that the machinery of Old Company and New Company is identical except for age; it is being depreciated on a straight-line basis over a ten-year period, with no salvage value. As a result, the annual income statements of the two companies show the following:

Income Statements	Old Company	New Company
Depreciation expense, machinery	$2,500	$4,925

Although assets of equal value are being depreciated, the income statements show that New Company's depreciation expense is 97% higher than is Old Company's. And, if all other revenue and expense items are the same, Old Company will appear more profitable than New Company. This is inconsistent with the fact that both companies own the same machines that are subject to the same depreciation factors. Furthermore, although Old Company will appear more profitable, it must pay more income taxes due to the apparent extra profits. Old Company also may not recover the full replacement cost of its machinery through the sale of its product.

Some of the procedures used in conventional accounting tend to reduce the impact of price-level changes on the income statement. Lifo inventory pricing and accelerated depreciation are examples. However, these are only partial solutions, since they do not offset the impact on both the income statement and the balance sheet.

Because of these deficiencies in conventional accounting practices, accountants have devoted increasing attention to alternatives that make comprehensive adjustments for the effects of price-level changes. This chapter discusses the two that have received the greatest attention. The first alternative involves adjusting conventional financial statements for changes in the general level of prices. This is called *constant dollar accounting,* or *general price-level adjusted accounting,* or sometimes *GPLA accounting.* Later, consideration is given to another alternative, *current cost accounting.* This makes adjustments for changes in the specific prices of the specific assets owned by the company.

UNDERSTANDING PRICE-LEVEL CHANGES

In one way or another, all readers of this book have experienced the effects of inflation, which is a general increase in the prices paid for goods and services. Of course, the prices of specific items do not all change at the same rate. Even when most prices are rising, the prices of some goods or services may be falling. For example, consider the following prices of four different items:

Item	Price/unit in 1980	Price/unit in 1981	Percent change
A	$1.00	$1.30	+30
B	2.00	2.20	+10
C	1.50	1.80	+20
D	3.00	2.70	−10
Totals	$7.50	$8.00	

What can be said to describe these price changes? One possibility is to state the percentage change in the price per unit of each item (see above). This information is very useful for some purposes. But, it does not show the average effect or impact of the price changes that occurred. A better indication of the average effect would be to determine the average increase in the per unit prices of the four items. Thus: $8.00/$7.50 − 1.00 = 6.7\%$[1] average increase in per unit prices. However, even this average may fail to indicate the impact of the price changes on most individuals or businesses. It is a good indicator only if the typical individual or business purchased an equal number of units of each item. But what if these items are typically purchased in the following ratio? For each unit of A purchased, 2 units of B, 5 units of C, and 1 unit of D are purchased. With a different number of each item being purchased, the impact of changing prices must take into account the typical quantity of each item purchased. Hence, the average change in the price of the A, B, C, D "market basket" would be calculated as follows:

Item	Units purchased	1980 prices		Units purchased	1981 prices	
A	1 unit × $1.00 =	$ 1.00		1 unit × $1.30 =	$ 1.30	
B	2 units × $2.00 =	4.00		2 units × $2.20 =	4.40	
C	5 units × $1.50 =	7.50		5 units × $1.80 =	9.00	
D	1 unit × $3.00 =	3.00		1 unit × $2.70 =	2.70	
Totals		$15.50			$17.40	

Weighted-average price change = $17.40/$15.50 − 1.00 = 12%

It may now be said that the annual rate of inflation in the prices of these four items was 12%. Of course, not every individual and busi-

---

[1] Throughout this chapter amounts are rounded to the nearest $1/10$ percent or to the nearest full dollar.

ness will purchase these four items in exactly the same proportion of 1 unit of A, 2 units of B, 5 units of C, and 1 unit of D. As a consequence, the stated 12% inflation rate is only an approximation of the impact of price changes on each buyer. But if these proportions represent the typical buying pattern, the stated 12% inflation rate fairly reflects the inflationary impact on the average buyer.

CONSTRUCTION OF A PRICE INDEX

When the cost of purchasing a given market basket is determined for each of several periods, the results can be expressed as a *price index*. In constructing a price index, one year is arbitrarily selected as the "base" year. The cost of purchasing the market basket in that year is then assigned a value of 100. For example, suppose the cost of purchasing the A, B, C, D market basket in each year is:

Year	Cost
1975	$ 9.00
1976	11.00
1977	10.25
1978	12.00
1979	13.00
1980	15.50
1981	17.40

If 1978 is selected as the base year, then the $12 cost for 1978 is assigned a value of 100. The index number for each of the other years is then calculated and expressed as a percent of the base year's cost. For example, the index number for 1977 is 85, or ($10.25/$12.00 $\times$ 100 = 85). The index numbers for the remaining years are calculated in the same way. The entire price index for the years 1975 through 1981 is presented in Illustration 16–1.

Having constructed a price index for the A, B, C, D market basket, it is possible to make comparative statements about the cost of purchasing these items in various years. For example, it may be said that the price level in 1981 was 45% (145/100) higher than it was in 1978, the price level in 1981 was 34% (145/108) higher than it was in 1979,

Year	Calculations of price level	Price index
1975	($9.00/$12.00) $\times$ 100 =	75
1976	($11.00/$12.00) $\times$ 100 =	92
1977	($10.25/$12.00) $\times$ 100 =	85
1978	($12.00/$12.00) $\times$ 100 =	100
1979	($13.00/$12.00) $\times$ 100 =	108
1980	($15.50/$12.00) $\times$ 100 =	129
1981	($17.40/$12.00) $\times$ 100 =	145

Illustration 16–1

and 12% (145/129) higher than it was in 1980. Stated another way, it may be said that \$1 in 1981 would purchase the same amount of A, B, C, D as would \$0.69 in 1978 (100/145 = 0.69). Also, \$1 in 1981 would purchase the same amount of A, B, C, D as would \$0.52 in 1975 (75/145 = 0.52).

USING PRICE INDEX NUMBERS

In accounting, the most important use of a price index is to restate dollar amounts of cost that were paid in earlier years into the current price level. In other words, a specific dollar amount of cost in a previous year can be restated in terms of the comparable number of dollars that would be incurred if the cost were paid with dollars of the current amount of purchasing power. For example, suppose that \$1,000 were paid in 1977 to purchase items A, B, C, D. Stated in terms of 1981 prices, that 1977 cost is \$1,000 × (145/85) = \$1,706. As another example, if \$1,500 were paid for A, B, C, D in 1978, that 1978 cost, restated in terms of 1981 prices, is \$1,500 × (145/100) = \$2,175.

Note that the 1978 cost of \$1,500 correctly states the number of monetary units (dollars) expended for items A, B, C, D in 1978. Also, the 1977 cost of \$1,000 correctly states the units of money expended in 1977. And, these two costs can be added together to determine the cost for the two years, stated in terms of the historical number of monetary units (units of money) expended. However, in a very important way, the 1977 monetary units do not mean the same thing as do the 1978 monetary units. A dollar (one monetary unit) in 1977 represented a different amount of purchasing power than did a dollar in 1978. Both of these dollars represent different amounts of purchasing power than a dollar in 1981. If one intends to communicate the amount of purchasing power expended or incurred, the historical number of monetary units must be adjusted so that they are stated in terms of dollars with the same amount of purchasing power. For example, the total amount of cost incurred during 1977 and 1978 could be stated in terms of the purchasing power of 1978 dollars, or stated in terms of the purchasing power of 1981 dollars. These calculations are presented in Illustration 16–2.

Year cost was incurred	Monetary units expended	Adjustment to 1978 dollars	Historical cost stated in 1978 dollars	Adjustment to 1981 dollars	Historical cost stated in 1981 dollars
1977	\$1,000	1,000 × (100/85)	\$1,176	1,176 × (145/100)	\$1,706*
1978	1,500	—	1,500	1,500 × (145/100)	2,175
Total cost	\$2,500		\$2,676		\$3,881

* Raised \$1 to correct for rounding. An alternative calculation is \$1,000 × (145/85) = \$1,706.

Illustration 16–2

SPECIFIC VERSUS GENERAL PRICE-LEVEL INDEXES

Price changes and price-level indexes can be calculated for narrow groups of commodities or services, such as housing construction material costs; or for broader groups of items, such as all construction costs; or for very broad groups of items, such as all items produced in the economy. A *specific price-level index*, as for housing construction materials, indicates the changing purchasing power of a dollar spent for items in that specific category, that is, to pay for housing construction materials. A *general price-level index*, as for all items produced in the economy, indicates the changing purchasing power of a dollar, in general. Two general price-level indexes are the Consumer Price Index for all urban consumers (prepared by the Bureau of Labor Statistics) and the Gross National Product (GNP) Implicit Price Deflator (prepared by the U.S. Department of Commerce).

USING PRICE INDEXES IN ACCOUNTING

There are at least two important accounting systems that use price indexes to develop comprehensive financial statements. Both are major alternatives to the conventional accounting system in general use in the United States. One alternative, called current cost accounting, uses specific price-level indexes (along with appraisals and other means) to develop statements that report assets and expenses in terms of the current costs to acquire those assets or services. Additional consideration is given to this alternative later in this chapter.

The other alternative is called general price-level-adjusted (GPLA) accounting or constant dollar accounting. It uses general price-level indexes to restate the conventional, unit-of-money financial statements into dollar amounts that represent current, general purchasing power. Most of the proposals for making constant dollar (GPLA) financial statements have suggested using the GNP Implicit Price Deflator because it is the broadest index of general price-level changes.[2] However, the FASB's recent *Statement No. 33* requires use of the Consumers' Price Index for all urban consumers. (CPI).[3] The following sections of this chapter explain how a general price index, such as the CPI, is used to prepare general price-level-adjusted (GPLA) financial statements.

---

[2] See, for example, APB "Financial Statements Restated for General Price Level Changes," *APB Statement No. 3* (New York: AICPA, 1969), par. 30; and also FASB, "Financial Reporting in Units of General Purchasing Power," *Proposed Statement of Financial Accounting Standards, Exposure Draft* (Stamford, Conn., 1974), par. 35.

[3] FASB, "Financial Reporting and Changing Prices," *Statement of Financial Accounting Standards No. 33* (Stamford, Conn., 1979), par. 39. Copyright © by the Financial Accounting Standards Board, High Ridge Park, Stamford, Conn. 06905, U.S.A. Quoted (or excerpted) with permission. Copies of the complete document are available from the FASB.

CONSTANT DOLLAR (GPLA) ACCOUNTING

Conventional financial statements disclose revenues, expenses, assets, liabilities, and owners' equity in terms of the historical monetary units exchanged when the transactions occurred. As such, they are sometimes referred to as *unit-of-money* or *nominal dollar financial statements*. This is intended to emphasize the difference between conventional statements and constant dollar or general price-level-adjusted (GPLA) statements. In the latter, the dollar amounts shown are adjusted for changes in the general purchasing power of the dollar.

Students should understand clearly that the same principles for determining depreciation expense, cost of goods sold, accruals of revenue, and so forth, apply to both unit-of-money statements and GPLA statements. The same generally accepted accounting principles apply to both. The only difference between the two is that GPLA statements reflect adjustments for general price-level changes; unit-of-money statements do not. As a matter of fact, GPLA financial statements are prepared by adjusting the amounts appearing on the unit-of-money financial statements.

CONSTANT DOLLAR (GPLA) ACCOUNTING FOR ASSETS

The effect of general price-level changes on investments in assets depends on the nature of the assets involved. Some assets, called *monetary assets*, represent money or claims to receive a fixed amount of money. The number of dollars owned or to be received is fixed in amount, regardless of changes that may occur in the purchasing power of the dollar. Examples of monetary assets are cash, accounts receivable, notes receivable, and investments in bonds.

Because the amount of money owned or to be received from a monetary asset does not change with price-level changes, the (GPLA) balance sheet amount of a monetary asset is not adjusted for general price-level changes. For example, if $200 in cash was owned at the end of 1980 and was held throughout 1981, during which time the general price-level index increased from 150 to 168,[4] the cash reported on both the December 31, 1980, and 1981, general price-level-adjusted (GPLA) balance sheets is $200. However, although no balance sheet adjustment is made, it is important to note that the investment in such a monetary asset held during a period of inflation does result in a loss of purchasing power. The $200 would buy less at the end of

---

[4] Observe that these index numbers, and those used in the remaining sections of the chapter, are different from those that were calculated on page 552. Since the earlier calculations were based on only four items (A, B, C, D), that index would not be appropriate to illustrate a general price index, which must reflect the prices of many, many items.

1981 than it would have at the end of 1980. This reduction in purchasing power constitutes a loss. The amount of the loss is calculated as follows:

Monetary asset balance on December 31, 1980	$ 200
Adjustment to reflect an equal amount of purchasing power on December 31, 1981: $200 × 168/150	$ 224
Amount of monetary asset balance on December 31, 1981	(200)
General purchasing power loss	$ 24

Nonmonetary assets are defined as all assets other than monetary assets. The prices at which nonmonetary assets may be bought and sold tend to increase or decrease over time as the general price level increases or decreases. Consequently, as the general price level changes, investments in nonmonetary assets tend to retain the amounts of purchasing power originally invested. As a result, the reported amounts of nonmonetary assets on GPLA balance sheets are adjusted to reflect changes in the price level that have occurred since the nonmonetary assets were acquired.

For example, say $200 was invested in land (a nonmonetary asset) at the end of 1980, and the investment was held throughout 1981. During this time the general price index increased from 150 to 168. The GPLA balance sheets would disclose the following amounts:

Asset	December 31, 1980, GPLA balance sheet	Adjustment to December 31, 1981 price level	December 31, 1981, GPLA balance sheet
Land	$200	$200 × (168/150)	$224

The $224 shown as the investment in land at the end of 1981 has the same amount of general purchasing power as did $200 at the end of 1980. Thus, no change in general purchasing power was recognized from holding the land.

CONSTANT DOLLAR (GPLA) ACCOUNTING FOR LIABILITIES AND STOCKHOLDERS' EQUITY

The effect of general price-level changes on liabilities depends on the nature of the liability. Most liabilities are monetary items, but stockholders' equity and a few liabilities are nonmonetary items.[5] *Monetary*

---

[5] Depending on its nature, preferred stock may be treated as a monetary item. If so, it is an exception to the general rule that stockholders' equity items are nonmonetary items.

liabilities represent fixed amounts that are owed, with the number of dollars to be paid not changing regardless of changes in the general price level.

Since monetary liabilities are unchanged in amounts owed even when price levels change, monetary liabilities are not adjusted for price-level changes. However, a company with monetary liabilities outstanding during a period of general price-level change will experience a general purchasing power gain or loss. Assume, for example, that a note payable for $300 was outstanding on December 31, 1980, and remained outstanding throughout 1981. During that time the general price index increased from 150 to 168. On the GPLA balance sheets for December 31, 1980, and 1981, the note payable would be reported at $300. The general purchasing power gain or loss is calculated as follows:

Monetary liability balance on December 31, 1980	$ 300
Adjustment to reflect an equal amount of purchasing power on December 31, 1981: $300 × (168/150)	$ 336
Amount of monetary liability balance on December 31, 1981	(300)
General purchasing power gain	$ 36

The $336 at the end of 1981 has the same amount of general purchasing power as $300 had at the end of 1980. Since the company can pay the note with $300, the $36 difference is a gain in general purchasing power realized by the firm. Alternatively, if the general price index had decreased during 1981, the monetary liability would have resulted in a general purchasing power loss.

Nonmonetary liabilities are obligations that are not fixed in amount. They therefore tend to change with changes in the general price level. For example, product warranties may require that a manufacturer pay for repairs and replacements for a specified period of time after the product is sold. The amount of money required to make the repairs or replacements tends to change with changes in the general price level. Consequently, there is no purchasing power gain or loss associated with such warranties. Further, the balance sheet amount of such a nonmonetary liability must be adjusted to reflect changes in the general price index which occur after the liability comes into existence. Stockholders' equity items, with the possible exception of preferred stock, are also nonmonetary items. Hence, they also must be adjusted for changes in the general price index.

Illustration 16–3 summarizes the impact of general price-level changes on monetary items and nonmonetary items. The illustration indicates what adjustments must be made in preparing a GPLA balance sheet and what purchasing power gains and losses must be recognized on a GPLA income statement.

Financial statement item	When the general price level rises (inflation)		When the general price level falls (deflation)	
	Balance sheet adjustment required	Income statement gain or loss	Balance sheet adjustment required	Income statement gain or loss
Monetary assets	No	Loss	No	Gain
Nonmonetary assets	Yes	None	Yes	None
Monetary liabilities	No	Gain	No	Loss
Nonmonetary equities and liabilities*	Yes	None	Yes	None

* However, a nonmonetary liability may require an additional adjustment to assure that the balance sheet shows the current estimated amount to satisfy the liability.

Illustration 16–3

PREPARING COMPREHENSIVE, CONSTANT DOLLAR (GPLA) FINANCIAL STATEMENTS

The previous discussion of price indexes and of GPLA accounting for assets, liabilities, and stockholders' equity provides a basis for understanding the procedures used in preparing comprehensive GPLA financial statements. In the following discussion, examples of these procedures are based on the unit-of-money (nominal dollar) financial statements for Delivery Service Company (Illustration 16–4).

Delivery Service Company
Balance Sheets
For Years Ended December 31, 1980, and 1981

	1980	1981
Cash	$ 8,000	$30,000
Land (acquired December 31, 1980)	12,000	12,000
Delivery equipment (acquired January 1, 1980)	25,000	25,000
Accumulated depreciation	(4,000)	(8,000)
Total assets	$41,000	$59,000
Note payable (issued July 1, 1980)	$ 5,000	$ 5,000
Capital stock (issued January 1, 1980)	30,000	30,000
Retained earnings	6,000	24,000
Total...................................	$41,000	$59,000

Delivery Service Company
Income Statement
For Year Ended December 31, 1981

Delivery revenues	$100,000
Depreciation expense	(4,000)
Other expenses..............................	(78,000)
Net income	$ 18,000

Illustration 16–4

Delivery Service Company was organized on January 1, 1980. Of the original $30,000 invested in the company, $25,000 was used to buy delivery trucks. The trucks are being depreciated over five years on a straight-line basis. They have a $5,000 salvage value. Since the company was organized, the general price index has changed as follows:

Date	Price index
December 1979	130
June 1980 (also average for 1980)	140
December 1980	150
Average for 1980	160
December 1981	168

Delivery Service Company's cash balance increased from $8,000 to $30,000 during 1981 and is explained as follows:

Beginning cash balance	$ 8,000
Revenues, earned uniformly throughout the year	100,000
Expenses, paid uniformly throughout the year	(78,000)
Ending cash balance	$ 30,000

Restatement of the balance sheet

In preparing a GPLA balance sheet, the account balances are first classified as being monetary items or nonmonetary items. Since monetary items do not change regardless of changes in the price level, each monetary item is placed on the GPLA balance sheet without adjustment. Each nonmonetary item, on the other hand, must be adjusted for the price-level changes occurring since the original transactions that gave rise to the item.

The restatement of Delivery Service Company's balance sheet is presented in Illustration 16–5. Observe that the monetary items "Cash" and "Note payable" are transferred without adjustment from the unit-of-money column to the price-level-adjusted column. All of the remaining items are nonmonetary and are adjusted. The land was purchased on December 31, 1980, when the price level was 150.[6] Thus, the historical cost of the land is restated from December 1980 dollars to December 1981 dollars (price index 168) as follows: $12,000 × (168/150) = $13,440. The delivery equipment was purchased on January 1, 1980, at the same time the capital stock was issued. Therefore, "De-

---

[6] Normally, price index numbers are determined for a period of time, such as one quarter or one month, and are not determined for a specific point in time, such as December 31. For example, the CPI for all urban consumers is prepared for each month. Thus, the index number for December is used to approximate the price level on December 31.

Delivery Service Company
Restatement of Balance Sheet
December 31, 1981

	Unit-of-money balances	Restatement factor from price index	GPLA Amounts
Cash	$30,000	—	$ 30,000
Land	12,000	168/150	13,440
Delivery equipment	25,000	168/130	32,308
Less accumulated depreciation	(8,000)	168/130	(10,338)
Total assets	$59,000		$ 65,410
Note payable	$ 5,000	—	$ 5,000
Capital stock	30,000	168/130	38,769
Retained earnings	24,000	(See discussion)	21,641
Total liabilities and stockholders' equity	$59,000		$ 65,410

Illustration 16–5

livery equipment," "Accumulated depreciation," and "Capital stock" are restated from January 1980 prices (index number 130) to December 1981 prices by applying the restatement factor of 168/130.

The retained earnings balance of $24,000 cannot be adjusted in a single step because this balance resulted from more than one transaction. However, the correct, adjusted amount of retained earnings can be determined simply by "plugging" the necessary amount to make the balance sheet balance, as follows:

Total assets, adjusted		$ 65,410
Less: Note payable	$ 5,000	
Capital stock	38,769	(43,769)
Necessary retained earnings		$ 21,641

The process of confirming this restated retained earnings amount is explained later in the chapter.

Students should recognize that Delivery Service Company is a simplified illustration; only two of its balance sheet amounts (cash and retained earnings) resulted from more than one transaction. In a more complex case, most account balances would reflect several past transactions that took place at different points in time. In such a situation, the adjustment procedures are more detailed. For example, suppose that the $12,000 balance in the Land account resulted from three different purchases of land, as follows:

January 1, 1980, purchased land for	$ 3,000
July 1, 1980, purchased land for	4,000
December 31, 1980, purchased land for	5,000
Total	$12,000

Under this assumption the following adjustments would be required to prepare the GPLA balance sheet, as of December 31, 1981:

	Unit-of-money balances	Adjustment factor from price index	Restated to December 31, 1981, general price level
Land purchased on:			
January 1, 1980	$ 3,000	168/130	$ 3,877
July 1, 1980	4,000	168/140	4,800
December 31, 1980	5,000	168/150	5,600
Total	$12,000		$14,277

Restatement of the income statement

The general procedure followed in preparing a GPLA income statement is that every individual revenue and expense transaction must be restated from the price index level on the date of the transaction to the price index level at the end of the year. The restated amounts are then entered on the GPLA income statement along with the purchasing power gain or loss that resulted from holding or owing monetary items.

The calculations to restate the 1981 income statement of Delivery Service Company from units of money to the price-level-adjusted amounts are presented in Illustration 16–6.

As previously mentioned, Delivery Service Company's revenues were received and its other expenses were incurred in many transactions that occurred throughout the year. To be completely precise, each of these individual transactions would have to be separately restated. However, these revenues and expenses occurred in a nearly uniform pattern throughout the year. Restating the total revenue and the total other expenses from the average price level during the year (160) to the end-of-the-year price level (168) is therefore an acceptable approximation procedure.

The unit-of-money amount of depreciation expense on delivery trucks ($4,000) was determined by taking 20% of the $25,000 — $5,000 cost to be depreciated. Since this cost was incurred on Janu-

Delivery Service Company
Restatement of Income Statement
For Year Ended December 31, 1981

	Unit-of-money amounts	Restatement factor from price index	GPLA amounts
Delivery service revenues	$100,000	168/160	$105,000
Depreciation expense	(4,000)	168/130	(5,169)
Other expenses	(78,000)	168/160	(81,900)
	$ 18,000		$ 17,931
Purchasing power loss (from Illustration 16–7)			(1,460)
Net income	$ 18,000		$ 16,471

Illustration 16–6

ary 1, 1980, the restatement of depreciation expense must be based on the price index for that date (130) and on the index number for the end of 1981 (168).

Purchasing power gain or loss

As was explained, the purchasing power gain or loss experienced by Delivery Service Company (shown in Illustration 16–6) stems from the amount of monetary assets held and monetary liabilities owed by the company during the year. During 1981, cash was the only monetary asset held by the company; the only monetary liability was a $5,000 note payable. The purchasing power gain or loss for these items is calculated in Illustration 16–7.

Note in Illustration 16–7 that the purchasing power loss from holding cash must take into account the changes in the cash balance that occurred during the year. First, the beginning cash balance of $8,000 is restated as an equivalent amount of general purchasing power at the end of the year. Since the December 1981 price index was 168 and the December 1980 price index was 150, the balance is restated as follows: $8,000 × 168/150 = $8,960. Next, each cash change is adjusted from the price level at the time the change occurred to the price level at the end of the year. In the example, cash receipts from revenues occurred uniformly throughout the year. Therefore, the average price index number for the year (160) is used to approximate the price level in effect when the revenues were received. The $100,000 cash received from revenues during the year is restated to the equivalent general purchasing power at the year's end, as follows: $100,000 × 168/160 = $105,000. Cash payments for expenses were also made uniformly throughout the year, so they are restated using the same index numbers. In other words, the $78,000 of cash expenses

Delivery Service Company
Calculation of Purchasing Power Gain or Loss
For Year Ended December 31, 1981

	Unit-of-money amounts	Restatement factor from price index	Restated to December 31, 1981	Gain or loss
Cash:				
Beginning balance	$ 8,000	168/150	$ 8,960	
Delivery revenue receipts	100,000	168/150	105,000	
Payments for expenses	(78,000)	168/160	(81,900)	
Ending balance, adjusted			$ 32,060	
Ending balance, actual	$ 30,000		(30,000)	
Purchasing power loss				$2,060
Note payable: beginning balance	$ 5,000	168/150	$ 5,600	
Ending balance, actual	$ 5,000		(5,000)	
Purchasing power gain				(600)
Net purchasing power loss				$1,460

Illustration 16–7

are restated as follows: $78,000 \times 168/160 = \$81,900$. With the initial cash balance and the cash changes restated into end-of-the-year purchasing power, the adjusted end-of-the-year purchasing power for cash is $32,060. Since the actual ending cash balance is only $30,000, the $2,060 difference represents a loss of general purchasing power.

The $5,000 note payable was issued on July 1, 1980, when the price index was 140. Nevertheless, the purchasing power gain associated with this monetary liability is calculated by adjusting the $5,000 from the beginning-of-1981 price level (index number 168). Since the calculation is being made for the purpose of preparing a 1981 GPLA income statement, only the purchasing power gain arising from inflation during 1981 should be included. The gain associated with the price index change from 140 to 150 occurred during 1980, and would have been included in the GPLA income statement for 1980.

Adjusting the retained earnings balance

The December 31, 1981, adjusted retained earnings balance was previously determined by "plugging" the amount necessary to make liabilities plus stockholders' equity equal to total assets (page 560). Alternatively, if a GPLA balance sheet for December 31, 1980, was available, the adjusted retained earnings balance on that date could be restated to the December 31, 1981, price level. Then the GPLA net income for 1981 could be added to determine GPLA retained earnings at December 31, 1981. For example, had GPLA financial statements been prepared for 1980, the $6,000 retained earnings balance in units of money (see Illustration 16–4) would have been adjusted to a December 31, 1980, general price-level-adjusted amount of $4,616.[7] With this additional information, the adjusted retained earnings balance for December 31, 1981, is calculated as follows:

	Restated to December 31, 1980, general price level	Factor from price index	Restated to December 31, 1981, general price level
Retained earnings, December 31, 1980	$4,616	168/150	$ 5,170
GPLA net income for 1981 (see Illustration 16–6)			16,471
Dividends declared during 1981			–0–
Retained earnings, December 31, 1981			$21,641

CONSTANT DOLLAR (GPLA) ACCOUNTING AND CURRENT VALUES

Early in this chapter, the fact that prices do not all change at the same rate was discussed. Indeed, when the general price level is rising, some specific prices may be falling. If this were not so, if prices all changed at the same rate, then constant dollar accounting would report current values on the financial statements. For example, suppose that a company purchased land for $50,000 on January 1, 1980, when the general price index was 130. Then the price level increased until December 1981, when the price index was 168. A GPLA balance sheet for this company on December 31, 1981, would report the land at $50,000 × 168/130 = $64,615. If all prices increased at the same rate during that period, the price of the land would have increased from $50,000 to $64,615, and the company's GPLA balance sheet would coincidentally disclose the land at its current value.

However, since all prices do not change at the same rate, the current value of the land may differ substantially from the GPLA amount of $64,615. For example, assume that the company obtained an appraisal of the land and determined that its current value on December 31, 1981, was $80,000. The difference between the original purchase price of $50,000 and the current value of $80,000 can be explained as follows:

[7] Notice that the $4,616 price-level-adjusted retained earnings on December 31, 1980, is smaller than the $6,000 units-of-money amount. This decrease was caused by the same factors that caused the adjusted net income for 1981 to be less than the units-of-money net income (see Illustration 16–6).

Unrealized holding gain	$80,000	$64,615	= $15,385
Adjustment for general price-level			
increase	$64,615	$50,000	= 14,615
			$30,000

In that case, the GPLA balance sheet would report land at $64,615, which is $15,385 ($80,000 − $64,615) less than its current value. This illustrates a very important fact concerning constant dollar (GPLA) accounting; it is not a form of current value accounting. Rather, GPLA accounting restates original transaction prices into equivalent amounts of current, *general* purchasing power. Only if current, *specific* purchasing power were the basis of valuation would the balance sheet display current values.

CURRENT VALUE ACCOUNTING

Constant dollar (GPLA) accounting often has been proposed as a way of improving accounting information. Proponents of GPLA accounting argue that conventional, unit-of-money financial statements have questionable relevance to decision makers. Conventional statements may even be misleading in a world of persistent, long-run inflation. Since GPLA accounting adjusts for general price-level changes, its proponents believe that GPLA financial statements provide a more meaningful portrayal of a company's past operations and financial position. And, they argue, GPLA accounting is sufficiently objective to allow its practical application without damaging the credibility of financial statements.

Other accountants argue that even GPLA accounting fails to communicate to statement readers the economic values of most relevance. They would design financial statements so that each item in the statements is measured in terms of current value.

Some arguments for current value accounting conclude that the current liquidation price or "exit value" of an item is the most appropriate basis of valuation for financial statements. However, other arguments, which appear to be more widely supported, conclude that the price to replace an item, its *current cost*, is the best basis of financial statement valuation.

CURRENT COST ACCOUNTING

Current costs on the income statement

In the current cost approach to accounting, the reported amount of each expense should be the number of dollars that would be required, at the time the expense is incurred, to acquire the resources consumed. For example, assume that the annual sales of a company included an item that was sold in May for $1,500 and the item had been acquired on January 1 for $500. Also, suppose that in May, at the time of the sale, the cost to replace this item was $700. Then the annual current cost income statement would show sales of $1,500 less cost of goods sold of $700. To state this idea more generally, when an asset is acquired and then held for a time before it expires, the historical cost of the asset likely will differ from its current cost at the time it expires. Current cost accounting requires that the reported amount of expense be measured at the time the asset expires.

The result of measuring expenses in terms of current costs is that revenue is matched with the current (at the time of the sale) cost of the resources that were used to earn the revenue. Thus, operating profit is not positive unless revenues are sufficient to replace all of the resources that were consumed in the process of producing those revenues. The operating profit figure is therefore thought to be an important (and improved) basis for evaluating the effectiveness of operating activities.

Current costs on the balance sheet

On the balance sheet, current cost accounting requires that assets be reported at the amounts that would have to be paid to purchase them as of the balance sheet date. Similarly, liabilities should be reported at the amounts that would have to be paid to satisfy the liabilities as of the balance sheet date. Note that this valuation basis is similar to GPLA accounting in that a distinction exists between monetary and nonmonetary assets and liabilities. Monetary assets and liabilities are fixed in amount regardless of price-level changes. Therefore, monetary assets need not be adjusted in amount. But all of the nonmonetary items must be evaluated at each balance sheet date to determine the best approximation of current cost.

A little reflection on the variety of assets reported on balance sheets will confirm the presence of many difficulties in obtaining reliable estimates of current costs. In some cases, specific price indexes may provide the most reliable source of current cost information. In other cases, where an asset is not new and has been partially depreciated, its current cost may be estimated by determining the cost to acquire a new asset of like nature. Depreciation on the old asset is then based on the current cost of the new asset. Clearly, the accountant's professional judgment is an important factor in developing current cost data.

FASB REQUIREMENTS FOR CONSTANT DOLLAR AND CURRENT COST INFORMATION

In October, 1979, the FASB issued *Statement No. 33,* which contains reporting requirements for both constant dollar and current cost information. These requirements are effective for financial statements issued after December 24, 1979, but with a one-year delay of the current cost requirements if a reporting company has difficulty implementing the requirements more quickly.[8] The requirements apply only to large companies with assets of more than $1 billion or inventories plus property, plant, and equipment (before deducting depreciation) of more than $125 million.[9]

Statement No. 33 does not affect the conventional financial statements; only supplemental information is required. The supplemental information to be presented includes:[10]

a. Income from continuing operations[11] adjusted for general price-level changes.

b. The general purchasing power gain or loss.

c. Income from continuing operations on a current cost basis.

d. Current cost of inventory at the end of the year.

e. Current cost of property, plant, and equipment at the end of the year.

f. The increase or decrease in the current cost of inventory, property, plant, and equipment, net of general price-level changes.

g. A five-year summary of selected financial data.

Examples of the required disclosures are presented in Illustrations 16–8 and 16–9. Compare the requirements listed as items a through f (above) with the information shown in Illustration 16–8. Each of the required items is disclosed.

Observe in Illustration 16–8 that the only restated income statement items are Cost of goods sold and Depreciation and amortization expense. These are the only income statement items (plus depletion expense, if any) which must be restated to meet the minimum FASB requirements. Net sales, Other operating expense, Interest expense, and Provision for income taxes do not have to be restated. These latter items may well have been affected by inflation. And the FASB would *permit* companies to adjust such items. But the Board does not require it.

Note that the general purchasing power gain or loss is called "gain from decline in purchasing power of net amounts owed." The FASB decided not to include this item in the calculation of income (loss) from continuing operations; instead, it is shown separately.

The five-year summary of financial data is shown in Illustration 16–

---

[8] *FASB Statement No. 33*, op. cit., par. 67–69.

[9] Ibid., par. 23.

[10] Ibid., par. 29–37.

[11] Income from continuing operations excludes the effects of accounting changes, extraordinary items, and income or loss from operations that are being discontinued. Detailed discussions of these items are left to a more advanced accounting course.

Statement of Income from Continuing Operations
Adjusted for Changing Prices
For the Year Ended December 31, 1980
(in 000s of dollars)

	As reported in the primary statements	Adjusted for general inflation	Adjusted for changes in specific prices (current costs)
Net sales and other operating revenues	$253,000	$253,000	$253,000
Cost of goods sold	197,000	204,384	205,408
Depreciation and amortization expense	10,000	14,130	19,500
Other operating expense	20,835	20,835	20,835
Interest expense	7,165	7,165	7,165
Provision for income taxes..................	9,000	9,000	9,000
	244,000	255,514	261,908
Income (loss) from continuing operations	$ 9,000	$ (2,514)	$ (8,908)
Gain from decline in purchasing power of net amounts owed.........................		$ 7,729	$ 7,729
Increase in specific prices (current cost) of inventories and property, plant, and equipment held during the year*			$ 24,608
Effect of increase in general price level			18,959
Excess of increase in specific prices over increase in the general price level			$ 5,649

* At December 31, 1980, current cost of inventory was $65,700 and current cost of property, plant, and equipment, net of accumulated depreciation was $85,100.
Source: *FASB Statement No. 33,* Appendix A, Schedule B, page 33.

Illustration 16–8

9. Observe that the constant cost and current cost information is shown for the years 1979 and 1980 only. This is because the requirements of *FASB Statement No. 33* apply only to financial statements issued after December 24, 1979.

Using recoverable amounts that are lower than current cost

In general, "current cost" is the cost that would be required to currently acquire (or replace) an asset or service. Current cost accounting involves reporting assets and expenses in terms of their current costs. However, the FASB recognizes an important exception to this general description of current cost accounting. That exception involves the use of recoverable amounts.

In the case of an asset about to be sold, the recoverable amount is its net realizable value. In other words, recoverable amount is the asset's expected sales price less related costs to sell. If an asset is to be used rather than sold, recoverable amount is the present value of future cash flows expected from using the asset. A recoverable amount

**Five-Year Comparison of Selected
Supplementary Financial Data Adjusted for Effects of Changing Prices**
(in 000s of average 1980 dollars)

	Years ended December 31,				
	1976	*1977*	*1978*	*1979*	*1980*
Net sales and other operating revenues.....................	265,000	235,000	240,000	237,063	253,000
Historical cost information adjusted for general inflation					
Income (loss) from continuing operations				(2,761)	(2,514)
Income (loss) from continuing operations per common share........................				$ (1.91)	$ (1.68)
Net assets at year-end				55,518	57,733
Current cost information					
Income (loss) from continuing operations				(4,125)	(8,908)
Income (loss) from continuing operations per common share........................				$ (2.75)	$ (5.94)
Excess of increase in specific prices over increase in the general price level				2,292	5,649
Net assets at year-end				79,996	81,466
Gain from decline in purchasing power of net amounts owed...............				7,027	7,729
Cash dividends declared per common share	$ 2.59	$ 2.43	$ 2.26	$ 2.16	$ 2.00
Market price per common share at year-end	$ 32	$ 31	$ 43	$ 39	$ 35
Average consumer price index	170.5	181.5	195.4	205.0	220.9

Source: *FASB Statement No. 33*, Appendix A, Schedule B, Page 34.

Illustration 16–9

is reported instead of current cost whenever the recoverable amount appears to be materially and permanently lower than current cost. Both the asset and the expense associated with using it (or selling it) should be measured in terms of the recoverable amount.[12]

The reason for using recoverable amounts emphasizes the value of an asset to its owner. The idea is that an asset should not be reported at an amount that is larger than its value to its owner. If the recoverable amount of an asset is less than its current cost, a business is not likely to replace it. A business would not be willing to pay more for an asset than it could expect to recover from using or selling the asset. Hence, the value of the asset to the business can be no higher than

[12] *FASB Statement No. 33*, op. cit., par. 62–63.

the recoverable amount. When value to the business is less than current cost, it is believed that current cost is not relevant to an analysis of the business. Following this line of reasoning, *Statement No. 33* calls for reporting current cost or recoverable amount, if lower.

Using recoverable amounts lower than historical cost in constant dollars

In constant dollar accounting, assets and their associated expenses are generally reported in terms of historical cost, adjusted for general price-level changes. However, the FASB requirements for constant dollar accounting involve the same "recoverable amount" exception as is applied in the case of current cost accounting. In other words, recoverable amounts must be substituted for historical costs in constant dollars if the recoverable amounts are lower. The Board argues that using recoverable amounts in such cases avoids overstating the "worth" of assets.[13]

THE MOMENTUM TOWARD MORE COMPREHENSIVE PRICE-LEVEL ACCOUNTING

The question of whether procedures of accounting for price-level changes should be implemented has been debated and discussed for many years. Granted, inflation (and taxes) has caused the expanded use of certain procedures such as Lifo. But the first significant requirements to report inflation-adjusted information were not imposed until 1976. At that time, the Securities and Exchange Commission (SEC) began to require certain large companies to report supplemental information on a replacement cost basis. They were required to estimate the

. . . current replacement cost of inventories and productive capacity at the end of each fiscal year for which a balance sheet is required and the approximate amount of cost of sales and depreciation based on replacement cost for the two most recent full fiscal years.[14]

To see an actual example of the disclosures required by the SEC, turn to the Appendix after this chapter which contains the 1978 financial statements of Masonite Corporation. Footnote 17 to those statements (pages 597 and 598) contains the replacement cost disclosures.

The SEC's replacement cost disclosure requirements generated many complaints and public statements of opposition by corporate managements. Time will tell whether the FASB's requirements are

---

[13] Ibid., par. 62, 195.

[14] Securities and Exchange Commission, *Accounting Series Release No. 190* (Washington, D.C., 1976).

more or less acceptable. Presumably, the SEC will withdraw its 1976 requirements and support those specified by the FASB.

The SEC's action was limited to large companies, and the required information was obviously much less than a complete set of financial statements prepared on a replacement cost basis. Nevertheless, the SEC action represented a major break with the U.S. tradition of relying totally on unit-of-money financial statements.

The recent FASB requirements constitute another major step toward improved accounting for price-level changes. While still limited to large companies and still substantially less than complete financial statements, they involve both constant dollar and current cost information, with important inclusions of income statement information. Whether or not current cost accounting and/or constant dollar accounting will eventually be required in most financial statements remains to be seen. No doubt, conventional, unit-of-money financial statements will continue to represent the primary basis of U.S. accounting in the near future. But a basic shift to one or the other inflation accounting alternative is a distinct possibility. Both constant dollar accounting and current cost accounting are being used in some countries. The strength of the calls for expanded usage of them in the United States will probably depend on how much future inflation as well as specific price changes undermine the perceived relevance of existing reporting methods.

GLOSSARY

Constant dollar accounting. Synonym for *general price-level adjusted accounting.*

Current value accounting. An accounting system that provides financial statements in which current values are reported; different versions of current value are possible, for example, current replacement costs or current exit values.

General price-level-adjusted (GPLA) accounting. An accounting system that adjusts unit-of-money financial statements for changes in the general purchasing power of the dollar. Also called *constant dollar accounting.*

General price-level index. A measure of the changing purchasing power of a dollar in general; measures the price changes for a broad market basket that includes a large variety of goods and services, for example, the Gross National Product Implicit Price Deflator or the Consumers Price Index for all urban consumers.

General purchasing power gain or loss. The gain or loss that results from holding monetary assets and/or owing monetary liabilities during a period in which the general price level changes.

Monetary assets. Money or claims to receive a fixed amount of money.

Monetary liabilities. Fixed amounts which are owed, with the number of dollars to be paid fixed in amount and not changing regardless of changes in the general price level.

Price index. A measure of the changes in prices of a particular market basket of goods and/or services.

Current cost. On the income statement, the numbers of dollars that would be required, at the time the expense is incurred, to acquire the resources consumed. On the balance sheet, the amounts that would have to be paid to replace the assets or satisfy the liabilities as of the balance sheet date.

Current cost accounting. An accounting system that uses specific price-level indexes (and other means) to develop financial statements that report items such as assets and expenses in terms of the current costs to acquire or replace those assets or services.

Specific price-level index. An indicator of the changing purchasing power of a dollar spent for items in a specific category; includes a much more narrow range of goods and services than does a general price index.

Unit-of-money financial statements. Conventional financial statements which disclose revenues, expenses, assets, liabilities, and owners' equity in terms of the historical monetary units exchanged at the time the transactions occurred.

QUESTIONS FOR CLASS DISCUSSION

1. Some people argue that conventional financial statements fail to adequately account for inflation. What is the general problem with conventional financial statements that generates this argument?
2. Are there any procedures used in conventional accounting that offset the effects of inflation on financial statements? Give some examples.
3. What is the fundamental difference in the price-level adjustments made under current cost accounting and under constant dollar accounting?
4. Explain the difference between an "average change in per unit prices" and a "weighted-average change in per unit prices."
5. What is the significance of the "base" year in constructing a price index? How is the base year chosen?
6. For accounting purposes, what is the most important use of a price index?
7. What is the difference between a specific price-level index and a general price-level index?
8. What is meant by "unit-of-money" financial statements?
9. Define "monetary assets."
10. Explain the meaning of "nonmonetary assets."
11. Define "monetary liabilities" and "nonmonetary liabilities." Give examples of both.
12. If the monetary assets held by a firm exceed its monetary liabilities

throughout a period in which prices are rising, which should be recorded on a GPLA income statement—a purchasing power gain or loss? What if monetary liabilities exceed monetary assets during a period in which prices are falling?

13. If accountants preferred to display current values in the financial statements, would they use constant dollar accounting or current cost accounting? Are there any other alternatives?

14. Describe the meaning of "operating profit" under a current cost accounting system.

15. "The distinction between monetary assets and nonmonetary assets is just as important for current cost accounting as it is for general price-level-adjusted accounting." Is this statement true? Why?

16. *FASB Statement No. 33* requires several specific disclosures of constant dollar items and current cost items. List the general disclosure requirements of *FASB Statement No. 33*.

CLASS EXERCISES

Exercise 16–1

Market basket No. 1 consists of 2 units of A, 5 units of B, and 3 units of D. Market basket No. 2 consists of 3 units of A, 2 units of B, and 4 units of C. The per unit prices of each item during 198A and during 198B are as follows:

Item	198A price per unit	198B price per unit
A	$1.50	$2.00
B	3.00	3.30
C	2.00	1.88
D	4.00	4.60

Required:

Compute the annual rate of inflation for market basket No. 1 and for market basket No. 2.

Exercise 16–2

The following total prices of a specified market basket were calculated for each of the years 198A through 198F:

Year	Total price
198A	$250
198B	400
198C	320
198D	480
198E	600
198F	640

Required:

1. Using 198D as the base year, prepare a price index for the six-year period.
2. Convert the index from a 198D base year to a 198F base year.

Exercise 16–3

Franklin Company's plant and equipment consisted of equipment purchased during 198A for $100,000, land purchased during 198C for $30,000, and a building purchased during 198D for $215,000. The general price index during these and later years was as follows:

198A	80
198B	95
198C	112
198D	125
198E	140
198F	154
198G	168

Required:

1. Assuming the above price index adequately represents end-of-the-year price levels, calculate the amount of each cost that would be shown on a GPLA balance sheet for *(a)* December 31, 198E, and *(b)* December 31, 198G. Ignore any accumulated depreciation.
2. Would the GPLA income statement for 198G disclose any purchasing power gain or loss as a consequence of holding the above assets? If so, how much?

Exercise 16–4

Classify the following items as monetary or nonmonetary.

1. Cash.
2. Investment in U.S. Government bonds.
3. Retained earnings.
4. Product warranties liability.
5. Accounts receivable.
6. Goodwill.
7. Salaries payable.
8. Common stock.
9. Prepaid fire insurance.
10. Common stock subscribed.
11. Delivery equipment.
12. Merchandise.
13. Accounts payable.
14. Patents.
15. Trademarks.
16. Unearned subscriptions revenue.

Exercise 16–5

The monetary items owned and owed by the J. Fields Company include cash, accounts payable, and a note payable. Calculate the general purchasing power gain or loss incurred by the company in 198B, given the following information:

Time period	Price index
December 198A	116
Average during 198B	125
December 198B	145

a. The balance in the Cash account on December 31, 198A, was $4,400. Cash sales were made uniformly throughout the year and amounted to $13,000. Payments on accounts payable were also made uniformly during the year and amounted to $6,400. Other expenses amounting to $3,000 were paid in cash and were evenly distributed during the year.

b. Accounts payable amounted to $800 on December 31, 198A. Credit purchases of merchandise amounting to $8,000 were spread evenly throughout the year, and $6,400 in cash was paid to accounts payable creditors.

c. A note payable of $5,000 was issued in June 198A when the price index was 110.

PROBLEMS

Problem 16–1

The costs of purchasing a common "market basket" in each of several years are as follows:

Year	Cost of market basket
198A	$18,000
198B....................	15,000
198C	21,000
198D	25,500
198E	27,000
198F....................	30,000
198G	33,000
198H	36,000

Required:

1. Construct a price index using 198F as the base year.
2. Using the index constructed in 1, what was the percent increase in prices from 198F to 198H?
3. Using the index constructed in 1, how many dollars in 198H does it take to have the same purchasing power as $1 in 198B?
4. Using the index constructed in 1, if $10,000 were invested in land during

198A, and $15,000 were invested in land during 198B, what would be reported as the total land investment on a GPLA balance sheet prepared in 198E? What would your answer be if the investments were in U.S. long-term bonds rather than in land?

Problem 16–2

Western Produce Company purchased equipment for $480,000 on January 4, 198B. The equipment was expected to last six years and have no salvage value; straight-line depreciation was to be used. The equipment was sold on December 31, 198D, for $340,000. End-of-the-year general price index numbers during this period of time were as follows:

198A 100
198B 125
198C 150
198D 175

Required:

1. What should be presented for the equipment and accumulated depreciation on a GPLA balance sheet dated December 31, 198B?
2. How much depreciation expense should be shown on the GPLA income statement for 198C?
3. How much depreciation expense should be shown on the GPLA income statement for 198D?
4. How much gain on the sale of equipment would be reported on the conventional, unit-of-money income statement for 198D?
5. After adjusting the equipment's cost and accumulated depreciation to the end-of-198D price level, how much gain in (loss of) general purchasing power was realized by the sale of the equipment?

Problem 16–3

The Laurleen Transit Company's only monetary asset or liability during 198D was cash, which changed during the year as follows:

Beginning balance	$ 3,500
Revenues received evenly throughout the year	25,000
Payments of expenses (spread evenly throughout the year)	(10,000)
Dividends declared and paid early in January 198D	(1,500)
Dividends declared and paid late in December 198D	(4,500)
Ending balance	$12,500

The unit-of-money income statement for 198D appeared as follows:

Sales		$25,000
Cash expenses	$10,000	
Depreciation expense, equipment	4,000	
Amortization expense, patents	3,000	
Total expenses		(17,000)
Net income		$ 8,000

The depreciation expense refers to equipment purchased in December, 198A, and the amortization expense refers to patents acquired in December, 198B. General price index numbers covering the periods of time mentioned above are as follows:

December 198A 120.0
December 198B 135.0
December 198C 150.0
December 198D 180.0
Average for 198D 160.0

Required:

1. Calculate the general purchasing power gain or loss experienced by Laurleen Transit Company in 198D.
2. Prepare a schedule that restates the income statement for 198D from units of money to GPLA amounts.

Problem 16–4

DeShazo Company's unit-of-money income statement for 198B and balance sheets for December 31, 198A, and December 31, 198B, are given below:

DESHAZO COMPANY
Income Statement for Year Ended December 31, 198B

Sales revenue		$250,000
Depreciation expense	$ 20,000	
Other expenses	200,000	220,000
Net Income		$ 30,000

DESHAZO COMPANY
Comparative Balance Sheets
December 31, 198A, and 198B

Assets	*198A*	*198B*
Cash	$ 60,000	$ 90,000
Accounts receivable	40,000	70,000
Equipment (net of depreciation)	95,000	75,000
Total assets	$195,000	$235,000

Liabilities and Stockholders' Equity		
Notes payable	$ 40,000	$ 50,000
Capital stock	100,000	100,000
Retained earnings	55,000	85,000
Total liabilities and stockholders' equity	$195,000	$235,000

Selected numbers from a general price-level index are as follows:

December 198A 75
Average during 198B 78
August 198B 80
December 198B 84

The increase in notes payable during 198B occurred on August 20, and the funds derived from the increase in notes payable were used to increase the cash balance. DeShazo Company purchased the equipment at a time when the general price index was 60. Revenue from sales was earned evenly throughout the year and was debited to Accounts Receivable. Cash receipts from receivables ($220,000) were also distributed evenly throughout the year, and expenses other than depreciation were paid in cash evenly throughout the year.

Required:

1. Calculate the purchasing power gain or loss incurred by DeShazo Company during 198B.
2. Prepare a general price-level-adjusted income statement for 198B.

Problem 16–5

Assume the same facts as were presented in Problem 16–4. In addition, DeShazo Company was organized at a time when the price index was 60. All of the capital stock ($100,000) was issued at that time.

Required:

1. Based on the above information and the data provided in Problem 16–4, prepare a GPLA balance sheet for DeShazo Company on December 31, 198B. (The retained earnings balance may be determined simply by "plugging" in the amount that is necessary to make the balance sheet balance.)
2. On DeShazo Company's GPLA balance sheet on December 31, 198A, retained earnings was $53,750. Also, assume that DeShazo Company reported a GPLA net income for 198B of $14,800. Present a calculation that confirms the retained earnings balance as it is reported on the GPLA balance sheet for December 31, 198B.

Problem 16–6

The December 31, 198B, and December 31, 198C, comparative balance sheets of Frost Company and its 198C income statement are presented below:

FROST COMPANY
Comparative Balance Sheets
December 31, 198B, and 198C

Assets	198B	198C
Cash	$15,000	$ 27,000
Accounts receivable	20,000	30,000
Inventory	7,000	9,000
Machinery	35,000	35,000
Accumulated depreciation	(5,000)	(10,000)
Investment in bonds of ABC Co.	25,000	25,000
Total assets	$97,000	$116,000

Liabilities and Stockholders' Equity

Accounts payable	$ 8,000	$ 10,000
Notes payable	5,000	5,000
Common stock	65,000	65,000
Retained earnings	19,000	36,000
Total liabilities and stockholders' equity ..	$97,000	$116,000

FROST COMPANY
Income Statement for Year Ended December 31, 198C

Sales		$80,000
Cost of goods sold:		
Beginning inventory	$ 7,000	
Purchases	40,000	
Total available merchandise	$47,000	
Ending inventory	9,000	38,000
Gross profit		42,000
Depreciation expense	$ 5,000	
Other expenses	18,000	23,000
Net income		$19,000

Additional information regarding Frost Company:

1. All sales are on credit and recorded to Accounts Receivable. Cash collections of Accounts Receivable occurred evenly throughout the year.
2. All merchandise purchases were credited to Accounts Payable and cash payments of Accounts Payable occurred evenly throughout the year. The beginning inventory was acquired when the price index was 112.
3. Other expenses ($18,000) were paid in cash evenly throughout the year.
4. Dividends of $2,000 were paid to stockholders in June 198C.
5. The machinery was acquired in January 198A. The Investment in Bonds of ABC Company was acquired on January 1, 198B. The outstanding stock was issued on January 1, 198A.
6. Sales and purchases of merchandise occurred evenly throughout the year.
7. The changes during the year in Cash, Accounts Payable, and Accounts Receivable accounts are as follows:

Cash

Beginning balance	15,000	Payments of accounts	38,000
Receipts from customers	70,000	Other expenses	18,000
		Dividend payments	2,000

Accounts Payable

Cash payments	38,000	Beginning balance	8,000
		Merchandise purchases	40,000

Accounts Receivable

| Beginning balance | 20,000 | Cash receipts | 70,000 |
| Credit sales | 80,000 | | |

Selected index numbers from a general price-level index are the following:

	General price index
January 198A	80
December 198A	100
December 198B........................	112
June 198C (also average for 198C)	125
December 198C	140

Required:

1. Calculate the purchasing power gain or loss to be reported on the GPLA income statement for 198C.
2. Prepare the GPLA income statement for 198C.
3. Prepare a GPLA balance sheet as of December 31, 198C. (Retained earnings may be determined by "plugging" in the amount necessary to make the balance sheet balance.)

ALTERNATE PROBLEMS

Problem 16–1A

The costs of purchasing a common "market basket" in each of several years are as follows:

Year	Cost of market basket
198A	$36,000
198B	31,500
198C	42,750
198D	45,000
198E	54,000
198F	58,500
198G	63,000
198H	60,750

Required:

1. Construct a price index using 198D as the base year.
2. Using the index constructed in 1, what was the percent increase in prices from 198E to 198H?
3. Using the index constructed in 1, how many dollars in 198G does it take to have the same purchasing power as $1 in 198D?
4. Using the index constructed in 1, if $16,000 were invested in land during 198A and $20,000 were invested in land during 198D, what would be reported as the total land investment on a GPLA balance sheet prepared

in 198G? What would your answer be if the investments were in corporate bonds (purchased at par) rather than in land?

Problem 16–2A

Clendinning Company purchased machinery for $300,000 on January 2, 198B. The machinery was expected to last five years and have no salvage value; straight-line depreciation was to be used. The machinery was sold on December 30, 198E, for $125,000. End-of-the-year general price index numbers during this period of time were the following:

198A.............	80
198B.............	96
198C.............	120
198D	112
198E.............	132

Required:

1. What should be presented for the machinery and accumulated depreciation on a GPLA balance sheet dated December 31, 198C?
2. How much depreciation expense should be shown on the GPLA income statement for 198D?
3. How much depreciation expense should be shown on the GPLA income statement for 198E?
4. How much gain on the sale of machinery would be reported on the conventional, unit-of-money income statement for 198E?
5. After adjusting the machinery's cost and accumulated depreciation to the end-of-198E price level, how much gain in (loss of) general purchasing power was realized by the sale of the machinery?

Problem 16–3A

The conventional, unit-of-money income statement of Jerry Hunt Enterprises for 198F appears as follows:

Sales....................................		$40,000
Cash expenses	$18,000	
Depreciation expense, building..........	7,000	
Amortization expense, trademark	6,000	
Total expenses		(31,000)
Net income		$ 9,000

Cash was the only monetary item held by the company during 198F, and the changes that occurred in the Cash account during the year were as follows:

Beginning balance	$10,000
Revenues received uniformly during the year	40,000
Payment of dividend on January 3, 198F	(5,000)
Payment of expenses evenly throughout the year	(18,000)
Purchase of land on December 28, 198F	(20,000)
Ending balance	$ 7,000

The only depreciable asset belonging to Jerry Hunt Enterprises is a building that was purchased early in January 198B. The trademark owned by the company was purchased in late December 198C. General price index numbers covering the periods of time mentioned above are as follows:

December 198A	80.0
December 198B.............	95.0
December 198C	105.0
December 198D	110.0
December 198E	108.0
December 198F.............	120.0
Average for 198F	112.0

Required:

1. Calculate the general purchasing power gain or loss experienced by Jerry Hunt Enterprises in 198F.
2. Prepare a schedule that restates the income statement for 198F from units of money to GPLA amounts.

Problem 16–4A

The directors of Cooke Company have expressed an interest in general price-level-adjusted financial statements and the concepts of purchasing power gains and losses. The price index in December 198A was 135, and in December 198B it was 146. The average price index during 198B was 140.

The unit-of-money financial statements for Cooke Company are presented below. The increase in notes payable during 198B occurred on May 15, at which time the reported price index was 138. The funds derived from the increase in notes payable were used to increase the cash balance. Cooke Company purchased the machinery several years ago when the price index was 100.

COOKE COMPANY
Comparative Balance Sheets
December 31, 198A, and 198B

Assets	198A	198B
Cash	$ 40,000	$100,000
Accounts receivable	75,000	75,000
Machinery (net of depreciation)	60,000	54,000
Total assets	$175,000	$229,000
Liabilities and Stockholders' Equity		
Notes payable	$ 25,000	$ 35,000
Capital stock	100,000	100,000
Retained earnings...............................	50,000	94,000
Total liabilities and stockholders' equity	$175,000	$229,000

COOKE COMPANY

Income Statement for Year Ended December 31, 198B

Sales revenue		$150,000
Depreciation expense	$ 6,000	
Other expenses	100,000	106,000
Net income		$ 44,000

Required:

1. Calculate the purchasing power gain or loss incurred by Cooke Company during 198B. You should assume that sales revenues were received in cash evenly throughout the year and that expenses other than depreciation were paid in cash evenly throughout the year.
2. Prepare a general price-level-adjusted income statement for 198B.

Problem 16–5A

Cooke Company, for which data were presented in Problem 16–4A, was organized at a time when the general price index was 100. All of the $100,000 capital stock was issued at that time.

Required:

1. Based on the above information and the data provided in Problem 16–4A, prepare a GPLA balance sheet for Cooke Company as of December 31, 198B. (The retained earnings balance may be determined simply by "plugging" in the amount that is necessary to make the balance sheet balance.)
2. On Cooke Company's GPLA balance sheet on December 31, 198A, retained earnings was reported as $36,000. Assume also that GPLA net income for 198B was $33,907. Present a calculation that confirms the retained earnings balance as it is reported on the GPLA balance sheet for December 31, 198B.

PROVOCATIVE PROBLEMS

Provocative problem 16–1
Sutter Company

Sutter Company has often been willing to consider new, innovative ways of reporting to its stockholders. For example, it has presented supplemental GPLA financial statements in its annual reports. The GPLA balance sheets of Sutter Company for December 31, 198A, and 198B, were as follows:

SUTTER COMPANY
GPLA Balance Sheets

Assets	As presented on December 31, 198B	As presented on December 31, 198A
Cash	$ 12,000	$ 5,000
Accounts receivable	20,000	10,000
Notes receivable	5,000	—
Inventory	6,429	3,250
Equipment	47,727	41,364
Accumulated depreciation	(13,636)	(5,909)
Land	37,987	23,636
Total assets	$115,507	$77,341

Liabilities and Stockholders' Equity		
Accounts payable	$ 17,000	$ 3,500
Notes payable	9,000	2,500
Common stock	68,182	59,091
Retained earnings	21,325	12,250
Total liabilities and stockholders' equity	$115,507	$77,341

A new member of Sutter Company's board of directors has expressed interest in the relationship between GPLA statements and unit-of-money statements. The board member understands that GPLA statements are derived from unit-of-money statements, but wonders if this process can be reversed. Specifically, you are asked to show how the GPLA balance sheets for December 31, 198A, and 198B could be restated back into unit-of-money statements.

Additional information:

1. The outstanding stock was issued in January 198A, and the company's equipment was purchased at that time. The equipment has no salvage value and is being depreciated over seven years.
2. The note receivable was acquired on June 30, 198B.
3. Notes payable consists of two notes, one for $2,500 which was issued on January 1, 198A, and the other for $6,500 which was issued on January 1, 198B.
4. The land account includes two parcels, one of which was acquired for $20,000 on January 1, 198A. The remaining parcel was acquired in June 198B.
5. Selected numbers from a general price-level index are:

January 198A	110
June 198A (also average for 198A)	120
December 198A	130
June 198B (also average for 198B)	140
December 198B	150

6. The inventory at the end of each year was acquired evenly throughout that year.

Provocative problem 16–2
Wilkins Development Company

Wilkins Development Company purchased a plot of land in 198A when the general price index was 98. The land cost $350,000 and was zoned for commercial use. In 198E the general price index is 128. However, a specific price index for commercial property in the general area of the land in question has risen from 90 in 198A to 138 in 198E.

Wilkins Development Company has no intention of building on the property. It is being held only as an investment and will eventually be sold. Some of the employees of Wilkins Development Company have been arguing over the matter of how the land should be presented in the balance sheet at the close of 198E and also over the amount of real economic benefit the company will have obtained from the investment if the land were to be sold immediately. Prepare an analysis which recognizes the alternative balance sheet valuation possibilities and which will help resolve the dispute.

appendix
Masonite Corporation
1978 Financial Statements

Report of Independent Public Accountants

To the Stockholders and Board of Directors of MASONITE CORPORATION:

We have examined the consolidated balance sheets of Masonite Corporation (a Delaware Corporation) and subsidiaries as of August 31, 1978 and August 31, 1977, and the consolidated statements of income, retained earnings and changes in financial position for the years then ended. Our examination was made in accordance with generally accepted auditing standards, and accordingly included such tests of the accounting records and such other auditing procedures as we considered necessary in the circumstances.

In our opinion, the accompanying consolidated financial statements present fairly the financial position of Masonite Corporation and subsidiaries as of August 31, 1978 and August 31, 1977, and the results of their operations and changes in their financial position for the years then ended, in conformity with generally accepted accounting principles applied on a consistent basis after giving retroactive effect to the change (with which we concur) in the method of accounting for certain lease transactions which had been entered into prior to January 1, 1977, as explained in Note 2 to the financial statements.

ARTHUR ANDERSEN & CO.

Chicago, Illinois,
October 12, 1978.

Consolidated Statements of Income and Retained Earnings

MASONITE CORPORATION and subsidiary companies

	Year Ended August 31	
	1978	1977
STATEMENT OF INCOME		
Net sales	$529,024,000	$450,081,000
Cost of sales (Note 4)	406,224,000	359,664,000
Selling, administrative, and research expenses	49,295,000	45,793,000
Income from operations	$ 73,505,000	$ 44,624,000
Other income (expense):		
Income from sale of timber	$ 4,703,000	$ 4,467,000
Income from oil operations, net	1,692,000	1,885,000
Income (loss) from foreign affiliates (Note 9)	879,000	(39,000)
Interest, net	1,443,000	(583,000)
Other, net	(1,333,000)	3,652,000
Income before income taxes	$ 80,889,000	$ 54,006,000
Provision for income taxes:		
Federal		
Current	$ 29,219,000	$ 15,993,000
Deferred	2,448,000	2,294,000
State	4,500,000	3,250,000
Deferred investment credit, net	233,000	1,669,000
Total income taxes (Note 15)	$ 36,400,000	$ 23,206,000
Net income	$ 44,489,000	$ 30,800,000
Per share	$ 2.73	$ 1.84
STATEMENT OF RETAINED EARNINGS		
Balance at beginning of year	$176,701,000	$156,011,000
Net income	44,489,000	30,800,000
Cash dividends declared ($.71 per share in 1978 and $.62 in 1977)	(11,489,000)	(10,110,000)
Balance at end of year (includes $7,613,000 and $6,734,000 of undistributed retained earnings of unconsolidated foreign affiliates at August 31, 1978 and 1977, respectively)	$209,701,000	$176,701,000

The accompanying notes are an integral part of these financial statements.

Consolidated Balance Sheets

MASONITE CORPORATION and subsidiary companies

	August 31	
	1978	1977
ASSETS		
Current Assets:		
Cash (Note 10)	$ 5,713,000	$ 2,309,000
Marketable securities, at cost (substantially market)	29,134,000	9,134,000
Receivables, less allowances of $1,665,000 in 1978 and		
$900,000 in 1977 (Note 14)	71,687,000	64,800,000
Inventories (Note 4)	50,966,000	53,547,000
Prepaid expenses	2,257,000	1,208,000
Total current assets	$159,757,000	$130,998,000
Property, Plant, and Equipment, at cost (Notes 5, 11 and 12):		
Land, timber, and roadways	$ 44,345,000	$ 42,168,000
Buildings	58,091,000	58,360,000
Machinery and equipment	287,473,000	282,488,000
	$389,909,000	$383,016,000
Less-Accumulated depreciation and depletion	203,404,000	192,390,000
	$186,505,000	$190,626,000
Investment in Foreign Affiliates (Note 9)	$ 10,628,000	$ 9,749,000
Other Assets, principally prepayments on cutting contracts	$ 7,419,000	$ 7,711,000
	$364,309,000	$339,084,000
LIABILITIES AND STOCKHOLDERS' EQUITY		
Current Liabilities:		
Current maturities of long-term debt (Notes 11 and 12)	$ 1,871,000	$ 3,409,000
Accounts payable	9,023,000	14,919,000
Cash dividend payable	3,133,000	2,772,000
Accrued liabilities –		
Payrolls	7,812,000	5,824,000
Taxes, other than Federal and state income taxes (Note 16)	8,333,000	6,689,000
Pension expense	1,041,000	1,086,000
Miscellaneous	10,630,000	7,978,000
Federal and state income taxes (Note 15)	17,678,000	5,148,000
Total current liabilities	$ 59,521,000	$ 47,825,000
Long-Term Debt (Note 11)	$ 2,869,000	$ 5,010,000
Obligations Under Capital Leases (Notes 2 and 12)	$ 3,931,000	$ 4,994,000
Deferred Federal Income Taxes (Note 15)	$ 30,615,000	$ 28,167,000
Deferred Compensation (Note 8)	$ 422,000	$ —
Commitments and Contingent Liabilities (Notes 12 and 20)		
Stockholders' Equity (Notes 8 and 13)		
Preferred stock, without par value, authorized 1,000,000		
shares; none issued		
Common stock, without par value, authorized 24,000,000		
shares; issued 16,756,763 shares in 1978 and 1977	$ 76,387,000	$ 76,387,000
Retained earnings	209,701,000	176,701,000
Less – Treasury stock – 1,091,300 shares at cost	(19,137,000)	—
	$266,951,000	$253,088,000
	$364,309,000	$339,084,000

The accompanying notes are an integral part of these financial statements.

Consolidated Statements of Changes in Financial Position

MASONITE CORPORATION and subsidiary companies

	Year Ended August 31	
	1978	1977
SOURCE OF FUNDS:		
Net income	$44,489,000	$30,800,000
Expenses (income) not affecting working capital:		
Depreciation	21,954,000	20,703,000
Investment tax credits amortized	(1,504,000)	(1,438,000)
Depletion	1,138,000	2,266,000
Foreign equity (income) loss	(879,000)	39,000
Provision for deferred Federal income taxes	2,448,000	2,499,000
Provision for deferred compensation	422,000	—
Working capital provided from operations	$68,068,000	$54,869,000
Long-term financing, including capital leases	665,000	1,434,000
Disposition of property, plant, and equipment	12,085,000	426,000
Investment tax credits deferred	1,737,000	3,107,000
Common stock issued under option plans	—	48,000
Dividends from foreign affiliates	—	512,000
Other sources	292,000	1,103,000
	$82,847,000	$61,499,000
DISPOSITION OF FUNDS:		
Property, plant, and equipment additions	$31,289,000	$27,862,000
Cash dividends	11,489,000	10,110,000
Long-term debt and capital lease maturities	3,869,000	3,087,000
Purchase of treasury stock	19,137,000	—
	$65,784,000	$41,059,000
INCREASE IN WORKING CAPITAL	$17,063,000	$20,440,000
ANALYSIS OF INCREASE IN WORKING CAPITAL:		
Increase (decrease) in current assets:		
Cash and marketable securities	$23,404,000	$ 6,484,000
Receivables	6,887,000	11,731,000
Inventories	(2,581,000)	2,211,000
Prepaid expenses	1,049,000	(609,000)
Decrease (increase) in current liabilities:		
Current maturities of long-term debt	1,538,000	(420,000)
Accounts payable and accrued liabilities	(704,000)	(7,387,000)
Federal and state income taxes	(12,530,000)	8,430,000
	$17,063,000	$20,440,000

The accompanying notes are an integral part of these financial statements.

Notes to Consolidated Financial Statements

1. STATEMENT OF ACCOUNTING POLICIES

Principles of Consolidation. The consolidated financial statements include the accounts of all domestic subsidiaries. All intercompany balances and transactions have been eliminated.

Investments in Foreign Affiliates. The investment in Masonite Canada Ltd. (50% owned) and Masonite (Africa) Limited (65% owned) is carried at cost, adjusted for equity in earnings net of estimated taxes on remittance and dividends received.

Depreciation and Depletion. Provision for depreciation is made on a straight-line basis on the estimated service lives of the various classes of property. Buildings are depreciated over a 10 to 50 year period, and machinery and equipment are depreciated over a 3 to 20 year period.
   Major replacements which extend the useful lives of units of equipment are capitalized and depreciated over the estimated remaining useful lives of the property. All other maintenance and repairs are expensed as incurred.
   Costs of property retired or otherwise disposed of, and the related accumulated depreciation, are removed from the accounts; the net gain or loss on retirements is credited or charged to earnings.
   Depletion of timberlands and roadways is computed on the cost of timberlands and roadways (less an allowance for land values) divided by the estimated recoverable timber to obtain overall average depletion rates.

Income Taxes. Investment tax credits on eligible property are amortized to earnings over the useful lives of the related assets. The unamortized amounts of investment tax credits are included in "Accumulated Depreciation and Depletion."
   Accelerated depreciation is used for tax purposes. Deferred taxes are provided on the difference between book and tax depreciation.

Inventories. Substantially all inventories are valued on the last-in, first-out cost basis. Other inventories are valued at the lower of first-in, first-out cost or market. Market is the lower of current replacement cost or net realizable value (sales price less cost to convert, sell and deliver). Appropriate allowances are made for overaged and obsolete inventory items. Quantities reflect physical counts at or near year end.

Retirement Plans. The company's policy is to fund retirement costs accrued under several retirement plans covering a majority of its employees, including unfunded past-service costs which are funded over a maximum of 30 years.

2. CHANGE IN ACCOUNTING FOR LEASES

During 1978 the company changed its method of accounting for certain leases entered into prior to January 1, 1977 to comply with Statement of Financial Accounting Standards No. 13, "Accounting for Leases." The new method requires that amounts related to lease agreements meeting the criteria for classification as capital leases be recorded as assets with the related lease obligations recorded as liabilities.
   The effect of this change was not significant in relation to net income of any year. The financial statements for 1977 have been restated for comparative purposes and include the charge of $198,000 ($.01 per share) representing the cumulative effect on retained earnings of retroactively applying this accounting method to years prior to 1977. Refer to the note on Lease Commitments for a discussion of leasing activity.

3. ACQUISITION

In December, 1977, the company acquired all of the net assets of Stuart Lumber Corporation, a particleboard manufacturer, in exchange for 450,000 shares of the company's common stock. This acquisition was accounted for as a pooling of interests. Accordingly, the prior-period consolidated financial statements have been restated to include the accounts of Stuart Lumber Corporation. The effect of the restatement on the consolidated financial statements was not material.

4. INVENTORIES

If the first-in, first-out method of inventory accounting had been used by the company, inventories would have been $19,369,000 and $13,724,000 higher than reported at August 31, 1978 and 1977, respectively.
   Inventories used in the determination of cost of sales are summarized as follows:

(000 omitted)	August 31, 1978	August 31, 1977	August 31, 1976
Finished stock	$26,605	$28,320	$26,654
Raw materials and supplies	24,361	25,227	24,682
Total	$50,966	$53,547	$51,336

5. PROPERTY, PLANT AND EQUIPMENT

Property, plant and equipment are stated at cost less accumulated depreciation and depletion, as follows:

(000 omitted)	Land	Timberlands & Roadways	Buildings	Machinery & Equipment	Construction in Progress	Investment Credit	Total
1977							
Cost basis, 9/1/76	$5,065	$33,050	$55,917	$255,053	$14,644		$363,729
Additions	166	3,532	488	1,206	22,470		27,862
Retirement or sales	(116)	(165)	(779)	(7,538)	16		(8,582)
Construction in progress transfers		440	2,494	29,365	(32,299)		—
Miscellaneous	74	122	240	(429)			7
Total	5,189	36,979	58,360	277,657	4,831		383,016
Less:							
Accumulated depreciation*, 9/1/76		10,218	22,344	135,275		$ 8,064	175,901
Depreciation* expensed during year		2,266	2,061	18,642			22,969
Adjustment for retirements, etc.			(332)	(6,414)			(6,746)
Investment credit deferred						3,107	3,107
Investment credit amortized						(1,438)	(1,438)
Miscellaneous		(1,311)	4	(96)			(1,403)
Total deductions		11,173	24,077	147,407		9,733	192,390
Balance, August 31, 1977	$5,189	$25,806	$34,283	$130,250	$ 4,831	$(9,733)	$190,626
1978							
Cost basis, 9/1/77	$5,189	$36,979	$58,360	$277,657	$ 4,831		$383,016
Additions	160	4,894		1,496	24,739		31,289
Retirements or sales	(169)	(2,540)	(2,609)	(18,709)	(138)		(24,165)
Construction in progress transfers			2,443	17,808	(20,251)		—
Miscellaneous	(70)	(98)	(103)	40			(231)
Total	5,110	39,235	58,091	278,292	9,181		389,909
Less:							
Accumulated depreciation*, 9/1/77		11,173	24,077	147,407		$ 9,733	192,390
Depreciation* expensed during year		1,138	1,504	20,450			23,092
Adjustment for retirements, etc.			(665)	(11,393)			(12,058)
Investment credit deferred						1,737	1,737
Investment credit amortized						(1,504)	(1,504)
Miscellaneous			(36)	(217)			(253)
Total deductions		12,311	24,880	156,247		9,966	203,404
Balance, August 31, 1978	$5,110	$26,924	$33,211	$122,045	$ 9,181	$(9,966)	$186,505

*Includes depletion and amortization

6. RETIREMENT PLANS

The total retirement plans expenses for 1978 and 1977 were approximately $4,600,000 and $4,200,000, respectively. The actuarially computed value of vested benefits for four of the plans exceeded the total of the assets of their retirement funds and balance sheet accruals as of August 31, 1978, by approximately $11,410,000. Unfunded past-service costs under the plans at August 31, 1978, approximated $11,277,000.

7. PROFIT SHARING PLAN

The Masonite Profit Sharing Stock Plan provides that each fiscal year the company contribute 2% of that part of the consolidated income before income taxes, as defined, of the divisions participating in the Plan, which is in excess of 6% of consolidated net worth of said divisions at the beginning of the fiscal year. To be eligible for participation, an employee must be a full-time salaried employee, permanently and continuously in the employ of the company for one year. The company's contributions for 1978 and 1977 were $1,315,000 and $798,000, respectively.

8. STOCK INCENTIVE PROGRAMS

The company's 1971 Incentive Plan for officers and key employees provides that options are granted at a price per share which is not less than 100% of market value on the date the options are granted. Qualified options expire five years after date of grant and non-qualified options expire ten years after date of grant. Terms of the options vary; but, in all cases for all options granted to date, a minimum service requirement of three years must be fulfilled before an option becomes exercisable.

At August 31, 1978 options for 147,440 shares were outstanding. By fiscal year of grant these outstanding options were: 1,500 in 1974; 135,940 in 1976; and 10,000 in 1977.

At August 31, 1978 and 1977, respectively, options for 147,440 shares and 271,753 were outstanding with market values at date of grant totaling $3,129,000 and $6,771,000. Prices of outstanding options ranged from $19.56 to $33.75 at August 31, 1978 and from $18.00 to $33.75 at August 31, 1977.

Options became exercisable as follows:

	1978	1977
Number of shares	3,180	10,660
Option price – Per share	$21.25	$19.19–$19.56
Total	$68,000	$208,000
Market value at date exercisable – Per share	$15.75–$15.88	$19.56–$24.00
Total	$50,000	$211,000

No options were exercised during 1978. During 1977, options for 2,100 shares, having an aggregate option price of $44,625, were exercised at a price per share of $21.25. At the date exercised, the aggregate market value was $49,350 and the market price per share was $23.50.

Also, the company's 1971 Incentive Plan provides for Performance Share Awards to officers and key employees. Awards of 23,580 common shares granted October 13, 1977 were earned based on fiscal 1978 results and will be paid in five annual installments providing the recipients are still employees of the company.

At August 31, 1978 and 1977, 240,532 and 163,379 shares, respectively, were reserved for future issuance under employee stock incentive programs.

The option price on options exercised has been credited to common stock. No charges or credits have been made to income for stock options.

The amount charged to income in 1978 for Performance Share Awards, based upon the year-end market value of the shares, was $528,000.

9. KEY DATA, UNCONSOLIDATED FOREIGN AFFILIATES (unaudited)

	Masonite Canada		Masonite (Africa)	
(000 omitted)	1978	1977	1978	1977
Current assets	$22,077	$16,665	$ 4,851	$ 4,801
Noncurrent assets	27,314	27,153	13,959	14,866
Current liabilities	11,126	5,673	4,191	5,053
Long-term debt	19,020	20,973	1,873	2,463
Other noncurrent liabilities	4,565	4,270	593	644
Shareholders' equity	14,680	12,902	12,153	11,507
Masonite Corporation's investment	5,632	5,016	4,996	4,733
Net sales	$56,071	$56,364	$14,157	$13,663
Net earnings	1,232	1,089	407	(897)
Masonite Corporation's equity in earnings	616	543	263	(582)

10. SHORT-TERM BORROWINGS

The company had no short-term borrowings during 1978 and at August 31, 1977. The maximum amount outstanding at any month-end for 1977 was $10,880,000, while the approximate average aggregate short-term borrowings payable for 1977 was $2,728,000. The approximate weighted average interest rate for these borrowings was 4.9%. The company maintains compensating balances of approximately 10% of its lines of credit pursuant to informal agreements with the lending banks. Normal daily deposits in the banks are sufficient to cover this arrangement, and none of the cash balances is legally restricted as to withdrawal. Lines of credit with banks for short-term borrowings support commercial paper borrowings when bank borrowings are not being utilized. Unused lines of credit for short-term borrowings aggregated $14,000,000 and $16,000,000 at August 31, 1978 and 1977, respectively. Such lines are not subject to contractual arrangements and can be withdrawn by the banks at anytime.

11. LONG-TERM DEBT

Property, plant and equipment with a cost of approximately $6,006,000 are pledged for notes, mortgages, and a land purchase contract outstanding at August 31, 1978. The obligations become due January 1, 1979 to March 31, 1994, and have interest rates ranging from .875% to 7.5%. Aggregate maturities on long-term debt are $1,220,000 (included in current liabilities), $665,000, $391,000, $280,000, and $243,000 for the years ending August 31, 1979 through August 31, 1983, respectively.

12. LEASE COMMITMENTS

The company has various lease agreements relating primarily to office space and transportation, data processing and office equipment that extend through 2015. The terms of the leases vary from one month to 40 years. Some of the leases also include renewal options for various terms and some require the company to pay contingent rentals based primarily on usage for data processing and office equipment and mileage for transportation equipment.

Capital Leases – The following is an analysis of the leased property under capital leases by major classes, as recorded in the financial statements.

	August 31	
	1978	1977
Buildings	$ 2,390,000	$ 3,401,000
Machinery and equipment	7,119,000	7,388,000
	$ 9,509,000	$10,789,000
Less: Accumulated amortization	5,407,000	5,344,000
	$ 4,102,000	$ 5,445,000

Amortization of assets recorded under capital leases is included with depreciation expense.

The following is a schedule by years of future minimum lease payments under capital leases together with the present value of the net minimum lease payments as of August 31, 1978:

Fiscal Periods	
1979	$1,160,000
1980	1,029,000
1981	1,025,000
1982	984,000
1983	902,000
Later Years	2,512,000
Total minimum lease payments	$7,612,000
Less amounts representing – Interest	1,340,000
– Estimated lessor executory costs	1,690,000
Present value of net minumum lease payments ($651,000 current and $3,931,000 long-term)	$4,582,000

Operating Leases — The following is a schedule by years of future minimum rental payments required under operating leases that have initial or remaining noncancellable lease terms in excess of one year as of August 31, 1978.

Fiscal Periods	
1979	$1,364,000
1980	1,010,000
1981	865,000
1982	662,000
1983	57,000
Later Years	222,000
Total minimum payments required	$4,180,000

Rental expense for 1978 and 1977 consisted of:

	1978	1977
Minimum rentals	$4,807,000	$3,449,000
Contingent rentals	1,142,000	1,193,000
Total	$5,949,000	$4,642,000

13. CAPITAL STOCK TRANSACTIONS

Transactions in the common stock account for the two years ended August 31, 1978, are summarized as follows:

	Common Stock		Treasury Stock	
	Shares	Amount	Shares	Amount
Balance at August 31, 1976, as previously reported	16,304,663	$76,264,000		
Shares issued for 1978 pooling of interests	450,000	75,000		
Balance at August 31, 1976, as restated	16,754,663	$76,339,000		
Exercise of stock options	2,100	48,000		
Balance at August 31, 1977	16,756,763	$76,387,000		
Purchase of treasury stock			1,091,300	$19,137,000
Balance at August 31, 1978	16,756,763	$76,387,000	1,091,300	$19,137,000

14. ACCOUNTS RECEIVABLE ALLOWANCES

Allowances for doubtful accounts, cash discounts and claims amounted to $1,665,000 at August 31, 1978 compared to $900,000 at August 31, 1977 (unchanged from August 31, 1976). The increase of $765,000 was charged to expense in 1978, as were bad debt write-offs, net of recoveries, amounting to $170,000, compared to $307,000 in 1977.

15. INCOME TAXES

The provision for deferred Federal income taxes results primarily from timing differences in the recognition of depreciation expense for book and tax purposes.

The difference between the statutory Federal income tax rate and the company's effective income tax rate is summarized as follows:

	1978	1977
Federal income tax rate	48.0%	48.0%
Increase (decrease) as a result of —		
Value of timber appreciation taxed at capital gains rates	(5.7)	(6.2)
State income taxes, net of Federal tax benefit	2.9	3.1
Other, including amortization of investment credit	(0.2)	(1.9)
Effective tax rate	45.0%	43.0%

16. SUPPLEMENTARY INCOME STATEMENT INFORMATION

Charged to expense during 1978 and 1977 were amounts shown in the table below for the indicated categories:

	1978	1977
Maintenance and repairs	$32,606,000	$30,036,000
Provision for:		
Depreciation of buildings and equipment	21,954,000	20,703,000
Depletion of timberlands and roadways	1,138,000	2,266,000
Taxes (other than Federal and state taxes on income):		
Real estate and personal property	4,084,000	3,513,000
Unemployment and old age benefit	8,209,000	7,065,000
Franchise, privilege, sales and use	1,406,000	1,248,000
Advertising costs	5,972,000	6,353,000
Research and development costs*	4,754,000	3,339,000

*Research and development costs include depreciation of $331,000 in 1978 and $262,000 in 1977.

17. REPLACEMENT COST DATA (unaudited)

General. The information presented herein does not necessarily represent the current value of existing assets or future costs of replacing them; nor should it be interpreted that the company presently has plans to replace its productive capacity or that replacement, if and when made, would occur in the form and manner assumed for purposes of developing the information. In reality, such replacement will take place over an extended period of time during which technology, price levels and competitive factors most likely will change. Additionally, the replacement cost information should not be used to impute the effects of inflation on the company's net income without considering such other factors as the impact of general price level changes, methods of financing and statutory taxing policies. Finally, the replacement cost information standing alone does not recognize customary relationships between changes in costs and changes in selling prices. Over the years, the company has attempted to adjust selling prices to maintain margins and, competitive conditions permitting, expects to do so in the future.

SUMMARY OF REPLACEMENT COST AMOUNTS AND RELATED HISTORICAL AMOUNTS

(000 omitted)	Historical Amounts Included In Financial Statements (a)	Land	Construction In Progress	Assets Which Will Not Be Replaced	Historical Amounts For Which Replacement Cost Information Is Provided	Replacement Cost Amounts (a)
For the Year Ended August 31, 1978:						
Inventories	$ 50,966			$ 2,351	$ 48,615	$ 69,206
Property, Plant and Equipment	$350,674	$5,110	$9,181	$ 5,149	$331,234	$639,096
Less:						
Accumulated Depreciation	181,127			3,399	177,728	319,375
	$169,547	$5,110	$9,181	$ 1,750	$153,506	$319,721
Cost of Sales Excluding Depreciation	$383,290			$18,831	$364,459	$369,833
Depreciation	$ 21,954			$ 699	$ 21,255(b)	$ 38,338(b)
For the Year Ended August 31, 1977:						
Inventories	$ 53,547			$ 1,473	$ 52,074	$ 68,093
Property, Plant and Equipment	$346,037	$5,189	$4,831	$ 8,721	$327,296	$592,907
Less:						
Accumulated Depreciation	171,484			4,719	166,765	283,721
	$174,553	$5,189	$4,831	$ 4,002	$160,531	$309,186
Cost of Sales Excluding Depreciation	$337,437			$10,072	$327,365	$333,366
Depreciation	$ 20,703			$ 554	$ 20,149(c)	$ 35,213(c)

The "Less: Items For Which Replacement Cost Information Is Not Provided" column group spans Land, Construction In Progress, and Assets Which Will Not Be Replaced.

(a) Historical and replacement cost information for timber and roadways and related depletion and forest management expenditures is excluded from this summary and discussed in the section captioned "Timberlands and Roadways."

(b) $18,197 historical cost and $33,670 replacement cost depreciation applicable to cost of sales.

(c) $16,984 historical cost and $30,146 replacement cost depreciation applicable to cost of sales.

METHODS USED TO DETERMINE 1978 AND 1977 REPLACEMENT COST

Inventories and Cost of Sales Excluding Depreciation. The replacement cost of inventories was estimated by applying the first-in, first-out (FIFO) method of inventory valuation. Inventories under the FIFO method reasonably approximate the most current production and purchase costs. Depreciation included as an element of inventory costs was adjusted to give effect to the replacement cost values of productive capacity.

In its financial statements, the company values substantially all of its inventories on the last-in, first-out (LIFO) method. Cost of sales under this method reasonably approximates cost of sales on a replacement cost basis. Also, the turnover rate of non-LIFO inventories is sufficiently rapid to approximate replacement cost. Accordingly, replacement cost of sales was estimated by using reported cost of sales, adjusted for the effect of the liquidation of prior years' LIFO layers, which were not material.

The estimated replacement cost amounts for inventory and cost of sales do not consider any cost savings that would result from replacing productive capacity.

Productive Capacity. Generally, replacement cost of productive capacity at August 31, 1978 was determined by indexing forward the August 31, 1977 replacement cost estimate and adjusting for additions and retirements made during the year.

At August 31, 1977, replacement cost was estimated as follows: (1) For buildings, by applying either internally developed construction costs on a per square foot basis to the applicable square footage or published construction cost indexes to the applicable historical cost or recent appraisal amounts; (2) For a significant portion of the company's machinery and equipment, using engineering estimates, vendor quotations or installation cost data, indexed forward if necessary; and (3) For the remaining machinery and equipment, by applying published indexes to historical costs or recent appraisal data.

Depreciation and Accumulated Depreciation. Estimated replacement cost depreciation was determined by applying historical cost composite depreciation rates on a straight-line basis to the estimated average replacement cost of composite asset groups. Estimated accumulated replacement cost depreciation was based upon the weighted-average historical lives of the composite asset groups. No adjustment was made for additional asset life that might result from technological improvements.

Operating Efficiencies. If the company's productive capacity were replaced in the manner assumed, costs other than depreciation (such as direct labor, repairs and maintenance, energy and certain other indirect costs) would be altered. Although these expected cost changes cannot be quantified with any precision, in the opinion of management the current level of operating costs other than depreciation would be reduced as a result of the technological improvements assumed in the hypothetical replacement, and would substantially offset the additional depreciation on a replacement cost basis.

Timberlands and Roadways. The company uses the sustained yield concept for managing its fee timberlands. Under this concept, timber harvested is replaced by new growth in order to maintain the fiber potential of these timberlands. Consistent with this sustained yield concept, the replacement cost of the company's fee timber was determined as reforestation costs plus forest management expenditures that would be required to bring timber holdings from a theoretically harvested state to a state of maturity equal to that existing at August 31, 1978 and 1977.

Accordingly, the total estimated replacement cost of the company's fee timber at August 31, 1978 and 1977 was calculated to be $94,534,000 and $86,523,000, respectively, of which $23,843,000 (1978) and $22,620,000 (1977) represent reforestation costs and $70,691,000 (1978) and $63,903,000 (1977) represent forest management expenditures. Timber replacement cost excludes replacement amounts for the land component of timberlands, minor amounts of acreage that will not be replaced and roadways. Estimated replacement cost amounts for timber harvested during 1978 and 1977, based on the replacement cost of fee timber and the amount of timber cut, were $2,696,000 and $3,343,000, respectively.

The above estimates are not comparable with the financial statement amounts for timberlands and roadways ($26,924,000 and $25,806,000 at August 31, 1978 and 1977, respectively) and depletion ($1,138,000 and $2,266,000 in 1978 and 1977, respectively). This is attributable primarily to the fact that forest management expenditures, amounting to $3,235,000 in 1978 and $3,036,000 in 1977, are charged to cost of sales as incurred for financial statement purposes.

Index

A

Accelerated depreciation, 314–15
  definition, 331
  price-level changes, 550
Account, 44
  adjusting, 80–87
  arrangement in ledger, 90–91
  asset, 46–47
  after closing, 126–30
  definition, 65
  liability, 47–48
  T-account, 44–45
Account balance, 45, 65
Account code numbers, 175–76
Account form balance sheet, 97–98
  definition, 98
Account number, 65
Account titles column, 163–65
Accounting
  auditing, 6–7
  definition, 25
  functions, 5
  governmental, 9
  management advisory services, 7
  private, 8
  profession, 6
  public, 6–8
  tax services, 7–8
Accounting concepts, 12–17
  definition, 25
Accounting cycle, 134–35
  definition, 135
Accounting equation, 19, 56
  business transaction, 19
  definition, 25
Accounting methods used, disclosure of, 254
Accounting period, 79
  definition, 98
Accounting principles, 12–17
  definition, 25
  sources of, 13

Accounting Principles Board (APB), 13, 24
  Opinions
    No. 10 "Disclosure of Accounting Policies," 254, 283
    No. 12 "Omnibus Opinion—1967," 315
    No. 15 "Earnings per Share," 533
    No. 16, 461, 464
    No. 17 "Intangible Assets," 331, 464
    No. 18 "Equity Method of Accounting for Investments in Common Stock," 461
    No. 19 "Reporting Changes in Financial Position," 494
    No. 20 "Accounting Changes," 284, 316
    No. 22 "Disclosure of Accounting Policies," 254, 283
    No. 29 "Accounting for Nonmonetary Transactions," 15, 324
  Statements
    No. 3 "Financial Statements Restated for General Price Level Changes," 554
    No. 4 "Basic Concepts and Accounting Principles Underlying Financial Statements of Business Enterprises," 5, 24, 280, 351
    No. 13 "Accounting for Leases," 364
Accounting Research Bulletins, 13
  No. 43, 94, 214, 279, 448
Accounting Research and Terminology Bulletin, Final Edition, 94, 214, 279, 285, 447
Accounting statements, 9–11
  balance sheet; *see* Balance sheet
  income statement; *see* Income statement
Accounts payable, 11, 47, 120, 257
  definition, 25
Accounts payable ledger, 251, 258–59
Accounts receivable, 11, 46
  aging, 244–45
  definition, 25
Accounts receivable account, 235

599

This book has been set in 10 and 9 point Gael, leaded 2 points. Part numbers and chapter titles are Vanguard Extra Light. Part titles are Vanguard Medium and chapter numbers are Vanguard Bold. The size of the text area is 27 by 48½ picas.